Health and
Health Care as
Social Problems

UNDERSTANDING SOCIAL PROBLEMS: AN SSSP PRESIDENTIAL SERIES

Understanding Social Problems is a textbook series published in collaboration with the Society for the Study of Social Problems, under the direction of the SSSP Editorial and Publications Committee. The anthologies introduce students to the principles for assessing social problems and to exemplary research studies in the field. Articles selected from the society's leading journal, *Social Problems,* are chosen for their coverage, their relevance, and their accessibility to students. Introductions written by each book's editors situate the issues raised by the articles into a broader sociological perspective.

All royalties from this series go to support the SSSP and its activities.

Social Problems across the Life Course

> Edited by Helena Z. Lopata and
> Judith A. Levy

Drugs, Alcohol, and Social Problems

> Edited by James D. Orcutt and
> David R. Rudy

Health and Health Care as Social Problems

> Edited by Peter Conrad and Valerie Leiter

Health and Health Care as Social Problems

EDITED BY
PETER CONRAD AND VALERIE LEITER

ROWMAN & LITTLEFIELD PUBLISHERS, INC.
Lanham • Boulder • New York • Toronto • Oxford

ROWMAN & LITTLEFIELD PUBLISHERS, INC.

Published in the United States of America
by Rowman & Littlefield Publishers, Inc.
A wholly owned subsidary of the Rowman & Littlefield Publishing Group, Inc.
4501 Forbes Boulevard, Suite 200, Lanham, Maryland 20706
www.rowmanlittlefield.com

P.O. Box 317, Oxford, OX2 9RU, United Kingdom

Copyright © 2003 by the Society for the Study of Social Problems

British Library Cataloguing in Publication Information Available

Library of Congress Cataloging-in-Publication Data

Health and health care as social problems / edited by Peter Conrad and
Valerie Leiter.
    p. cm. — (Understanding social problems)
Includes bibliographical references and index.
  ISBN 0-7425-2856-1 (cloth : alk. paper) — ISBN 0-7425-2857-X (pbk. :
alk. paper)
  1. Social medicine. I. Conrad, Peter, 1945– II. Leiter, Valerie,
1965– III. Series.
  RA418.H3865 2003
  362.1—dc21

                                                          2003008906

Printed in the United States of America

♾™ The paper used in this publication meets the minimum requirements of American
National Standard for Information Sciences—Permanence of Paper for Printed Library
Materials, ANSI/NISO Z39.48-1992.

Contents

Introduction

Peter Conrad and Valerie Leiter

Health and health care have become central concerns in American society over the past fifty years. The health care sector has grown enormously in this time: in 1950, 4.2 percent of our gross national product (GNP) went to health care; by the year 2002, it was nearly 14 percent. One of the major public dilemmas in U.S. society is how to provide broad access to medical care while simultaneously controlling costs.

Medicine's ability to make a significant impact on health is a twentieth-century phenomenon. In 1900, the life expectancy in the United States was forty-seven years; in 2000, it is 76.9 years. While much of this increase is the result of improvements in public health (e.g., sanitation, clean water) and a rising standard of living (McKinlay and McKinlay 1977), it is also the result of important advances in medical care. Although medicine is one of the oldest professions, the success and prestige of medical intervention is a relatively recent phenomenon. L. J. Henderson noted, "Somewhere between 1910 and 1912 in this country, a random patient, with a random disease, consulting a doctor chosen at random, had for the first time in the history of mankind, a better than fifty-fifty chance of profiting from the encounter" (Blumgart 1964). By the late twentieth century, organ transplantation, cardiac bypass, neonatal infant care, improved cancer treatment, and new families of drugs (e.g., antibiotics, immunizations, and psychoactive) had given physicians a great medical armory with which to treat patients. Despite the successes of medicine, it does have some glaring problems—particularly regarding access to care, the costs of care, inequalities in health outcomes, and the emergence of chronic health problems.

Access to health care is distributed very unevenly across the U.S. population. Roughly forty-four million Americans have no health insurance, and even more are underinsured for their medical needs. Those who have higher incomes are much more likely to be insured: 34 percent of individuals living in poverty have no health insurance, compared with 9 percent of those who have income at 200 percent or more above the poverty level are uninsured. While other countries have long had some form of universal health care, the United States has not implemented such a system. Our system is a mixture of public financing for some people who are elderly, disabled, or poor, and a private system for those who can obtain health insurance through employment. But even those with insurance are often not covered completely, especially for prescription drug costs (one of the fastest rising parts of health costs) or long-term care.

Medical care has become hugely expensive. As noted, health care in the United States now assumes 14 percent of the GNP, and it continues to rise. In the 1970s, the main problem around health care was defined as "access" to care. But with the sky-rocketing health care costs, attention has shifted to controlling the costs. Managed care has become the major mode of health care organization. Under managed care, patients have fairly easy access to primary care but restricted access to specialized care. Managed care organizations limit patients' use of specialists' care, hospital treatment, and other specialty medical goods and services by having a designated primary care provider act as a gatekeeper to more specialized (and expensive) specialty care. Most attempts at controlling costs, including managed care, have had only limited success, as health costs have continued to rise in the past two decades. Ever-expanding developments in medical technology and drugs have contributed to this growth in costs, as managed care organizations struggle to rein in the costs associated with access to expensive improvements in care. One of the problems with managed care is that it sometimes pits patients, doctors, and insurance companies against one another when patients attempt to obtain services (Light 1993). Doctors are placed in the middle of managed care organizations' attempts to control access to care and their patients' medical needs. As a result, patient trust of physicians has eroded (Mechanic 1996) because, first, managed care creates incentives for providers to undertreat patients by restricting services and, second, because it makes the "business" side of medicine more evident.

Huge inequalities in health outcomes continue to exist in the United States. Sociologists have called social inequality a fundamental cause of disease in society (Link and Phelan 1995). Numerous studies have demonstrated the inverse relationship between social class and illness: the lower the social class, the higher the rates of illness and death. People in lower classes have higher rates of infectious diseases, infant mortality, and disability, as well as lower life expectancy and higher death rates (Robert and House 2000). Race in the United States exemplifies health inequalities. In the United States, racial minorities are usually poorer than the population in general. For example, infant morality rates among African-Americans are almost double those of whites, a disparity that remains constant even when infant mortality declines. Overall mortality rates are also higher for African-Americans at all ages. Life expectancy for African-Americans has actually decreased since the 1980s (Smaje 2000). The causes of these disparities are complex, but social disadvantage is exacerbated by racism and discrimination (Williams 1999).

Over the past three decades, the burden of disease has changed, with a shift from acute to chronic illnesses. For example, previously unknown diseases like HIV/AIDS have become epidemics in certain populations; disorders like chronic fatigue syndrome have emerged to become contested illnesses; tuberculosis, once thought cured, has reoccurred in more resistant forms; and asthma has more than doubled in prevalence in the past two decades. While reduction in smoking has helped reduce lung cancer and heart disease, obesity affects over 30 percent of Americans and raises the risk for heart disease and diabetes. The social causes and responses to these problems have become prominent features as medicine and society work to reduce the risk of disease.

A social problems perspective to health and health care can help us understand that health is not merely a medical issue, but a fundamentally social one as well. This volume introduces a social problems approach, providing a broad lens with which to view not only health problems but the social and medical responses to them.

The metaphor of upstream/downstream approaches to health (see McKinlay 2001) can help us conceptualize a social problems approach in form of a story. Imagine a river. In that river, there are dozens of people drowning. Lifesavers are diving in and pulling the victims from the water, administering CPR and consequently saving a number of them. But the lifesavers are exhausted from continually pulling out drowning individuals, and their efforts are not always successful. A bystander might ask, "Why aren't we looking further upstream to see who is pushing these folks in?" or "How did these people all end up in trouble downstream?" The metaphor suggests that our current medical system (i.e., clinical medicine) focuses downstream on all the drowning (i.e., sick) people without fully examining what is making them sick. Couldn't we prevent the problems by intervening further upstream? To offer just two examples: First, if we want to find the causes of obesity (a major risk factor for heart disease), we should, rather than focus on individuals after they become overweight, examine the food industry and their advertising, as well as the fat-laden, high-carbohydrate junk foods served in public schools. Second, if we want to reduce deaths from lung cancer and emphysema (as well as heart disease), we need to look beyond stop-smoking programs and smokeless areas to examine the cigarette companies that make a business of increasing their markets by getting people to smoke. Not all health problems are amenable to upstream approaches; but when we adopt such a perspective, we turn health problems into social problems with a broader set of public solutions.

A social problems approach to health can sometimes align with medical perspectives, which is particularly true when health problems are examined from a public health perspective. Here we can focus on understanding the development of health problems in the social and physical environment. This focus includes, in particular, occupationally and environmentally induced diseases, whether they are black lung disease among coal miners (Smith 1981) or environmentally induced breast cancer or asthma (Brown et al. 2001). A public health perspective also includes interventions concerning behavior and lifestyle: for example, HIV/AIDS with safer sex or needle exchange, or changes in diet and exercise to reduce the risk for cardiovascular disease. When a social problems approach aligns with more medical-specific approaches, the emphasis is not only on the social production of disease and illness but also on the interventions in the social structure or culture as ways of preventing or even treating the maladies.

A social problems approach to health care rests on a number of assumptions and raises important issues. Some of the most significant ones include the following:

1. All people have a right to access to quality medical care. Financial and other barriers restrict some individuals from getting proper health care. Concern regarding access to care is reflected in public debates over universal health insurance, which would eliminate the large number of uninsured.
2. Social environments can have a significant impact on health and illness. Clinical approaches tend to focus on individual patients and their bodies as the locus of intervention. But researchers are increasingly finding that social environments (e.g., social inequality) can be primary causes of disease. Here the concern becomes how

to intervene in the social environment to prevent disease and promote health. Some analysts have suggested a focus on "upstream" approaches. For example, current standards for the treatment of asthma stress the importance of prevention through controlling environmental irritants and triggers and through educating the patient in self-care, not simply through the control of acute symptoms via pharmaceutical treatment.

3. The social inequities in society are reflected in health and health care. One of the fundamental findings of social research on disease is the inverse relationship between social class and illness. The lower the social class, the higher the rates of illness—and vice versa. Another example is that blacks suffer from twice the infant mortality (death before the age of one) than do whites. Evidence suggests that this phenomenon is socially produced and related to social inequalities.

4. What is considered health and illness in any society changes over time and circumstance. Medicine has made great inroads in the twentieth century in controlling infectious disease; however, as people live longer, chronic diseases like cancer, stroke, and heart disease become the major causes of death. As the burden of disease changes, so do medical approaches and the attendant problems they may bring. Medical care was previously decided by doctors and hospitals to cover the most visible diseases and symptoms; now, however, we witness not only consumer-driven health services (e.g., cosmetic surgery) but also restrictions on care as driven by insurance companies and managed care.

5. More health care is not always better. While there is undertreatment of some important health problems, there may be overtreatment of others. This imbalance is reflected in a concern about turning all human problems into medical problems, or what is now called the "medicalization" of life. For example, hormone replacement therapy has been used extensively to "treat" menopause in older women. Only recently have medical researchers found that such therapy may actually cause health problems that are far more serious than menopausal symptoms.

6. The way that medicine is organized can create problems with health and illness. Even though medical professionalization has had certain benefits, it has also created a profession with little public accountability. In the last two decades, with the coming of managed care, the public has seen an increased corporatization of medicine, both in terms of insurance companies' increased influence over health care providers and in the rise of for-profit medicine. This trend has encouraged an increase in profitable kinds of treatments and a restriction in other kinds of care.

7. Lay people and professionals may conflict in the way they view health problems, which may be in terms of cause, such as with the debates of environmental causes of breast cancer or Gulf War syndrome (Brown et al. 2001), or whether a particular ailment really is a disease, such as with chronic fatigue syndrome. Some conflicts reflect the patients' and doctors' divergent views on treatment, such as when doctors want patients to follow medical regimens while patients are more focused on managing the contingencies of their everyday lives (Conrad 1985). Patients and their advocates are much more likely to challenge medical authority today than they were three decades ago.

8. Increased medical technology has made important contributions to improving health and health care. There have been significant developments in genetics, brain and body scanners, pharmaceutical interventions, microsurgery, and life extension

technology. Yet new problems come with these technologies: We can extend the quantity of life, but can we also extend the quality? Who is to pay for expensive new technologies and to whom will they be available? Can society afford to spend ever-increasing amounts on medical technological interventions?

A social problems approach to health and health care recognizes that advances in medical knowledge and technology may create as well as solve human problems—thus, the two principles of this approach: first, that health and illness are at least partly socially produced; second, that health care is not an unfettered good and often brings with it serious social problems.

In this volume we examine six sets of social problems in health and health care. Parts I and II take what sociologists call a social constructionist perspective by examining the medicalization of human problems and the social construction of health problems. Part III shows how social movements can affect the understanding and treatment of medical problems. Part IV explores the role of gender in health and illness. Part V addresses the roles that race and class play in the provision of health care, and part VI addresses the issue of medical accountability in society. Taken together, the essays in this volume demonstrate the depth and richness of a social problems approach to health and health care, and the critical perspective it can bring to our understanding of health and illness in U.S. society.

References

Blumgart, H. L. 1964. "Caring for the Patient." *New England Journal of Medicine* 270: 449–56.

Brown, Phil, Stephen M. Zavestoski, Sabrina McCormick, Joshua Mandelbaum, Theo Luebke. 2001. "Print Media Coverage of Environmental Causation of Breast Cancer." *Sociology of Health and Illness* 23: 747–75.

Conrad, Peter. 1985. "The Meaning of Medications: Another Look at Compliance." *Social Science and Medicine* 20: 29–37.

Light, Donald R. 1993. "Countervailing Power: The Changing Character of the Medical Profession in the United States." In *The Changing Medical Profession: An International Perspective*, edited by F. W. Hafferty and J. B. McKinlay, 69–80. New York: Oxford University Press.

Link, Bruce G., and Jo C. Phelan. 1995. "Social Conditions as Fundamental Causes of Disease." *Journal of Health and Social Behavior*. Extra issue: 80–94.

Mechanic, David. 1996. "Changing Medical Organization and the Erosion of Trust." *The Milbank Quarterly* 74: 171–89.

McKinlay, John B. 2001. "A Case for Refocusing Upstream: The Political Economy of Illness." In *The Sociology of Health and Illness: Critical Perspectives,* 6th ed., edited by Peter Conrad, 516–29. New York: Worth Publishers.

McKinlay John B., and Sonja M. McKinlay. 1977. "The Questionable Contribution of Medical Measures to the Decline of Mortality in the United States in the Twentieth Century." *Milbank Memorial Quarterly* 55: 405–28.

Robert, Stephanie A., and James S. House. 2000. "Socioeconomic Inequalities in Health: An Enduring Sociological Problem." In *The Handbook of Medical Sociology*, 5th ed., edited by Chloe Bird, Peter Conrad, and Allan Fremont, 79–97. Upper Saddle River, NJ: Prentice Hall.

Smaje, Chris. 2000. "Race, Ethnicity and Health." In *The Handbook of Medical Sociology*, 5th ed., edited by Chloe Bird, Peter Conrad, and Allan Fremont, 114–29. Upper Saddle River, NJ: Prentice Hall.

Smith, Barbara Ellen. 1981. "Black Lung: The Social Production of Disease." *International Journal of Health Services* 11: 343–59.

Williams, David R. 1999. "Race, SES and Health: The Added Effects of Racism and Discrimination." *Annals of the New York Academy of Science* 896: 173–88.

Part I

MEDICALIZATION

Over the past century, an increasing number of human problems have become defined as medical problems. Sociologists have called this process "medicalization," which literally means "to make medical." The key to medicalization is defining a problem as an illness, which often includes mandating that the doctors do something about it. Medicalization has occurred with "normal life events" such as birth, death, aging, and menopause; forms of "deviance" such as madness, alcoholism, homosexuality, obesity, addictions, eating disorders, child abuse, and attention deficit hyperactivity disorder (ADHD); and common human problems like learning difficulties, infertility, and sexual dysfunction. While a wide range of problems have been medicalized, it is important to recognize that there are degrees of medicalization. For instance, although problems such as childbirth are almost completely medicalized, problems such as sexual addiction are contested and have been (at best) marginally medicalized.

Numerous analysts have been concerned with the consequences of medicalization. By expanding the medical jurisdiction, medicalization has increased the social control function of medicine. That is, medicine has become more directly involved with the social control of deviance and other problems in society. While this participation may have some social benefits, such as providing a more therapeutic rather than punitive approach to social problems, some analysts are troubled by a particular underside. With its "clinical gaze," medicalization can turn social problems into individual problems, often taking the problems out of their social context. For example, with ADHD, restless children become a clinical entity to be diagnosed and treated with medications; however, the school and the classroom—precisely where the problems are identified— are frequently ignored. Furthermore, medicalization reduces individual responsibility.. If alcoholism is a disease, then, under the medicalized label, the alcoholic may not be deemed responsible for deviant drinking. Finally, to reduce deviance or improve common human problems, medicine may be ultimately asked to use powerful forms of social control that could not be used otherwise—including psychoactive medications, types of surgery, or perhaps even genetic engineering.

The articles in part I reflect different issues around medicalization. Joseph W. Schneider, in "Deviant Drinking as a Disease: Alcoholism as a Social Accomplishment," examines how deviant drinking became seen as a disease. In particular, he focuses on the role of the Alcoholics Anonymous, the Yale Center, and the Jellineck proposition in promoting the disease model of alcoholism. Here we have a major case of medicalization where lay and medical interests aligned in the expansion of medicalization. The disease model continues to dominate alcoholism treatment to this day.

With the reinstitution of capital punishment, numerous states passed laws instituting execution by lethal injection. In the second article, *Primum Non Nocere: Chemical Execution and the Limits of Medical Social Control,* Herb Haines shows how, in the case of chemical executions, physicians can resist social pressures for medicalization and medical social control. The medical profession perceived this phenomenon as a threat to its professional interests, and thus most physicians attempted to dissociate themselves from this procedure.

The final article, "From Hyperactive Children to ADHD Adults: Observations on the Expansion of Medical Categories," by Peter Conrad and Deborah Potter, traces the rise of adult attention deficit hyperactivity disorder. Childhood ADHD, previously termed "hyperactivity," became a common diagnosis for children's problem behavior in the 1970s, but it wasn't until the 1990s that the adult ADHD was diagnosed and treated. This article shows how once a medical diagnosis is established, the range of medicalized problems can increase through what can be called "diagnostic expansion." The authors ask whether this diagnostic expansion is a new manifestation of the disorder or a form of "the medicalization of underperformance."

CHAPTER 1

Deviant Drinking as Disease
ALCOHOLISM AS A SOCIAL ACCOMPLISHMENT

Joesph W. Schneider

This paper presents a brief social history of the idea that certain kinds of deviant drinking behavior should be identified by the label "disease." The historical location is the United States since roughly the end of the eighteenth century. I define the claim that such behavior is a disease as a social and political construction, warranting study in its own right (Berger and Luckmann, 1966; MacAndrew, 1969; Mulford 1969; Freidson, 1790; Spector and Kitsuse, 1977). Whether such drinking "really" is a disease and, as such, what its causes might be, are not at issue. The analysis will trace the connection between ideas and social structures which appear to support or "own" them (Gusfield, 1975). This study is an investigation of the social bases of an assertion about a drinking behavior. More generally, this discusstoin is a case example of the medicalization of deviance and social control (Pitts, 1968; Szasz, 1970; Freidson, 1970:244–247; Kittrie, 1971; Zola, 1972; Conrad, 1976) wherein a form of non-normative behavior is labelled first a "sin," then a "crime," and finally a "sickness."[1]

Clarification of the Problem

To those who treat problems caused by alcohol, debates about the definition of alcoholism as a disease are tedious and academic. After all, if one is employed in a hospital clinic treating alcoholics, then alcoholism must be a disease. However, whether something is a disease depends on significant portions of the medical community accepting the definition or not opposing its use by those in other fields. Because physicians represent the dominant healing profession in most industrialized societies, they have control over the use of the labels "sickness," "illness," and "disease," even if they are sometimes unable to treat those conditions effectively (Freidson, 1970:251). As such, these designations become political rather than scientific achievements (Spector and Kitsuse, 1977). Zola (1972) captures the expansive quality of medical jurisdiction clearly:

> My contention is that if anything can be shown in some way to effect the inner workings of the body and to a lesser extent the mind, then it can be labeled an "illness" or jurisdictionally a "medical problem."

This becomes particularly likely when the effect Zola describes are defined as negative rather than positive. The label "sick," although free from the opprobrium and implied culpability of "criminal," nevertheless involves a clearly disvalued moral condition, a deviation from "health, and a threat to the on-going network of interaction" (Parsons, 1951). This common moral dimension provides the foundation for the historical shift from one system of social control (the church and state) increasingly to another (science and medicine).

Although it is clear that what is usually called "deviant drinking" fits Zola's description, I am here concerned with only a small segment of the medical model of alcohol: I focus on the idea that a particular pattern of repetitive, usually heavy, and always consequential drinking behavior should, of itself, be considered an instance of disease. A closely related yet distinct issue is the belief that some prior condition, usually identified as "pathological," causes the drinking which is seen as a "symptom" of this prior, and analytically distinct, pathology. Nor am I concerned with medicine's jurisdiction over the pharmacological, physiological, or psychological effects on the body, although this jurisdiction is, nonetheless, political.[2] I am concerned with the assertion that there is a disease called alcoholism that is identifiable independent of the specification of any conditions believed to be causes or effects of it.

Colonial Foundations and Origins of the Disease Concept

Drinking in seventeenth and eighteenth century America was normative and although disapproved, drunkenness was far from rare (Lender, 1978; Levine, 1978; Paredes, 1976; Keller 1976). If anything was "bad" about drinking it was not drink itself, which even prominent clergy called a "good creature of God." Churches and drinking houses, as social centers of the community, were often close together. Concern about public drunkenness was expressed by a small few scholarly, aristocratic church leaders who warned against the sin of drunken excess, sometimes attributed to the work of the Devil. Punishment was initially a clerical admonition, followed by the extreme sanction of suspension, and finally by excommunication as the ultimate, although probably infrequently used, religious control. Civil authorities affirmed the church's judgment and meted out various forms of public degradation: fines, ostracism, whippings, and imprisonment (Lender, 1973).

The colonists, like their ancestors and descendents, distinguished between being drunk and habitual drunkenness. The latter not only made the drinker a public spectacle but had deleterious effects on health, family, and the larger community. Historically, it is this puzzling—and apparently irrational—pattern of repeated, highly consequential drinking that calls for an explanation (MacAndrew, 1969). The proposed solution reflects the interests and ideologies of the time as well as the "world views" of specialists charged with providing such answers (Holzner, 1972:122–162). The religious heritage of the colonies defined such behavior as due to the drinker's will, freely operating in terms of a rational, hedonistic calculus. This kind of drinking, if repeated, was often taken as an indicator of moral degeneration. The "ownership" of the problem of drunkenness during this period fell to leading clergy and civil authorities, joined occasionally by prominent citizens concerned about the use of spiritous liquors among workers, farmhands, and other persons of lesser station.

The idea the extended drunkenness might be the joint result of the drink and qualities of the drinker that might be beyond his control, was first synthesized by the highly respected physician, Benjamin Rush, in his *An Inquiry of the Effects of Ardent Spirits upon the Human Body and Mind,* published originally in 1784 (Levine, 1978; Wilkerson, 1966:42–20). Rush studied the bodily effects on various forms of alcoholic drink and provided what is probably the first systematic, clinical picture of intoxication. Most significant is Rush's description of inebriety was the connection between drinker and drink defined as an "addiction" to distilled liquors. He believed the disease developed gradually and was progressive, ultimately producing a "loss of control" over drinking. He called inebriety a "disease of the will," assuming that one's will and desire were independent of each other and that the former became weakened and ultimately debilitated by excessive drink. The first step in treatment was abstinence from alcohol.

Although Rush did not specify the mechanisms by which this disease of the will developed, his ideas provided an alternative to the traditional morality of the church. In trying to solve the puzzle of habitual drunkenness, some physicians began to employ science as a framework in which new solutions might be found. They avoided the traditional description of the drinker's "love" of drink and supplied new terms, such as "craving," and "insatiable desire" to describe the link between the individual and alcohol. Important for questions of individual responsibility, this conceptualization implied that since such persons are not willful in their chronic drunkenness, punishment is not an appropriate strategy of control. Treatment and therapy, allegedly employed in the individual's and the community's interest, became the "reasonable" and humanitarian solution. The historical trend whereby persons deemed incapable of willful criminal or wrong intent have been subjected to "treatment" rather than punishment has been called the "divestment" of the criminal justice system and the rise of the "therapeutic state" (Kittrie, 1971; Szasz, 1970). Rush's concept of alcohol addiction represents the beginning of this divestment process for habitual deviant drinking behavior in America.

The Disease Concept and the American Temperance Movement

Rush and his fellow "temperance physicians" provided two themes that became particularly important in the nineteenth century temperance movement. First, they established that alcohol causes both deviant physiology and deviant behavior. Their descriptions became grist for the temperance mill. Facing arguments on both physical and social grounds, the "social drinker" found it more difficult to resist the temperance call. The second theme was the statement that inebriety is a disease, which quickly became a slogan of the movement (Levine, 1978).

The plausibility of Rush's interpretation depended on the decline of the philosophy of free will and the rise of the idea that one's behavior could be determined by forces beyond one's control; that one's will and desire were distinct (Levine, 1978). Demonic possession was an unacceptable solution. The apparently irrational nature of repetitive drunkenness remained a puzzle. However, science slowly provided some solutions. Although crude by contemporary standards, medical explanations referred to natural laws in an "objective," non-mystical fashion. Loss of control was increasingly assumed to be the result of an unknown but natural disease process, an idea that supplied at least the borders of the habitual drunkenness puzzle.

Such a characterization allowed temperance leaders to draw on a cultural universal. Disease, however defined, is undesirable. It should be opposed, controlled, and if possible, eradicated, and by logical extension, so should all known or suspected causes of disease. The physicians who called inebriety a disease provided the movement with an evil more pervasive than sin itself. Rush's prescription of abstinence was also turned to use as "the" temperance solution for any problem drinking. An important consequence of the use, politically, of the disease concept was that the idea was not examined as an intellectual or scientific claim during most of the nineteenth century. As a moral slogan it allowed advocates both to pity the sick inebriate who required treatment and to rail against "Demon Rum" and even moderate drinking as something that demanded control.

An intellectually noteworthy but politically inconsequential exception did occur toward the end of the century. Trying to succeed where traditional intuitions such as prisons and mental asylums had failed, a small group of physicians founded the inebriate asylum: a special place to provide physical and moral care to regenerate inebriates' diseased wills. The first was opened in Binghamton, New York, in 1867, although the Washingtonian Home for inebriates in Boston had begun operation about two decades before. By 1900, there were more than fifty such institutions operating in the United States (Wilkerson, 1966:142–151). They were regarded skeptically both by the temperance movement and the medical community; the general public was even more hostile because of the use of public monies (Jellinek, 1960). It was not until 1872, when the superintendent physicians formed an association to study and combat the problem of inebriety as a disease caused by sinful indulgence, that the National Temperance Society issued its reserved endorsement:

> The Temperance press always regarded drunkenness as a sin and a disease—
> a sin first, then a disease; and we rejoice that the Inebriate Association are
> now substantially on the same platform (Quoted in Levine, 1978).

The physician-superintendents and a number of interested colleagues, mostly psychiatrists, began to publish a journal devoted to the belief that inebriety is a disease. The *Journal of Inebriety* was first published in 1876, and continued, on a precarious basis, until 1914. Its approach was distinctly psychiatric. It reinforced the idea that inebriety was a special kind of mental illness. Neither the *Journal* nor the association received the support of the psychiatric community or medical profession. Although one explanation of this reception might be the poor quality of research reported in the journal, it is more insightful to consider: the relatively low status of psychiatry or alienism in American medicine; the moral stigma attached to working with and in support of inebriates; the political controversy surrounding the inebriate hospitals coupled with the weak position of the medical profession in the public consciousness. Regardless of the scientific quality of the disease-advocates' work, these conditions would preclude professional and popular support.

The Post-Prohibition Rediscovery: The Yale Center, Alcoholics Anonymous, and the Jellinek Model

As Gusfield (1975) has suggested, there was virtually no organized interest in the disease concept from the end of the nineteenth century until after prohibition. There was considerable interest, however, in science and the professionalization of scientific research in American universities (Ben-David, 1971:139–168). As the moral crusade against alcohol waned, science and scientific work became established. This trend had a great impact on the solutions Americans would pose for a variety of problems. It was not likely that alcohol, popular and again legal after 1933, would be seen as the source of deviant drinking. Intoxication and drunkenness, when requiring control, were problems assigned to civil authorities or the state. But with the rise and achievements of science, the apparent irrationality of chronic drunkenness became a more intriguing and less tolerable mystery.

In this context even more than during Rush's time, science and medicine seemed to hold promise. Three developments, all beginning within a decade after repeal, provided the foundation on which a "new" conceptualization of chronic deviant drinking was to rise in the twentieth century: The Yale research center; the self-help group, Alcoholics Anonymous; and a more careful, largely non-psychiatric, specification of the claim "alcoholism is a disease," referred to here as the Jellinek model. These developments provided the moral and political foundation for the subsequent rise of the more than two hundred million dollar federal bureaucracy, the National Institute on Alcohol Abuse and Alcoholism (NIAAA), and an "alcoholism industry" (Trice and Roman, 1972:11–12) of professional and other workers devoted to treating this disease.

THE YALE RESEARCH CENTER

The major body coordinating support for scientific work in the mid-1930s was the Research Council on Problems of Alcohol, organized shortly after repeal (Keller, 1976). This council was composed disproportionately of physicians and natural scientists interested in finding the causes of alcoholism. One member of the committee was Howard Haggard, the physician-director of the Laboratory of Applied Physiology at Yale University. Although the Council was unsuccessful in raising substantial monies for alcohol research, the prominence of its members gave the work scientific respectability. One grant, however, was consequential. It was for a review of the literature on the biological effects of alcohol on humans. The Council called on E.M. Jellinek, who had been doing research on neuroendocrine schizophrenia, to administer the project.

Haggard and his colleagues at Yale Laboratory were involved in alcohol metabolism and nutritional research, a study which was gaining attention through the journal he founded in 1940, *The Quarterly Journal of Studies on Alcohol*.[3] As this work became more interdisciplinary within the natural sciences, Haggard came to believe that adequate study required an even more comprehensive approach. He invited E.M. Jellinek to Yale where he became the director of a truly multidisciplinary Yale Center for Alcohol Studies. The Center, the Laboratory, and the *Journal* became the core of American research on alcohol.[4] One of the Center's most significant contributions to the idea that alcoholism is a disease was its Summer School program, begun in 1943. These annual sessions were educational programs for concerned citizens from around the country who were involved in policy formation in their local communities. A common concern was what to do about alcoholism and alcohol-related problems. Straus (1976) and Chafetz and Demone (1962) suggest that the slogan "alcoholism is a disease" was introduced intentionally by Center staff in an attempt to reorient local and state policy and thinking about "alcoholics." These summer sessions were a good opportunity to disseminate the idea and point out its moral and political implications for treatment and cure. Although only a small segment of the summer program was devoted to the disease question, it soon became a topic of interest among the lay audience. Critics of this idea (Seeley, 1962; Pattison, 1969; Room, 1972; Robinson, 1976) suggest that its appeal must be seen in historical perspective and should be understood in terms of its practical, humanitarian, and administrative consequences rather than on the basis of scientific merit.[5]

These sessions also provided an established organizational foundation for the rise of the National Council of Alcoholism, the leading voluntary association in the United States devoted to public education about the disease (Chafetz and Demone, 1962; Paredes, 1976). The National Council, known initially as the National Committee for Education on Alcoholism, was established in 1944 by three women: a former alcoholic, a journalist, and a psychiatrist. Mrs. Marty Mann, a one-time member of Alcoholics Anonymous, saw the National Committee as supplementing the work of A.A. for public education against ignorance about alcoholism's disease status. In the spring of 1944, these women met with Jellinek and determined that the National Committee "plan" be introduced in the Yale Summer School program. At the time of the original incorporation of the National Committee, its close connection with the Yale Center is evidenced by the Committee's officers: Howard Haggard was named President; E.M. Jellinek was Chairman of the Board; Professor Seldon Bacon of Yale was secretary, and Professor Edward Baird, also of Yale, was the Committee's legal counsel (Chafetz and Demone, 1962:142):

> NCA then began to search for a formula, something which would translate the basic facts of alcoholism into easily understood and remembered phrases. This resulted in the well known concepts or credo: Alcoholism is a disease and the alcoholic a sick person. The alcoholic can be helped and is worth helping. This is a public health problem and therefore a public responsibility.

ALCOHOLICS ANONYMOUS

In 1935 Alcoholics Anonymous was founded by two men, one of whom was a physician. Another physician, Dr. W. D. Silkworth, suggested to these founders the idea that alcoholism is an allergy of the body, the result of a physiological reaction to alcohol (Jellinek, 1960:160). Although medical opinion was generally skeptical of this questionable formulation (Jellinek, 1960:86–88), the concept of alcoholism as a mark of physiological sensitivity rather than moral decay was appealing and the allergy concept came to occupy a central although implicit place in A.A. ideology. This theory had an additional advantage over other versions of the disease concept common during the early decades of the century that suggested alcoholism was a mental illness, a notion opposed strongly by A.A. (Trice and Roman, 1970). The appeal of allergy rests precisely in its identity as a bona fide medical or "disease" condition; people with allergies are victimized by, not responsible for, their condition. Trice and Roman (1970) suggest that much of the apparent success of A.A. involves the process of removing a stigmatized label and replacing it with a socially acceptable identity, such as "sick," "repentant," "recovered," or "controlled."

Two themes relevant to A.A.'s implicit disease concept are found in the first and third of the famous "Twelve Steps" to recovery, printed originally in *Alcoholics Anonymous* (1939). The first and most important step is, "We admitted we were powerless over alcohol—that our lives had become unmanageable." This is precisely the concept of "loss of control," a key idea in the early writing on alcoholism as a disease. Step three is "(We) have made a decision to turn our will and our lives over to the care of God as we understood him." Representatives of A.A. are quick to note that although this language sounds traditionally religious, such terms are to be interpreted broadly and on the basis of the individual's own biography. In discussing the interpretation of step three, Norris (1976) says:

> This turning over of self direction is akin perhaps to the acceptance of a regimen prescribed by a physician for a disease. The decision is made to accept reality, to stop trying to run things, and to let the "Power greater than ourselves" take over.

This partial description of the role of A.A. recalls Parson's (1951) discussion of the sick role. Norris's suggestion that "God" might be interpreted to be a physician is perhaps not an extreme exaggeration given a doctor's control over the legitimacy of sickness and disease designations and admission to treatment.

The success attributed to the A.A. program in helping drinkers "recover" from alcoholism has become part of popular wisdom and is largely unchallenged, despite the lack of systematic empirical evidence. The effect of A.A. programs and ideology on thinking about alcoholism has been humanitarian and educational. The generally high regard for the program throughout the country serves to reinforce the disease concept implied in its approach. This pattern of regard is evidenced by recent research showing that a majority of physicians who agreed that alcoholism is a disease felt that referring such cases to A.A. was the best professional strategy (Jones and Helrich, 1972).

THE JELLINEK MODEL

The Yale Center and Alcoholics Anonymous provided important structural vehicles for the spread and popularization of the disease definition. Without the research and writing of Jellinek, and later Mark Keller (neither of whom, incidentally, are physicians), this idea would probably have remained largely undeveloped. By comparison with previous efforts, Jellinek's work on the disease concept was brilliant and stimulated further research and writing. His reputation as a medical researcher, coupled with his being the director of the Yale Center, established his work as worthy of serious consideration. Excluding Howard Haggard, no one of Jellinek's stature since Rush had chosen to address the question at length.

In a series of articles beginning shortly after his arrival in New Haven and subsequently in a comprehensive manuscript, *The Disease Concept of Alcoholism* (1960), Jellinek (1941, 1946, 1952) set out his understanding of what it meant to call alcoholism a disease. In the early paper with psychiatrist Bowman (1941) as first author, Jellinek raised the question of alcoholism as an addiction. Using data obtained from a questionnaire in an issue of the A.A. *Grapevine,*[6] he constructed his well-known phase progression of the disease (Jellinek, 1946). A revision and extension was published in 1952 titled "The Phases of Alcohol Addiction," which appeared initially under the auspices of the Alcoholism Subcommittee of the World Health Organization, of which Jellinek was a member. Five phases of the progressive disease of alcohol addiction[7] were presented in terms of characteristic drinking and drinking-related behaviors. A major purpose of this paper, beyond presenting the phase progression, was to resurrect and clarify a distinction central to the disease concept. Drinking behavior that results in problems of living, or problem drinking, while important in its own right, was to be kept quite distinct from drinking behavior indicative of disease.[8] Such a distinction is important for the viability of the disease view: first because it serves to define the boundaries within which medicine could (and should, according to Jellinek) operate; second, because it suggests that forms of deviant drinking not properly called disease should be "managed only on the level of applied sociology, including law enforcement" (Jellinek, 1952). Non-disease forms of drinking behavior are here defined as moral problems to be met on moral terms; disease forms are, by contrast, medical problems and deserve the attention and treatment of the medical profession. Without defining alcoholism,[9] Jellinek proposes two subcategories of this larger entity: "alcohol addicts" and "habitual symptomatic excessive drinkers." Although both types have "underlying psychological or social pathology" that leads to drinking, only the former, after a number of years, develops a "loss of control," becomes addicted to alcohol, and is therefore diseased.

"Loss of control" as the distinction between the disease and non-disease types of alcoholism is elaborated in Jellinek's major work, *The Disease Concept of Alcoholism* (1960), which provides and exhaustive review of relevant research and a clearer description of the kinds of behaviors typically called "alcoholism." Using Greek letters to designate distinct types, Jellinek describes four major categories: Alpha, Beta, Gamma, and Delta (1960:36–39). The first two, Alpha and Beta, are not distinct disease entities: Alpha is the symptomatic drinking discussed in the 1952 essay; Beta refers specifically to all physical disease conditions resulting from pro-longed substantial drinking, for example, polyneuropathy, gastritis, and cirrhosis of the liver. Only the Gamma and Delta types qualify as disease entities and are de-fined by four key elements three of which are unambiguously physiological and common to both: 1) acquired increased tissue tolerance to alcohol, 2) adaptive cell metabolism, and 3) withdrawal symptoms. These three conditions lead to "craving" or physical dependence on alcohol. In addition, Gamma alcoholics lose control over how much they drink, which involves a progression from psychological to physiological dependence. Jellinek identified this type as most typical of the United States; as causing the greatest personal and social damage; and as the type of alco-holism recognized by Alcoholics Anonymous. The Delta alcoholic differs from Gamma in losing control not over quantity of intake, but rather over the ability to abstain for a significant period. As a result, this type of alcoholic, while suffering from the disease of alcoholism, rarely experiences the devastating consequences of the Gamma type. Jellinek suggests that the Delta drinking pattern is characteristic in certain European countries, particularly France. Although the disease is seen as a product of drinking, in neither case are the initial causes important in identifying the disease itself.

Jellinek's explicit development of addiction as the defining quality of the disease was a necessary condition for the contemporary medicalization of deviant drinking. Although addiction is itself not a particularly precise concept (see Coleman (1976) and Grinspoon and Bakalar (1976:177–178) for recent critiques), its contemporary associ-ation with narcotics and their physiological effects renders it a medicalized condition. Use of the term serves to locate the above forms of alcoholism in the body,[10] thus iden-tifying them as legitimate problems for medial attention and intervention. Medicine reluctantly assumed responsibility. In 1956, The American Medical Association's Com-mittee on Alcoholism (A.M.A., 1956) issued its well known statement encouraging medical personnel and institutions to accept persons presenting the syndrome of alco-holism defined by excessive drinking and "certain signs and symptoms of behavioral, personality, and physical disorder." A key sentence in the statement asserts:

> The Council on Mental Health, its Committee on Alcoholism, and the pro-fession in general recognizes this syndrome of alcoholism as illness which justifiably should have the attention of physicians (A.M.A., 1956:750).

State and local medical societies soon created their own committees on alcoholism based on this reaffirmation of an idea that had already achieved a certain degree of official recognition. Keller (1976a) notes that "Alcohol Addiction" and "Alco-holism" were included in the first volume of the Standard Classified Nomenclature of Disease issued by the National Conference on Nomenclature of Disease in 1933 and approved by the American Medical Association. The significance of the 1956 statement was to reiterate this and other previous definitions. Regardless of how many American physicians agreed with the A.M.A. statement, the formal re-endorsement of the idea that alcoholics fall properly within medical jurisdiction be-came compelling "evidence" in support of the disease concept.[11] In this context,

Jellinek's (1960:12) comments on whether his Gamma and Delta types are "really" diseases are instructive:

> Physicians know what belongs in their realm. . . . a disease is what the medical profession recognizes as such. . . . the medical profession has officially accepted alcoholism as an illness, whether a part of the public likes it or not, and even if a minority of the medical profession is disinclined to accept the idea.

Almost impatiently, the concept's leading proponent argues that diseases are what physicians say they are and since physicians, as represented by their major professional organization, have said so, alcoholism is a disease and that should settle the matter!

Since Jellinek's death in 1963, the leading spokesman for the disease concept has been Mark Keller, longtime colleague of Jellinek at the Yale Center and editor of the *Journal of Studies on Alcohol,* a position he has held since its inception in 1940.[12] In two early essays, Keller (1958, 1962) attempted to develop a definition of alcoholism consistent with the disease view but useful also in epidemiological and survey research. In the first essay, he defines alcoholism as a "chronic behavioral disorder" in which repeated drinking exceeds "dietary and social uses of the community" and causes harm to the drinker's health and social and economic functioning. The two key and familiar elements are that the drinking is deviant and causes harm. Although ambiguous on the question of disease, Keller agrees with Jellinek's position that persons apparently addicted to alcohol suffer from the disease of alcoholism. In a subsequent essay, Keller (1962) provides a "medical definition" of alcoholism as a "psychogenic dependence on or a physiological addition to" alcohol, the defining characteristic of which is "loss of control." He translates the latter idea in behavioral terms: "Whenever an alcoholic starts to drink it is not certain that he will be able to stop at will." In an attempt to show the links between harm due to drinking, loss of control, and the existence of disease, Keller gives revealing insight into the intellectual core of the idea that chronic drunkenness is a disease:

> The key criterion, for all ill effects, is this: Would the individual be expected to reduce his drinking (or give it up) in order to avoid the injury or its continuance? If the answer is yes and he does not do so, it is assumed—admitting it is only an assumption—that he cannot, hence that he has "lost control over drinking," that he is addicted to or dependent on alcohol. This inference is the heart of the matter. Without evident or at least reasonably inferred loss of control, there is no foundation for the claim that "alcoholism is a disease," except in the medical dictionary sense of diseases . . . caused by alcohol poisoning . . . (Keller, 1962).

In order to extend the research use of the disease concept, Keller applies canons of reason and medicine to the behavioral puzzle of repeated, highly consequential drinking: (1) If one drinks in an excessive, deviant manner, (2) so as to bring deprivation and harm to self and others (3) while remaining impervious to pleas and admonitions based on this "obvious" connection, (4) the person is assumed not to be in control of his or her will (regardless of desire); (5) such lack of control is then "explained" by the medical concept disease and the medicalized concept addiction, inherent in which is the presumption of limited or diminished responsibility. Resting on the inference of loss of control in a cultural system in which values of rationality, personal control, science, and medicine are given prominence, the assertion that alcoholism is a disease becomes an affirmation of dominant cultural and institutional values on which empirical data are never brought to bear. Indeed, it is precisely this quality of the question that holds the key to its viability as well as its controversy: it is a statement not for scientific scrutiny but for political debate.

Keller's (1976a) most recent defense of the idea supports this contention. In a style at once more polemical and less cautious that that of his mentor Jellinek, Keller reiterates that alcoholism is a "dysbehaviorism" typified by deviant drinking that causes harm; that "It is the same as alcohol addiction and classified as a chronic disease of uncertain etiology and undetermined site." Wishing to base his argument on logic, Keller defines disease to mean the same as "disablement" of physical or mental functioning, in effect saying that alcoholism is a behavior disorder that impairs typical functioning and is therefore a disease because disease is a disablement. Using this circular and inclusive argument Keller proceeds to defend the disease concept against all detractors, both real and imagined, taking liberty with the critical arguments he chooses to cite.[13] Keller's defense has a particularly *ad hominem* quality illustrated by the following remarks concerning skeptic's motives (1976a):

> It is possible that some people look with envy—unconscious, of course—at those fellows who are having an uproariously good time at everybody else's expense, getting irresponsibly drunk and then demanding to be cared for and coddled—at public cost yet.
> Another motive is apparent in those who, not being M.D.'s, think they know better than doctors how to treat alcoholism. . . . It is understandable that some people would feel uncomfortable—they might even perceive it to be illegal—to be treating a disease without a license to practice medicine. But if only it is not a disease—why, then they are in business![14]

Not only are the critics' characters under attack, but, as Keller's discussion makes clear, they also run the risk of definition as anti-medical, unhumanitarian, and, perhaps worst, modern day moral crusaders. His attempts at "logic" notwithstanding, Keller is primarily a disciple arguing that the disease formulation is revealed truth, and that skeptics and detractor, whether physicians or social scientists, are heretics. Such, of course, is the quality of ideological debate.

Conclusions

The purpose of this paper has been to develop a social historical overview of the major structural and cultural supports of the idea that certain forms of deviant drinking behavior should be considered as instances of disease. I have not attempted to defend the empirical validity of this idea. Indeed, such an attempt would produce a tautological discussion. The question of whether or not a given condition constitutes a disease involves issues of politics and ideology—questions of definition, not fact. The disease concept of alcoholism has a long history in America and has been supported both by medical and non-medical people and organizations for a wide variety of reasons. That certain forms of deviant drinking are now or have been for more than one hundred and fifty years medicalized is not due to a medical "hegemony," but reflects the interests of the several groups and organizations assuming, or being given, responsibility for behaviors associated with chronic drunkenness in the United States. The disease concept owes its life to these variously interested parties, rather than to substantive scientific findings. As such, the disease concept of alcoholism is primarily a social rather than a scientific or medical accomplishment.

Notes

1. The medicalization of a variety of forms of deviance and social control is discussed in Conrad and Schneider (1980), which contains a considerably expanded version of this paper.

2. Seldon Bacon has pointed out to me that the recent controversy over alcohol use among pregnant women attests to the political nature of even these "obvious" medical questions.

3. This journal, which in 1975 became *The Journal of Studies on Alcohol* and is issued monthly, is perhaps the key international publication on alcohol research, its tenure of continuous publication being second only to the *British Journal of Addiction*, which began in 1892 as *The British Journal of Inebriety*.

4. In 1962 the Yale Center was moved to Rutgers—the State University, where it remains one of the most prestigious of the few such centers in the world. Straus (1976) provides some insight into the social and political history leading to this move. He suggests that the wide publicity the Yale Center received was an embarrassment to the University because of the substance of the Center's work, and that its interdisciplinary quality was perceived as inappropriate in the context of the traditional departmental structure of the University.

5. Trice and Roman (1968) suggest some unintended consequences of adopting the sick role that may serve to perpetuate and perhaps reinforce the individual's self-definition as one who cannot control his or her drinking.

6. The A.A. *Grapevine* began publication in 1944 and continues as a monthly magazine comprised of items written mainly, although not exclusively, by alcoholics themselves about A.A. and alcoholism (Norris, 1976).

7. Jellinek called these phases the prealcoholic symptomatic phase, the prodromal phase, the crucial phase (wherein loss of control develops), and the chronic phase. The retrospective "discovery" of these phases is not unlike similar discovery processes discussed recently for hyperactivity (Conrad, 1976) and child abuse (Pfohl, 1977). Analysis of such diagnostic categories from a sociology of knowledge perspective suggests that they represent a particular organization of information that serves or reinforces values, assumptions, or beliefs held by the discoverers. Using disease as his guiding assumption, Jellinek decidedly increased the probability of "discovering" phase movement and progression, given the processural, temporal imagery that this concept conveys (Fabrega, 1972; Room, 1974).

8. Recent research by Cahalan and Room (1974) on problem drinking among American men suggests the importance of distinctions between "problem drinkers" and "alcoholics" to be less than once thought and perhaps misleading in terms of the typical history of drinking problems. This and previous research (Trice and Wahl, 1958) also questions the popular notice of the inevitable progression of alcoholism. For a thorough, critical review of these and other disease propositions, see Pattison, et al. (1977).

9. In avoiding a conceptual definition of alcoholism, Jellinek is not unlike many if not most students of the problem (see Bacon, 1976, for a complete and critical discussion of the definitional chaos in this field of study).

10. The medicalization of deviance does not depend solely on the presence of physiological dimensions. Other conditions, such as the availability of relevant and efficacious technology, moral and ethical considerations, and a supportive political context, must be considered (see Conrad, 1976:92–100, for preliminary discussion).

11. Fingarette (1970) discusses the impact of the disease concept of alcoholism in the law and in key United States Supreme Court ruling based thereon.

12. Keller has recently assumed the position of editor emeritus for the *Journal.*

13. For example:

> Sociologists, no less humane [than social workers], object to classifying alcoholism as a disease because that involves labeling people. This concern is especially touching in the case of alcoholism and alcoholics, labels that tend to stigmatize (Keller, 1976a).

Keller gives no citation to support this allegation and although frequent reference is made to "social scientist" critics, work cited in this regard appears to be by psychiatrists and other physicians, e.g., Thomas Szasz.

14. Keller's (1967a) faith in the disease status of alcoholism and physician's abilities to diagnose it is steadfast: ". . . I have never met a physician who could not diagnose alcoholism if he was willing."

References

Alcoholics Anonymous. 1939. Alcoholics Anonymous. New York: A.A. World Services.

The American Medical Association. 1956. "Report of the board of trustees: Hospitalization of patients with alcoholism." Journal of The American Medical Association 162(October 20):750

Bacon, Selden D. 1976. "Concepts." Pp. 57–134 in W. Filstead, J. Rossi, M. Keller (eds), Alcohol and Alcohol Problems. Cambridge, Massachusetts: Ballinger.

Ben-David, Joseph. 1971. The Scientist's Role in Society. Englewood Cliffs, N.J.: Prentice-Hall.

Berger, Peter L., and Thomas Luckmann. 1966. The Social Construction of Reality. Garden City, N.Y.: Anchor.

Bowman, K.M., and E.M. Jellinek. 1941. "Alcohol addiction and chronic alcoholism." Quarterly Journal of Studies on Alcohol 2:98–176.

Cahalan, Don, and Robin Room. 1974. Problem Drinking Among American Men: A Mongraph. New Brunswick, N.J.: Rutgers Center for Alcohol Studies.

Chafetz, Morris E., and Harold W. Demone, Jr. 1962. Alcoholism and Society. New York: Oxford University Press.

Coleman, James W. 1976. "The myth of addiction." Journal of Drug Issues 6(Spring):135–141.

Conrad, Peter. 1976. Identifying Hyperactive Children: The Medicalization of Deviant Behavior. Lexington, Massachusetts: D.C. Heath.

Conrad, Peter and Joseph W. Schneider. 1980. Deviance and Medicalization: From Badness to Sickness. St. Louis: Mosby.

Fabrega, Horacio Jr. 1972. "Concepts of disease: Logical features and social implications." Perspectives in Biology and Medicine 15(Summer):583–616.

Fingarette, Herbert. 1970. "The perils of Powell: In search of a factual foundation for the 'disease concept of alcoholism'." Harvard Law Review 83:793–812.

Freidson, Eliot. 1970. The Profession of Medicine. New York: Dodd, Mead.

Grinspoon, Lester, and James B. Bakalar. 1976. Cocaine. New York: Basic Books.

Gusfield, Joseph. 1975. "Categories of ownership and responsibility in social issues: alcohol use and automobile use." Journal of Drug Issues 5(Fall):285–303.

Holzner, Burkart. 1972. Reality Construction in Society. Revised Edition. Cambridge, Mass.: Schenkman.

Jellinek, E.M. 1946. "Phases in the drinking history of alcoholics." Quarterly Journal of Studies on Alcohol 7:1–88.

———. 1952. "Phases of alcohol addiction." Quarterly Journal of Studies on Alcohol 13:673-684.

———. 1960. The Disease Concept of Alcoholism. Highland Park, N.J.: Hillhouse.

Jones, R. W., and A.R. Helrich. 1972. "Treatment of alcoholism by physicians in private practice: a national survey." Quarterly Journal of Studies on Alcohol 33:117–131.

Keller, Mark. 1958. "Alcoholism: nature and extent of the problem." The Annals of the American Academy of Political and Social Science 315:1–11.

———.1962. "The definition of alcoholism and the estimation of its prevalence." Pp. 310–329 in D.J. Pittman and C.R. Synder (eds), Society, Culture and Drinking Patterns. New York: Wiley.

———.1976. "Problems with alcohol: An historical perspective." Pp. 5–28 in W. Filstead, J. Rossi, M. Keller (eds.), Alcohol and Alcohol Problems. Cambridge, Massachusetts: Ballinger.

———.1976a. "The disease concept of alcoholism revisited." Journal of Studies on Alcohol 37(September): 1694–1717.

Kittrie, Nicholas. 1971. The Right to be Different. Baltimore: Johns Hopkins Press

Lender, Mark. 1973. "Drunkenness as an offense in early New England: A study of Puritan attitudes." Quarterly Journal of Studies on Alcohol 34:353–366.

Levine, Harry Gene. 1978. "The discovery of addiction: Changing conceptions of habitual drunkenness in America." Journal of Studies on Alcohol 39(January):143–174.

MacAndrew, Craig. 1969. "On the notion that certain persons who are given to frequent drunkenness suffer from a disease called alcoholism. Pp. 483–501 in S.C. Plog and R.B. Edgerton (eds.), Changing Perspectives in Mental Illness. New York: Holt, Rinehart and Winston.

Mulford, Harold. 1969. "Alcoholics," "Alcoholism" and "Problem Drinkers": Social Objects in the Making. Washington, D.C.: National Center for Health Statistics, Department of Health, Educaiton and Welfare.

National Conference on Nomenclature of Disease. 1933. A Standard Classified Nomenclature of Disease. H.B. Logie (ed). New York: Commonwealth Fund.

Norris, John L. 1976. "Alcoholics anonymous and other self-help groups." Pp. 735–776 in R. Tarter and A. Sugerman (eds.), Alcoholism. Reading, Massachusetts: Addison-Wesley.

Paredes, Alfonso. 1976. "The history of the concept of alcoholism." Pp. 9–52 in R. Tarter and A. Sugerman (eds.), Alcoholism. Reading, Massachusetts: Addison-Wesley.

Parsons, Talcott. 1951. The Social System. New York: The Free Press.

Pattison, E.M. 1969. "Comment on the alcoholic game." Quarterly Journal of Studies on Alcohol 30:953.

Pattison, E.M., Mark Sobell, and Linda Sobell. 1975. Emerging Concepts of Alcohol Dependence. New York: Springer.

Pfohl, Stephen J. 1977. "The 'discovery' of child abuse." Social Problems 24(February): 310–323.

Pitts, Jesse. 1968 "Social control: the concept." International Encyclopedia of the Social Sciences, no. 14. New York: Macmillian.

Robinson, David. 1976. From Drinking to Alcoholism: A Sociological Commentary. New York: Wiley.

Roman, Paul M., and H.M. Trice. 1968. "The sick role, labelling theory, and the deviant drinker." International Journal of Social Psychiatry 14:245–251.

Room, Robin. 1972. "Drinking and disease: Comment on 'the alcohologist's addiction'." Quarterly Journal of Studies on Alcohol 33(December):1049–1059.

———.1974. "Governing images an the prevention of alcohol problems." Preventive Medicine 3:11–23.

Seeley, John R. 1960. "Alcoholism is a disease: implications for social policy." Pp. 586–593 in D.J. Pittman and C.R. Snyder (eds.), Society, Culture and Drinking Patterns. New York: Wiley.

Spector, Malcolm, and John I. Kitsuse. 1977. Constructing Social Problems. Menlo Park, California: Cummings.

Straus, Robert. 1976. "Problem drinking in the perspective of social change 1940–1973." Pp. 29–56 in W. Filstead, J. Rossi, M. Keller (eds.), Alcohol and Alcohol Problems. Cambridge, Massachusetts: Ballinger.

Szasz, Thomas. 1969. The Manufacture of Madness. New York: Dell.

Trice, H.M., and Paul Roman. 1972. Spirits and Demons at Work: Alcohol and Other Drugs on the Job. Ithaca, New York: New York State School of Industrial and Labor Relations, Cornell University.

———.1970 "Delabeling, relabeling, and alcoholics anonymous." Social Problems 17:538–546.

Trice, H.M., and Richard J. Wahl. 1958. "A rank order analysis of the symptoms of alcoholism."

Wilkerson, A.E. 1966. A History of the Concept of Alcoholism as a Disease. Unpublished doctoral dissertation, University of Pennsylvania.

Zola, Irving K. 1972. "Medicine as an institution of social control." Sociological Review 20:487–504.

CHAPTER 2

Primum Non Nocere

CHEMICAL EXECUTION AND THE LIMITS OF MEDICAL SOCIAL CONTROL

Herb Haines

On the morning of 7 December 1982, the state of Texas executed Charlie Brooks by injecting him with a mixture containing a sedative, a muscle relaxant, and a paralytic agent. He was the first convict in history to die by lethal injection rather than by the older methods of hanging, electrocution, lethal gas, or firing squad. At the time of Brooks' death, five states had officially adopted this method of executing prisoners (Reinhold 1982), but a total of 17 states had made similar provisions by 1986 (Zimring and Hawkins 1986).

Capital punishment by lethal injection has been the subject of intense moral and political debate since it employs what is usually seen to be a healing technology to, instead, kill people. To the delight of the death penalty's supporters and the horror of its opponents, injection apparently renders execution more palatable to many who find other methods unacceptable. But in addition to the ethical dilemmas involved, lethal injection raises an interesting theoretical issue pertaining to the medicalization of social control.

Past scholarship has tended to portray medical and mental health professionals primarily as entrepreneurs who have eagerly sought to expand their domains into arenas where medial discourse was not deemed relevant (but see Schneider and Conrad 1980; Conrad and Schneider 1980). But organized medicine has not always been eager to include new problems under its aegis. For example, it has been hesitant to embrace the disease model of alcoholism as set forth by Alcoholics Anonymous. Similarly, the idea that medical personnel and technology should be used to help the State dispose of condemned criminals—an idea that came from outside the health professions—generated immediate and intense resistance from health-related organizations.

In this paper, I describe the reaction of organized medicine to lethal injection statutes and discuss the dilemma they pose for the medical profession. I discuss the nature of medicalization and medical social control; describe how lethal injection and statutes to support it emerged in the United States since 1977; consider the resistance to lethal injection and these laws by state medical societies and national medical groups; and suggest the implications of these events for understanding the limits of medical social control.

Medicalization, Medical Social Control, and Execution by Lethal Injection

A wide variety of deviant behaviors and other human problems previously understood in moral terms have come to be reconceptualized as "disorders" and "illnesses." This process has been termed the "medicalization of deviance." Behavioral categories that have been medicalized more or less successfully include childhood hyperactivity (Conrad 1975), child abuse and family violence (Pfohl 1977; Tierney 1982; Kurz 1987), alcohol dependency (Schneider 1978), mental disorders (Conrad and Schneider 1980:38–72), homosexuality (Conrad and Schneider 1980:179–193), transexualism (Billings and Urban 1982), religious cult membership (Robbins and Anthony 1982), compulsive gambling (Rosecrance 1985), homelessness (Snow et al. 1986; Wright 1988), learning disabilities (Carrier 986) and "sexual compulsivity" (Levind and Troiden 1988).

In addition to a cognitive shift, the medicalization of deviance recasts social control as a form of "treatment" and assigns oversight to health-related personnel—physicians, psychiatrists, psychologists, public health officials, and the like. This transformation of control strategies and personnel follows from the prior reconceptualization of the behavior. Accordingly, it makes no more sense to punish a person for alcoholism than it does to punish one who suffers from tuberculosis. Nor does it make sense to hold the sufferer responsible for his or her condition/behavior in the fully moral sense of the term.

From within medicine, medicalization and medical social control are, simply, scientific enlightenment. Through a series of "discoveries," previously misunderstood behavior patterns are seen in their true light and, at long last, approached in a manner befitting a thoroughly modern, civilized society. Sociologists, however, have approached medicalization using entrepreneurial models of deviance definition, models that assume that political and professional initiative rather than objective discovery are chiefly responsible for the social construction of these new illness categories. The definition of problematic behaviors as illnesses is thus seen as not so much the inevitable consequence of scientific progress, but rather the outcome of moral and scientific crusading.

It has been noted that medicalization depoliticizes moral problems by reconceptualizing them in medial and scientific terms that are considered to be "above" morality., i.e., in the realm of "facts" and scientific certainty. Once this transformation is made, it is only a short step of logic to argue that the matters at hand, once robustly moral and open to more general popular debate, are now best left to medical experts who presumably act in the patient's best interests. In addition, as also has been noted in the case of alcoholism, those assigned to "treat" and care for (i.e., control) the newly sick can occupy a considerably more sanguine public identity. The physician or therapist enjoys more positive cultural characterizations (Kittrie 1971; Zola 1975) than, for instance, the jailor or executioner; enlightened "treatment" of sickness is preferable to brutal and harsh punishment.

In addition to enterprising physicians and health personnel, however, the parallel activities of interested parties outside medicine who may wish to support and encourage the medicalization and medical social control of deviance also can be consequential for the process. Attempts to secure official recognition for medical concepts and control strategies typically involve a range of entrepreneurial groups (Conrad and Schneider 1980), many of which are not made up of medical professionals; e.g., pharmaceutical corporations, government agencies, and diverse lay self-help groups.

Medical culture and metaphors are not the sole property of professional medicine (Schneider and Conrad 1980). This would seem to set the stage for medicine and its personnel to be appropriated by those outside interests having sufficient power and influence to do so. Dilemmas of control and legitimacy *within* medicine, then, can arise as a rather direct consequence of the expansion of the medical domain. In short, medicalization is not without its perils for the profession. Schneider and Conrad (1980) noted that the annexation of new behaviors into the domain of therapeutic control may, under some circumstances, threaten the profession's credibility, require medical personnel to deal with undesirable patients, and place doctors in the role of "double agent"—i.e., in a position in which the patient's interests do not come first.

Perhaps more than any other development, the advent of chemical execution poses such a dilemma for the profession. With the return of capital punishment in the United States, doctors have been asked to lend their expertise, their tools, or both, to assist the state in executing criminals. Paradoxically, lethal injection can be interpreted both as a logical extension and a supreme contradiction of therapeutic social control. It is logical extension of medicalization in that the physician's authority is allowed to encompass the ultimate legal sanction. It is the supreme contradiction of medicalized social control in that it brings about the death of a human being.

The Emergence of Lethal Injection as an Execution Technology

Every modern innovation in the technology of capital punishment, from the guillotine to electrocution and the gas chamber, had its origins in concerns that existing methods failed to provide quick and relatively painless deaths. Such concerns over death by hanging led a New York physician to propose in 1888 that condemned criminals be killed with morphine. Injection was also formally considered and rejected by a British Royal Commission in the late 1940s and early 1950s. The next widely publicized recommendation for chemical executions came from California Governor Ronald Reagan. Reagan likened the execution of criminals to the destroying of an injured horse, in which case a simple act by a veterinarian allows the owner to avoid the unpleasant task of shooting the animal (Zimring and Hawkins 1986).

Actual adoption of lethal injection laws did not occur until after the 1976 Supreme Court decision in *Gregg v. Georgia,* which effectively reinstated the death penalty in the United States. Facing the prospect of expensive repairs on its electric chair or the even more expensive option of constructing a gas chamber, the state of Oklahoma passed a law in 1977 calling for execution by means of a "continuous, intravenous administration of a lethal quantity of an ultrashort-acting barbiturate in combination with a chemical paralytic agent" (Bedau 1982). As the state's first scheduled execution approached, the Warden of McAlester Prison left his post rather than participate (Jendrzejczyk 1982).

Texas adopted a similar bill the day after Oklahoma did. The legislature in Texas was persuaded more by a humanitarian argument than a fiscal one (Malone 1979). The bill's Senate sponsor introduced the bill to end the circus-like atmosphere that surrounded electrocutions in that state, in the aftermath of a district judge's decision—later reversed—that electrocutions could be televised. If executions were going to be on television, he reasoned, the least gruesome of the available technologies should be employed (Bonavita 1982). Similar lethal injection statues were passed during the late 1970s and early 1980s in Idaho, New Mexico, and Washington. Sixteen other states followed suit by 1985 (Bureau of Justice Statistics 1986).

In general, procedures for lethal injections are comparable in all the states that have adopted the method. The convict is strapped to a gurney in an execution chamber, a catheter is inserted into a vein in the arm, and a saline drip is begun. Following the reading of the death warrant, the flow of the lethal mixture is started by one or more executioners. The convict is first rendered unconscious by a massive dose of barbiturates, then killed with a paralytic agent and potassium chloride, which stop breathing and induce cardiac arrest (see Finks 1983). New Jersey's lethal injection statute, passed in 1983, contained one unique feature: it called for the condemned person to be sedated prior to execution (Norman 1983).

ARGUMENTS FOR LETHAL INJECTION

Advocates of execution by lethal injection have mustered four major arguments in its favor. One of these, as mentioned in the above discussion of Oklahoma's death penalty law, rests on economy; executions by injection are relatively cheap, costing an estimated ten to fifteen dollars per "event" (Malone 1979:5; Annas 1985). The other arguments for lethal injection center around humanitarianism, political feasibility, and constitutionality. Since these are related to the medical profession's reaction to the method, I will briefly review each.

More Humanitarian

The point most frequently raised by proponents of lethal injection is that the method, if properly carried out, assures a quick and painless death. In state after state, legislative debates over lethal injection included graphic descriptions of hangings, electrocutions, and gassings, followed by assurances that the "death needle" is a dignified and peaceful procedure in which a convict simply "goes to sleep." When New Jersey was in the process of reinstating capital punishment, for instance, a major factor in choosing injection over electrocution was the work of a legal assistant to the governor. The assistant, Stephen L. Carnes, was strongly affected by an article in the *Ohio State Law Journal* (Gardner 1978) that described other methods of execution in gruesome detail and made lethal injection appear much more humane (Norman 1983). There is, in fact, dispute over whether or not lethal injection is actually a humane method of death.

Some physicians have charged that it is not. Moreover, two inmates filed a petition in early 1981 asking that the Food and Drug Administration ban the substances used on the grounds that they may not be "safe and effective" in bringing about a quick, painless demise. Although the FDA had previously evaluated drugs used to put animals to sleep, the agency refused to rule. In June of 1985, the Supreme Court found in *Cheney v. Heckler* that the FDA was free not to exercise its authority unless Congress ruled otherwise. Consequently, states were free to continue with pharmaceutical executions (Hagar 1985; Annas 1985).

In other states, the adoption of lethal injection was closely related to particularly scandalous electrocutions. The method's prospects in Alabama received a boost after John Evans required three jolts of electricity on 22 April 1983 before being pronounced dead. Some charged that Evans had been "tortured" and "burned alive" (Sikora 1983), and a prison spokesman said afterwards, "Based on what I saw, I would think that everybody would rather have a different method." Critics contrasted the execution with Texas lethal injection of Charlie Brooks the previous year (Gordon 1983). Botched executions were also cited in support of the method in Indiana, where a lethal injection bill had been turned down in 1985 (Bell 1986; Headden 1986), and in Mississippi (Brennan 1984).

Politically Feasible

Many other proponents of lethal injection favor it not because of their own concern for condemned prisoners, but rather to achieve the acquiescence of those who would otherwise oppose capital punishment. "Humane and effective or not," writes Hugo Bedau (1982:18), "lethal injection is undeniably attractive to a society that wants to keep the death penalty but does not want its executions to repel those who must authorize, administer, and witness them, lest it thereby turn those officials . . . into fervent abolitionists." Similarly, it has been argued that the availability of lethal injection would result in a greater willingness by jurors in capital cases to impose the death penalty (Curran and Casscells 1980). Sponsors of death penalty bills in the New Mexico, New Jersey, and Alabama legislatures used this argument openly (Malone 1979; Norman 1983; Martin 1984). Death penalty opponents are indeed placed in a difficult position with respect to lethal injection. Many are tempted to support it on the grounds that relatively humane techniques are preferable to brutal ones if executions are unavoidable. On the other hand, most oppose it because it makes the death penalty more acceptable (Schwarzchild 1982).

Constitutionally Sound

Closely related to the political issue, at least during the late 1970s, was the fact that lethal injection seemed less likely than other methods to be declared unconstitutionally "cruel and unusual" (Curran and Casscells 1980). This point figured prominently in the Arkansas legislative debate (Matlack 1983), and subsequent judicial decisions seem to have borne it out.

State Medical Association Resistance

Doctors have been involved in executions in one way or another for a long time. The guillotine, for instance, was invented by a French physician, and doctors have always been required to provide an official certification of death following an execution. Declaring a convict dead is a passive act undertaken only after legal authorities have killed him. But lethal injection is different. It draws medicine more deeply into capital punishment than ever before, since it requires a direct application of biomedical knowledge and technology. Moreover, it potentially calls for a direct role for physicians in the death chamber itself, in ways that would be part and parcel of the official killing (Curran and Casscells 1980; Finks 1983).

None of the laws enacted by the states specified that a doctor must actually perform the catheterization or start the lethal flow, although the original Oklahoma law did require a physician to order the necessary drugs and to inspect the catheter and equipment in advance. But neither did any of the early laws explicitly prohibit doctors from becoming executioners, and there were at the time no assurances that they would not be asked to do so in the near future (Bristow 1979; Hirsh 1984:3). What would happen, for instance, if technicians couldn't find a suitable vein for catheterization, due to damage from drug use? Would the attending physician have to do a venous cutdown? This would compromise the doctor's historical healing role and violate the Hippocratic tenet, *primum non nocere*—first, do no harm.

The profession's response was swift, coinciding with the first serious considerations of lethal injection in Oklahoma and Texas. The medical director of Oklahoma's prison system, Dr. Armond Start, stated that he would not participate in any aspect of a lethal injection except to pronounce death and that he would prohibit members of his staff from doing so (Rempel 1981). He was later quoted as saying that it was a "sordid procedure" that was not truly medical in nature (Bolsen 1982:518–19). State medical societies in each of the first four states that adopted lethal injection (Oklahoma, Texas, Idaho, and New Mexico) quickly resolved that medical participation beyond the pronouncement of death is ethically unacceptable (Casscells and Curran 1982). And each of these state medical societies fought for and won legislative assurances that a physician would never be asked to insert the needle in a chemical execution (Malone 1979:6)

The motives for this lobbying were not always solely moralistic; the Texas Medical Association expressed concerns about possible malpractice suits should a physician ever act as an executioner (Brennan 1984). Similar assurances were insisted upon and obtained in New Jersey (Norman 1983; Hirsh 1984:4), North Carolina (May 1983), Missouri (Goodrich 1983), Arkansas (Matlack 1983; Smith 1983), and Delaware (Sharpe 1983). In some instances it later proved necessary to amend laws concerning prescription drugs, since under existing statutes only licensed physicians could obtain them or authorize others to do so (Finks 1983; Bolsen 1982).

In several states, doctors testified against lethal injection bills (for example, see Hoover 1983; Egler 1983; Headden 1986), and state organizations in Kansas and Illinois announced that their members would refuse to participate even if legally required to do so (Finks 1983). When Idaho state prison physicians, nurses, and medical assistants vowed not to assist in executions, it appeared possible that the state would be unable to perform a lethal injection in the manner specified by law. In response, the legislature was forced in 1982 to reinstate the firing squad as an optional method (Schmidt 1982).

Professional societies on the state level were also responsible for stalling the passage of lethal injection statutes, as seems to have been the case in Illinois (Finks 1983), or in defeating such bills. Florida anesthesiologists and other physicians, for example, spoke out forcefully against lethal injection, and were instrumental in the bill's defeat (Bedau 1982). They emphasized the distinct possibility that technical difficulties and unforeseen complications might cancel the supposed humanitarian advantages of the method. An insufficient dosage of barbiturate, for example, might cause the prisoner to awaken before the execution was completed.

National Professional Resistance

As physicians were rushing to distance themselves from the emerging machinery of execution in their respective states, lethal injection was being transformed into an issue of professional ethics on the national level as well. Statements of opposition to participation in capital punishment were voiced in the medical journals and through national and international professional organizations.

MEDICAL ETHICISTS SPEAK OUT

The first physician to write on the ethical dilemmas of lethal injection was Dr. Lonnie R. Bristow. In June 1979 article in *Forum on Medicine,* Bristow emphasized how lethal injection entailed an insidious form of symbolic manipulation. The injection of intravenous drugs by medical personnel is understood in our society to be a healing act, almost by definition. But when the injection is intentionally employed to bring about a person's death, killing is elevated into something pseudo-therapeutic. Bristow noted the irony of the fact that Charlie Brooks' arm was swabbed with alcohol before he was executed, as though there were some need to avoid infection.

Like many other writers and practitioners after him, Bristow concluded that health professionals should not take any active part in executions, but his major concern was not so much society's use of physicians as it was the appropriation of the physicians' instruments. "At times medicine appears to be developing tools and techniques in rapid fashion"—including not only lethal injection but also genetic engineering and related biotechnologies—"and turning them over to an ill-prepared society while absolving itself of responsibility, beyond the day-to-day practice of the healing arts, for how those tools and techniques are used" (Bristow 1979:418). Bristow asserted that this dangerous trend can be slowed only by including medical ethicists and bioethicists more centrally in the development of social policy. Similar points were made later by Finks (1983) in *The Journal of Legal Medicine.* He stressed that lethal injection, in addition to avoiding disfigurement of the convict and other unpleasant features of older methods, also replaces "the monster-like figure of the executioner" with the "more benign, if no less deadly, appearance of the medical professional" (Finks 1983:382).

In January 1980, a lawyer and a physician from the Harvard Medical School co-authored a broader attack on lethal injection in the *New England Journal of Medicine.* Curran and Casscells (1980) began by describing the new capital statutes that recently had been adopted and the roles of doctors as called for in those laws. They argued that medical participation in this new form of execution was clearly inconsistent with universally accepted medical ethics, and cited four major source of authority: (1) The Hippocratic Oath, which specifically prohibits the administration of poisons or the use of medical skills for harmful purposes; (2) the World Medical Association's (WMA) Declaration of Geneva, which was adopted partly in reaction to the misdeeds of Nazi doctors during the Second World War; (3) a declaration of the medical commission of the Conference for the Abolition of Torture; and most importantly, (4) the WMA's Declaration of Tokyo, which prohibits doctors from assisting in inhumane or degrading procedures, permitting their instruments or knowledge to be used in such procedures, or even being present at their administration. Curran and Casscells concluded that all forms of medical participation in lethal injection should be unequivocally condemned, including the insertion of the needle, the preparation of the lethal substance, the supervision of the preparation or administration of the substance by others, and even the continuous monitoring of the prisoner's condition in order to pronounce death. Such continuous monitoring, they asserted, "would be so intimately a part of the whole action as to deny any consideration as a separate medical service" (Curran and Casscells 1980:229).

In addition to commenting on the ethical issues of death by injection, medical writers also noted the possible technical difficulties that might complicate such procedures (Hastings Center 1982; Finks 1983; Hirsh 1984). First, they noted that it may be difficult to locate a suitable vein. According to Casscells, as many as one out of every four prisoners present this difficulty due to pigmentation, obesity, or damage from drug use (quoted by Kotulak 1982). In fact, it took technicians 40 minutes to get the needle into the arm of Stephen Peter Morin, a drug user who was executed in March 1985 in Texas. In some cases it might prove necessary to perform a "cutdown," i.e., a surgical penetration to locate a vein; presumably, only a physician would be qualified to do so properly. Second, this cutdown procedure would result in excruciating pain for the convict if an incompetent technician struck an artery rather than a vein. And if the catheter missed a vein and went into subcutaneous tissue, the sodium thiopental would probably wear off too soon, causing the person to awaken in the midst of suffocation. Finally, the determination of proper dosages and drug proportions can be difficult if the convict had a history of alcohol or drug abuse. Each of these risks is minimized if the executioner is a physician.

Some of the early executions by lethal injection provided evidence that tended to support the position that the new method was not as clean and sanitary as had been claimed. Charlie Brooks took seven minutes to die, and four reporters claimed that he appeared to have suffered some pain (Reinhold 1982). At the March 1984 execution of James Autry in Texas, the drugs failed to take effect until fifteen minutes had elapsed, during which time he complained of pain (Hager 1985).

THE AMERICAN MEDICAL ASSOCIATION
HOUSE OF DELEGATES RESOLUTION

The American Medical Association (AMA) took its first decisive action on the matter of lethal injection in July 1980. The Judicial Council produced a report that noted the receipt of numerous inquiries on the issue from doctors and medical societies. Opinions within the profession were mixed, and mostly corresponded to more general attitudes on capital punishment. The Judicial Council acknowledged the possible validity of the sundry arguments both for and against chemical executions, but maintained that the concept of *primum non nocere* ("first, do no harm") was decisive. The report stopped well short of a blanket condemnation of lethal injection, nothing only that "capabilities in pharmacology, toxicology, catheterization, or injection" are not exclusively the provinces of medical doctors and thus "the active participation by physicians in executions is not required" (American Medical Association 1980:85). The report concluded that:

> (1) an individual's opinion on capital punishment is the personal moral decision of the individual; (2) a physician, as a member of a profession dedicated to preserving life when there is hope of doing so, should not be a participant in a legally authorized execution; and (3) a physician may make a determination or certification of death as currently provided by law in any situation (American Medical Association 1980:86).

The Judicial Council Report was presented to the House of Delegates as a resolution and, somewhat surprisingly, it was passed. According to one account (Jendrzejczyk 1982), the adoption came at the urging of Dr. Armond Start, the prison medical officer from Oklahoma who had condemned lethal injection when his state had become the first to adopt it in 1977. But the new AMA policy statement was quite limited. First, as noted above, the resolution condemned neither capital punishment in general nor lethal injection specifically. It left these issues to the individual conscience, coming out only against direct participation by physicians. Second, the House of Delegates' policies are merely guidelines, binding only on AMA members, and in all likelihood the AMA would be unable to do anything to a member who violated them (Hirsh 1984). A member of the AMA's Office of General Counsel later acknowledged, in response to a written inquiry, that while a physician who directly participated in an execution would be in violation of medical ethics, he or she would not be subject to any disciplinary action (Devlin 1982). In 1986, the AMA Council of Ethical and Judicial Affairs restated the House of Delegates' resolution virtually verbatim, without resolving any of the ambiguities of the earlier document (American Medical Association 1986).

The most important limitation on the AMA resolution, however, was its failure to define specifically those forms of direct physician participation in executions that were prohibited, other than to exempt the certification of death. Thus, many issues remain unresolved. Finks noted in the *Journal of Legal Medicine* (1983:390–92) that medical involvement may be "explicit," "implicit," and "inherent." Explicit involvement includes legally required participation by doctors, and it is just such explicit roles that were prevented by the lobbying activities of state medical societies. Implicit medical involvement is involvement at a distance. An example would be a physician training others in the administration of the substances, overseeing the equipment and procedures, authorizing the obtaining of the drugs from pharmaceutical sources, performing a cut-down to facilitate catheterization, or performing any sort of emergency procedures in the event the execution did not go off routinely. State laws regarding restricted drugs and other medical prerogatives appear to make such roles likely. Inherent medical involvement refers to the simple fact that lethal injection itself depends upon "the use of medical knowledge, research, and expertise in the destruction of human life" (1983:392). Since this expertise was originally developed by doctors for medical use, it might be argued that doctors have a certain proprietary claim on it and thus ought to consider whether its use in killing "entagle[s] medicine in a conflict with its own ethical standards" (Finks 1983:392).

DR. RALPH GRAY AND THE BROOKS' EXECUTION

The loose ends left by the AMA became quite apparent with the first execution by lethal injection. Dr. Ralph Gray, he medical director of the Texas Department of Correction, emerged as an important figure in the execution. He supplied the drugs for the lethal mixture, provided the medical technicians from his own staff to administer the drugs, and examined Brooks' veins. His role seemed to some to have exceeded the AMA guidelines, and it set off a furor. The Chairman of the AMA Judicial Council stated that Gray had not violated medical ethics since he himself neither prepared nor injected the substance, and did not give the actual order to administer it (Boffey 1982). But others disagreed. An associate of the Hastings Center, a New York think tank specializing in medical and bioethical issues, said that Gray appeared to have facilitated the execution. He was not released from responsibility by his indirect role in the execution, and the difference between inspecting Brooks' veins and actually inserting the catheter was so small as to be insignificant (Boffey 1982). William J. Curran, a Harvard law professor and co-author of the widely circulated article in the *New England Journal of Medicine*, called for an investigation of Gray's activities and complained that the AMA and Texas Medical Association (TMA) policies on lethal injection were not intended to be interpreted so narrowly as to allow for such involvement. He urged the TMA to seek revocation of Gray's license (Kotulak 1982).

Gray was anything but defensive in his reaction to these charges. In fact, he noted that he would have preferred to have performed the injection himself, since the technicians, who had not performed an intravenous injection in years, experienced difficulty with it and splattered Brooks' blood in the process (Weiner 1983). Gray also reportedly said that the removal of criminals from society is equivalent to the surgical removal of tissue from a sick patient and that physicians are thus entitled to assist society by performing lethal injections (Schwarzchild 1982). Such a statement is particularly chilling to physicians, since just such an analogy was used to justify the physicians' role in the Nazi holocaust (Lifton 1986).

Many of these same ethical issues were raised at a Harvard Medical School conference on the death penalty in early 1982, jointly sponsored by several organizations including the Massachusetts Civil Liberties Union, the Massachusetts American Medical Students Association, and a group called Massachusetts Physicians Against the Death Penalty. Participants included noted authorities and abolitionists, such as Hugo Bedau and the American Civil Liberty Union's Henry Schwarzchild, as well as concerned physicians. A symposium on physicians and the death penalty was held a few months later, in conjunction with the commencement exercises of Harvard Medical School. Physicians at that symposium argued that lethal injection is not the only issue doctors should confront. Rather, they should take a firm stand against the death penalty in all its forms (Bolsen 1982; Reilly 1982). Michael Nelson, a psychiatrist and founding member of Massachusetts Physicians Against the Death Penalty, urged doctors to investigate the consequences of executions and particularly the possibility that the death penalty may contribute to the broader problem of violence and homicide (telephone interview, 24 January 1989).

Professional Interests and Medical Social Control

The advent of execution by lethal injection can be seen as both a logical extension and an ultimate contradiction of medicalized control. For over a century, doctors in America have battled to solidify and expand their authority. They have done so first by undermining the legitimacy claims of competing groups, such as midwives and chiropractors, and second, by trying to extend medical authority over hitherto nom-medical arenas such as mental illness and substance abuse. Both forms of expansion have brought not only greater public acceptance of medical truth-claims, but also greater power for medicine to intervene in human affairs and to influence social control strategies.

But the advent of lethal injection is, to date, the clearest instance in which an expansion of medical authority is widely perceived by professional medicine not as a victory but as a threat to its interests. Political authorities in this instance did not have to be cajoled into relying more heavily on medical expertise as they had been in earlier instances of medicalization (e.g., the case of child abuse; see Pfohl 1977). Moreover, the impetus for medicalizing capital punishment came *entirely* from non-medical interest groups—especially pro-capital punishment politicians—with their own agendas. Their campaigns to replace other forms of execution with lethal injections betrayed both an ignorance of medicine's ethical codes and, in some cases, a cynical and manipulative stance toward the physician's enterprise.

The psychiatric profession has also been forced to confront a difficult ethical dilemma due to the Supreme Court's 1986 decision in *Ford v. Wainwright*. In *Ford*, the Court held that the execution of a person who has become legally insane while on death row is in violation of the Eighth Amendment ban on cruel and unusual punishment (Sargent 1986). The decision elevated an existing common law rule to constitutional status, and put psychiatrists in a position of having to make final evaluations of a convict's competency to be put to death. Arguably, this makes them "participants" and thus violators of medical ethics. At the time of this writing, the American Psychiatric Association has still produced no more than a vague policy statement similar to that of the AMA (American Psychiatric Association 1980; Council on Psychiatry and Law 1987).

The resistance of physicians and psychiatrists to recent death penalty innovations reinforces a simple point that is often overlooked in the literature of medicalizaiton, namely, that the expansion of professional turf is not always desirable for the professionals involved. The establishment of professional authority over an issue and the concomitant exclusion of outsiders from participating in decisions, which I have termed "social problem enclosure" (Haines 1979), may threaten the targeted profession by forcing it to take actions which, arguably at least, contradict its own principles. Examples include active euthanasia, abortion (see Imber 1986) and fetal tissue research (Fine 1988).

Lethal injection illustrates a situation in which an attempt is made to "thrust" an issue into a profession's domain to serve the interests of outsiders. Chemical execution is attractive to its advocates largely because it weakens abolitionist arguments and clothes a potentially objectionable policy in the morally neutral trappings of medical science. In so doing, it appears to use medicine to legitimate the state's execution of criminals. The attempt to medicalize capital punishment may be an unintended result of medicine's success over the past two centuries in expanding public acceptance of its world view. But this attempt has met with incomplete success, owing first to physicians' sensitivity to other cooptations of doctors (the crimes of the Nazi doctors [Lifton 1986] and the participation of physicians in torture under authoritarian regimes) and, more fundamentally, to the inherent difficulty of reconciling a healing ideology with a procedure ending in the intentional death of an unwilling "patient."

References

American Medical Association. 1980. "Report A of the Judicial Council," Proceedings of the House of Delegates. Chicago: American Medical Association, 85–86, 254.

———. 1986. Current Opinions of the Council on Ethical and Judicial Affairs of the AMA, Paragraph 2.06. Chicago: American Medical Association.

American Psychiatric Association. 1980. "Position statement on medical participation in capital punishment." American Journal of Psychiatry 137:1487.

Annas, George J. 1985. "Killing with kindness: why the FDA need not certify drugs used for executions safe and effective." American Journal of Public Health 75:1096–99.

Bedau, Hugo Adam. 1982. The Death Penalty in America. 3rd edition. Oxford: Oxford University Press.

Bell, Robert N. 1985. "House vote to substitute lethal injections for chair." Indianapolis Star, January 22.

Billings, Dwight B., and Thomas Urban. 1982. "The socio-medical construction of transsexualism: an interpretation and critique." Social Problems 29:266–82.

Boffey, Philip M. 1982. "Experts debate ethics of doctor's execution role." New York Times, December 8.

Bolsen, Barbara. 1982. "Strange bedfellows: death penalty and medicine." Journal of the American Medical Association 248:518–19.

Bonavita, Fred. 1982. "Author of lethal injection law satisfied with results." Houston Post, December 8.

Brennan, Tom. 1984. "Lethal injection now considered more humane." (Jackson, Miss.) Clarion Ledger, August 26.

Bristow, Lonnie R. 1979. "Medical ethics: quo vadis?" Forum on Medicine, June:417–18.

Bureau of Justice Statistics. 1986. "Capital Punishment." Bureau of Justice Statistics Bulletin, November.

Carrier, James G. 1986. Learning Disability: Social Class and the Construction of Inequality in American Education. Westport, Conn.: Greenwood Press.

Casscells, Ward, and William J. Curran. 1982. "Doctors, the death penalty, and lethal injections." New England Journal of Medicine 307:1532–33.

Council on Psychiatry and Law (American Psychiatric Association). 1987. "The council on psychiatry and law." American Journal of Psychiatry 144:411–12.

Conrad, Peter. 1975. "The discovery of hyperkinesis: notes on the medicalization of deviant behavior." Social Problems 23:12–21.

Conrad, Peter and Joseph W. Schneider. 1980. Deviance and Medicalization: From Badness to Sickness. St. Louis, Mo.: C.V. Mosby.

Curran, William J. and Ward Casscells. 1980. "The ethics of medical participation in capital punishment by intravenous drug injection." New England Journal of Medicine 302:226–30.

Devlin, Mary M. 1982. "Capital punishment." Journal of the American Medical Association 248:3031.

Egler, Daniel. 1983. "Execution by injection becomes law." Chicago Tribune, September 9.

Fine, Alan. 1988. "The ethics of fetal tissue transplants." Hastings Center Report, June/July:5–8.

Finks, Thomas O. 1983. "Lethal injection: an uneasy alliance of law and medicine." The Journal of Legal Medicine 4:382–403.

Gardner, Martin R. 1978. "Executions and indignities—an eighth amendment assessment of methods of inflicting capital punishment." Ohio State Law Journal 39:96–130.

Goodrich, Robert. 1983. "Lethal injection ban sought for doctors." St. Louis Post-Dispatch, March 8.

Gordon, Tom. 1983. "Evans death to spur change from chair?" Birmingham News, April 24.

Hager, Philip. 1985. "Justices uphold executions by lethal drugs." Los Angeles Times, March 21:4.

Haines, Herbert H. 1979. "Cognitive claims-making, enclosure, and the depoliticization of social problems." The Sociological Quarterly 20:119–30.

Hastings Center. 1982. "On lethal injections and the death penalty." Hastings Center report (October):2–3.

Headden, Susan. 1986. "Unlikely coalition gives death sentence to lethal injection." Indianapolis Star, February 5.

Hirsh, Harold L. 1984. "Physicians as executioners." Legal Aspects of Medical Practice, March:1–4, 8.

Hoover, Daniel, C. 1983. "Tranquil killer draws turbulent reaction." (Raleigh) News and Observer, April 20.

Imber, Jonathan B. 1986. Abortion and the Private Practice of Medicine. New Haven: Yale University Press.

Jendrzejczyk, Mike. 1982. "'Sanitized' execution is still dirty." New York Times, January 10.

Kittrie, Nicholas. 1971. The Right to be Different: Deviance and Enforced Therapy. Baltimore: Johns Hopkins University Press.

Kotulak, Ronald. 1982. "Execution by injection: The doctor's dilemma." Chicago Tribune, December 12.

Kurz, Demie. 1986. "Emergency department responses to battered women: resistance to medicalization." Social Problems 34:69–81.

Levine, Martin P., and Richard R. Troiden. 1988. "The myth of sexual compulsivity." The Journal of Sex Research 25:347–63.

Lifton, Robert Jay. 1986. The Nazi Doctors: Medical Killing and the Psychology of Genocide. New York: Basic Books.

Malone, Patrick. 1979. "Death row and the medical model." Hastings Center Report, October 5–6.

Martin, Virginia. 1984. "Lethal injection increasingly popular means of carrying out death sentences." Montgomery Advertiser, April 29.

Matlack, Carol. 1983. "House votes injection bill." Arkansas Gazette, February 22.

May, A.L. 1983. "Lethal injection option endorsed for inmates sentenced to death." (Raleigh, N.C.) News and Observer, May 27.

Norman, Michael. 1983. "Why Jersey is leaning to executions by injection." New York Times, May 18.

Pfohl, Stephen, J. 1977. "The 'discovery' of child abuse." Social Problems 24:310–23.

Reilly, Phillip. 1982. "Injection laws latest ground in death penalty fight." American Medical News, July 23:32.

Reinhold, Robert. 1982. "Execution by injection stirs fear and sharpens debate." New York Times, December 8.

Rempel, William C. 1981. "Execution by injection: is it best?" Los Angeles Times, June 5.

Robbins, Thomas, and Dick Anthony. 1982. "Deprogramming, brainwashing and the medicalization of deviant religious groups." Social Problems 29:283–97.

Rosecrance, John. 1985. "Compulsive gambling and the medicalization of deviance." Social Problems 32:275–84.

Sargent, Douglas A. 1986. "Treating the condemned to death." Hastings Center Report, December:5–6.

Schmidt, William E. 1982. "Idaho officials wrestle with death row problems." New York Times, April 20.

Schneider, Joseph W. 1978. "From deviant drinking to disease: alcoholism as a social accomplishment." Social Problems 25:361–72.

Schneider, Joseph W. and Peter Conrad. 1980. "The medical control of deviance: contests and consequences." Research in the Sociology of Health Care, 1:1–53. Greenwich, Conn.: JAI Press.

Schwarzchild, Henry. 1982. "Homicide by injection." New York Times, December 23:15.

Sharpe, Rochelle. 1983. "House approves death by injection." Wilmington Evening Journal, June 1.

Sikora, Frank. 1983. "Huntsville senator renews pitch that injection best way to execute." Birmingham News, April 26.

Smith, Doug. 1983. "Pharmacy college's dean resents role in execution thrust unasked on school." Arkansas Gazette, March 5.

Snow, David A., Susan G. Baker, Leon Anderson, and Michael Martin. 1986. "The myth of pervasive mental illness among the homeless." Social Problems 33:407–23.

Tierney, Kathleen J. 1982. "The battered women movement and the creation of the wife beating problem." Social Problems 29:207–20.

Weiner, Tim. 1983. "Injections: civilizing executions." Philadelphia Inquirer, January 30.

Wright, James D. 1988. "The mentally ill homeless: what is myth and what is fact?" Social Problems 35:182–91.

Zimring, Franklin E., and Gordon Hawkins. 1986. Capital Punishment and the American Agenda. New York: Cambridge University Press.

Zola, Irving K. 1975. "In the name of health and illness: on some socio-political consequences of medical influence." Social Science and Medicine 9:83–87.

CHAPTER 3

From Hyperactive Children to ADHD Adults

OBSERVATIONS ON THE EXPANSION OF MEDICAL CATEGORIES

Peter Conrad and Deborah Potter

Over the past thirty years there has been keen sociological interest in the medicalization of deviance and social problems (Conrad 1992, 2000; Conrad and Schneider 1992; Zola 1972). By now, there are dozens of case examples of medicalization and a body of literature has accumulated that has loosely been called "medicalization theory" (see Williams and Calnan 1996). At this point, it is important to build on this corpus of knowledge to better understand different aspects of medicalization. Medicalization is, by definition, about the extension of medical jurisdiction or the expansion of medical boundaries. In different situations, medical professionals (Halpern 1990), political reformers (Haines 1989), lay activists (Schneider 1978), or social movements (Scott 1990) have promoted boundary expansion. Most medicalization studies focus on how nonmedical problems become defined as medical problems, usually as illnesses or disorders. But there has been less examination of how medicalized categories themselves can be subjects of expansion, thus, engendering further medicalization.

It seems clear by now that medicalization of social problems is not an either/or phenomenon, but that it is better conceptualized in terms of degrees of medicalization. Some conditions are almost fully medicalized (e.g., death, childbirth), others are partly medicalized (e.g., opiate addiction, menopause), and still others are minimally medicalized (e.g., sexual addiction, spouse abuse). One dimension of the degree of medicalization is the elasticity of a medical category. "While some categories are narrow and circumspect, others can expand and incorporate a number of other problems" or be applied to new populations (Conrad 1992, p. 221). For example, Alzheimer's Disease (AD) was once an obscure disorder, but with the removal of "age" as a criteria (Fox 1989), there was no longer a distinction between AD and senile dementia. This sharply increased the number of cases of AD, now including cases of senile dementia over 60 years old. As a result, AD has become one of the top five causes of death in the United States.

Psychiatric and medical diagnoses are the product of socio-historical circumstances and the claims-making of particular interest groups. New diagnoses rarely emerge simply as a result of new scientific discoveries. Medicalization studies have demonstrated that agents such as self-help and advocacy groups, social movements, health-related organizations, pharmaceutical companies, academic researchers, and clinicians can be central in creating specific diagnoses.

Medicalization is usually a product of collective action, rather then a result of "medical imperialism" (Conrad 1992). Whatever the extent of medicalization, it is not simply doctors colonizing new problems of labeling feckless patients. Reissman (1983) and others have asserted the patients and other lay people can be active collaborators in their own medicalization, although sympathetic professionals are usually needed for successful claims-making (Brown 1995). Numerous studies show how affected parties can make critical contributions to the medicalization process. Conrad and Schneider (1992) outlined the role of organized lay interests in the medicalization of alcoholism and the demedicalization of homosexuality. Other studies demonstrate the importance of the mobilization of people who are diagnosed in collectively promoting and shaping their medical diagnoses. This kind of diagnostic advocacy is often accomplished by or directly connected to an extant social movement: premenstrual syndrome (PMS) with the women's movement (Reissman 1983; Figert 1996); post traumatic stress disorder (PTSD) with the Vietnam Veterans movement (Scott 1990); and AIDS treatment with the Gay and Lesbian movement (Epstein 1996). In each case, an explicit politicization of the medical diagnosis and the active mobilization of the social movement apparatus propelled the new category forward. Self-help and patient advocacy groups are legion, and some of these have been active in promoting the acceptance of their own illness categories. But the difficulty that supporters of multiple chemical sensitivity disorder (MCSD) (Kroll-Smith 1997) or sexual addiction (Irvine 1995) have encountered in their attempts to achieve acceptance as medical diagnoses highlights some limits of lay advocacy. Without being able to draw upon the resources of a larger movement, lay claims about medical diagnosis seem to have more difficulty becoming medically acknowledged and institutionalized.

A wide range of new medical categories that did not exist previously have emerged in the past four decades: attention deficit/hyperactivity disorder (ADHD), anorexia and eating disorders, chronic fatigue syndrome (CFS), repetition strain injury, fibromyalgia, PMS, PTSD, and MCSD. Many of these diagnoses have been promoted actively by sufferers and their advocates, with some achieving substantial medical acceptance while others remain contested or controversial (Singer, et al. 1984). By the close of the 20th century, patients have become more engaged in their own treatment and more demanding in what they want from physicians (Guadagnoli and Ward 1998). Moreover, as Barsky and Boros (1995) point out, the American public's tolerance for mild symptoms and benign problems has decreased, which may be leading to a further medicalization of ills.

There are numerous reasons for seeking new medical diagnoses. Life's troubles are often confusing, distressing, debilitating, and difficult to understand. Michael Balint (1957) pointed out many years ago that a medical diagnosis transforms an "unorganized illness," an agglomeration of complaints and symptoms that may be unclear, unconnected, and mysterious, into an entity that is a more understandable "organized illness." As Broom and Woodward (1996) show with CFS, sufferers will often seek a diagnosis, which will both legitimate their troubles and provide them with an understanding of their problem. In some instances a diagnosis can be a kind of self-labeling that provides a new public identity as having a particular illness or disorder. In other cases, it may facilitate medical treatments that can have a substantial impact on individuals' lives. When these occur, it is hardly surprising to see sufferers embracing medicalization.

The emergence of so many new medical categories raises the question of what happens to them over time. It is likely that some just become established and a part of regular medical practice, others may be challenged, disappear or become vestigial from nonuse, while others may expand in new ways. Medical diagnostic categories, perhaps especially psychiatric categories (Horwitz 2002), are often fluid and subject to expansion or contraction. The extension of established diagnoses is especially interesting for it can occur almost unnoticed as a part of regular medical practice and, at the same time, expand the realm of medicalization in significant ways. To examine this phenomenon, we can find a similar process in the social constructionist frame for studying social problems.

"Domain expansion" describes a process by which definitions of social problems expand and become more inclusive (Best 1990; Loseke 1999). Domain expansion encompasses claims-making work that extends the definitional boundaries of an established social problem to include similar or related conditions. Best (1990) examined the emerging definitions of child abuse and found that "by 1976, the issue encompassed a much broader array of conditions threatening children. The more general term 'child abuse' had replaced the earlier, narrower concept of 'battered child' and the even broader expression 'child abuse and neglect' had gained currency among professionals" (Best 1990, p. 67). Jenness (1995) has argued how activism by the gay and lesbian movement brought attention to the scope and consequences of anti-gay and lesbian violence. She suggests that domain expansion accompanied social movement growth and was key in reframing violence against gays and lesbians as a "hate crime" and as a specific public issue in the United States. While domain expansion need not always be linked to a social movement, the activities of champions and claims-makers are likely to be critical to the expansion of definitional boundaries.[1]

This paper examines an analogous process for medicalization, focusing on the emergence of the diagnosis of Attention Deficit-Hyperactivity Disorder (ADHD) in adults in the 1990s. How did hyperactivity, which was deemed largely a disorder of childhood, become adult ADHD? This research follows on Conrad's study of the medicalization of hyperactivity published in the 1970s (Conrad 1975, 1976). Our interest here, however, is also to investigate this case as an example of how medicalized categories, once established, can expand to become broader and more inclusive. This category expansion is one means for increasing medicalization and provides us with an opportunity to explore how this aspect of medicalization operates. This paper will focus on key claims and counter-claims made by mental health and medical professionals, as well as lay leaders, support groups, and conferences.[2] After reviewing the state of childhood hyperactivity as a medicalized diagnosis in the 1970s, we trace the emergence of "adult hyperactives" among those whose childhood symptoms persisted into adulthood, and then examine how this was transformed into the category "ADHD adults." We show how lay, professional, and media claims helped establish the expanded diagnosis. We identify particular aspects of the social context that contributed to the rise of adult ADHD, and then outline some of the consequences of the medicalization of ADHD in adults and the social implications of expanding diagnostic categories.

The DSM as a Categorical Touchstone

Psychiatric diagnoses are historically and culturally situated. Certain diagnostic categories appear and disappear over time, reflecting and reinforcing particular ideologies within the "diagnostic project" (the professional legitimization of diagnoses), as well as within the larger social order (Cooksey and Brown 1998, p. 550). As numerous researchers have noted, psychiatric diagnoses are not necessarily indicators of objective conditions, but are a product of a negotiated interactive process influenced by sociopolitical factors (Caplan 1995; Cooksey and Brown 1997; Kirk and Kutchins 1992; Kutchins and Kirk 1997). Diagnoses related to behavior or involving cognitive symptoms are frequently contested or controversial and, as such, diagnosis of "functional diseases" can "represent and implicitly negotiated solution to the problem of idiosyncratic suffering that is not explainable by specific pathology" (Aronowitz 1998, p.16).

Most psychiatric disorders become legitimated in the American Psychiatric Association's *Diagnostic and Statistical Manual* (DSM), the official guidebook for psychiatric diagnoses. Although DSM does not contain all medical diagnoses, when it comes to behavior, it can be seen as a repository of medicalized categories. Despite psychiatric claims, it is not a scientific document, but a "mix of social values, political compromise, scientific evidence and material for insurance forms" (Kutchins and Kirk 1997, pp. 11, x). As the authoritative voice of psychiatry, the DSM has been used as a mechanism to "secure psychiatric turf" (Kirk and Kutchins 1992) and to sanction psychiatric categories.

The various revisions of DSM have reflected distinct approaches taken by mental health professionals toward understanding human troubles as psychiatric conditions. In 1952, the original version of the DSM reflected the dominance of psychoanalytic thought and sought to "provide a broader set of labels which would be inclusive of the whole society" (Cooksey and Brown 1998, p. 530). A major shift in psychiatric thinking occurred with the publication of DSM-III in 1980, when the largely psychoanalytic orientation was abandoned and replaced with an avowedly biomedical and categorical approach to diagnosis. "The fundamental premise of DSM-III was that different clusters of symptoms indicated distinct underlying diseases such as schizophrenia, depression, panic disorder and substance abuse" (Horwitz 2002, p. 2). The "diagnostic project" was now heralded as a scientific endeavor, a claim that has increased with the publication of DSM-IV (1994), a revision that identifies nearly 400 distinct medical diagnostic entities.

The DSM provides a useful touchstone for the sociological task of understanding how behaviors are defined medically, especially for documenting how criteria for diagnosing a problem change over time and through various revised editions. In this way, we can track some of the elasticity of a diagnosis such as ADHD.

Hyperactivity in the 1970s

Although ADHD's roots are often traced to early in the twentieth century (Goldman, et al. 1998), it only emerged as a diagnostic category in the 1950s (see Conrad 1975). It was termed at various times Minimal Brain Dysfunction (MBD), Hyperactive Syndrome, Hyperkinesis, Hyperactive Disorder of Childhood, among several other diagnostic categories. While there were slight differences among the categories, in practice, they were interchangeable. The terms Hyperactivity and MBD were most commonly used.

Beginning in 1968, the DSM-II identified "minimal brain damage" and other problems such as "hyperkinetic reaction" as a childhood disorder "characterized by overactivity, restlessness, distractibility, and short attention span, especially in young children; the behavior usually diminishes in adolescence" (APA, 1968, p. 50). The disorders, thus, were defined by both hyperactivity and inattention, two distinguishing features that would persist in various combinations throughout the next 30 years (see also, Stewart, et al. 1966; Stewart 1970; Wender 1971). Although this official classification clearly placed the hyperactivity within the realm of childhood psychiatric illnesses, it also allowed for the possibility of persistence into adolescence. For example, hyperactive behavior "usually" (but not always) "diminished" (though not necessarily disappeared) by the time the patient entered adolescence. While there was no solid evidence of biological causation, there was an assumption that there was some type of organic pathology.

The most significant criterion for diagnosis was a child's behavior, especially at school. The emphasis in identification was on hyperactive and disruptive behaviors (Conrad 1976). The major treatments for hyperactivity were stimulant medications, especially Ritalin. During the 1960s, the disorder became increasingly well known, due, in part, to publicity it received concerning controversies about drug treatment. By the middle 1970s, it had become the most common childhood psychiatric problem (Gross and Wilson 1974) and special clinics to identify and treat the disorder were established, although most children were diagnosed by their pediatrician or primary care physician.

While there were no methodologically sound epidemiological studies in the 1970s, it was widely estimated that 3–5% of elementary school students were hyperactive (occasionally estimates were as high as 10%). Frequently mentioned estimates suggested between 250,000 and 500,000 children were identified as hyperactive. The disorder was believed to affect boys more often than girls, perhaps at a ratio of 8 to 1. In sum, hyperactivity was seen, fundamentally, as a disorder of childhood, typically identified in the early years of school, which most children were expected to "outgrow" by adolescence.

The Emergence of "Adult Hyperactives"

Beginning in the late 1970s, several cohort studies were published which followed children who had been originally diagnosed with hyperactivity a decade or more earlier and traced their development into adulthood. These studies established that for some hyperactive children, the symptoms persisted into adolescence and even into adulthood. Thus emerged the notion of what we call "adult hyperactives," hyperactive children who did not "outgrow" their symptoms and still manifested some problems as adults.

Weiss and colleagues (1979) followed 75 hyperactive children and 45 matched controls for 15 years. When compared to a matched cohort, they found that clear symptoms persisted for many hyperactive children into adulthood; 66 percent had at least one symptom (Weiss and Hechtman 1986). Most notable was the persistence of restlessness and poor concentration. Despite criticisms that only 60 percent of the children were followed into adulthood, the study remains widely cited, and mis-cited.[3] A second prospective study found 31 percent were still diagnosable as hyperactive in late adolescence (Gittleman, et al. 1985; see also Mannuzza, et al. 1991; 1998). A follow-up at young adulthood, however, showed a significant decrease of ADD symptoms, to about one-third the rate reported by Weiss. The media has tended to focus on the higher prevalence rates reported in the Weiss data.

Following the publication of these seminal studies, other researchers investigated the persistence of symptoms into adulthood (e.g., Biederman, et al., 1996) to further identify what they believed to be confounding factors (such as co-morbidity with other disorders). These studies reflect the dominant thinking of the late 1980s: any diagnosis of Attention Deficit Disorder (ADD, as the diagnosis was renamed) was found only among adults whose disorder persisted from childhood and, thus, was *not* a disorder that was either "missed" during childhood or was of adult onset. All ADD adults were hyperactive children grown-up.

The 1980 update, DSM-III, both reflected and facilitated an interest in hyperactivity beyond childhood.[4] First, in line with the general trend in DSM-III to define disorders by symptoms, rather than etiology, the updated manual reclassified the disorder according to its primary symptoms: either hyperactivity *or* inattention. Thus, the diagnosis focused on *attention* deficits with two major subtypes: Attention-Deficit Disorder with Hyperactivity and Attention-Deficit Disorder without Hyperactivity (deemed the less severe of the two categories). The symptoms were focused largely on children's activities (e.g., "runs about or climbs on things excessively," "frequently calls out in class," "has difficulty concentrating on schoolwork or other tasks requiring sustained attention"). To be diagnosed, patients needed to exhibit symptoms before age seven.

Secondly, the range of behaviors included within the official diagnosis became more comprehensive. Some symptoms were related to school-based behavior, such as "frequently calls out in class"; whereas others were more interpersonal and ephemeral in nature, e.g., "often acts before thinking" or "is easily distracted." These changes in the diagnostic category meant that individuals who may not have "qualified" for a diagnosis of hyperkinetic reaction or minimal brain damage under DSM-II, could now be thought of as having ADD under DSM-III. Both subtypes of ADD permitted courses of the disorder in which "all symptoms persist into adolescence or adulthood" or that "hyperactivity disappears, but other signs persist into adolescence or adulthood" (APA 1980, p. 42). Thus, the DSM-III definition expanded the diagnostic criteria in terms of necessary "symptoms," while allowing for the possibility for persistence into adulthood.

The Development of "ADHD Adults"

In the 1987 revision, DSM-IIIR, ADD was renamed "Attention Deficit Hyperactivity Disorder" (ADHD) to reassert the condition of hyperactivity as one possible, but not mandated, symptom of the disorder. ADHD enabled children who were hyperactive and impulsive, but less inattentive to meet the diagnostic criteria. Over 50% more children received ADHD diagnoses under these criteria (Newcorn, et al. 1989). The revised diagnostic criteria did not refer to the disorder in adulthood, but opened the door slightly for an expanded definition beyond "adult hyperactives" to "ADHD adults" who had no childhood diagnosis. For example, the environment in which ADHD symptoms occurred had expanded to the workplace: "In the classroom or workplace, inattention or impulsiveness are evidenced . . ." (APA 1987, p. 50). There was less emphasis on school-aged behaviors: "frequently calls out in class" (DSM-III) became "often blurts out answers to questions before they have been completed." The criteria of exhibiting symptoms before age seven was retained, and although the revision obliquely acknowledged the possibility of post-childhood ADHD, adult ADHD was not highlighted in the manual.

Early Claims

In the same year that DSM-IIIR was published, two publications aimed at lay readers heralded a new category of "ADHD Adults"—adults who had not been diagnosed as children, but had suffered from symptoms. Although later claims would be made by those who could not trace their suffering to their youth, these early claims were made either by or for those who, retrospectively, could identify signs of ADHD in their childhood.

In 1987, Paul Wender, a longtime hyperactivity researcher, published a book that examined hyperactivity throughout the life span. Although the book was entitled, *The Hyperactive Child, Adolescent and Adult,* only one chapter described adults with ADHD symptoms. Nonetheless, the book targeted a lay audience and would be cited frequently in subsequent years.

The same year, Frank Wolkenberg (1987), a free-lance photographer and picture editor, wrote a first-person account in the *New York Times Magazine* about his discovery that he had ADHD despite his apparently successful life. When he sought treatment for depression and suicidal ideation, he was diagnosed with ADHD by a psychologist whose specialty was learning disorders. Wolkenberg then began reinterpreting several clues from early in his life (e.g., impulsivity, distractibility, disorganization, and emotional volatility) as signs of the disorder. This highly visible testimony of someone not previously diagnosed with ADHD as a child put the idea of "ADHD Adults" into the public realm. No one had diagnosed him as hyperactive as a child, yet now, he was attributing "seemingly inexplicable failures . . . all unnecessary and many inexcusable" (p. 62) to ADHD. He suggested it was a neurobiological dysfunction "of genetic origin," thus attributing his life problems to a chemical imbalance.

As the notion of ADHD in adulthood was filtering into the public, the psychiatric profession was also turning attention to this new problem. Clinics for adults with ADHD were established at Wayne State University in 1989 and two years later at the University of Massachusetts in Worcester (Jaffe 1995).

In 1990, Dr. Alan Zametkin of the National Institute of Mental Health and several of his colleagues published an often-cited article in the *New England Journal of Medicine.* Using positron-emission tomography (PET) scanning to measure brain metabolism, Zametkin demonstrated different levels of brain activity in individuals with ADHD compared to those without the disorder, providing new evidence for a biologic basis for ADHD. Because of the risks inherent in research involving radiologic images, the researchers used adult subjects who both had childhood histories of hyperactivity and were biological parents of hyperactive children. Although not their intention, Zametkin's work became one of the key professional sources cited by others to demonstrate the presence of ADHD in adults (e.g., Bartlett 1990; and *Newsweek,* December 3, 1990), since it appeared to bolster claims that ADHD could persist into or develop during adulthood.[5] While the study made national headlines, additional follow-up studies which did not confirm the strength of the initial study's findings, received no widespread publicity from the professional and lay press.[6]

ADULT ADHD IN THE PUBLIC SPHERE

Writing about ADHD as a disorder in adults has been increasing in the professional literature for years. As can be seen in Table 3.1, by the middle 1980s there were over 40 articles in the medical literature and about a dozen in the psychological literature published per year (with some overlap). Many of these articles were minor and nearly all dealt with the persistence of symptoms in hyperactive children as they reached adulthood. The issue of "ADHD adults" *per se* did not reach the popular media until the 1990s (see Table 3.1) and in a moderate, but growing number of articles. But the idea that adults could have ADHD did spread with the help of a variety of media.

By the early 1990s, several books written for a popular audience looking specifically at ADHD adults were published. Psychologist Lynn Weiss (1992) identified her adult subjects as those who were diagnosable with ADHD, not merely grown-up

Table 3.1.   Adult ADHD in the Professional and Lay Media Mean Articles per year, 1975–1999 (in five year intervals)*

	Professional Media		Lay Media		
	Medline	Psychinfo	Academic Universe		
Year			Wire Service	NE Regional	Magazines
1975–1979	34.4	3.4	0	0	0
1980–1984	41.6	7.6	0	0	0
1985–1989	43.6	11.4	0	0.4	0.2
1990–1994	50.0	13.8	5.8	6.0	0.4
1995–1999	95.6	42.6	25.2	28.6	3.2

*For this table, we do not distinguish between articles on "adult hyperactives" or "ADHD Adults." Search criteria: *Medline and Psychinfo databases:* adult and (ADHD or "attention deficit hyperactivity disorder" or "attention deficit disorder" or hyperkinesis). *Academic Universe:* in text search for: "Attention deficit disorder or ADHD or hyperkinesis" and in headline or lead paragraph: "adult." Sources are divided among wire service (e.g., *Associated Press, United Press International*). New England Regional Newspapers (e.g., *Boston Globe, New York Times*), and Popular Magazines (e.g., *Ladies Home Journal, Newsweek*).

hyperactive children having remnants of they symptoms carried over from an earlier condition. Another popular book quickly followed with the provocative title of, *You Mean I'm Not Lazy, Stupid or Crazy?!* (Kelly and Ramundo 1993), emphasizing the shift in responsibility that being diagnosed with adult ADHD can bring. Thom Hartmann (1994), writing in a somewhat esoteric, but essentially sociobiological frame, associated ADHD with an evolutionary adaptation to the social environment. He likened those with ADHD to hunters (who are nomadic, scanning the environment for sustenance, seeking of sensation, reacting quickly and decisively) adapting to a more modern farming community (which requires greater stability and focus). This hypothesis, by its nature, supports the notion of ADHD adults.

Further support came from the television news media reports on the spread of ADHD in adults. Major news shows put their own spin on the prevalence of the disorder. For example on "20/20," Catherine Crier attributed ADHD to a "biologic disorder of the brain" in adults (September 2, 1994). Dr. Timothy Johnson on "Good Morning America" (March 28, 1994) was quoted as saying that experts estimate as many as 10 million adult Americans may have ADHD (Vatz and Weinberg 1997, p. 77). The new face of the disorder was not limited to hyperactive children grown-up, but included a new group of "ADHD adults" who came to reinterpret their current and previous behavioral problems in light of an ADHD diagnosis.

The message was reiterated in popular magazines. A feature article in *Newsweek,* for example, described a 38-year old security guard who held more than 128 jobs since leaving college after being enrolled in the academic institution for 13 years (Cowley and Ramo 1993). He finally "received a diagnosis that changed his life" at the adult ADHD clinic at the University of Massachusetts in Worcester. Similarly, an article in *Ladies Home Journal* (Stich 1993) described a husband who would continually be fired from job after job, constantly interrupted his wife, and forgot details of conversations. Then "Two years ago, the Pearsons discovered there was a medical reason for Chuck's problems. After their son was diagnosed with attention deficit disorder (ADD) . . . they learned Chuck also had the condition" (Stich 1993, p. 74). The article does not mention the fact that Chuck, who was diagnosed at age 54, also went on to found the Adult Attention Deficit Foundation, which acts as a clearinghouse for information about adult ADHD (Wallis 1994, p. 47).

Adult ADHD was given a great boost in 1994 with the publication of a bestselling book *Driven to Distraction* by Edward Hallowell and John Ratey (1994), two psychiatrists with prestigious organizational affiliations. Hallowell offered his own experience as the springboard for the book: although successful as a medical student, and later as a practicing psychiatrist, he came to believe he had ADHD. Ratey also stated he had ADHD. The book has become a crucial touchstone among the lay public. Using their clinical experience as the basis for their book, Hallowell and Ratey (1994) argue that ADHD takes various forms. Based upon their clinical experience, Hallowell and Ratey propose "suggested diagnostic criteria for attention deficit disorder in adults" (p. 76). These criteria recognize the disorder without hyperactivity. They present thirteen sub-types of the disorder, a set of "suggested diagnostic criteria," and offer a 100-question test (with elusive criteria[7]) for readers to assess whether or not they may need to seek evaluation for ADHD. The authors urge readers not to self-diagnose, but seek professional assessment of their condition. Neither Hallowell nor Ratey is a hyperactivity researcher—Ratey published only one article on the topic in a professional journal (Ratey, et al. 1992) and Hallowell, none. Both remain very active in promoting their work in public circles. Their affiliation with Harvard Medical School gave them some academic legitimacy, but they came to the area of ADHD adults more as professional advocates than as scientific researchers. In a sense, they are moral entrepreneurs for the adult diagnosis (Leffers 1997).

The cover of July 18, 1994 *Time* magazine issued a clarion call for ADHD adults: "Disorganized? Distracted? Discombobulated? Doctors Say You Might Have ATTENTION DEFICIT DISORDER. It's not just kids who have it." The 9-page article disseminated the criteria and possibilities of ADHD in adults to a wide audience, including speculations that Ben Franklin, Winston Churchill, Albert Einstein, and Bill Clinton may have had the disorder (Wallis 1994).

Organizational Stake-holders

Over the years a number of parents and advocacy groups emerged around ADHD in children, inlcuding those involved in the learning disabilities movement (Erchak and Rosenfeld 1989). The largest ADHD support group, Children and Adults with Attention Deficit Disorder (Ch.A.D.D.), has grown significantly over the last decade and owes much of its growth to its adult membership, specifically, those adult members with ADHD. In its activities, as well as its framing of ADHD, the organization has helped expand the categorization to include adults. In 1990, the parent organization sponsored a national meeting that featured three adults with ADD and four professionals as speaker (Jaffe 1995). In 1993, the organization added the "and adults" to its name to reflect its broadened focus. In May 1993, a Ch.A.D.D.-sponosred national conference entitled, "The Changing World of Adults with ADD," attracted representatives from 30 states and two Canadian provinces. The organization now sees education and support of adults with ADHD as part of its core mission. For example, on its web page, the organization proclaims, "With relative certainty, we can predict that AD/-HD will continue to influence the behavior and attitude of an individual throughout his or her life . . ." (http://www.CHADD.org/attention/attnv5n4p12.htm). In addition to lobbying for educational service for children, Ch.A.D.D. advocates legislation that provides workplace protection for adults with ADHD.[8] In all official publications and communications, Ch.A.D.D. has positioned ADHD as a medical condition, a "neurobiological disorder," rather than as a psychiatric or behavioral disorder (Diller 1997, p. 130; http://www.CHADD.org), so it can be perceived as having a more legitimate claim to disability entitlements.

Ch.A.D.D. played a significant role in bringing the lay and professional claims-makers together to promote better understanding, acceptance, and treatment of ADHD (Leffers 1997). Additionally, not only does Ch.A.D.D. promote the existence of adult ADHD to the public, the organization legitimates the disorder for sufferers, almost as much as the individual diagnosis does. Similar to other controversial illnesses (e.g., Kroll-Smith and Floyd 1997), the organization is both a haven and advocate for those who believe they suffer from the disorder.

Another organizational stakeholder is the pharmaceutical firm of Ciba-Geigy that manufactures Ritalin (methylphenidate), the drug most widely prescribed for treating ADHD. Ciba-Geigy has long been involved in promoting hyperactivity and now, ADHD as a medical disorder (Conrad 1975; Schrag and Divoky 1976). As early as 1971, Ritalin provided as much as 15 percent of Ciba's gross profits (Conrad 1976, p. 16). While the original patent on the drug has long expired, and methylphenidate is available in generic formulations, Ritalin is still the most commonly prescribed medication for ADHD (Arnst 1999) and one of the three most commonly prescribed stimulants (Ballard, et al. 1997). The amount of methylphenidate manufactured has increased sharply in the 1990s. From 1990 through 2000, the production of methylphenidate in the United States grew by 800% (Wen 2000).[9] One national survey of physicians' diagnoses, based on 1993 data, found that of the 1.8 million persons receiving medications for ADHD, 1.3 million were taking methylphenidate (cited in Diller 1996, p. 12). Other sources have variously estimated that 2.6 million children (Guistolise 1998) and 729,000 adults received prescriptions for Ritalin (Breggin 1998, p. 160). The potential market, with 3 million children and 4 million adults in the U.S. diagnosed with ADHD (Arnst 1999), has untapped pockets.[10] By redefining ADHD as a lifetime disorder, the potential exists for keeping children and adults on medication indefinitely. A recent review article noted, "The eightfold increase in the use of stimulants in the United States over the past decade stems from several increase in the use of stimulants in the United States over the past decade stems from several factors, including the continuation of treatment from childhood into adolescence and the treatment of adults" (Zametkin and Ernst 1999, p. 45). While it is difficult to accurately assess what proportion of this huge increase of Ritalin use is for ADHD adults, it is likely to be a substantial proportion.

These organizational stake-holders have worked both independently and in consort. Ciba-Geigy reportedly has provided significant financial assistance through a variety of support mechanisms that assist adults with ADHD, including the support group Ch.A.D.D. and a video produced for the Office of Special Education Programs (OSEP) (Diller 1996). In 1995, The Merrow Report, a public radio talk show, reported that Ch.A.D.D. received significant financial contributions from Ciba-Geigy (PBS 1995). The public outcry and media attention questioned the neutrality of this group. Since then, Ch.A.D.D. continued to claim that the percentage of its funding from pharmaceutical companies never exceeded 17% and has been decreased to less than 10%, and is used only for educational programs (www.CHADD.org/presso4-13-98.htm).

DIAGNOSTIC INSTITUTIONALIZATION

By 1994, DSM-IV reflected the growing consensus that adults could be diagnosed with ADHD, provided they had exhibited symptoms as children before the age of seven. Two (out of the five) diagnostic criteria were clearly relevant to adults. First, DSM-IV required that "some impairment must occur in at least 2 settings." While for children, these settings usually mean school and home, the range of settings may be greater for adults and include home, school, work, and other vocational or recreational settings. Secondly and related, "there must be clear evidence of interference with developmentally appropriate social, academic, or occupational functioning." The inclusion of work environments in the criteria section of the manual reflected the central and relatively uncontroversial position that the diagnosis of ADHD in adults now occupied.[11]

The new definition allowed for more variations of symptomatic behavior across and within settings. "It is very unusual for an individual to display the same level of dysfunction in all settings or within the same setting at all times" (APA 1994, p. 79). Adults who might be quite successful at work, but highly inattentive in particular interpersonal relationships and recreational activities, could now be diagnosed with ADHD. As the more expansive criteria in DSM-IV gained acceptance among mental health professionals, some advocated eliminating the requirement that adults be able to retrospectively reconstruct a history of ADHD (Barkley and Biederman 1997). This would permit even greater expansion of the adult ADHD category.

Reports from the American Medical Association (AMA) and the National Institutes of Health (NIH) supported an expanded ADHD diagnosis. In 1997, the Council of Scientific Affairs of the AMA issued recommendations for treating ADHD, which were published in *JAMA* (April 8, 1998). The article noted:

> The criteria of what constitutes ADHD in children have broadened, and there is a growing appreciation of the persistence of ADHD into adolescence and adulthood. As a result, more children (especially girls), adolescents, and adults are being diagnosed and treated with stimulant medication, and children are being treated for longer periods of time (Goldman, et al. 1998, p. 1100).

The report concluded there was "little evidence of widespread overdiagnosis or misdiagnosis of ADHD or of widespread overprescription of methylphenidate by physicians" (Goldman, et al., 1998, p. 1100). In November 1998, NIH convened a Consensus Conference on the Diagnosis and Treatment of Attention Deficit Hyperactivity. While little new emerged from the conference, two papers explicitly focused on adults with ADHD. Overall, the conference report affirmed the validity of ADHD, although recognizing scientific controversies, the need fore more basic and longitudinal research, and a lack of consensus on optimal treatment (http://odp.od.nih.gov/consensus/cons/110/110_statement.htm).

Further institutional support for the ADHD diagnosis in adults has come from prestigious professional publications. A lead editorial in the *American Journal of Psychiatry* (Shaffer 1994) and major review articles in *New England Journal of Medicine* (Elia, et al. 1999 and Zametkin and Ernst 1999), which included discussions of ADHD in adults, symbolized the acceptance of the diagnostic category in medical circles.

It is clear that by 1994, the clinical diagnosis of ADHD had expanded to include adolescence and adulthood and had become institutionalized in psychiatry and medicine. One longtime researcher called it "the most common chronic undiagnosed psychiatric disorder in adults" (Wender 1998, p. 671).

Diagnosis

One of the starkest contrasts to the earlier history of ADHD with children is the vast amount of self-diagnosis of ADHD among adults. Virtually all children were referred by parents or schools to physicians (Conrad 1976). Among adults self-referrals are the norm, and many patients come to physicians apparently seeking an ADHD diagnosis. Frequently, adults who encounter a description of the disorder, sense that "this is me" and go on to seek professional confirmation of their new identity. Another common path to self-diagnosis occurs when parents bring a child to a physician for treatment and remark, "I was the same when I was a kid . . ." and thus, begin to see themselves and their own difficulties through the lens of ADHD. While this trend appears to have been precipitated by some of the popular press (e.g., Hallowell and Ratey 1994), it continues with legitimization provide by support groups designed for adults with ADHD such as Ch.A.D.D.

Anecdotes in the popular literature suggest that adults who self-diagnose, may recognize the condition in a popular media article or book. Hallowell and Ratey (1994) tell of one woman who noted, "My husband showed me this article in the paper" (p. 26). Comments on Internet sites state directly that it was one of the books on adult ADHD that led individuals to physicians for a diagnosis. Diller (1997) relates that one of his patients came to self-diagnosis after reading *Driven to Distraction*. Diller points out that, while the physician who is presented with such a self-diagnosed patient may have difficulty establishing the existence of symptoms in their childhood (as opposed to a checklist of symptoms absorbed through reading), the self-diagnosis, itself, becomes an element that the professional diagnosis must take into account. One psychiatrist wrote a colleague, "Adult ADHD has now become the foremost *self-diagnosed* condition in my practice. I fear that the condition allows a patient to find a biological cause that is not always reasonable, for job failure, divorce, poor motivation, lack of success, and chronic depression" (Shafer 1994, p. 638).

Diagnosis-seeking behavior is an integral feature of the emergence of Adult ADHD. This is kind of self-labeling, information exchange, and pursuit of diagnosis fuels the social engine medicalizing certain adult troubles. Without it, the spread of Adult ADHD would be seriously limited.

CRITICS, SKEPTICS AND COUNTER-CLAIMS

Even with well-established diagnoses such as ADHD in children, there may be skeptics and critics who dismiss the validity of diagnoses, criticize over-diagnosis, or enumerate the dangers of pharmacological treatment. Although such attempts to rein in medicalization have had little impact on Adult ADHD, they remain a reservoir of counter-claims that could affect diagnostic expansion.

Some therapists who treat those with ADHD believe that the diagnosis is becoming too prevalent. "Certainly, some people diagnosed with ADHD are neurologically impaired and need medication. But the disorder is also being named as the culprit for all sorts of abuses, hypocrisies, neglects, and other societal ills that have nothing to do with ADHD"

(Bromfield 1996, p. 32). Alan Zametkin, a leading researcher on ADHD, has become quite critical of what he has called "a cottage industry of adult ADD" (Kolata 1996).

Beginning in the late 1980s, the Church of Scientology launched a major media campaign against the use of Ritalin with children. Although the controversial church remained an outsider in the debate, for several years they offered continuous public criticism about ADHD (Leffers 1997). Furthermore, a number of popular books critical of the "epidemic" of ADHD and Ritalin usage have been published: *Running on Ritalin* (Diller 1997), *Ritalin Nation* (DeGrandpre 1999), and *Talking Back to Ritalin* (Breggin 1998). While most of the books focused their critiques on the diagnosis and drug treatment of children, they offered some skepticism about the disorder in general.

The popular media that had been actively involved in publicizing the prevalence of the disorder among adults in 1993 and 1994 has become more critical in subsequent years. Leading the challenge was a prominent, front-page article in *Time Magazine* (Wallis 1994); the synopsis banner read, "Doctors say huge numbers of kids and adults have attention deficit disorder. Is it for real?" "60 Minutes" (December 10, 1995) produced segments that highlighted the absence of a definitive test for ADHD. Other major news shows focused on controversies about the subjectivity of ADHD diagnoses and the over-prescription of Ritalin (e.g., The "Today" Show on October 24, 1995; CNN on November 2, 1995; "20/20" on December 20, 1995; and "ABC Evening News" on March 28, 1996—reported in Vatz and Weinberg 1997).

Most of the criticism has been about the overdiagnosis and treatment among children. And even in this context, there are also a steady number of articles supportive of treating the disorder (e.g., Gladwell 1999). Only a small amount of the criticism has been directed against notions of adult ADHD. Yet, ironically, controversy about ADHD raises the public's awareness and increases the diffusion of information about the disorder, which can indirectly contribute to diagnostic expansion.

The Social Context for the Rise of Adult ADHD

The expansion of the hyperactivity diagnosis to adults is not, primarily, the result of new scientific discoveries about the biomedical nature of the disorder. While a number of studies indicated that symptoms in children diagnosed as ADHD could persist beyond childhood, the studies also showed that this occurred in perhaps a third of the cases (Weiss, et al. 1979). To the best of our knowledge, there were no breakthrough epidemiological or clinical studies that identified a population of adults as having ADHD who were not previously diagnosed in childhood. Yet it is clear that "adult ADHD" has become a more common and accepted diagnosis in recent years. What would bring adults to physicians seeking such a diagnosis and what spurs physicians to treat them? Several social factors appear to have contributed to the diagnostic expansion.

THE PROZAC ERA

Since the introduction of chlorpromazine in 1955, there has been a pscyhopharmacological revolution in psychiatry (Healy 1997). Psychoactive medications played a major role in deinstitutionalization and became regular parts of physicians' treatment protocols for various life problems, especially anxiety (e.g., Valium). American psychiatrists preferred drugs that would be useful in office psychiatry, rather than medications limited to inpatient populations (Healy, p. 70).

In 1987, Prozac (fluoxetine) was introduced as a new type of medication to treat depression. This drug is a selective serotonin reuptake inhibitor that directly affected a different group of neurotransmitters with fewer unpleasant side effects than previous types of antidepressants. This drug quickly became a phenomenon in itself, and led to a whole new class of drugs for treating psychiatric and life problems. Peter Kramer's book, *Listening to Prozac* (1993) and the subsequent news media coverage (e.g., cover stories in *Newsweek* and *New York* magazines, and dozens of TV and radio appearances), piqued the public interest in this new drug. Prozac was increasingly depicted as a medication that was a psychic energizer and that could make people feel, in Kramer's terms, "better than well." Prozac was not seen as a medication only for the seriously disturbed, but was a formulation that could improve the lives of people with minor disturbances and distresses.

The introduction and popularity of Prozac (and a series of related medications) created a context whereby taking medications for life problems was more acceptable (cf., Diller 1996). Prozac was seen as a drug that was appropriate for a range of psychic difficulties, and whose use could even make an OK life better. It led numerous people to redefine their life woes in terms of mild depression and seek treatment. A person did not have to be severely disturbed to benefit from Prozac. Similarly, Ritalin was now available to adults who had not been diagnosed as hyperactive in childhood, but who were now redefining their life difficulties as related to "inattention," "impulsivity," and "restlessness." The possibility that adults could "have" ADHD became common in parts of the culture and many individuals "recognized" that they, too, suffered from the disorder and sought treatment from physicians. For example, Hallowell and Ratey (1994) recount a case in which a patient demanded Ritalin for their as-yet-to-be officially diagnosed condition. As physicians have come to view ADHD symptoms as not limited to children, they are likely to offer an ADHD diagnosis and a "trial on Ritalin" to adults with certain kinds of life difficulties. The key here, however, is that our culture seems to be moving away from "pharmacological Calvinism" (Klerman cited in Healy 1997) to the idea that designer drugs might improve the functioning of most anyone.

GENETICS

Genetics is the rising paradigm in medicine and an increasing number of human problems are being attributed to genetic associations, markers, or causes (Conrad 1999). Some experts have long believed that there is a genetic component to ADHD and its predecessor, hyperactivity, but to date, evidence is only suggestive, even though the claims of inheritance date back at least 25 years (Cantwell 1975; Wender 1971; Wood, et al. 1976). After reviewing extant evidence, researchers noted, "Family, twin, adoption, and molecular genetic studies show that it has a substantial genetic component" (Faraone and Beiderman 1998. p. 951). Recent research has focused on a genetically induced imbalance of dopamine. Researchers posit a potential link between ADHD and three genes: D4 dopamine receptor gene, the dopamine transporter gene, and the D2 dopamine receptor gene (Faraone and Beiderman 1998). The thinking is that people who carry the gene overproduce dopamine, which impairs self-control. Some suggested that genetic inheritance might account for as much as 80 percent of the likelihood that one has ADHD (Barkley 1997, p. 39). Despite the research and much published testimony (e.g., parents reiterating about their ADHD child, "I was just like that when I was his age"), the genetic nature of ADHD is still contested. However, the greater the medical and public acceptance of a genetic component of ADHD, the more adult ADHD becomes a social reality. If the disorder is genetic, then it is deemed an intrinsic characteristic of people with the gene. This supports the notion that ADHD is a lifelong disorder, and the position that adults could have the disorder, even though they were never diagnosed as children.[12]

THE RISE OF MANAGED CARE

Managed care affects all aspects of medicine, including psychiatry. Health insurance imposes strict limits on the amount of psychotherapy for individual patients. Psychiatrists, now, must make use of utilization review, participate in medication management, consultation, or administering "carve-out programs" (Domino, et al. 1998). Mental health advocates and some researchers argue that, under managed care, there is a growing reliance upon various forms of prescription therapies to treat all types of psychiatric and life problems (Johnson 1998). A recent study found that managed care might fuel growth in the pharmaceutical industry (Murray and Deardorff 1998). Undoubtedly, there are now greater incentives for psychiatrists and other physicians to treat all potential mental health problems with medication, rather than with some form of talking or psychotherapy. Managed care tends to replace psychiatrists with primary care physicians who are less versed in "talking therapies" (Stoudemire 1996), and thereby, increasing the potential for relying on medication for treatment. Searight and Mclaren (1998) describe a "pragmatic assessment and treatment" that occurs when primary care physicians diagnose and treat ADHD children with pharmaceuticals. In fact, there is some evidence that ADHD children are treated with stimulant medications to the exclusion of other "talking therapies" (Woolraich, et al. 1990). It is likely there are similar trends with adult ADHD.

Furthermore, this apparent treatment preference may encourage the expansion of drug treatable diagnoses, since these are reimbursable under managed care. It is feasible that problems that might have been diagnosed differently two decades ago (e.g., adult adjustment reaction) or seen as life dissatisfaction, now can be diagnosed and treated as ADHD. While we do not claim that managed care has caused the rise of adult ADHD, it is part of the context that makes ADHD a more likely diagnosis than in the past.

Some Consequences of the Adult ADHD Diagnosis

In a paper over two decades ago, Conrad (1975) outlined some of the ramifications of the medicalization of hyperactive behavior. These included: (1) the problem of expert control; (2) the uses of medical social control; (3) the individualization of social problems; and (4) the depoliticization of deviant behavior. To these, he later added the dislocation of responsibility from the individual to the nether world of biophysiological functioning (Conrad and Schneider 1992). Most of these can be applied to adult ADHD as well. The self-initiated and even self-diagnosed nature of most adult ADHD puts a different emphasis on some of these issues (e.g., depoliticization) but does not neutralize them. With adult ADHD, it may be the shift from personal responsibility and the individualization of life problems that are most critical. Creating a "medical excuse" directs attention away from social forces to biogenic ones and shifts blame from the person to the body. Thus, adult ADHD carries with it some unique consequences, especially since most cases are self-referred adults.

THE MEDICALIZATION OF UNDERPERFORMANCE

What is interesting about adult ADHD is that many of the individuals who are given the diagnosis are, by some measures, successful individuals. Ratey and Hallowell, for example, are both psychiatrists affiliated with a major medical school and authors of a best-selling book, yet identify themselves as having ADHD. Frank Wolkenberg was a successful free-lance artist. In a widely publicized and controversial article, James Trilling (1999) characterized both himself (a professor and author) and his late father, the renowned literary critic, Lionel Trilling, as suffering from ADHD. Both lay and professional accounts of adult ADHD commonly provide examples of adults who have achieved success by many conventional social measures (e.g., Hallowell and Ratey 1994; Leffers 1997). There are, of course, individuals with limited achievement who are also defined as ADHD, but the issues remain similar. In fact, Hallowell and Ratey see their audience as "chronic underachievers" whose difficulties are caused, not by a lack of self-discipline, but by an inborn neurological condition.

For adults, the issue surrounding ADHD is performance, not behavior. As Diller (1997, p. 277) notes:

> In broadest terms, moving from childhood to later life for those with ADD involves a shift from problems with behavior to problems with performance. The simple fact of hyperactivity or impulsivity is not the chief concern for teens and adults: rather, it's their disorganization, irresponsibility, procrastination, and inability to complete tasks.

The adult ADHD diagnosis often stems from a perception of underperformance. This underperformance can be reflected in how tasks are accomplished, continual problematic adaptation, or the level of success achieved. Individuals feel that they could/should be doing better and seek help in improving their performance. The ADHD diagnosis provides a medical explanation for their underperformance, allows for the re-evaluation of past behavior, and by shifting responsibility for problems reduces self-blame. A man who has come to see his ADHD as underlying the chaos in his life said, "I always though I was stupid" (quoted in Hales and Hales 1993, p. 64). Laura, a minister, "always did very well, was always at or near the top of her class through high school, and seminary. . . . But now, she told [the psychiatrist], academics had always been a struggle for her" (Hallowell and Ratey 1994, pp. 83–84). Another woman reflected, "I had 38 years of thinking I was a bad person. Now I'm rewriting the tapes of who I thought I was to who I really am" (Wallis 1994, p. 43).

But beyond an explanation, Ritalin provides a strategy for improving the underperformance. Ritalin has been credited with saving marriages, rebuilding faltering careers, and transforming what had been problematic personalities. For example, "once Sam's ADD was diagnosed, he started on Ritalin at a dosage of 10 mg three times a day, and it worked well in helping him focus and reducing his mood swings" (Hallowell and Ratey 1994, p. 111). A 43-year-old woman reports, "I was able to sit down and listen to what my husband had done at work. Shortly after, I was able to sit in bed and read while my husband watched TV" (Wallis 1994, p. 49). Some even describe a personal epiphany after first taking Ritalin. "The first day after starting to take the medication, walking down the Brooklyn street on which I then lived, I noticed the sky through the leaves of a tree and stopped to look at it. After a minute, it struck me that, for the first time in my life, I was looking at something with no sensation of having to stop and move on" (Wolkenberg 1987, p. 82).

A NEW DISABILITY

A diagnosis of ADHD puts an individual into the larger category of having a "disability," which can serve as a gateway to potential claims to certain benefits and accommodations. Within this "rights" framework, the diagnosis has been interpreted, primarily, as a learning disorder (rather than a psychiatric disorder). While previous research has analyzed the role of ADHD-based claims to rights within children's education (cf., Searight and Mclaren 1998), the expansion of the diagnosis permits the medicalization of adult ADHD to gain further legal legitimization within the institutions of medicine, as well as employment and adult education.

As ADHD was coming to be identified as a disorder among adults in the early 1990s, individuals began to pursue legal actions to lay claim to rights under legislation such as the American with Disabilities Act and the Rehabilitation Act of 1973. Although rights are guaranteed under these statutes, they are only enforceable through civil suit. ADHD is not one of the conditions explicitly covered under the ADA, yet advocates have argued that the disorder falls under the umbrella of the law. When ADHD is of sufficient severity to affect an otherwise qualified individual by limiting a major life activity, protections are afforded under the ADA (Latham and Latham 1995). Individuals with ADHD have field suits so that they might receive reasonable accommodations in education and in the workplace (Jaffe 1995). For example, a search using the legal database of Lexis-Nexis, identified 211 cases in federal labor law between 1980 and 1999 that concern ADHD (many of which include school boards or universities).

Clearly a diagnosis of adult ADHD carries with it a certain currency in the public sphere. The public is aware of these disability-related issues. A key article appeared in the *Wall Street Journal* in 1993 that outlined workplace and criminal justice issues for those with ADHD. A book on ADD-related disability law was published for advocates in 1992 (Latham and Latham 1992). Not only are individuals with ADHD the potential beneficiaries of a "medical excuse" for their life problems, but they may be eligible for specific benefits under the ADA. Individuals who, prior to diagnosis, would not have seen themselves having a disability find themselves reaping the benefits of disability legislation. Under the ADA, individuals with ADHD are entitled to "reasonable accommodations" if their disorder is sufficiently severe to interfere with tasks that they are otherwise qualified to perform. Accommodations could include untimed tests, oral versus written administration of tests or instructions, additional time to complete tasks, structured work assignments with written instructions, extra clerical support, more frequent performance appraisals, checklists for multi-stage tasks, diminished capacity arguments in criminal suits, and protection against discrimination (taken from Latham and Latham 1995; Nadeau 1995). The 1997 guidelines from the Equal Employment Opportunity Commission (EEOC) led to a list of accommodations for ADHD-diagnosed employees, including special office furniture, equipment such as tape recorders and laptops, and "organizational schemes (color coding, buddy systems, alarm clocks, and other 'reminders') designed to keep such employees on track" (Eberstadt 1999).

On Adult ADHD and Medicalized Category Expansion

Adult ADHD offers a clear example of how a medicalized category can expand to include a wider range of troubles within its definition. ADHD's expansion was, primarily, accomplished by refocusing the diagnosis on inattention, rather than hyperactivity and stretching the age criteria. This allowed for the inclusion of an entire population of people and their problems that were excluded by the original conception of hyperactive children.

The expanded category, adult ADHD, has become what Ian Hacking (1995, p. 96) terms "an object of knowledge" with discernable symptoms, putative causes, and particular treatment and care. Adult ADHD is recognized widely as an entity that is real, a "natural category" that only needs proper application. While thirty years ago adult ADHD might have been an oxymoron, today it is deemed a discrete disorder that can be claimed and diagnosed.

What is particularly interesting about the adult ADHD case is the role of lay groups in promoting the expansive medicalization. The lay-professional alliance (see also, Leffers 1997), best exemplified by Ch.A.D.D., but also evident in the media presentations, suggests an alignment between the claims of sufferers and professionals. This contrasts sharply with the case of multiple chemical sensitivity disorder where there is a clear-cut disjunction between lay claim-makers and skeptical professionals (Kroll-Smith and Lloyd 1997) and chronic fatigue syndrome, where individuals may have a difficult time getting their symptoms medically legitimated (Cooper 1997). The lay promotion of adult ADHD and the predominance of self-diagnosis contradict some of the basic premises of the labeling theory of psychiatric diagnosing (Scheff 1984), which suggests a fundamental conflict between social control agents and putative deviants. In the adult ADHD case, the diagnosis is embraced and promoted by the people who receive it. This suggests that this may be a different kind of psychiatric diagnosis from those sociologists typically study, one that is sought out by the very people to whom it is to be applied. In this case, medication treatment may be seen as much as an enhancement as a form of social control.

Studies have shown that the interaction of lay and professional claims-makers, rather than "medical imperialism," typically underlies the medicalization process. But the case of adult ADHD indicates that popularization may also play a part in diagnostic expansion. Media, including TV, popular literature, and now the Internet, spread the word quickly about illnesses and treatment. This popularization of symptoms and diagnosis can create new "markets" for disorders and empower previously unidentified sufferers to seek treatment as new or expanded medical explanations become popularly available. The widespread popular acceptance of entities as illnesses suggests a *feedback loop* among professionals, claims-makers, media, and the public in terms of the creation, expansion, and application of illness categories. Just as medicalization research has moved from focusing primarily on the claims and activities of physicians, to examining the interplay of professional and lay claims-makers, it behooves us to investigate how medical diagnoses penetrate in the public consciousness and become "taken-for-granted as an objective natural entity" in the public sphere (Horwitz 2002). Such medical diagnostic entities are often accepted without recognizing their history and with an assumption of their universal categorical significance regardless of cultural context. Within an increasingly medically aware public reside individuals who take identified "symptoms" as revealing an underlying disease condition and, in cases like adult ADHD, may seek to attain their diagnosis of choice.

But in terms of diagnostic expansion, the ADHD case is not unique. We can point to other cases where medicalized categories, which were originally developed and legitimated for one set of problems, were extended or reframed to include a broader range of problems. Several examples come to mind. Post-Traumatic Stress Disorder (PTSD) was originally conceived of as a disorder of returning Viet Nam war veterans who suffered from the aftereffects of brutal combat experience (e.g., with flashbacks, sleep problems, intense anxiety, etc.) (Scott 1990; Young 1995). But in recent years, PTSD has been applied to rape and incest survivors, disaster victims, and witnesses to violence. Alcoholism was medicalized, in large part, due to the efforts of AA (Conrad and Schneider 1992), but the medicalization has expanded to include adult children of alcoholics, enablers, and especially "codependency" (Irvine 1999). Child abuse, which was originally limited to battering, has expanded to include sexual abuse and neglect, and to lesser extent, child pornography and exploitation (cf., Best 1990 and 1999) and, to a degree, spawned the larger domain of domestic violence (including woman battering and elder abuse). In 1972, multiple personality disorder was a rare diagnosis (estimated at less than a dozen cases in 50 years); by 1992, thousands of multiples were diagnosed. This "epidemic" resulted from the diagnostic reconceptualization to "dissociative identity disorder" in DSM-IIIR with less restrictive criteria and an association with child abuse (Hacking 1995).[13]

Definitional categories are potentially elastic and can be stretched to include more phenomena within their realm. This may be particularly true with medicalized categories because of the social advantages of medical definitions (e.g., mitigation of personal blame, medical excuse, health insurance, or disability benefits), although fiscal constraints of medicine may set limits on certain applications (Conrad 2000). While, in general, the expansion of medical categories may be limited by the carrying capacity of the medical profession and the health insurance industry (cf., Hilgartner and Bosk 1988), it appears that with active claims-makers, committed stake-holders, and receptive potential clients, diagnostic expansion can occur readily and with minimal opposition. Similar to domain expansion, diagnostic expansion begins with established disorders and moves toward more problematic claims. One legitimated medical category can beget others.

It is interesting to consider whether a parallel process of diagnostic contraction may take place. Some have suggested this narrowing has occurred for serious mental illness. With the increased reliance on primary care providers in managed care, for example, some research has suggested an underrecognition of some serious mental disorders (Stoudemire 1996). Others have noted that the "medical necessity" standard has altered, not only treatment, but also diagnosis (Ford 1998). It stands to reason that, in the age of managed care, shrinkage of the medical domain is a likely outcome. Yet as noted in the adult ADHD example, managed care may have paradoxically played a role in the emergence of this new category. Whatever the ultimate outcome of problem definitions, it seems clear the flexibility of certain medical diagnoses allows for expansion and, thus, the increase of medicalization in our society.

Notes

1. More recently, Best (1999) has drawn on the work of Stallings (1990) to make a distinction between "domain expansion" and "domain elaboration," the latter being a process related to domain expansion, which "involves the identification of new aspects of a problem" (Best, 1999, p. 169). The terms "domain elaboration" and "domain expansion" overlap considerably in their meaning and both refer to the way in which expanding categories of social problems results in additional claims-makers and advocates identifying with the problem, promoting its continued problematization, and keeping the problem alive in the public eye. To maintain consistency throughout this paper, we have chosen to use the more familiar term "domain expansion.

2. A recent study by Leffers (1997) focuses on how individuals with ADHD come to understand their problems and how the social construction of the disorder affects this understanding. The present paper is more of a sociological account of the expansion of the ADHD diagnosis to adults.

3. For example, although the cohort continued to exhibit signs of hyperactivity, a twenty-year follow-up found 36% of the cohort symptomatic—a less widely reported statistic (e.g., *Newsweek,* 1990). Even "experts" (such as Edward Hallowell) are cited in the popular literature referring to "seventy percent of the kids who have it continue to suffer symptoms as adults" (Stich 1993, p. 77). The figure of 70% appears to come from a study published by Wender in 1995, but is not the most accepted estimate of persistence of symptoms.

4. DSM-III, the third revision, aimed for more rigorous diagnoses and represented the dominance of the biopsychiatric viewpoint in psychiatry over other perspectives (Cooksey and Brown 1998).

5. Referencing the work of others, Zametkin noted that "the disorder is probably inherited in certain families" and "symptoms persist into adulthood in 40 to 60 percent of the persons with childhood hyperactivity," but these claims were primarily in the context of justifying using an adult sample (Zametkin, et al. 1990, p. 1361).

6. The follow-up studies using adolescent populations produced varied results (e.g., Ernst, et al. 1994; Zametkin, et al. 1993). Additionally, with more evidence in, scientists are less sure that PETs establish a clear marker of ADHD—in children or in adults.

7. Questions include: "Do you change the radio station in your car frequently?" and "Are you always on the go, even when you don't really want to be?" The authors provide no normative standards against which to judge the answers.

8. As a claims-maker, Ch.A.D.D. spans several significant sectors, Ch.A.D.D. is buttressed by both the academic and business sectors of the ADHD community. The board of directors of Ch.A.D.D. includes well-known academic researchers and physicians working in the area of ADHD.

9. Production rates do not tell the entire story: while not all of the methylphenidate production is consumed in this country, a sizable portion is. According to the United Nations 1993 statistics, the U.S. produces and consumes more than 80% of all the methylphenidate (Guistolise 1998), but the DEA has estimated that the U.S. consumes over 90 percent of the 8.5 tons produced worldwide (Livingston 1997).

10. For many years, Ciba-Geigy actively proclaimed the benefits of Ritalin in advertisements. It is interesting that we have been unable to locate drug advertising for Ritalin for ADHD adults in major psychiatric or medical journals. Either Ciba-Geigy advertises Ritalin for ADHD through other channels—e.g., "detail" representatives who call on physicians or through conferences—or they have not promoted Ritalin for adult ADHD. Given the potential market, this is curious and worthy of further investigation.

11. In keeping with the approach begun with DSM-III, however, such markers are not seen as establishing the etiology of the disorder. Rather, they are diagnostic in nature. While the manual asserted that no biologic markers currently exist ("There are no laboratory tests that have been established as diagnostic . . ."), through the absence of such makers, the manual gives creditability to such tests. Therefore, in refuting the absence of any such tests, the manual may have laid the groundwork for the next version of the DSM to consider laboratory tests such as PET or SPECT. In fact, lay as well as professional claims-makers have been asserting the presence of genetic, as well as other biologic, markers of ADHD.

12. A recent article reported a sharp increase in Ritalin use among 2–4-year-old children enrolled in two Medicaid programs (Zito, et al. 2000). While safety and efficacy for such young children is unknown, and diagnostic validity even more problematic, this suggest that ADHD may be expanding in two directions age-wise, creating a lifelong disorder.

13. In a different domain the medicalization of childbirth has been the gateway to the medicalization of infertility, pregnancy, the post-natal period, and contributed to the medicalization of sexuality and sexual dysfunction.

References

American Psychiatric Association, The Committee on Nomenclature and Statistics. 1968. *DSM-II. Diagnostic and Statistical Manual of Mental Disorders,* Second Edition. Washington, DC: APA.

———. 1980. *DSM-III. Diagnostic and Statistical Manual of Mental Disorders,* Third Edition. Washington, DC: APA.

———. 1987. *DSM-III-R. Diagnostic and Statistical Manual of Mental Disorders,* Third Edition revised. Washington, DC: APA.

———. 1994. *DSM-IV. Diagnostic and Statistical Manual of Mental Disorders,* Fourth Edition. Washington, DC: APA.

Arnst, Catherine. 1999. "Attention deficit: Is it in the genes?" *Business Week* (November 22):70.

Aronowitz, Robert. 1998. *Making Sense of Illness: Science, Society and Disease.* Cambridge, UK: Cambridge University Press.

Balint, Michael. 1957. *The Doctor, His Patient, and the Illness.* New York: International Universities Press.

Ballard, Shirley, Morna Bolan, Michael Burton, Sherry Snyder, Claire Pasterczyk-Seabolt, and Don Martin. 1997. "The neurological basis of Attention Deficit Hyperactivity Disorder." *Adolescence* 32:855–862.

Barkely, Russell A. 1997. *ADHD and the Nature of Self-Control.* New York : Guilford Press.

Barkely, Russell A. and Joseph Biederman. 1997. "Toward a broader definition of the age-of-onset criterion for Attention-Deficit Hyperactivity Disorder." *Journal of the American Academy of Child and Adolescent Psychiatry* 36:1204–1210.

Barsky, Arthur J. and Jonathan F. Boros. 1995. "Somatization and medicalization in the era of managed care." *Journal of American Medical Association* 274:1931–1934.

Bartlett, K. 1990. "Attention deficit: Scientists move toward understanding of brain disorder once thought limited to children." *Houston Chronicle* (December 2):6G.

Best, Joel. 1990. *Threatened Children: Rhetoric and Concern about Child Victims.* Chicago: University of Chicago Press.

———. 1999. *Random Violence: How We Talk About New Crimes and New Victims.* Berkeley: University of California Press.

Biederman, Joseph, Stephen Faraone, Sharon Milberger, Jessica Guite, Eric Mick, Lisa Chen, Douglas Mennin, Abbe Marrs, Cheryl Ouellette, Phoebe Moore, Thomas Spencer, Dennis Norman, Timothy Wilens, Ilana Kraus, and James Perrin. 1996. "A prospective four-year follow-up study of Attention-Deficit Hyperactivity and related disorders." *Archives of General Psychiatry* 53:437–446.

Breggin, Peter. 1998. *Talking Back to Ritalin.* Monroe, ME: Common Courage Press.

Bromfield, Richard. 1996. "Fad or disorder?" *American Health* (June):32.

Broom, Dorothy H. and Roslyn V. Woodward. 1996. "Medicalization reconsidered: Toward a collaborative approach to care." *Sociology of Health and Illness* 18:357–378.

Brown, Phil. 1995. "Naming and framing: The social construction of diagnosis and illness." *Journal of Health and Social Behavior* (extra issue):34–52.

Cantwell, D. P. 1975. "Psychiatric illness in the families of hyperactive children." *Archives of General Psychiatry* 27:414–417.

Caplan, Paula. 1995. *They Say You're Crazy: How the World's Most Powerful Psychiatrists Decide Who's Normal.* Reading, MA: Addison-Wesley.

Conrad, Peter. 1975. "The discovery of Hyperkinesis: Notes on the medicalizaiton of deviant behavior." *Social Problems* 23:12–21.

———. 1975. *Identifying Hyperactive Children: The Medicalization of Deviant Behavior.* Lexington, MA: D.C. Heath.

———. 1992. "Medicalization and social control." *Annual Review of Sociology* 18:209–232.

———. 1999. "A mirage of genes." *Sociology of Health and Illness* 21:228–241.

———. 2000. "Medicalization, genetics, and human problems." In *The Handbook of Medical Sociology,* Fifth Edition, Chloe Bird, Peter Conrad, and Allen Fremont, eds., 322–333. Upper Saddle River, NJ: Prentice Hall.

Conrad, Peter and Joseph W. Schneider. 1992. *Deviance and Medicalization: From Badness to Sickness,* Expanded Edition. Philadelphia: Temple University Press.

Cooksey, Elizabeth and Phil Brown. 1998. "Spinning on its axes: DSM and the social construction of psychiatric diagnosis." *International Journal of Health Services* 28:525–554.

Cooper, Cooper. 1997. "Myalgic Encephalomyelities and the medical encounter." *Sociology of Health and Illness* 19:186–207.

Cowley, Geoffrey and Joshua Cooper Ramo. 1993. "The not-young and the restless." *Newsweek* (July 26):48–49.

DeGranpre, Richard. 1999. *Ritalin Nation: Rapid-Fire Culture and the Transformation of Human Consciousness.* New York: W. W. Norton and Company.

Diller, Lawrence H. 1996. "The run on Ritalin: Attention Deficit Disorder and stimulant treatment in the 1990s." *The Hastings Center Report* (March–April):12–18.

———. 1997. *Running on Ritalin.* New York: Bantam Books.

Domino, M. E., David S. Salkever, Deborah A. Zarin, and Harold Alan Pincus. 1998. "The impact of managed care on psychiatry." *Administration and Policy in Mental Health* 26:149–157.

Eberstadt, Mary. 1999. "Why Ritalin rules." *Policy Review* 94:24–40.

Elia, Josephine, Paul J. Ambrosini, and Judith L. Rapoport. 1999. "Treatment of Attention-Deficit-Hyperactivity Disorder." *New England Journal of Medicine* 340:780–788.

Epstein, Steven. 1996. *Impure Science: AIDS, Activism, and the Politics of Knowledge.* Berkeley: University of California Press.

Erchak, Gerald M. and Richard Rosenfeld. 1989. "Learning disabilities, dyslexia, and the medicalization of the classroom." In *Images of Issues,* Joel Best, ed. New York: Aldine de Gruyter.

Ernst, Monique, Robert M. Cohen, Laura L. Liebenauer, P.H. Jons, and Alan J. Zametkin. 1997. "Cerebral glucose metabolism in adolescent girls with Attention-Deficit/Hyperactivity Disorder." *Journal of the American Academy of Child and Adolescent Psychiatry* 36:1399–1406.

Ernst, Monique, Laura L. Liebenauer, A. C. King, G. A. Fitzgerald, R. M. Cohen, and Alan J. Zametkin. 1994. "Reduced brain metabolism in hyperactive girls." *Journal of the American Academy of Child and Adolescent Psychiatry* 33:858–868.

Faraone, Stephen V. and Joseph Biederman. 1998. "Neurobiology of Attention-Deficit Hyperactivity Disorder." *Biology and Psychiatry* 44 (Novemeber 15):951–958.

Figert, Anne E. 1996. *Women and the Ownership of PMS: The Structuring of a Psychiatric Disorder.* New York: Aldine de Gruyter.

Ford, W. E. 1998. "Medical necessity: Its impact in managed mental health care." *Psychiatric Services* 49:183–184.

Fox, Patrick. 1989. "From senility to Alzheimer's disease: The rise of the Alzheimer's movement." *Milbank Quarterly* 67:58–101.

Gittleman, Rachel, Salvatore Mannuzza, Ronald Shenker, and Noreen Bonagura. 1985. "Hyperactive boys almost grown up." *Archives of General Psychiatry* 42:937–947.

Gladwell, Malcolm. 1999. "Running from Ritalin." *New Yorker* (February 15):80–86.

Goldman, Larry S., Myron Genel, Robecca J. Bezman, and Priscilla J. Slanetz. 1998. "Diagnosis and treatment of Attention-Deficit/Hyperactivity Disorder in children and adults." *Journal of the American Medical Association* 279:1100–1107.

Gross, Mortimer B. and William E. Wilson. 1974. *Minimum Brain Dysfunction.* New York: Burnner Mazel.

Guadagnoli, Edward and Patricia Ward. 1998. "Patient participation in decision-making." *Social Science and Medicine* 47:329–39.

Guistolise, Jodi. 1998. "Special section: Attention Deficit Disorder: The Ritalin epidemic." *Home Education Magazine* 15 (May–June):30–31.

Hacking, Ian. 1995. *Rewriting the Soul: Multiple Personality and the Sciences of Memory.* Princeton, NJ: Princeton University Press.

Haines, Herb. 1989. "Primum non nocere: Chemical execution and the limits of medical social control." *Social Problems* 36:442–454.

Hales, Dianne and Robert E. Hales. 1993. "Pay attention: Hyperactivity isn't just for children anymore." *American Health* 12 (September):62–65.

Hallowell, Edward M. and John J. Ratey. 1994. *Driven to Distraction.* New York: Pantheon Books.

Halpern, Sydney A. 1990. "Medicalization as a professional process: Postwar trends in pediatrics." *Journal of Health and Social Behavior* 31:28–42.

Hartmann, Thom. 1994. *Attention Deficit Disorder: A Different Perception.* New York: Underwood Books.

Healy, David. 1997. *The Anti-Depressant Era.* Cambridge, MA: Harvard University Press.

Hilgartner, Stephen and Charles Bosk. 1988. "The rise and fall of social problems." *American Journal of Sociology* 94:53–78.

Horwitz, Allan V. 2002. *Creating Mental Illnesses: Diagnostic Psychiatry and the Proliferation of Mental Disease.* Chicago: University of Chicago Press.

http://odp.od.nih.gov/consensus/cons/110/110_statement.htm. 1998. Diagnosis and Treatment of Attention Deficit Hyperactivity Disorder. NIH Consensus Statement Online (Nov.16–18) 16, 2:1–37.

http://www.adders.org. n.d. "Your success stories and top tips for adults."

http://www.chadd.org. n.d. "Children and adults with Attention Deficit/Hyperactivity Disorder."

http://www.chadd.org/attention/attnv5n4p12.htm. n.d. "You and your AD/HD: Partners for life."

http://www.chadd.org/press04-13-98.htm. 1998. "Ch.A.D.D. 'talks back' to Peter Breggin." (Press release, April 14.)

Irvine, Janice M. 1994. "Regulated passions: The invention of inhibited sexual desire and sexual addiction." In *Deviant Bodies: Critical Perspectives on Science and Popular Culture,* Jacqueline Urla and Jennifer Terry, eds. Indianapolis: Indiana University Press.

Irvine, Leslie. 1999. *Codependent Forevermore: The Invention of Self in a Twelve Step Group.* Chicago: University of Chicago Press.

Jaffe, Paul. 1995. "History and overview of adulthood ADD." In *A Comprehensive Guide to Attention Deficit Disorder in Adults: Research, Diagnosis, and Treatment,* Kathleen G. Nadeau, ed. New York: Brunner/Mazel:3–17.

Jenness, Valerie. 1995. "Social movement growth, domain expansion and framing process: The gay/lesbian movement and violence against gays and lesbians as a social problem." *Social Problmes* 43:145–163.

Johnson, Dale L. 1998. "Are mental health services losing out in the U.S. under managed care?" *PharmacoEconomics* 14:597–601.

Kelly, Kate and Peggy Ramundo. 1993. *You Mean I'm Not Lazy, Stupid or Crazy?! A Self-Help Book for Adults with Attention Deficit Disorder.* Cincinnati: Tyrell and Jerem Press.

Kirk, Stuart A. and Herb Kutchins. 1992. *The Selling of DSM: The Rhetoric of Science in Psychiatry.* New York: Aldine de Gruyter.

Kolata, Gina. 1996. "Boom in Ritalin sales raises ethical issues." *The New York Times, Late New York edition* (May 15):C8.

Kramer, Peter. 1993. *Listening to Prozac.* New York: Penguin

Kroll-Smith, Steve and H. Hugh Floyd. 1997. *Bodies in Protest: Environmental Illness and the Struggle over Medical Knowledge.* New York: NYU Press.

Kutchins, Herb and Stuart A. Kirk. 1997. *Making Us Crazy: DSM: The Psychiatric Bible and the Creation of Mental Disorders.* New York: The Free Press.

Latham, Patricia H. and Peter S. Latham. 1992. *Attention Deficit Disorder and the Law: A Guide for Advocates.* Washington, DC: JKL Communications.

Latham, Peter S. and Patricia H. Latham. 1995. "Legal rights of the ADD adult." In *A Comprehensive Guide to Attention Deficit Disorder in Adults,* Kathleen G. Nadeau, ed., 337–350. New York: Brunner/Mazel Publishers.

Leffers, Jeanne Mahoney. 1997. The Social Construction of a New Diagnostic Category: Attention Deficit Disorder in Adults (Medicalization). Unpublished Ph.D. dissertation. Brown University.

Livingston, Ken. 1997. "Ritalin: Miracle drug or cop-out?" *Public Interest* 127 (Spring):3–18.

Loseke, Donileen R. 1999. *Thinking About Social Problems.* New York: Aldine de Gruyter.

Mannuzza, Salvatore, Rachel Gittleman, and Klein and Kathy A. Addalli. 1991. "Young adult mental status of hyperactive boys and their brothers: A prospective follow-up study." *Journal of the American Academy of Child and Adolescent Psychiatry* 30:743–751.

Mannuzza, Salvatore, Rachel G. Klein, Abrah Bressler, Patricia Malloy, and Maria LaPadula. 1998. "Adult psychiatric status of hyperactive boys grown up." *American Journal of Psychiatry* 155:493–498.

Maser, J.D., C. Kaebler, and R.E. Weise. 1991. "International use and attitudes toward DSM-III and DSM-III-R: Growing consensus in psychiatric classification." *Journal of Abnormal Psychology* 100:271–279.

McDowell, Jim. 1997. "A hyperactive way to make more money: Teens with Ritalin prescriptions can supply drug-abusing classmates." *British Columbia Report* 8, 28:34–35.

Murray, M. D., and F. W. Deardorff. 1997. "Does managed care fuel pharmaceutical industry growth?" *PharmacoEconomics* 14:341–348.

Nadeau, Kathleen G. 1995. "ADD in the workplace: Career consultation and counseling for the adult with ADD." In *A Comprehensive Guide to Attention Deficit Disorder in Adults: Research, Diagnosis, and Treatment,* Kathleen G. Nadeau, ed. New York: Brunner/Mazel.

Newcorn, Jeffery H., Jeffery M. Halperin, James M. Healey, John D. O'Brien, Daisy M. Pascualvaca, Lorraine E. Wolf, Allen Morganstein, Vanshdeep Sharma, and J. Gerald Young. 1989. "Are ADDH and ADHD the same or different?" *Journal of the American Academy of Adolescent Psychiatry* 285:734–738.

Newsweek. 1990. "A New View on Hyperactivity." (December 3): 61.

New York Times. 1999. "For school nurses, more than tending the sick." *Late New York edition* (January 28):A20.

Public Broadcasting Service (PBS). 1995. "ADD: A dubious diagnosis." *Merrow Report* (October 20). New York, NY.

Ratey, John J., Mark S. Greenberg, Jules R. Bemporad, and Karen J. Lindem. 1992. "Unrecognized Attention-Deficit Hyperactivity Disorder in adults presenting for outpatient psychotherapy." *Journal of Child and Adolescent Psychopharmacology* 2:267–275.

Reissman, Catherine. 1983. "Women and medicalization: A new perspective." *Social Policy* 14:3–18.

Scheff, Thomas J. 1984. *Being Mentally Ill: A Sociological Theory,* Revised Edition. Chicago: Aldine de Gruyter.

Schneider, Joseph W. 1978. "Deviant drinking as disease: Alcoholism as a social accomplishment." *Social Problems* 25:361–372.

Schrag, Peter and Dian Divoky. 1976. *Myth of the Hyperactive Child.* New York: Pantheon.

Scott, Wilbur J. 1990. "PTSD in DSM-III: A case of the politics of diagnosis and disease." *Social Problems* 37:294–310.

Searight, H. Russell and A. Lesley McLaren. 1998. "Attention-Deficit Hyperactivity Disorder: The medicalization of misbehavior." *Journal of Clinical Psychology in Medical Settings* 5:467–495.

Shaffer, David. 1993. "Attention Deficit Hyperactivity Disorder in adults." *American Journal of Psychiatry* 151:633–638.

Singer, Merrill, Carol Arnold, Maureen Fitzgerald, Lynn Madden, and Christa Voight von Legat. 1984. "Hypoglycemia: A controversial illness in U.S. society." *Medical Anthropology* 8:1–35.

Stallings, Robert A. 1990. "Media discourse and the social construction of risk." *Social Problems* 37:80–95.

Stewart, Mark A. 1970. "Hyperactive children." *Scientific American* 222 (April):794–798.

Stich, Sally. 1993. "Why can't your husband sit still?" *Ladies Home Journal* (September):74, 77.

Stoudemire, A. 1996. "Psychiatry in medical practice: Implications for the education of primary care physicians in the era of managed care. Part 1." *Psychosomatics* 37:502–508.

Trilling, James. 1999. "My father and the weak-eyed devils." *American Scholar* 68, 2:17–41.

Vatz, Richard E. and Lee S. Weinberg. 1997. "How accurate is media coverage of Attention Deficit Disorder?" *USA Today* 127 (July):76–77.

Wallis, Claudia. 1994. "Life in overdrive." *Time Magazine* (July 18):43–50.

Weiss, Gabrielle and Lily Trokenberg Hechtman. 1986. *Hyperactive Children Grown Up: Empirical Findings and Theoretical Considerations.* New York: Guilford Press.

Weiss, Gabrielle, Lily Trokenberg Hechtman, Terrye Perlman, Joyce Hopkins, and Albert Wener. 1979. "Hyperactives as young adults: A controlled prospective 10-year follow-up of the psychiatric status of 75 children." *Archives of General Psychiatry* 36:675–681.

Weiss, Lynn. 1992. *Attention Deficit Disorder in Adults: Practical Help for Sufferers and Their Spouses.* Dallas: Taylor Press.

Wen, Patricia. 2000. "As easy to get as candy? A new Massachusetts study finds wide teen abuse of Ritalin." *Boston Globe* (October 29):A1.

Wender, Paul H. 1971. *Minimal Brain Dysfunction in Children.* New York: Wiley.

———. 1987. *The Hyperactive Child, Adolescent and Adult: Attention Deficit Disorder Throughout the Lifespan.* New York: Oxford University Press.

———. 1995. *Attention Deficit Hyperactivity Disorder in Adults.* New York: Oxford University Press.

———. 1998. "Attention-Deficit Hyperactivity Disorder in adults." *Psychiatry Clinic North America* 21:761–774.

Williams, Simon J. and Michael Calnan. 1996. "The 'limits' of medicalization: Modern medicine and the lay populace in 'late modernity.'" *Social Science and Medicine* 42:1609–1620.

Wolkenberg, Frank. 1987. "Out of a darkness." *The New York Times* (October 11):62, 66, 68–70, 82–83.

Wood, D. R., F. W. Reimherr, Paul H. Wender, and G. E. Johnson. 1976. "Diagnosis and treatment of minimal brain dysfunction in adults." *Archives of General Psychiatry* 33:1453–1460.

Woolraich, Mark L., Scott Lingren, A. Stromquist, R. Milich, C. Davis, and D. Watson. 1990. "Stimulant medication use by primary care physicians in the treatment of Attention Deficit Hyperactivity Disorder." *Pediatrics* 86:95–101.

Young, Alan. 1995. *The Harmony of Illusions: Inventing Post-Traumatic Stress Disorder.* Princeton: Princeton University Press.

Zametkin, Alan J. and Monique Ernst. 1999. "Problems in the management of Attention-Deficit-Hyperactivity Disorder." *New England Journal of Medicine* 340:40–46.

Zametkin, Alan J., Laura L. Liebenauer, G. A. Fitzgerald, A. C. King, D. V. Minkunas, P. Herscovitz, Em Yamada, and Robert M. Cohen. 1993. "Brain metabolism in teenagers with Attention-Deficit Hyperactivity Disorder." *Archives of General Psychiatry* 50:333–340.

Zametkin, Alan J., Thomas E. Nordahl, Michael Gross, A. Catherin King, William E. Semple, Judith Rumsey, Susan Hamburger, and Robert M. Cohen. 1990. "Cerebral glucose metabolism in adults with hyperactivity of childhood onset." *New England Journal of Medicine* 323 (November 15):1361–1366.

Zito, Julie Magno, Daniel J. Safer, Susan dos Reis, James F. Gardner, Myde Boles, and Francis Lynch. 2000. "Trends in the prescribing of psychotropic medications to preschoolers." *Journal of the American Medical Association* 283:1025–1030.

Zola, Irving Kenneth. 1972. "Medicine as an institution of social control." *Sociological Review* 20:487–504.

PART II

SOCIAL CONSTRUCTION OF HEALTH PROBLEMS

When and why do some health issues become health problems, worthy of public intervention? A social problems perspective on health provides a framework for answering this question, helping us to focus on the identity and motivation of actors who make claims regarding health problems, the proposed causes and solutions of the purported health problems, and the overall social process through which a health issue is transformed into a health problem.

The three cases in part II illustrate the wide range of issues that can be framed as social problems, with consequences for our understanding of health problems and for the allocation of public resources to "solve" those problems. In all three cases, professional interests take a role in shaping the social process through which health issues become framed as social problems. In the cases of child abuse and poison control, physicians claimed that epidemiological patterns of health experiences were in fact larger social problems, which should therefore be solved through professionally determined policy intervention. In contrast, parent organizations were at the forefront of claiming that sudden infant death syndrome (SIDS) was a social problem, while health professionals lagged behind in claiming public resources for investigating the causes of SIDS, thereby playing a supporting rather than leading role.

Pediatric radiologists defined child abuse as a social problem in the 1950s, according to Stephen Pfohl's article "The 'Discovery' of Child Abuse." Here, Pfohl argues that pediatric radiologists were in a better position than emergency room physicians to claim that the injuries they saw were due to parents' behavior because the radiologists had more social and professional distance from the parents. The radiologists' "discovery" of child abuse also served their professional interests: it improved their prestige within the field of medicine and allowed them to form coalitions with other physicians and with social organizations, thus resulting in widespread state legislation prohibiting child abuse in the 1960s.

Parent organizations, not physicians, were the driving force behind the recognition of sudden infant death syndrome, according to Michael Johnson and Karl Hufbauer. In their article, "Sudden Infant Death Syndrome as a Medical Research Problem since 1945," Johnson and Hufbauer show that even though SIDS was recognized as a medical problem in 1945, it was not until parent groups organized in the 1960s and lobbied Congress in the early 1970s that federal child health agencies began a significant national research effort to investigate the causes of SIDS. Parents had a much larger stake than physicians in promoting this research, as their children's deaths were sometimes attributed to their own child care actions.

In Robert Broadhead's article, "Officer Ugg, Mr. Yuk, Uncle Barf . . . Ad Nausea: Controlling Poison Control, 1950–1985," pediatricians were instrumental in the definition of poison control as a social problem. In response to these concerns, hospitals developed poison control centers and telephone hotlines. Yet over time, hospitals realized that it was not in their institutional interests to maintain poison control centers. They were costly, and they reduced the demand for emergency care. Thus, hospitals relinquished poison control to consolidated, government-funded regional centers.

CHAPTER 4

The "Discovery" of Child Abuse

Stephen J. Pfohl

Despite documentary evidence of child beating throughout the ages, the "discovery" of child abuse as deviance and its subsequent criminalization are recent phenomena. In a four-year period beginning in 1962, the legislatures of all fifty states passed statutes against the caretaker's abuse of children. The paper is a study of the organization of social forces which gave rise to the deviant labeling of child beating and which promoted speedy and universal enactment of criminal legislation. It is an examination of certain organized medical interests, whose concern in the discovery of the "battered child syndrome" manifestly contributed to the advance of humanitarian pursuits while covertly rewarding the groups themselves.

The structure of the present analysis is fourfold: First, an historical survey of social reaction to abusive behavior prior to the formulation of fixed labels during the early sixties, focusing on the impact of three previous reform movements. These include the nineteenth-century "house-of-refuge" movement, early twentieth century crusades by the Society for the Prevention of Cruelty to Children, and the rise of juvenile courts. The second section concentrates on the web of cultural values related to the protection of children at the time of the "discovery" of abuse as deviance. A third section examines factors associated with the organizational structure of the medical profession conducive to the "discovery" of a particular type of deviant label. The fourth segment discusses social reaction. Finally, the paper provides a sociological interpretation of a particular social-legal development. Generically it gives support for a synthesis of conflict and labeling perspectives in the sociology of deviance and law.

The History of Social Reaction: Preventative Penology and "Society Saving"

The purposeful beating of the young has for centuries found legitimacy in beliefs of its necessity for achieving disciplinary, educational or religious obedience (Radbill, 1968). Both the Roman legal code of "Patria Patistas" (Shepard, 1965), and the English common law

(Thomas, 1973), gave guardians limitless power over their children who, with chattel-like status, had no legal right to protection.

The common law heritage of America similarly gave rise to a tradition of legitimized violence toward children. Legal guardians had the right to impose any punishment deemed necessary for the child's upbringing. In the seventeenth century, a period dominated by religious values and institutions, severe punishments were considered essential to the "sacred" trust of child-rearing (Earle, 1926:119–126). Even in the late eighteenth and early nineteenth centuries, a period marked by the decline of religious domination and the rise of rationalism and a proliferation of statutes aimed at codifying unacceptable human behavior, there were no attempts to prevent caretaker abuse of children. A major court in the state of North Carolina declared that the parent's judgment of need for a child's punishment was presumed to be correct. Criminal liability was said to exist only in cases resulting in "permanent injury" (*State v. Pendergass*, in Paulsen, 1966b:686).

I am not suggesting that the American legal tradition failed to recognize any abuse of discipline as something to be negatively sanctioned. A few cases resulting in the legal punishment of parents who murdered their children, have been recorded. But prior to the 1960's sociolegal reactions were sporadic, and atypical of sustained reactions against firmly labeled deviance.

Beginning in the early nineteenth century, a series of three reform movements directed attention to the plight of beaten, neglected and delinquent children. These included the nineteenth century "house-of-refuge" movement, the turn of the century crusades by the Society for the Prevention of Cruelty to Children and the early twentieth century rise of juvenile courts. Social response, however, seldom aimed measures at ameliorating abuse of correcting abusive parents. Instead, the child, rather than his or her guardians, became the object of humanitarian reform.

In each case, the primary objective was not to save children from cruel or abusive parents, but to save society from future delinquents. Believing that wicked and irresponsible behavior was engendered by the evils of poverty and city life, these movements sought to curb criminal tendencies in poor, urban youths by removing them from corrupt environments and placing them in institutional settings. There they could learn order, regularity and obedience (Rothman, 1970). Thus, it was children, not their abusive guardians, who felt the weight of the moral crusade. They, not their parents, were institutionalized.

THE "HOUSE OF REFUGE" MOVEMENT

Originating in the reformist dreams of the Jacksonian era, the so-called "House of Refuge Movement" sought to stem the social pathologies of an industrializing nation by removing young people, endangered by "corrupt urban environments," to institutional settings. Neglect statutes providing for the removal of the young from bad home lives were originally enacted to prevent children from mingling freely with society's dregs in alms houses or on the streets. In 1825, the first statute was passed and the first juvenile institution, the New York House of Refuge, was opened. Originally privately endowed, the institution soon received public funds to intervene in neglectful home situations and transplant children to a controlled environment, where they shared a "proper growing up" with other vagrant, abandoned and neglected youths as well as with delinquents who had violated criminal statutes. Similar institutions were established in Philadelphia and Boston a year later, in New Orleans in 1845, and in Rochester and Baltimore in 1849.

The Constitutionality of the neglect statutes, which formed the basis for the House of Refuge Movement, was repeatedly challenged on the ground that it was really imprisonment without due process. With few exceptions court case after court case upheld the policy of social intervention on the Aristotelian principle of "parens patriae." This principle maintained that the State has the responsibility to defend those who cannot defend themselves, as well as to assert its privilege in compelling infants and their guardians to act in ways most beneficial to the State.

The concept of preventive penology emerged in the wording of these court decisions. A distinction between "delinquency" (the actual violation of criminal codes) and "dependency" (being born into a poor home with neglectful or abusive parents) was considered irrelevant for "child saving." The two were believed to be intertwined in poverty and desolation. If not stopped, both would perpetuate themselves. For the future good of both child and society, "parens patriae" justified the removal of the young before they became irreparably tainted (Thomas, 1972:322–323).

The underlying concept of the House of Refuge Movement was that of preventive penology, not child protection. This crusade registered no real reaction against child beating. The virtue of removing children from their homes was not to point up abuse or neglect and protect its victims, it was to decrease the likelihood that parental inadequacies, the "cause of poverty," would transfer themselves to the child and hence to the next generation of society (Giovannoni, 1971:652). Thus, as indicated by Zalba (1966), the whole nineteenth century movement toward institutionalization actually failed to differentiate between abuse and poverty and therefore registered no social reaction against beating as a form of deviance.

MARY ELLEN, THE SPCC, AND A SHORT-LIVED SOCIAL REACTION

The first period when public interest focused on child abuse occurred in the last quarter of the nineteenth century. In 1875, the Society for the Prevention of Cruelty to Animals intervened in the abuse case of nine-year-old girl named Mary Ellen who had been treated viciously by foster parents. The case of Mary Ellen was splashed across the front pages of the nation's papers with dramatic results. As an outgrowth of the journalistic clamor, the New York Society for the Prevention of Cruelty to Children was formed. Soon incorporated under legislation that required law enforcement and court officials to aid agents of authorized cruelty societies, the NYSPCC and other societies modeled after it undertook to prevent abuse.

Though the police functions of the anti-cruelty societies represented a new reaction to abuse, their activities did not signify a total break with the society-saving emphasis of the House of Refuge Movement. In fact, three lines of evidence suggest that the SPCC enforcement efforts actually withheld a fixed label of deviancy from the perpetrators of abuse, in much the same manner as had the House of Refuge reforms. First, the "saving" of the child actually boosted the number of children placed in institutions, consequently supporting House of Refuge activities (Thomas, 1972: 311). Second, according to Falks (1970:176), interorganizational dependency grew between the two reform movements; best evidenced by the success of SPCC efforts in increasing public support to childcare institutions under the auspices of House of Refuge groups. Finally, and perhaps most convincingly, natural parents were not classified as abusers of the great majority of the so-called "rescued children." In fact, the targets of these saving missions were cruel employ-ers and foster or adopted parents (Giovannoni, 1971:653). Rarely did an SPCC inter-vene against the "natural" balance of power between parents and children. The firmness of the SPCC's alleged social action against abuse appears significantly dampened by its reluctance to shed identification with the refuge house emphasis on the "industrial sins of the city" and to replace it with a reaction against individuals.

The details of the SPCC movement is often attributed to lack of public interest, funding problems, mergers with other organizations and the assumption of protection services by public agencies (Felder, 1971:187). Its identification with the House of Refuge Movement also contributed to its eventual demise. More specifically, the House of Refuge emphasis on the separation of child from family, a position adopted and reinforced by the SPCC's activities, came into conflict with perspectives advocated by the newly-emerging professions of social work and child psychology (Kadushen, 1967:202f). Instead of removing the child from the home, these new interests em-phasized efforts to unite the family (Thomas, 1972). This latter position, backed by the power of professional expertise, eventually undercut the SPCC's policy of preven-tive policing by emphasizing the protection of the home.

The erosion of the SPCC position was foreshadowed by the 1909 White House Conference on Children. This Conference proclaimed that a child should not be re-moved from his or her home for reasons of poverty alone, and called for service pro-grams and financial aid to protect the home environment. Yet, the practice of preven-tive policing and institutionalization did not vanish, due, in part, to the development of the juvenile court system. The philosophy and practice of this system continued to identify abuse and neglect with poverty and social disorganization.

THE JUVENILE COURT AND THE CONTINUED SHADOW OF ABUSE

The founding of the first juvenile court in Illinois in the 1899 was originally heralded as a major landmark in the legal protection of juveniles. By 1920, courts were estab-lished in all but three states. Nonetheless, it is debatable that much reform was ac-complished by juvenile court legislation. Coalitions of would-be reformers (headed by various female crusaders and the commissioners of several large public reformatories) argued for the removal of youthful offenders from adult institutions and advocated al-teration of the punitive, entrepreneurial and sectarian "House of Refuge" institutions (Fox, 1970:1225–29). More institutions and improved conditions were demanded (Thomas, 1972:323). An analysis of the politics of juvenile court legislation suggests, however, that successful maneuvering by influential sectarian entrepreneurs resulted in only a partial achievement of reformist goals (Fox, 1970: 1225–26). Legislation did remove juveniles from adult institutions. It did not reduce the House of Refuge Movement's control of juvenile institutions. Instead, legislation philosophically supported and financially reinforced the Movement's "society-saving" operation of sectarian industrial schools (Fox, 1970:1226–27).

The channeling of juvenile court legislation into the "society-saving" mold of the House of Refuge Movement actually withheld a deviant label from abusive parents. Even the reformers, who envisioned it as a revolution in child protection, did not see the court as protection from unfit parents. It was meant instead to prevent the development of "lower class" delinquency (Platt, 1969) and to rescue "those less fortunate in the social order" (Thomas, 1972:326). Again, the victims of child battering were characterized as pre-delinquents, as part of the general "problem" of poverty. These children, not their guardians, were the targets of court action and preventive policies. The courts, like the House of Refuge and SPCC movements before them, constrained any social reaction which would apply the label of deviant to parents who abused their children.

Social Reaction at Mid-century: The Cultural Setting for the "Discovery" of Abuse

THE DECLINE OF PREVENTATIVE PENOLOGY

As noted, preventative penology represented the philosophical basis for various voluntary associations and legislative reform efforts resulting in the institutionalization of neglected or abused children. Its primary emphasis was on the protection of society. The decline of preventive penology is partially attributed to three variables: the perceived failure of "institutionalization," the impact of the "Great Depression" of the 1930's, and a change in the cultural meaning of "adult vices."

In the several decades prior to the discovery of abuse, the failure of institutionalization to "reorder" individuals became increasingly apparent. This realization undermined the juvenile courts' role in administering a pre-delinquency system of crime prevention. Since the rise of juvenile courts historically represented a major structural support for the notion of preventative penology, the lessening of its role removed a significant barrier to concern with abuse as an act of individual victimization. Similarly, the widespread experience of poverty during the Great Depression weakened other beliefs in preventive penology. As impersonal economic factors impoverished a great number of citizens of good moral credentials, the link between poverty and immorality began to weaken.

Another characteristic of the period immediately prior to the discovery of abuse was a changing cultural awareness of the meaning of adult vice as indices of the future character of children. "Parental immoralities that used to be seen as warnings of oncoming criminality in children [became] acceptable factors in a child's homelife" (Fox, 1970:1234). Parental behavior such as drinking, failing to provide a Christian education, and refusing to keep a child busy with useful labor, were no longer classified as unacceptable nor deemed symptoms of immorality transmitted to the young. Hence, the saving of society from the tainted young became less of a mandate, aiding the perception of social harm against children as 'beings" in themselves.

ADVANCE OF CHILD PROTECTION

Concurrent with the demise of "society-saving" in the legal sphere, developments in the fields of child welfare and public policy heightened interest in the problems of the child as an individual. The 1909 White House Conference on Children spawned both the "Mother's Aid" Movement and the American Association for the Study and Prevention of Infant Mortality. The former group, from 1910 to 1930, drew attention to the benefits of keeping children in the family while pointing out the detrimental effects of dehumanizing institutions. The latter group then, as now, registered concern over the rate of infant deaths.

During the first half of the twentieth century, the Federal Government also met the issue of child protection with legislation that regulated child labor, called for the removal of delinquent youths from adult institutions, and established, in 1930, a bureaucratic structure whose purpose revolved around child protection. The Children's Bureau of HEW immediately adopted a "Children's Charter" promising every child a home with love and security plus full-time public services for protection from abuse, neglect, exploitation or moral hazard (Radbill, 1968:15).

Despite the growth of cultural and structural dispositions favoring the protection and increased rights of children, there was still no significant attention given to perpetrators of abuse, in the courts (Paulsen, 1966:710), in the legislature (DeFrancis, 1967:3), or by child welfare agencies (Zalba, 1966). While this inactivity may have been partly caused by the lack of effective mechanisms for obtaining data on abuse (Paulsen, 1966:910), these agencies had little social incentive for interfering with an established power set—the parent over the child. As a minority group possessing neither the collective awareness nor the elementary organizational skills necessary to address their grievances to either the courts or to the legislators, abused and neglected children awaited the advocacy of some other organized interest. This outside intervention would not, however, be generated by that sector of "organized helping" most closely associated with the protective needs of children—the growing web of child welfare bureaucracies at State and Federal levels. Social work had identified its professional advance with the adoption of the psychoanalytic model of casework (Zalba, 1966). This perspective, rather than generating a concern with political inequities internal to the family, focused instead on psychic disturbances internal to its members. Rather than challenging the strength of parents, this served to reinforce the role of powerful guardians in the rearing of young.

Nor would advocacy come from the public at large. Without organized labeling interests at mid-century, child abuse had not become an issue publicly regarded as a major social problem. In fact, a fairly general tolerance for abuse appeared to exist. This contention is supported by the findings of a nationwide study conducted by NORC during the period in which laws against abuse were actually being adopted (Gil & No-bel, 1969). Despite the widescale publicizing of abuse in this "post-discovery" period, public attitudes remained lenient. Data revealed a high degree of empathy with con-victed or suspected perpetrators (Gil, 1970): 63–67). These findings are understand-able in light of cultural views accepting physical force against children as a nearly uni-versally applied precept of intrafamilial organization (Goode, 1971). According to the coordinator of the national survey, "Culturally determined permissive attitudes toward the use of physical force in child rearing seem to constitute the common core of all physical abuse of children in American society" (Gil, 1970:141).

While the first half of the twentieth century is characterized by an increasing con-cern for child welfare, it developed with neither an organizational nor attitudinal reac-tion against child battering as a specific form of deviance. The "discovery" of abuse, its definition as a social problem and the socio-legal reaction against it, awaited the coali-tion of organized interests.

The Organization of Social Reaction against the "Battered Child Syndrome"

What organization of social forces gave rise to the discovery of abuse as deviance? The discovery is not attributable to any escalation of abuse itself. Although some authors have recently suggested that the increasing nuclearization of the family may increase the victimization of its offspring (Skolnick & Skolnick, 1971), there has never been any evidence that, aside from reporting inflation due to the impact of new laws, bat-tering behavior was actually increasing (Eads, 1972). The attention here is on the or-ganizational matrix encouraging a recognition of abuse as a social problem. In ad-dressing this issue I will examine factors associated with the organizational structure of the medical profession leading to the discovery of abuse by pediatric radiologists rather than by other medical practitioners.

The "discovery" of abuse by pediatric radiology has often been described chrono-logically (Radbill, 1968:15; McCoid 1965:2–5; Thomas, 1972:330). John Caffey (1946) first linked observed series of long bone fractures in children with what he termed some "unspecific origin." Although his assumption was that some physical dis-turbance would be discovered as the cause of this pattern of "subdural hematoma," Coffey's work prompted a series of further investigations into various bone injuries, skeletal trauma, and multiple fractures in young children. These research efforts lead pediatric radiology gradually to shift its diagnosis away from an internal medical ex-plication toward the ascription of social cause.

In subsequent years it was suggested that what was showing up on x-rays might be the results of various childhood accidents (Barmeyer, et al., 1951), of "parental careless-ness" (Silverman, 1953), of "parental conduct" (Bakwin, 1956), and most dramatically, of the "indifference, immaturity and irresponsibility of parents" (Wooley & Evans, 1955). Surveying the progression of this research and reviewing his own investigations, Coffey (1957) later specified "misconduct and deliberate injury" as the primary etiological factors associated with what he had previously labeled "unspecific trauma." The discovery of abuse was on its way. Both in scholarly research (McCoid, 1966:7) and journalistic outcry (Radbill, 1968:16), the last years of the fifties showed dramatically increased concern for the beaten child.

Why did pediatric radiologists and not some other group "see" abuse first? Legal and social welfare agents were either outside the scene of abusive behavior or inside the constraining vision of psychoanalytically committed casework. But clinicians, particularly hospital physicians and pediatricians, who encountered abused children more immediately, should have discovered "abuse" before the radiologists.

Four factors impeded the recognition of abuse (as it was later labeled). First, some early research maintained that doctors in emergency room settings were simply unaware of the possibilities of "abuse" as a diagnosis (Bain, 1963; Boardman, 1962). While this may be true, the massive symptoms (blood, burns, bruises) emergency room doctors faced far outweighed the lines appearing on the x-ray screens of radiologic specialists. A second line of evidence contends that many doctors were simply psychologically unwilling to believe that parents would inflict such atrocities on their own children (Elmer, 1960; Fontana, Donovan, & Wong, 1963; Kempe et al., 1963). This position is consistent with the existing cultural assumptions pairing parental power with parental wisdom and benevolence. Nonetheless, certain normative and structural elements within professional medicine appear of greater significance in reinforcing the physician's reluctance to get involved, even diagnostically. These factors are the "norm of confidentiality between doctor and client" and the goal of professional autonomy.

The "norm of confidentiality" gives rise to the third obstacle to a diagnosis of abuse: the possibility of legal liability for violating the confidentiality of the physician-patient relationship (Boardman, 1962). Interestingly, although some research connotes doctors' concern over erroneous diagnosis (Braun, Braun & Simonds, 1963), physicians primarily view the parent, rather than the child, as their real patient. On a strictly monetary level, of course, it is the parent who contracts with the doctor. Additional research has indicated that, particularly in the case of pediatricians, the whole family is viewed as one's clinical domain (Bucher & Strauss, 1961:329). It is from this vantage point that the impact of possible liability for a diagnostic disclosure is experienced. Although legal liability for a diagnosis of abuse may or may not have been the risk (Paulsen, 1967b:32), the belief in such liability could itself have contributed to the narrowness of a doctor's diagnostic perceptions (McCoid, 1966:37).

A final deterrent to the physician's "seeing" abuse is the reluctance of doctors to become involved in a criminal justice process that would take both their time (Bain, 1963:896) and ability to guide the consequences of a particular diagnosis (Boardman, 1962:46). This deterrent is particularly related to the traditional success of organized medicine in politically controlling the consequences of its own performance, not just for medical practitioners but for all who come in contact with a medical problem (Freidson, 1969:106; Hyde, et al., 1954).

The political control over the consequences of one's profession would be jeopardized by the medical diagnosis of child abuse. Doctors would be drawn into judicial proceedings and subordinated to a role as witnesses. The outcome of this process would be decided by criminal justice standards rather than those set forth by the medical profession. Combining this relatively unattractive alternative with the obvious and unavoidable drain on a doctor's financial earning time, this fourth obstacle to the clinician's discovery of abuse is substantial.

FACTORS CONDUCIVE TO THE DISCOVERY OF ABUSE BY PEDIATRIC RADIOLOGY

Why didn't the above factors inhibit the discovery of abuse by pediatric radiologists as well as by clinicians? First it must be recognized that the radiologists in question (Caffey, Barmeyer, Silverman, Wooley and Evans) were all researchers of children's x-rays. As such, the initial barrier becomes irrelevant. The development of diagnostic categories was a consequence rather than a pre-condition of the medical mission. Regarding the psychological denial of parental responsibility for atrocities, it must be remembered that the dramatic character of a beating is greatly reduced by the time it reaches an x-ray laboratory. Taken by technicians and developed as black and white prints, the radiologic remnants of abuse carry with them little of the horror of the bloody assault.

With a considerable distance from the patient and his or her family, radiologists are removed from the their obstacle concerning legal liabilities entailed in violating the doctor-patient relationship. Unlike pediatricians, radiologists do not routinely regard the whole family as one's clinical domain. Of primary importance is the individual whose name or number is imprinted on the x-ray frames. As such, fears about legal sanctions instigated by a parent whom one has never seen are less likely to deter the recognition of abuse.

Given the irrelevance of the first three obstacles, what about the last? Pediatric radiologists are physicians, and as such would be expected to participate in the "professional control of consequences" ethos. How is it that they negotiate this obstacle in favor of public recognition and labeling of abuse?

THE DISCOVERY: AN OPPORTUNITY FOR ADVANCEMENT WITHIN THE MEDICAL COMMUNITY

To ask why the general norm of "professional control of consequences" does not apply equally to radiologists as to their clinical counterparts is to confuse the reality of organized medicine with its image. Although the medical profession often appears to outsiders as a separate and unified community within a community (Goode, 1957), and although medical professionals generally favor the maintenance of this image (Glaser, 1960), it is nonetheless more adequately described as an organization of internally competing segments, each striving to advance its own historically derived mission and future importance (Bucher & Strauss, 1961). In analyzing pediatric radiology as one such segment, several key variables facilitated its temporary parting with the dominant norms of the larger medical community. This parting promoted the elevation of its overall status within that community.

The first crucial element is that pediatric radiology was a marginal specialty within organized medicine. It was a research-oriented subfield in a profession that emphasized face-to-face clinical interaction. It was a safe intellectual endeavor within an overall organization which placed a premium on risky pragmatic enterprise. Studies of value orientations among medical students at the time of the "discovery" of abuse have suggested that those specialties which stress "helping others," "being of service," "being useful," and "working with people" were ranked above those which work "at medical problems that do not require frequent contact with patients" (Cahalan, 1957). On the other hand, intellectual stimulation afforded very little prestige. Supporting this conclusion was research indicating that although forty-three percent of practicing physicians selected "close patient relations" as a mandate of their profession, only twenty-four percent chose "research" as worthy of such an evaluation (Philips, 1964). Pairing this ranking system with the profession's close knit, "fraternity-like" communication network (Hall, 1946), one would expect research-oriented radiologists to be quite sensitive about their marginal evaluation by colleagues.

Intramedical organizational ranking extends along the lines of risk-taking as well as patient-encounters. Here, too, pediatric radiologists have traditionally ranked lower than other medical specialties. Becker's (1961) study of medical student culture suggests that the most valued specialties are those which combine wide experiences with risk and responsibility. These are most readily "symbolized by the possibility of killing or disabling patients in the course of making a mistake" (Freidson, 1969:107). From this perspective, it is easy to understand why surgery and internal medicine head the list of the most esteemed specialties. Other research has similarly noted the predominance of surgeons among high elected officials of the American Medical Association (Hall, 1946). Devoid of most risk-taking, little involved in life or death decisions, pediatric radiologists are again marginal to this ethos of medical culture.

The "discovery" of child abuse offered pediatric radiologists an alternative to their marginal medical status. By linking themselves to the problem of abuse, radiologists became indirectly tied into the crucial clinical task of patient diagnosis. In addition, they became a direct source of input concerning the risky "life or death" consequences of child beating. This could represent an advance in status, a new basis for recognition within the medical profession. Indeed, after initial documentation of abuse, literature in various journals of radiology, roentgenology and pediatrics, articles on this topic by Wooley and Evans (1955) and Gwinn, Lewin and Peterson (1961) appeared in the *Journal of the American Medical Association*. These were among the very few radiologic research reports published by that prestigious journal during the time period. Hence, the first factor conducive to the radiological discovery of abuse was a potential for intraorganizational advance in prestige.

THE DISCOVERY: AN OPPORTUNITY FOR COALITION WITHIN THE MEDICAL COMMUNITY

A second factor encouraging the discovery of abuse by relatively low-status pediatric radiologists concerns the opportunity for a coalition of interests with other more prestigious segments within organized medicine. The two other segments radiologists joined in alliance were pediatric and psychodynamically oriented psychiatry. By virtue of face-to-face clinical involvements, these specialties were higher ranking than pediatric radiology. Nevertheless each contained a dimension of marginality. Pediatrics had attained valued organizational status several decades prior to the discovery of abuse. Yet, in an age characterized by preventive drugs and treatments for previously dangerous or deadly infant diseases, it was again sliding toward the margins of the profession (Bucher & Strauss, 1961). Psychodynamic psychiatry (as opposed to its psychosomatic cousin) experienced marginality in dealing with non-physical problems.

For both pediatrics and psychodynamic psychiatry, links with the problem of abuse could partially dissipate the respective marginality of each. Assuming a role in combating the "deadly" forces of abuse could enlarge the "risky" part of the pediatric mission. A symbolic alliance of psychodynamic psychiatry with other bodily diagnostic and treatment specialties could also function to advance its status. Neither of these specialties was in a position to "see" abuse before the radiologists. Pediatricians were impeded by the obstacles discussed above. Psychiatrists were blocked by the reluctance of abusive parents to admit their behavior as problematic (Steele & Pollock, 1968). Nonetheless, the interests of both could perceivably be advanced by a coalition with the efforts of pediatric radiologists. As such, each represented a source of potential support for pediatric radiologists in their discovery of abuse. This potential for coalition served to reinforce pediatric radiology in its movement toward the discovery of abuse.

THE DISCOVERY: AN OPPORTUNITY FOR THE APPLICATION OF AN ACCEPTABLE LABEL

A crucial impediment to the discovery of abuse by the predominant interest in organized medicine was the norm of controlling the consequences of a particular diagnosis. To diagnose abuse as social deviance might curtail the power of organized medicine. The management of its consequences would fall to the extramedical interests of formal agents of social control. How is it then, that such a diagnosis by pediatric radiology and its endorsement by pediatric and psychiatric specialties, is said to have advanced these specialties within the organization of medicine? Wasn't it more likely that they should have received criticism rather than acclaim from the medical profession?

By employing a rather unique labeling process the coalition of discovery interests were able to convert the possible liability into a discernible advantage. The opportunity of generating a medical, rather than socio-legal label for abuse provided the radiologists and their allies with a situation in which they could both reap the rewards associated with the diagnosis and avoid the infringement of extramedical controls. What was discovered was no ordinary behavior form but a "syndrome." Instead of departing from the tradition of organized medicine, they were able to idealize its most profound mission. Possessing a repertoire of scientific credibility, they were presented with the opportunity "to label as illness what was not previously labeled at all or what was labeled in some other fashion, under some other institutional jurisdiction" (Freidson, 1971:261).

The symbolic focal point for the acceptable labeling of abuse was the 1962 publication of an article entitled "The Battered Child Syndrome" in the *Journal of the American Medical Association* (Kempe, et al., 1962). This report, representing the joint research efforts of a group of radiologic, pediatric, and psychiatric specialists, labeled abuse as a "clinical condition" existing as an "unrecognized trauma" (Kempe, 1962:17). It defined the deviance of its "psychopathic" perpetrators as a product of "psychiatric factors" representing "some defect in character structure" (Kempe, 1962:24). As an indicator of prestige within organized medicine, it is interesting to note that the position articulated by these labelers was endorsed by the editorial board of the AMA in that same issue of JAMA.

As evidenced by the AMA editorial, the discovery of abuse as new "illness" reduced drastically the intra-organizational constraints on doctors' "seeing" abuse. A diagnostic category has been invented and publicized. Psychological obstacles in recognizing parents as capable of abuse were eased by the separation of normatively powerful parents from non-normatively pathological individuals. Problems associated with perceiving parents as patients whose confidentiality must be protected were reconstructed by typifying them as patients who needed help. Moreover, the maintenance of professional autonomy was assured by pairing deviance with sickness. This last statement is testimony to the power of medical nomenclature. It was evidenced by the fact that (prior to its publication) the report which coined the label "battered child syndrome" was endorsed by a Children's Bureau conference which included social workers and law enforcement officials as well as doctors (McCoid, 1965:12).

THE GENERATION OF THE REPORTING MOVEMENT

The discovery of the "battered child syndrome" was facilitated by the opportunities for various pediatric radiologists to advance in medical prestige, form coalitions with other interests, and invent a professionally acceptable deviant label. The application of this label has been called the child abuse reporting movement. This movement was well underway by the time the 1962 Children's Bureau Conference confirmed the radiological diagnosis of abuse. Besides foreshadowing the acceptance of the sickness label, this meeting was also the basis for a series of articles to be published in *Pediatrics* which would further substantiate the diagnosis of abuse. Soon, however, the reporting movement spread beyond intraorganizational medical maneuvering to incorporate contributions from various voluntary associations, governmental agencies, as well as the media.

Extramedical responses to the newly discovered deviance confirmed the recognition of abuse as an illness. These included reports by various social welfare agencies which underscored the medical roots of the problem. For instance, the earliest investigations of the problem of social service agents resulted in a call for cooperation with the findings of radiologists in deciding the fate of abusers (Elmer, 1960:100). Other studies called for "more comprehensive radiological examinations" (Boardman, 1962: 43). That the problem was medical in its roots as well as consequences was reinforced by the frequent referral of caseworkers to themselves as "battered child therapists" whose mission was the "curing" of "patients" (Davoren, 1968). Social welfare organizations, including the Children's Division of the American Humane Association, the Public Welfare Association, and the Child Welfare League, echoed similar concerns in sponsoring research (Children's Division, 1963; DeFrancis, 1963) and lobbying for "treatment based" legislative provisions (McCoid, 1965).

Not all extramedical interests concurred with treatment of abusers as "sick." Various law enforcement voices argued that the abuse of children was a crime and should be prosecuted. On the other hand, a survey of thirty-one publications in major law journals between 1962–1972 revealed that nearly all legal scholars endorsed treatment rather than punishment to manage abusers. Lawyers disagreed, however, as to whether reports should be mandatory and registered concern over who should report to whom. Yet, all concurred that various forms of immunity should be granted reporters (Paulsen, 1967; DeFrancis, 1967). These are all procedural issues. Neither law enforcers nor legal scholars parted from labeling abuse as a problem to be managed. The impact of the acceptable discovery of abuse by a respected knowledge sector (the medical profession) had generated a stigmatizing scrutiny bypassed in previous eras.

The proliferation of the idea of abuse by the media cannot be underestimated. Though its stories were sensational, its credibility went unchallenged. What was publicized was not some amorphous set of muggings but a "syndrome." Titles such as "Cry rises from beaten babies" (*Life*, June 1963), "Parents who beat children" (*Saturday Evening Post*, October 1962), "The shocking price of parental anger" (*Good Housekeeping*, March 1964), and "Terror struck children" (*New Republic*, May 1964) were all buttressed by an awe of scientific objectivity. The problem had become "real" in the imaginations of professionals and laymen alike. It was rediscovered visually by ABC's "Ben Casey," NBC's "Dr. Kildare," and CBS's "The Nurses," as well as in several other television scripts and documentaries (Paulsen, 1967: 488–89).

Discovered by the radiologists, substantiated by their colleagues, and distributed by the media, the label was becoming widespread. Despite this fact, actual reporting laws were said to be the cooperative accomplishments of zealous individuals and voluntary associations (Paulsen, 1967:491). Who exactly were these "zealous individuals"?

Data on legislative lobbyists reveal that, in almost every state, the civic committee concerned with abuse legislation was chaired by a doctor who "just happened" to be a pediatrician (Paulsen, 1967:491). Moreover, "the medical doctors who most influenced the legislation frequently were associated with academic medicine" (Paulsen, 1967:491). This information provides additional evidence of the collaborative role of pediatricians in guiding social reaction to the deviance discovered by their radiological colleagues.

LACK OF RESISTANCE TO THE LABEL

In addition to the medical interests discussed above, numerous voluntary associations provided support for the movement against child abuse. These included the League of Women Voters, Veterans of Foreign Wars, the Daughters of the American Republic, the District Attorneys Associations, Council of Jewish Women, State Federation of Women's Clubs, Public Health Associations, plus various national chapters of social workers (Paulsen, 1967:495). Two characteristics emerge from an examination of these interests. They either have a professional stake in the problem or represent the civic concerns of certain upper-middle class factions. In either case the labelers were socially and politically removed from the abusers, who in all but one early study (Steele and Pollock, 1968), were characterized as lower class and minority group members.

The existence of a wide social distance between those who abuse and those who label, facilitates not only the likelihood of labeling but nullifies any organized resistance to the label by the "deviant" group itself. Research findings which describe abusers as belonging to no outside-the-family associations or clubs (Young, 1964) or which portray them as isolates in the community (Giovannoni, 1971) reinforce the conclusion. Labeling was generated by powerful medical interests and perpetuated by organized media, professional and upper-middle class concerns. Its success was enlarged by the relative powerlessness and isolation of abusers, which prevented the possibility of organized resistance to the labeling.

The Shape of Social Reaction

I have argued that the organizational advantages surrounding the discovery of abuse by pediatric radiology set in motion a process of labeling abuse as deviance and legislating against it. The actual shape of legislative enactments has been discussed elsewhere (DeFrancis, 1967; Paulsen, 1967). The passage of the reporting laws encountered virtually no opposition. In Kentucky, for example, no one even appeared to testify for or against the measure (Paulsen, 1967:502). Any potential opposition from the American Medical Association, whose interests in autonomous control of the consequences of a medical diagnosis might have been threatened, had been undercut by the radiologists' success in defining abuse as a new medical problem. The AMA, unlikely to argue against conquering illness, shifted to support reporting legislation which would maximize a physician's diagnostic options.

The consequences of adopting a "sick" label for abusers is mirrored in two findings: the low rate of prosecution afforded offenders and the modification of reporting statutes so as exclusively to channel reporting toward "helping services." Regarding the first factor, Grumet (1970:306) suggests that despite existing laws and reporting statutes, actual prosecution has not increased since the time of abuse's "discovery." In support is Thomas (1972) who contends that the actual percentage of cases processed by family courts has remained constant during the same period. Even when prosecution does occur, convictions are obtained in only five to ten percent of the cases (Paulsen, 1966). And even in these cases, sentences are shorter for abusers than for other offenders convicted under the same law of aggravated assault (Grumet, 1970:307).

State statutes have shifted on reporting from an initial adoption of the Children's Bureau model of reporting to law enforcement agents, toward one geared at reporting to child welfare or child protection agencies (DeFrancis, 1970). In fact, the attention to abuse in the early sixties has been attributed as a factor in the development of specialized "protective interests" in states which had none since the days of the SPCC crusades (Eads, 1969). This event, like the emphasis on abuser treatment, is evidence of the impact of labeling of abuse as an "illness."

References

Bain, Katherine. 1963. "The physically abused child." Pediatrics 31(June): 895–897.

Bakwin, Harry. 1956. "Multiple skeletal lesions in young children due to trauma." Journal of Pediatrics 49(July): 7–15.

Barmeyer, G.H., L.R. Anderson and W.B. Cox. 1951. "Traumatic periostitis in young children." Journal of Pediatrics 38(Feb): 184–90.

Becker, Howard S. 1963. The Outsiders. New York: The Free Press.

Becker, Howard S. et al. 1961. Boys in White. Chicago: University of Chicago Press.

Boardman, Helen. 1962. "A project to rescue children from inflicted injuries." Journal of Social Work 7(January): 43–51.

Braun, Ida G., Edgar J. Braun and Charlotte Simonds. 1963. "The mistreated child." California Medicine 99(August): 98–103.

Bremner, R. 1970. Children and Youth in America: A Documentary History. Vol. I. Cambridge, Mass.: Harvard University Press.

Bucher, Rue and Anselm Strauss. 1961. "Professions in process." American Journal of Sociology 66(January): 325–334.

Caffey, John. 1946. "Multiple fractures in the long bones of infants suffering from chronic subdural hematoma." American Journal of Roentology 56(August): 163–173.

———. 1957. "Traumatic lesions in growing bones other than fractures and lesions: clinical and radiological features." British Journal of Radiology 30(May): 225–238.

Cahalan, Don. 1957. "Career interests and expectations of U.S. medical students." 32: 557–563.

Chambliss, William J. 1964. "A sociological analysis of the law of vagrancy." Social Problems 12(Summer): 67–77.

Children's Division. 1963. Child Abuse—Preview of a Nationwide Survey. Denver: American Humane Association (Children's Division).

Davoren, Elizabeth. 1968. "The role of the social worker." Pp. 153–168 in Ray E. Helfer and Heny C. Kempe (eds.), The Battered Child. Chicago: University of Chicago Press.

DeFrancis, Vincent. 1963. "Parents who abuse children." PTA Magazine 58(November): 16–18.

———. 1967. "Child abuse—the legislative response." Denver Law Journal 44(Winter): 3–41.

———. 1970. Child Abuse Legislation in the 1970's. Denver: American Humane Association.

Eads, William E. 1969. "Observations on the establishment of child protection services in California." Stanford Law Review 21(May): 1129–1155.

Earle, Alice Morse. 1926. Child Life in Colonial Days. New York: Macmillan.

Elmer, Elizabeth. 1960. "Abused young children seen in hospitals." Journal of Social Work 3(October): 98–102.

Felder, Samuel. 1971. "A lawyer's view of child abuse." Public Welfare 29: 181–188.

Folks, Homer. 1902. The Case of the Destitute: Neglected and Delinquent Children. New York: Macmillan.

Fontana, V., D. Donovan and R. Wong. 1963. "The maltreatment syndrome in children." New England Journal of Medicine 269(December): 1389–1394.

Fox, Sanford J. 1970. "Juvenile justice reform: an historical perspective." Stanford Law Review 22(June): 1187–1239.

Freidson, Eliot J. 1968. "Medical personnel: physicians." Pp. 105–114 in David L. Sills (ed.), International Encyclopedia of the Social Sciences. Vol. 10. New York: Macmillan.

———. 1971. The Profession of Medicine: A Study in the Sociology of Applied Knowledge. New York: Dodd, Mead and Co.

Gil, David. 1970. Violence Against Children. Cambridge, Mass.: Harvard University Press.

Gil, David and John H. Noble. 1969. "Public knowledge, attitudes and opinions about physical child abuse." Child Welfare 49(July): 395–401.

Giovannoni, Jeanne. 1971. "Parental mistreatment." Journal of Marriage and the Family 33(November): 649–657.

Glaser, William A. 1960. "Doctors and politics." American Journal of Sociology 66(November): 230–245.

Goode, William J. 1957. "Community within a community: the profession." American Sociological Review 22(April): 194–200.

———. 1971. "Force and violence in the family." Journal of Marriage and the Family 33(November): 424–436.

Grumet, Barbara R. 1970. "The plaintive plaintiffs: victims of the battered child syndrome." Family Law Quarterly 4(September): 296–317.

Gusfield, Joseph R. 1963. Symbolic Crusades. Urbana, Ill.: University of Illinois Press.

Gwinn, J.J., K.W. Lewin and H.G. Peterson. 1961. "Roetenographic manifestations of unsuspected trauma in infancy." Journal of the American Medical Association 181(June): 17–24.

Hall, Jerome. 1952. Theft, Law and Society. Indianapolis: Bobbs-Merrill Co.

Hall, Oswald. 1946. "The informal organization of medicine." Canadian Journal of Economics and Political Science 12(February): 30–41.

Hyde, D.R., P. Wolff, A. Gross and E.L. Hoffman. 1954. "The American Medical Association: power, purpose and politics in organized medicine." Yale Law Journal 63(May): 938–1022.

Kadushin, Alfred. 1967. Child Welfare Services. New York. Macmillan.

Kempe, C.H., F.N. Silverman, B.F. Steele, W. Droegemuller and H.K. Silver. 1962. "The battered-child syndrome." Journal of the American Medical Association. 181(July): 17–24.

Lemer, Edwin M. 1974. "Beyond Mead: the societal reaction to deviance." Social Problems 21(April): 457–467.

McCoid, A.H. 1965. "The battered child syndrome and other assaults upon the family." Minnesota Law Review 50(November): 1–58.

Paulsen, Monrad G. 1966. "The legal framework for child protection." Columbia Law Review 66(April): 679–717.

———. 1967. "Child abuse reporting laws: the shape of the legislation." Columbia Law Review 67(January): 1–49.

Philips, Bernard S. 1964. "Expected value deprivation and occupational preference." Sociometry 27(June): 15–160.

Platt, Anthony M. 1969. The Child Savers: The Invention of Juvenile Delinquency. Chicago: University of Chicago Press.

Quinney, Richard. 1970. The Social Reality of Crime. Boston: Little Brown.

Radbill, Samuel X. 1968. "A history of child abuse and infanticide." Pp. 3–17 in Ray E. Helfer and Henry C. Kempe (eds.), The Battered Child. Chicago: University of Chicago Press.

Rothman, David J. 1971. The Discovery of the Asylum: Social Order and Disorder in the New Republic. Boston: Little Brown.

Shepard, Robert E. 1965. "The abused child and the law." Washington and Lee Law Review 22(Spring): 182–195.

Silverman, F.N. 1965. "The roentgen manifestations of unrecognized skeletal trauma in infants." American Journal of Roentgenology, Radium and Nuclear Medicine 69(March): 413–426.

Skolnick, Arlene and Jerome H. Skolnick. 1971. The Family in Transition. Boston: Little Brown.

Steele, Brandt and Carl F. Pollock. 1968. "A psychiatric study of parents who abuse infants and small children." Pp. 103–147 in Ray E. Helfer and Henry C. Kempe (eds.), The Battered Child. Chicago: University of Chicago Press.

Sutherland, Edwin H. 1950. "The diffusion of sexual psychopath laws." American Journal of Sociology 56(September): 142–148.

Thomas, Mason P. 1972. "Child abuse and neglect: historical overview, legal matrix and social perspectives." North Carolina Law Review 50(February): 293–249.

Woolley, P.V. and W.A. Evans Jr. 1955. "Significance of skeletal lesions in infants resembling those of traumatic origin." Journal of the American Medical Association 158(June): 539–543.

Young, Leontine. 1964. Wednesday's Children: A Study of Child Neglect and Abuse. New York: McGraw-Hill.

Zalba, Serapio R. 1966. "The abused child. I. A survey of the problems." Social Work 11(October): 3–16.

CHAPTER 5

Sudden Infant Death Syndrome as a Medical Research Problem Since 1945

Michael P. Johnson and Karl Hufbauer

For millennia, when a sleeping baby died suddenly and unexpectedly, its death was often attributed to accidental suffocation. The victim's parents were frequently criticized for overlying the baby or for neglecting to take proper precautions with the baby's bedding (Hansen, 1979; Johnson, 1981; Le Roy Ladurie, 1978:210; Savitt, 1975, 1979). Between 1945 and 1961, a small number of forensic pathologists in the United States discredited the suffocation theory and hypothesized that some mysterious disease agent, possibly a virus, caused the deaths. Their research did not produce conclusive evidence of a disease agent or process, and it attracted little funding and few new researchers. However, the disease hypothesis gave parents of victims reason to believe that they were not responsible for their babies' deaths and a basis for hope that such deaths could be prevented with more research.

Between 1962 and 1974, three major groups of bereaved parents organized around the issue. They counseled parents of new victims, sponsored local and regional research projects, and persuaded Congress to pass the Sudden Infant Death Syndrome Act of 1974, which required the National Institute of Child Health and Human Development (customarily abbreviated NICHD) to stimulate and support research on the problem. Although scientists, NICHD, and Congress actively participated in these developments, the parents' groups played the decisive role. They focused attention on the social significance of sudden infant death syndrome (SIDS)—popularly known as "crib death"—and insisted that research on the problem deserved top priority. Together with researcher and government officials, the parents transformed SIDS in the 1970s from an obscure medical mystery into an important medical research problem that attracted new researchers and additional funds, thereby contributing to a new research hypothesis: that SIDS victims suffer from neurological abnormalities that probably arise during fetal development.[1]

Forensic Pathologists and "Smothered" Infants: 1945–1961

In the early twentieth century, when a baby was found dead in its bed in the United States, a policeman or coroner was often called in to rule out foul play and to assign a cause of death. Parents were sometimes suspected of criminal neglect or even infanticide (Bergman, 1973). More commonly, sudden infant deaths were attributed to suffocation and considered unfortunate accidents. The grief-stricken parents were wracked with guilt and with questions about why their babies had died, but they were not usually charged with a crime.

Since the babies were considered victims of accidental suffocation, their deaths did not seem to require special medical attention. Unlike infants with recognizably life-threatening illnesses, crib death victims were not in a hospital when they died. Instead, they were being cared for by their parents at home. Because physicians considered crib deaths as accidents rather than the result of a disease, they did little more than caution parents about the dangers of suffocation.

Only forensic pathologists holding positions in large university medical centers or appointments as medical examiners in major cities were likely to encounter many cases of sudden infant death. Since autopsies did not conclusively establish suffocation as the cause of death, a few pathologists tried to learn more about why these babies died. In the mid-1930s they began to express doubts that suffocation was the cause of death (Farber, 1934).

Evidence that these doubts were well founded was first published in 1947 by Jacob Werne, a New York City medical examiner, and his wife Irene Garrow, a pathologist at St. John's Long Island City and Flushing Hospitals. Autopsies that they had conducted during the preceding 15 years on 167 infants who had apparently suffocated revealed that a quarter of these deaths were cased by mastoiditis, heart disease, or pneumonia. All the remaining cases showed signs of "fulminating respiratory disease" (Werne and Garrow, 1947:677). Since these signs were absent in babies known to have suffocated, Werne and Garrow concluded that it was wrong for coroners and medical examiners to attribute sudden infant deaths to accidental suffocation. Determined to eliminate this error and the parental suffering it engendered, Werne and Garrow recommended that the American Public Health Association "appoint a commission consisting of pediatricians, pathologists, and health officers for the comprehensive study of this important problem of sudden death during infancy" (1947:687).

Parents of victims added unexpected impetus to Werne and Garrow's recommendation. In February 1948, *Women's Home Companion* published "Death in the Bassinet," an anonymous account by a father who was convinced that his infant son had suffocated because, on the advice of a pediatrician, he had been allowed to sleep on his stomach. Rebuffed by physicians for trying to understand better why his son had died, the father commissioned a private research firm to collect information about other children in the Los Angeles area whose deaths were attributed to suffocation. The firm reported that nearly all of the infants had died lying face down. The children's editor of *Women's Home Companion* reinforced the father's message with a warning to parents about the dangers of accidental suffocation during sleep (*Women's Home Companion,* 1948). The description of medical ignorance and inertia that threatened babies' lives alarmed many readers, who subsequently wrote to the United State Public Health Service (USPHS) to insist that it make a greater effort to alert parents to the risks of suffocation.

In response to public pressure, Katherin Bain, a pediatrician with the Children's Bureau—the federal agency responsible at that time for safeguarding the interests of children (Steiner, 1976)—obtained National Institutes of Health (NIH) funding for a conference on sudden infant death. Bain recruited Sidney Farber, a professor of pathology at Harvard who was an early proponent of the respiratory disease hypothesis, to chair the conference. Bain, Farber, five other pathologists (including Werne), a pediatrician, an epidemiologist, and five NIH officials met in Washington in November 1949 and set the agenda for research on sudden infant death and for educating physicians and parents about the problem (Children's Bureau, 1949).

USPHS RESEARCH CONTRACTS

The conference readily accepted Werne and Garrow's case against accidental suffocation and discussed how to organize research to pursue the respiratory disease hypothesis. Coroners were in the best position to obtain clinical material, but most of them were elected officials with no training in pathology; in 41 states coroners were not even required to be physicians (Moritz et al., 1944). Consequently, coroners usually assigned an uncontroversial cause to sudden infant deaths rather than troubling to arrange for an autopsy by a pathologist (Helpern, 1977:5; *Journal of the American Medical Association,* 1946:349; Moritz et al., 1944). Farber suggested that a nationwide research project would help boost "the standards in the practice of pathology as a whole" by alerting coroners to the need for a careful autopsy by a well-trained pathologist (Children's Bureau, 1949:17). The conference decided that such an ambitious undertaking was unrealistic because of the widespread legal impediments to post-mortem research, the shortage of experienced forensic pathologists, and the scarcity of laboratories capable of delivering reproducible viral studies. Instead, the conference proposed a few parallel studies in cities that already had forensic pathologists and first-rate facilities (Children's Bureau, 1949).

In 1950 the USPHS sponsored four investigations. The contracts went to Werne and Garrow and to three young forensic pathologists who had been Farber's research fellows in Harvard's legal medicine program: Richard Ford, a medical examiner in Boston; Russell S. Fisher, Maryland's chief medical examiner, in Baltimore; and Lester Adelson, a forensic pathologist who was a deputy coroner in Cleveland (Landing, 1979). The outcome of the four studies was uneven. Though Werne and Garrow published their prior research (Werne and Garrow, 1953a,b), they dropped out of the USPHS project when New York City officials charged Werne with neglecting his duties as medical examiner (*New York Times,* 1955:48). Ford never mounted a study, evidently because he was unable to overcome unexpected legal obstacles to post-mortem research (Adelson, 1979). Fisher and his colleagues completed their study and wrote a report, but it was so inconclusive that they decided against publication (Fisher et al., 1954).

Only Adelson in Cleveland lived up to the project's expectations. He received the cooperation of his employer, Cuyahoga County Coroner Samuel R. Gerber, an officer of the National Association of Coroners, who was eager to prove that a good coroner's office could do research in forensic pathology equal to that of a medical examiner's staff (Gerber, 1948). Adelson was also encouraged by his former teacher, Alan R. Moritz, a leader in the American Medical Association's campaign to replace coroners with medical examiners trained in forensic medicine (Moritz et al., 1944). Moritz had recently left his position in legal medicine at Harvard to direct the Institute of Pathology at Case Western Reserve University in Cleveland (Adelson, 1979).

During the two-year study, Adelson and Eleanor Roberts Kinney, a microbiologist and research associate in pathology at Case Western Reserve, performed autopsies on 126 victims of sudden infant death. Their results came to be regarded as the classic characterization of such cases. Like Werne and Garrow (1947; 1953), they demonstrated "that mechanical asphyxia by bedclothes is not a serious consideration" and presented pathological evidence "that in the majority of infants and children who die suddenly and unexpectedly there is an inflammatory process in some portion of the respiratory tract" (Adelson and Kinney, 1956:693). However, they were unable to determine the exact mechanism by which respiratory inflammation caused death. During the next five years Adelson's friend Eli Gold, an assistant professor of pediatrics at Case Western Reserve, headed a group that searched for a viral cause for the respiratory inflammation and subsequent deaths. Their finds proved inconclusive (Gold et al., 1961).

DISSEMINATING THE RESPIRATORY DISEASE HYPOTHESIS

How to combat the pervasive belief in the suffocation hypothesis was a subject of concern at the 1949 conference. Werne pointed out that physicians "in routine medical practice" were ignorant of recent research (Children's Bureau, 1949:21). Farber agreed that the evidence against suffocation was not familiar "to the medical profession and certainly not the general public" (1949:18). Paul R. Cannon, chair of pathology at the University of Chicago, suggested that, as a first step toward communicating with the professional audience, a statement should be published in the *Journal of the American Medical Association.* Farber prepared the report which served as the basis for the journal's lead editorial a few moths later. Entitled "Infant Deaths From Suffocation," it summarized the case against accidental suffocation, described a typical instance of sudden infant death, and recommended:

> Efforts to prevent sudden death of infants should be directed toward diminishing exposure to known sources of infection during this highly vulnerable period of infant life and to the education of parents in the early signs of acute respiratory disease and their significance (*Journal of the American Medical Association,* 1950:1296).

About the same time, Bain was trying to reach a lay audience by publishing an account of Werne and Garrow's findings and the conference deliberations in the magazine

The Child (Bain, 1950). Two years later, after Adelson's research was underway, the American Medical Association's magazine for the general public, *Today's Health,* featured a progress report entitled "Babies Rarely Smother" (Bruner, 1952). A similar message was conveyed to an even larger audience in a *McCall's* article, "Babies Don't Smother," which also contained Bain's endorsement of "this reassuring report of the 'smothering superstition'" (Stern, 1952:44). All of these articles told parents not to worry about accidental suffocation but instead to be on the alert for signs of respiratory infections. Furthermore, they told parents of victims to request an autopsy. The *Today's Health* article quoted Adelson's insistence that an autopsy should be conducted any time a child died of an infection that was not ordinarily fatal. Parents who had just suffered the loss of a baby were understandably reluctant to consent to an autopsy and were likely to ask what good it would do; Adelson emphasized that an autopsy was "the only way to learn the real cause of death" (Bruner, 1952:71). Only with the consent of bereaved parents could researchers perform the autopsies needed to make progress in understanding and preventing these deaths. Adelson also explained how an autopsy could benefit the parents:

> In most cases, I believe it will eliminate the possibility of accident. I know what great measure of comfort it will give to parents to know that they were not responsible for their baby's death, and that their doctor was also powerless to save his life. Otherwise, they would torture themselves with feelings of guilt or blame their doctor for negligence (Bruner, 1952:71).

Despite the lay readership of *McCall's, The Child,* and *Today's Health,* few parents of victims were likely to see the articles. The most effective way to disseminate the new research to parents of victims was through practicing physicians, especially pediatricians. With knowledge of the recent work on the problem, physicians would be better prepared to advise grief-stricken parents. In addition, physicians needed to resist the strong temptation to assign a vague and unsubstantiated cause of death in such cases. At the 1949 conference Rustin McIntosh, Director of Pediatrics at Columbia University's Babies Hospital, pointed out that physicians often assigned a cause of death on the basis of inadequate evidence in order, "as we know, to avoid publicity in the family, so an explanation is given as 'bronchopneumonia'" (Children's Bureau, 1949:16). Pediatricians, like parents, had to be convinced that an autopsy was necessary.

The descriptions of sudden infant death in the standard *Textbook of Pediatrics* provide evidence of the slow diffusion of the respiratory disease hypothesis. The 1942 edition listed "asphyxia from overlying" first in a long list of possible causes of sudden infant death and discounted the then widely held belief that these deaths were often the result of an enlargement or dysfunction of the thymus (Griffith and Mitchell, 1942:142). The 1945 edition dropped suffocation to fourth in the list of seven major possible causes of sudden infant death and pointed out that although "many deaths have been falsely attributed to suffocation resulting from entanglement in bedclothes," it was actually a "rare occurrence" whose "importance has been greatly overemphasized" (Nelson, 1945:209). This description remained unchanged in the next two editions (Nelson, 1950:374; 1954:299). In the 1959 edition, suffocation was dropped to the last of six possible causes of sudden infant death and the account closely followed

Adelson's conclusions: evidence of suffocation was "difficult or impossible to obtain;" unless there was "unequivocal" evidence of homicide or strangulation, death should not be attributed to suffocation nor should such a diagnosis be made "simply because an infant is found face down in bed;" and finally, "in the absence of irrefutable evidence to the contrary, the family should be made to understand that they were in no manner responsible for the death of their child" (Nelson, 1959:350).

By the early 1960s there had been substantial progress toward the goals of the 1949 conference. Adelson and his colleagues had clinched the case against suffocation. Diffusion of this finding among physicians, medical examiners, and coroners was slowly increasing the fraction of victims' parents receiving sympathy rather than blame for their babies' deaths. Yet there had been virtually no headway in determining the cause of sudden infant death. The infectious disease hypothesis suggested that the solution might emerge from viral studies. But with few promising leads, researchers had little basis for claiming that their endeavors warranted increases in attention and funding.

Bereaved Parents Take the Initiative: 1962–1969

Although forensic pathologists believed that proper dissemination of their findings would result in parental "reassurance and peace of mind" (Adelson and Kinney, 1956:694), not all bereaved parents found the message comforting. Some wanted to know why, if they were not to blame, modern medical science lacked the knowledge to protect their babies. In the early 1960s, the Roes in Greenwich, Connecticut, the Dores in Seattle, Washington, and the Goldbergs in Baltimore, Maryland, organized groups to counsel bereaved parents, to disseminate information, and to sponsor research on crib death.

THE ROES

The depth of parental concern about medical ignorance of sudden infant death is revealed by the response of Jedd and Louise Roe to the death of their six-month-old son Mark in their Greenwich, Connecticut, home in October 1958. The Roes' pediatrician, J. Frederick Lee, doubted that Mark had suffocated, even though he had been discovered dead in his bed, burrowed under his blanket. Lee insisted on an autopsy and, when fluid was found in the lungs, decided that Mark had probably died from acute bronchial pneumonia. Lee was aware that the pathological evidence was not conclusive, however, and the Roes were tortured by doubts. Louise Roe later recalled: "I kept asking myself, 'Why? Why did this happen to us? Why?' And no one could give me an answer" (Cadden, 1963:102). Over the next six months the Roes heard of five similar cases. Resolving to find out what was known about sudden infant death, Jedd Roe eventually contacted Rustin McIntosh, a participant in the 1949 conference. McIntosh confirmed that the cause of sudden infant death was still a mystery, but reported that some promising research was underway. The Roes decided to set up a foundation in memory of their son that would support research and serve as a clearing house for the latest information. In August 1962 they read in *Newsweek* that Renate Dische, a pathologist at New York University's Bellevue Medical Center, was about to begin a study of sudden infant death in Manhattan, with the cooperation of Milton Helpern, the city's chief medical examiner, and funding from the New York Health Research Council (*Newsweek,* 1962). Jedd Roe immediately met with Dische, who encouraged the plans for a foundation (Cadden, 1963). Within two weeks the Roes founded the Mark Addison Roe Foundation "to promote, stimulate, and support research in the diagnosis, treatment, and cure of sudden, unexpected death in infants" (Mark Addison Roe Foundation, 1965).

Using funds contributed by the Roes, parents of other victims, and sympathizers, the foundation made small grants to Dische and to two other researcher during its first year of existence (Mark Addison Roe Foundation, 1965). To help researchers collect data, it supported the development of a standard form for reporting the medical details about each victim and, beginning in mid-1965, distributed the forms through medical examiners and interested physicians and parents. As bereaved parents continued to contact the foundation for information, the Roes and the other trustees realized that a national network of local parents groups was needed to help parents cope with the death of their babies and to distribute information about sudden infant death. The first chapter was formed on Long Island in the spring of 1966. Shortly thereafter, the Roes moved to Denver, Colorado, and formed another chapter (Mark Addison Roe Foundation, 1966). As chapters continued to spring up across the United States, the Mark Addison Roe Foundation changed its name in mid-1967 to the National Foundation for Sudden Infant Death (NFSID).

THE DORES

Fred and Mary Dore of Seattle became aware of sudden infant death in September 1961 when they lost their three-month-old daughter Christine to "acute pneumonitis" (Dore, 1980). The coroner's pathologist told them that researchers had no idea how to prevent the disease, which in King County, Washington, alone claimed up to 50 babies a year. Their pediatrician was equally discouraging about the prospects for prevention. But he did recall that his colleague, Sherod M. Billington, had chaired a subcommittee on sudden infant death for the Washington State Medical Association. The Dores decided to discuss the problem with Billington once they regained their composure; in the meantime they joined other bereaved families in extending sympathy to families of new victims in the Seattle area.

When the Dores met with Billington in June 1962, they learned that his subcommittee had been formed seven years earlier by a few Seattle pediatricians acting on the request of parents of victims. The subcommittee had tried to educate physicians about the problem and to obtain autopsies of victims, but their efforts had stalled when they could not even raise enough funds to transport victims from the morgue to Children's Orthopedic Hospital for detailed autopsies by the University of Washington medical faculty. Hoping to overcome this obstacle, Fred Dore, a Democratic state senator, approached the new coroner of King County, Leo Sowers, a Republican. Sowers revealed that he too had lost a baby to crib death, and offered to help. With Sowers' cooperation, the Dores built a bipartisan coalition in the Washington state legislature to promote research on sudden infant death. In March 1963 a state law authorized county coroners to transfer all sudden death victims under three years of age to the University of Washington; the state would pay for transportation and the university for the cost of the autopsies (Billington, 1980; Dore, 1980; Spencer, 1966; Washington Association for Sudden Infant Death Study, 1965).

The new law obliged the pediatrics and pathology departments of the University of Washington to become acquainted with current thinking about the problem. Neither department included an expert on sudden infant death, but the chair of pediatrics, Ralph J. P. Wedgwood, had recently come to Seattle from Case Western Reserve and was aware of Adelson's work. Wedgwood and Earl P. Benditt, the chair of pathology, agreed that a conference with the researchers from Cleveland would be the best way to begin. They obtained funding for the conference from the National Institute of Child Health and Human Development (NICHD), which was just getting organized under its first director, Robert A. Aldrich, a former member of the pediatrics department at the University of Washington. In September 1963 the experts from Cleveland and elsewhere met in Seattle and reviewed the recent research. They were not optimistic about the prospects for a quick breakthrough in understanding the cause of sudden infant deaths. Benjamin H. Landing, a professor of pathology and pediatrics at the University of Southern California, proposed that researchers emphasize how little was known about the cause of sudden infant death by labeling it a "syndrome" and thereby "imply the existence of a constellation of properties in the patient which need not have the same cause" (Aldrich, 1979; Benditt and Wedgwood, 1964; Landing 1966:1; 1979; *Time*, 1963; Wedgwood and Benditt, 1966).

Since none of the conference participants from the University of Washington volunteered to run the state autopsy program, Benditt recruited J. Bruce Beckwith, a young pediatric pathologist who had been working with Landing collecting data on sudden infant death in Los Angeles (Beckwith, 1980). Soon after he arrived in Seattle, Beckwith was joined by Abraham B. Bergman, a recent recruit to the university's pediatrics department who had learned about Adelson's research as a medical student at Case Western Reserve in the mid-1950s (Bergman, 1974). Beckwith and Bergman drew up a proposal for a three-year study of "the sudden death syndrome in infancy" and submitted it to the National Institute of Child Health and Human Development (Magnuson, 1965:23451). They proposed to study victims brought to Seattle's Children's Orthopedic Hospital under the state-mandated program. NICHD funded the proposal in August 1965 (Magnuson, 1965), and Beckwith and Bergman went on to organize a comprehensive research program, enlisting, among others, the virologist C. George Ray and the epidemiologist Donald R. Peterson. By the late 1960s, Seattle had replaced Cleveland as the center of sudden infant death research in the United States.

In addition to providing the impetus for the research program at the University of Washington, the Dores cooperated with the researchers in founding the Washington Association for Sudden Infant Death Study in January 1965. The association provided information and support for bereaved families and helped obtain the parents' consent for their babies to be studied by the Seattle researchers (Washington Association for Sudden Infant Death Study, 1965). The association also kept in touch with the Mark

Addison Roe Foundation and with another new parents group in Baltimore (Washington Association for Sudden Infant Death Study, 1966).

THE GOLDBERGS

Saul and Sylvia Goldberg's two-month-old daughter Suzanne Elysa died suddenly at their home in Baltimore in December 1963. Seeking an answer to why their baby had died, they wrote to authors of medical articles to which their pediatrician referred them. They discovered how little was known and how little was being spend to learn more. At the time their daughter died, a copy of *Redbook* with an article about the Mark Addison Roe Foundation was in their home, and early in 1964 they wrote to the foundation suggesting that they might organize a branch in Baltimore. When the foundation replied with printed material and a request for a contribution, the Goldbergs were put off. They wanted to join a grass-roots organization of parents who would help counsel bereaved families of new victims, yet the Mark Addison Roe Foundation was, at that time, essentially a board of trustees rather than a membership organization. In addition, the foundation's name did not mention sudden infant death. The Goldbergs decided to form their own organization in Baltimore. In November 1964 they met with other parents and sympathizers and founded the Guild for Infant Survival to provide support, counseling, and information to parents of victims and to work to prevent sudden infant death (Goldberg and Goldberg, 1982; Leblanc, 1973).

Soon after founding the Guild for Infant Survival, the Goldbergs met with Russell Fisher, Maryland's chief medical examiner who had held one of the USPHS contracts for research into sudden infant death in the early 1950s. Fisher was trying to raise funds for new facilities, three rooms of which would be devoted to research on sudden infant death. The Goldbergs immediately decided to raise money from their acquaintances in Baltimore and to lobby the state legislature for building funds. They also made small annual grants to support Fisher's continuing research and, like the Seattle parents, contacted bereaved parents and helped them cope with their loss (Krehnbrink, 1973). However, less than a year after forming the Guild, the Goldbergs concluded that private resources were simply insufficient for a full-scale attack on sudden infant death and that major federal funding was necessary. With the help of the Maryland congressional delegation, the Goldbergs sought out the National Institute of Child Health and Human Development staff members who were monitoring research on sudden infant death. The Goldbergs received a sympathetic hearing and were assured that NICHD was supporting research on the problem (Goldberg and Goldberg, 1982).

The principal activity of the Guild for Infant Survival was organizing parent volunteers to counsel parents of new victims in the Baltimore area and, by phone, throughout the nation. Parents who had been counseled often set up a local guild in their area. To reflect this steady expansion, the organization changed its name in 1968 to the International Guild for Infant Survival (Goldberg and Goldberg, 1982; U.S. Congress: Senate, 1973a).

The Goldbergs corresponded regularly with the National Institute of Child Health and Human Development during the late 1960s, but became increasingly frustrated when NICHD's expressions of concern about the problem did not translate into more attention or funding for research. After Sylvia Goldberg met with NICHD director Gerald LaVeck in 1968 and was told that the institute's primary interest was mental retardation, the Goldbergs gave up on NICHD and decided to lobby Congress. Aided again by the Maryland delegation to Congress, Saul Goldberg managed to secure a place on the agenda of the hearings of Senator Warren Magnuson's Senate Appropriations Subcommittee on Labor, Health, Education and Welfare on December 2, 1969 (Goldberg and Goldberg, 1982).

EMPHASIZING THE SOCIAL SIGNIFICANCE
OF SUDDEN INFANT DEATH

When Goldberg appeared before Magnuson's committee, he used an argument about the social significance of SIDS that parents and their supporters had developed during the previous few years. At the time of the 1949 conference, researcher estimated that about 2,000 infants were victims of sudden infant death in the United States every year, a few hundred more than the number of infants reported as dying each year of accidental suffocation (Children's Bureau, 1949). During the late 1950s and early 1960s it became clear that the incidence of crib death was much greater. Since such deaths were frequently attributed to pneumonia and other causes, mortality statistics minimized the incidence and made it difficult to estimate precisely the total number of crib deaths in the nation. However, forensic pathologists assumed that the national death rate was approximately the same as that discovered in the few cities with research projects—about three deaths per thousand live births (Valdes-Dapena, 1967).

To parents and members of the press who reported on the activities of the parents groups, the significance of such numbers was difficult to grasp. Parents and the press wanted a dramatic and understandable measure of how many children were struck by this mystery killer. They though death-rate statistics obscured the gravity of the problem. At first they stated the incidence of crib death in terms of the annual number of victims in the United States. *Redbook,* for example, used the estimate that Landing gave to the 1963 Seattle conference (Landing, 1963) and reported that "each year in this country an estimated 25,000 apparently healthy babies die inexplicably" (Cadden, 1963:59). By the mid-1960s this numerical estimate was translated into a statement about the social significance of sudden infant death by pointing out that it was the nation's foremost killer of babies over one week old. In 1966, for example, the *Saturday Evening Post* explained that "this silent invisible killer [is] the leading cause of death among infants between the ages of one week and one year" (Spencer, 1966:79).

About the same time researchers began to emphasize the scale of the problem. Bergman and his colleagues in Seattle reported that sudden infant death was "the greatest single cause of death in infancy, beyond the first week of life" (Bergman et al., 1966:711). The first review essay on the problem opened with the statement that since crib death claimed 15,000 to 25,000 children every year in the United States, "the phenomenon may well be considered a health problem of major magnitude" (Valdes-Dapena, 1967:123). Such claims suggested that the resources allocated for research on sudden infant death were not proportional to its social significance. At the Second International Conference on causes of Sudden Infant Death, held in Seattle in 1969, Bergman and his colleagues observed that it "says something about our assignment of research priorities [that], considering the magnitude of the problem, [such] a miniscule amount of scientific effort is being expended on sudden infant death" (Berman et al., 1970:ix).[2]

Goldberg, who had attended the 1969 conference at his own expense, echoed these observations in his testimony before the Magnuson committee:

> I speak to you now [in the name of] the tens and hundreds of thousands—perhaps millions—of innocent babies who have died suddenly and unexpectedly in years past. I speak to you also in the name of the 15,000–25,000 normal, healthy babies in our 50 states who are dying in this same bizarre manner in this year of 1969 (Goldberg, 1972:78).

On behalf of the International Guild for Infant Survival, Goldberg urged Congress to increase research funding until it was "commensurate with the magnitude and scope of these deaths" (Goldberg, 1972:81).

Government Responds to Parental Pressure: 1970–1974

During the late 1960s, bereaved parents, prompted by the growing parents organizations, subjected the National Institute of Child Health and Human Development to a steady barrage of letters demanding more attention and funding for SIDS research. In December 1970, the Goldbergs told Roger O. Egeberg, assistant secretary of the Department of Health, Education and Welfare (HEW), that parents were frustrated by NICHD's passivity and that they were going to Congress to get action (Goldberg and Goldberg, 1982). NICHD responded to these pressures during the winter of 1970–71 by considering how to expand their research program (Hasselmeyer and Hunter, 1975:226; Lane et al., 1979:15).

Prior to 1970, NICHD had funded every proposal that appeared to have some prospect of advancing or diffusing scientific knowledge of SIDS; the 1963 and 1969 conferences in Seattle, nine investigations of SIDS etiology and epidemiology, and the first review essay on the problem (U.S. Congress: Senate, 1972a:4, 1978:28). To the NICHD officials responsible for SIDS research, Eileen G. Hasselmeyer and Jehu C. Hunter, it seemed that the best way to improve on this record was to attract the interest of researchers from a broad spectrum of medical sub-specialties. They decided to host a planning workshop on SIDS to recruit new investigators and to identify promising approaches for research (Lane et al., 1981:79).

The planning workshop was held in August 1971. It brought together Beckwith, Bergman, two other SIDS researcher funded by NICHD, and four specialists in sleep physiology, cardiopulmonary pediatrics, neonatal pathology, and comparative medicine. The workshop participants, especially the sleep physiologist M. Barry Sterman, urged NICHD to expand the research program beyond the early weeks of life to all developmental stages, from conception through the sixth month after birth. Sterman argued that this would encourage exploration of the possibility that SIDS was "closely tied to an aberrant developmental and maturational phenomenon," particularly in "the interactions of sleep physiologic mechanisms and autonomic regulatory processes" (U.S. Congress: Senate, 1973a:269, 273). Hasselmeyer and others at NICHD agreed with this general emphasis and soon afterward began negotiations for research contracts with Sterman and other workshop participants (U.S. Congress: Senate, 1972a:7).

1972 SENATE HEARING AND RESOLUTION

During the last six months of 1971, parental pressure continued to mount for a congressional hearing on SIDS. In June the Guild[3] surveyed the chief medical officers of every state to determined how SIDS deaths were reported and how many had occurred within the previous year. The survey revealed that 16 different names were used for SIDS, that no uniform system of classification existed for reporting SIDS deaths, and that as a result only 1,155 cases were reported for 1970, about one tenth the number that researchers estimated actually occurred (International Council for Infant Survival, 1973:4; U.S. Congress: Senate, 1972a:72,77). To this evidence of the need for federal action Richard H. Raring, a newly bereaved parent, added his voice. After losing his son in February 1971, Raring wrote Senator Edward M. Kennedy expressing his anger that NICHD was not sponsoring an aggressive research program. Kennedy passed Raring's letter to Senator Walter F. Mondale, who chaired the Senate Subcommittee on Children and Youth (U.S. Congress: Senate, 1972a:91). The Guild had already been lobbying for a hearing before Mondale's committee (Goldberg and Goldberg, 1982). The National Foundation for Sudden Infant Death, which had just absorbed the Washington Association for Sudden Infant Death Study, added its weight to the demand of Raring and the Guild, and a hearing was scheduled for January 1972.

The purpose of the hearing, Mondale said, was to review "our efforts to discover the medical cause of [this] frightening disease that takes the lives of at least 10,000 infants each year . . . and ways to prevent . . . these deaths" (U.S. Congress; Senate, 1972a:2). As testimony was presented at the hearing, the senators began to express their dissatisfaction with NICHD's performance. Kennedy declared: "I don't think there is any question but there can and needs to be a dramatic and more effective program developed with the agencies of Government in respect to SIDS" (U.S. Congress: Senate, 1972a:63). Mondale agreed that 'it is pretty obvious that we have here another example of [an] enormous, compelling human need being largely ignored, particularly in terms of medical research" (U.S. Congress: Senate, 1972a:75).

A few weeks after the hearing, Mondale announced that he would seek a $10 million appropriation for SIDS research (*Washington Post,* 1972). As a first step, he persuaded the Committee on Labor and Public Welfare to propose a resolution "to assure that the maximum resources and effort be concentrated on medical research into sudden infant death syndrome and on the extension of services to families who lose children to the disease" (U.S. Congress: Senate, 1972a:85). The resolution also directed NICHD "to designate the search for a cause and prevention of [SIDS] as one of [its] tops priorities" and it called on HEW to disseminate information about SIDS to coroners, medical examiners, and others who dealt with bereaved parents (U.S. Congress: Senate, 1972a:85). The resolution gathered co-sponsors during the spring of 1972 and was adopted on June 7 without a single dissenting vote (U.S. Congress: Senate, 1972b).

NICHD EXPANDS ITS SIDS RESEARCH PROGRAM

In response to the Senate hearing and resolution, Hasselmeyer and Hunter took steps to encourage SIDS research. Between May and August of 1972 they hosted five research workshops in which SIDS researchers conferred with specialists in potentially related fields (Lane et al., 1979:21, 1981:81). They also identified seven areas of investigation for special emphasis—giving first priority to "developmental neurophysiology, [particularly] abnormal sleep patterns" (U.S. Congress: Senate, 1973a: 13). They intensified their recruitment of SIDS researchers by announcing NICHD's "expanded research program" in 30 medical journals (Hasselmeyer, 1972: 386). By August 1973, NICHD had received 21 SIDS grant proposals, more than in all the years through 1971 (U.S. Congress: House, 1973:42; U.S. Congress: Senate, 1978:31). In addition to the five new research proposals that were funded, NICHD awarded six research contracts, one to Sterman for research on "Developmental Phenomena and the Occurrence of SIDS" and another to Bergman for a survey of the management of SIDS throughout the nation (U.S. Congress: Senate, 1973a:43, 183, 190). Funding for SIDS research increased dramatically, from a total of $46,000 in the fiscal 1971–72 to $604,000 in 1973–74 (U.S. Congress: Senate, 1978: 28).

1973 CONGRESSIONAL HEARINGS AND 1974 SIDS ACT

NICHD's expanded research program was scrutinized closely in August and September of 1973 in hearings before the House Subcommittee on Public Health and Environment and the Senate Subcommittees on Health and on Children and Youth (U.S. Congress: House, 1973; U.S. Congress: Senate, 1973a). The committees were considering legislation to require NICHD to emphasize SIDS research far more than it had done so far. Bergman and Saul Goldberg, spokesmen for the national parents groups, testified in favor of the proposed law. The National Institutes of Health opposed it, arguing that it duplicated their existing authority and that, given their current research program, it was unnecessary.

The bills proposed by the two committees were quite different. The Senate committee reported that it was "disappointed and not satisfied with the magnitude and the scope of the SIDS research program" and recommended a law providing $24 million for SIDS research and $12 million for counseling bereaved parents over three years (U.S. Congress: Senate, 1973b: 2, 8; 1973c). The House bill, in contrast, contained no special appropriation for SIDS research but provided $6 million for counseling (U.S. Congress: House, 1974a,b). The bill that emerged from the Senate-House conference committee followed the House proposal and implicitly acknowledged NICHD's defense of its SIDS research program. It authorized $9 million for counseling but did no more than assign NICHD responsibility for SIDS research and require the Department of Health, Education and Welfare to report annually on the SIDS research projects it was supporting. The bill passed both houses and the Sudden Infant Death Syndrome Act of 1974 was signed by President Richard Nixon on April 22, 1974, as Public Law 93–270.

The new law did not satisfy the Goldbergs and other parents because it did not require NICHD to set aside a substantial budget exclusively for SIDS research (Goldberg and Goldberg, 1982; Steiner, 1973:221). Nonetheless, by lobbying Congress the parents groups generated pressure on NICHD that intensified its SIDS research efforts. With the passage of the 1974 SIDS Act the parents achieved congressional recognition of their conviction that SIDS was a significant social problem and deserved high priority on the nation's medical research agenda.

Consequences of the New Research Policy

UNPRECEDENTED RESEARCH ACTIVITY

Passage of the 1974 SIDS Act combined with NICHD's expanded research program to stimulate SIDS research activity to unprecedented levels. Between 1974 and 1976, NICHD reviewed nearly four times as many SIDS proposals (61) and funded six times as many SIDS grants (30) as during the entire period from 1964 to 1971 (U.S. Congress: Senate, 1978:31). NICHD spent $6.5 million on SIDS research between 1974 and 1976, nearly nine times more than the total funding for SIDS research between 1964 and 1971 (U.S. Congress: Senate, 1978:28). In 1965, five SIDS research articles appeared in the medical literature in the United States; in 1971 eight articles were published; and in 1976 the number of publications quadrupled to 35. Since 1976 the number and variety of SIDS research papers have become so great that review articles must be selective (Valdes-Dapena, 1980).

A NEW RESEARCH HYPOTHESIS

Much of the recent research has explored a new hypothesis that SIDS victims are not normal, healthy babies but instead suffer from some developmental abnormality. This hypothesis grew out of the research of Alfred Steinschneider (1972), a pediatrician at the State University of New York in Syracuse, and Richard L. Naeye (1973), the chair of pathology at Pennsylvania State University. The two researchers confirmed NICHD's expectation that developmental neurophysiology would be an important area of research.

Steinschneider attended the 1969 Seattle conference at the invitation of Bergman, his former colleague at Syracuse where he was working on autonomic reactivity of infants. At the conference, Steinschneider participated in discussions on sleep apnea, that is, episodes of breathing cessation during sleep (Berman et al., 1970: 202, 205, 219). Impressed by the magnitude of the SIDS problem, he returned from the conference and notified the staff at the State University Hospital of the Upstate Medical Center that he was interested in seeing babies who were subject to apnea (Steinschneider, 1982). In 1972, Steinschneider reported five case histories of babies who had more frequent and prolonged episodes of sleep apnea than normal babies. After these infants were released from the hospital, two of the five died in their sleep. Steinschneider suggested that these cases supported "the hypothesis that prolonged apnea, a physiological component of sleep, is part of the final pathway resulting in sudden death" (Steinschneider, 1972:652).

Naeye read Steinschneider's article and reasoned that if prolonged apnea were a factor in SIDS, then victims should show signs of oxygen deficiencies caused by recurrent apneic episodes (Steinschneider, 1982). Using clinical material provided by Fisher in Baltimore, Naeye compared SIDS victims with children who lived at high altitudes and had been killed in accidents. He found that many SIDS victims, like the control sample, had an unmistakable sign of chronic hypoxia (oxygen deficiency)—hypertrophy (thickening) of the small pulmonary arteries (Naeye, 1973). Over the next few years, Naeye located six other "tissue markers" for hypoxia and hypoxemia in SIDS victims (Naeye, 1980; Valdes-Dapena, 1980:602).

NICHD did not fund the research Steinschneider reported in his 1972 article (Steinschneider, 1982) and its support for Naeye's initial work was for the study of lung maturation rather than SIDS (U.S. Congress: Senate, 1973a:181). However, NICHD quickly recognized the importance of their research and promoted further investigations. In 1973 Steinschneider received NICHD's largest SIDS grant for a study of sleep apnea (U.S. Congress: senate, 1973a:184). Naeye's research was funded with grants focused on possible causes of SIDS (U.S. Congress: Senate, 1978:140).

NICHS aggressively promoted the new hypothesis, which was avidly pursued by the rapidly growing SIDS research community in the Unites States; a review article referred to NICHD's efforts as a "near crusade" (Valdes-Depena, 1980:611). Since 1974, researchers have attempted to locate developmental abnormalities in SIDS victims, to discover why they occur, to find physiological indicators that can be used to identify high-risk infants, and to develop home monitors that will warn parents of dangerous apneic crises (Valdes-Dapena, 1980). In 1976 Steinschneider moved to the University of Maryland to direct the new SIDS Institute, a multidisciplinary research center funded in 1977 by a $2.84 million grant from NICHD (Steinschneider, 1982; U.S. Congress: Senate, 1978:365).

PARENTS GROUPS

Members of NFSID and the Guild were proud of their successful lobbying campaign in Congress and pleased that NICHD was sponsoring a vigorous research program. However, the counseling centers created under the 1974 SIDS Act took over some of the functions of the parent groups, and the latest research has disturbing implications about possible parental responsibility for SIDS deaths.

The counseling program authorized by the 1974 Act was operating in 27 states in 1978 (U.S. Congress: Senate, 1978:9). To help provide information and support for parents not served by these SIDS centers, the government awarded a non-competitive $264,000 contract in September 1976 to NFSID's successor, the National Sudden Infant Death Syndrome Foundation (Staats, 1981:45). Although parents in the Guild and NSIDSF continued to counsel bereaved parents, the professional counselors hired by the funded SIDS centers assumed many of the jobs formerly done by parent volunteers. In hearings on March 1, 1978, before the Senate Subcommittee on Child Health and Human Development which was considering the renewal of the 1974 Act, Guild representatives Nancy Lefebvre and Saul Goldberg questioned whether scarce funds should be used to replace parent volunteers with professional counselors when these monies might be better spent on research (U.S. Congress: Senate, 1978: 217). Furthermore, Lefebvre pointed out that "professionalization has usually meant an alienation of the very Guild members who sought projects and eagerly anticipated a productive, cooperative relationship" (U.S. Congress: Senate, 1978:219). Despite this testimony, when Congress renewed the SIDS Act in 1979 as Public Law 96–142, the most notable alteration was the extension of professionally staffed SIDS centers to all 50 states.

Working as ancillaries to professional counseling staffs, the parents' groups lost some of their autonomy and much of their morale and momentum. Representatives of NSIDSF and the Guild met in Dallas in 1978 to discuss the possibility of consolidating into one national organization (Council of Guilds for Infant Survival, 1978). The merger did not materialize and relations between the two groups deteriorated (Goldberg and Goldberg, 1982), further weakening both organizations.

While parents can still be reassured that they did not smother their babies, they are confused and upset by the new research (U.S. Congress; Senate, 1977:86). The hypothesis that SIDS victims suffer from some developmental abnormality suggests that something about the pregnant mother and her environment may well contribute to her baby's death, a possibility that is chilling and unsettling for parents. Furthermore, attempts to identify high-risk babies and design home monitors suggest that, with sufficient vigilance, parents can prevent SIDS. Parents organizations have continued to support SIDS research, hoping for an effective method of prevention. But the initiative is no longer in their hands. Instead, as the pace of research has accelerated, parents have been shunted to the sidelines where they have become interested, but essentially passive, bystanders.

Summary

After 1945 forensic pathologists overturned the hypothesis that babies who died suddenly and unexpectedly were suffocated. They proposed a new hypothesis based on respiratory infection, but they did not produce conclusive evidence of infectious disease. Their work did not lead to sustained interest in sudden infant death among new researchers or in the National Institutes of Health. Between the studies of the Cleveland group in the 1950s and the passage of the Sudden Infant Death Syndrome Act of

1974, parents of SIDS victims were the most active and influential proponents of SIDS research. They promoted the studies in Seattle; they developed a persuasive argument for a national commitment to study SIDS; and they pressured Congress to focus attention on SIDS and require the National Institute of Child Health and Human Development to foster SIDS research. Since 1974 the parents' influence in SIDS research has sharply diminished as researchers have taken custody of the problem.

Notes

1. For other studies of SIDS research policy in the United States, see Lally, 1977; Lane et al., 1981; Raring, 1975; Steiner, 1976; and Wade, 1974. For social and historical studies of other medical research problems, see Redman, 1973; Rettig, 1977; Strickland, 1972; and Studer and Chubin, 1980.

2. At this conference Bergman and Beckwith also launched their successful campaign for the current name and acronym for crib death: "sudden infant death syndrome" and "SIDS" (Bergman et al., 1970:ix, 14).

3. In October 1972, the International Guild for Infant Survival changed its name to the International Council for Infant Survival. Although this remains the official name, the organization began referring to itself as the Council of Guilds for Infant Survival in the late 1970s. Because these name changes did not alter the character of the organization, we have chosen, for the sake of simplicity, to refer to it here and subsequently as "the Guild."

References

Adelson, Lester. 1979. Interview with authors (October 4).

Adelson, Lester, and Eleanor Roberts Kinney. 1956. "Sudden and unexpected death in infancy and childhood." Pediatrics 17 (May):663–697.

Aldrich, Robert A. 1979. Letter to authors (October 23).

Bain, Katherine. 1950. "When a baby dies unexpectedly." The Child 14 (March):130–131.

Beckwith, J. Bruce. 1980. Letter to authors (June 5).

Benditt, Earl P., and Ralph J. P. Wedgwood. 1964. "Sudden-death syndrome." Science 143 (January 10):156–158.

Bergman, Abraham B. 1973. "The management of sudden infant death syndrome (SIDS) in the United States." Report in pp. 324–762 of U.S. Congress: Senate, Sudden Infant Death Syndrome Hearings. Committee on Labor and Public Welfare, Subcommittees on Health and on Children and Youth, 93rd Congress, 1st session, September 20, 1973. Washington, D.C.: U.S. Government Printing Office.

———. 1974. "Humanizing Society." Pp. 303–308 in Robert R. Robinson (ed.), SIDS 1974: Proceedings of Francis E. Camps International Symposium on Sudden and Unexpected Deaths in Infancy. Toronto: Canadian Foundation for the Study of Infant Deaths.

Bergman, Abraham B., J. Bruce Beckwith, and C. George Ray (eds.). 1970. Sudden Infant Death Syndrome: Proceedings of the Second International Conference on the Causes of Sudden Death in Infants. Seattle and London: University of Washington Press.

Bergman, Abraham B., Joyce D. Miller, and J. Bruce Beckwith. 1965. "Sudden death syndrome: The physician's role." Clinical Pediatrics 5 (December):711–713.

Billington, Sherod M. 1980. Letter to authors (April 10).

Bruner, Louise. 1952. "Babies rarely smother." Today's Health 30 (July):32–33, 70–72.

Cadden, Vivian. 1963. "Why babies die." Redbook 122 (November):58–59, 100–104.

Children's Bureau. 1949. "Conference on sudden death in infants, November 30, 1949." Transcript of proceedings. In authors' possession.

Council of Guilds for Infant Survival. 1978. G.I.S. Outcry, Spring 1978. Newsletter. In author's possession.

Dore, Mary. 1980. Letters to authors (March 16).

Farber, Sidney. 1934. "Fulminating streprococcus infections in infancy as a cause of sudden death." New England Journal of Medicine 211 (July 26):154–158.

Fisher, Russell S., S. S. Katz, and W. V. Lovitt, Jr. 1954. "Sudden death in infancy: A sociopathic study." Unpublished manuscript. In authors' possession.

Gerber, Samuel R. 1948. "Adequate medical examination in unexpected and violent deaths." Journal of the American Medical Association 138 (December 18):1190–1191.

Gold, Eli, David H. Carver, Hannelore Heineberg, Lester Adelson, and Frederick C. Robbins. 1961. "Viral infection: A possible cause of sudden, unexpected death in infants." New England Journal of Medicine 264 (January 12):53–60.

Goldberg, Saul. 1971. Testimony before the Senate Appropriations Subcommittee on Labor, Health, Education, and Welfare, December 2, 1969. First published in pp. 78–81 of U.S. Congress: Senate, Rights of Children: Examination of the Sudden Infant Death Syndrome Hearings. Committee on Labor and Public Welfare, Subcommittee on Children and Youth, 92nd Congress, 2nd session, January 25, 1972. Washington, D.C.: U.S. Government Printing Office.

Goldberg, Saul and Sylvia Goldberg. 1982. Interview with authors (March 14).

Griffith, J. P. C., and A. G. Mitchell (eds.). 1942. Textbook of Pediatrics, 3rd edition. Philadelphia: W. B. Saunders Co.

Hansen, Elizabet deG. R. 1979. " 'Overlaying' in 19th-century England: Infant mortality or infanticide?" Human Ecology 7 (December):333–352.

Hasselmeyer, Eileen G. 1972. "The sudden infant death syndrome." Obstetrics and Gynecology Annual 4:213–236.

Helpern, Milton, with Bernard Knight. 1977. Autopsy: The Memoirs of Milton Helpern, The World's Greatest Medical Detective. New York: St. Martin's Press.

International Council for Infant Survival. 1973. G.I.S. Newsletter, Winter 1973. In authors' possession.

Johnson, Michael P. 1981. "Smothered slave infants: Were slave mothers at fault?" Journal of Southern History 67 (November):493–520.

Journal of the American Medical Association. 1946. "The office of coroner." Editorial, volume 130 (February 9):349.

———. 1950 "Infant death from suffocation." Editorial, volume 142 (April 22):1296–1297.

Krehnbrink, Rebecca. 1973. "The tragedy of crib death." Baltimore Magazine, (September):20, 64–67.

Lally, J. J. 1977. "Social determinants of differential allocation of resources to disease research: Comparative analysis of crib death and cancer research." Journal of Health and Social Behavior 18 (June):125–138.

Landing, Benjamin H. 1966. "Review of the problem." Pp. 1–9 in Ralph J. P. Wedgwood and Earl P. Benditt (eds.), Sudden Death in Infants: Proceedings of the Conference on Causes of Sudden Death in Infants, September 1963, Seattle, Washington. Washington, D.C.: United States Public Health Service and National Institute of Child Health and Human Development.

———. 1979. Letter to authors (September 20).

Lane, Henry W., Rodney G. Beddows, and Paul R. Lawrence. 1981. Managing Large Research and Development Programs. Albany: State University of New York Press.

Lawrence, Paul R. 1979. "The sudden infant death syndrome." Unpublished manuscript. Department of Business Administration, Harvard Business School, Cambridge, Mass. 02163.

Leblanc, Rena Dictor. 1973. "Somebody help my baby." Good Housekeeping 177 (July):16–26.

LeRoy Ladurie, Emmanuel. 1978. Montaillou: Promised Land of Error. New York: G. Braziller.

Magnuson, Warren G. 1965. "Grant to the children's orthopedic hospital and medical center in Seattle for research on the sudden death syndrome in infancy." U.S. Congress: Senate, Congressional Record, 89th Congress, 2nd session, September 10, 111:23451–23452.

Mark Addison Roe Foundation. 1965. "Sudden unexpected infant death." Brochure. In authors' possession.

———. 1966. Newsletter #2, August. In authors' possession.

Moritz, Alan R., Edward R. Cunniffe, J. W. Holloway, Jr., and Harrison S. Martland. 1944. "Report of committee to study the relationship of medicine and law." Journal of the American Medical Association 125 (June 24):577–583.

Naeye, Richard L. 1973. "Pulmonary arterial abnormalities in the sudden infant death syndrome." New England Journal of Medicine 289 (November 29):1167–1170.

———. 1980. "Sudden infant death." Scientific American 242 (April):56–62.

Nelson, Waldo E. (ed.). 1945. Textbook of Pediatrics, 4th edition. Philadelphia: W. B. Saunders Co.

———. 1950. Textbook of Pediatrics, 5th edition. Philadelphia: W. B. Saunders Co.

———. 1954. Textbook of Pediatrics, 6th edition. Philadelphia: W. B. Saunders Co.

———. 1959. Textbook of Pediatrics, 7th edition. Philadelphia: W. B. Saunders Co.

New York Times. 1955. "City medical aide suicide in Queens." April 15:48.

Newsweek. 1962. "Why babies die." August 20:80.

Raring, Richard H. 1975. Crib Death: Scourge of Infants—Shame of Society. Hicksville, N.Y.: Exposition Press.

Redman, Eric. 1973. The Dance of Legislation. New York: Simon and Schuster.

Rettig, Richard A. 1977. Cancer Crusade: The Story of the National Cancer Act of 1971. Princeton, N.J.: Princeton University Press.

Savvitt, Todd L. 1975. "Smothering and overlaying of Virginia slave children: A suggested explanation." Bulletin of the History of Medicine 49 (Fall):400–404.

———. 1979. "The social and medical history of crib death." Journal of the Florida Medical Association 66 (August):853–859.

Spencer, Steven M. 1966. "Crib death: Search for a mystery killer." Saturday Evening Post 239 (November 13):79–80, 82.

Staats, Elmer B. 1981. The Sudden Infant Death Syndrome Program Helps Families But Needs Improvement. Washington, D.C.: General Accounting Office.

Steiner, Gilbert Y., with Pauline H. Milius. 1976. The Children's Cause. Washington, D.C.: The Brookings Institution.

Steinschneider, Alfred. 1972. "Prolonged apnea and the sudden infant death syndrome: Clinical and laboratory observations." Pediatrics 50 (October): 646–654.

———. 1982. Interview with authors (March 22)

Stern, Edith. 1952. "Babies don't smother." McCall's 80 (June):44, 115, 118.

Strickland, Stephen P. 1952. Politics, Science, and Dread Disease: A Short History of United States Medical Research Policy. Cambridge: Harvard University Press.

Studer, Kenneth E., and Daryl E. Chubin. 1980. The Cancer Mission: Social Context of Biomedical Research. Beverly Hills, Calif., and London: Sage Publications.

Time. 1963. "Sudden death syndrome." October 4:88.

U.S. Congress: House of Representatives. 1973. Sudden Infant Death Syndrome Hearings. Committee on Interstate and Foreign Commerce, Subcommittee on Public Health and Environment, 93rd Congress, 1st session, August 2. Washington, D.C.: U.S. Government Printing Office.

———. 1974a. Sudden Infant Death Syndrome Act of 1974: Report to Accompany H.R. 11386. Committee on Interstate and Foreign Commerce, 93rd Congress, 2nd session, H. Rept. 758. Washington, D.C.: U.S. Government Printing Office.

———. 1974b. "Amending Public Health Service Act respecting sudden infant death." Congressional Record, 93rd Congress, 2nd session, January 21, 120:105–109.

U.S. Congress: Senate. 1972a. Rights of Children: Examination of the Sudden Infant Death Syndrome Hearings. Committee on Labor and Public Welfare, Subcommittee on Children and Youth, 92nd Congress, 2nd session, January 25. Washington, D.C.: U.S. Government Printing Office.

———. 1972b. "Sudden infant death syndrome." Congressional Record, 92nd Congress, 2nd session, June 7, 118:19985–19992.

———. 1973a. Sudden Infant Death Syndrome Hearings. Committee on Labor and Public Welfare, Subcommittees on Health and on Children and Youth, 93rd Congress, 1st session, September 20. Washington, D.C.: U.S. Government Printing Office.

———. 1973b. Sudden Infant Death Syndrome Act of 1973: Report to Accompany S. 1745. Committee on Labor and Public Welfare, 93rd Congress, 1st session, Sen. Rept. 606. Washington, D.C.: U.S. Government Printing Office.

———. 1973c. "Sudden Infant Death Syndrome Act of 1973." Congressional Record, 93rd Congress, 1st session, December 11, 119:40627–40634.

———. 1977. Sudden Infant Death Syndrome Hearings. Subcommittee of the Committee on Appropriations, 95th Congress, 1st session, April 7. Washington D.C.: U.S. Government Printing Office.

———. 1978. Sudden Infant Death Syndrome Act Extension Hearings. Committee on Human Resources, Subcommittee on Child Health and Human Development, 95th Congress, 2nd session, March 1. Washington, D.C.: U.S. Government Printing Office.

Valdes-Dapena, Marie A. 1967. "Sudden and unexpected death in infancy: A review of the world literature, 1954–1966." Pediatrics 39 (January):123–138.

———. 1980. "Sudden infant death syndrome: A review of the medical literature 1974–1979." Pediatrics 66 (October):597–614.

Wade, Nicholas. 1974. "Crib death: Foremost baby killer long ignored by medical research." Science 184 (April 26):447–449.

Washington Association for Sudden Infant Death Study. 1965. "The history of sudden infant death study in Washington state." Mimeograph. In authors' possession.

———. 1966. Newsletter, February. In authors' possession.

Washington Post. 1972. "Mondale to seek 'crib death' action." February 15:sec.A, p. 2.

Wedgwood, Ralph J. P., and Earl P. Benditt (eds.). 1966. Sudden Death in Infants: Proceedings of the Conference on Causes of Sudden Death in Infants, September 1963, Seattle, Washington. Washington, D.C.: United States Public Health Service and National Institute of Child Health and Human Development.

Werne, Jacob, and Irene Garrow. 1947. "Sudden death of infants allegedly due to mechanical suffocation." American Journal of Public Health and the Nation's Health 37 (June):675–687.

———. 1953a. "Sudden apparently unexplained death during infancy." American Journal of Pathology 29 (July–August): 633–675.

———. 1953b. "Sudden apparently unexplained death during infancy." American Journal of Pathology 29 (September–October):817–851.

Women's Home Companion. 1948. "Death in the bassinet." Volume 38 (February):113–115.

CHAPTER 6

Officer Ugg, Mr. Yuk, Uncle Barf . . . Ad Nausea

CONTROLLING POISON CONTROL, 1950–1985

Robert S. Broadhead

Health care in the United States has often been described as a "nonsystem"—an unplanned conglomeration of overlapping services and organizations competing for certain patient populations. Free enterprise discouraged voluntary coordination of different levels and varieties of services, and, due to resultant distortions, the government was forced periodically to initiate various regulatory measures. Efforts to plan and consolidate health services have always been hotly contested and resisted, particularly by the American Medical Association and other health provider associations. As Starr (1982:407) quipped, "In health reform, a little known law of nature seems to require that every move toward regulation be followed by an opposite move toward litigation." Critics have even argued that distortions in services were caused by the disorganized and redundant efforts of planning agencies themselves (Bice, 1980).

As a component of the health care "system," poison control services exhibited the same erratic development and disorganization as the larger health industry. Following the "discovery" of acute poisoning as a social problem in the early 1950s, hospitals throughout the United States rushed to implement poison control centers (PCCs) as adjuncts to their emergency departments. Essentially, centers consist of telephone hotlines, staffed 24 hours a day by health professionals who provide advice to physicians and the public on how to manage poison crises that occur in the home or workplace. Although centers occasionally have physicians as directors, their main staff is composed primarily of licensed pharmacists and nurses who have had some (frequently only minimal) training in toxicology.

Beginning in 1953 with the establishment of the first hotline, PCCs emerged suddenly, resulting in over 500 centers nationwide within 10 years and peaking at 641 by 1976 (Simpson and Simpson, 1976; U.S. FDA, 1982). Centers competed with one another in promoting their hotline numbers and logos, such as "Uncle Barf," "Mr. Yuk," "Pinkie the Elephant," and "Officer Ugg." Some states had over 100 centers, others had only one or none. As Krenzelok (1980:33) observed:

> The movement . . . developed in a rather haphazard fashion since the inception of the concept. Early on no consideration was given to regional needs and some cities, such as Minneapolis, had as many as 11 designated centers.

However, in contrast to the larger world of health care, poison control centers since the late 1970s have been in a widespread process of consolidation and regionalization. By 1979 the number of centers nationwide had decreased to around 500, 454 by 1981, 395 by 1983, and 319 by 1985 (*Emergency Medicine,* 1985; U.S. FDA, 1981, 1983). Hospitals have been withdrawing their designation as poison centers, abolishing their logos and telephone hotline numbers, and instructing their emergency room staff to refer calls to specialized, regional PCCs. These centers are not adjuncts of emergency departments of any particular hospital but are "free-standing" providers that offer hotline consultation to many communities and refer patients, on an "as needed" basis, to hospitals that are closest to the crisis situation. While there are still several hundred adjunct centers in the United States, the American Association of Poison Control Centers (AAPCC) estimates that 60 regional centers can provide complete coverage for the entire country. As I discuss below, all signs indicate that continuing professional and governmental efforts at "controlling poison control" will successfully bring about a consolidation of services nationwide.

With respect to the larger health care "system," therefore, what is evolving is highly unusual. Not only is there uncustomary cooperation among conventional health providers to relinquish involvement in poison control and defer to a regionalized system, but this is all happening while the incidence of acute poisoning is high and increasing, at least according to health experts. Poison control leaders would have it that regionalization is occurring in this one component of the health system because it makes "good clinical sense." If this were a sufficient reason it would seem that the larger world of medicine would also be consolidating. The central finding of the analysis below is that regionalization is occurring because conventional health providers have come to see that, irrespective of increasing demand, the provision of poison control services is inconsistent with their own professional and economic interests. In fact, such inconsistencies have become more obvious and pressing as demands increased for poison control services.

This analysis is part of a larger participant observation study which I conducted for one year, beginning in the fall of 1983, at an official, state poison control center on the East coast. The qualitative data, which include tape recordings of more than 300 telephone exchanges, bear on the interactional dynamics of managing acute poisonings over the telephone (Broadhead, 1986). I focus here on the history of the poison control movement, and the evolution of the larger structural context within which the provision of telephone poison services occur. Thus, while I occasionally draw upon the qualitative data, my analysis is based largely on official documents and statistics from the federal government, and studies in the various medical journals, from the 1940s to the present. Articles in lay periodicals, particularly through the 1950s, were also analyzed for changes in the public's concern about the risk of acute poisoning.

The first section of the analysis traces the promotion of acute poisoning as a social problem in the 1950s. Early medical concerns about the incidence of poisoning made dramatic news in popular periodicals. Poison control as a social movement took organizational shape as hospitals nationwide began promoting their own hotlines. I examine several organizational opportunities that hospitals perceived in the "business" of poison control. I describe the arrival in the early 1970s of acute poisoning as a permanent social problem, and the arenas within which poison hotlines competed with one another for public visibility and prominence.

The second section examines several reasons why, notwithstanding the alleged magnitude of the social problem, hospitals have come to see that catering to the growing demand of poison control services in inconsistent with their own interests: PCCs reduce the utilization of emergency rooms, generate expenses in their own right, vastly increase the number of nonproblems and noncrises that emergency room staff must manage, and increase the professional and legal liabilities of hospitals. I conclude with a discussion of the forces, particularly governmental, that are transforming poison control into a coordinated, regionalized system—an anomaly in this age of corporate transformation of the health care "system."

The Promotion of Poison Control

Poison is an ancient evil but, since the mid-twentieth century, it has been perceived in distinctly modern ways. Previously, poison was associated with deadly substances found in nature—toxic plants, insects or snake venom—or human concoctions invented for villainy or suicide. But, since the mid-1950s, poison has come to be defined as virtually *any* substance or material, however innocent. Physicians even remind one another in professional journals of several categories of "nontoxic" substances that are of special medical concern: "Caution must be exercised since no product or drug is entirely safe: all products can produce undesirable effects if ingested in sufficiently great concentration or amount" (Mofenson et al., 1984:587–88).

Traditionally, poison was assumed to be a threat mainly to adults, due either to their drug usage or their interpersonal conflicts. But a survey conducted by a committee of the American Academy of Pediatrics in 1951 found that "accidental poisoning accounted for more than half of all emergencies handled by pediatricians" (DuShane, 1960:1221). Since then, it has become an accepted fact that children account for approximately 80 percent of all reported poisonings—virtually all of them accidental, but some related to neglect or abuse (Rogers, 1981). Eighty to 90 percent of all child poisonings occur in children under the age of five (Bernstein et al., 1983). Finally, the threat of acute poisoning has changed from being seen as a danger which individuals can reasonably guard against through their own prudent efforts and common sense, into a social problem—that is, a danger perceived as chronic and pervasive that requires the formal intervention of experts (Spector and Kitsuse, 1977).

These major changes in the public's perception of poison were stimulated and shaped by the poison control movement. The latter was originally sparked by the efforts of pediatricians as they attempted to expand their professional boundaries and areas of expertise (Pawluch, 1983). Similar to the "discovery" of child abuse (Pfohl, 1977), pediatricians were the first to draw attention to poisoning as an alarming danger to children. The above-mentioned 1951 survey of the American Academy of Pediatrics led to the formation of the first poison control center in 1953. Indeed, the first center "was organized in the city of Chicago under the sponsorship of the Illinois chapter of the American Academy of Pediatricians" (Cann and Verhulst, 1958:719). DuShane (1960:1221) noted that "The center became a focus of community effort in the prevention of poisoning. . . . Other major cities followed Chicago's lead, and by 1956 centers had been established in 38 cities." Reviewing the development of poison control five years after the first center was established, Cann and Verhulst (1958:717), writing in *The Journal of the American Medical Association,* noted that "Probably the most noteworthy of these developments is the realization by the medical profession, especially by pediatricians, that poison accidents constitute a major health problem." Other developments had also occurred: nearly 200 PCCs had been established by 1958; a federal clearinghouse was created in 1957 that began monthly publication of the poison control center *Bulletin;* the AAPCC was formed in 1958; and a number of professional conferences and papers publicized the threat of acute poisoning (Bain, 1954; Cann and Verhulst, 1958).

All of this professional activity generated news stories which cast the threat of acute poisoning into a new and more compelling light. Most of these stories emphasized the indispensability of poison centers to manage a crisis of epidemic proportions involving the acute poisoning of children.

ACUTE POISONING AS NEWS

There were no stories about poison control centers in lay periodicals from the end of the Second World War through 1955. Of 40 articles cited under "poison" in the *Reader's Guide to Periodic Literature,* roughly 75 percent were informational pieces about poisonous plants: where and how they grow, how to identify them, and methods of treatment following exposure. Some typical titles were, "Hands off those gay autumn leaves," "Hidden enemies in the garden," and "Poisonous plants in school." During this 10 year period, 12 articles appeared on human poisoning under titles such as "Toxic limits to potable water," "Home poisons may kill," "Protect from poisoning," "Many cases of poisoning are unnecessary," and "Mother, lock up your poisons." These articles apparently were not particularly newsworthy since almost all of them appeared in obscure periodicals such as *Consumers Research Bulletin* and *Science Newsletter.* Characteristically, none of the articles spoke of an alarming rise in the incidence of accidental poisoning—let alone an epidemic—or claimed that children were at a far greater risk than any other group. The underlying message, as the titles suggest, is that caution in handling and storing medicines and household products, and awareness of common plants, is sufficient to manage the risk of accidental poisoning.

However, in September 1956 the first article on poison control centers appeared in a popular periodical. The article exemplifies how acute poisoning subsequently became dramatized as a social problem. First published in *Parents Magazine* under the title "Poison control centers," the article was quickly reprinted in the same month's issue of *Reader's Digest* under the new title, "First aid for poisoned children." It begins by proclaiming that accidental poisonings kill more children than polio, scarlet fever, and diptheria together; that over 200,000 children a year are poisoned; and that "child poisoning could be immensely reduced overnight if parents would take the simplest precautions. . . . Meantime, a poison control center can help everyone—sick child, frantic mother, busy doctor" (James, 1956:61). Certain themes in this article became more pronounced in subsequent articles published from the fall of 1956 through 1957, many of them appearing in very popular periodicals such as *Good Housekeeping, Saturday Evening Post,* and *Newsweek.*

The link between acute poisoning and the need for poison control centers was drawn with a sense of urgency. An article in *Newsweek* (1957), "Tragedy at fingertips," emphasized that poisonings can happen so quickly and easily that even children whose parents exercise caution are still at great risk. The article also proclaimed a national crisis: every 24 hours, 50 children are poisoned due to "curiosity," and at least one dies. An article in the *Saturday Evening Post* featured action photographs of emergency medical teams and personalized the tragedy of accidental poisoning by describing the misfortune of four individual children and their parents. It concluded with a dramatic overview of the scope of the social problem:

> Heartbreaking stories multiply day after day in the files of America's spreading poison-control centers. They tell of children killed, blinded and permanently disabled by unguarded patent medicines, by furniture polish, cleaning fluids, disinfectants, bleaches, insect sprays, paint thinner—by some 250,000 or more packaged items sold in this country for home use, and with the list of new brands constantly growing (Berger, 1957:24).

The notion that "everything is poison" was also emphasized at length in an article in the May 1957 issue of *The New Yorker,* which saw the dependency of physicians on poison center experts as due to the lack of content information printed on the packaging of thousands of products:

> Doctors don't have to guess at the nature of the toxic substance in the box or bottle with the fancy label. All they have to do is step to the telephone. They know that we will probably have the answer (Roueche, 1957:147).

Thus, since the end of 1957, the perspective promoted in popular periodicals has been that acute poisoning of children occurs in crisis proportions year after year; the threat is imminent because everything is poisonous and accidents happen instantaneously; neither the vigilance of parents nor the expertise of physicians is sufficient to prevent or treat the problem; and therefore, a fully developed, nationwide system of poison control centers, staffed with trained poison experts, is indispensable for managing the crisis.

In promoting acute poisoning as a social problem the poison control movement laid the groundwork for a massive expansion in control centers that continued for more than a decade. The official justification for the expansion was, of course, medical need. The explosion in services was claimed to reflect the Baby Boom of the 1950s (i.e., the increased number of children who began "putting things in their mouths"), and the rapid growth of the peacetime economy which flooded the civilian market with thousands of new products. However, the rapid emergence and expansion of services was more than a simple response to a perceived medical crisis. Health care institutions, particularly hospitals, responded to several attractive opportunities that poison control seemed to offer.

OPPORTUNITIES OF POISON CONTROL

Community hospitals throughout the nation rushed into poison control in order to take advantage of an impressive public relations opportunity. The urgency of poison control seemed consistent with the "Wild West" ethos of American medicine, as Dubos (1959) described it; an ethos in which physicians are modern-day cowboys whose style is to ride into situations *after* things have gotten out of hand, and to rely on "magic bullets" and the latest hardware. The drama of poison control, like the western thriller, seemed to involve daring acts in life and death situations. Combined with the idea of saving the lives of innocent children, it proved to be an effective appeal for community support and fund raising. As Dr. Alan Done (1978:132) of Children's Hospital of Detroit said:

> Hospitals found very early that nothing would get them public support more quickly than the stories and statistics that can be gleaned from a poison center and there are still very few problems from which you can get as much PR mileage.

Second, hospitals thought that the PR would be theirs for free. Hospitals assumed that they could establish a poison control center by simply advertising the telephone number of their emergency room as a poison hotline and making more efficient use of their already existing staff and facilities. Their ERs were already staffed 24 hours, seven days a week. Given a staff of licensed practitioners, the responsibility for answering hotline calls would not have to fall on any one member or even require a new position; the responsibility could be shared pragmatically by all—whoever was closest to the phone could answer it. Thus, as Done (1978:132) described, most centers consisted "of the same emergency room that existed all along, now provided with perhaps a little additional information and a new title. The number of poison centers that arose as a result of a real change in activity or a new endeavor was . . . relatively small." Similarly, Chi (1982:68) noted that "any hospital with a telephone and a poison information book can call itself a poison control center." Thus, establishing a center was attractive because it did not seem to require any real expansion of facilities or personnel.

Finally, hospitals rushed to implement poison control services in order to maintain their competitive edge in the emergency room marketplace. As an adjunct to emergency rooms, the poison hotline would presumably serve as a patient referral mechanism. With the bandwagon of poison control gaining momentum, hospitals saw a risk of losing their fair share of emergency work if they failed to jump aboard: "For the hospitals, there was also the element of fear that because nearly everyone seemed to be getting into the act they were somehow not providing full services if they did not make themselves into poison centers" (Done, 1978:132). Given what appeared to be a growing epidemic in accidental poisoning, a hospital that had no hotline was hardly in the position to funnel patients to its own emergency room; nor could it expect the poison hotline in other hospitals to do so. On the other hand, with a hotline number prominently displayed in the telephone directory of the surrounding community, a hospital could not help but increase patient utilization of its emergency department—

of so it seemed. In short, hospitals perceived clear opportunities in the "business" of poison control, and equally clear risks if they chose to ignore it.

THE ARRIVAL OF POISON CONTROL

Within five years, the poison control movement was in full swing. The approximately 200 poison control centers established by 1958 doubled to over 400 centers by 1960 (DuShane, 1960). In 1961, the U.S. Congress, following fact-finding conferences in the House and the Senate, authorized President Kennedy to declare the third week of March as "National Poison Prevention Week," which he did in September. By 1976, there were 641 poison centers. The "system," composed almost entirely of centers that were adjuncts to hospital emergency rooms, resembled the larger health care industry:

> Throughout the 1960s, poison centers developed rapidly and, to a large degree, without coordination. The policy of the National Clearinghouse was to recognize any poison center designated by the state health department. This policy resulted in erratic development. . . . Some states had only one center, whereas others had more than 100 (Manoquerra and Temple, 1984:562).

In those areas of the country containing a glut of centers, conspicuous competition occurred among them for public visibility. Poison logos of different centers flourished, giving rise to "Mr. Yuk" versus "Uncle Barf," and so on. As recently as 1982, one expert observed: "Across the country, a legion of such logos exist, reflecting the state of poison control today—a crazy quilt of services with no centralized authority to guide the orderly development of centers or to set standards to ensure that quality care is provided" (Chi, 1982:68). Another arena of competition was poison hotline listings in telephone directories. For example, my examination of all area telephone directories in one eastern state for 1984 revealed brisk competition between the state's officially designated poison control center (SPCC) and centers in several area hospitals. In the "Community Services" listings (in the front of directories) for one metropolitan area, SPCC competed with the hotline numbers of two other hospital centers; in the white pages, under "Poison," SPCC was also listed with the two other hotlines, but one of the centers had had their listing specially highlighted and enlarged; SPCC had not purchased a listing in the yellow pages, but both of the other hotlines had. I found similar patterns of competition in 10 of the 25 other area directories in the state. In all, SPCC competed with 13 other poison hotline numbers, many of them listed in several sections in different area directories.

In the 1970s, the competition for public visibility and attention between PCCs was so lively that an entrepreneur in Pittsburgh saw it as a market ripe for organizing under a private franchising scheme. It emerged in 1973 as the *National Poison Control Network*. Centers that affiliated with the network (some 55 in 40 states) by paying a yearly membership fee became eligible to bear the "Mr. Yuk" logo, a symbol that quickly became highly visible and well known. They also received promotional literature and "Mr. Yuk" stickers for mass distribution (Chi, 1982). The stickers, which prominently listed the hotline number of each center, were generously distributed to area residents to be affixed to containers of medicines and dangerous substances in their homes, and to their telephone for ready reference. Hundreds of other poison centers engaged in similar promotional efforts, including mass mailings, public service spots on television and radio, and news releases of dramatic poison cases. Such promotion was obviously influential and helps account for the increase in hotline traffic that many centers experienced within a relatively short time. The public was made increasingly sensitive to, if not anxious about, the risk of hundreds of common products in the home and workplace, and became aware that free medical consultation was available to them at virtually any time, regardless of how trivial the reason.

The point, however, is that the existence of hundreds of poison control centers, competing with one another over visibility and PR, signaled the arrival of acute poisoning as a fully institutionalized social problem by the 1970s. Today, it is seen as a permanent problem requiring widespread public and governmental concern, and ongoing professional effort to combat.

The Retreat from Poison Control

Almost as quickly as centers emerged in the mid-1950s, they began to disappear 20 years later. By 1980, the poison clearinghouse *Bulletin* (U.S. FDA, 1982:2) reported that 175 centers had disappeared, leaving 466, and that "regionalization in states such as Illinois, Minnesota, and West Virginia [was] responsible for the decline." By 1983, nearly 100 more centers had closed (U.S. FDA, 1983) and, by 1985, only 319 centers remained—a 50 percent decline in 10 years (*Emergency Medicine*, 1985). The retreat is still occurring.

ECONOMIC DISAPPOINTMENTS

Hospitals have discovered that poison control centers do not increase the utilization of their emergency rooms. Although they were seen initially as a way of maintaining a competitive edge with other hospitals, a realization gradually emerged that poison control services reduce the utilization of emergency rooms, not slightly but overwhelmingly. For example, Fry and McIntire (1979:75) found in their utilization study of Omaha's Children's Memorial Hospital that, since the inception of the poison control center in 1963, a "significant increase in PCC utilization by telephone calls was accompanied by significant decreases in hospitalization and outpatient visits." Similarly, a 1980 study in Massachusetts found that:

> If parents or their family physicians do not call the poison center, they are much more apt to visit an emergency room than if the poison center is called. This result reinforces studies . . . [that] found that poison center use results in a 15% to 19% reduction of immediate visits to the hospital. Our study suggests that the impact of poison center use may be even twice what

has been previously estimated (Chafee-Bahamon and Lovejoy, 1983:167; also see Veltri, 1980).

The impact of poison control in reducing visits to emergency rooms is now widely accepted within medicine. While the public continues to see acute poisoning of children as a major social problem, and thousands of hotline calls are made every day, poison control experts recognize that the actual number of serious episodes is extremely small. For example, the Massachusetts PCC reported: "Only 10% of exposures result in signs and symptoms, 2% in hospitalization, and less than 1% in death" (Chaffee-Bahamon and Lovejoy, 1983:164); Rocky Mountain PCC noted: "Our experience indicates that 80% to 90% of pediatric patients can be treated at home over the telephone, and most of the cases are ingestions rather than poisonings" (Rumack, 1980:123); and, National Capitol PCC found that "nearly 80% of poison exposures can be safely treated at home, with appropriate follow-up" (Litovitz and Elshami, 1982:348).

Thus, rather than helping hospitals maintain their competitive edge in the medical marketplace, poison hotlines work to keep patients out of emergency rooms, thus substantially saving the public thousands of dollars in treatment costs. But, for hospitals, poison control has become a financial drain: "PCCs don't generate income but are an expense to the institutions housing them, although they do provide a public relations value" (Chi, 1982:68).

DEMANDS ON STAFF

The retreat from poison control has also occurred because of the heavy demands placed on hospitals' staff to manage hotline traffic. Essentially, hundreds of hospitals over the years maintained their PCCs by making do with existing facilities and simply stretching the role responsibilities of their available ER staff. Staffs had to improvise ways to manage poison hotlines. Basically, PCCs have been "bootstrap" operations, manufactured out of nothing but sheer staff efforts to deliver more services with existing organizational resources. Apparently, such arrangements worked reasonably well for some PCCs over the last two decades because they received very few calls. A survey in the 1970s indicated that many PCCs received less than two calls a day (U.S. FDA, 1982). ER staff could easily "wing it" in handling so few calls, although hotlines that virtually never rang hardly provided those hospitals with sufficient rewards to remain in the "business" of poison control.

However, for hundreds of hospitals whose PCCs experienced a significant rise in hotline traffic, reaching annual totals into the thousands, bootstrap operations became unworkable. They could not be viably sustained by simply making more efficient use of existing ER staff and facilities. Although the vast bulk of hotline calls concern benign exposures which callers can handle at home, it takes appreciable time and effort for a staff member to make a confident determination of the severity of any given call. As Done (1978:138) explained, "The bulk of poisoning cases, in fact, are not of great consequence and do not require more than home treatment. But this is a judgment that can only be made by an expert." To do so requires a telephone interview, which frequently must begin by calming the caller down. Detailed information about the "history" of the episode must be obtained, poison literature may have to be consulted, and calculations made to determine the level of toxicity involved, if any. All of this must occur before an exposure can be dismissed as being either a nonproblem or something that can be safely handled at home, which is almost always the case.

In short, the assumption collapsed that ER staff can squeeze in scores of hotline calls a day while they go about their own acute care duties. Hospitals began retreating from poison control, in part, because centers became an expense in their own right, one that could not be managed by simply expanding the role of available staff or "banking" on their expertise.

POISON CONTROL AS LO-TECH MEDICINE

Third, hospitals initially thought that poison control offered a new market for the provision of hi-tech, acute care medicine. The perceived drama and urgency of poison crises complemented the ethos of American medicine and its fascination with specialists, sophisticated technology, and intensive care. However, hospitals eventually discovered that the challenge of poison control was less than dramatic. For example, of the 300 hotline calls that I recorded, only a fraction required the staff to do anything more than tell parents to give their child a glass of milk and to expect to see a possible upset stomach and some diarrhea. Of the 15,500 calls received by SPCC in 1984–85 involving poison exposures, 82 percent were managed at home—which meant that the staff was required to provide reassurance to a caller that nothing of any significance had happened or, at the most, to give instructions on how to induce vomiting with "Syrup of Ipecac" and assist the victim through an unpleasant but quite safe ordeal. Of course, an appreciable measure of expertise was required to "read" the severity of all those thousands of calls and to know the toxicological effects of thousands of substances. Staff also had to be adept at making calculations of chemical strengths and volumes to body weights, and at interviewing anxious people over the phone. However, hospitals found that, rather than entrée into a new health market involving hi-tech, acute care medicine, poison control centers drastically increase the volume of nonemergencies and nonproblems that medical staff must wade through—a problem that has always been the bane of emergency departments anyway (Shah et al., 1980). But, what else could have been expected? Since the beginning of poison control, the public has been given the simplest means and the strongest encouragement to call their nearest poison control center if they have any questions or anxieties, no matter how trivial. Thousands of people do just that everyday, and the trend continues. Hospitals have discovered that such a demand provides few opportunities for the practice of flashy medicine.

LEGAL LIABILITIES

Hospitals have also been retreating from poison control since the 1970s because, as hotline traffic increased, liabilities in providing poison services have grown. While hospitals originally offered the public free poison consultations because, they thought, the service was free for them to offer, legal liabilities have evolved which pose high risks for doing so. One problem is that, in gratuitously offering to render assistance or service, hospitals assume a "duty to care" to the public for which they can be held liable; that is, they become legally bound to respond to requests for help, and to meet clients' expectations that expert assistance is available and can be relied on. As Winokur and Weiss (1978:322) explained, "An important factor in the imposition of liability has been the reliance of the public on the availability of emergency services where the hospital has 'held itself out' as providing such services." Poison control introduces all kinds of risks for hospitals in consistently meeting their duty to care: breakdowns in providing 24-hour, seven-day-a-week service; difficulties in promptly responding to calls; and staff errors in determining the seriousness of a situation, or in providing clinical advice. The latter are particularly tricky because those decisions are "complicated for the poison center staffer by the fact that the victim is not physically present for first-hand observation and the information received by phone is, as often as not, inaccurate or incomplete" (Winokur and Weiss, 1978:322). "Duty to care" thus means that hospitals must ensure a consistent provision of service that any given caller can reasonably expect in seeking help.

In addition, poison centers also introduce liabilities surrounding "standards of care." Hospitals have now become vulnerable if the quality of the poison services they offer falls below established standards. In the early days of poison control, those standards were virtually unknown. However, as some centers took the lead in advancing the field, standards have emerged against which all centers can be judged. As Done (1978:132) explained:

> Now that clinical toxicology and poison center functions have become better defined and recognized, there's every reason to expect that institutions choosing to designate themselves as poison centers will be held to a standard of care beyond that to be expected of a similar hospital not so designated.

Hospital offering poison services ultimately may be expected to conform to the "highest possible standards" in the field, even if some of those standards are still not clearly known.

For example, in February 1984, a jury issued a $3.6 million judgment against the Arizona PCC for negligence in the advice it gave a physician. The physician had called the center because his nurse had accidently injected a 10-year-old patient with a massive dose of liquid cocaine instead of acetaminophen, as had been prescribed. The jury found against the PCC not because it failed to give the physician the correct information about the toxicological effects of acute cocaine ingestion, but because it did not tell the physician to take the patient immediately to a hospital (Brink, 1984). The standard at the root of the jury's decision caught the larger world of poison control by complete surprise. It means that poison centers are now expected to make clinical decisions *for* physicians on how to handle a case and what they should do. Such an expectation becomes even more problematic since, as mentioned earlier, most poison control staff are not physicians but nurses and pharmacists. In the Arizona case, it was a pharmacist who "failed" to tell the physician what clinical steps he should take in handling the case.

Thus, the legal liabilities for offering poison control services have grown substantially. Gone are the lightheaded days when hospitals assumed that poison services could be offered by advertising a hotline and expecting calls to be answered by any emergency staff member who just happened to be closest to the phone.

PROFESSIONAL EMBARRASSMENT

Liabilities of a professional nature have also stimulated hospitals' retreat from poison control. Evidence has been accumulating that the quality of services provided by adjunct centers is significantly below that of free-standing, regional poison centers. For example, an evaluation of regional and adjunct centers was singled out for special attention in the editorial column of the *New England Journal of Medicine*. The commentary reinforced the professional pressure on hospitals to dismantle their adjunct poison centers:

> In this issue of the *Journal* Thompson et al. (1983) demonstrate that regional poison-centers are far more proficient than nonregional centers in the evaluation and treatment of potential salicylate intoxication of a young child. . . . Appropriate treatment was recommended in 93 percent of calls to regional centers but in only 67 percent of the calls to nonregional centers. Archaic or hazardous treatment, such as saline emesis, was recommended in over one third of the responses by nonregional centers (McIntire and Angle, 1983:220).

In addition, several prominent leaders in poison control disparagingly refer to adjunct centers as "renegades," "fly-by-nights," and "outlaws," and even exaggerate their alleged incompetence in professional journals. For example, Done (1978:138) said that "an inferior [read, adjunct] center probably refers closer to 80% of its inquiries either to an emergency room or to a private physician." In fact, the data indicate that "inferior" centers recommend treatment less often than regional centers (Thompson et al., 1983). In another article in the *New England Journal of Medicine*, Lovejoy et al. (1979) praised the establishment of regional centers and, by implication, attempted to hasten the disappearance of adjunct centers located in the ERs of hospitals. A physician in Georgia who apparently failed to appreciate the underlying message wrote a letter to the editor commending Lovejoy et al. but adding, "The only improvement that I can suggest is that the regional poison centers should be placed in hospital emergency rooms" (Haddad, 1979:1223). Another letter appeared shortly thereafter, signed by 20 physicians in poison control, that classified Dr. Haddad's recommendation as out of touch with the major developments in poison control (Aldrich et al., 1979).

Clearly, hospitals are abandoning poison control partly because of professional embarrassment, and because hotlines are at odds with their own legal and economic interests. The cost to hospitals of maintaining poison centers has come to far outweigh the benefits. As Done (1978:132) said, "They don't even pay off anymore in PR when you really look at the costs and the efforts involved."

Conclusion

Due to the inadequacies of public planning up to and through the 1970s, U.S. health care spawned services and organizations that were wasteful, overlapping, and ultimately unaffordable. According to Starr (1982:449), such a situation portended what is now happening:

> The failure to rationalize medical services under public control meant that sooner or later they would be rationalized under private control. Instead of public regulation, there will be private regulation, and instead of public planning, there will be corporate planning.

Such private regulation has been leading to spectacular processes of corporate consolidation and integration of health services and organizations, although as Starr (1982) cautioned, it would be a mistake to assume that corporate planning incentives will reward efficiency. Nor will they work toward eliminating distortions in services: "Profit-making enterprises are not interested in treating those who cannot pay. . . . A system in which corporate enterprises play a larger part is likely to be more segmented and more stratified" (Starr, 1982:448).

However, in one component of the health care "system"—poison control—a very different regulatory shift has been occurring. Due to gross distortions spawned by the competition among hospitals as they jockeyed for a market in poison control, a similar nonsystem of duplication and waste developed. But, as hospitals now retreat from poison control, planning by "free-for-all" has given way to a consortium of governmental and professional efforts that are ushering in a coordinated, regionalized system of poison control. As the recent editor of *Emergency Medicine* observed, "Today, well over a third of states have shifted to state-designated or regional poison control systems, which is evidence of a national trend toward regionalization" (Wagner, 1985:11). Other uniformities in services are also beginning to appear, such as a standardized logo which most centers now use, replacing the mish-mash of previous symbols. The new logo is thought to offer a more sober and universal warning than does, say, "Mr. Yuk": it resembles the classic logo in bearing a skull, but no cross-bones.

Interestingly, the very reasons for hospitals' retreat have become incentives for greater governmental investment in the "business" of poison control, particularly at the state level. First, although the vast majority of hotline calls are about inconsequential exposures, poison centers significantly reduce the number of emergency room visits to which such "crises" can lead. State governments, in response to strong federal pressure, are now taking more determined steps to reduce waste and excessive use of medical services—a major incentive to implement single, statewide poison centers. Physicians are also exhorting one another to support regionalized services. For instance, the editor of *Emergency Medicine* offered the following advice to readers:

> Regionalization cannot be done without funding, which in this age of federal cutbacks means the burden must fall on the states and that community

physicians must be the prime movers to get the state legislatures to appropriate (Wagner, 1985:11).

Second, although hospitals found that poison control did not generate revenues, either directly or indirectly, their "loss" demonstrated to government that poison control can reduce overall expenditures in health care dollars. The former editor of *Emergency Medicine* advised his colleagues that the issue of saving money was "particularly worthy of the attention of legislators and others who might be instrumental in obtaining necessary funding for regionalizing programs. . . . There probably is no place where more health care costs could be eliminated than in the field of poison control" (Done, 1978:138).

Finally, although poison control may offer little to hospitals in the way of PR, it offers a lot to government. In this era of dwindling social services and supports, government officials are increasingly anxious to assure the public that "safety nets" and essential services remain in place. The growing provision of hotlines generally—poison, suicide, family crisis, police—can serve as an important method of maintaining public confidence that care is there even though daily experience may suggest otherwise.

Thus, in light of program retrenchment and revenue scarcity, state governments have absolutely no difficulty in finding justifications for funding an emerging network of regional poison control centers, although they may have some difficulty in finding the money. While the vast majority of hotline calls appear to be overreactions to trivial exposures—well into several million a year—the magnitude of the social problem now exerts tremendous pressure on government to maintain optimum services. In addition to the weight of medical opinion, the Surgeon General even set 1990 as the date when at least 90 percent of the nation's population should live within access to a regionalized center certified by the AAPCC (Wagner, 1985). With pressure also to reduce waste and funding of health and social services, state investment in "controlling poison control" will be a significant step toward meeting those conflicting goals.

References

Aldrich, Franklin D (with 19 signatories). 1979. "Poison-control centers." New England Journal of Medicine 301:334.

Bain, Katherine. 1954. "Death due to accidental poisoning in young children." Journal of Pediatrics 44:616–23.

Berger, Meyer. 1957. "Help for the poisoned child." Saturday Evening Post 230 (November 16):24–25.

Bernstein, Judith, Lewis Goldfrank, Mary Ann Howland and Richard Weisman. 1983. "New York City's poison control center: a systematic approach to a complex problem." Urban Health 12:37–43.

Bice, Thomas, W. 1980. "Health services planning and regulation." Pp. 325–54 in Stephen J. Williams and Paul R. Torrens (eds.), Introduction to Health Services. New York: Wiley.

Brink, Carla J. 1984. "Jury verdict raises questions about practice standards in poison centers." American Journal of Hospital Pharmacy 41:1268–69.

Broadhead, Robert S. 1986. "Directing intervention from afar: the telephone dynamics of managing acute poisonings." Journal of Health and Social Behavior 27: 303–16.

Cann, Howard M. and Henry L. Verhulst. 1958. "Control of accidental poisoning—a progress report." Journal of the American Medical Association 168:717–24.

Chaffee-Bahamon, Claire and Frederick H. Lovejoy. 1983. "Effectivenes of a regional poison center in reducing excess emergency room visits for children's poisonings." Pediatrics 72:164–69.

Chi, Judy. 1982. "Poison control centers." Drug Topics 10:68–72.

Done, Alan K. 1978. "The toxic emergency: the case for regionalizing poision centers." Emergency Medicine 15:131–32.

Dubos, Rene. 1959. Mirage of Health. Garden City, NY: Doubleday.

DuShane, G. 1960. "Middleground." Science 132:1221.

Emergency Medicine. 1985. "Directory of poison control centers." Emergency Medicine 17:11–12.

Fry, David K. and Matilda S. McIntire. 1979. "Poison control and cost containment." Veterinary and Human Toxicology 79:73–76.

Haddad, Lester M. 1979. "Emergency physicians and poison control." New England Journal of Medicine 300:1223.

James, Selwyn. 1956. "First aid for poisoned children." Readers' Digest 69:58–61.

Krenzelok, Edward. 1980. "The poison information center comes of age." Journal of Emergency Medical Services 5:33–37.

Litovitz, Toby L. and Jane E. Elshami. 1982. "Poison center operations: the necessity of follow-up." Annals of Emergency Medicine 11:348–52.

Lovejoy, Frederick H., Debra L. Caplan, Thomas Rowland and Louis Fazen. 1979. "A statewide plan for care of the poisoned patient: the Massachusetts Poison Control Center." New England Journal of Medicine 300:363–65.

Manoquerra, Anthony S. and Anthony R. Temple. 1984. "Observations on the current status of poison control centers in the United States." Clinics in Laboratory Medicine 4:561–73.

McIntire, Matilda S. and Carol R. Angle. 1983. "Regional poison-control centers improve patient care." New England Journal of Medicine 308:219–21.

Mofenson, Howard C., Joseph Greensher and Thomas R. Caraccio. 1984. "Ingestions considered nontoxic." Clinics in Laboratory Medicine 4:587–602.

Newsweek. 1957. "Tragedy at fingertips." Newsweek 50 (September 2):56.

Pawluch, Dorothy. 1983. "Transitions in pediatrics: a segmental analysis." Social Problems 30:449–65.

Pfohl, Stephen J. 1977. "The 'discovery' of child abuse." Social Problems 24:310–23.

Rogers, John. 1981. "Recurrent childhood poisoning as a family problem." Journal of Family Practice 13:337–40.

Roueche, Berton. 1957. "The most delicate thing in the world." The New Yorker 33 (May 4):146–61.

Rumack, Barry H. 1980. "The poison control center: answers not antidotes." Hospital Practice 15:123–29.

Shah, C.P., T.J. Egan and H. W. Bain. 1980. "An expanded emergency service: role of telephone services in the emergency department." Annals of Emergency Medicine 9:617–23.

Simpson, T.R. and T.R. Simpson III. 1976. "Poison control revisited." Journal of the American Pharmaceutical Association 16:659–63.

Spector, Malcolm and John I. Kitsuse. 1977. Constructing Social Problems. Menlo Park, CA: Cummings.

Starr, Paul. 1982. The Social Transformation of American Medicine. New York: Basic Books.

Thompson, Dennis F., Harold L. Trammel, Nancy J. Robertson and J. Routt Reigart. 1983. "Evaluation of regional and nonregional poison centers." New England Journal of Medicine 308:191–94.

United States Food and Drug Administration (FDA). 1981. National Clearinghourse for Poison Control Centers Directory. Rockville, MD: Department of Health and Human Services.

———. 1982. National Clearinghouse for Poison Control Centers Bulletin 26 (January/March). Rockville, MD: Department of Health and Human Services.

———. 1983. Directory of the United States Poison Control Centers 1983. Rockville, MD: Department of Health and Human Services.

Veltri, Demaris Gullekson. 1980. "Alternatives to the Intermountain Regional Poison Control Center." Veterinary and Human Toxicology 22:323–25.

Wagner, Douglas W. E. 1985. "Editorial." Emergency Medicine 17:11–12.

Winokur, James L. and Robert Weiss. 1978. "Some thoughts on minimizing legal liability of poison control centers." Clinical Toxicology 12:319–34.

Part III

SOCIAL MOVEMENTS

Social movements are important vehicles for social change. They frequently include organizations that channel social discontent into concrete actions. In general, social movements emerge either outside of or on the edges of the mainstream, and they work to change aspects of that society. Major social movements include the civil rights, environmental, women's, gay and lesbian, and antiwar movements.

In the areas of health and health care, more specific social movements have emerged. Among the most well-developed of these are the disability rights, women's health, and HIV/AIDS movements. Each of these movements is made up of numerous social movement organizations, and each has a different focus. For example, the organizations in the disability rights movement seek greater accessibility and equal rights for people with disabilities. One of the great successes of the movement was the passage of the Americans with Disabilities Act. The breast cancer prevention movement is a part of the larger women's movement, and it has goals to improve the prevention, treatment, and cure for breast cancer. This movement has been crucial to raising public and political awareness about breast cancer and to supporting new research. Since the emergence of HIV/AIDS in the early 1980s, a number of organizations, mostly stemming from the gay community, have been active in supporting people with the disease. Their actions have included lobbying the government to allocate more funds for research on prevention and treatment, and working to reduce the stigma associated with AIDS. Along with medical advances, this HIV/AIDS movement has been important in improving prevention and treatment and in helping people live longer lives with and despite HIV infection.

In "Silence, Death, and the Invisible Enemy: AIDS Activism and Social Movement 'Newness'" Josh Gamson focuses on the organization ACT UP (AIDS Coalition to Unleash Power), one of the most activist of all AIDS organizations, called by some the "shock troops" of the AIDS movement. ACT UP engages in strategic public actions to bring attention to their issues, and it has attempted to both increase public awareness and change social responses to and resources available for AIDS. In the period Gamson studied ACT UP, members felt they were literally fighting for the lives of people with AIDS. While the situation in the United States has improved, the ACT UP organization remains an exemplar of the possibilities of health-orientated movements.

While gay social movement organizations quickly included AIDS as part of their change mandate, black and civil rights organizations were slower to embrace AIDS as part of their movement agenda. Ernest Quimby and Samuel R. Friedman present a case study of one city in "Dynamics of Black Mobilization against AIDS in New York City." Despite a long and successful history of black activism, Quimby and Friedman examine how and why in the first decade of the AIDS epidemic, black churches and civil rights organizations did not respond to the increasing AIDS epidemic in the black community. They suggest that these organizations could have made a difference in the early years had they mobilized the black population toward HIV/AIDS prevention.

As Maren Klawiter shows in "Racing for the Cure, Walking Women, and Toxic Touring: Mapping Cultures of Action within the Bay Area Terrain of Breast Cancer," health social movements can assume many different strategies. She illustrates how three specific breast cancer "cultures of action" have varying relationships to medicine and differing goals as to how to treat or prevent breast cancer. These organizations have widely contrary views about breast cancer activism, but together (along with other groups) they make up a large movement that has been very successful at mobilizing resources to improve the situation of breast cancer in the United States.

CHAPTER 7

Silence, Death, and the Invisible Enemy

AIDS ACTIVISM AND SOCIAL MOVEMENT "NEWNESS"

Josh Gamson

Shea Stadium is packed. As the Mets play the Astros, New York AIDS activists scream and shout along with the rest of the fans. Their cheers are somewhat unusual: "ACT UP! Fight back! Fight AIDS!" Their banners, unfurled in front of the three sections they have bought out, shout plays on baseball themes: "No glove, no love," "Don't balk at safer sex," "AIDS is not a ball game." The electronic billboard flashes some of their messages as well. The action gets wide coverage the following day. Later, in a *Newsweek* (1988a) article on the activist group ACT UP, a baseball fan complains, "AIDS is a fearful topic. This is totally inappropriate."

The fan is right, on both counts; in fact, I would suggest, he inadvertently sums up the point of the action. He also calls attention to the oddities: Why fight AIDS at a baseball game? Why mix fear and Americana? Who or what is the target here?

Susan Sontag and others have noted that the AIDS epidemic fits quite smoothly into a history of understanding disease through the "usual script" of the plague metaphor: originating from "outside," plagues are visitations on "them," punishments of both individuals and groups, they become stand-ins for deep fears and tools for bringing judgments about social crises. "AIDS," Sontag (1988:89) suggests, "is understood in a premodern way."

Yet the plague of AIDS has brought with it understandings and actions that are hardly "premodern": civil disobedience at the Food and Drug Administration protesting the sluggish drug approval process, guerrilla theater and "die-ins," infiltrations of political events culminating in the unfurling of banners protesting government inaction, media-geared "zaps," illegal drug research and sales, pickets and rallies. AIDS has given rise to a social movement. This is not, in fact, part of the usual script.

Perhaps, then, AIDS can be understood as part of a different script as well. Much has been written in the past decade about "new social movements" (NSMs); perhaps AIDS activism follows an outline particular to contemporary movements. This classification presents its own difficulties: social movements literature has a hard time clarifying exactly what is "new" about contemporary social movements and can, through its fuzziness, easily accommodate yet another social movement without shedding new light.

In this paper, I examine AIDS activism—by which I mean an organized "street" response to the epidemic—through the activities of ACT UP (the AIDS Coalition to Unleash Power), its most widespread and publicly visible direct-action group.

ACT UP, which began in New York, has chapters in Chicago, Boston, Atlanta, Los Angeles, Houston, Rochester, Madison, Nashville, San Francisco, and a number of other cities. The groups are loosely federated under the umbrella of the AIDS Coalition to Network, Organize and Win (ACT NOW). New York is by far the largest ACT UP, with weekly meeting attendance in the hundreds and membership estimated at nearly 3,000, while the others are smaller. San Francisco, with a membership of over 700, averages 50 people at general meetings. My comparisons between ACT UP in San Francisco and chapters in New York and other cities are based on a national conference in Washington, DC, internal publications, informal discussion and interviews, and newspaper reports.

Using data from six months of participant-observation research (September 1988 through February 1989) in San Francisco's ACT UP, coupled with local and national internal documents and newspaper writings about the group, I develop an analysis intended both to sharpen focus on the struggle over the meaning of AIDS and to challenge some of the hazy understandings of social movement newness. The analysis here treats ACT UP not as an exemplar but rather as an anomaly, asking what unique conditions constitute the case and how the case can aid in a reconstruction of existing theory. Micro- and macro-level analyses are linked through seeking out an "explanation for uniqueness" such that "we are compelled to move into the realm of the 'macro' that we observe in face-to-face interaction" (Burawoy 1989:7).

In the first part of the paper I briefly review approaches to contemporary social movements, locating ACT UP within this literature. I then turn to ACT UP's activities and internal obstacles, looking at their response to the plague script, the alternative scripts, they propose and their strategies for doing so, and the difficulties they face in this process. I argue that asking "who is the enemy?" provides a fruitful direction for making sense of these dynamics because ACT UP members often have trouble finding their "enemies." The paper continues with an examination of why this may be so, and what light it may shed on contemporary movements. Borrowing from Michel Foucault (1979), I turn to an examination of the forms of domination to which ACT UP members respond. I argue that, in addition to visible targets such as government agencies and drug companies, much of what ACT UP is fighting is abstract, disembodied, invisible: control through the creation of abnormality. Power is maintained less through direct force or institutionalized oppression and more through the delineation of the "normal" and the exclusion of the "abnormal." I suggest that this "normalizing" process, taking prominence in a gradual historical shift, is increasingly unlocked from state oppression in recent decades. State figures and institutions—though certainly still deeply involved in this domination—are now less apt to contribute to the production and dissemination of labels, making the process itself, abstracted, the hazy focus of protest. The paper then traces how responses to normalization play themselves out in ACT UP activities: activists use the labels to dispute the labels, use their abnormality and expressions of gay identity to challenge the process by which this identity was and is defined.

Finally, I suggest directions this framework provides for analyzing contemporary movement.

The Theorectical Context: What's New?

Among the shifts provoked by the rise of massive social movements in the 1960s and 1970s was a rupture in theorizing about social movements. Until that time, the dominant paradigm of collective behavior theory treated noninstitutional movements as essentially nonrational or irrational responses by alienated individuals to social strain and breakdown (for example, Smelser 1963). Many 1960s activists did not fit the mold. Neither anomic nor underprivileged nor responding to crises with beliefs "akin to magical beliefs" (Smelser 1963:8), they in fact came together largely from the middle class, with concrete goals and rational calculations of strategies. The predictions of classical social movement theory regarding who made up social movements and how they operated had broken down (see Cohen 1985, McAdam 1982).

In the last two decades, attempts to retheorize social movements have moved in two major directions. North American resource mobilization theory accounts for large scale mobilizations by emphasizing rational calculations by actors, focussing on the varying constraints and opportunities in which they operate and the varying resources upon which they draw (see McCarthy and Zald 1977, Oberschall 1973, Tilly 1978, and Jenkins 1981). This paradigm, directly challenging the assumptions of collective behavior theory, insists on the rationality of collective action. European theorists, on the other hand, have argued that rational-actor models are inappropriately applied to new groups seeking identity and autonomy. The movements of the 1960s and their apparent descendants—the peace movement, for example, or feminist, ecological, or local-autonomy movements—have been taken together by theorists as "new" phenomena to be accounted for; it is their nonrational focus on identity and expression that these theories emphasize as distinctive. They attempt to outline the characteristics shared by contemporary movements and to discern the structural shifts that might account for new dimensions of activity (see Kitschelt 1985, Cohen 1985, Eder 1985, Habermas 1981, Offe 1985, and Touraine 1985).

With some exceptions (see, for example, Doug McAdam's 1982 study of black insurgency), American theory, with its insistence on instrumental rationality, tends to pass over these distinctive characteristics—feminist attention to "consciousness," for example, and black and gay "pride"—to which European theories of "new social movements" (NSMs) direct attention. The European literature, then, in that it attempts to explain these apparently new characteristics found also in AIDS activism, provides the stronger conceptual tools with which to approach ACT UP. Yet what is actually "new" according to European NSM theory is both disputed and unclear. Most agree that a middle-class social base is distinctive (see Eder 1985 and Kreisi 1989); indeed, the fact that that NSMs are *not* working-class movements focussed primarily on economic distribution seems to be a characteristic on which there is clarity and agreement. From here, the range of characteristics expands and abstracts; NSMs claim "the sphere of 'political action within civil society' as [their] space" (Offe 1985:832); they use different tactics from their predecessors (Offe 1985); their conflicts concern not "problems of distribution" but "the grammar of forms of life," arising in "areas of cultural reproduction, social integration and socialization" (Habermas 1981:33); they "manifest a form of middle-class protest which oscillates from moral crusade to political pressure group to social movement" (Eder 1985:879); they are "both culturally oriented and involved in structural conflicts" (Touraine 1985:766), and involve a "self-limiting radicalism" that "abandons revolutionary dreams in favor of the idea of structural reform, along with a defense of civil society that does not seek to abolish the autonomous functioning of political and economic systems" (Cohen 1985:664).

Common to this list is a recognition that the field of operation has shifted, broadly put, to "civil society" and away from the state; that culture has become more of a focal point of activity (through "lifestyle" and "identity" movements, for example); and that this shift has to do with broad changes in the "societal type" to which movements respond and in which they act. Common to the list is also an unclear answer to the question of how new the shift really is; as Jean Cohen (1985:665) points out, the theme of defending civil society does not in itself imply something new—the question "is whether the theme has connected to new identities, forms of organization, and scenarios of conflict." New social movement theorists—even those like Touraine and Cohen who address these questions directly—seem to be unclear on what these shifts and changes really are: What exactly is the "cultural field" of "civil society" and what do these movements actually do there? What is it that is different about contemporary society that accounts for the characteristics of new social movements? When and how did these changes take place?

ACT UP as a New Social Movement

ACT UP provides an opportunity both to examine some of these issues concretely and to offer new hypotheses. The AIDS activist movement appears to share the most basic characteristics of "new social movements": a (broadly) middle-class membership and a mix of instrumental, expressive, and identity-oriented activities. Rather than exclusively orienting itself towards material distribution, ACT UP uses and targets cultural resources as well. What, this examination asks, does ACT UP do on the cultural terrain? What light does their activity shed on the question of "newness"? How can a study of this group contribute to an understanding of shifts in the nature of social movements and in the nature of the social world in which they operate?

The answer begins with the group's overall profile. ACT UP/San Francisco grew out of the 1987 San Francisco AIDS Action Pledge, becoming ACT UP in the fall of that year after New York's ACT UP began to gain recognition. In addition to planned and spontaneous actions, the group meets weekly in a church in the predominantly gay Castro neighborhood. ACT UP/San Francisco is made up almost exclusively of white gay men and lesbians, mostly in their 20s and 30s. The core membership—an informal group of about 25 activists—draws from both established activists (gay rights,

Central American politics, etc.) and those newly politicized by AIDS.[1] Some, but by no means all, of ACT UP's membership has either tested positive for HIV antibodies or been diagnosed with AIDS. As one member said, "I'm here because I'm angry and I'm tired of seeing my friends die." The membership is typically professional and semi-professional: legal and health care professionals, writers, political organizers, students, artists with day jobs. ACT UP/New York and ACT UPs in other cities exhibit similar profiles (Green 1989).

Self-defined in their flyers and media kits as "a nonpartisan group of diverse individuals united in anger and committed to direct action to end the AIDS crisis" (ACT UP 1988a), ACT UP pushes for greater access to treatments and drugs for AIDS-related diseases; culturally sensitive, widely available, and explicit safe-sex education; and well-funded research that is "publicly accountable to the communities most affected" (ACT UP 1988a). Moreover, the group pushes for the participation of people with AIDS (PWAs) in these activities (ACT UP 1989). The idea here is to change the distribution of resources and decision-making power; the principle guiding actions are strategic, aimed at affecting policy changes. "People have been fighting for social justice in this country for centuries," says one member (September 1988). "We're going to get aerosol pentamidine [a treatment drug for pneumocystis pneumonia] a lot quicker than we're going to get social justice."

ACT UP is also often involved in actions, however, whose primary principle is expressive. They focus inward on "building a unified community" (the gay and lesbian community and, increasingly, a sub-community of PWAs and the HIV-infected), and on the "need to express the anger and rage that is righteous and justified" from the community outward. They organize at times around actions in which AIDS is not the central issue or in which AIDS activism is incorporated into the project of "recreating a movement for gay and lesbian liberation." This orientation towards identity and expression, while not excluding older-style strategic actions, is one key characteristic cited by students of post-60s social movements.

Most interestingly, though, one hears and sees in ACT UP a constant reference to theater. ACT UP operates largely by staging events and by carefully constructing and publicizing symbols; it attacks the dominant representations of AIDS and of people with AIDS and makes attempts to replace them with alternative representations. At times, ACT UP attacks the representations alone; at times the attack is combined with a direct one on cultural producers and the process of AIDS-image production.

Another action principle weaves through ACT UP. As *Newsweek* (1988a) puts it, ACT UP has often "deliberately trespassed the bounds of good taste": throwing condoms, necking in public places, speaking explicitly and positively about anal sex, "camping it up" for the television cameras. This trespassing or boundary-crossing—and we can include in it the infiltration of public and private space (the Republican national convention, for example, where activists posing as participants unfurled banners)—both uses and strikes at the cultural field as well. In this case, rather than reacting to images of AIDS, activists use a more general tactic of disturbing "good taste"—and, in a point *Newsweek* quite characteristically misses, calling attention to the connection between cultural definitions and responses to AIDS. Boundary-crossing, along with theatrical and symbolic actions, makes clear

that ACT UP operates largely on the cultural field where theorists situate new social movements.[2] It also suggests that an examination of the specific patterns of culturally oriented actions may be especially revealing. By focussing on the cultural activities of AIDS activists as a key *distinctive* element, I by no means want to suggest
that this activism is primarily cultural. In fact, treatment issues, needle-exchange
programs, and access to health care, for instance, are all common subjects of action.
Pursuing this examination via ACT UP's peculiarities, I hope to generate possibilities for grounding and developing social movement theory.

ACT UP's Internal Obstacles

The examination turns, then, to ACT UP's distinctive characteristics. ACT UP's
strong cultural orientation has already been noted. In addition, buried in its various
strategies are three fundamental confusions. First, ACT UP's orientation towards the-
atrics suggests a clear delineation of performer from audience, yet actions are often
planned by ACT UP members without an articulation of whom they're meant to influence. If one wants to affect an audience—for example, by invoking a symbol whose
meaning is taken for granted and then giving it a different meaning—one clearly needs
a conception of who that audience is. In ACT UP planning meetings, there is often an
underlying confusion of audiences, and more often the question of audience is simply
ignored. When activists in New York infiltrated a Republican women's cocktail party
and later unfurled banners ("Lesbians for Bush," read one), the response of the cocktail partiers, a defensive singing of "God Bless America" (reported in "Workshop on
Creative Actions," ACT NOW Conference, Washington, DC, October 8, 1988), was
important not for what it showed about the Republicans' AIDS consciousness, which
came as no surprise. Instead, it was important for what it showed the activists about
their own power. They were, effect, their own audience, performing for themselves and
making others perform for them. In "brainstorms" for new actions, there is almost
never a mention of audience, and action ideas with different audiences proliferate.
ACT UP protested Dukakis, for example, with no media coverage, Dukakis nowhere
in sight, and no one to witness the protest but passing cars (San Francisco, September
30, 1988). In the meeting I observed, I commonly heard suggestions for actions that
bypassed any actual event, heading straight for the at-home audience through "photo
opportunities," mixed in with suggestions for actions that almost no one would see.
Much of this confusion is exacerbated by an openness of exchange and decentralized
decision making born of ACT UP's democratic structure (in San Francisco, decisions
are made consensually). The loose organizational structure acts against focussed planning and action. I argue, however, that the roots are deeper.

A second point of confusion is that, while ACT UP professes to be inclusive, and
ideas are often brought up that target non-gay aspects of AIDS (issues of concern to intravenous drug-users, for example, or access to health care for those who cannot afford
it), there are few signs that ACT UP in fact succeeds at including or actively pursues non-
gay members. This does not mean that the membership is exclusively gay men; in fact, a
good portion of the activists are women.[3] The formation of coalitions is sometimes

brought up as a good idea—"we need to join with others in solidarity around common suffering and common enemies," said the keynote speaker at the ACT NOW conference in October 1988—but generally not effected. Cooperative actions with other groups generate little excitement in San Francisco meetings. Actions are aimed mainly at targets with particular relevance to lesbians and gays; there are few black or Hispanic members, gay or straight. Despite the goal of inclusiveness, ACT UP continues to draw from and recreate the white, middle-class gay and lesbian community.

A third and related problem is perhaps ever more fundamental: AIDS politics and gay politics stand in tension, simultaneously associated and dissociated. ACT UP is an AIDS activist organization built and run by gay people. Historically, this is neither surprising nor problematic; among the populations first hit hardest by AIDS, gay people were alone in having an already established tradition and network of political and self-help organizations. Still, this tradition has meant that "AIDS groups have found it very difficult to establish themselves as non-gay, even where they have deliberately presented themselves as such" (Altman 1986:90). AIDS activists find themselves simultaneously attempting to dispel the notion that AIDS is a gay disease (which it is not) while, thorough their activity and leadership, treating AIDS as a gay problem (which, among other things, it is).

While this dilemma is in part due to the course the disease itself took, how it plays itself out in ACT UP is instructive. For some, particularly those members who are not newly politicized, ACT UP *is* gay politics, pure and simple, a movement continuous with earlier activism. They emphasize the need for "sex positive" safe-sex education, for example, linking AIDS politics to the sexual liberation of earlier gay politics. The main organizer of a November 1988 election night rally in San Francisco's Castro district for the gay community to "Stand Out and Shout" about results envisioned it as a return to the good old days of gay celebration. In planning speakers for the rally, he and others quickly generated a long list of possibles—from the gay political community. Here, AIDS issues often get buried.

For others, it's important to maintain some separation, albeit a blurry one, between the two sets of issues. In New York, for example, when a newspaper calls ACT UP a "gay organization," ACT UP's media committee sends out a "standard letter" correcting the error ("Media Workshop" at ACT NOW Conference in Washington, DC, October 8, 1988). The ACT UP agenda, when the balance is towards distinctive AIDS politics, often focuses more narrowly on prevention and treatment issues as in, for example, a San Francisco proposal for an "AIDS treatment advocacy project" which argued that "whether it is an entire family with AIDS in Harlem or an HIV+ gay man in San Francisco, treatment is ultimately the issue they are most concerned with" (ACT UP 1988b:1). More commonly, though, ACT UP actions don't fall on one side or the other, but combine an active acceptance of the gay-AIDS connections with an active resistance to that connection.

Visible and Invisible Enemies

Why do these particular confusions occur? They eventually will come to make sense as the particularities of ACT UP's actions are examined. These three confusions within

ACT UP, which seem to give its action a somewhat unfocussed character, in fact will prove to be core elements of the group's being. Explaining ACT UP's confusions, and those of social movements like it, hinges on the answer to a pivotal question: Who is the enemy? Asking this question of ACT UP, one often finds that the enemies against which their anger and action are directed are clear, familiar, and visible: the state and corporations. At other times, though, the enemy is invisible, abstract, disembodied, ubiquitous: it is the very process of "normalization" through labelling in which everyone except one's own "community" of the de-normalized (and its supporters) is involved. At still other times, intermediate enemies appear, the visible institutors of the less visible process: the media and medical science.

This second enemy forms the basis of my core theoretical claims: that ACT UP is responding to a gradual historical shift towards a form of domination in which power is maintained through a normalizing process in which "the whole indefinite domain of the non-conforming is punishable" (Foucault 1979:178). Through labelling, or socially organized stigmatization, behaviors and groups are marked as abnormal; in the last two centuries, the norm has largely replaced the threat of violence as a technique of power. As Michel Foucault (1979:183) argues, individuals are differentiated

> In terms of the following overall rule: that the rule be made to function as a minimum threshold, as an average to be respected or as an optimum towards which one must move. It . . . hierarchizes in terms of values the abilities, the level, the "nature" of individuals. It introduces, through this "value-giving" measure, the constraint of a conformity that must be achieved. Lastly, it traces the limit that will define difference in relation to all other differences, the external frontier of the abnormal.

In this process, the dominator becomes increasingly abstracted and invisible, while the dominated, embodied and visible (and, importantly, "marked" through stigmatization), becomes the focus of attention. In effect, people dominate themselves; rather than being confronted with a punishment (physical, material) as a mechanism of control, they confront themselves with the threat of being devalued as abnormal.

These ideas are not incompatible with those put forward by the sociology of deviance and discussions of stigmatization (e.g., Lemert 1967, Goffman 1963), which, of course, call attention to the process of labelling and its impact on the "deviant." However, the various forms of labelling theory have also been challenged by collective action since the 1960s. Those theories, by studying how one "becomes deviant," and the defensive reaction of "deviants" to an identity defined for them—the "management of spoiled identities" (Goffman) and "secondary deviation" as a "means of defense" against the "problems created by the societal reaction to primary deviation" (Lemert 1967:17)—are ill-equipped to explain the organization of the stigmatized into social movements. As John Kitsuse (1980:5) argues, the accomodative reactions analyzed by deviance sociology (retreat into a subculture, nervously covering up or denying aberrations) do not "account for, nor do they provide for an understanding of, the phenomenal number of self-proclaimed deviant groups that have visibly and vocally entered the politics" of recent decades. Earlier theories are hard-pressed to account for historical change, and for the assertive building of collective movements based on self-definitions that *reject* the dominant definitions. Foucault, on the other hand, treats pressure for conformity not as a given problem for the "deviant," but as a technique of power with a variable history.

Identity strategies are particularly salient and problematic within this domination form. When power is effected through categorization, identity is often built on the very categories it resists. ACT UP's expressive actions, in this light, are part of a continuing process of actively forging a gay identity while challenging the process through which it is formed *for* gay people at a time when the stigma of disease has been linked with the stigma of deviant sexuality. ACT UP members continue to organize around the "deviant" label, attempting to separate label from stigma. Identity-oriented actions accept the labels, and symbolic actions disrupt and resignify them.

Identity actions and representational strategies thus stand in awkward relationship: they are increasingly linked in the attack on the normalization process itself. In a simpler identity politics—in the celebration of gay liberation, for example—labels are important tools for self-understanding. That sort of politics involves what John Kitsuse (1980:9) calls "tertiary deviation," the "confrontation, assessment, and rejection of the negative identity . . . and the transformation of that identity into a positive or viable self-conception." ACT UP members, however, push past this "new deviance" to use stigmas and identity markers as tools against the normalization process. The representation of oneself as abnormal now becomes a tool for disrupting the categorization process; the labels on which group identity is built are used, in a sense, against themselves.

Why, though, is this response to normalizing power coming into its own now? Stigmatization is certainly not new. Foucault, in *Discipline and Punish*, traces a shift in the eighteenth and nineteenth centuries, a shift that takes place primarily in technologies of control: the rise of surveillance techniques and the constitution of the subject by "experts" and scientific discourse. This shift has arguably solidified in this century in Western societies. Yet, while state institutions and actors in the twentieth century certainly have still been involved in the normalization process (as well as in direct repression), they have evidently been less involved in the latter half of this century (or, stated less strongly, less visibly involved). One sees this in the history of civil rights: racism continues while state-sponsored racism and racist policies become less acceptable (see Omi and Winant 1986:89ff). Similarly, state definitions of women's "roles" have been liberalized, as the state has withdrawn somewhat from prescribing "normal" female behavior. One sees this as well in the response to AIDS; the federal government, while conservative or split in its policies, has over time become somewhat more liberal in terms of labelling. Public health officials advertise AIDS as an "equal opportunity destroyer"; the Surgeon General warns against treating AIDS as a gay disease and argues in favor of protections against discrimination; the Presidential Commission calls for "the reaffirmation of compassion, justice, and dignity" and indicts, among other things, "a lack of uniform and strong antidiscrimination laws" (Johnson and Murray 1988). State institutions increasingly refuse to "discriminate," that is, to set policies based on social labels. As the state becomes less directly involved in normalization, the process itself necessarily becomes more an independent point of attack by the de-normalized and resisted as a process. It is within this overall historical shift in methods of domination, this study proposes, that ACT UP's social movement activity makes sense.

ACT UP and Normalization

How does this resistance play itself out? What is the link between enemies and actions? Let's begin with the old forms of domination, which are very much still at work. The state is certainly involved in the domination of people with AIDS, as it is in the repression of sexual minorities. For example, the Federal Food and Drug Administration approves drugs and has been sluggish in approving AIDS-related drugs; it is perceived as allowing bureaucracy to get in the way of saving or prolonging lives (*Newsweek* 1988b). In October 1988, ACT NOW organized a conference, teach-in, rally, and day of civil disobedience in Washington, DC, to "seize control of the FDA" (Okie 1988, Connolly and Raine 1988). The Reagan and Bush administrations have been notoriously inattentive to the AIDS epidemic. Reagan first mentioned AIDS publicly at a time when over 36,000 people had already been diagnosed and over 20,000 had died from the disease. While subsequently calling AIDS "America's number one health problem," the administration consistently avoided initiating a coordinated, adequately financed attack on that problem (see Shilts 1988). Reagan and Bush have become common targets of ACT UP "AIDSgate" signs and t-shirts, of "zaps," of posters charging that "the government has blood on its hands," of disruption and protest during campaign speeches. In this case, specific state institutions and actors are targeted, mostly through conventional protest actions and media-geared actions. In these cases, it is quite clear who is responsible for needless death and who is controlling resources, and ACT UP functions as a pressure group to protest and effect policy decisions. Here, AIDS politics and gay politics are quite separable and separated.

Similarly, pharmaceutical companies are manifest enemies; they control the price of treatment drugs and make decisions about whether or not to pursue drug development. That drug company decisions are guided by considerations of profit (Eigo et al. 1988) is a direct and visible instance of oppression and represents an embodied obstacle to the physical survival of people with AIDS. For example, AZT (azidothymidine, the only drug approved at this writing for treatment of AIDS illnesses) cost $13,000 a year in 1987. Again, ACT UP attacks these targets with pressure tactics: boycotting AZT manufacturer Burroughs-Wellcome, zapping that company and others with civil disobedience actions, publicizing government-drug company relations (Eigo et al. 1988). In this example, again, the focus is specifically on issues of relevance to all people with AIDS.

Yet AIDS has also been from the outset a stigma, an illness constructed as a marker of homosexuality, drug abuse, moral deficiencies—stigmas added to those of sexual transmission, terminal disease and, for many, skin color.[4] AIDS has

> come to assume all the features of a traditional morality play: images of cancer and death, of blood and semen, of sex and drugs, of morality and retribution. A whole gallery of folk devils have been introduced—the sex-crazed gay, the dirty drug abuser, the filthy whore, the blood drinking voodoo-driven black—side by side with a gallery of "innocents"—the hemophiliacs, the blood transfusion "victim," the new born child, even the "heterosexual" (Plummer 1988:45).

Associated most commonly with the image of the male homosexual or bisexual AIDS "victim" or "carrier" who is vaguely responsible through deviant behavior for his own demise, AIDS has been appropriated to medicalize moral stances: promiscuity is medically unsafe while monogamy is safe; being a member of certain social groups is dangerous to one's health while being a member of the "general population" is dangerous only when the un-general contaminate it. As Simon Watney (1987:126) notes, in AIDS "the categories of health and sickness . . . meet with those of sex, and the image of homosexuality is reinscribed with connotations of contagion and disease, a subject for medical attention and medical authority."

The construction and reconstruction of boundaries has been, then, an essential aspect of the story of AIDS. The innocent victim is bounded off from the guilty one, pure blood from contaminated, the general population from the AIDS populations, risk groups from those not at risk. Those who span the boundaries arguably become the most threatening: the promiscuous bisexual, the only one who can "account for and absolve the heterosexual majority of any taint of unlawful desire" (Grover 1987:21) and the prostitute, with her longstanding position as a "vessel" of disease (Grover 1987:25).

Who achieves this demarcation of boundaries? Who has made AIDS mean what it does? Who is the enemy? Two manifest producers of stigmas appear (in addition to certain public figures who disseminate them): the mass media, on whose television screens and newspaper pages the stigmatized are actually visible, and medical science, which translates the labels into risk-group categories. ACT UP thus challenges the medical establishment, largely by undermining the expertise claimed by them. Activists keep up to date on and publicize underground and foreign treatments (e.g., Eigo et al. 1988), sell illegal treatment drugs publicly, yell the names of known AIDS-illness drugs in front of the FDA ("Show them we know!" the organizer calls). They wear lab coats and prepare a "guerilla slide show" in which they plan to slip slides saying "He's lying" and "This is voodoo epidemiology" into an audio-visual presentation by a health commissioner.

ACT UP also sets up challenges to the media. An ongoing San Francisco battle had ACT UP shutting down production and members negotiating with producers over the script of an NBC drama, "Midnight Caller." In that script a bisexual man with AIDS purposely infects others and is shot and killed in the end by one of his female partners. It was objected to by ACT UP members as playing on "the great fear of the 'killer queer'"[5] and implying that, as an ACT UP representative put it, "basically it's justifiable to kill a person with AIDS" (Ford 1988). A similar response has been discussed for the San Francisco filming of Randy Shilts's *And The Band Played On*, a controversial history of the American AIDS epidemic. The media are usually treated by ACT UP as allies in the public relations operation of garnering coverage. As one New Yorker put it (October 1988), "the media aren't the enemy, the media are manipulated by the enemy, and we can manipulate them too." When actively involved in the labelling of people with AIDS as murderers, however, the media become the enemies to be fought. This ambivalence makes sense: the media, as the institutional mechanism through which normalization is most effectively disseminated, are both a visible enemy and a necessary link to a more abstract form of domination.[6]

The question of who is behind the generation and acceptance of stigmas, though, for the most part doesn't get asked as activists plan and argue, perhaps because the answer is experienced daily: everyone and no one. No one actually does it and everyone participates in it—your family and your neighbors as well as the blatant bigots far away. It's a process that appears usually as natural, as not-a-process.

Playing with Labels, Crossing the Boundaries

Fighting this largely hidden process calls for different kinds of strategies, mostly in the realm of symbols. Examining the symbolic maneuverings of ACT UP, we can begin to see how fighting the process calls for particular strategies. ACT UP's general strategy is to take a symbol or phrase used to oppress and invert it. For example, ACT UP makes explicit challenges, guided by other AIDS activists and particularly PWAs, on the kind of language used to discuss AIDS. In place of the "AIDS victims" they speak of "people with AIDS" or "people living with AIDS." In place of "risk groups," they insert the category of "risk practices." They talk about blood and semen rather than "bodily fluids," and they challenge the exclusionary use of "general population" (see Grover 1987).

The strategy runs much deeper than speech, however. The visual symbol most widely publicized by American AIDS activist—"SILENCE=DEATH" written in bold white-on-black letters beneath a pink triangle, the Nazi emblem for homosexuals later co-opted by the gay movement—provides a snapshot look at this process. Here, ACT UP takes a symbol used to mark people for death and reclaims it. They reclaim, in fact, control over defining a cause of death; the banner connects gay action to gay survival, on the one hand, and homophobia to death from AIDS, on the other. ACT UP's common death spectacles repeat the inversion. In AIDS commentary death is used in a number of ways (Gilman 1987); it is either a punishment (the image of the withered, guilty victim), an individual tragedy (the image of the lonely, abandoned dying), or a weapon (the image of the irresponsible "killer queer"). A "die in," in which activists draw police-style chalk outlines around each other's "dead" bodies, gives death another meaning by shifting the responsibility: these are deaths likened to murders, victims not of their own "deviance," but shot down by the people controlling the definition and enforcement of normality. You have told us what our deaths mean, their actions say, now we who are actually dying will show you what they mean.

A similar shift of responsibility takes place around the symbol of blood. In popular discussions, blood is talked about in terms of "purity" and a benevolent medical establishment working to keep "bad blood" out of the nation's blood supply. In many ACT UP activities, "blood" is splattered on t-shirts (San Francisco, October 3, 1988) or doctor's uniforms (Washington, DC, October 11, 1988). Members want to shoot it out of squirt guns, blood-balloon it onto buildings, write "test this" with it on walls ("Creative Actions" workshop, Washington, DC, October 8, 1988). Here, on one level, they use the established discourse of purity against its users as an angry weapon: "infected" blood is everywhere. On another level, though, the frame is shifted from purity (in which the blood supply is "victimized") to crime (in which PWAs are victimized). The blood becomes evidence not of infection, but of murder; the activists are blood-splattered victims, as was made explicit in posters originally directed at Mayor Koch in New York and later translated into an indictment of the federal government. "The government has blood on its hands," the sign says, "One AIDS death every half hour." Between the two phrases is the print of a large, bloody hand. In a San Francisco rally against Rep. William Dannemeyer's Proposition 102 (October 3, 1988), which would have required by law that doctors report those infected and those "suspected" of infection, require testing at the request of doctors, employers or insurers, and eliminate confidential testing, ACT UP carried a "Dannemeyer Vampire" puppet. The vampire, a big ugly head on a stick, with black cape and blood pouring from its fangs, was stabbed with a stake later in the action. Here, ACT UP activates another popular code in which blood has meaning—the gore of horror movies—and reframes blood testing as blood sucking. It's not the blood itself that's monstrous, but the vampire who would take it. By changing the meaning of blood, ACT UP activists dispute the "ownership" of blood; more importantly, they call attention to the consequences of the labels of "bad" blood and "purity" and implicate those accepting the labels in the continuation of the AIDS epidemic.

Boundary-crossing, though tactically similar, goes on the offensive while inversions are essentially reactive. The spectacle of infiltration and revelation runs through real and fantasized ACT UP actions. Members speak of putting subversive messages in food or in the pockets of suit jackets, of writing messages on lawns with weed killer, of covering the Washington monument with a giant condom, of replacing (heterosexual) bar ashtrays with condom-shaped ashtrays. They place stickers saying "Touched by a Person with AIDS" in phone booths and stage a mock presidential inauguration through the San Francisco streets during rush hour (January 1989). The idea, as one activist put it, is to "occupy a space that's not supposed to be yours," to "usurp public spaces." San Francisco's underground graffiti group, specializing in "redecorating" targeted spaces, sums up the principle in its humorous acronym, TANTRUM: Take Action Now to Really Upset the Masses.

The ideas that charge brainstorming sessions and the eventual choices of visual and theatrical activity at actions are not arbitrary. The selections are revealing. Spaces and objects are chosen that are especially American (that is, middle American—lawns, cocktail parties, baseball games, patriotic symbols, suits) and presumably "safe" from the twin "threats" of homosexuality and disease. ACT UP here seizes control of symbols that traditionally exclude gay people or render them invisible, and take them over, endowing them with messages about AIDS; they reclaim them, as they do the pink triangle, and *make them mean* differently. In so doing, they attempt to expose the system of domination from which they reclaim meanings and implicate the entire system in the spread of AIDS.

It is important to notice that ACT UP's identity-oriented actions often revolve around boundary-crossing and label disruption. These are strategies for which these mostly white, middle-class gay people are particularly equipped, largely because their stigma is often invisible unlike, for example, the stigmatized person of color. They can draw on a knowledge of mainstream culture born of participation rather than exclusion and, thus, a knowledge of how to disrupt it using its own vocabulary. Here the particular cultural resources of ACT UP's membership become important; they are re-sources that other movements (and gay people from other races or classes) may not have to the same degree or may not be able to use without considerable risk.

Gay campiness, raunchy safe-sex songs in front of the Department of Health and Human Services, straight-looking men in skirts wearing "Fuck Me Safe" t-shirts (Wash-ington, DC, October 1988), lesbians and gay men staging "kiss-ins," a general outra-geousness that "keeps the edge"—these actions simultaneously accept the gay label, build a positive gay identity, challenge the conventional "deviant" label, connect stigmatization to AIDS deaths, and challenge the very process of categorization. This is the power of the pink triangle and "SILENCE=DEATH"; the building of an identity is linked with the resistance of a stigma as the key to stopping the AIDS epidemic. "We are everywhere," says a sign at the DC ACT NOW rally, a sign common at gay political demonstrations, and the noisy expressions of collective anger and identity add up to the same claim. Here, the gay "we" and the AIDS "we" are melded; the destabilizing effect of the suddenly re-vealed homosexual is joined with the fear that suddenly no space is safe from AIDS. A chant at several San Francisco protests captures the link between asserting an identity and challenging the labels: "We're fags and dykes," the activist chant, "and we're here to stay." Meaning we are what you say we are, and we're not what you say we are. "We're here," they chant, "We're queer, and we're not going shopping."

What exactly is being challenged in these symbolic inversions? Certainly, in symbols like the Dannemeyer vampire and the bloody hand attributed to the government, the old and consistent enemy, the state, is mixed in; but it isn't exclusive. ACT UP disrupts sym-bolic representation, heeding the call to "campaign and organize in order to enter the amphitheater of AIDS commentary effectively and unapologetically on our own terms" (Watney 1987:54). It does so, moreover, often through symbols that are not tied to the state but to "mainstream" American culture. In the case of inversions, AIDS and gay la-bels are not necessarily linked: any oppressive marker is taken over. In the case of bound-ary-disruption AIDS and gay labels are connected; the fear of gay people and the fear of AIDS, now linked in the normalization process, are used to call attention to themselves. In both cases, the *process* of stigmatization, by which symbols become markers of abnor-mality and the basis for decisions about "correcting" the abnormal, is contested.

Strategies and Obstacles Revisited

The mix of strategies, then, can be seen in terms of the visiblity of enemies. More fa-miliar, instrumental pressure-group strategies attempt to change the distribution of re-sources by attacking those visibly controlling distribution. Identity-forming strategies are particularly crucial and problematic when the struggle is in part against a society rather than a visible oppressor. Label disruption—contained in identity-forming strategies, and the core of symbolic strategies—is a particular operation on the cultural field. It is made necessary by a form of domination that operates through abstractions, through symbols that mark off the normal. (I am not suggesting, of course, that these are discrete types in concrete actions; actions are always mixed exactly because the forms of domination are simultaneous.)

We can also make sense of ACT UP's internal obstacles through this lens. It's not surprising that the question of audience becomes a difficult one to address. First of all, the audience often is the group itself when identity formation becomes a key part of struggle. Yet at the same time, we have seen that identity struggles involve pushing at the very labels on which they're based, and here the audience is the entire society. Actions are thus often founded on a confusion of audiences. More commonly, the question of audience is simply lost because the underlying target of action is the normalization process. While it might be more "rational" for ACT UP activists to try to spell out the particular audience each time they design an action, the struggle in which they are involved makes the particularity of an audience difficult to see. When stigmatization is being protested, the audience is the undifferentiated society—that is, audience and enemy are lumped together, and neither is concretely graspable.

Understanding that ACT UP is attacking this particular form of domination, we can also see why ACT UP is caught between the association and dissociation of AIDS politics from gay politics. Clearly, PWAs and gay people are both subject to the stigmatization process; this process, as it informs and supports responses to AIDS, has become literally lethal for PWAs, gay and non-gay, and dangerous for those labelled as "risk group" members, gay men (and often by an odd extension, lesbians), drug users, prostitutes, blacks, and Hispanics. Socially organized labels that, before AIDS, were used to oppress, are now joined with the label of "AIDS victim." This form of domination is *experienced* by ACT UP members as a continuous one. AIDS is a gay disease because AIDS has been made to attribute viral disease to sexual deviance. Separating AIDS politics from gay politics would be to give up the fight against normalization.

Yet joining the two politics poses the risk of losing the fight in that it confirms the very connection it attempts to dispel. This is a familiar dilemma, as Steve Epstein (1987:19) points out, and one that is not at all limited to the gay movement: "How do you protest a socially imposed categorization, except by organizing around the category?" Organizing around a resisted label, in that it involves an initial acceptance of the label (and, in identity-oriented movements, a celebration of it), can tend to reify the label. Identity politics thus contain a danger played out here: "If there is perceived to be such a thing as a 'homosexual person,' then it is only a small step to the conclusion that there is such a thing as a 'homosexual disease,' itself the peculiar consequence of the 'homosexual lifestyle'" (Epstein 1987:48). The familiarity of the dilemma, though, should not obscure its significance. This is neither a dilemma attributable simply to the random course of AIDS nor to mistakes on the part of activists, but to the form of domination to which social movements respond.

In this light, it's not surprising that ACT UP has difficulty including non-gays and forming coalitions. In some ways, ACT UP is driven towards inclusiveness since AIDS is affecting other populations and since the fight includes more broad-based struggles over resources. But, as we have seen, resistance to labelling involves accepting the label but redefining it, taking it over. Group identity actions are bound up with this resistance. This drives ACT UP strongly away from inclusiveness. The difficulty in walking these lines—between confirming and rejecting the connection between gay people and AIDS, between including and excluding non-gays—is built into the struggle against normalization in which ACT UP is involved.

Bodies and Theories

I have argued that ACT UP responds to the script of the AIDS plague by undermining that script, resisting the labelling through which contemporary domination is often effectively achieved. This seems to be missed by most observers of AIDS, who interpret the politics of AIDS on the model of conventional politics. Randy Shilts's 1988 bestseller, for example, ignores the development of grassroots AIDS activism even in its updating epilogue. AIDS serves as a particularly vivid case of disputed scripts in American politics in that the epidemic of disease, as others have noted, has occurred simultaneously with an "epidemic of signification"; AIDS exists "at a point where many entrenched narratives intersect, each with its own problematic and context in which AIDS acquires meaning" (Treichler 1987:42, 63). ACT UP illustrates this, treating the struggle over the narratives opened and exposed by AIDS as potentially life-saving.

ACT UP also illustrates major effects of an historical shift. If, as I've proposed in drawing on Foucault, domination has gradually come to operate less in the form of state and institutional oppression and more in the form of disembodied and ubiquitous processes, it is hardly surprising that diseased bodies become a focal point of both oppression and resistance. As the enemy becomes increasingly disembodied, the body of the dominated—in this case, primarily the diseased, gay male body—becomes increasingly central. The AIDS epidemic itself fits this process so well as to make it seem almost inevitable: the terror of the disease is that it is an enemy you cannot see, and, like the labels put to use in normalizing power, it is spread invisibly. AIDS activism in part struggles against this disembodied type of power by giving that body—its death, its blood, its sexuality—new, resistant meanings. The plague script meets here with the script of new social movements.

But what does this tell us about theorizing new social movement? First, it calls into question the value of "newness" as a reified category of analysis. In suggesting that the history of enemies and types of domination is central to understanding ACT UP, this study points to a gradual shift rather than a radical break in movement activity; "newness" militates towards a focus on a moment (the 1960s) rather than a history that reaches back into, for example, the eighteenth and nineteenth centuries (as in the historical transformation that Foucault describes). It obscures what may be instructive continuities across time. Secondly, this study points towards ways of distinguishing *among* contemporary movements. To assert that ACT UP exemplifies contemporary movements would clearly be to overstate the case; rather, this analysis demonstrates the insufficiency of analyzing different movements as like phenomena simply because of a shared cultural and identity focus. Operating on the "cultural field" means something more specific than focussing on problems that "deal directly with private life" (Touraine 1985:779) or even targeting and using narrative and artistic representation. ACT UP's cultural strategies reclaim and resignify oppressive markers. Orienting actions towards identity formation means something more specific than "defend[ing] spaces for the creation of new identities and solidarities" (Cohen 1985:685). Identity assertions in ACT UP point up boundaries, using the fear of the abnormal against the fearful. These are specific operations that may be shared by other contemporary social movements—those subject to stigmatization, for example, and which are also in a position to "shock"—and not by others. Stigmatization, moreover, may take different forms and give rise to different types of movement activity. Whether in Shea Stadium or at the FDA, discerning the types of enemies to whom movements are responding is a task for analysts of social movements as well as for activists within them.

Notes

1. Unless otherwise noted, quotations and descriptions of actions are drawn from the author's field notes from September 1988 through January 1989 (ACT UP weekly general meetings; Media Committee weekly meetings and activities, and other committee meetings; ACT NOW AIDS Activism Conference, October 8–11, 1988. Washington, DC; ACT UP/San Francisco actions). For a sampling of published reporting on ACT UP, see Green 1989, *US News & World Report* 1989, Linebarger 1989, Tuller 1988, Ford 1988, Johnson 1988, Okie 1988, Connolly and Raine 1988, Morgan 1988.

2. By way of comparison, it's important to notice that most AIDS politics does not operate according to this description, but according to a more conventional political model. "Most AIDS politicking," as Dennis Altman (1986:105) describes it, "has involved the lobbying of federal, state and local governments. . . . [This] has meant dependence upon professional leaders able to talk the language of politicians and bureaucrats."

3. Why so many women are attracted to the AIDS movement is an interesting question to which I've accumulated only brief, speculative answers: some because their friends are dying, some because of a history of working in health politics through women's health issues. One woman suggested an answer that seems to run deeper and along the lines suggested by this study. Oppression through AIDS, she said, is the most severe end of a spectrum of violence to which "all gay people are subject." For her, while silence might not mean literal death, it would mean a symbolic death (not being allowed to live as "me").

4. The activist response of black communities to AIDS has, though, differed greatly from that in gay communities, and this merits careful examination not allowed for here. The lag in black and Hispanic activism has been attributed by one observer to a combination of lack of material and political resources (minority PWAs are disproportionately lower class or underclass) and "denial" on the part of minority leadership (because of the dangers posed by feeding racism with the stigma of disease, and because of strong anti-gay sentiments in black and Hispanic cultures); (see Goldstein 1987).

5. The figure of the irresponsible killer-victim was popularized by Randy Shilts in the character of Gaetan Dugas, an airline steward Shilts labels "Patient Zero." Shilts charges that Dugas knowingly spread the virus throughout the continent. For a critique of Shilts, see Crimp, 1987b.

6. The mass media clearly play a very central and complex role in contemporary activism (see, for example, Gitlin 1980), an examination of which is unfortunately beyond the scope of this paper. It's quite likely that much of the escalation of symbols comes from the need by social movements to compete for attention in an increasingly message-dense environment; this does not explain the content of those symbols, though, nor does it explain why the media at times become explicit enemies.

References

ACT UP/San Francisco. 1988a. "Our goals and demands." Informational flyer.
———. 1988b. "The AIDS treatment advocacy project." Proposal drafted for ACT NOW Conference. September.

————. 1989. "ACT UP PISD caucus." Informational flyer.

Altman, Dennis. 1986. AIDS in the Mind of America. Garden City, NY: Anchor Press/Doubleday.

Burawoy, Michael. 1989. "The extended case method." Unpublished manuscript.

Cohen, Jean L. 1985. "Strategy or identity: new theoretical paradigms and contemporary social movements." Social Research 52:663–716.

Connolly, Mike and George Raine. 1988. "50 AIDS activists arrested at FDA." San Francisco Examiner, October 11:A1.

Crimp, Douglas, ed. 1987a. AIDS: Cultural Analysis/Cultural Criticism. Cambridge, MA: MIT Press.

————. 1987b. "How to have promiscuity in an epidemic." Pp. 237–71 in Douglas Crimp (ed.), AIDS: Cultural Analysis/Cultural Criticism. Cambridge, MA: MIT Press.

Eder, Klaus. 1985. "The 'new social movements': moral crusades, political pressure groups, or social movement?" Social Research 52:869–90.

Eigo, Jim, Mark Harrington, Iris Long, Margaret McCarthy, Stephen Spinella, and Rick Sugden. 1988. "FDA action handbook." Unpublished manuscript prepared for October 11 action at the Food and Drug Administration.

Epstein, Steven. 1987. "Gay politics, ethnic identity: the limits of social constructionism." Socialist Review 17:9–54.

Ford, Dave. 1988. "'Midnight caller' script provokes gay activists' ire." San Francisco Sentinel, October 21:4–5.

Foucault, Michel. 1979. Discipline and Punish. New York: Vintage Books.

Gilman, Sander. 1987. "AIDS and syphilis: the iconography of disease." Pp. 87–107 in Douglas Crimp (ed.), AIDS: Cultural Analysis/Cultural Criticism. Cambridge, MA: MIT Press.

Gitlin, Todd. 1980. The Whole World Is Watching: Mass Media in the Making of the New Left. Berkeley, CA: University of California Press.

Goffman, Erving. 1963. Stigma: Notes on the Management of Spoiled Identity. Englewood Cliffs, NJ: Printice-Hall, Inc.

Goldstein, Richard. 1987. "AIDS and race." Village Voice. March 10:23–30.

Green, Jesse. 1989. "Shticks and stones." 7 Days, February 8:21–26.

Grover, Jan Zita. 1987. "AIDS: keywords." Pp. 17–30 in Douglas Crimp (ed.), AIDS: Cultural Analysis/Cultural Criticism. Cambridge, MA: MIT Press.

Habermas, Jürgen. 1981. "New social movements." Telos 49:33–37.

Jenkins, J. Craig. 1981. "Sociopolitical movements." Pp. 81–153 in Samuel Long (ed.), Handbook of Political Behavior. New York: Plenum Press.

Johnson, Clarence. 1988. "Gays attack KRON building." San Francisco Chronicle, December 12:A2.

Johnson, Diane and John F. Murray. 1988. "AIDS without end." New York Review of Books. August 18:57–63.

Kitschelt, Herbert. 1985. "New social movements in West Germany and the United States." Political Power and Social Theory 5:273–324.

Kitsuse, John I. 1980. Coming out all over: deviants and the politics of social problems." Social Problems 28:1–13.

Kreisi, Hanspeter. 1989. "New social movements and the new class in the Netherlands." American Journal of Sociology 94:1078–1116.

Lemert, Edwin. 1967. Human Deviance, Social Problems, and Social Control. Englewood Cliffs, NJ: Prentice-Hall, Inc.

Linebarger, Charles. 1989. "All the rage: angry AIDS activist pump up the volume on deaf policy-makers." San Francisco Sentinel, February 23:3–5.

McAdam, Doug. 1982. Political Process and the Development of Black Insurgency 1930–1970. Chicago: University of Chicago Press.

McCarthy, John and Mayer Zald. 1977. "Resource mobilization and social movement: a partial theory." American Journal of Sociology 82:1212–40.

Morgan, Thomas. 1988. "AIDS protesters temper their tactics as a way to reach the mainstream." New York Times. July 22:A12.

Newsweek. 1988a. "Acting up to fight AIDS." June 6:42.

———. 1988b. "The drug-approval dilemma." November 14:63.

Oberschall, Anthony. 1973. Social Conflict and Socal Movements. Englewood Cliffs, NJ: Prentice-Hall.

Offe, Claus. 1985. "The new social movements: challenging the boundaries of institutional politics." Social Research 52:817–68.

Okie, Susan. 1988. "AIDS coalition targets FDA for demonstration." The Washington Post, October 11:A4.

Omi, Michael, and Howard Winant. 1986. Racial Formation in the United States. New York: Routledge and Kegan Paul.

Plummer, Ken. 1988. "Organizing AIDS." In Peter Agleton and Hilary Homans, (eds.), Social Aspects of AIDS. London: The Falmer Press.

Shilts, Randy. 1988. And the Band Played On: Politics, People and the AIDS Epidemic. New York: Penguin Books.

Smelser, Neil. 1963. Theory of Collective Behavior. New York: The Free Press.

Sontag, Susan. 1988. "AIDS and its metaphors." New York Review of Books, October 27:89–99.

Tilly, Charles. 1978. From Mobilization to Revolution. Reading, MA: Addison-Wesley.

Touraine, Alain. 1985. "An introduction to the study of social movements." Social Research 52:749–87.

Treichler, Paula A. 1987. "AIDS, homophobia, and biomedical discourse: an epidemic of signification." Pp. 31–70 in Douglas Crimp (ed.), AIDS: Cultural Analysis/Cultural Criticism. Cambridge, MA: MIT Press.

Tuller, David. 1988. "AIDS protesters showing signs of movement's new militancy." San Francisco Chronicle, October 27:A4.

U.S. News and World Report. 1989. "The artists' diagnosis." March 27:62–70.

Watney, Simon. 1987. Policing Desire: Pornography, AIDS and the Media. Minneopolis, MN: University of Minnesota Press.

CHAPTER 8

Dynamics of Black Mobilization against AIDS in New York City

Ernest Quimby and Samuel R. Friedman

Black persons' relationships to the threat of AIDS vary widely. Those who are gay men, intravenous (IV) drug users, or sexual partners of IV drug users are directly at risk. Other blacks not in these categories may be at much lower risk. Nevertheless, blacks and Latinos are disproportionately likely to get AIDS (Bakeman, Lumb, and Smith 1986, Centers for Disease Control, personal communication 1988; Friedman et al. 1987b, Friedman et al. in press, Morbidity and Mortality Weekly Report [MMWR] 1986, 1988; Rogers and Williams 1987; Selik, Castro, and Pappaioanou 1988). In spite of this, African-American groups and communities have been slow to mobilize to reduce risks, affect political and budgetary decisionmaking, or organize volunteer services for the sick.

Common models of intervention against AIDS emphasize education as the way to reduce risk. The role and potential of community mobilization as a form of intervention is given less importance (Bayer 1988, Osborn 1988). Tilly (1978:69) defines mobilization as "the process by which a group goes from being a passive collection of individuals to an active participant in public life." Such participation by both white and black gays against AIDS has helped accomplish a wide variety of goals, ranging from education and dialogue, to support for new, lower risk behaviors, to care for the ill, to community defense against threatening public policies dealing with AIDS (Altman 1986, Patton 1985; Stall, Coates, and Hoff 1988).

Research shows that community initiatives do not necessarily get implemented by the communities that most need them (J. Friedman 1973, 1977), and it is a truism in social movement literature that the most oppressed people often are not the ones who mobilize to confront their problems. This said, however, the task of specifying the obstacles to minority mobilization around AIDS remains. In this paper we pursue this task for such mobilization in New York City. We hope to develop a deeper understanding of how social processes and structures affect responses to group problems, and suggest possible strategies for strengthening minority efforts against AIDS.

Although blacks and Latinos are overrepresented among people with AIDS, public impressions and most scientific reports about AIDS issues generally come from non-blacks. Insights from black experience thus easily can be ignored and omitted from this knowledge and understanding. In particular, analyses by non-blacks may underestimate the extent to which black organizational reactions to AIDS develop out of an contribute to an on-going history of struggle for survival and development. This paper is authored by an African-American and a white investigator, each of whom has participated (as organizer, presenter, researcher and activist) in AIDS-related activities. It draws on data gathered in 1987–88, primarily in New York City, but also in Atlanta, Boston, Philadelphia, New Jersey, and Washington, DC.

Material was obtained from conference proceedings, formal interviews, informal discussions, participation in meetings and events, transcripts of public events, media reports, scientific reports, legal documents, and educational and training sessions. Sources include diverse community leaders; clients, members, and leaders/staff from organizations concerned with AIDS, drug abuse, civil and legal rights, gay rights, and black politics; and representatives of the media and business. To protect anonymity and confidentiality, we generally have not used people's names in this paper. All undocumented quotations and references are personal communications to the authors. In what follows, we describe the impact of the AIDS epidemic on African Americans and Latinos, detail black mobilization efforts in New York City, and discuss the obstacles these efforts faced. We close by drawing out implications of our findings for understanding how mobilization occurs.

AIDS in Minority Populations

AIDS case data show a disproportionate number of blacks and Latinos with AIDS. Table 8.1 gives the racial distribution of AIDS cases for the United States by categories of risk behaviors. While blacks and Latinos constitute only about 20 percent of the U.S. population, they are 41 percent of all AIDS cases, 76 percent of pediatric AIDS cases, 80 percent of cases among intravenous (IV) drug users without male/male sexual contact, and [69] percent of heterosexual transmission cases. Among homosexual and bisexual males with AIDS who do not report IV drug use, 26 percent are black or Latino, as are 39 percent of homosexual and bisexual males who report IV drug histories. Among women with AIDS, 71 percent are black or Latino (Centers for Disease Control, personal communication 1988). New York City data, seen in Table 8.2, show that blacks and Latinos are overrepresented in city AIDS cases due to IV drug use or heterosexual transmission, although not for male/male sexual transmission.

These data probably understate the extent of the racial disparities among AIDS cases. For example, many IV drug users die of "non-AIDS" HIV-related diseases before developing the specific opportunistic infections that define AIDS. A number of studies (Des Jarlais, Friedman and Hopkins 1985; Des Jarlais, Friedman and Stoneburner 1988; Slim et al. 1988; Ruggeri, Sathe, and Kapila 1988; Klein et al. 1988, Selwyn et al. 1988, Stoneburner et al. 1988a, Stoneburner et al. 1988b, Galli et al. 1988) have indicated that among IV drug users many "non-AIDS" infections such as bacterial pneumonias, endocarditis, and tuberculosis are based on HIV-induced immunosuppression. Between 1980 and 1986 in New York City, we have estimated that more IV drug users died from diseases resulting from HIV infection than from

Table 8.1.   AIDS Cases by Race (within Each Risk Category), United States, December 12, 1988

	Race				Total
Risk	Black	White	Hispanic	Other	Cases
Adult Cases					
Male/Male Sex	16%	73%	10%	1%	49,023
IV Drug Use	50	20	30	0	15,690
IV Drug Use and Male/Male Sex	25	60	14	0	5,717
Heterosexual Cases[a]	46	30	23	1	2,249
Total adult cases[b]	26	58	15	1	79,247
Children under 13 years of age					
Parent with/at risk of AIDS	61	15	24	0	1,002
Other pediatric cases[b]	26	54	18	1	289
Total pediatric cases	53	24	23	1	1,291
Total	26	58	15	1	80,361[c]

Notes:

a. CDC data have been adjusted to remove 1,229 cases without other identified risk who are classified as heterosexual transmission cases because they were born in countries in which heterosexual transmission is believed to play a major role (although precise means of transmission have not been fully defined). In performing this calculation, the authors assumed that all these 1,229 cases were among blacks—since they are overwhelmingly Haitian, and the major other countries in which heterosexual transmission occurs on a large scale are in sub-Saharan Africa.

b. These include hemophilia/coagulation disorder, transfusion/blood components, and undetermined cases.

c. In addition, 177 cases had been reported whose race was unknown.

Source:

Personal communication, Centers for Disease Control.

Table 8.2.   New York City Adult AIDS Case Surveillance Data Percent within each Risk and Gender by Race October 12, 1988

	Race			
Males	White	Black	Latino	Total Number All races[a]
Sex with male	63%	19%	17%	8,705
IV drug use	15	43	41	4,445
IV drug use & sex with male	34	37	29	728
Total	44	29	25	14,710
	(6530)	(4322)	(3713)	

	Race			
Females	White	Black	Latino	Total Number All races[a]
Sex with male	13%	39%	47%	478
IV drug use	14	54	31	1,206
Total	15	52	33	2,031
	(298)	(1058)	(644)	
N.Y.C. Population 1980 (U.S. Census)	52%	24%	20%	

Note:

a. Total includes Native Americans, Asians, Pacific Islanders, and undetermined.

diagnosed AIDS (Stoneburner et al. 1988b). In this same period, blacks accounted for 65 percent of the deaths from bacterial pneumonia, endocarditis, and tuberculosis and 45 percent of the AIDS deaths; Latinos for 19 percent and 34 percent respectively; and whites for 10 percent and 13 percent (Friedman et al. in press). Although these differences await fuller epidemiologic analysis, it appears that deaths from HIV-associated diseases are even more racially disproportionate than AIDS statistics indicate.

Early Black Response to AIDS

In the epidemic's early days, media reports that AIDS was a disease of white gay men reduced the attention blacks paid to it. In general, blacks denied AIDS was a problem that affected them and blamed white gay men for it. According to Gil Gerald (personal communication, April 6, 1988), the National AIDS Network's former director of minority affairs, during this early period there was a dominant heterosexual view that "we don't have gays in our community," an attitude of some black gay men that "you only get AIDS if you sleep with white men," and a belief held by some other black gays that "only whites who slept with whites got AIDS."

By 1985, however, some leaders of the minority gay and lesbian community began to challenge this denial, and helped set up some of the first minority-focused AIDS events. A primarily gay Third World AIDS Advisory Task Force, with the assistance of the city health department and the University of California, organized a western regional conference on AIDS in Racial and Ethnic Minority Communities in April 1986, in San Francisco. Also in 1986, the National Coalition of Black Lesbians and Gays held a conference in Washington, DC.

Differences among national African American groups in their response to AIDS are related to their broader goals and ideologies. The Southern Christian Leadership Conference (SCLC), the Urban League, and the National Association for the Advancement of Colored People (NAACP), long connected to civil rights activities, tend to see AIDS in the context of the broader problems of poverty, drug addiction, inadequate education, and unemployment. Their approaches tend to be non-confrontational and assimilationist. SCLC and the Urban League have issued reports and prepared pamphlets on AIDS and blacks. In May 1986, SCLC held a national conference on AIDS and blacks. In New York, the center of the black AIDS epidemic in America, Urban League activity appears to be mainly limited to distribution of its AIDS report, "AIDS in the Black Community" (New York Urban League Black Papers, n.d.). The NAACP, so far, has not highlighted the epidemic. Many black elected political leaders ignore AIDS and instead focus on matters related to housing, schooling, jobs, and access to health care.

African-Americans Against AIDS, a more single-issue organization whose members are health professionals, conceptualize issues in terms of racial oppression. Nationalists and militant AIDS and health activists criticize the efforts of the established civil rights groups and politicians for being too tied to governmental and corporate structures. Several leading AIDS educators and health workers, such as Dr. Janet Mitchell of Harlem Hospital and Suki Ports, former director of the New York City-based Minority Task Force on AIDS, talk of by-passing traditional leaders because of their failure to aggressively acknowledge and attack the AIDS problem among blacks. They challenge these "establishment" leaders to get more involved in the growing war.

Some respondents argued that public response to race-related HIV issues was delayed because health officials did not highlight them until 1986, even though the Centers for Disease Control (CDC) data showed associations between race and AIDS as early as 1983. At the same time, some AIDS organizations and civil rights groups such as the Brooklyn-based Haitian Coalition on AIDS had earlier criticized the CDC and the media for emphasizing the disease's connection to gays and Haitians. They argued that labeling and singling out such "risk groups" led to discrimination.

One unintended consequence of this early critique might have been to make public health officials reluctant to focus on AIDS and racial minorities. Indeed, minority organizations have been faced with a similar dilemma. Given the disproportionate numbers of blacks and Latinos among AIDS cases, highlighting the connection risks increasing racial discrimination, but ignoring it could slow risk reduction among these groups.

In August 1987, CDC sponsored and organized a national conference on AIDS in minority communities. Its stated aim was to gather researchers and activists in order to collectively identify AIDS-related issues and problem-solving strategies. Despite some vocal opposition to the conference's structure and agenda, the meeting served as an opportunity for blacks and Latinos to network. It also gave minority AIDS issues prominent national and local media attention. This conference sparked a considerable effort by black organizations in New York City to mobilize the black community against AIDS. Barriers to its success are the focus of the rest of this paper.

Minority Attempts to Mobilize Against AIDS

By 1987, some black medical and substance abuse personnel who had not been activists on these issues became more interested and involved. Emerging CDC evidence of black heterosexual transmission and pediatric AIDS cases heightened this concern and made continued avoidance difficult. Inaction by public officials was called "genocidal" and "racist" by many respondents whom we interviewed in 1987 and 1988, particularly health educators and drug abuse treatment personnel. Church and political leaders initially did not use such severe terms.

At that time, various lay and professional groups began to hold meetings to inform, strategize, and secure financial resources. To some extent, however, they were reactions to the initiatives, requests, or funding opportunities presented by non-black institutions. In the months after the August 1987 CDC Atlanta conference, many meetings were held in New York City to try to mobilize a black response (see Table 8.3). This attempted mobilization is most evident in the involvement of churches, politicians, and drug treatment personnel in these efforts.

Local black churches began to openly address AIDS in late 1987. On October 7, a prominent Brooklyn civil rights activist, Rev. Herbert Daughtry, sponsored a forum, "AIDS and the African-American Community," at his House of the Lord Church. Although only about 25 people turned out, they expressed much interest and the forum illustrated growing clergy and lay concern. Three months later, when Brooklyn's prestigious Concord Baptist Church held the first major church-sponsored AIDS conference, over 200 people, mainly African-American, attended. Both events concentrated on basic AIDS education.

Manhattan Borough President David Dinkens was perhaps the earliest and most active black politician to stress that AIDS is also a black people's problem. His office and numerous city-wide labor, health, and civic organizations sponsored and organized a well-attended "Community Dialogue on AIDS" on October 31, 1987, in Harlem. Particular efforts were made to address youth, the hearing-impaired, local residents, and non-profesionals. Its content was both educational and motivational. New York Congressman Charles Rangel, who chairs the House Select Committee on Narcotic Abuse and Control, convened hearings on drugs and AIDS (September 1987) and held a hearing in Harlem on pediatric AIDS (July 1987). He also co-sponsored AIDS health care legislation and opposed needle exchanges in which users can trade in used syringes for sterile ones. New York State Assemblyperson Ed Towns held a community forum in Brooklyn (October 1987). Since 1987, central Brooklyn assemblypersons Roger Green, chair of the Caucus of new York State Elected Black and Latin Political Officials, and Al Vann, of Bedford-Stuyvesant, have made personal pleas for more effective policies aimed at reducing drug abuse, improving the plight of "boarder babies," and establishing better foster care services both generally and as they relate to AIDS.

Vann's political organization in central Brooklyn sponsored a standing-room only conference on January 29, 1988, at Interfaith Medical Center's Brooklyn Jewish Hospital on "AIDS and the Black Community." New York City Health Commissioner Dr. Stephen Joseph said at that conference that, unlike a year ago, denial by blacks had been replaced with interest and actions to eliminate the epidemic, adding that now he couldn't keep up with the many AIDS meetings and conferences in the black community.

These efforts aside, most elected black political officials have not taken on AIDS as a health issue. No elected political leader attended the Brooklyn AIDS Task Force's conference, and only Dinkens prepared testimony for Public Health Hearings of the New York State Governor's Advisory Committee for Black Affairs.

Drug abuse professionals became involved in AIDS issues before the CDC conference in 1987. The Association for Drug Abuse Prevention and Treatment, Inc. (ADAPT) is a Brooklyn-based voluntary group of former addicts and professional substance abuse workers. Originally formed in the pre-AIDS era, it had become inactive. In 1985, it was revived to deal with AIDS-related issues, and in 1986 an Hispanic woman assumed its leadership. Many other leading members of ADAPT are black ex-users or treatment personnel. The organization has mobilized volunteer efforts to educate IV drug users on how to decontaminate injection equipment; has taken bottles

Table 8.3.   Selected Meetings and Conferences on Minorities and AIDS

National Events

Sponsor	Purpose or Title	Place and Date
Third World Advisory Task Force	"AIDS in Racial and Ethnic Minority Communities"	San Francisco, April 1986
National Coalition of Black Lesbians and Gays	Publicize AIDS impact on minorities	Washington DC, 1986
Southern Christian Leadership Conference (SCLC)	Publicize and discuss AIDS and blacks	Atlanta, GA, May 1986
SCLC	"AIDS and the Black Community"	Savannah, GA, May 1987
SCLC	National conference on AIDS and the black community	Washington DC, May 1987
Centers for Disease Control (CDC)	"AIDS and Minorities"	Atlanta, GA, August 1987
CDC	Preventing HIV infection and AIDS among U.S. minorities	Washington DC, August 1988

New York City Events

Sponsor	Purpose or Title	Place and Date
Congressman Charles Rangel	Hearings on pediatric AIDS in Harlem	New York City, July 1987
Various women's groups (especially National Women's Health Network)	Women and AIDS	New York City, September 1987
NY State Governor's Advisory Committee on Health	Public hearing on health issues of blacks	Brooklyn, October 1987
National Institute on Drug Abuse Technical Review	"Minority Issues Regarding intravenous Drug Abuse and AIDS"	Brooklyn (Addiction Research and Treatment Co.), October 1987
House of the Lord Church	"AIDS and the African-American Community	Brooklyn, October 1987
Minority Women in Crisis; NY State Division for Women; Minority Task Force on AIDS; Women's Center of John Jay College	AIDS and minority women	New York City, October 1987
Brooklyn AIDS Task Force	Community conference	Brooklyn, October 1987
Assemblyman Ed Towns	Community forum	Brooklyn, October 1987
Manhattan Borough President's Office	"Community Dialogue on AIDS"	Manhattan, October 1987
Concord Baptist Church	Forum on AIDS and blacks	Brooklyn, January 1988
ACT UP; ADAPT	Demonstrations at City Hall and at NY State Office Building (in Harlem)	Manhattan, April 1988

of bleach, condoms, and educational messages into the "shooting galleries," often in
abandoned buildings, where users rent injection equipment and get high; and has been
a major advocate of needle exchanges.

Addiction Research and Treatment Corporation (ARTC) is a primarily black
methadone maintenance treatment center with main offices in Brooklyn and clinics in
Brooklyn and Manhattan. In 1986, ARTC expanded its AIDS-related research, education, counseling, and prevention. It was the site of a 1987 National Institute on
Drug Abuse (NIDA) Technical Review of AIDS among minorities, which was an important indicator of NIDA's growing awareness of the issue. ARTC's president, Dr.
Beny Primm, a member of the President's Commission on HIV Infection, has been
particularly critical of the research establishment's lack of minority researchers.

A "Women and AIDS" conference organized by the National Women's Health
Network took place on September 26, 1987, at St. Peter's Church in Manhattan. Black
participants whom we interviewed thought that while the event was often emotionally
moving, the composition of speakers and the concerns expressed were "too white." It
seemed to illustrate the predicament of politically voiceless women depending on others who were more organized, better connected, and financially endowed. On October
16, a conference exclusively on "AIDS and Minority Women" co-sponsored by a working alliance of women's groups, Women in Crisis, the New York State Division for
Women, the Minority Task Force on AIDS, the Hispanic AIDS Forum, and the AIDS
Institute, was held at John Jay College of Criminal Justice in New York City. Its tone
and content were multicultural, as was the list of speakers. Outreach workers told us
that they felt a sense of empowerment both from what was said and by seeing numerous women of color as potential role models.

Conflicts and Problems in Black Mobilization

Attempts at mobilization often provoke strategic dilemmas and conflicts that illuminate social schisms among potential participants, all of which can divide movement.
Here, we present a few examples of such conflicts in New York City that have inter-
fered with AIDS mobilization in the black community.

Joint action between anti-establishment gays and blacks around AIDS could
strengthen efforts to combat the epidemic. The possibility of such cooperation was exemplified during the meeting at Brooklyn Jewish Hospital sponsored by Assemblyperson Vann. Members of ACT UP, a white AIDS activist group, were extremely critical
of perceived racial discrimination concerning limited minority access to experimental
drugs and protocols other than AZT. Although Vann did not support these critiques,
many black audience members applauded them.

When gay activist groups ACT UP, ACT NOW, and GRAN FURY held "Spring
AIDS Action '88," "nine days of nationwide AIDS related actions and protests," no
black politicians endorsed them or took part. However, ADAPT did take part, and
ACT UP and ADAPT held joint demonstrations at City Hall, agitating for free dis-
tribution of sterile needles for drug addicts, and held a demonstration at the New York
State Office Building in Harlem the next day.

One emerging obstacle to grassroots cooperation between gay and minority activists is a disagreement over how to approach questions of HIV transmission epidemiology. Some black and white gay spokespersons in New York City agencies such as the Commission on Human Rights and the Health Department see the growing public and professional attention to AIDS among IV drug users as a threat to their interests. Several black gay respondents argued that there is a growing official and media emphasis on transmission from intravenous drug users (IVDUs) to heterosexuals that downplays risks to black gays and bisexuals. One respondent criticized "buying into a myth alleging that responding to AIDS is responding to intravenous drug use." He added that politicians and the media see IVDU transmission as a safer and "far more socially acceptable" issue than either bisexuality or homosexuality. And a black gay AIDS educator called the association of IVDU and HIV a "two-edged problem": "It denies the needs and responses of those who have AIDS and who may be gay or bisexual. It slows down prevention efforts or adds to actions which may be misdirected."

One black gay respondent said that well-placed black health professionals incorrectly and dangerously claim "the gay community has taken care of the gay HIV issue." He added that the focus on AIDS in women and children is the main source of concern about AIDS among IV drug users:

> There is no empathy for intravenous drug users themselves. . . . Intravenous drug addicts are seen as "criminals," but their partners are viewed as "victims." So they and only they deserve compassion and care. There is no corresponding empathy for drug users. But underlying social and economic conditions that lead to and keep people in harmful or risky lifestyles are ignored. These conditions include lack of opportunities, inadequate education, IVDU support systems, and motivation to not have to look at drugs as a way of dealing with life.

To the extent that AIDS activity in the black community is initiated by groups like ADAPT that are involved with IV drug users' issues, this emerging competition between IV-drug-user and gay-focused needs could disrupt efforts at cooperation.

The issue of needle exchanges for IV drug users also has sparked considerable controversy, particularly after the New York State Department of Health announced its approval in early 1988 of a small-scale experimental needle exchange proposed by the N.Y.C. Department of Health. Among the ardent critics were Dr. Lorraine Hale, a Harlem-based AIDS/substance abuse service provider, and Congressman Charles Rangel. Hale, Rangel, Dr. Beny Primm, officials of most black churches, and many black physicians have charged that supplying sterile needles encourages and endorses IV drug use and that it will be substituted for actual rehabilitation and opening up of more drug treatment slots. Minority opponents of needle exchanges have been extremely visible on this issue, and indeed many have tried to mobilize opposition to needle exchanges more forcefully than they have acted in other AIDS-related matters.

ADAPT and many black and Latino drug users support needle exchanges. They argue that drug addicts are responding reasonably to information about sharing and cleaning needles. Yolanda Serrano, ADAPT's executive director, notes that needle distribution, coupled with drug treatment and counseling, works in other countries and appears to have helped slow the spread of AIDS.[1] The controversy over the needle exchange shows the extent to which actions that might slow HIV transmission have been hindered by hostility to drug users. In San Francisco, where there is less polarization between city government and blacks, most black spokespersons have supported a proposed needle exchange.

LIMITED MOBILIZATION

The efforts described above led to little "mobilization" around AIDS by the black population of New York City. Considerable networking did occur among organizational elites, and hundreds of black persons attended conferences that informed them about AIDS and how it is transmitted. Relatively little mobilization, however, took place. Overwhelmingly what we observed is the lack of connection between those who held the public meetings, and indeed even those who attended, and the poor and working class blacks most at risk of HIV infection. There are two main strands of evidence for this conclusion.

First, although a few new projects did develop that involved adolescents in creating and distributing videos or posters, and volunteers did outreach in high drug-use areas, non-gay black neighborhood groups have not formed to conduct local AIDS education, to provide pressure and support for risk reduction, or to provide support services for infected or ill persons. Similarly, new AIDS activist groups (akin to ACT UP) did not form in minority communities, and ADAPT did not gain much additional strength through these meetings. Further, already existing groups of lower or working class blacks have not gotten significantly involved in AIDS issues. This is probably most obvious in the continued lack of involvement by storefront churches.

Second, the attendance at the pubic meetings that did occur was primarily middle class. This has also been a problem for white gay AIDS organizations, but the greater extent to which HIV infection among blacks affects working class or poor persons makes middle class meetings even less effective for black communities. Persons who spoke from the floor, or with whom we spoke privately at the meetings and conferences we attended, were almost all college graduates or currently taking college courses. Exceptions were the ex-addict AIDS outreach workers employed by ADAPT or by Narcotic and Drug Research, Inc. and people at the small meeting held at House of the Lord Church in October 1987.

Discussion

The failure of the considerable effort by sincerely concerned persons to spark black mobilization around AIDS issues in New York City is intriguing. Here, we can only speculate about factors that may have retarded mobilization, and suggest some implications for the AIDS epidemic and the sociological analysis of community and social movements.

Churches have often taken a major role in mobilizing black communities, as was the case in the civil rights movement (Morris 1984). Many black churches espouse a moralistic version of Christianity which condemns the behaviors, such as gay male sex, intravenous drug use, and multiple partner heterosexual sex, that transmit HIV. Indeed, working class black churches, for whose parishioners intravenous drug use and heterosexual transmission are most relevant, may be most intolerant of and moralistic toward these risk activities. In addition, black churches—especially working class ones—usually have low budgets and thus are vulnerable to fears that taking controversial stands could cause a decline in member contributions, reducing funds for church operation and programs, imperiling the ability of the church to survive.

Black political officials face a similar situation. Many of their constituents have strong moral views opposed to homosexuality and drug use. Many black New Yorkers resent the effects of widespread drug use on their lives—as is reflected in the sign that was commonly posted on lampposts in Harlem: "When will all the junkies die so the rest of us can go on living?" Many middle class black interviewees saw the drug issue as a reflection of an inadequacy of the black community to confront "improper" behavior by community members, allowing conduct sure to increase the stigma and racism blacks experience.

AIDS is a high-risk political issue. It is not surprising that many politicians shy away from it. A full black community mobilization against AIDS would involved organizing and activating large numbers of lower income and working class people, a constituency that could turn against black officials who have been elected with the support of middle class black voters. The gay organizations and AIDS groups have not regularly and publicly attacked racism and other black concerns may have further distanced AIDS from the agendas of black political leaders.

Drug treatment programs specialize in getting users to quit using drugs. Efforts aimed at promoting safer ways to inject drugs seem to betray their primary goal. Furthermore, treatment programs face a shortage of staff and facilities relative to demand. And one recurrent problem is difficulty in finding sites where neighbors will allow a program to operate. AIDS brings more stigma to users and treatment programs, making it even harder to get neighborhood forbearance. Hence, in addition to the psychological dynamics that lead treatment staff to deny the impact of AIDS, tactical considerations lead many programs to take a low profile.

The black population of New York City came into the AIDS era with many divisions. Blacks may seem unified on the basis of a similar history of oppression and struggles. Diversity among blacks, however, has led to different experiences with white domination and the struggle against it. These differences have created varying interpretations of events, diverse forms of organization, and different traditions of mobilization. Thus, to talk of "the" black community in New York City can be as misleading as to talk about "the" gay community. It consists of African-Americans, documented and undocumented Caribbean immigrants, Caribbean-Americans, Africans, Muslims, Jews, Christians, and Ratafarians, men and women, heterosexuals, gays, lesbians, and bisexuals, different classes, nationalists, socialists, Democrats and Republicans, and so on.

Efforts at health education are complicated by hostility, cultural diversity, minimal resources, and limited power. Diversity of interests and concerns means that the relatively small number of persons involved in public affairs is torn among the wide variety of issues that beset an already-embattled population. AIDS has to compete for the attention and time of activists, would-be activists, and the public.

Although the black civil rights movements of the 1960s won many changes in laws, government structure, and social and corporate policies (Piven and Cloward 1977), it did not leave behind the kinds of institutions, subcultures, and activists that white gays managed to maintain (Bloom 1987, Blumberg 1984, Adam 1987, Shilts 1987, Altman 1986, Friedman et al. 1987a, Patton 1985, Geschwender 1978). This gay "movement [fleet] in being" (Mahan 1957 [1890]) was an important source of active, trained, and at least somewhat organized personnel (Friedman 1982, 1985) that could be mobilized against AIDS. On the other hand, when it became clear that AIDS was disproportionately affecting blacks, the black population and its activists had few existing resources to call upon, quite unlike those that have been available in the gay community. And to the extent such resources do exist in the black community—such as churches, elected officials, and drug treatment programs—they face ideological and practical difficulties in confronting AIDS.

Attempts to mobilize people around a public health issue such as AIDS may be decisively affected by structures of power and influence among the population in question. In particular, the New York City efforts were mounted by the leaders of middle class churches, professional drug treatment personnel, political leaders, and professional staff in government health and substance abuse agencies. Although they were able to attract hundreds of black people to community meetings, most of these people were middle class. The people most at risk, blacks who are or who interact with IV drug users, or who are gay, did not get involved. This pattern of elite activists failing to mobilize non-elites is common in politics and in social movements (Friedman 1984/1985).

Since such top-down efforts have not succeeded in mobilizing the black population against AIDS, what should be done? We suggest attempts to mobilize and empower persons at risk and people in their neighborhoods. We have been involved in attempts to organize IV drug users around risk reduction, support for the sick, and other issues (Friedman and Casriel 1988) and have shown that it is possible to hold weekly meetings with IV drug-using prostitutes in one Latino community, although it is still too soon to know if these efforts lead either to sustained risk reduction or to independent mobilization and empowerment (Friedman et al. 1989). In addition, innovative community action to mobilize volunteers and hire people to provide education and support services for the sick should be attempted. These efforts are likely to be an effective way not only to educate but to involve black sex partners of IV drug users and black gays. While ostensibly public health measures, they will be strengthened by understanding that they also are political ones. The outcomes will be shaped by how such attempts at mobilization impact and draw on existing black agendas, institutions, and cultures.

Note

1. Serrano's claim is supported by research by Buning et al. 1988, van den Hoek et al. 1988, Alldritt et al. 1988, Wolk et al. 1988, Ljungberg et al. 1988, Fuchs et al. 1988. Evaluation data

on the first needle exchange in North America, in Tacoma, Washington, are presented in Hagan et al. 1989 and in Des Jarlais et al. 1989.

References

Adam, Barry D. 1987. The Rise of a Gay and Lesbian Movement. Boston, MA: Twayne.

Alldritt L., K. Dolan, M. Donoghoe, and G.V. Stimson. 1988. "HIV and the injecting drug user: clients of syringe exchange schemes in England and Scotland." Paper presented at the IV International Conference on AIDS, Stockholm, June 12–16. Abstract 8511.

Altman, Dennis. 1986. AIDS in the Mind of America. Garden City, NY: Doubleday.

Bakeman R., J.R. Lumb, and D.W. Smith. 1986. "AIDS Statistics and the risk for minorities." AIDS Research 2:249–52.

Bayer, Ronald. 1988. "AIDS and the ethics of public health challenges posed by a maturing epidemic." AIDS 2, supplement:S217–22.

Bloom, Jack M. 1987. Class, Race, and the Civil Rights Movement. Bloomington, IN: Indiana University Press.

Blumberg, Rhoda Lois. 1984. Civil Rights: The 1960s Freedom Struggle. Boston, MA: Twayne.

Buning E.C., C. Hartgers, A.D. Verster, G.W. van Santen, and R.A. Coutinho. 1988. "The evaluation of the needle/syringe exchange in Amsterdam." Paper presented at the IV International Conference on AIDS, Stockholm, June 12–16. Abstract 8513.

Des Jarlais, D.C., S.R. Friedman, and W. Hopkins. 1985. "Risk reduction for the acquired immunodeficiency syndrome among intravenous drug users." Annals of Internal Medicine 103:755–59.

Des Jarlais, D.C., S.R. Friedman, and R.L. Stoneburner. 1988. "HIV infection and intravenous drug use." Reviews of Infectious Diseases 10:151–58.

Des Jarlais, D.C., H. Hagan, D. Purchase, T. Reid, and S.R. Friedman. 1989. "Safer injection among participants in the first North American syringe exchange program." Paper presented at the Fifth International Conference on AIDS, Montreal.

Friedman, Judith J. 1973. "Structural constraints on community action." Social Problems 21:230–45.

———. 1977. "Community action on water pollution." Human Ecology 5:329–53.

Friedman, Samuel R. 1982. Teamster Rank and File. New York: Columbia University Press.

———. 1984/1985. "Mass organizations and sects in the American student movement and its aftermath." Humboldt Journal of Social Relations 12:1–24.

———. 1985. "Worker opposition movements." Research in Social Movements, Conflicts and Change 8:133–70.

Friedman, Samuel R. and Cathy Casriel. 1988. "Drug users' organizations and AIDS policy." AIDS and Public Policy 3:30–36.

Freidman, Sameul R., Don C. Des Jarlais, Jo L. Sotheran, Jonathan Garber, Henry Cohen, and Donald Smith. 1987a. "AIDS and self-organization among intravenous drug users." International Journal of the Addictions 22:201–19.

Friedman Samuel R., Jo L. Sotheran, Abu Abdul-Quader, Beny J. Primm, Don C. Des Jarlais, Paula Kleinman, Conrad Mauge, Douglas S. Goldsmith, Wafaa El-Sadr, and Robert Maslansky. 1987b. "The AIDS epidemic among blacks and Hispanics." The Milbank Quarterly 65, supplement 2:455–99.

Friedman, Samuel R., Yolanda Serrano, Luis Torres, Meryl Sufian, Pat Nelson, and Frank Tardalo. 1989. "Organizing intravenous drug users against AIDS." Paper presented at the Fifth International Conference on AIDS, Montreal, June.

Friedman S.R., E. Quimby, M. Sufian, A. Abdul-Quader, and D.C. 1988. In Press. "Racial aspects of the AIDS epidemic." California Sociologist 11:55–68.

Fuchs, Dietmar, B. Unterweger, H. Hinterhuber, M.P. Dierich, S.H. Weiss, H. Wachter et al. 1988. "Successful preventive measures in a community of IV drug addicts." Paper presented at the IV International Conference on AIDS, Stockholm, June 12–16. Abstract 8524.

Galli M., M. Carito, V. Cruccu, L. Zampini, D. Ciacci, A. Villa, S. Pacini, G. Zaihi, L. Corsi, G. Codini, and A. Saracco. 1988. "Causes of death in I.V. dug abusers (IVDAs)." Paper presented at the IV International Conference on AIDS, Stockholm, June 12–16.

Geschwender, James A. 1978. Racial Stratification in America. Dubuque, IA: William G. Brown.

Hagan, Holly, D.C. Des Jarlais, D. Purchase, T. Reid, and S.R. Friedman. 1989. "Drug use trends among participants in the Tacoma syringe exchange." Paper presented at the Fifth International Conference on AIDS, Montreal, June.

Klein R.S., P. Selwyn, D. Maude, C. Pollard, and G. Schiffman. 1988. "Response to pneumococcal vaccine (PV) among HIV infected drug users (IVDU) and heterosexual patners (SP) of persons with AIDS." Paper presented at the IV International Conference on AIDS, Stockholm, June 12–16.

Ljungberg B., B. Andersson, B. Christensson, M. Hugo-Persson, K. Tunving, and B. Ursing. 1988. "Distribution of sterile equipment to IV drug abusers as part of an HIV prevention program." Paper presented at the IV International Conference on AIDS, Stockholm, June 12–16. Abstract 8514.

Mahan, Alfred Thayer. [1890]. The Influence of Seapower upon History. New York: Hill and Wang. 1957.

Morbidity and Mortality Weekly Report. 1986. "Acquired immunodeficiency syndrome (AIDS) among blacks and Hispanics—United States." MMWR 35:655–66.

———. 1988. Reports on Selected Racial/Ethnic Groups. October 24.

Morris, Alden. 1984. The Origins of the Civil Rights Movement. New York: Free Press.

Osborn, June E. 1988. "AIDS prevention: issues and strategies." AIDS 2, supplement:S229–35.

Patton, Cindy. 1985. Sex and Germs: The Politics of AIDS. Boston, MA: South End Press.

Piven, Frances Fox and Richard A. Cloward. 1977. Poor People's Movements. New York: Vintage Books.

Rockwell, Richard C. 1988. "Social impacts of the AIDS epidemic." AIDS 2, supplement: S223–28.

Rogers M.F. and W.W. Williams. 1987. "AIDS in blacks and Hispanics: implications for prevention." Issues in Sciences and Technology (Spring):89–94.

Ruggeri P., S.S. Sathe, and R. Kapila. 1988. "Changing patterns of infectious endocarditis (IE) in parenteral drug abusers (PDA) with human immunodeficiency virus (HIV) infections." Paper presented at the IV International Conference on AIDS, Stockholm, June 12–16.

Selik R.M., K.G. Castro, and M. Pappaioanou. 1988. "Racial/ethnic differences in the risk of AIDS in the United States." American Journal of Public Health 79:1539-45.

Selwyn P.A., A.R. Feingold, D. Hartel, E.E. Schoenbaum, M.H. Alderman, R.S. Klein, and G.H. Friedland. 1988. "Increased risk of bacterial pneumonia in HIV-infected intravenous drug users without AIDS.: AIDS 2:267–72.

Shilts, Randy. 1987. And the Band Played On: Politics, People, and the AIDS Epidemic. New York: St. Martin's Press.

Slim, J., J. Boghossian, G. Perez, and E. Johnson. 1988. "Comparative analysis of endocarditis in HIV(+) and HIV(-) intravenous drug abusers." Paper presented at the IV International Conference on AIDS, Stockholm, June 12–16.

Stall, Ron D., Thomas J. Coates, and Colleen Hoff. 1988. "Behavioral risk reduction for HIV infection among gay and bisexual men." American Psychologist 43:878–85.

Stoneburner R.L., S. Laussucq, D. Benezra, J.L. Sotheran, and D.C. Des Jarlais. 1988a. "Increasing pneumonia mortality in NYC, 1980–1986: evidence for a larger spectrum of HIV-related disease in intravenous drug users." Paper presented at the IV International Conference on AIDS, Stockholm, June 12–16.

Stoneburner, R.L., D.C. Des Jarlais, D. Benezra, L. Gorelkin, J.L. Sotheran, S.R. Friedman, S. Schultz, M. Marmor, D. Mildvan, and R. Maslansky. 1988b. "A larger spectrum of severe HIV-related disease in intravenous drug users in New York City." Science 242:916–19.

Tilly, Charles. 1978. From Mobilization to Revolution. Reading: Addison-Wesley.

Van den Hoek, Johanna A.R., H.J.A. von Haastrecht, J. Goudsmit, and R.A. Coutinho. 1988. "Influence of HIV-AB testing on the risk behaviour of IV drug users in Amsterdam." Paper presented at the IV International Conference on AIDS, Stockholm, June 12–16.

Wolk, W.S., A. Wodak, J.J. Guinan, A. Morlet, J. Gold, E. Wilson, and D. Cooper. 1988. "HIV seroprevalence in syringes of intravenous drug users using syringe exchange in Sydney, Australia, 1987." Paper presented at the IV International Conference on AIDS, Stockholm, June 12–16. Abstract 8504.

CHAPTER 9

Racing for the Cure, Walking Women, and Toxic Touring

MAPPING CULTURES OF ACTION WITHIN THE BAY AREA TERRAIN OF BREAST CANCER

Maren Klawiter

> The main function of public spaces is that of rendering visible and collective the questions raised by movements.
>
> Alberto Melucci (1994:189)

Beginning in the second half of the 1980s and gathering momentum in the 1990s, new forms of cancer organizing, activism, and community began to proliferate across the United States. Within a decade, a wide range of networks, projects, organizations, foundations, coalitions, and public events arose that expanded and challenged the way that cancer, and breast cancer in particular, had been publicly framed and institutionally managed. Although this was not the first time that cancer had entered the "universe of discourse" (Bourdieu 1977) and been transformed into an object of political debate and public scrutiny,[1] the cultures of action that mushroomed in the late 1980s and expanded during the 1990s introduced onto the historical landscape a new set of social actors, cultural practices, and political logics. Unlike earlier historical moments in which cancer as a broad category had occupied center stage, this time it was breast cancer that moved to the center, and it was breast cancer survivors and activists who moved it there.[2]

In 1993 the breast cancer movement—or at least one slice of it—arrived on the cover of the *New York Times Magazine (NYT)*. The cover of the August 15 issue featured a self-portrait of the breast cancer activist and artist Matushka with one half of the bodice of her elegant white dress cut away to expose a mastectomy scar where her right breast had been. The cover story, entitled "'You Can't Look Away Anymore': The Anguished Politics of Breast Cancer" (Ferraro 1993), focused on the rapid rise and remarkable success of the National Breast Cancer Coalition (NBCC), a Washington DC-based feminist lobbying organization founded in 1991.[3] In the *NYT* article, the agenda of the breast cancer movement—with NBCC as its symbolic representative—was defined as raising public awareness, increasing the influence of breast cancer survivors, and expanding the federal budget for breast cancer research.

This issue of the *New York Magazine* received four times the usual volume of letters to the editor (Batt 1994). Interestingly enough, it seemed to be the cover photo, as much as the content of the article, that inspired the flurry of letter-writing. The image of Matushka—the public display of her one-breasted body—had struck a powerful chord. The range and intensity of responses to this article and to Matushka's style of embodied activism suggested that widespread support for the general goals of the NBCC might be concealing important differences within the broader terrain of breast cancer activism.

In 1994, I began studying how breast cancer was being publicly reshaped and politicized in the San Francisco Bay Area. But instead of studying the dynamics of change and challenge within national lobbying campaigns, I chose to explore the local terrain of action. In the Bay Area I discovered a multifaceted movement that was in full swing. However, within this arena, the National Breast Cancer Coalition—the force consistently defined by itself and the media as *the* breast cancer movement—was organizationally absent and discursively marginal. What I discovered instead was a dynamic, diverse, and expanding field of local grassroots activity.

This paper contributes to scholarship on the breast cancer movement and to theorizing at the juncture of culture and social movements. Through participant observation[4] I develop thick descriptions, or representations, of three social movement spectacles and analyze them as loci for the production, performance, and circulation of new social actors, cultural practices, and political logics—or what I conceptualize as three different *cultures of action*. I use the concept *culture of action* to emphasize that culture within social movements is publicly produced and performed through an assembly of practices that are enacted, enunciated, emoted, and embodied.[5]

By paying attention to the different ways in which breast cancer is enacted, enunciated, emoted, and embodied, I disaggregate the Bay Area field of breast cancer activism into three different cultures of action. The first, represented by Race for the Cure®, draws upon biomedicine and private industry and emphasizes individual agency, honor, and survival. It connects breast cancer to the display of normative femininities, mobilizes hope and faith in science and medicine, and promotes biomedical research and early detection. The second, represented by the Women & Cancer Walk, draws upon multicultural feminism, the women's health movement, and AIDS activism. It connects breast cancer to other women's cancers, challenges the emphasis on survival and the hegemonic display of heteronormative femininities, emphasizes the effects of institutionalized inequalities, mobilizes anger against the institutions of biomedicine, and promotes social services and treatment activism. The third, represented by the Toxic Tour of the Cancer Industry, draws upon the feminist cancer and environmental justice movements and broadens the focus to include all cancers and environmentally-related illnesses. It represents breast cancer as both the product and source of profits of a global cancer industry, mobilizes outrage against corporate malfeasance and environmental racism, and replaces the emphasis on biomedical research and early detection with demands for corporate regulation and cancer prevention.

In the next two sections I locate my study within the sociological literature on breast cancer activism and within the literature on culture and social movements. I then proceed, in the following three sections, to develop a comparative analysis of the publicly-enacted cultures of the three cancer events discussed above, all of which were held in San Francisco, on an annual basis, during the mid-1990s.

Feminist Approaches to Breast Cancer Activism

Only a small number of scholars have studied the breast cancer movement and they have analyzed it by posing questions that engage most directly with the sociology of emotions (Montini 1996), the sociology of gender (Taylor and Van Willigen 1996), and the sociology of science (Anglin 1997). The first study, conducted by Montini (1996), examined the wave of breast cancer informed consent legislation that swept across the United States during the 1980s. In twenty-two states, legislation was introduced that required physicians to inform their patients of treatment options and obtain their consent before proceeding. In each state, the legislative effort constituted a small-scale phenomena that involved only a handful of former breast cancer patients who operated in isolation from broader social movement communities. Montini showed how these breast cancer activists strategically drew upon conservative norms of heterofemininity in their media presentations and public testimonies. As part of their script, they positioned themselves as the victims of callous surgeons and who were in need of state protections; the avoided the public display of anger—although they expressed it in private—and they displayed instead the gender-normative emotions of fear and grief. Montini argued that, in so doing, they reproduced conservative norms of femininity and extended them to a new political subject: the breast cancer patient. Although informed consent legislation was successfully passed in sixteen states by 1989, breast cancer activism in the eighties remained narrowly focused on specific legislative goals, and was sustained by a handful of individuals rather than by broader social movements.

Taylor and Van Willigen (1996) published the first sociological study of the breast cancer movement of the nineties. Drawing upon Taylor's research on the postpartum depression movement and VanWilligen's research on the breast cancer movement, they traced the genealogies of both mobilizations to the cultural and political repertoires of self-help groups and to the larger phenomena of women's self-help movements of the past two decades. Taylor and Van Willigen argued that women's self-help movements had, in recent years, been maligned as "apolitical" by one strand of scholars within feminism and dismissed as "not a social movement" by many scholars within sociology. They used their research to construct a counter-narrative demonstrating that breast cancer activists challenged the gender order by identifying themselves as "breast cancer survivors," refusing to wear breast prostheses, demanding access to medical information, challenging the boundaries of allopathic medicine, and creating new social networks and supportive spaces. Taylor and Van Willigen thus argued that the breast cancer and postpartum depression movements—and women's self-help movements in general—challenged the institution of gender along three different dimensions: as a process; a hierarchy; and a structure.[6]

Finally, Anglin (1997) used her ethnography of a breast cancer organization to explore the ways in which treatment activism during the early 1990s challenged the power relations embedded within science and medicine. Whereas Montini's activists in the eighties were positioned as individual, victimized patients operating outside the context of a broader social movement, Anglin's breast cancer activists belong to just such a movement, made up of more than three hundred breast cancer organizations united in their demands for more research and better treatment alternatives. Anglin drew primarily upon literature within the sociology of knowledge and science to analyze the challenges posed by breast cancer treatment activism to structures of power within science and medicine. At the same time, she used her case study to argue that treatment activism was being narrowly defined from the privileged social, medical, and cultural location of a predominantly white and middle class constituency.

My analysis touches upon themes that have been identified and explored by these scholars. For example, I analyze the ways in which gender styles and emotions are publicly mobilized and enacted (Montini 1996; Taylor and Van Willigen 1996). I also explore some of the ways that breast cancer activism discursively engages the authority and priorities of science and medicine (Anglin 1997; Taylor and VanWilligen 1996). And I pay attention to the workings of power and to questions of position, representation, and exclusion (Anglin 1997). But instead of identifying commonalities and developing an analysis of the breast cancer movement as a whole,[7] I seek to identify, disentangle, and analyze different strands of activism around breast cancer. Thus, instead of situating my analysis within the sociology of emotions (Montini 1996), gender and social movements (Taylor and Van Willigen 1996), or the sociology of science (Anglin 1997), I approach the local terrain of breast cancer activism from an angle of vision opened up by recent developments at the juncture of culture and social movements.

Theorizing at the Juncture of Culture and Social Movements

This article draws upon and contributes to a recent trend in the study of social movements—what Ingalsbee (1993) has referred to as a shift towards "the semiotics of collective action," or what many others have referred to, simply, as the "turn towards culture." This turn towards culture is reflected in the work of leading scholars in the field and by the growing number of books and collections of essays that incorporate cultural factors and analyses into the study of social movements (cf. Ferree and Martin 1996; Johnston and Klandermans 1995; Laraña, Johnston and Gusfield 1994; McAdam, McCarthy, and Zaid 1996; Morris and Mueller 1992). These volumes open new ground for theorizing and research, but they do so by moving in different directions.

Culture has most often been conceptualized within social movements theory in terms that emphasize its mental and cognitive dimensions. This tends to be true whether the object in question has been conceptualized using Marxist terminology—as consciousness or ideology, as the collective identities of symbolic interactionists and "new social movements" theorists, or as the discourses of cultural and postmodern theory. The concept that I use—cultures of action—expands the focus from the realm of disembodied cognition to include the emotional and physical dimensions of social movements. As such, my approach to studying culture is most indebted to the analytic insights and conceptualizations that have been developed in scholarship on practices and performance. Several contributors to *Social Movements and Culture* (Johnston and Klandermans 1995) analyze culture from his performative and practice-oriented angle.

In an essay entitled "Cultural Power and Social Movements" Swidler (1995) synthesizes developments within cultural theory and social movements scholarship and affirms that social movements "are the sites where new cultural resources, such as identities and ideologies, are most frequently formulated" (30). She notes that "altering cultural codings is one of the most powerful ways social movements actually bring about change" (33), and that, because most movements lack political power, "they can reshape the world more effectively through redefining its terms rather than rearranging its sanctions" (34). Swidler argues that cultural theory is a rich source of insights for the study of social movements, but she also cautions against the tendency of social movements researchers to rely on a Weberian approach that locates culture in the thoughts, ideas, and worldviews of individual activists. While acknowledging that this approach is easier for researchers to work with and operationalize, she points out that "cultural theory is moving in the other direction" (1995:31). Drawing on the work of Foucault (1977, 1980, 1983), Bourdieu (1977, 1984), and others, Swidler argues that an abundance of work now indicates "that culture should be seen as socially organized practices rather than individual ideas or values, that culture can be located in public symbols and rituals rather than in ephemeral subjectivities, and that culture and power are fundamentally linked" (1995:31). Swidler summarizes these developments in cultural theory as a shift towards thinking about culture in terms of "publicness, practices, and power" (1995:27).

This shift toward publicness, practices, and power is evident in several other essays in this volume (Fantasia and Hirsch 1995; Fine 1995; Jenson 1995; Lofland 1995; Taylor and Whittier 1995). These contributors theorize social movements as staging areas for the production of culture, as contested terrains infused with power relations, and as sites in which discourses and symbolic objects are continuously negotiated, transformed, and contested. Drawing upon Swidler's and others' insights, I have focused on public events and have analyzed these public events as ritualized performances. In doing so, I pay attention to the narrative conventions and discursive practices that feature prominently within them and I observe the ways in which these rituals function to produce and transform the emotions that create solidarity and strengthen participation (Fine 1995; Jenson 1995; Lofland 1995; Taylor and Whittier 1995). My study of the local terrain of breast cancer activism thus embraces what many of the contributors to *Social Movements and Culture* seem to share—a tendency to shy away from removing culture from context, frames from feelings, and discourses from practices. However, I also seek to push this one step further. Re-embedding culture within context, frame within feelings, and discourses within practices allows the body—as a site of cultural contestation, a flexible signifier of identities and meanings, a vehicle for the expression of emotion, and an anchor of political logics—to emerge more clearly into the field of analytic vision. By incorporating the body into the study of culture and social movements, I seek to flesh out the disembodied conceptions of culture that define much of social movements scholarship. Thus, in the analysis that follows, I pay explicit attention to the ways that social movement culture is not only enacted, enunciated, and emoted, but also, and importantly, embodied.

THE SAN FRANCISCO RACE FOR THE CURE®[8]

Background

The Susan G. Komen Breast Cancer Foundation, inventor of Race for the Cure, was established in 1982 by Dallas socialite Nancy Brinker and named in honor of her sister, Suzy, who died from breast cancer in 1980 at the age of thirty-six. Two years after founding the organization, Nancy Brinker was herself diagnosed with breast cancer. But Brinker was luckier than her sister. She became a "breast cancer survivor" and remained the driving force behind the Komen Foundation.

The Komen Foundation has played a paradoxical role in the breast cancer movement, acting as both a ground-breaking pioneer and a force of conservatism. In the early 1980s, at a time when no other nonprofit organizations were focusing exclusively on breast cancer, Nancy Brinker mobilized her tremendous economic, social, and political capital to raise money for the promotion of breast cancer research and early detection campaigns.[9] Brinker and the Komen Foundation thus carved out a new terrain for breast cancer advocacy and played a pioneering role in helping transform breast cancer from a hidden and unspeakable disease into a household word, a corporate language, a social problem, and a legislatable issue. On the other hand, the Komen Foundation has adopted an uncritical stance toward the medical and research establishments—raising money for them, but never challenging their authority or priorities.[10] And while the Komen Foundation has been at the forefront of redefining cultural meanings and representations of women with breast cancer, they have done so by tying these to norms of white, heterosexual, middle-class, consumerized feminity.[11]

Although the national organization is headquartered in Texas, a network of volunteers working through local chapters spans the country. The San Francisco chapter of the Komen Foundation was formed in 1987. It was not until 1991, however, that the Komen Foundation became an important source of local funding. In 1991, the San Francisco chapter of the Komen Foundation became one of fifteen cities to host Race for the Cure. The San Francisco Race raised $232,000 and these funds were used to support biomedical research and to launch a program, administered by the University of California, San Francisco, of mobile mammography vans that provide free screening to "the medically underserved" (Chater 1992). Since 1991, the Race has been held annually in San Francisco, and biomedical research and early detection have remained the core mission of the local chapter, as well as the national organization.[12] In October 1996, as part of National Breast Cancer Awareness Month, the sixth annual Race for the Cure was held in San Francisco's Golden Gate Park. The event drew almost 9,000 participants and raised over $400,000 (*San Francisco Chronicle*, October 21, 1996).

The 1996 Race for the Cure

It is a beautiful October morning in San Francisco. In Golden Gate Park, the atmosphere of a carnival prevails. The sixth annual Race for the Cure, sponsored by the Susan G. Komen Breast Cancer Foundation, is coming to life. Corporate booths line the outskirts of Sharon Meadow. Inside the booths, staffers display their wares. Dressed in running attire, thousands of women, children, and men meander about. The crowd is about 75 percent white and 75 percent women, most of whom are towing clear plastic Vogue bags that contain free hair products, cosmetics, lotions, and perfumes. The bags are rapidly filling up with more free items—pins of the newly issued breast cancer awareness stamp, pink ribbons, and breast self-exam brochures. *Tropicana Orange Juice*, one of the national sponsors of the Race, offers some encouraging news about how to avoid breast cancer. We're told: "Don't gamble with the odds. If you play it smart, you can beat them." *Tropicana* even provides a set of diet tips and orange juice recipes to help us do it. The brochure explains that being overweight and not getting enough vitamin C are "risk factors" for the development of breast cancer. Individual risk factors and breast health practices are consistent themes throughout the Race.

In addition to the booths of the corporate sponsors (*Chevron, Genentech, JC Penney, American Airlines, Ford, Pacific Bell, Vogue, Nordstrom, Wells Fargo, BankAmerica*), the medical care industry is in attendance, among those represented are: Kaiser Permanente: California Pacific; Davies Medical Center; UCSF-Mount Zion; the UCSF Mobile Mammography Van; and Marin General Hospital. In an increasingly competitive industry, women with insurance are a market that no one can afford to ignore. And in the breast cancer capital of the world, breast cancer is a big ticket item for the health care industry.[13] The last few years have witnessed a whirlwind of sales, closures, and mergers, and the medical centers that remain have reorganized their services and repackaged their messages better to appeal to the concerns and demands of female baby-boomer consumers. Old-fashioned hospitals and general medical centers have been replaced by women's health centers, breast health and breast cancer centers, and the less specialized, more old-fashioned cancer centers. One breast health center distributes an 11-page handout listing 34 services, groups, and programs for women with breast cancer and "breast health" concerns.

Last but certainly not least, the fitness, nutrition, beauty, and fashion industries are here in abundance. They offer an amazing array of services and top-of-the-line accessories tailored to the special needs of women in treatment for cancer and women who have survived breast cancer treatment. There are nutrition consultants, fitness experts, and hair stylists. There are special lotions and cremes. There are special swimsuits, wigs, scarves, make-up, clothing, and vitamins. There are customized breast prostheses beginning at $2100 and created from a cast of a woman's breast before it is surgically removed. There are partial prostheses for women with less radical surgeries. For the physically active crowd, there are sports bras, biker pants, and baseball caps—with or without attached ponytails. There is sexy lingerie and lots of it. And in a stroke of marketing genius, a women's fashion catalogue weds the breast cancer patient's pursuit of femininity to the baby boomers' feminist sensibilities. The catalogue cover features a quote attributed to Simone de Beauvior: "One is not born a woman, one becomes one." Inside are the means of (re)becoming a woman—prostheses, lingerie, ponytails, and fitness wear. This is the style of embodiment that is given center stage at the Race.

Adding to the festive atmosphere are the shiny new automobiles parked in the middle of the meadow, adorned with balloons, courtesy of *Ford* and *Lincoln-Mercury* dealerships—national sponsors of the Race. In every direction, purple and aqua balloons dance in the air. Also bobbing about in the crowds and easily noticeable from a distance, are women in bright pink visors. These visors signal a special status and are worn with pride. On each visor, below the corporate logos, the following message is stitched in black: "I'm a survivor." The visors are distributed from a special booth, situated in the center of the meadow—the Breast Cancer Survivors' Station. Here, more than a dozen queues have formed with women standing six deep, chatting, socializing, and awaiting their turn to receive the complimentary pink visor that marks them as a breast cancer survivor. As each woman dons her visor and mingles with the crowd, she proudly, voluntarily, and publicly marks herself as a breast cancer survivor, visually embodying an identity not otherwise apparent. This is an act of social disobedience—a collective "coming out," a rejection of stigma and invisibility, and a simultaneous appropriation of the traditional color of femininity for the survivor identity. Later, after the Race had been run and walked, there is an official ceremony during which all the breast cancer survivors who wish to be recognized are asked to ascend the main stage. They are honored for their courage in fighting breast cancer and for their willingness to demonstrate to other women, through their rejection of the cultural code of silence and invisibility, that breast cancer is not shameful, that it is survivable, and that it is neither disfiguring nor defeminizing.

One way of publicly remembering and honoring women with breast cancer is provided at the registration tables. Instead of the standard numbered forms pinned to the contestant's backs, participants can choose to wear "In Honor of" and "In Memory of" forms displaying the names of women—both living and dead—whom they wish to publicly honor and acknowledge or mourn and remember. Like the visors, these forms are pink and they mark their wearers with a particular status.

In choosing to display these forms, the participants identify themselves as part of the expanding circle of those whose lives have been touched by breast cancer. These moving displays generate powerful effects and enhance the intensity of the experience of moving en masse through the park with thousands of strangers to raise money for breast cancer. One encounters these pink signs here, there, and everywhere. The practice of wearing a sign is a way of enacting community, including oneself, in this sea of runners who have suffered at the hands of this disease and who are working together to raise awareness of breast cancer and money for mammograms and a cure. They are powerful visual reminders of the pervasiveness of this disease. These signs, like the visors, signify the public display of private losses and triumphs. Wearing them is an emotional act at once painful, brave, and hopeful.

There are three more ways in which breast cancer is visually coded, packaged, and displayed. All three are stationed at one end of the meadow, apart from the booths. The first display is in the form of a large vertical cloth banner. The banner is imprinted with thousands of pink ribbons—the symbol of breast cancer awareness. Many of these ribbons are filled in with handwritten names. Everyone is invited to write a name on a ribbon. The second display is "The Breast Cancer Quilt." Modeled after the AIDS Quilt but in smaller dimensions, each quilt—and there are several on display—contains approximately twenty 12 × 14-inch panels. Unlike the AIDS quilt, which recognizes those who have died, the Breast Cancer Quilt recognizes survival. Each panel is created by a breast cancer survivor—or by a women who, at least at the time of the quilt-making, was still a survivor. Not far from the Breast Cancer Quilt is the "Wall of Hope." This display contains a long series of panels. Each panel is comprised of fifteen 8 × 10-inch "glamour photos" of breast cancer survivors. The survivors are photographed in full make-up and adorned in brightly-colored evening gowns, sparkling jewelry, and even feather boas. Most of the survivors are white. Women of color stand out in a sea of light faces, their visages poorly captured by a photographer accustomed to working with lighter hues. Each woman is identified by name and year of diagnosis or number of years of survival. Frozen in time, all of these women are survivors—even those, unidentified, who are now dead.

The message of the official program, conducted on stage by a woman in a pink visor, is clear and concise; the solution to breast cancer lies in two directions—biomedical research and early detection. The audience is informed that the Komen Foundation, sponsors of this Race and 66 others being organized by local chapters throughout the country, has contributed more money for breast cancer research, screening, and early detection than any other private organization dedicated solely to breast cancer in the world. The audience learns that the Susan G. Komen Breast Cancer Foundation was established in 1982 by Nancy Brinker in memory of her sister, Suzy, who died from breast cancer at age thirty-six. "Back then," says the speaker, "there was no follow-up therapy, no radiation, no chemotherapy, no pill."[14] Those were the dark ages of medicine.

The speaker continues with her story of individual control and medical progress: Nancy Brinker learned from her sister's experience "that early detection is the key." This knowledge served her well. As a result, she was vigilant and proactive in her own "breast health practices" and was soon thereafter diagnosed with early stage breast cancer. She is now a survivor. This is a story of success. The speaker concludes: "This is what every woman here needs to know. All women should get a baseline mammogram at age 35, every two years after age 40, and yearly after age 50. And every woman should practice monthly breast self-exam." The message here is clear: biomedical research has led to advances in breast cancer treatments that, in combination with breast self-examination and mammography are saving a new generation of breast cancer patients and transforming them into breast cancer survivors.

This is the archetypal story of Race for the Cure and National Breast Cancer Awareness Month. It is a story of individual triumph and responsibility. There is nothing sad or tragic about Brinker's encounter with breast cancer. Rather, her story is a narrative of unqualified success. It is also, of course, a story of failure and in this sense it serves as a cautionary tale. Suzy was not aware of, or did not practice, early detection. Suzy's breast cancer was diagnosed too late. She did not have access to radiation and chemotherapy. She died. In its morality tale the proactive survive and only the unaware and the irresponsible die. Responsibility exists solely within the context of detection, not within the context of causation. In fact, questions of causality are unspeakable in the terms of this discourse. In the discourse of the Race, survival is a matter of individual choice and responsibility. Regular mammograms never fail to diagnose breast cancer early and women diagnosed early never die.[15] For those who practice breast health, breast cancer may constitute a momentary set-back but it is not a debilitating, recurring, or chronic disease. In the discourse of the Race, breast cancer is part of each survivor's historical biography. A finished chapter. In this discourse, breast cancer is a disease of universal, individual, ahistorical, resilient, reconstructable, heterofeminine, biologically female bodies. Thus, the story told by Race for the Cure and enacted by the participants gathered together is a story of individual control and survivor pride, a narrative of hope, and a declaration of faith in the steady progress of science and medicine.

In addition to breast cancer survivors, there is a second category of women who are singled out for special attention. These women are constituted as "the medically underserved." Although the medically underserved are not visibly marked or present at the Race, except as signified indirectly by the UCSF Mobile Mammography Van, they are discursively constituted in official Komen publicity (brochures and registration forms) and by speakers who refer to programs supported by money raised by the Race. Still, it is not clear who they are or why they are medically underserved. Like the simultaneously individualizing and universalizing category of the breast cancer survivor, the medically underserved are not situated as members of particular racial, ethnic, cultural, social, sexual, generational, or geographic categories or communities. In the biomedical discourse of the Race, the medically underserved are represented as individual women whose needs can be met and managed by mammograms and breast health education.

THE BAY AREA WOMEN & CANCER WALK

Background[16]

In the summer of 1991, three white lesbians, recent immigrants to the Bay Area, organized the first meeting of the Women & Cancer Project. The inspiration for this meeting, and the genesis of the cancer project itself, came from several places: the organizers' histories of involvement in feminist, and lesbian and gay communities; the recent cancer history of one of the organizers; and the powerful example and inspiration provided by the San Francisco gay community's ability to rally around and organize services for people with AIDS. The gay community's remarkable mobilization around AIDS led all three women to question the absence of a parallel mobilization around women's health. They saw that breast cancer was gaining ground in the media but, at the same time, nothing seemed to be happening in their community—no fundraising, no activism, no attention.

The first meeting of the Project included representatives from an array of women's health organizations whose foci ranged from breast cancer exclusively, to women's health more generally. Representatives from Breast Cancer Action, the Women's Cancer Resource Center, the National Latina Health Organization, the Bay Area Black Women's Health Project, and the Vietnamese Community Health Promotion Project were present at the first meeting. Thus, from the beginning, an explicitly "multicultural" vision and network informed the development of the Women & Cancer Project; and, although breast cancer was the starting point, from the beginning it was linked, both discursively and organizationally, to cancer as a broader category, and to women's health more generally.

The first Walk was held in 1992 and it has been held on an annual basis ever since. Every year proceeds from the Walk are divided evenly among the beneficiary organizations. Proceeds have ranged from a 1995 high of $7000 per organization ($115,000 total raised), to a 1996 low of $2500 for each organization. By 1995, the number of beneficiary groups had grown from six to thirteen.[17] The steering committee, in theory comprised of at least one volunteer representative from each beneficiary organization, was in reality made up of whomever could come to meetings and work on the event. In practice, most of the volunteer labor and leadership was performed by a handful of white women who were connected to grassroots cancer organizations.

The project has hovered on the edge of collapse for the last few years.[18] Even after several years, a consistent, reliable template of systematization and procedure has not quite emerged. With no permanent paid staff or office space, rotating fiscal sponsors, low levels of institutionalization and organization, and the work burden carried by a few volunteers, most of whom are working full-time jobs elsewhere and are perpetually on the brink of burnout, every year the wheel, to some extent, must be reinvented.

Many of the walking teams hail from feminist or lesbian organizations and small, progressive businesses, and many of the individual supporters and volunteers also come from these networks and connections. But the project has been unsuccessful at more effectively harnessing the resources of these communities; and, although there is a great deal of discussion about tapping into the resources of the gay male community, with a few notable exceptions, this had not happened. Yet another problem has to do with publicity and media messages. Many of the organizations do not focus specifically on cancer because they address the broader health needs of their communities. The Walk, in turn, has had difficulty developing effective ways of framing its focus and philosophy. Although in AIDS organizing it is common to fund community-based organizations that provide community-based, direct services and advocacy, the discursive terrain of breast cancer—the "universe of political discourse" (Jenson 1987)—has been effectively colonized by the discourses of research and early detection. The Walk has been unable to effectively communicate an alternative vision. Despite these obstacles, the actual number of participants in the Women & Cancer Walk has grown steadily, if slowly, each year, with many returning and familiar faces.

1996 Women & Cancer Walk

It is a crisp fall morning in San Francisco. Gradually a crowd of between six and eight hundred assembles in front of a temporary stage in Golden Gate Park. This is the fifth annual Women & Cancer Walk. Like Race for the Cure, this is a fund-raiser; but whereas the Komen Foundation funds biomedical research and screening mammograms for medically underserved individuals, proceeds from the Women & Cancer Walk support the work of a multicultural set of grassroots women's health and advocacy organizations. The Women & Cancer Walk takes place in the same meadow as Race for the Cure, and like the Race, it seeks to create a festive atmosphere; but the same meadow that held 9000 participants and scores of booths and displays seems almost empty with fewer than 800 participants, a modest stage, a few folding tables and colorful splashes of artwork here and there. Neither balloons nor pink ribbons are in abundance. There is no sign of pink visors.

Like the Race, the Walk constructs and celebrates a particular symbolic community. But the symbolic community constructed by the Walk is quite different from that of the Race. The beauty, fashion, and fitness industries are absent. So too, for the most part, is the health care industry. Instead, the community is comprised of dozens of volunteers, performers, speakers, walkers, and the thirteen beneficiary organizations. The beneficiaries include three feminist cancer organizations and six women's health advocacy organizations—two Latina, two African American, one Vietnamese, and one older women's. It also includes three community health clinics—one lesbian, one Native American, and one serving a cross-section of poor people in San Francisco's Mission neighborhood. But, although the Walk tries to construct a multicultural and multiracial community, the links within this community are visibly weak. Several of the beneficiary organizations are present in name only.

Like the Race, women, and white women in particular, predominate at the Walk. Many of the women here, however, hail from a different social location. Certainly, there are women here who would blend in easily at the Race, but they are neither the most visible nor the majority. At the Walk, there is a broad range of non-normative "corporeal styles" (Butler 1990:272) on display that, together, create a different kind of body politic. Though there are certainly active and athletic women in this crowd, they do not set the standard. Soft bodies in comfortable shoes replace hard bodies in exercise attire. There is a strong lesbian, feminist, queer, and counter-cultural presence. It is signaled by styles of dress, hair, and adornment; by the decentering of normative heterofemininity and the visibility of queer and lesbian relationships and sexualties. At the Walk, there are women with disabilities, large women, women for whom walking a mile will be an effort and for whom running a race would be out of the question. There are women with body piercings and tattoos. There are women with dread-locks, short-hair, and no hair at all.

Hair provides an interesting twist on standards of deviance and normality. Whereas at the Race, companies market feminine wigs, scarves, and hats to women seeking to disguise the effects of chemotherapy, at the Walk women who have lost their hair *involuntarily* blend in with women who have cropped their hair or shaved their heads *deliberately*, as part of a lesbian and/or queer aesthetic. The line between health and illness is more difficult to discern in a context where, instead of donning wigs to blend into the dominant norms of femininity, the norms are reconfigured so that bald women and women with very short hair move from the margins to the center and women with carefully-coifed corporate styles appear unusual.

On the other hand, there are women at the Walk whose breast cancer histories set them apart from other women in ways that are visible to the discerning eye.

Whereas at Race for the Cure the identities of breast cancer survivors are stitched in black upon the bills of their pink visors, the breast cancer histories of some women at the Walk are inscribed upon their bodies in a way that is at one and the same time more subtle and, for many, more disquieting. Beneath their shirts it is possible to discern the outline of one breast, but not two. These women are not wearing breast prostheses and they have not undergone surgical reconstruction. Theirs is a doubly-loaded act of defiance. Not only are they rejecting the code of invisibility, but the way in which they are doing so directly challenges dominant norms of beauty, sexuality, and femininity. And it disrupts, quite visibly, attempts to tie the discourse of survival to the display of unmarred bodies.

This form of body politics is carried still further by RavenLight, an exhibitionist, sex radical, lesbian, feminist, and cultural worker. RavenLight describes her work as "educating the s/m community about breast cancer and educating women with breast cancer about sexuality." At the Walk she is wearing a skin tight black and white dress, black hose, and high heels. Hardly the picture of normative femininity, however, one half of her dress is pulled downward and secured in back, starkly revealing the evidence of her breast cancer history. The smooth, pale surface is exaggerated by the fullness of her remaining breast. As I accompanied RavenLight on the one mile walk through the park, a woman in her late fifties approached us from behind. As she pulled up beside us and peered across, she exclaimed, "Oh good! That's what I thought! Well then—I'm going to take my shirt off too!" She then removed the two shirts she wore that were covering a sleeveless, skintight, gray unitard that showed off the asymmetry of her chest and made it clear that she, too, had had a mastectomy. Here, in the context of the Walk and in the company of a fellow traveler, this woman was moved to publicly reveal her breast cancer history, to display an otherwise hidden form of embodiment, and to celebrate an alternative style of femininity.

For the past couple of years, "Walkers of Courage" have been named and honored on stage. Sometimes they are women with breast cancer histories. Just as often they are women currently living with metastatic disease. But always, they are women who are singled out for their service and activism rather than for their survival. Last year Gracia Buffleben, a woman then living with advanced metastatic breast cancer, was honored as a Walker of Courage. During the previous year, Buffleben and other breast cancer activists, following in the footsteps of Elenore Pred—one of the founders of Breast Cancer Action—had worked with AIDS activists to graft ACT UP tactics onto breast cancer activism. In December they had organized civil disobedience against Genentech, a powerful Bay Area biotech company, in order to win "compassionate use" access to a promising new drug then in clinical trials. When Buffleben ascended the Women & Cancer Walk stage to accept her award, ACT UP activists, dressed in black, stood behind her holding signs with rows of gravestones. The signs read: "Don't Go Quietly to the Grave. Scream for Compassionate Use!" In form and structure, this ceremony was no different from Race for the Cure's on-stage recognition of breast cancer survivors. The contrast in images and meanings, however, was telling: pink versus black; survival versus death; gratitude versus anger.

As in previous years, this year's program is deliberately multicultural and multiracial—more so than the audience. Sign language interpretation is provided on stage. The pre-walk warm-up is led by an Afro-Brazilian dancer and masseuse. The disk jockey is well-known with the lesbian club scene. And live music is performed by an African American woman and a white man who are local jazz musicians. The discursive performances are similarly diverse.

The first speaker, a Walk organizer, begins by noting that women's health concerns have been "systematically ignored and underfunded" and that "health care and social services are least accessible to the women who need them most." At the same time, the speaker notes, cancer rates have continued to rise to epidemic proportions and "one in three women will be diagnosed with cancer in her lifetime." This is the same discourse that circulates on the pledge sheets and event programs. It broadens the terms of the discourse from breast cancer to all cancers that affect women, and from breast cancer early detection to broader concerns about women's health and access to health care.

Next, San Francisco Mayor Willie Brown gives a brief speech. This is the first time that a politician of such stature has addressed the Women & Cancer Walk and it is not entirely clear how the audience feels about his presence. The Mayor affirms his commitment to solving the problem of breast cancer and he publicizes and promotes the upcoming Mayor's Summit on Breast Cancer. Then, misjudging at least part of his audience, he segues into a sound bit on prostate cancer and reminds the audience that men get cancer too, and that he intends to address the growing problem of prostate cancer. Some women in the audience applaud. Others hiss and shake their heads. The woman I am standing next to, a staff person at a feminist cancer agency, turns to me, rolls her eyes and says: "Does he have any clue about the issues? Does he have any idea who he's talking to? Does he realize that this is the *Women* and Cancer Walk!?"

One of the two main speakers is the director of the Native American Health Center in Oakland. She begins by speaking about the devastation of the environment and its negative impact on the well-being of the earth and all of its inhabitants. She speaks about the large impact on the well-being of the earth and all of its inhabitants. She speaks about the large Native American community in Oakland that she belongs to and describes the lack of access to basic health care services and cancer support programs. She then describes the uses to which the money donated to her health center by the Women & Cancer Walk has been put. These funds paid for cabfare to the hospital for a woman receiving chemotherapy but too sick to take the bus across town. It paid for phone service for a woman dying of cancer so that she could talk to her family in the Southwest during her final weeks. It bought Christmas toys for the children of a third woman with cancer. It paid for therapy for a fourth woman, also dying; and it helped pay her burial expenses. Each woman's story is narrated with compassion and respect.

These are stories of desperation, hardship, loss, and death. The subjects of these stories do not speak for themselves—they are spoken of; but they are spoken of, and discursively constituted, as women with complicated commitments and biographies—these are women with their own needs, histories, priorities, and desires. They are individuals, but individuals embedded within particular cultures, communities, and institutionalized inequalities. These women are not passive, but certainly they are victims—victims of multiple institutionalized inequalities—and cancer is just one of many obstacles that they are up against. Perhaps some will become long-term survivors, but this is not where the logic of the narrative leads. This is a narrative of harsh realities, poverty, and dislocation, not a discourse of individual choice and responsibility, or hope and triumph.

Although the Women & Cancer Walk focuses on services and advocacy for women with cancer, in recent years it has joined this to an environmental justice discourse of cancer prevention. This year the final speaker is an Italian woman who has never been diagnosed with cancer but who is an environmental activist and crusader for cancer prevention. She delivers an impassioned speech that at key moments, elicits enthusiastic applause from the audience. She weaves together the global connections between rising cancer rates, profit-driven industries, and environmental racism.

THE TOXIC TOUR OF THE CANCER INDUSTRY

Background[19]

In the summer of 1994, a handful of Bay Area activists convened an informal meeting to network, learn about each other's work, identify areas of overlap, and explore the possibility of working together on issues of mutual interest. These activists came from four organizations: Breast Cancer Action; Greenpeace; West County Toxics Coalition; and the Women's Cancer Resource Center. At their second meeting, they decided to formalize the collaboration and christened themselves the Toxic Links Coalition (TLC). The formation of the Toxic Links Coalition thus represented a local synthesis of the feminist cancer and environmental justice movements.[20]

During the first two meetings, as they shared information and educated one another, they decided to focus their energies on challenging the pristine image and hegemonic discourse produced and circulated by National Breast Cancer Awareness Month (NBCAM). Invented in 1985 by the London-based Imperial Chemicals Industry (ICI) and later taken over by its subsidiary, Zeneca Pharmaceuticals, NBCAM was viewed by these activists as a wolf in sheep's clothing—a public relations campaign that accomplished three things: 1) it expanded the market for treatment drugs and detection technologies; 2) it legitimized early detection programs as the only conceivable public health approach to breast cancer; and 3) it effectively concealed from the public the fact that multinational corporations, assisted by their allies, were profiting by *causing* cancer on the one hand, and detecting and treating it on the other. In other words, as TLC activists would say, "they getcha coming and going."

The basis of these claims was simple. Zeneca Pharmaceuticals not only bankrolls and controls the publicity for NBCAM's breast cancer early detection campaigns, but they also, through their parent company ICI, manufacture the pesticides and insecticides that contribute to causing it. Adding more fuel to the fire, Zeneca is the manufacturer of tamoxifen (brandname Nolvadex), the world's best-selling breast cancer treatment drug (categorized by the World Health Organization as a carcinogen) and the owner of Salick, Inc., a management company that runs a dozen cancer treatment centers across the country—including a cancer center just down the road from the

TLC meeting place. ICI/Zeneca/NBCAM/Salick thus represented a textbook case of vertical integration. And every October, through a series of public and private partnerships and in combination with hundreds of thousands of posters, pamphlets, radio spots, newspaper ads, and promotional videos, NBCAM promoted the message that "Early detection is your best protection." Neither the word "carcinogen" nor "cause" had ever appeared in NBCAM publicity.[21]

NBCAM thus seemed like the perfect target. Its discourse of early detection and its refusal to speak of carcinogens and prevention was understood by TLC activists as a campaign of miseducation, obfuscation, and shameless profiteering. Therefore, as part of their project of reeducation, the TLC declared that October was no longer National Breast Cancer Awareness Month but was instead renamed Cancer Industry Awareness Month. TLC's first collective action was to set up an informational picket at the 1994 Race for The Cure in Golden Gate Park. They targeted the Race because its sponsor, the Komen Foundation, was a participant in NBCAM and because the Komen Foundation, like NBCAM, avoided any mention of causality, carcinogens, or the environment in its publicity. This action was followed, within a couple weeks, by the first Toxic Tour of the Cancer Industry—the invention of the TLC. The Cancer Industry Tour quickly became the signature of this group and the focus of their energy in years to come.

1996 Cancer Industry Tour

It is noon on Wednesday, and in downtown San Francisco a crowd has gathered on Market Street, in front of Chevron's corporate headquarters. Metal barriers and uniformed police line the sidewalk and street for about 100 feet, separating the courtyard, sidewalk, and street traffic from the protesters who are assembling inside the barriers. A large banner identifies the coordinators of the event. It reads "Toxic Links Coalition—United for Health and Environmental Justice." Another large banner reads "Stop Cancer Where It Starts!" The demonstrators begin walking in an elongated circle, carrying signs aloft and loudly chanting "Stop Cancer Where it Starts!, Stop Corporate Pollution!," and "Toxins Outside! Cancer Inside! Industry Profits! People Suffer!," and "People Before Profits!"

The 1996 Cancer Industry Tour is the third annual event and it draws approximately 150 to 200 participants. As in previous years, the Toxic Tour is designed as a one-hour *tour de force* that moves through downtown San Francisco and stops at specific "targets" along the way. The 1996 targets are *Chevron, Pacific Gas & Electric*, Senator Dianne Feinstein, Burson Marsteller (a public relations firm), *Bechtel* (builder of nuclear power plants), and the American Cancer Society. The Cancer Industry Tour shifts the focus even further away from the universal, feminine, individual frames of Race for the Cure. Although the Tour is similar to the Walk in that many of the speakers locate themselves as members of particular communities, in the Toxic tour, the focus of their political discourse shifts *away* from their community and group identities in order to constitute and draw attention to the local outposts of the global cancer industry.

The theme of the Tour is "Make the Link!" and the Tour is choreographed so that each stop along the way represents a link in the chain of the cancer industry. TLC publicity materials assert that "the cancer industry consists of the polluting industries, public relations firms, [and] government agencies that fail to protect our health, and everyone that makes cancer possible by blaming the victims and not addressing the real sources." This is a smear campaign, a strategy of public shaming, an attack on corporate images. At each stop a culprit is identified and their name is bellowed out over a bullhorn. A description of corporate practices destructive to human health and the environment follows. Literally and figuratively, the cancer industry is mapped through the delivery of speeches, the display of props and signs, and the movement from site to site. The speakers call for a politics of cancer prevention and an end to environmental racism.

There are clear lines separating "them" from "us," and those lines are reinforced by the uniformed police escort and barricade. This is street theater. It is ritualized confrontation and condemnation. And it creates opportunities for the mobilization and expression of oppositional identities. Like the Race and the Walk, about three-quarters of the participants are white and three-quarters are women, but many—perhaps one-half—of the authorized speakers are people of color, both women and men. They speak not as individuals, but as members and representatives of environmental justice organizations. There are also speakers from feminist cancer organizations—Breast Cancer Action, the Women's Cancer Resource Center, Impart, Inc. (a breast implant activist organization), and individual activists living with cancer. All of the speakers express anger, outrage, and injustice and these emotions are mirrored and affirmed by the Toxic Tour participants. Although some speakers identify themselves as "living with cancer" and "breast cancer survivors," many do not. Like the Race and the Walk, men are in the minority at the Tour. But unlike the Race and the Walk, men speak from positions of entitlement equal to those of the women speakers. There are no men, however, who identify themselves as cancer survivors or living with cancer and speak from either of those subject positions.

This is not primarily an expression of solidarity with, or sympathy for, people with cancer. It is a collective expression of rage at the cancer industry's destruction of the health of all people, but particularly those living in communities affected by environmental racism. Like the Race and the Walk, breast cancer occupies a privileged position in speakers' narratives and in the visual signs and signifiers. But just as the Walk decentered breast cancer by connecting it to other forms of cancer that affect women, the Toxic Tour decenters breast cancer by linking it to cancers affecting men, women, and children, and further still, to a host of environmentally-related health conditions such as reproductive, respiratory, and auto-immune diseases. In this context, everyone is part of the inner circle of the aggrieved; but it is not grief that is mobilized, it is anger.

The bright orange flyers distributed along the way announce that one-third of U.S. women and one-half of U.S. men will be diagnosed with cancer in their lifetime. It states that the lifetime risk for breast cancer is 1 in 8 and rising, that the Bay Area has the highest rates of breast cancer in the world; and that African-American women living in Bayview-Hunters Point—a low-income and predominantly African American community—have breast cancer rates double that of the rest of San Francisco. The orange flyer also states that "we are all exposed in increasing doses to industrial chemicals and radioactive waste *known* to cause cancer, reproductive, and developmental disorders" and that "big profits are made from the continued production of cancer-causing chemicals."

Last year, the 60 or so protesters carried handmade signs painted with slogans, miniature coffins, and gravestones emblazoned with a handwritten name, a lifespan, and the letters "R.I.P." This year, there are more than twice as many participants as last year and the coffins and gravestones are nowhere to be seen. Instead, two show-stealing props have appeared: The first prop is a gigantic puppet with moving arms, deftly operated by a team of three. The twenty-foot puppet is a papier-mâché woman with blue skin and a mastectomy scar dripping blood where her second breast should be. In each of her gigantic moveable hands she holds a container of toxic substances, painted with a skull and crossbones. The second prop is a tall, narrow float on wheels, one side of which is painted as a man in a business suit—but without a head; the other side of the float is a skyscraper with an assortment of corporate insignias: *Chevron; PG&E; Dow; Dow Corning; Monsanto; UNOCAL; US Ecology.* This float is known as the Tower of Evil. Images of death, deformity, and destruction abound at the Toxic Tour.

One woman holds high an exhibit of photographs of women's nude torsos. They include startling images of disfigured women with double mastectomies—some of them with the concave chests characteristic of the Halsted radical mastectomy, a particularly mutilating and in some cases debilitating surgical procedure performed by American surgeons from the 1880s until the 1980s. Other women distribute vivid color photographs of ruptured implants and mutilated chests—the result of negligence on the part of Dow Corning, inc., the manufacturers of silicone implants. It is just these sorts of images that Race for the Cure seeks to banish from the collective consciousness. But here they are resurrected and pasted onto sandwich boards and donned by angry women marching through downtown San Francisco.

There are no freebies distributed at this event—none of the beauty products, pink ribbons, or breast health brochures that abound at the Race. There are no corporate sponsors. Although Chevron and the American Cancer Society are present at both the Race and the Tour, they are participants and sponsors of the Race whereas they are targets of the Tour. At the American Cancer Society, for example, Judy Brady—a breast cancer activist and self-described "cancer victim"—delivers a series of withering accusations which she substantiates by distributing copies of a recent internal ACS memo marked "Confidential." The memo comes from the national office and instructs local offices to ignore and suppress a brochure on cancer and pesticides created and distributed by a small office in the Great Lakes region. She charges the ACS with miseducating the public, ignoring cancer prevention, refusing to take a stand against industrial and agricultural pollution, and colluding with the corporate stakeholders to hide evidence of corporate carcinogens. Brady's assertion of her identity as a cancer victim is loaded with significance. It reclaims a highly stigmatized identity that the breast cancer survivor identity was designed to displace. At the same time, it resignifies this identity by disconnecting it from earlier associations with passivity and connecting it instead to an in-your-face, confrontational politics. The association with victimization is deliberately reasserted, but instead of being victimized by a random, terrorizing disease, the person with cancer is resituated as a victim of the brutal cancer industry.

At the Toxic Tour, there is no call for more research to uncover the mysteries of tumor biology or discern the patterns of cancer epidemiology. There are no visions of more or better science, or for more or better social and medical services. There is no call for women to be vigilant, to practice breast self-exam and get mammograms. Mammography *is* invoked—but as an example of false promises and corporate profiteering. These activists do not promote the ideology of early detection. They do not promote the notion that disease growing within community bodies can be mapped onto the genetic structures and "risk factors" of individual lifestyles. "Cancer," they stress, "is not a lifestyle choice." Instead of mapping the biomedical geography of individual women's bodies and behaviors, as in the Race, or mapping the social geography of communities and health services, as in the Walk, the Toxic Tour maps the political economy and geography of the cancer industry—the hidden maze of linkages and networks connecting the bodies of state agencies, politicians, charities, and profit-driven corporations to the unhealthy bodies of people involuntarily exposed to toxins and living in contaminated communities. The Toxic Tour maps the sickness and disease of toxic bodies and the body politic onto the corporate corpus. Cancer prevention, they make clear, requires a different kind of cartography.

Comparative Summary and Theoretical Implications

This paper responds to the call for comparative research on social movements (McAdam, McCarthy, and Zald 1996) and the call for rich descriptions of social movement culture (Lofland 1995) by proposing the concept cultures of action and using it to develop a comparative, descriptive analysis of differences within the field of breast cancer activism in the San Francisco Bay Area. It does so by analyzing three social movement events—each of which crystallizes a different culture of action. Although all three events were designed to educate and motivate—to "raise awareness" and mobilize action—each event sought to raise awareness and reshape the social terrain by creating a different culture of action.

First, whereas Race for the Cure singled out breast cancer, the Women & Cancer Walk expanded the category to include all cancers affecting women, and the Toxic Tour of the Cancer Industry expanded the category still further, to include cancer in general and other environmentally-related diseases. Second, whereas the Race drew upon biomedicine and represented breast cancer as a universal, ahistorical disease of biologically female bodies that could be controlled through salvationist science, surveillance medicine, and individual vigilance, the Walk drew upon multicultural feminism and represented cancer as a body-altering, life-threatening source of suffering that was compounded by institutionalized inequalities in access to health care and social services. The Toxic Tour, on the other hand, drew upon the environmental justice movement and discourses of environmental racism to represent breast cancer as the product and source of profit of a predatory cancer industry. In Race for the Cure, the most privileged and honored identity was that of the breast cancer survivor. The Women & Cancer Walk, on the other hand, created more space for the identities of women "living with cancer" and women dying from the disease. Finally, the Toxic Tour decentered women as a category, gender as a lens of analysis and even, to some extent, the identities of participants altogether. Instead, the Toxic Tour highlighted the identities and relationships of specific industries and organizations, and discursively constituted, from these linked identities, an entity that they named the cancer industry. Finally, the Race called for more biomedical research and early detection, and supported the provision of mammograms to the medically underserved; the Walk called for better health care and social services, and supported the work of community clinics and women's health advocacy and activism; and the Toxic Tour called for cancer prevention instead of early detection, for more corporate regulation instead of more research, and supported the work of coalition members on behalf of environmental health and justice.

All three social movement events produced and promoted different cultures of action not only by articulating—or enunciating—them, but by physically enacting them. Clearly, the activities of *racing* for the cure for breast cancer, *walking* for women with cancer, and *touring* the cancer industry are symbolically loaded, but part of this symbolic charge came not just through naming and framing, but through physical participation. Participation in collective action, after all, is a physical and emotional experience as well as a cognitive and mental one—and the latter may well be balanced on the knees of the former. Consciousness, ideologies, mentalities, discourses, and collective action frames are enabled not simply through abstract mental processes, but through practices of participation that work on and through bodies. Indeed, as Louis Althusser wrote, quoting Pascal, "Kneel down, move your lips in prayer, and you will believe" (1970:168).

In terms of emotional expression—which is also an embodied experience—all three events mobilized feelings of togetherness and solidarity. But beyond this, they diverged. The Race mobilized hope and faith in biomedicine, while also mobilizing the respect of Race participants *for* women with histories of breast cancer and mobilizing self-pride *among* breast cancer survivors. The Walk, on the other hand, mobilized anger against the same institutions celebrated and trusted by the Race—the institutions of biomedicine and the health care system. At the same time, the Walk mobilized respect for the work of cancer activists and women's health organizations, and it privileged the identities of women dealing with cancer—but it did so by positioning them as fighting women and suffering women, rather than as victors who believed they had defeated breast cancer and put it behind them. Finally, the Toxic Tour mobilized a deep sense of injustice and choreographed the expression of anger and outrage against the cancer industry and its destruction of human health and the environment.

Each culture of action represented breast cancer through the lens of a particular conception of the body, and in each case its corporeal model was reinforced by particular corporeal styles. The Race, ironically enough, embraced a corporeal model that cancer historian Richard Proctor (1995) has referred to elsewhere as "body machismo." Proctor uses this term to illustrate the tendency of industry allies and anti-environmentalists to conceptualize the human body as a "macho body" that is able to withstand repeated environmental insults, detoxify potential carcinogens, and repair genetic damage (1995:171). Race for the Cure, interestingly enough, promoted a feminized and domesticated version of this "macho body" and connected it to medical technologies rather than environmental carcinogens. In Race for the Cure the macho body morphed into the heterofeminne, resilient body—the repaired, reconstructed body beautiful—responsive to medical treatment and safe from the specter of recurrence. The corporeal styles that were produced and promoted at the Race were those that represented and reinforced this corporeal model—unmarred bodies, fitness activities, visually marked survivor identities, and the reassertion of heteronormative femininities. Thus, in the context of the Race, the absent breast was flawlessly concealed by prostheses and reconstructive surgeries and the only indication that breast cancer could result in altered bodies was found in the corporate booths, where wigs and prostheses circulated as free-floating commodities.

The corporeal model undergirding the analysis of the Toxic Tour of the Cancer Industry, on the other hand, embraced what Proctor has termed "body victimology" (1995:171). This corporeal model focuses on the vulnerability of the body to toxic assaults and its weakness in the face of repeated exposures to carcinogens. His use of the term accurately describes the corporeal model undergirding the Toxic Tour. Indeed, some cancer activists in the Toxic Tour directly challenged the implicit corporeal model of the breast cancer survivor identity and explicitly asserted the identity of cancer victim. In turn, the victimized body was visually represented at the Tour through pictures of mutilated bodies, ruptured implants, props with mastectomy scars dripping blood, canisters of poison, R.I.P. signs, and coffins. At the Toxic Tour, the vulnerable, victimized body was represented in the form of death and mutilation.

The Women & Cancer Walk also embraced a corporeal model of body victimology, but it developed a different variation on this theme. In the case of the Walk, it was the physical effects of cancer treatments that were represented through the visual display of altered bodies. In the Walk, cancer recurrences and metastases were not banished from the collective consciousness, and health and recovery were represented as tentative and possibly temporary. Here, women living with cancer could feel comfortable not concealing their chemically and surgically-altered bodies. Here, the absent breast was actually "present" as an absence—directly challenging the corporeal model of resilient, reconstructed bodies and the display of unmarred bodies. The subtly-altered bodies of the Walk also posed a challenge to the Toxic Tour's representation of the victimized, graphically mutilated body. And even RavenLight's overtly exhibitionist style of body activism drew attention to the sexuality and beauty of one-breasted women and mobilized pride and self-acceptance. She did not represent herself as victimized and mutilated, and the mastectomy scar she exposed was thin and healed, not the gory and mutilating scars on display at the Toxic Tour. Thus, as in the case of the Race and the Toxic Tour, the Walk's political vision was anchored in a set of interpretations of women's bodies and these interpretations were mobilized and reified through different styles of embodiment.

Until recently, the hegemonic model for interpreting and acting with regard to breast cancer, in the United States, has been the biomedical model developed by scientific medicine and delivered by the health care industry. Race for the Cure, while embracing many of the assumptions and visions of this biomedical perspective, was able to challenge successfully some of its stigmatizing practices and effects by redeeming and revalorizing the social identities of women with breast cancer. The biomedical model has been challenged in more radical ways, however, by the local women's cancer movement and by the environmental justice movement. The women's cancer movement, represented by the Women & Cancer Walk, challenged the narrowness of the biomedical model by insisting that the problems of breast cancer be examined from a wide-angle lens that extended beyond the parameters of the clinic and screening procedures and into the communities in which women actually live, and struggle to live, with cancer post-diagnosis. The Toxic Tour of the Cancer Industry, the synthesis of the feminist cancer community and the environmental justice movement, challenged the biomedical model from a different angle. Whereas the Walk directed attention beyond the medical clinic and drew attention to struggles and problems that occur *after* the moment of diagnosis, the Toxic Tour redirected the focus to a point in time *before* the moment of diagnosis and *before* the practices of screening and early detection. The environmental justice movement, represented by the Toxic Tour, reframed the agenda around the politics of cancer *prevention*. In so doing, however, the needs of women actually living with breast cancer were pushed back into the margins.

The cultures of action created and deployed in the Women's Walk and the Toxic Tour of the cancer industry have been misrepresented and ignored by dominant media representations of the breast cancer movement. They have been silenced and dismissed by the state, the health care system, and the forces of corporate capital. By amplifying the voices and making visible the cultures of action that have been minimized by dominant representations, this article also seeks to recover some of these "subjugated knowledges" (Foucault 1980) and to represent some of the "stories less told" (Darnovsky 1992). At the same time, I am also interested in drawing attention to aspects of culture within social movements that have received short shrift within the sociological literature. Here, too, there are subjugated knowledges and stories less told, and these stories have to do with the ways that meanings are not only collectively enacted and enunciated, but are shaped and informed by profoundly emotional and embodied dimensions of experience and participation. This article thus attempts to complicate narratives of the breast cancer movement and, at the same time, to complicate sociological narratives of culture within social movements. It does so, in part, by paying attention to the ways in which bodies figure not only as sites of disease, but as the vehicles and products of social movements, and as anchors and signifiers of contested meanings.

Notes

1. See Patterson (1987) for a cultural history of cancer in the United States from the 1880s to the early 1980s, and see Stacey (1997) for a feminist, cultural analysis of cancer in postmodern societies. See Ross (1987) for an organizational history of the American Cancer Society, Rettig (1977) for a political history of the National Cancer Act of 1971, and Breslow and Breslow (1995) for an historical perspective on cancer control campaigns. Proctor (1995) provides a political history of scientific knowledge about cancer, while Yadlon (1997) constructs a Foucaultian analysis of discourses of individual risk and responsibility, and Fosket, LaFia and Karran (2002)

analyze representations of breast cancer in popular women's magazines. See Agran (1977), Epstein (1978), and Moss (1982) for early muckraking analyses of the industrial production of cancer, the growth of the cancer establishment, and the corporate shaping of cancer policy and Markle, Petersen and Wagenfeld (1978) for a study of the laetrile controversy. See Altman (1996), Batt (1994), Brady (1991), Clorfene-Casten (1996), Linden (1995), Soffa (1994), and Stocker (1991, 1993) for feminist perspectives on the politics of breast cancer and women's cancer activism in the nineties. See Carson (1962), Kushner (1975, 1984), Lorde (1980), and Rennie (1977) for pioneering contributions that laid the groundwork for breast cancer activism in the nineties. Finally, Colburn et al. (1996), and Steingraber (1997) offer recent contributions that are feeding into contemporary mobilizations around cancer and the environment. Studies of breast cancer activism have been published by Montini (1996), Taylor and Van Willigen (1996), and Anglin (1997), and are addressed in the next section of this paper.

2. Some of the factors that distinguish recent forms of cancer activism from those of the past are: 1) the fragmentation of the category of cancer into the narrower and more specialized categories of particular *types* of cancer; 2) the movement of *breast* cancer, in particular, into a politically and discursively privileged position; 3) the prominence of new subjectivities and collective identities (e.g., breast cancer survivors, breast cancer warriors, women living with cancer; women at risk); and, 4) the scale and scope of activism and the density of networks and linkages between proliferating organizations, campaigns, and coalitions.

3. Susan Ferraro's (1993) article in the *New York Times Magazine* detailed the early lobbying success of the National Breast Cancer Coalition. In its first year of lobbying, the Coalition secured a $43 million increase in national funds for breast cancer research—an increase of almost fifty percent. The following year, it won an additional $300 million. More recently, NBCC's own publications indicate that between 1991 and 1997, the federal budget for research on breast cancer increased fivefold as a result of its lobbying efforts—from less than $90 million to more than $500 million.

4. More than three yeas of participant observation in the San Francisco Bay Area began in the fall of 1994. Field research included the observation of four different cancer support groups (ranging from two months to two years), ongoing volunteer work at a feminist cancer resource center, and participant observation in a range of networks, projects, fund-raisers, cultural evens, educational forums, environmental protests, street theater, public hearings, early detection campaigns, and various conferences and symposia. My research also included more than forty taped interviews with cancer and breast cancer experts, advocates, and activists. Although this paper grew out of a broader framework of fieldwork, it draws most directly upon my participant observation of the three events in question—Race for the Cure®, the Women & Cancer Walk, and the Toxic Tour of the Cancer Industry. I conducted participant observation at four consecutive Race for the Cure events held in San Francisco (1994 to 1997), I helped organize and staff two Women & Cancer Walks (1995–96). I also participated in three consecutive Toxic Tours of the Cancer Industry (1995–97) and attended TLC meetings beginning shortly after the group's formation in 1994.

5. The concept *culture of action* should not be confused with Ann Swidler's theory of culture in her 1986 essay "Culture in Action: Symbols and Strategies." Swidler developed the concept of culture as a "tool kit" in order to explain how culture influences individual action—hence, culture *in* action. In Swidler's formulation, culture functions as a set of tools, or resources, that are used to fashion action repertoires and innovations. My concept of cultures of action does not address the question of *how* culture (the independent variable in Swidler's formulation) influences action (the dependent variable). I am seeking, instead, to develop a comparative analysis of how systems of embodied meanings are produced within different, representative episodes of collection action. In my analysis, cultures of action are the assembly of practices *and* the product.

6. Taylor and Van Willigen's (1995) three-dimensional conceptualization of gender as an institution is based on the work of Judith Lorber (1994).

7. This identification of commonalities is accomplished in different ways, and with different purposes, in each of the three studies under discussion. Montini (1996) creates a category comprised of a representative sample of women activists from each of the states that attempted to pass breast cancer informed consent legislation. She then uses grounded theory to analyze her interview data and looks for what is common, or generalizable. Taylor and Van Willigen (1996) use diverse sources of data to develop an analysis of the breast cancer movement as a whole so that they can position it and the postpartum depression movement as representative of self-help movements in general. They, like Montini (1996), look for commonalities and generalizable characteristics rather than dissimilarities and distinctions. Anglin (1997) positions her case study of a breast cancer organization as representative of the breast cancer movement as a whole. She then develops a critique of the movement by drawing upon texts produced and circulated within arenas outside of it.

8. "Race for the Cure" is a registered trademark. For the sake of easier reading, I have eliminated the trademark symbol (®) in the remainder of the text.

9. Brinker's husband, Norman Brinker, is a tremendously wealthy and well-connected businessman—a founder of three national restaurant chains—and active in Republican politics. Through her husband's connections, Brinker became acquainted with the Bushes, Quayles, the Reagans, and other powerful Republicans whose support and name-recognition she was able to enlist in her breast cancer work (Altman 1996; Love 1995).

10. Although the Komen Foundation has steered away from challenging the medical profession and the research establishment, it spearheaded the movement to force the health insurance industry to cover baseline and screening mammograms. As far back as 1987, for example, Komen volunteers successfully lobbied members of the Texas state legislature for insurance coverage of baseline mammograms, thus setting a precedent for legislation in many other states, and federally (Altman 1996).

11. For example, Brinker and the Komen Foundation pulled out of the committee that issued the call for, and guided the formation of, the feminist National Breast Cancer Coalition. One interview subject told me that, at this meeting, "the Komen ladies, dripping in diamonds, sat on one side of the table, and across from them were some women from the Mary Helen Mautner Project for Lesbians and Cancer." According to the story told by this interviewee—a story I have often heard repeated in activist circles—the Komen ladies (and they are always referred to as "ladies") decided to pull out of the NBCC as it was in the process of formation because they did not want to work with feminists and lesbians. The repetition of this narrative within certain networks speaks to a particular set of cultural and political divisions that the Komen Foundation is seen as representing.

12. Komen publicity materials specify that 25 percent of the proceeds from the San Francisco Race for the Cure go to support the work of the national office in Dallas and to fund the National Grants program for breast cancer research. The remaining 75 percent of the net proceeds stay in the host community to fund local projects, especially education and early detection programs for medically underserved women.

13. For the past 20 years, the San Francisco Bay Area has had the highest documented rates of breast cancer in the world. The figures available in 1994 showed that the rate was "about 50% higher than in most European countries and five times higher than in Japan" (Northern California Cancer Center 1994).

14. "The pill" refers to tamoxifen, a hormonal, systemic treatment for women who have been diagnosed with breast cancer (and approved in September 1998 by the FDA as a "preventative" treatment for healthy women at "higher risk" for developing breast cancer). Although the

speaker at the Race referred to the early eighties as a time when neither tamoxifen, chemotherapy, nor radiation were available to women with breast cancer, this is not entirely accurate. All three treatment modalities were available and used during the early eighties, although tamoxifen and chemotherapy were typically reserved for women with later stage disease (De Gregorio and Wiebe 1994; Moss 1995). But the details and accuracy of the speaker's narrative are less important than the trope of medical progress.

15. According to even the most conservative estimates, mammograms (and the radiologists who interpret them) fail to diagnose breast cancers large enough to be visualized by this technology at least 15 percent of the time—even more among premenopausal women ("Fact Sheet on Breast Cancer." Office of Women's Health, U.S. Public Health Service n.d.). Most breast cancers do not appear on mammograms and cannot be "seen" by radiologists until they have been growing for about eight years (Love and Lindsey 1995:265).

16. The historical data for this background section is based on an interview (1997) with Abby Zimberg, one of the founders and key organizers of the Women & Cancer Walk. The rest of the analysis is based upon my participant observation of organizing meetings and activities during 1995 and 1996, and my participant observation during the actual events.

17. The beneficiary organizations were: Bay Area Black Women's Health Project; Breast Cancer Action; Cancer Support Community; Charlotte Maxwell Complementary Clinic; Lyon-Martin Women's Health Services; Mission Neighborhood Health Center; Mujeres Unidas Y Activas; National Latina Health Organization: National Black Leadership Initiative Against Cancer; Native American Health Centers; Older Women's league; Vietnamese Community Health Promotion Project; and Women's Cancer Resource Center.

18. As a result of a series of complicated developments the Women & Cancer Walk was not held in 1997 and it seems unlikely that it will be held again.

19. The information about the first two meetings of the Toxic Links Coalition (TLC) is based upon interviews with cancer activist Judy Brady and the public recounting of this history at various events. I began doing participant-observation of the TLC in the early stages of its formation—in October 1994—so most of this information comes from my notes on those meetings and from early events, including the 1994 demonstrating at Race for the Cure.

20. During the next few months, the Coalition grew to include a handful of unaffiliated individuals and more than 20 organizations—mostly from the environmental movement community.

21. This is information that circulates orally within the feminist cancer and environmental justice movements and has been reproduced, on dozens of occasions, in feminist cancer and environmental movement newsletters (e.g., the newsletters of Breast Cancer Action [San Francisco], the Women's Cancer Resource Center [Berkeley], the Women's Community Cancer Project [Cambridge], and *Rachel's Environmental Weekly*—published by the Environmental Research Foundation), in leftist magazines (cf. Paulsen 1993, 1994), in books written by investigative journalists (Batt 1994; Clorfene-Casten 1996), and in scholarly publications (Proctor 1995).

References

Agran, Larry. 1977. The Cancer Connection—And What We Can Do About It. Boston. Mass.: Houghton Mifflin.

Althusser, Louis. 1971. Lenin and Philosophy and Other Essays. New York: Monthly Review Press.

Altman, Roberta. 1996. Waking Up, Fighting Back: The Politics of Breast Cancer. New York: Little, Brown and Company.

Anglin, Mary K. 1997. "Working from the inside out: Implications of breast cancer activism for biomedical policies and practices." Social Science and Medicine 44:1403–1415.

Batt, Sharon. 1994. Patient No More: The Politics of Breast Cancer. Charlottetown, Canada: Gynergy Books.

Bourdieu, Pierre. 1977. Outline of a Theory of Practice, Cambridge, Mass.: Cambridge University Press.

———. 1984. Distinction: A Social Critique of the Judgment of Taste. Cambridge, Mass.: Harvard University Press.

Brady, Judy (ed.). 1991. 1 in 3: Women with Cancer Confront an Epidemic. San Francisco, Calif.: Cleis Press.

Breslow, Lester, and Devra Miller Breslow. 1995. "Historical perspectives on cancer control." In Readings in American Health Care: Current Issues in Socio-Historical Perspective, ed. William G. Rothstein, 364–374. Madison, Wisc.: University of Wisconsin Press.

Butler, Judith. 1990. "Performative acts and gender constitution: An essay in phenomenology and feminist theory." In Performing Feminisms: Feminist Critical Theory and Theatre, ed. Sue-Ellen Case, 270–282. Baltimore, Mass.: The Johns Hopkins University Press.

Carson, Rachel. 1962. Silent Spring. New York: Houghton Mifflin Company.

Chater, Veronica. 1997. "The run of their lives." Northern California Woman (October).

Clorfene-Casten, Liane. 1996. Breast Cancer: Poisons, Profits and Prevention. Monroe, Maine: Common Courage Press.

Colborn, Theo, Dianne Dumanoski, and John Peterson Myers. 1996. Our Stolen Future: Are We Threatening Our Fertility, Intelligence, and Survival?—A Scientific Detective Story. New York: A Dutton Book.

Darnovsky, Marcy. 1992. "Stories less told: Histories of US environmentalism." Socialist Review 22:11–54.

Epstein, Samuel S., M.D. 1978. The Politics of Cancer. Garden City, N.Y.: Anchor Books.

Fantasia, Rick, and Eric L. Hirsch. 1995. "Culture in rebellion: The appropriation and transformation of the veil in the Algerian revolution." Culture and Social Movements, eds. Hank Johnston and Bert Klandermans, 144–162. Minneapolis, Minn.: University of Minnesota Press.

Ferraro, Susan. 1993. "'You can't look away anymore': The anguished politics of breast cancer." New York Times Magazine (August 15):24–27, 58–62.

Ferree, Myra Marx, and Patricia Yancey Martin (eds.). 1995. Feminist Organizations: Harvest of the New Women's Movement. Philadelphia: Temple University Press.

Fine, Gary Alan. 1995. "Public narration and group culture: Discerning discourse in social movements." In Culture and Social Movements, eds. Hank Johnston and Bert Klandermans, 127–143. Minneapolis: University of Minnesota Press.

Fosket, Jennifer, Christine LaFia, and Angie Karran. 2002. "Breast cancer in popular women's magazines from 1913 to 1996." In Breast Cancer: Society Shapes an Epidemic, eds. Susan J. Ferguson and Anne S. Kasper. New York: St. Martins Press.

Foucault, Michel. 1973. The Birth of the Clinic: An Archaeology of Medical Perception. New York: Vintage Books.

———. 1977. Discipline and Punish: The Birth of the Prison. New York: Vintage Books.

———. 1978. History of Sexuality, Volume I. New York: Pantheon Books.

———. 1980. "Two lectures." In Power and Knowledge: Selected Interviews and Other Writings 1972–1977, ed. Colin Gordon, 78–108. New York: Pantheon.

———. 1983. "Afterword: The subject and power." In Michel Foucault: Beyond Structuralism and Hermeneutics, eds. Hubert Dreyfus and Paul Rabinow, 208–226. Chicago: University of Chicago Press.

Ingalsbee, Timothy. 1993. "Resource and action mobilization theories: The new social psychological research agenda." Berkeley Journal of Sociology 38:139–156.

Jenson, Jane. 1987. "Changing discourse, changing agendas: Political rights and reproductive policies in France." In The Women's Movements of the United States and Western Europe: Consciousness, Political Opportunity, and Public Policy, eds. Mary Fainsod Katzenstein and Carol McClurg Mueller, 64–88. Philadelphia: Temple University Press.

———. 1995. "What's in a name? Nationalist movements and public discourse." In Social Movements and Culture, eds. Hank Johnston and Bert Klandermans, 107–126. Minneapolis: University of Minnesota.

Johnston, Hank, and Bert Klandermans (eds.). 1995. Social Movements and Culture, Volume 4. Minneapolis: University of Minnesota Press.

Kushner, Rose. 1975. Breast Cancer: A Personal History and an Investigative Report. New York: Harcourt Brace Jovanovich.

———. 1984. Alternatives. Cambridge, Mass.: The Kensington Press.

Larana, Enrique, Hank Johnston, and Joseph Gusfield (eds.). 1994. New Social Movements: From Ideology to Identity. Philadelphia: Temple University Press.

Linden, Ruth. 1995. "Writing the breast: Contests over screening mammography, 1973–1995." History and Philosophy of Science Colloquium. Stanford University. (April 27)

Lofland, John. 1995. "Charting degrees of movement culture: Tasks of the cultural cartographer." In Culture and Social Movements, eds. Hank Johnston and Bert Klandermans, 188–216. Minneapolis: University of Minnesota Press.

Lorber, Judith. 1994. Paradoxes of Gender. New Haven, Conn.: Yale University Press.

Lorde, Audre. 1980. The Cancer Journals. San Francisco, Calif.: Aunt Lute Books.

Love, Susan, and Karen Lindsey. 1995. Dr. Susan Love's Breast Book. (2nd ed.) New York: Addison-Wesley Publishing Company.

Markle, Gerald E., James C. Peterson, and Morton O. Wagenfeld. 1978. "Notes from the cancer underground: Participation in the laetrile movement." Social Science and Medicine 12:31–37.

McAdam, Doug, John D. McCarthy, and Mayer N. Zald. 1996. "Opportunities, mobilizing structures, and framing processes: Toward a synthetic, comparative perspective on social movements." Comparative Perspectives on Social Movements: Political Opportunities, Mobilizing Structures, and Cultural Framings, eds. Doug McAdam, John D. McCarthy and Mayer N. Zald. New York: Cambridge University Press.

Melucci, Alberto. 1994. "Paradoxes of post-industrial democracy everyday life and social movements." Berkeley Journal of Sociology 38:185–192.

Montini, Theresa. 1991. "Women's activism for breast cancer informed consent laws." Unpublished doctoral dissertation. University of California, San Francisco.

———. 1996. "Gender and emotion in the advocacy of breast cancer informed consent legislation." Gender and Society 10:9–23.

Morris, Aldon, and Carol McClurg Mueller (eds.). 1992. Frontiers in Social Movement Theory. New Haven: Yale University Press.

Moss, Ralph W. 1982. The Cancer Syndrome. New York: Grove Press, Inc.

———. 1995. Questioning Chemotherapy. New York: Equinox Press.

Northern California Cancer Center. 1994. "Greater Bay Area Cancer Registry Report." 5(1).

Office on Women's Health. 1997. "Fact sheet on breast cancer." U.S. Public Health Service: Washington D.C., distributed at Women's Health and Emerging Issues: California Perspective Conference; co-sponsored by California Public Health Association-North and the Office of Women's Health, California Department of Health Services. (October 24)

Patterson, James T. 1987. The Dread Disease: Cancer and Modern American Culture. Cambridge, Mass.: Harvard University Press.

Paulsen, Monte. 1993. "The politics of cancer." UTNE Reader (November/December).
———. 1993. "The cancer business." Mother Jones (May/June).
Proctor, Robert N. 1995. Cancer Wars: How Politics Shapes What We Know and Don't Know About Cancer. New York: BasicBooks.
Rennie, Susan. 1977. "Mammography: X-rated film." Chrysalis 5:21–33.
Rettig, Richard A. 1977. Cancer Crusade: The Story of the National Cancer Act of 1971. Princeton, N.J.: Princeton University Press.
Ross, Walter S. 1987. Crusade: The Official History of the American Cancer Society. New York: Arbor House.
San Francisco Chronicle. 1996. Bay Area Section. (October 21):C1.
Soffa, Virginia M. 1994. The Journey Beyond Breast Cancer: Taking an Active Role in Prevention, Diagnosis, and Your Own Healing. Rochester, Vermont: Healing Arts Press.
Stacey, Jackie. 1997. Teratologies: A Cultural Study of Cancer. New York: Routledge.
Steingraber, Sandra. 1997. Living Downstream: An Ecologist Looks at Cancer and the Environment. New York: Addison-Wesley Publishing Company.
Stocker, Midge (ed.). 1991. Cancer as a Women's Issue: Scratching the Surface. Volume 1. Chicago: Third Side Press.
———. 1993. Confronting Cancer, Constructing Change: New Perspectives on Women and Cancer, Volume 2. Chicago: Third Side Press.
Swidler, Ann. 1995. "Cultural power and social movements." In Social Movements and Culture, eds. Hank Johnston and Bert Klandermans, 25–40. Minneapolis: University of Minnesota Press.
———. 1986. "Culture in action: Symbols and strategies." American Sociological Review 51:273–286.
Taylor, Verta, and Marieke Van Willigen. 1996. "Women's self-help and the reconstruction of gender: The postpartum support and breast cancer movements." Mobilization: An International Journal 1:123–143.
Taylor, Verta, and Nancy Whittier. 1995. "Analytical approaches to social movement culture: The culture of the women's movement." Social Movements and Culture, eds. Hank Johnston and Bert Klandermans. 163–187. Minneapolis: University of Minnesota Press.
Yadlon, Susan. 1997. "Skinny women and good mothers: The rhetoric of risk, control, and culpability in the production of knowledge about breast cancer." Feminist Studies 23:645–677.

PART IV

GENDER

Health differences between men and women are the result of sex differences in physiology and socially constructed gender roles. While biomedical explanations of gender differences stress the physical differences between men and women, sociologists point to the ways in which gender roles shape individuals' life experiences. Men's and women's choices of occupations determine the degree to which they will be exposed to different sets of health hazards—for instance, physical dangers or toxic chemicals in the case of construction or heavy factory work, or repetitive fine-motor motions in the case of clerical work. Gender roles thereby affect individuals' health indirectly through the choices they make regarding occupations, family life, lifestyle habits, and use of health care.

Gender roles may also affect the ways that health issues are socially constructed and the ways that health care is provided. A social problems approach to gender and health helps us to analyze where and why some health issues become so strongly associated with gender roles. Much of the scholarship regarding gender and health has focused on the interaction between health issues and women's gender roles, especially the ways that women's life experiences are defined as medical problems and thus subject to medical intervention. The articles included in part IV illuminate some of the ways that gender roles and health issues may interact, including the ways that medicine has been used to "help" women fulfill their traditional roles and functions in society.

In yet another medical "discovery," physicians defined menopause as a deficiency disease in the 1950s, according to Frances McCrea's article on "The Politics of Menopause: The 'Discovery' of a Deficiency Disease." The development of synthetic estrogens contributed to this definition, as it allowed physicians to prescribe and pharmacists to distribute estrogens to women, thereby holding off the biological (and social) effects of menopause. In contrast, feminists defined menopause as a normal aging process, stating that social roles, not hormones, make aging problematic for women.

Cosmetic surgery is "normal" and "natural" for women, according to the women patients and cosmetic surgeons interviewed for Diana Dull and Candace West's article, "Accounting for Cosmetic Surgery: The Accomplishment of Gender." Women are seen as "objectively" needing repair, to keep up a youthful appearance, while the few men who considered cosmetic surgery did so because of job-related concerns. Cosmetic surgery, therefore, helps individuals (especially women) fulfill their gender roles.

According to C. Amanda Rittenhouse's analysis in "The Emergence of Premenstrual Syndrome as a Social Problem," women's hormones were defined (once more) as problematic in the 1980s. Rittenhouse examines how the definition of premenstrual syndrome was shaped by the interaction of medical, popular, and feminist literature, resulting in debates regarding the effect that women's reproductive capacities have on women's behavior and abilities (particularly in the public sphere) and on their appropriate gender roles.

CHAPTER 10

The Politics of Menopause
THE "DISCOVERY" OF A DEFICIENCY DISEASE

Frances B. McCrea

In the 1960s the medical profession in the United States hailed the contraceptive pill as the "great liberator" of women, and estrogens in general as the fountain of youth and beauty. Prominent gynecologists "discovered" that menopause was a "deficiency disease," but promised women that estrogen replacement therapy would let them avoid menopause completely and keep them "feminine forever." Yet within a few years, U.S. feminists in the vanguard of an organized women's health movement defined the health care system, including estrogen treatment, as a serious social problem. The male-dominated medical profession was accused of reflecting and perpetuating the social ideology of women as sex objects and reproductive organs. Treating women with dangerous drugs was defined as exploitation and an insidious form of social control.

These issues raised several questions: How did such diametrically opposed definitions evolve? How, under what conditions, and by whom does a certain behavior become defined as deviant or sick? In what context does a putative condition become defined as a social problem?

I believe that definitions of health and illness are socially constructed and that these definitions are inherently political. "Deviant behaviors that were once defined as immoral, sinful or criminal," according to Conrad and Schneider (1980:1), "have now been given new medical meanings" which are "profoundly political in nature" and have "real political consequences." Indeed "in many cases these medical treatments have become a new form of social control."

I interpret the definition of menopause from this framework. During the 19th century, Victorian physicians viewed menopause as a sign of sin and decay; with the advent of Freudian psychology in the early 20th century, it was viewed as a neurosis; and as synthetic estrogens became readily available in the 1960s, physicians treated menopause as a deficiency disease (McCrea, 1981). Perhaps more important than these differences, however, are four themes which pervade the medical definitions of menopause. These are: (1) women's potential and function are biologically destined; (2) women's worth is determined by fecundity and attractiveness; (3) rejection of the feminine role will bring physical and emotional havoc; (4) aging women are useless and repulsive.

In this paper I first analyze the rise of the disease definition of menopause and show that this definition reflects and helps create the prevailing ageism and sexism and of our times. Then I show how the disease definition has been challenged from inside the medical community. Finally I examine how feminists outside the medical community have also challenged the disease model, claiming that menopause is normal and relatively unproblematic.

Menopause as Disease

The roots of the disease definition of menopause can be traced back to the synthesis of estrogens. The earliest interest in these hormones grew out of efforts to find a cure for male impotence (Buxton, 1944; Page, 1977). In 1889, Charles Édouard Brown-Sequard, a French physiologist, reported to the Société de Biologie in Paris that he experienced renewed vigor and rejuvenation after injecting himself with extracts from animal testicles. Four years later another French scientist, Regis de Bordeaux, used an ovarian extract injection to treat a female patient for menopausal "insanity." And in 1896 a German physician, Theodore Landau, used desiccated ovaries to treat menopausal symptoms at the Landau Clinic in Berlin. In the late 1920s, Edgar Allen and Edward Doisey isolated and crystallized theelin (later known as estrone) from the urine of pregnant women. In 1932 Samuel Geist and Frank Spielman described in the *American Journal of Obstetrics and Gynecology* their efforts to treat menopausal women with theelin. Such treatments, however, were expensive and supplies of the drug limited, since it was derived from human sources. These problems were solved in 1936 when Russell Marker and Thomas Oakwood developed a synthetic form of estrogen known as diethylstilbesteral (DES). This cheap and potent hormone substance could be made readily available to a large number of women and paved the way for the development of the contraceptive pill. The last step in the development of hormone therapy occurred in 1943 when James Goodall developed an estrogen extract from the urine of pregnant mares. Termed conjugated equine estrogen and manufactured by Ayerst under the brand name Premarin, it was only about half as potent as synthetic estrogen, but it created fewer unpleasant side effects.

By the early 1960s exogenous estrogen (that is, estrogen originating outside the human body) was widely available in the United States, and was inexpensive and easy to administer. It was used to treat various conditions of aging. But if estrogens were to become the cure, what was to be the disease?

> [Medicine] is active in seeking out illness. . . . One of the greatest ambitions of the physician is to discover and describe a "new" disease or syndrome and to be immortalized by having his name used to identify the disease. Medicine, then, is oriented to seeking out and finding illness, which is to say that it seeks to create social meanings of illness where that meaning or interpretation was lacking before. And insofar as illness is defined as something bad—to be eradicated or contained—medicine plays the role of what Becker called the "moral entrepreneur" (Friedson, 1970:252).

The moral entrepreneur who, during the 1960s, led the crusade to redefine menopause as a disease was the prominent Brooklyn gynecologist Robert A. Wilson.

As founder and head of the Wilson Foundation, established in New York in 1963 to promote estrogens and supported by $1.3 million in grants from the pharmaceutical industry (Mintz and Cohn, 1977), Wilson's writings were crucial to the acceptance of menopause as a "deficiency disease" and the large-scale routine administration of Estrogen Replacement Therapy (ERT). He claimed that menopause was a hormone deficiency disease similar to diabetes and thyroid dysfunction. In an article published in the *Journal of the American Medical Association*, Wilson (1962) claimed that estrogen prevented breast and genital cancer and other problems of aging. Even though his methodology was weak,[1] this article launched a campaign to promote estrogens for the prevention of menopause and age-related diseases.

A year later, writing with his wife Thelma in the *Journal of the American Geriatrics Society*, Wilson and Wilson (1963) advocated that women be given estrogens from "puberty to grave." Crucial to the popular acceptance of the disease model of menopause was Robert Wilson's widely read book *Feminine Forever* (1966a), which claimed that menopause is a malfunction threatening the "feminine essence." In an article summarizing his book, Wilson described menopausal women as "living decay" (1966b:70) but said ERT could save them from being "condemned to witness the death of their womanhood" (1966b:66). He further proclaimed that menopause and aging could be allayed with ERT and listed 26 physiological and psychological symptoms that the "youth pill" could avert—including hot flashes, osteoporosis (thinning of bone mass), vaginal atrophy (thinning of vaginal walls), sagging and shrinking breasts, wrinkles, absent-mindedness, irritability, frigidity, depression, alcoholism, and even suicide.

Wilson also was aware of the physician's potential and even mandate for social control. The first paragraph of a chapter title "Menopause—The Loss of Womanhood and Good Health" states:

> . . . I would like to launch into the subject of menopause by discussing its *effect on men*. Menopause covers such a wide range of physical and emotional symptoms that the implications are by no means confined to the woman. *Her husband, her family, and her entire relationship to the outside world* are affected almost as strongly as her own body. Only in this broader context can the problem of the menopause—as well as the benefits of hormonal cure—be properly appreciated (emphasis added, 1966a:92).

Wilson gives an example of how he helped a distressed husband who came to him for help with the following complaint:

> She is driving me nuts. She won't fix meals. She lets me get no sleep. She picks on me all the time. She makes up lies about me. She hits the bottle all day. And we used to be happily married (1966a:93).

This man's wife, Wilson says, responded well to "intensive" estrogen treatment and in no time resumed her wifely duties (1966a:94). In another chapter Wilson conjures up visions of Ira Levin's (1972) novel *The Stepford Wives*:

> In a family situation, estrogen makes women adaptable, even-tempered, and generally easy to live with. Consequently, a woman's estrogen carries significance beyond her own well-being. It also contributes toward the happiness

of her family and all those with whom she is in daily contact. Even frigidity in women has been shown to be related to estrogen deficiency. The estrogen-rich woman, as a rule, is capable of far more generous and satisfying sexual response than women whose femininity suffers from inadequate chemical support (Wilson, 1966:64).

From Wilson's own words it is obvious that the disease label is not neutral. This label, like any disease label, decreases the status and the autonomy of the patient while increasing the status and power of the physician. When seen as part of a political process,

> knowledge and skill are claimed by a group to advance its interests. True or false the knowledge, disinterested or interested the motive, claims of knowledge function as ideologies. . . . insofar as claims to knowledge and skill are essential elements in a political process . . . it is highly unlikely that they can remain neutrally descriptive (Freidson, 1971:30).

By individualizing the problems of menopause, the physician turns attention away from any social structural interpretation of women's conditions. The locus of the solution then becomes the doctor-patient interaction in which the physician is active, instrumental, and authoritative while the patient is passive and dependent. The inherent authority of physicians is institutionalized in ways that minimize reliance on explanation and persuasion. This clinical mentality is "intrinsically imperialistic, claiming more for the profession's knowledge and skill, and a broader jurisdiction than in fact can be justified by demonstrable effectiveness" (Freidson, 1971:31). Such imperialism is independent of the particular motivation of the physician. Not only could it function as "crude self-interest," but also as "a natural outcome of the deep commitment to the value of his work developed by the thoroughly socialized professional" (1971:31).

A number of prominent U.S. physicians supported Wilson's claims. Robert Greenbelt (1974), former president of the American Geriatrics Society, claimed that about 75 percent of menopausal women are acutely estrogen-deficient and advocated ERT for them, even if they were without symptoms. Another crusader for ERT, Helen Jern, a gynecologist at the New York Infirmary, wrote a book of case studies proclaiming the miraculous recoveries made by elderly women placed on ERT:

> I know the remarkably beneficial effect of estrogen as energizer, tranquilizer and anti-depressant. I know that it stimulates and maintains mental capacity, memory, and concentration, restores zest for living, and gives a youthful appearance. . . . Hormone therapy, once begun, should be continued throughout a woman's lifetime. It is my firm belief that many female inmates of nursing homes and mental institutions could be restored to full physical and mental health through adequate hormone therapy (Jern, 1973:156).

David Reuben proclaimed in his best-selling book *Everything You Wanted To Know About Sex*:

> As estrogen is shut off, a woman comes as close as she can to being a man. Increased facial hair, deepened voice, obesity, and decline of breasts and female genitalia all contribute to a masculine appearance. Not really a man but no longer a functional woman, these individuals live in a world of intersex. Having outlived their ovaries, they have outlived their usefulness as human beings (Reuben, 1969:287).

But women need not despair. Reuben (1969:290) proclaimed that with estrogen replacements women can "turn back the clock," and adequate amounts of estrogens throughout their lives will protect them against breast and uterine cancer.

Throughout the late 1960s and early 1970s, Wilson's book was excerpted widely in traditional women's journals, and over 300 articles promoting estrogens appeared in popular magazines (Johnson, 1977). During the same period an aggressive advertising campaign, capitalizing on the disease label, was launched by the U.S. pharmaceutical industry. ERT products were widely advertised in medical literature and promotional material as amelioratives for a variety of psychological, as well as somatic, problems. One advertisement depicted a seated woman clutching an airline ticket, with her impatient husband standing behind her glancing at his watch. The copy read:

> Bon Voyage? Suddenly she'd rather not go. She's waited thirty years for this trip. Now she doesn't have the "bounce." She has headaches, hot flashes, and she feels tired and nervous all the time. And for no reason she cries (Seaman and Seaman, 1977:281).

Another advertisement promoted ERT "for the menopausal problems that bother him the most" (Seaman and Seaman, 1977:281). Yet another advertisement stated: "Any tranquilizer might calm her down . . . but at her age, estrogen may be what she really needs" (Seaman and Seaman, 1977:281). Such advertisements paid off; between 1963 and 1973 dollar sales in the United States for estrogen replacements quadrupled (U.S. Bureau of the Census, 1975). As one Harvard researcher stated, "few medical interventions have had as widespread application as exogenous estrogen treatment in post-menopausal women" (Weinstein, 1980). By 1975, with prescriptions at an all-time high of 26.7 million (Wolfe, 1979), estrogens had become the fifth most frequently prescribed drug in the United States (Hoover *et al.*, 1976). A 1975 survey in the Seattle-Tacoma area of Washington State revealed that 51 percent of all post-menopausal women had used estrogens for at least three months, with a median duration of over 10 years (Weiss *et al.*, 1976).

Indeed, 1975 was a watershed year for estrogen therapy: sales were at an all-time high and physicians routinely used estrogens to treat a wide variety of purported menopausal symptoms. Yet within a few years this trend changed as estrogen therapy came under attack from inside and outside the medical community.

Medical Controversy

Researchers had suspected an association between estrogens and cancer since the 1890s (Johnson, 1977). Experimental animal studies, conducted in the 1930s and

1940s, claimed that estrogenic and progestinic substances were carcinogenic (Cook and Dodds, 1933; Gardner, 1944; Perry and Ginzton, 1937). Novak and Yui (1936) warned that estrogen therapy might cause a pathological buildup of endometrial tissue.

Most investigators trace the roots of the ERT controversy back to 1947. In that year Dr. Saul Gusberg, then a young cancer researcher at the Memorial Sloane-Kettering Hospital and Columbia University in New York City, made a histologic link between hyperplasia (proliferation of the cells) and adenocarcinoma in the female endometrium (lining of the uterus). After finding a significant increase in endometrial cancer among estrogen users, Gusberg (1947:910) wrote:

> Another human experiment has been setup in recent years by the widespread administration of estrogens to post-menopausal women. The relatively low cost of stilbestrol [synthetic estrogen] and the ease of administration have made its general use promiscuous.

Why was more attention not paid to these early warnings? In addition to the low cost and ease of administering estrogens mentioned by Gusberg, most scientists judged these early cancer studies to be scientifically unsound: those based on animal studies were dismissed as not applicable to humans. Perhaps most importantly, physicians found estrogens to be remarkably effective in alleviating vasomotor disturbances (hot flashes) and vaginal atrophy (Page, 1977:54). In his book *The Ageless Woman*, Sherwin Kaufman (1967:61) described menopausal symptoms as the result of hormone deficiency, and lamented:

> Many women are obviously in need of estrogen replacements but are so afraid of "hormones" that it requires a good deal of explanation to persuade them that estrogen does not cause cancer and may, on the contrary, make them feel much better.

Kaufman regretted that some of his colleagues also share this unwarranted fear of cancer:

> Some doctors prescribe estrogens reluctantly. . . . Historically, and too often hysterically, estrogens have been endowed with malignant potentialities. Paradoxically, it has been pointed out that even conservative physicians may not hesitate to give sedatives or tranquilizers, yet they stop at the suggestion of estrogen replacement therapy. This is baffling to a good many doctors (1967:67).

Kaufman confessed that "Years ago, I used to discontinue such treatment [ERT] after a few months," but "today I am in no rush to stop" (1967:64).

The ERT controversy erupted in 1975 when two epidemiological studies, by research teams from Washington University (Smith *et al.*, 1975) and The Kaiser-Permanente Medical Center in Los Angeles (Ziel and Finkle, 1975), found a link between post-menopausal estrogen therapy and endometrial cancer. The two studies, according to Ziel,[2] were written independently of each other and published side by side in the prestigious *New Eng-*

land Journal of Medicine. By 1980, nine more studies, all done in the United States, concluded that women on ERT were four to 20 times more likely to develop endometrial cancer than non-users (Ziel, 1980). Moreover, the risk of cancer purportedly increased with the duration and dose of estrogens. Indeed, according to Gusberg (1980:729), endometrial cancer has "superseded cervical cancer as the most common malignant tumor of the female reproductive tract."

At a 1979 Consensus Development Conference on Estrogen Use and Post-Menopausal Women, sponsored by the National Institute on Aging, researchers unanimously concluded that ERT substantially increases the risk of endometrial cancer.[3] The final report of the conference concluded that ERT is only effective in the treatment of hot flashes and vaginal atrophy, and, if used at all, should be administered on a cyclical basis (three weeks of estrogen, one week off), at the lowest dose for the shortest possible time.[4] Any candidate for post-menopausal estrogen, the report recommended, "should be given as much information as possible about both the benefits and risks and then, with her physician, reach an individualized decision regarding whether to receive estrogens" (Gastel *et al.*, 1979:2).

Not only has the treatment of menopause come under criticism, the disease label has also been challenged by medical researchers. Saul Gusberg, who first warned of the ERT-cancer link, called the deficiency disease label for menopause "nonsense," adding "People are beginning to be more sensible about this, and realize that not a great trauma has happened to the average woman going through the menopause" (quoted in Reitz, 1977:198). Research presented at the Consensus Development Conference in 1979 claimed that although ovarian production of estrogen declines after the menopause, older women need less estrogen. Moreover, production of the hormone by the adrenal glands partially compensates diminished ovarian production for most women (Ziel and Finkle, 1976). Furthermore, only 10 to 20 percent of women experience severe or incapacitating symptoms, and even those are generally temporary and decline over time (Gastel *et al.*, 1979; McKinley and Jeffreys, 1974).

Researchers have also criticized the disease model on ideological grounds. Ziel and Finkle (1976:737), two well-known cancer researchers, argued that the disease model was based on a traditional view of women's role:

> Because they desire the preservation of cosmetic youth and the unflagging libido of the patients, physicians have championed estrogen replacement therapy in the hope of attaining a maximal quality of life for their patients.

The female patient, in turn, "is readily deluded by her wish to preserve her figure and her physician's implication that estrogen promises eternal youth" (1976:739).

Despite a strong consensus in the research community that ERT increases the risk of endometrial cancer, practicing physicians continued to prescribe the drug. As one San Francisco gynecologist stated after the 1975 cancer studies were published:

> I think of the menopause as a deficiency disease like diabetes. Most women develop some symptoms whether they are aware of them or not, so I prescribe estrogens for virtually all menopausal women for an indefinite period (quoted in Brody, 1975:55).

Even though U.S. prescriptions for ERT have steadily declined since the 1975 cancer studies, some 16 million were written in 1978 (Wolfe, 1979). Indeed, a 1978 Detroit-area survey showed that two-thirds of all women who saw their physicians about menopausal complaints received estrogens and 50 percent received tranquilizers (Dosey and Dosey, 1980). In fact, a 1978 drug analysis by the U.S. Food and Drug Administration (FDA) concluded that menopausal estrogens, even after a major decline, were still "grossly overused" (Burke *et al.*, 1978). My analysis[5] of 1979 estrogen replacement prescriptions revealed that 31 percent were still written for such vague diagnostic categories as "symptoms of senility," "special conditions without sickness," and "mental problems"—in violation of FDA specifications.[6]

Other measures of physicians' endorsement of ERT are authoritative references which describe menopause as a morbid condition for which estrogen therapy is indicated. For example, *The Merck Manual* (Berkow, 1980), a book of diagnosis and therapy widely used by physicians, lists menopause under "Ovarian Dysfunction." Modell's (1980) *Drugs of Choice* lists it under "Diseases of the Endocrine System." Both sources advocate estrogens for treatment. *Drugs of Choice* states that "objective studies" evaluating the risks and benefits are "not currently available" (1980:540). Likewise, *Current Medical Diagnosis and Treatment* (Krupp and Chatton, 1980:731) lists menopause under "Endocrine Disorders" and notes that "estrogen therapy has been recommended for life" but "the advisability of this practice remains unsettled." *Current Therapy* (Kantor, 1980:839) lists as benefits of ERT "improvement of disposition and unreasonable outburst of temper" and "avoidance of the shrinking and sagging of breasts." Attention is called to recent cancer claims, but "when doses are small and administration is in interrupted courses, any potential risk is indeed small and perhaps theoretic." But a patient who has been frightened by "magazine articles" or "Food and Drug Administration bulletins" may "psychologically block the benefits" of ERT (Kantor, 1980:839).

U.S. physicians have viewed the use of ERT as a political issue, and their endorsement of the therapy as an exercise of professional control. Editorials in the *Journal of the American Medical Association* have been critical of outside interference in the doctor-patient relationship. A 1979 editorial criticized the FDA Commissioner for mandating a "biased" warning: "In doing so he has officially expressed his distrust of the medical profession" (Landau, 1979:47). A 1980 editorial castigated the FDA for creating unnecessary "public anxiety." Contradicting almost all the then-current U.S. research, the editorial concluded that "Estrogens already rank among the safest of all pharmaceuticals" (Meier and Landau, 1980:1658).

Menopause as Normal

In the late 1960s and early 1979s, U.S. feminists began to challenge medical authority by questioning the legitimacy of the disease model of menopause. They argued that menopause is not a disease or sickness but a natural process of aging, through which most women pass with minimum difficulty.[7] The medical problems that do arise can be effectively treated or even prevented by adequate nutrition and exercise combined with vitamin supplements. According to feminists, the menstrual and menopausal myths are a form of social control. If women are perceived as physically and emotionally handicapped by menstruation and menopause, they cannot and may not compete with men. The health care system legitimates sexism, under the guise of science, by depicting women's physical and mental capabilities as dependent on their reproductive organs.

Schur (1980:6) calls these struggles over collective definitions "stigma" contests, wherein subordinate groups reject their deviant label. Although economic, legal, and political power are often involved in stigma contests, "what is essentially at stake in such situations is the power of moral standing or acceptability." Thus, stigma contests are always partly symbolic, since prestige and status are important issues (Gusfield, 1966; 1967). Stigmatized individuals must rectify a "spoiled identity" (Goffman, 1963) through collective efforts. In the United States, feminist have tried to neutralize stigma by claiming that menopause is a normal experience of normal women.

On these ideological grounds, feminists have opposed the routine use of ERT. For example, an article, published in *Ms.* in 1972, before strong medical evidence against ERT was uncovered, maintained that menopause was not a traumatic experience for most women. Because menopause freed women from the risk of pregnancy, it was viewed as a sexually liberating event. ERT, seen as an attempt to keep women "feminine forever," was thus viewed as a male exploitation, relegating women to the status of sex objects (Solomon, 1972). Four years later, offering a feminist interpretation of the menstrual and menopausal taboo, Delaney *et al.* (1976:184) stated that "the main fault of *Feminine Forever* lies not in the medicine but in the moralizing."

After medical evidence became available to strengthen the ideological arguments, feminist criticism became widespread. In *Women and the Crisis in Sex Hormones* (Seaman and Seaman, 1977), the ERT controversy received a 70-page analysis titled "Promise Her Anything But Give Her . . . Cancer." These authors warned against the increasing medicalization of normal female functions:

> Pregnancy or non-pregnancy are hardly diseases; and neither is menopause. The latter is a normal developmental state wherein reproductive capacity is winding down; the temporary hot flashes some women experience may be compared to the high-to-low voice register changes adolescent boys evidence when their reproductive capacity is gearing up. We no longer castrate young boys to preserve their male sopranos, nor should we treat hot flashes with a cancer-and-cholesterol pill (1977:xi).

In a collection of feminist critiques, Grossman and Bart (1979:167), two social scientists, make a similar claim in a chapter entitled "Taking Men Out of Menopause":

> . . . [the] actions of the medical and pharmaceutical groups dramatize the sexism and general inhumanity of the male-dominated, profit-oriented U.S. medical system. A "deficiency disease" was invented to serve a drug that could "cure" it, despite the suspicion that the drug caused cancer in women. That the suspicion has been voiced for so many years before anyone would investigate it is yet another example of how unimportant the well-being of women is to men who control research and drug companies who fund much of it.

The 1981 edition of *The Ms. Guide to a Woman's Health* warns women that "Estrogen replacement therapy (ERT) is a dangerously overused treatment. Avoid it if at all possible" (Cooke and Dworkin, 1981:310). The chapter on menopause repeatedly states that the change of life is not a disease but a normal process. Similarly, *The New Woman's Guide to Health and Medicine* states "The truth is that menopause is a positive or at least neutral experience for many women" (Derbyshire, 1980:269). Several other U.S. feminist publications, such as *Majority Report* (Lieberman, 1977) and *Off Our Backs* (Moira, 1977), have taken strong stances against ERT. *Mother Jones* condemned ERT in an article entitled "Feminine Straight to the Grave" (Wolf, 1978).

Though most of the criticism has been voiced by younger feminists, some older women have also opposed ERT. Reitz (1977:181) referred to ERT as "The No. 1 Middle-Age Con" and proclaimed:

> I accept that I'm a healthy woman whose body is changing. No matter how many articles and books I read that tell me I'm suffering from a deficiency disease, I say I don't believe it. I have never felt more in control of my life than I do now and I feel neither deficient nor diseased. I think that people who are promoting this idea—that something is wrong with me because I am 50—have something to gain or are irresponsible or stupid.

Collins (1977:3), in an article in *Prime Time*, a publication devoted to ageist issues, stated:

> Even today the literature . . . defines menopause as a deficiency disease. Of course that may sell estrogen, and we'll stay out of the controversy over whether that's a good thing or not. But it certainly echoes once more the male prejudice against menopausal and post-menopausal women.

Health-related associations and consumer groups have also joined feminists in their opposition to ERT. *Consumer Reports* (1976), the official publication of Consumers Union, published a lengthy article warning women of the risks; Citizens Health, Ralph Nader's organization, opposes (and regularly testifies against) ERT (Wolfe, 1979). Smaller groups such as Coalition For the Medical Rights of Women (Brown, 1978), and National Action Forum for Older Women (1979), have all warned women of the risks of ERT and advocated alternate treatment (diet, exercise, and vitamin supplements) for menopause. Menopause workshops and self-help groups have sprung up across the United States (Page, 1977).

After the 1975 cancer studies several feminist and consumer groups, including the National Women's Health Network and Consumers Union, began to pressure the FDA to warn consumers of the dangers of ERT. On July 22, 1977, after two years of public hearings, the FDA issued a ruling that a "patient package insert" (PPI), warning of the risk of cancer and other dangers, be included with every estrogen and progesterone prescription. On October 5, 1977, in an effort to block this regulation, the Pharmaceutical Manufacturing Association—together with the American College of Obstetricians and Gynecologists, the National Association of Chain Drug Stores, the American Society of Internal Medicine, and various state and county medical societies—responded by filing a civil suit in the Wilmington, Delaware, Federal District Court against the FDA. The plaintiffs charged that the FDA lacked statutory authority to require the patient package insert warning, and that such a requirement was an unconstitutional interference with the practice of medicine. They also asserted that such a regulation is "arbitrary, capricious [and] an abuse of discretion" (*Pharmaceutical Manufacturers Association v. Food and Drug Administration*, 1980).

To represent the interest of women patients, the National Women's Health Network, Consumers Union, Consumers Federation of America, and Women's Equity Action League filed as interveners in the lawsuit in support of the FDA. Three years later, in 1980, Federal District Judge Walter K. Stapleton upheld the FDA decision, giving estrogen replacements the distinction of being one of only four classes[8] of drugs which require such patient package inserts in the United States (*Pharmaceutical Manufacturers Association v. Food and Drug Administration, 1980*). Regulation, however, does not mean compliance, and the feminist victory appears more symbolic than instrumental. A 1979 FDA survey of 271 drug stores in 20 U.S. cities revealed that only 39 percent of all ERT prescriptions were accompanied by the required insert (Morris *et al.*, 1980). Moreover, under the administration of President Ronald Reagan, the FDA has suspended all proposed PPI regulations and is reconsidering existing ones (National Women's Health Network, 1981).[9]

Conclusion

In this article I have characterized the medical-feminist struggle over the collective definition of menopause as a stigma contest. Feminists have attempted to show that menopause is not an event that limits women's psychological or physical capacities, but a natural part of aging. Physicians have tried to explain the problems of middle-aged women through a medical model. In so viewing the life course, including menopause, physicians have tended to see problems experienced during menopause as either "all in the head" or the result of a deficiency disease, to be treated with tranquilizers or hormones.

The aging woman has a particularly vulnerable status in our society. She is no longer the object of adoration and romanticism that youthful women frequently are. Menopause usually comes at a time when children leave home, and husbands frequently seek younger sexual partners. Physical changes taking place in her body might be compounded, and negatively interpreted, by the loss of status and primary social role. Clearly, such women are vulnerable to the promise of a "youth" pill which purports to allay the aging process. Yet to blame all the problems that aging women experience on menopause is a classic case of blaming the victim. The medical model individualizes the problem, and deflects responsibility from the social structure which assigns aging women to a maligned and precarious status.

The vulnerable status of women makes fertile ground for medical imperialism. A health care system, based on fee-for-service, is conducive to defining more and more life events as illnesses. A disease definition of menopause has served the interests of both the medial profession and the pharmaceutical industry. Until these structural arrangements change, the hormone deficiency definition of menopause, or some equivalent to it, is likely to prevail.

Feminists, particularly those in the women's health movement (Ruzek, 1979) have exposed the sexism in women's health care. Publications such as *Our Bodies, Ourselves* (Boston Women's Health Collective, 1976) offered a new definition of women's role in health care. No longer passive consumers of male-dominated medicine, women asserted the right to control their own bodies. Feminists in the health movement have begun to demystify menopause and have made it a topic for discussion. By making their stigma contest part of a broad-base social movement, feminists have been able to define women's health care as a social problem (Mauss, 1975).

Yet in their efforts to fight off the stigma of menopause, some feminists have inadvertently contributed to ageism. Most criticisms have been voiced by younger feminists who have not gone through menopause. Their main focus has been on the medicalization of childbirth and menstruation, and they have extrapolated their analysis to menopause without adequate appreciation of the problems of aging women. By emphasizing the natural and unproblematic nature of menopause, they have overlooked the minority of women who do need medical attention. Such women might feel shame or guilt for suffering through what others claim is normal or unproblematic (Posner, 1979).

Moreover, most feminist studies of menopause have ignored structural factors, restricting their analyses to ideological and social psychological issues. Most feminists in the health movement see women's oppression rooted in arguments of biological inferiority. Feminists have tried to settle the nature-nurture debate by showing that differences in socialization, not biology, account for women's inferior status. In their attempt to overthrow the dictum "biology is destiny," feminists have argued that menstruation, childbirth, and menopause are natural events and, in most cases, do not warrant medical intervention. They charge that myths surrounding these events function as social control. In so doing, feminists have attempted to substitute a new ideology (biology is irrelevant) for an old one (biology is destiny).

The women's health movement, largely middle-class, has approached the problems of women's health care from a point most visible to the middle-class consumer: the private office of the gynecologist or psychiatrist. Focusing on doctor-patient interaction, they have advocated self-help outside the established health care system. Admirable though these actions are, they are not sufficient to change the collective status of women. Nor will the call by radical feminists for self-help, alternative health care accomplish this goal; it only takes the struggle to the margins of the established order (Fee, 1975).

Neither ideological nor social-psychological analyses challenge the private health care system or the economic and social infrastructure which support it. What is needed are studies which elucidate the structural affinities between the economics of health care and the status of women. Such scholarship might point the way toward more meaningful change.

Notes

1. For example, Wilson (1962) stated that 86 of the 304 women had undergone a total hysterectomy either before or during treatment without giving a reason for the hysterectomy (Johnson, 1977).

2. Harry Ziel, February 1, 1983: personal communication.

3. Other U.S. studies claimed that ERT increased the risk of breast cancer, atherosclerosis, myocardial infarction, pulmonary emboli, thrombophlebitis, gall bladder disease, and diabetes (Gastel *et al.*, 1979).

4. In Great Britain researchers are skeptical of the cancer link. They claim that sequential therapy (the addition of progestin for the last five to 13 days of a 20-to-30-day course of estrogen) would eliminate the potential risk of cancer. U.S. researchers claim that sequential treatment may not prevent endometrial cancer (Ziel, 1980:451) and the dangers associated with progestins have not been fully evaluated (Gastel *et al.*, 1979). British researchers also promote ERT for the prevention of osteoporosis (loss of bone mass), but U.S. researchers contend more research is needed on osteoporosis and, at this time, the established cancer risk outweighs the potential benefit of the treatment. For a discussion of the cancer and osteoporosis debates, see McCrea and Markle (1984).

5. The data for this analysis are proprietary, and were obtained from the IMS National Disease and Therapeutics Index, IMS America, Ltd., Ambler, Pennsylvania. IMS collects these data from a representative panel of 1,500 physicians who, four times a year, report case history information on private patients seen over a 48-hour period. For each prescription written, physicians report their diagnosis.

6. The FDA has found menopausal estrogens "effective" only for the treatment of vasomotor symptoms and atrophic vaginitis, and "probably" effective for "estrogen deficiency-induced osteoporosis, and only when used in conjunction with other important therapeutic measures such as diet, calcium, physiotherapy, and good general health-promoting measures." Furthermore, the FDA states that estrogens are not effective for nervous symptoms or depression "and should not be used to treat such conditions" (*Physicians Desk Reference*, 1982:641).

7. Although the majority of U.S. feminists, particularly those in the women's health movement, have defined menopause as unproblematic, there are notable exceptions. For example, Posner (1979:189) charges that feminists ". . . have been led into the ideological trap of denying their own hormones." Lock (1982) argues that physicians ought to pay more attention to physiology, and not dismiss women's medical complaints as psychological. British feminists also want more medical services made available in the treatment of menstruation and menopause (McCrea and Markle, 1984; Sayers, 1982).

8. The other three are oral contraceptives, progestational drug products, and isoproterenol inhalation preparations used by asthmatics.

9. This was confirmed by the FDA official in charge of the PPI program, Louis Morris, May 11, 1983: personal communication.

References

Berkow, Robert. 1980. The Merck Manual of Diagnosis and Therapy. 13th edition. Rahway, N.J.: Merck and Company.

Boston Women's Health Book Collective. 1976. Our Bodies, Ourselves. New York: Simon and Schuster.

Brody, Jane. 1975. "Physicians' views unchanged on use of estrogen therapy." New York Times, December 5:55.

Brown, Sheryl. 1978. "The second forty years." Second Opinion 1:1–10.

Burke, Laurie, Dianne Crosby, and Chang Lao. 1978. "Estrogen prescribing in menopause." Paper presented at the annual meeting of the American Public Health Association, Washington, D.C., November 2, 1977. Updated June 23, 1978.

Buxton, C.L. 1944. "Medical therapy during the menopause." The Journal of Endocrinology 12:591–596.

Collins, Marjorie. 1977. "We are witness to ageism in the medical profession." Prime Time 5:3–5.

Conrad, Peter, and Joseph W. Schneider. 1980. Deviance and Medicalization: From Badness to Sickness. St. Louis: Mosby.

Consumer Reports. 1976. "Estrogen therapy: The dangerous road to Shangri La." Consumer Reports 5:642–645.

Cook, J. W., and E. C. Dodds. 1933. "Sex hormones on cancer-producing compounds." Nature 131:205.

Cooke, Cynthia, and Susan Dworkin. 1981. The Ms. Guide to a Woman's Health. New York: Berkeley Publishing.

Delaney, Janice, Mary Lupton, and Emilly Toth. 1976. The Curse. New York: E. P. Dutton and Co.

Derbyshire, Caroline. 1980. The New Woman's Guide to Health and Medicine. New York: Appleton Century Croft.

Dosey, Mary, and Michael Dosey. 1980. "The climacteric women." Patient Counseling and Health Education 2 (First Quarter):14–21.

Fee, Elizabeth. 1975. "Women and health care: A comparison of theories." International Journal of Health Services 5:397–415.

Freidson, Eliot. 1970. Profession of Medicine. New York: Harper and Row.

———. 1971. The Professions and Their Prospects. Beverly Hills: Sage.

Gardner, W. U. 1944. "Tumors in experimental animals receiving steroid hormones." Surgery 16:8.

Gastel, Barbara, Joan Coroni-Huntley, and Jacob Brody. 1979. "Estrogen use and postmenopausal women: A basis for informed decisions." Summary Conclusion, National Institute on Aging Consensus Development Conference. Bethesda, Maryland, September 13–14.

Geist, Samuel H., and Frank Spielman. 1932. "Therapeutic value of theelin in menopause." American Journal of Obstetrics and Gynecology 23:701.

Goffman, Erving. 1963. Stigma. Englewood Cliffs, N.J.: Prentice Hall.

Greenblatt, Robert. 1974. The Menopausal Syndrome. New York: Medcom Press.

Grossman, Marilyn, and Pauline Bart. 1979. "Taking men out of menopause." Pp. 163–184 in Ruth Hubbard, Mary Sue Henifin, and Barbara Fried (eds.), Women Looking at Biology Looking at Women. Boston: G. K. Hall and Co.

Gusberg, Saul. 1947. "Precursors of corpus carcinoma estrogens and adenomatous hyperplasia." American Journal of Obstetrics and Gynecology 54:905–926.

———. 1980. "Current concepts in cancer." New England Journal of Medicine 302:729–731.

Gusfield, Joseph. 1966. Symbolic Crusade. Urbana: University of Illinois Press.

———. 1967. "Moral passage: The symbolic process in public designations of deviance." Social Problems 15:175–188.

Hoover, Robert, Laman Gray, Philip Cole, and Brian MacMahon. 1976. "Menopausal estrogens and breast cancer." New England Journal of Medicine 295:401–405.

Jern, Helen. 1973. Hormone Therapy of the Menopause and Aging. Springfield, Ill.: Charles C. Thomas Publishers.

Johnson, Anita. 1977. "The risks of sex hormones as drugs." Women and Health 1:8–11.

Kantor, Herman. 1980. "Menopause." Pp. 838–840 in Howard F. Conn (ed.), Current Therapy. Philadelphia: W.B. Saunders and Co.

Kaufman, Shirwin. 1967. The Ageless Woman. Englewood Cliffs, N.J.: Prentice-Hall.

Krupp, Marcus, and Milton Chatton. 1980. Current Medical Diagnosis and Treatment. Los Altos, Cal.: Lange Medical Publications.

Landau, Richard. 1979. "What you should know about estrogens." Journal of the American Medical Association 241:47–51.

Levin, Ira. 1972. The Stepford Wives. New York: Random House.

Lieberman, Sharon. 1977. "But you will make such a feminine corpse . ." Majority Report 6 (February 19–March 4):3.

Lock, Margaret. 1982. "Models and practice in medicine: Menopause as syndrome or life transition?" Culture, Medicine and Psychiatry 6:261–280.

McCrea, Frances. 1981. "The medicalization of normalcy? Changing definitions of menopause." Paper presented at the International Interdisciplinary Congress on Women, Haifa, Israel, December 28–January 1, 1982.

McCrea, Frances, and Gerald Markle. 1984. "Estrogen replacement theraphy in the United States and Great Britain: Different answers to the same questions?" Social Studies of Science 14:1–26.

McKinley, Sonja M., and Margot Jeffreys. 1974. "The menopausal syndrome." British Journal of Preventive and Social Medicine 28:108–115.

Mauss, Armand. 1975. Social Problems as Social Movements. Philadelphia: J. B. Lippincott.

Meier, Paul, and Richard Landau. 1980. "Estrogen replacement therapy." Journal of the American Medical Association 243:1658.

Mintz, Morton, and Victor Cohn. 1977. "Hawking the estrogen fix." The Progressive 41:24–25.

Modell, Walter. 1980. Drugs of Choice, 1980–1981. St. Louis: Mosby.

Moira, Fran. 1977. "Estrogens forever: Marketing youth and death." Off Our Backs (March): 12.

Morris, Louis, Ann Meyers, Paul Gibbs, and Chang Lao. 1981. "Estrogen PPIs: A survey." American Pharmacy 20 (June):318–322.

National Action Forum for Older Women. 1979. "Forum." Newsletter of the National Action Forum for Older Women 2(2):8.

National Women's Health Network. 1981. "Network fights to save PPI program." National Women's Health Network Newsletter 6(6):1–2.

Novak, Emil, and Enmei Yui. 1936. "Relation of endometrial hyperplasia to adenocarcinoma of the uterus." American Journal of Obstetrics and Gynecology 321:596–674.

Page, Jane. 1977. The Other Awkward Age: Menopause. Berkeley, Cal.: Ten Speed Press.

Perry, I. H., and L. L. Ginzton. 1937. "The development of tumors in female mice treated with 1:2:5:6 dibenzanthracone and theelin." American Journal of Cancer 29:680.

Physicians' Desk Reference. 1982. Physicians' Desk Reference. 36th Edition. Oradell, N.J.: Medical Economics Company, Inc.

Posner, Judith. 1979. "It's all in your head: Feminist and medical models of menopause (strange bedfellows)." Sex Roles 5:179–190.

Reitz, Rosetta. 1977. Menopause: A Positive Approach. Radnor, Penn.: Chilton Book Co.

Reuben, David. 1969. Everything You Always Wanted to Know About Sex But Were Afraid To Ask. New York: David McKay Co.

Ruzek, Sheryl Burt. 1979. The Women's Health Movement. New York: Praeger.

Sayers, Janet. 1982. Biological Politics. London: Tavistock Publications, Ltd.

Schur, Edwin. 1980. The Politics of Deviance. Englewood Cliffs, N.J.: Prentice Hall.

Seaman, Barbara, and Gideon Seaman. 1977. Women and the Crisis in Sex Hormones. New York: Rawson Association Publishers, Inc.

Smith, Donald D., Prentice Ross, J. Thompson Donovan, and Walter L. Herrmann. 1975. "Association of exogenous estrogen and endometrial carcinoma." New England Journal of Medicine 293:1164–1167.

Solomon, Jean. 1972. "Menopause: A rite of passage." Ms. (December) 1:16–18.

U.S. Bureau of the Census. 1975. Pharmaceutical Preparations, Except Biologicals. Current Industrial Reports, Series Ma-28G(73)-1. Washington, D.C.: U.S. Government Printing Office.

Weinstein, Milton. 1980. "Estrogen use in post-menopausal women—costs, risk and benefits." New England Journal of Medicine 303:308–316.

Weiss, Noel S., Daniel Szekely, and Donald F. Austin. 1976. Increasing incidence of endometrial cancer in the United States. New England Journal of Medicine 294:1259–1262.

Wilson, Robert. 1962. "Roles of estrogen and progesterine in breast and genital cancer." Journal of the American Medical Association 182:327–331.

———. 1966a. Feminine Forever. New York: M. Evans.

———. 1966b. "A key to staying young." Look (January):68–73.

Wilson, Robert, and Thelma Wilson. 1963. "The fate of nontreated post-menopausal woman: A plea for the maintenance of adequate estrogen from puberty to the grave." Journal of the American Geriatrics Society 11:347–361.

Wolfe, Sidney. 1978. "Feminine straight to the grave.: Mother Jones (May):18–20.

———. 1979. Women in Science and Technology Equal Opportunity Act, 1979. Testimony before the Committee on Labor and Human Resources, Subcommittee on Health and Scientific Research. 96th Congress, 1st session. Washington, D.C.: U.S. Government Printing Office.

Ziel, Harry K. 1980. "The negative side of long-term postmenopausal estrogen therapy." Pp. 450–452 in Louis Lasagna (ed.), Controversies in Therapeutics. Philadelphia: W.B. Saunders.

Ziel, Harry K., and William D. Finkle. 1975. "Increased risks of endometrial carcinoma among users of conjugated estrogens." New England Journal of Medicine 293:1167–1170.

———. 1976. "Association of estrone with the development of endometrial carcinoma." American Journal of Obstetrics and Gynecology 134:735–740.

CASE CITED

Pharmaceutical Manufacturers Association v. Food and Drug Administration, 484 F. Supp. 1179, 1980.

CHAPTER 11

Accounting for Cosmetic Surgery
THE ACCOMPLISHMENT OF GENDER

Diana Dull and Candace West

Within the United States, physicians claim a professional mandate to define the nature and treatment of disease (Hughes 1958:78; Thorne 1973:36–37). For most surgeons, this mandate includes the right to evaluate patients' complaints, to determine what should be done about them, and to assess post-operative results.[1] For plastic surgeons, however, the mandate is not so clear. The field of plastic surgery encompasses two categories of operations: (1) reconstructive procedures, which restore or improve physical function and minimize disfigurement from accidents, diseases, or birth defects, and (2) cosmetic procedures, which offer elective aesthetic improvement through surgical alterations of facial and bodily features (American Society of Plastic and Reconstructive Surgeons 1988). In the case of reconstructive surgery, the professional mandate rests on the surgeon's ability to improve physical function and minimize disfigurement. But in the case of cosmetic surgery, the evaluation of patients' complaints, the determination of what should be done about them, and the assessment of post-operative results must be negotiated in relation to *what* "aesthetic improvement" might consist of, and to *whom*. This, then, is the central dilemma of cosmetic surgery.

The disproportionate number of women who undergo cosmetic operations suggests the importance of gender to understanding how this dilemma is resolved. For example, in 1988 more than half a million people in the United States had cosmetic surgery, with the available evidence indicating that the vast majority were women.[2] Although official statistics do not distinguish between cosmetic and reconstructive operations, they do indicate a decided bias. In 1985, 61 percent of all rhinoplasty (nose surgery), 86 percent of all eyelid reconstruction, and 91 percent of all face-lifts were performed on women (U.S. National Center for Health Statistics 1987). The American Society of Plastic and Reconstructive Surgeons estimates that 90,000 men opted for cosmetic surgery in 1988, but that number represents only 16 percent of the total cosmetic operations identified.

Our purpose in this paper is to examine how those involved in cosmetic operations resolve the central dilemma of cosmetic surgery. Our analysis of surgical screening and decision making focuses on how the medical profession comes to enter a terrain that would seem so clearly beyond its mandate—that is, constructing appearances and performing surgery that, by its own definition, is unnecessary. We show how surgeons who perform cosmetic procedures justify their entry into this terrain and how people who elect such procedures make sense of their decisions to do so. Finally, in conjunction with these activities, we show how women are constituted as the primary frontier for this territorial expansion through the accomplishment of gender—in this context, the assessment of "good candidates" for surgery in relation to normative conceptions of men's and women's "essential natures" (Fenstermaker, West, and Zimmerman 1990; West and Fenstermaker 1993; West and Zimmerman 1987).

Methods

Our primary data consist of interviews with surgeons who perform cosmetic surgery and with individuals who have undergone such operations. By law, any licensed medical doctor may perform cosmetic surgery, but we limited our study to surgeons certified to do so through boards recognized by the American Board of Medical Specialties. Eight of the ten surgeons in this sample are certified by the American Board of Plastic Surgery and two, by the American Board of Otolaryngology. We obtained these interviews through a snowball sample, yielding one woman and nine men surgeons, all white. With the exception of one surgeon outside California (whom we interviewed by phone), we conducted all our physician interviews in person at surgeons' offices. Each interview was recorded on audiotape and lasted approximately one hour.

Given the sensitive nature of the topic, we gave people who had undergone cosmetic surgery two interview options. The first option, chosen by 7 of the total 23, was to be interviewed on audiotape face to face. The second option, chosen by 16 of the 23, was to complete an open-ended questionnaire with a follow-up discussion over the phone if clarification was needed. In the analysis that follows, we found no differences among people's perspectives on cosmetic surgery according to which of the options they selected. These interviews were also obtained through a snowball sample.

Nineteen of the 23 persons interviewed were women whose surgical experiences included face lifting, upper and lower eyelid reduction, rhinoplasty, chin implantation, breast augmentation, breast reduction, and liposuction of the hips, thighs and knees. Two of the interviews were with men who had undergone eyelid reduction or face lifting. Our secondary data consist of two further interviews with men who ultimately decided against cosmetic surgery. Given that both had seriously contemplated aesthetic rhinoplasty and were among only for men we were able to locate who had ever consulted plastic surgeons, we decided to include their views with those of our other interviewees—setting them off in our analysis as anomalous cases.[3] Four of the women and one of the men had undergone more than one surgery, and in at least two cases later operations were performed in order to correct the results of an earlier procedure.

At the time we interviewed them, individuals in this sample ranged in age from 24 to 67. Nine had had surgery before turning 35; seven more, between 35 and 50; and seven more, when they were 51 years old or older. While facelifts were confined to those who were 50 and over, the other procedures were reported by people across different age groups.

Six people were single, two were divorced, and ten were married (with five failing to indicate marital status). Nine of them, including one who was single, had children. All of them were white; two identified their ethnicity as Jewish and one, as Italian. They held a variety of jobs, including those of dentist, bookkeeper, and administrative assistant. One, a retired medical assistant, had formerly been employed in the offices of two different cosmetic surgeons; another, also retired, had worked as a medical editor in a large health care facility.

Our analysis of these data is qualitative and inductive. In the tradition of grounded theory (Glaser and Strauss 1967), we did not set out to test specific hypotheses but rather to generate them from the entire corpus of material.

Surgery as a "Normal, Natural" Pursuit

In routine descriptions of their circumstances and activities, people provide names, formulations, characterizations, excuses, explanations, and justifications for the circumstances and activities, thereby situating them in a social framework (Heritage 1984:136–137). Among those who had undergone cosmetic surgery, many described their desires for such surgery as "normal" and "natural," explicitly comparing their inclination to buying makeup and having their hair done. They extolled the benefits of cosmetic surgery by characterizing their actions as what anyone would do. Hence, patients' descriptions of their activities were formulated as justifications for those activities. For example, a woman who underwent breast augmentation observed,

> In this age, with all the technology possible, changing something less than perfect about one's looks seems so easy, so normal. It's unfair that cost keeps such a wonderful thing from so many people. . . . I would recommend this procedure to anyone.

A woman who underwent a facelift stated,

> I mean, if it is your body and you want to have it done, why not? And if it helps your vanity, what's wrong with it? . . . Women buy makeup and have their hair done—what's the difference?

We might expect such descriptions from people who have undergone cosmetic surgery, insofar as they are accounting for having done so in the course of being interviewed. However, such descriptions were not unique to former patients. Many surgeons also categorized cosmetic surgery as a "normal," "natural" pursuit. For example,

> *There is a certain natural order to things.* (Italics added.) A person who is twenty-five years old does not need a facelift, but they need a breast augmentation.—Well, "need" is relative, obviously, but for purposes of discussion . . . there's a certain order of what you go through psychologically and what you might need. . . . If it makes them happy and gives them a boost, then it's no different than going on a two-week vacation as far as I'm concerned.

Or, as another surgeon remarked, "It's not any vainer than wearing makeup or changing your hairstyle. If you think those things are vain, then plastic surgery is vain too."

To be sure, those descriptions contained numerous contradictions. First, some patients who characterized their surgery as what anyone would do nonetheless reported that they agonized over their decisions to have surgery. Second, surgeons and former patients who compared cosmetic surgery with other mundane activities often advanced claims with defensive overtones (for instance, assessing surgery as "no vainer than" other attentions to one's appearance). Third, even while surgeons and former patients referred to the desire for surgery as "normal" and "natural," they implied that the desire was only "normal" and "natural" for women. They did not, for example, draw parallels between cosmetic procedures and shaving one's face or trimming one's beard. Thus, the claim that cosmetic surgery was a "normal," "natural" pursuit was a deceptively simple one.

"Objective" Indicators

A more complex picture began to emerge as interviewees described "criteria" for particular surgical procedures as if these were objective indicators for surgery. As Zimmerman (1979:11) observes, we can examine "properties of social life which seem objective, factual, and transsituational" as "managed accomplishments or achievements of local processes." Such examination provides a preliminary understanding of how surgeons and former patients could reach the conclusion that cosmetic surgery was "normal" and "natural," namely, by formulating facial or bodily features as "objectively" problematic.

For example, like the surgeon who suggested that a 25-year-old person does not "need" a facelift, many patients alluded to "self-evident indicators" for surgery in accounts of their decisions. One woman "explained" her upper eyelid reduction by noting that

> At about forty-five [your eyelids] start to come down. And that's when you start to notice that you're losing elasticity and you get the fold in your upper eye . . . by the time you get to be my age, it was certainly time to do it.

The same woman described her subsequent decision to undergo liposuction under her chin by adding,

> In your late fifties and sixties you start to get a lot of "crepeyness" in your neck. Just all of a sudden it's just there. And it's just, you know, not attractive. And your jowls, of course. Mine weren't that bad, but they were coming down.

In these excerpts, we find a concrete empirical description of the "natural order of things" described earlier. While this woman's description is perhaps more chronologically detailed than most, other patients were just as explicit in their references to "heavy eyelids," "droopy necks," and "baggy chins" as "objective" grounds for their decisions to have surgery.

Interestingly, surgeons were the ones who suggested that "objective" signs of aging—and their relationship to cosmetic surgery—might not be so objective. For example, when asked about the relationship between age and cosmetic surgery, many intimated that "age" was in the eye of the beholder. While a 20-year-old woman might look terrific to the person on the street, she may well look "too old" if she is competing in front of the camera:

> The youngest lady I've done was a younger lady in her twenties who was a model and was losing it to the teenagers. So I did her face and eyes. . . . To you and me, she looked great. But to the camera and the people who wanted to shoot the teenage look, she looked too old. . . . It was a modest facelift, but it was enough to put her right back there on the front page of the magazine. . . . She was perfectly realistic. She showed me her shots and shots of the kids and said, "This is where the industry is going, and I want to stay in it." You see, the perceived deformity relates to that person's particular situation in life. Their jobs or their perceived role.

Although many surgeons acknowledged that procedures such as facelifts were more easily and effectively performed on someone who is young, one surgeon remarked:

> You're never too old for it. The best answer to the question of when you need it or when you should do it, is when you need it. . . . I've done a facelift on a ninety-three-year-old.

Thus, the surgeons took patients' individual perceptions and livelihoods into account in their perspectives on "objective" signs of aging. Surgeons were not always so sociologically reflective when it came to other dimensions of identity such as race and ethnicity. For example, more than a few of them averred that patients' racial or ethnic features constituted "objective" problems. Through references to what people, particularly women, of color "have" and "need," these surgeons invoked race and ethnicity as factual, transsituational grounds for surgical interventions in appearance (cf. Zimmerman 1987):

> I've had one Black patient . . . it was a lip reduction. . . . I guess there are more Black people that have big lips than white people. . . . I had a lot of Black patients back in [the South] . . . breast reduction was a tremendously common procedure . . . because . . . a lot of Black women have huge breasts. . . . The usual cosmetic procedures were, with the exception of rhinoplasty, very uncommon. You know, Black women don't usually have the aging changes that white women have—they don't get the fine wrinkles. . . . Orientals don't either.

Or, as another surgeon remarked,

> The Black people that I have operated on have had . . . mostly their noses [done]. The Black people have big flared nostrils and would like that smaller. The Orientals don't seem to have much of a bridge, so they, you know, [have] kind of a dish face.

On the other hand, some surgeons implied that "problems" with racial and ethnic features were—at least in part—subjectively determined. They acknowledged, for example, that patients' conceptions of their racial features were often derived from their groups:

> There are not that many Black flat women compared to Caucasians. . . . But another flipside—how many flat Asians do you see? Females? Lots! They're all over the place. For them, that's accepted. I do very few Asians. Very few Blacks. And my theory is that most of the Blacks don't need it. And my theory is for Asians, flat is still in.

One surgeon contended that whatever a patient's racial or ethnic features, the surgeon's task was to improve the appearance of the individual patient, rather than to force fit it according to some universal criteria:

> I saw a Black lady today who I had done her eyelids and a facelift. And she came back, and she wanted a forehead lift. And uh, you know . . . that was fine. . . . But this was just to make this lady look better. . . . Basically, it is just trying to make them look better, rather than to have them fit a mold.

In this regard, the most complicated claims we heard were those that acknowledge "objective" differences between the racial or ethnic "characteristics" of different groups, but attributed desires for changes in such characteristics to the patients' individual perceptions—not to the characteristics themselves. Changes in such characteristics might result in a "different" appearance but not necessarily a "better" appearance:

> I mean, if you've got a great big old honker, and it looks like somebody hit it with three passes of the sword and it comes down you face like a "Z" or a "W," you want to look better. . . . Now, contrariwise, if you just happen to have a big nose because you come from an Armenian background or some very recognizable ethnic appearance and you want to change it, that's cosmetic surgery. . . . Michael Jackson is leading the way on changing Negroid characteristics to Caucasian characteristics.

Patients' descriptions of their surgeries in relation to their ethnic backgrounds were more complex still. They expressed their desires for surgery through references to subtle alterations—rather than total transformations—of their "ethnic features." For example, one woman of Italian descent said that prior to her rhinoplasty,

> I didn't like my nose in photographs. [Now] I have a cute profile and my nose is not tiny but in proportion to my face. . . . I think I look softer [now] and not as exotic as before.

A Jewish woman said of her pre-operative consultation with a surgeon for rhinoplasty, "He wasn't going to give me a cute little WASPy nose, but one in proportion to my face. I was very satisfied." Through such carefully worded descriptions, patients implied that they were essentially satisfied with their "ethnic appearances," despite their desires to have particular features surgically changed. Notwithstanding these nuanced claims, we observed that surgeons and former patients only specified "problems" with racial and ethnic features in the marked case; in the case of individuals who were not white, Anglo Saxon, and Protestant. Some former patients referred to their "big Jewish" noses, but none ever referred to their "puny gentile" ones. Some surgeons alluded to "Caucasian" eyelids or lips, but only when contrasting them with "Oriental" or "Negroid" ones. Thus, even in these carefully worded descriptions, race and ethnicity were invoked as "objective," transsituational grounds for surgery.

Of course, patients' class backgrounds might also be seen as "objective" indicators for cosmetic surgery insofar as these determine who is—and who is not—able to afford it. Since insurance companies, health maintenance organizations, and state-funded health care programs exclude virtually all elective aesthetic procedures from their provisions for patients' care, prospective patients must be prepared to pay for their surgeries themselves.[4] A woman to whom $2,000 is "nothing" is in a far better position to finance her upper eyelid reduction than a person to whom $2,000 is substantial—or inconceivable—outlay. For example, one patient reported that

> In South America, they say that everyone in the upper class has had this surgery. I mean, it's automatic, like you go to the dentist. And to me, it was like, you buy a car. You pay eight thousand to twelve thousand dollars for a car, and four years later, it's worth nothing. . . . So what's two thousand dollars? Nothing. And it's going to last a lot longer than a car.

Or, as another patient put it,

> It's sort of like wearing braces—it's sort of a status thing. Everybody's doing it. If one of [your] friends does it and looks good, well, how are [you] going to let her get away with that? [You're] going to have it done too. It is a status thing: "I had so and so do mine"—"Oh, did you? How did you like him? I had so and so do mine."

But our data indicate that while limited economic resources may *hinder* the pursuit of cosmetic surgery, they do not necessarily *prevent* that pursuit. For instance, one woman who underwent breast augmentation took out a personal loan for $3,000 to finance her operation, a loan she worked very hard to pay off for a year following her surgery. Another woman received her breast augmentation "as a present" from her husband for her thirty-second birthday after ten years of wanting it. Other people we interviewed scrimped and saved for their operations on their modest salaries as bank tellers or secretaries. Thus, although class differences influenced people's perceptions of their operations as "luxuries" or "investments," they did not explain people's desires to pursue surgery in the first instance.

Assessing "Good Candidates"

As surgeons described their screening procedures, they revealed a complex sequence of assessments with a course they did not determine by themselves. For example, most described their first task as finding out what patients "really want," as opposed, presumably, to what patients think they want or say they want. Some surgeons employ computerized questionnaires to help them elicit such information, but even then, they cannot rely on what patients tell them as prima facie evidence for surgery. Like surgeons who function without computers, they then assess whether patients' expectations are "realistic," that is, consistent with what surgeons expect they can do for patients. Though photographs may be employed as visual aids, it becomes clear that "having realistic expectations" results from extensive negotiations *between* surgeons and their prospective patients:

> The first thing I've got to find out is what the patient really wants. Then I have to find out whether the expectations are realistic or not. That sort of goes into what they want and what I can do for them. Once we've established that, then I tell them the way I do it . . ., and I give them real informed consent . . ., [discussing] potential complications, the kind of procedures and what they're going to be going through. Then they have to make up their mind whether they're going to go ahead with it.

As another surgeon put it, gauging whether a patient has realistic expectations is not a one-shot determination he makes by himself, but a "two-way interview" with the patient. If surgeons *can* establish that prospective patients "have realistic expectations," they can then solicit patients' informed consent and accept them as candidates for surgery. Even then, as many surgeons note, would-be patients have to make up their minds to go through with it.

What we see in such descriptions is the central dilemma of cosmetic surgery. As we noted earlier, where cosmetic procedures are concerned, the surgeons' mandate rests solely on their ability to provide elective "aesthetic improvement." Thus, surgeons involved in cosmetic procedures must negotiate the evaluation of patients' complaints, the determination of what should be done about them, and the assessment of postoperative results in relation to *what* "aesthetic improvement" might consist of, and *to whom*. Even individuals who are not deemed as "in need" of aesthetic improvement by the first surgeon prior to their operations, with several indicating that they had been refused surgery by the first surgeon they consulted. Our data suggest that the determination of *what* "aesthetic improvement" might consist of revolves in large part around patients' displays of "appropriate" levels of concern.

Appropriate Levels of Concern

All of the surgeons advanced the view that there were "appropriate" and "inappropriate" levels of concern for particular patient problems. They advanced this view with explicit references to when patients should exhibit concern—and how much concern patients should exhibit—for the specific problems that bring them to the surgeon's office. They saw it as inappropriate, for example, for patients to wait until they were middle-aged before seeking surgical alteration of features that had bothered them all their lives:

> Say they're fifty years old—why have the waited until now? There may be some good reason—maybe they couldn't afford it or they couldn't get the

time off. But the reason may also be that this woman's husband is leaving her, and she thinks it may be her nose and puts undue attention on this one thing without paying attention to the other things—it can be very danger-ous to operate on someone like that.

Moreover, they saw it as very inappropriate for patients to display concern for prob-lems that were insignificant in relation to the whole:

> Say some absolutely gorgeous woman has some eeny-teeny little wrinkle right here and she's just invested her whole life to getting that wrinkle away—well, I know almost one hundred and ninety-nine percent that no matter what hap-pens to that little wrinkle, she's going to fix on something else afterwards to uh, grope after. And those are real tough patients to help out.

Of course, one of the dangers involved in doing surgery on patients who show "in-appropriate" levels of concern is the possibility of subsequent suits for malpractice. Plastic surgeons are among the four types of surgical specialists (the others are neuro-surgeons, obstetrician/gynecologists, and orthopedic surgeons) most likely to lose mal-practice insurance due to lawsuits or negligence (Schwartz and Mendelson 1989). Among surgeons we interviewed, there was general consensus that "problem" patients (cf. Lorber 1975) who display "inappropriate" levels of concern are, most often, men. For example, when asked why so few men sought cosmetic surgery, surgeons re-sponded:

> I think that male patients are more difficult. They're harder to deal with. Ten years ago when I was beginning to train, the dictum was "you don't do male cosmetic surgery" because they're all problems. They all have enough emotional instability to one, either sue you, or two, be a surgical disaster.

And,

> I've turned a couple of males down. They were just totally unrealistic—totally secretive, which is fairly typical for males. Didn't have a good sense for what they wanted at all. Just totally edgy, jumpy sorts of people.

Such descriptions suggest that surgeons rely on a proportionate analysis of pa-tients' concerns in relation to patients' sex categories and surgeons' own perceptions of patients' problems. The claim that there are "appropriate" levels of concern for specific problems sustains the belief in objective, factual, transsituational grounds for aesthetic improvement—even as these are constructed from the particulars of the case at hand.

Doing It for Themselves

More complex still was the determination of *to whom* a particular surgical intervention might constitute an "aesthetic improvement." Surgeons implied that they determined this on the basis of evidence that prospective patients were seeking cosmetic surgery "for themselves." They described "good candidates" for surgery as those who think surgery will increase their self-esteem and improve their self-image, not those who think it will help them attract a younger lover or maintain their spouse's attention. Through these means, surgeons located the impetus for aesthetic improvement within patients themselves. As one surgeon explained:

> Married female patients, especially with breast enlargements, have a lot of antagonism from their husbands. . . . [A husband may say,] "You look fine to me. I don't know why you want to do this." The comment the ladies make is, "I don't feel good about myself, that's why I want to do it. I've had two or three babies, and I used to have a nice figure and now I don't, and I just don't feel good about myself and I'm having my breasts increased."

However, surgeons' expressed preferences for patients who "do it for themselves" were not without contradiction. For instance, most surgeons acknowledged that it is perfectly reasonable for someone to seek surgery in order to meet the requirements of their job:

> You know, I do a lot of theatrical people. . . . [Those] who earn a living by their appearance are pretty legitimate. I've had many of them tell me . . . that they wouldn't do this unless it were important for them to make a living.

Moreover, many former patients indicated that they were influenced in their decision to seek surgery by significant others. One woman who had undergone rhinoplasty at 14 years of age said,

> My father was physically and psychologically abusive to me, and part of his abuse was about how ugly I was, how I didn't deserve to be alive, [and] how he wished I was dead. But a lot of it was on my looks, and I looked identical to him. I probably even had the same size nose as he did—that's where I got my nose—and he used to say that I looked so much like his mother. . . . He hated his mother.

Another woman who had worked for two different plastic surgeons told the following story:

> The first doctor I worked for . . . one day he came into my office—this was after I had been there about three or four years—and he sat there and he looked at me and said, "One thing I have found out,"—And I looked at him and said, "And that is?"—And he said, "*Every* surgeon in town has done his girls." And I was the only girl! So he said, "When are we going to do you?" . . . Well, he never let me alone! Finally, I let him [perform a facelift]. I just figured, "Well, if it'll make him happy and it will help his practice, I'll do it . . ." because he needed an example to show patients. He was thrilled to have done me . . . , and I just loved him and his family, but I tell you, I would *not* have had it done.

Finally, surgeons' own accounts indicated that under some conditions, they might advise their would-be patients to consider particular surgical procedures that they did not "come in for." For example, one surgeon confided,

> I personally feel that the patient should tell me what procedures they want—what they feel a need for, that's what they should tell me. Now, if they ask me if there's anything else that I feel could use improvement, I'll give them an opinion.

Thus, our data show that patients "with realistic expectations" do not always generate those expectations from within. Surgeons' stated preferences for patients who are "doing it for themselves" obscure a range of outside influences (including friends, family members, and employers) on people's decision to seek "aesthetic improvement." Moreover, once in the surgeon's office, those considering surgery may be influenced by further recommendations as to what they might "need." Through these means, "patients with realistic expectations" are *created* as well as "found" (cf. Conrad 1976; Conrad and Schneider 1980).

Reducing the Body into Parts

For the surgeons and former patients we interviewed, a primary means of creating patients with realistic expectations was the reduction of would-be patients' faces and bodies to a series of component parts. To be sure, reductionism is a key to scientific, and therefore medical, reasoning, and surgeons are encouraged to develop the capacity for it in the course of their professional training. Given that surgical practice is predicated on the subdivision of patient "parts," it would be odd if the surgeons we interviewed did *not* display an orientation toward reductionism in their descriptions of their activities (cf. Guillemin and Holmstrom 1986; Scully 1980). But our data indicate that surgeons also look for evidence of this orientation in prospective patients. One surgeon explained his approach as follows:

> There's two groups of people. One that will come in and say, "Make me beautiful"—those are very poor candidates. And somebody [who comes in] and says, "I don't like my nose." And you say, "What don't you like?" And he says, "Well, I don't like the lump and it's too long"—if they can describe what bothers them, and you know that it can be surgically corrected, then those are excellent candidates for surgery.

Most former patients provided ample evidence of their orientation toward seeing their bodies in parts. For example, one woman described her "pre-rhinoplasty" appearance as follows:

> I had a very Roman nose, straight, kind of broad. I mean, it was perfect, but kind of big. When the first guy operated, I had scars in here (pointing to nostrils in the drawing she has made of her nose). There was more of a

> stereotype of Jewish women [and] big noses. . . . So I thought, what better
> thing to do than have my nose made smaller?

Another woman specified the benefits of her facelift in this way:

> I got what I wanted. A clear forehead, no heavy eyelids and bags under my
> eyes (my eyes weren't too bad to begin with [but] my forehead was heavily
> lined). No furrows around my mouth. No wrinkles. Neck is great.

Still another itemized the pluses and minuses of her breast augmentation by saying:

> I am very pleased with the results. Sometimes I fluctuate on wondering if I
> should have chosen an even larger size in breasts, but I inevitably return to
> the same conclusion: that this is perfect proportionately. I see no scar what-
> soever on the left nipple; there is a slight trace of scar along the edge of the
> right nipple, but I don't think anyone would ever notice, it is so slight.

Here, patients demonstrate such well-honed abilities to reduce their bodies to parts that they can offer pre- and post-operative drawings of the parts in question, itemize the benefits of their procedures part by part, and even identify subtle traces of scars that no one else would notice. Clearly, reductionism plays an important part in these patients' own views of their experiences.[5]

We might ask why this orientation becomes so central to accounts of people who undergo cosmetic surgery and those who perform it. Our data suggest that reduction-ism is essential to problematizing the part (or parts) in question and establishing their "objective" need for repair. For example, throughout these interviews, surgeons and pa-tients alike alluded to technically normal features as "flaws," "defects," "deformities," and "correctable problems" of appearance. Surgeons referred to patients as "needing" facelifts and breast augmentations, while patients referred to the specific parts (or parts of parts) that they had "fixed." Through such terminology, they constitute *cosmetic* sur-gery as a *reconstructive* project. Ultimately, they may even dissolve the distinction be-tween the two categories of plastic surgery—suggesting, for example, that to someone with "an ugly nose or prominent ears," cosmetic surgery may be "just as important as reconstructing somebody after cancer removal." Thus, reductionism provides a means of resolving the central dilemma of cosmetic surgery—defining the nature and treat-ment of "disease." By jointly reducing patients' bodies to a series of parts and focusing on the parts that require "correction," surgeons and patients forge a *mutual* basis for evaluating patients' complaints, determining what should be done about them, and as-sessing post-operative results.

Of course, there were minor variations on this theme. For example, one surgeon argued that *patients* were the ones who perceived their features as deformed, not him:

> I'm perceiving it as a shape, a structure, as whatever you want to call it . . .
> this *person* perceives it as a deformity. I just perceive it as the way they look.
> And they're asking me, "Can you change the way I look to something I
> don't perceive as a deformity?" So I'm basically treating their attitude to-
> wards their own appearance.

Two other surgeons characterized their work as "improving the patient's self esteem" and "giving them more confidence." However, whether surgeons conceptualized the deformity as on the patient or in the patient's head, they took surgical means to repair it.[6]

There are several apparent inconsistencies in the evidence we have presented so far. For example, if the pursuit of cosmetic surgery is—as surgeons and patients claim— "normal" and "natural," why are objective indicators needed to justify it? And if the objective grounds for surgery are sociologically variable, what sense does it make to describe them as "objective" in the first place? Finally, if surgeons prefer patients who are doing it for themselves, why do they accept patients whose decisions to have surgery are clearly influenced by others' (including surgeons') opinions on their problems? Below, we address what we see as the "missing link" in our analysis so far, namely, the accomplishment of gender.

The Accomplishment of Gender

Elsewhere, we advance an ethnomethodological view of gender as an *accomplishment*, that is, an achieved property of situated social action (Fenstermaker, West, and Zimmerman 1990; West and Fenstermaker 1993; West and Zimmerman 1987). From this perspective, gender is not simply something one is; rather, it is something one does in ongoing interaction with others. Following Heritage (1984:179), we argue that to the extent that members of society know their actions are accountable, they will design their actions with an eye to how others might see and characterize them. Moreover, insofar as sex categories (e.g., "girl" or "boy," "woman" or "man") are omnirelevant to social life (Garfinkel 1967:111; Goffman 1977:324), they provide an ever-ready resource for characterizing social action (e.g., as consistent with women's or men's "essential nature"). Accordingly, "people involved in virtually *any* activity may hold themselves accountable and be held accountable for their performance of that activity *as women* or *as men*" (West and Fenstermaker 1993:7).

In the data presented in this paper, we find that accounts of cosmetic surgery rest ultimately on the accomplishment of gender. For example, throughout our interviews with surgeons and former patients, we found implicit claims that what was "normal" and "natural" for a woman was *not* normal or natural for a man. Surgeons were united in the view that women's concerns for their appearance are *essential* to their nature as women. They observed that women are, after all, taught to look good and disguise their real or imagined "defects." Hence, they said, it is taken for granted that a woman "wants to primp and look as pretty as she can." Her desire may not be biologically ordained—as they noted, she *is* a product of our society and how she was brought up. But, they pointed out, by the time a woman has been "brought up," her consciousness of her appearance as a matter of self image is "intrinsic" to her nature *as a woman* (cf. Cahill 1982; 1986a; 1986b).

By contrast, surgeons characterized men's concerns for their appearance as extrinsic to their nature as men. They observed that men are taught "to deal with little defects here and there," and that therefore, "they don't have the psychological investment in it that women do." They further observed that men must rely on their wives to buy their clothes or tell them what looks good, and that men only attend to their appearance in instrumental fashion, for example, to attain a more prestigious job.

> Women are more concerned about the appearance than men are as a basic rule. Now that is not something you can apply to every person. Obviously you'll see that the success level is related to their appearance level. People who don't take some care in how they appear don't seem to be in supervisory or professional positions. And I guess people, as they're educated, I guess, as they attempt to reach some goal in life, find that their appearance relates to achieving those goals. Women, conversely, are intrinsically . . . concerned about their appearance, not just in a goal-oriented fashion, but as a matter of self image.

Here, a surgeon notes that educated "people" (meaning men) may discover that their appearance has an impact on their "attempt to reach some goal in life," but he does not attribute that discovery to any natural order of things. In fact, a concern for appearance is so unnatural for men that, as another surgeon notes, some men may deliberately misrepresent it in surgeons' offices, for example, complaining that they "can't breathe" to cover up their wishes for "a better-looking nose."

Our interviews with former patients also suggested that what was "normal" and "natural" for a woman was not normal or natural for a man. As noted above, women referred to cosmetic surgery as what "anyone" would do, extolled its benefits for "everyone," and compared it to "wearing makeup" or "having your hair done." By contrast, the only grounds on which men characterized the pursuit of cosmetic surgery as "normal" were job-related concerns. One man, a cosmetologist who underwent upper eyelid reduction, felt his upper lids were a distraction in his work. Another, who had undergone a facelift, explained that as a dentist, he felt patients liked "younger persons working on them." Still another man we spoke with who underwent reconstructive rhinoplasty for a deviated septum—but decided against cosmetic alteration—stated that he would only consider cosmetic surgery if he "were disfigured or something." And a man who consulted a surgeon about cosmetic rhinoplasty—but then decided against it—told us,

> I like my nose. It's a little on the large side, and I was teased about it when I was younger, but it's the nose I grew up with. . . . Besides, would I lie to the kids I have some day? They're going to grow up with these noses and say, "Where did this come from?" My philosophy is that you work with what you've got.

Of course, the men in the last two excerpts were accounting for something they did not do, while those in the first two excerpts were accounting for something they did. We can, therefore, understand why the last two excerpts would emphasize good reasons for not having surgery, and the first two, good reasons for having it. But what is noteworthy in all four descriptions is the assumption that a desire for aesthetic improvement must be *justified* (either on the basis of job-related concerns or in the case of "disfigurement"). Clearly, it was not seen as "natural."

Our interviewees further distinguished women from men in their descriptions of "objective" indicators for surgery. Many surgeons acknowledge that our culture and its double standard of aging are responsible for women's and men's differential experiences as they get older. Thus, they explained the fact that a man with wrinkles looks "acceptable" while a woman with wrinkles does not on the basis of cultural conceptions, rather than any objective standard. Surgeons, however, relied *on those same cultural conceptions* to select candidates for surgery:

> Our society has got a very strange double standard and it can be summarized that when a man gets old, he gets sophisticated, debonair [and] wise; but when a woman gets old, she gets old. A man with a wrinkly face doesn't necessarily look bad in our society. A woman with a wrinkly face looks old. So when a man comes in and he wants a facelift, I have to be able to get considerably more skin than I would on a woman. . . . And usually there is something else going on. . . . Usually, they're getting rid of their wife.

In requiring "considerably more [excess] skin" for men than women, the surgeon constructs an "objective indicator" for doing surgery—as well as "objective differences" between women and men.

Another surgeon contended that there *are* objective differences that make women more likely to "need" surgery:

> Men don't seem to have the lipodystrophy (i.e., deposition of fat in tissue) that women do. They don't have subcutaneous fat layers and uh . . . I guess I've only done one man with love handles . . . I think it is more of a gender-related difference than uh, psychological. . . . Men dermabrade their face with a razor every morning. You have thick hair follicles that support the skin so it doesn't get wrinkled . . . like your upperlip, for instance. Men hardly ever have any problem with that and women, sometimes by age 50, need their lip peeled or something.

Our concern here is *not* the physiological differences this surgeon attests to (although we note that he ignores potbellies in this description). Rather, we are interested in how these differences are invoked to legitimize one course of activity and discredit another. If women's bodies are seen as *essentially* "in need of repair," then surgery on women can be seen as a moral imperative instead of an aesthetic option. But if men "hardly ever have any problem with that," then surgery on men will require elaborate justification.

Such justification was apparent in our interviews with men who had undergone cosmetic surgery. For example, in contrast to the woman patient who said that "when your eyelids start to come down" and "you start to get that 'crepeyness' in your neck" it is simply "time to do it," one man said that *his wife's appearance* motivated him to have a facelift, as he did not want his wife "to look much younger." Here, he eschewed a description of "objective" signs of aging for an explanation of how he might appear in relation to his spouse. Another man stated that following his upper eyelid reduction, he "once again looked like [his] old self." As a result, he indicated he "felt better" and did not "get as tired," attributing the difference to psychological effect.

The notion of gender as an interactional accomplishment also advances our analysis of how race and ethnicity were constituted as "objective" grounds for surgery. References to Michael Jackson notwithstanding, the descriptions of most surgeons focused on what *women* in various racial and ethnic groups "have" and "need," not on men. Even while former patients relied on white, Anglo Saxon, Protestant features as the unmarked case, they described their post-operative benefits not only as looking "less exotic," but also, "prettier" and "more attractive to men."

In short, we contend that our interviewees' accounts would not have been possible without the accomplishment of gender. This is the mechanism that allows them to see the pursuit of elective aesthetic improvement as "normal" and "natural" for a woman, but not for a man. The accountability of persons to particular sex categories provides for their seeing women as "objectively" needing repair and men as "hardly ever" requiring it. The fact that gender is an *interactional* accomplishment explains why surgeons prefer patients who are "doing it for themselves" but actively participate in the construction of patients' preferences.

The evidence indicates that the selection of "good candidates" for cosmetic surgery relies not merely on the creation of patients with "appropriate" levels of concern and the reduction of patients' faces and bodies to a series if component parts. It also relies on the simultaneous accomplishment of gender. Following Berk (1985), we contend that there are actually *two* processes here: (1) the selection of "good candidates" for surgery, and (2) the accomplishment of gender. The "normal," "natural" character of each process is made sensible in relation to the other, and since they operate simultaneously, the relationship between the two processes and their outcomes "is virtually impossible to question" (West and Fenstermaker 1993:14). Thus, the assessment of "appropriate levels of concern" ensures patients who will agree with a surgeon's perceptions of their problems, and at the same time, it furnishes the opportunity to affirm the pursuit of cosmetic surgery as an essentially "gendered" activity:

> A lot of guys come in and the classic one is that they want their nose fixed. And you look at the guy and he's got this big, God-awful nose. So does Anthony Quinn! Uh, a man can get away with that kind of nose. So what is normal for a man would not be . . . well, let's say what is *acceptable* for a man would not necessarily be acceptable for a woman.

The point, then, is not merely that pursuing cosmetic surgery is seen as something women do, but that for a woman to seek it while a man does not displays the "essential" nature of each.

Conclusion

Sociologists have had little to say about cosmetic surgery. Although an impressive body of literature has documented the expansion of medicine into nonmedical terrain, this literature has focused primarily on the medicalization of deviance, redefining "badness" as "sickness" (Conrad and Schneider 1980; Ehrenreich and Ehrenreich 1978; Zola 1972), and the medicalization of natural processes, moving activities such as childbirth from home to hospital (Ehrenreich and English 1978; Reissman 1983; Wertz and Wertz 1977). Other research has treated the social and historical construction of the body as a subject of inquiry (Connell 1987; Glassner 1988; Turner 1984; Wilson 1987), but it has not yet addressed cosmetic surgery as a primary object of investigation. With the exception of feminist analyses of "the politics of appearance" (Chapkis 1986; Freedman 1986; Lakoff and Scherr 1984; Millman 1980), most scholarly interest in the topic has been limited to psychological studies of interpersonal attractiveness (Berscheid and Gangestad 1982; Berscheid and Walster 1969) and clinical studies of patients' motivations for surgery (Crikelair, Druss, and Symonds 1971; Edgerton and Knorr 1971).

In this paper, we have examined how surgeons who do cosmetic operations account for their activities and how people who elect such operations make sense of their decisions to do so. Our data indicate that surgeons and patients "explain" their involvement in these activities by extending the definition of reconstructive surgery to include cosmetic procedures. By reducing patients' faces and bodies to a series of component parts, surgeons and patients together establish the problematic status of the part in question and its "objective" need of "repair." This process affords them a mutual basis for negotiating the evaluation of patients' complaints, the determination of what should be done about them, and the assessment of post-operative results. But this process operates in tandem with the accomplishment of gender, allowing surgeons and patients to see the pursuit of cosmetic surgery as "normal" and "natural" for a woman and *not* for a man. Without the accountability of persons to sex categories, women could not be established as "objectively" in need of repair, nor men, as "objectively" acceptable.

We advance our findings as hypotheses rather than generalizations. Indeed, we present them in a spirit of invitation—with the hope of stimulating among sociologists a broader range of interest in the topic we sought to address. We do not know, for example, how prevalent these processes are among surgeons and patients at large. Nor do we know how these processes might operate in other clinical domains, such as orthodontia (for some suggestive leads, see Davis 1980) or cosmetic dentistry.

We do know that our findings contribute to the existing literature on medicalization by identifying a new frontier for expansion of the medical mandate. Beyond work on the appropriation of "bad" behavior and on the usurpation of natural processes, our findings point to the expropriation of the aesthetic realm as a third area of medicalization. We also know that our findings yield a new direction for research on the social construction of the body; illustrating that bodies are not merely adorned and altered, but physically *reconstructed* in accord with prevailing cultural conceptions. Finally, we know that at least among the surgeons and patients we interviewed, accounting for cosmetic surgery depends on the accomplishment of gender (West and Zimmerman 1987). In offering accounts of their pursuit of surgery, patients enact their "essential natures" as women or men. In offering accounts of their surgical decision-making, surgeons uphold normative attitudes and activities for particular sex categories and, hence, become co-participants in the accomplishment of gender. In addition, surgeons act as technological facilitators of gender's accomplishment and as cultural gatekeepers in the fine tuning of gender's presentation. Thus, cosmetic surgery emerges as an institutional support for "doing gender."

Notes

1. The surgeon's mandate to assess post-operative results works in at least two ways. First, it affords surgeons the authority to appraise likely outcomes of operations in advance of their occurrence (and thereby, to determine whether operations should be performed). Second, it affords surgeons the authority to judge results of particular procedures after the face (and thus, to pronounce procedures as "successful"). The latter mandate is especially important in cases of malpractice suits, where the expert testimony of other surgeons weighs heavily in litigation.

2. This figure should be treated as a conservative estimate, insofar as it only includes operations performed by the 2,550 active physician members of the American Society of Plastic and Reconstructive Surgeons. However, statistics on the actual incidence of cosmetic surgery are virtually impossible to maintain. For example, the U.S. National Center for Health Statistics reports figures independently of physicians' and surgeons' Board affiliations and society memberships, but it does not include operations performed outside hospitals. Since 95 percent of cosmetic procedures are said to be performed in private offices or clinics (American Society of Plastic and Reconstructive Surgeons 1988), the National Center for Health Statistics offers an even less reliable estimate of their actual incidence.

3. Ideally, we also would have obtained interviews with women who consulted plastic surgeons, but decided against cosmetic surgery. We were unable to locate such women through our snowball sample. However, insofar as the accomplishment of gender involves the *accountability* of persons to particular sex categories (not deviance or conformity per se), this "gap" in our data does not constitute a problem for our analysis.

4. Until July of 1990, military personnel and their families were an exception to this rule. Prior to that time, military physicians and surgeons performed aesthetic procedures on members of the U.S. Armed Forces under the general provisions for health care of those personnel "to sharpen their skills as surgeons in preparation for wartime duty" (*Parade Magazine* 1990:14). The Pentagon has introduced new regulations to prevent the use of appropriated funds except for "the correction of birth defects, the repairing of injuries, or the commission of breast-reconstruction procedures following mastectomies."

5. Of course, the capacity for reductionism has received considerable attention in feminist analyses of the politics of appearance. Freedman (1986:25–29), for example, suggests that women develop an overall image of their bodies from the detailed scrutiny of particular parts. In cases where women suffer from "poor body image," they "generalize from one bad feature to their whole appearance, while ignoring the ways they are attractive" (25).

6. Here, we do not mean to be glib. But these surgeons' claims to be engaged in "surgery of the self image" are belied by their own participation in formulation of patients' preferences and by their limited expertise in techniques of psychological assessment. For example, most surgeons said that "specific" psychiatric and/or psychological training had not been a part of their medical education and that patient selection was ultimately a "judgment call," based on their "gut feelings."

References

American Society of Plastic and Reconstructive Surgeons. 1988. Press Release: "Estimated number of cosmetic procedures performed by ASPRS members." Department of Communications, Arlington Heights, Ill.

Berk, Sarah F. 1985. The Gender Factory: The Apportionment of Work in American Households. New York: Plenum.

Berscheid, Ellen and Steve Gangestad. 1982. "The social psychological implications of facial physical attractiveness." Clinics in Plastic Surgery 9:289–296.

Berscheid, Ellen and Elaine H. Walster. 1969. Interpersonal Attraction. Reading, Mass.: Addison-Wesley.

Cahill, Spencer E. 1982. "Becoming boys and girls." Ph.D. dissertation. Department of Sociology, University of California, Santa Barbara.

———. 1986a. "Childhood socialization as recruitment process: Some lessons from the study of gender development." In Sociological Studies of Child Development, ed. Patricia and Peter Adler, 163–186. Greenwich, Conn.: JAI Press.

———. 1986b. "Language practices and self-definition: The case of gender identity acquisition." The Sociological Quarterly 27:295–311.

Chapkis, Wendy. 1986. Beauty Secrets: Women and the Politics of Appearance. Boston: Southend Press.

Connell, R.W. 1987. "The Body and Social Practice." In Gender and Social power: Society, The Person and Sexual Politics, 66–88. Stanford, Calif.: Stanford University Press.

Conrad, Peter. 1976. Identifying Hyperactive Children: The Medicalization of Deviant Behavior. Lexington, Mass.: Lexington Books.

Conrad, Peter and Joseph W. Schneider. 1980. Deviance and Medicalization: From Badness to Sickness. St. Louis, Mo.: Mosey.

Crikelair, George F., Richard G. Druss, and Francis C. Symonds. 1971. "The problems of somatic delusions in patients seeking cosmetic surgery." Plastic and Reconstructive Surgery 48:246–250.

Davis, Peter. 1980. The Social Context of Dentistry. London: Croom Helm Ltd.

Edgerton, Milton T. and Norman J. Knorr. 1971. "Motivational patterns of patients seeking cosmetic surgery." Plastic and Reconstructive Surgery 48:551–557.

Ehrenreich, Barbara and John Ehrenreich. 1978. "Medicine and social control." In the Cultural Crisis of Modern Medicine, ed. John Ehrenreich, 39–79. New York: Monthly Review Press.

Ehrenreich, Barbara and Deirdre English. 1978. For Her Own Good: 150 Years of the Experts' Advice to Women. Garden City, N.Y.: Anchor/Doubleday.

Fenstermaker, Sarah, Candace West, and Don H. Zimmerman. 1990. "Gender inequality: New conceptual terrain." In Gender, Family and Economy: The Triple Overlap, ed. Rae Lesser Blumberg, 289–307. Beverly Hills: Sage.

Freedman, Rita. 1986. Beauty Bound. Lexington, Mass.: D.C. Heath and Company.

Garfinkel, Harold. 1967. Studies in Ethnomethodology. Englewood Cliffs, N.J.: Prentice Hall.

Glaser, Barney and Anselm Strauss. 1967. The Discovery of Grounded Theory. Chicago: Aldine.

Glassner, Barry. 1988. Bodies: Why We Look the Way We Do (and how we feel about it). New York: Putnam.

Goffman, Erving. 1977. "The arrangement between the sexes." Theory and Society 4:301–331.

Guillemin, Jeanne H. and Lynda L. Holmstrom. 1986. Mixed Blessings: Intensive Care for Newborns. New York: Oxford University Press.

Heritage, John. 1984. Garfinkel and Ethnomethodology. Cambridge, England: Polity Press.

Hughes, Everett C. 1958. Men and Their Work. Glencoe, Ill.: The Free Press.

Lakoff, Robin T. and Raquel L. Scherr. 1984. Face Value: The Politics of Beauty. Boston: Routledge & Kegan Paul.

Lorber, Judith. 1975. "Good patients and problem patients: Conformity and deviance in a general hospital." Journal of Health and Social Behavior 16:213–225.

Millman, Marcia. 1980. Such a Pretty Face: Being Fat in America. New York: Norton.

Parade Magazine. 1990. "Cosmetic surgery curbed." August 26, 1990:14.

Reissman, Catherine Kohler. 1983. "Women and medicalization." Social Policy 14:3–18.

Schwartz, William B. and D.N. Mendelson. 1989. "Physicians who have lost their malpractice insurance. Their demographic characteristics and the surplus-lines companies that insure them." Journal of the American Medical Association 262:1335–41.

Scully, Diana. 1980. Men Who Control Women's Health: The Miseducation of Obstetrician-Gynecologists. Boston: Houghton Mifflin.

Thorne, Barrie. 1973. "Professional education in medicine." In Education for the Professions of Medicine, Law, Theology and Social Welfare (a report of the Carnegie Commission on Higher Education), by Everett C. Hughes. Barrie Thorne. Agostino M. DeBaggis. Arnold Gurin and David Williams, 17–99. New York: McGraw Hill.

Turner, Bryan S. 1984. The Body of Society: Explorations in Social Theory. Oxford: B. Blackwell.

U.S. National Center for Health Statistics. 1987. Detailed Diagnoses and Surgical Procedures. Washington, D.C.: U.S. Government Printing Office.

Wertz, Richard W. and Dorothy C. Wertz. 1977. Lying In: A History of Childbirth in America. New York: Schocken Books.

West, Candace and Sarah Fenstermaker. 1993. "Power, inequality and the accomplishment of gender: An ethnomethodological view." In Theory on Gender/Feminism on Theory, ed. Paula England. New York: Aldine.

West, Candace and Don H. Zimmerman. 1987. "Doing gender." Gender & Society 1:125–151.

Wilson, Elizabeth W. 1987. "Gender and Identity." In Adorned in Dreams: Fashion and Modernity, 117–133. Berkeley: University of California Press.

Zimmerman, Don H. 1978. "Ethnomethodology." The American Sociologist 13:6–15.

Zola, Irving K. 1972. "Medicine as an Institution of Social Control." Sociological Review 2:487–504.

CHAPTER 12

The Emergence of Premenstrual Syndrome as a Social Problem

C. Amanda Rittenhouse

In the early 1980s premenstrual syndrome (PMS) became a household term. Popular press articles told women how to "beat the blues," overcome the "premenstrual uglies," and negotiate interpersonal relations during "that time of the month." Clinicians and researchers met at international conferences to discuss the definition, etiology, and possible treatments for a syndrome estimated by some to affect 80 percent of all women. Feminists and legal scholars debated the validity of the term, its medical definition, and its use as a defense for criminal behavior.

Since premenstrual tension (PMT), as PMS was first termed, has been in the medical discourse since Frank (1931) associated it with hormone imbalances, we may ask why PMS did not capture the attention of the public discourse until the early 1980s. This paper examines the influence of cultural contexts on the emergence of PMS as a social problem: a "putative condition or situation that (at least some) actors label as a 'problem' in the arenas of public discourse and action, defining it as harmful and framing its definition in particular ways" (Hilgartner and Bosk 1988:70). I trace the process by which PMS emerges as a social problem through a content analysis of medical, popular, and feminist literature. From this analysis, I develop a model to explain the emergence of premenstrual syndrome as a social problem and answer the following research questions: What set of events or social contexts triggered the emergence of PMS as a social problem in the early 1980s? How did constructions of PMS shift over time based upon the interaction of the three bodies of literature reviewed?

Setting the Stage—Theoretical and Conceptual Definitions

Classic social problems analysis follows a "natural history" model (Blumer 1971; Fuller and Meyers 1941; and Spector and Kitsuse 1973, 1977) that describes stages through which a social problem moves. Hilgartner and Bosk (1988) have formulated an alternative model in which public attention is treated as a scare resource. Therefore, the process of competition and selection for public attention plays a key role in determining whether or not an issue emerges as a social problem. For each issue, public attention depends on certain "principles of selection," which include drama, culture, politics, and institutional rhythms. This approach improves upon the natural history model identifying the specific combination of background and events which cause an issue to be defined as a social problem in a particular time and place.

Using this basic framework, I identify the principles of selection for public attention that played a leading role in the emergence of PMS as a social problem. Two key principles are identified: (1) drama, in this case specific dramatic events; and (2) important cultural factors, specifically contending beliefs about the role that a woman's reproductive capacities play in affecting her behavior and abilities and about her appropriate role.

The specific dramatic events were a set of British murder trials held in 1980 and 1981. The courts reduced to manslaughter the sentences of two women charged with murder on the grounds that severe PMS reduced their capacity to control their behavior. These trials stimulated public debate within the popular and feminist arenas, initiating a new phase in the conceptionalization of PMS and more generally of women's bodies.

The second important variable is the cultural context in which PMS emerged. The debate over the definition and influence of PMS in women's lives emerged at a time when women were increasingly making in-roads into the paid labor force as well as demanding greater equality and opportunities. These economic and political changes brought to the fore conflicting late twentieth century beliefs about the "appropriate" role of women in the culture's economic and political life—old beliefs deeply rooted in the culture and newer beliefs sparked by feminism and rising rates of women's labor force participation. Discussions about PMS thus came to revolve, sometimes subtly and sometimes blatantly, around contrasting assessments of the competence of women to participate equally with men in economic and political arenas.

Thus, the larger context in which PMS emerged as a social problem involves two alternative social constructions of the effects of biology. The first and older construction portrays women's menstrual cycles as limiting their ability to participate on a par with men in economic and political life. Hilgartner and Bosk (1988) describe such ideas as pre-existing "deep mythic themes." With PMS these mythic themes existed prior to the British trials and played a role in the debate over the emerging constructions. In fact, almost a century ago, these beliefs played a similar part in the public discourse on hysteria (Smith-Rosenberg 1972) and menstruation (Clarke 1989).

The newer construction of women's biology reflects a reinterpretation of these myths as articulated by women's health movement activists in the 1960s and 1970s. These activists updated the nineteenth-century feminist discourse on women's bodies. This updated and recent construction of women's biology revolves around the perspective that economic and political participation by women is not limited by their reproductive ability (e.g., Friedan 1965; Ruzek 1978, 1980.) Once public attention was drawn to the issue by the use of PMS as a defense in the British murder trials, these two views of women were part of the context in which the public debate over the definition of PMS and its simultaneous emergence as a social problem proceeded.

Methodology

The public debate about PMS was both reflected in and partly shaped by the articles contained in the popular and professional journals and periodicals. Because PMS would not have become a social problem without the influence of these publications, I use a content analysis of this literature to understand the emergence of this phenomenon and to provide a systematic and objective means to quantify and analyze both manifest and latent content in a text of any sort. Such an analysis allows a researcher to study the phenomenon over time.[1] I reviewed literature from 1931 when Frank first labeled premenstrual tension through 1987.[2]

THE MEDICAL LITERATURE

I reviewed *Index Medicus*, which lists all published articles on a given topic, from 1931 to 1987. The search focused on U.S. articles in the last six decades—most of them generally accessible—which were considered to be legitimate within a given field and which included "premenstrual changes," PMS(T), or a synonym in the title. I analyzed 51 articles from the following sources: *American Journal of Obstetrics and Gynecology* (21 articles), the *American Journal of Psychiatry* (13 articles), *Psychosomatic Medicine* (13 articles), and *Research in Nursing and Health* (4 articles).

THE POPULAR LITERATURE

In order to locate at least two popular magazines with articles on PMS over the last four decades, I reviewed *The Readers' Guide to Periodical Literature* from 1931 through 1987. Articles on PMS did not appear until 1954, and from 1954 to 1980, there were only 24 articles on PMS. Two magazines were selected because they published articles over several decades, reflecting changes over time. These were *Ladies Home Journal* (4 articles) and *Reader's Digest* (3 articles). Four other magazines were included because they provided breadth in the intended audience. These were *Essence,* a magazine for African-Americans (3 articles); *Mademoiselle,* a fashion magazine for young women (9 articles); *Newsweek,* a weekly news magazine (2 articles); and *Psychology Today,* a popular psychology magazine aimed at a well educated audience (3 articles).

THE FEMINIST LITERATURE

The process for choosing and defining what represented "feminist" literature was more complicated than the process for categorizing medical or popular literature. Since there is no set of "feminist" journals, a researcher must set out clear definitional guidelines for inclusion. A consideration of feminism is a political perspective and feminist theory as a scholarly approach resulted in the following criteria for inclusion: (1) The author must question what has become the dominant attitude toward PMS research.

This does not mean that an author must totally refute a medical approach but that she must consider a perspective that includes not only medical/physiological factors in the etiology of PMS but must also look at personal, social, or cultural factors; (2) The writer must question the implications of commonly cited views and constructions of premenstrual changes for individual women and women as a group, bringing these women's experiences of premenstrual changes and their meaning into consideration. (See Acker, Barry, and Esseveld [1983], Koeske [1983], Rittenhouse [1989] for further references on feminism and what constitutes a feminist perspective on PMS.)

Using this definition, I located and reviewed 15 articles representing the feminist discourse on PMS. Of the 15 articles, five came from book chapters, eight from journals, and two from newsletters. Generally, I did not review more than one article by a given author unless it represented a different analysis or approach to the topic.[3]

METHOD

Articles were coded to reflect study design, symptoms listed, etiology, definition of PMS, impact of PMS on women's lives, imagery/ideology of PMS, and the view of women who suffer from PMS. (See Rittenhouse [1989] for the complete coding categories.) After coding categories were developed from the articles, I coded each article twice to insure that all categories were included. (See Appendix A for a list of all articles reviewed.)

Results

The content analysis documented three constructions of premenstrual changes which shifted over time as they were influenced by one another and various external events. The shifts represented gradual changes in the manner in which PMS was discussed and defined. Prior to the trials in 1980, only a popular and medical discourse existed. PMS was viewed primarily as a private matter and as a medical problem. After the trials and the subsequent popularization of PMS in the popular literature, a feminist discourse emerged to challenge portrayals of premenstrual women and the dominant medical definition of premenstrual changes. Finally, a third shift in constructions of PMS was just beginning as this content analysis was being conducted. This third shift is represented by a moderation of a singular construct of premenstrual syndrome in the medical literature and less focus on the unpredictable nature of women in the popular literature. The feminist literature during this period becomes less reactive to the medical and popular literature and begins to create its own definitions of premenstrual changes.

The primary catalyst for the first shift from PMS being a medical and private matter to it emerging as a social problem were the trials in Britain. In the popular and feminist discourse, the influence that the trials had upon the growth of interest in PMS is vivid. Every article in the popular literature which dealt with more than just advice on weight gain or exercise for premenstrual symptoms mentioned the murder trials either as a way of legitimating concern for PMS (Angier and Witzleben 1983; Lauersen and

Stukane 1982) or as a start off point for a discussion of what PMS means for women and their lives and opportunities (Cantarow 1983; Hopson and Rosenfeld 1984; Press and Clausen 1982; Sommer 1984). The influence of the trials is less clear in the medical arena since this research focuses on a biomedical level and generally does not analyze social or cultural variables. None of the medical literature discussed the trials. However, several articles mentioned a concern abut potential violence by premenstrual women as a reason for the increased interested in premenstrual syndrome as a research topic (Berlin et al. 1982; Reid 1986; Reid and Yen 1981).

The British trials stimulated the first public debate about the influence of premenstrual symptoms on women's behavior. Although these issues were discussed within the popular and to a lesser extent the medical discourse prior to 1980, they did not elicit the response that the trials did. These trials influenced discussions about PMS world wide and triggered several cases in the U.S., none of which resulted in the successful use of PMS as a defense (Chait 1986; Press and Clausen 1982).

The trials forced PMS into public discourse in a very particular context; the murder trials of women who had killed men and claimed that their premenstrual symptoms had contributed to their actions. The particular context in which PMS was publicized forced it to be thought of as a potential social problem.

At the same time that the PMS defense stimulated discussion abut women's roles and the influences of biology, the unprecedented numbers of women entering the paid labor force brought renewed emphasis concerning lingering questions about sex roles, gender differences, and whether or not gender differences make women less able to function in some roles than men.

THE MEDICAL LITERATURE

Prior to the increased interest in PMS in 1980–1981, references to premenstrual symptoms—labeled as premenstrual tension (PMT), premenstrual tension syndrome (PMTS), or PMS—appeared fairly constantly in the medical literature between 1931 and 1980. Authors generally constructed PMS as a medical phenomenon requiring management and treatment by a physician or a psychiatrist/psychologist. However, PMS was not seen as a major problem for the majority of women. For those women who viewed it as a problem, various treatments were offered, for example mood medications and vitamin B6. Hormonal drugs did not appear in the medical literature until the 1980s, which is surprising since hormonal remedies for menstrual difficulties were recommended throughout the period reviewed in other medical literature (Frank 1931).

Medical discussion of PMS occurred in a context in which women's menstrual cycles were generally viewed as problematic and in need of control. The medical literature did not discuss premenstrual women negatively, yet authors did describe their cycles as disabling or handicapping (Lamb et al. 1953; Moos 1968). This distinction differentiates the medical discourse from the popular literature which problematizes both women and their cycles. For the majority of women, premenstrual symptoms were handled as a private matter. However, for women who sought out advice and relief from doctors, their symptoms came to be defined within medical terms.

Starting in the early 1980s, there began a gradual increase in the numbers of articles published on PMS in the medical literature. From 1980–1987, there were 267 articles published on PMS in English language journals, compared to 83 in the 1970s. From approximately 1980 to 1985, PMS was discussed at conferences, in forums, and in the literature. It came to be viewed as a potential medical problem for menstruating women in general. This is reflected in reported incidence rates of up to 100 percent of all menstruating women. The term PMS was used generally to define all changes which occurred during the premenstrual and even the early menstrual phase. Also, there was very little attempt to separate out severity and type of symptom.

By 1985, PMS researchers began to shift their focus from a singular concept of PMS to a differentiation between PMS and premenstrual symptoms. Two articles exemplify these shifts (Brooks-Gunn 1986; Reid 1986). Brooks-Gunn states that while most medical literature generalized premenstrual changes into one category, she saw two different phenomena were occurring: (1) "the existence of premenstrual symptoms," and (2) "the more specific designation of a premenstrual syndrome [or possibly syndromes]" (1986:385). Reid (1986), a PMS researcher throughout the 1980s, further explored the implications of the generalization of premenstrual symptoms into one singular syndrome for healthy women who were categorized as suffering from a condition that may "have significant implications regarding their health and functioning in society" (1986:922). Reid realized the potential socio-cultural consequences of the generalized use of the term PMS and alerted researchers and clinicians to these issues.

These writers illustrate a shift in focus for PMS researchers who no longer use the term PMS to describe all changes related to menstruation but only those most severe changes. Thus, the view was that most women experience mild to moderate cyclical changes which do not greatly interfere with their lives, but a minority of women suffer more severe symptoms which may constitute a medical problem requiring a physician's management. This shift is significant since it is the first time authors in the medical literature attempted more narrowly to define PMS and to recognize that premenstrual changes do not fit under a single construct but form a continuum that is different in each woman and even from cycle to cycle in a single woman. This shift is also important from a socio-cultural standpoint since it implies that not all women who experience premenstrual symptoms have a syndrome that necessitates medical intervention and treatment. Premenstrual symptoms can be seen as a "normal" part of a woman's monthly cycle.

THE POPULAR LITERATURE

Similar to the medical literature, most popular publications prior to 1980 focused on definitions and management of PMS within a medical paradigm. The popular literature reflected the ambiguities regarding the etiology and treatment of PMS that were found in the medical literature which generally hypothesized that premenstrual syndrome was caused by a malfunction of the hypothalmic-pituitary-ovarian axis or the adrenal cortex. Yet there was no agreement across the literature reviewed on the specific cause or the best treatment. Popular authors generalized medical studies and tended to focus on the symptoms and not the causes of PMS. Such writers, for the most part, uncritically accepted that PMS existed as a medical condition and was a problem for the majority of women. Their discussions, therefore, focused on what could be done to prevent, relieve, or treat premenstrual distress.

There are two key differences between the media and popular literatures prior to 1980. In the popular literature, unlike the medical literature, women were portrayed negatively. For instance, women who suffered from moderate to severe premenstrual changes were called "once-a-month-witches" suffering from the "needless misery" of "monthly blues." Also, the popular literature tended to take for granted that the majority of women suffered from PMS.

In the early 1980s, the popular construction of PMS began generally to avoid the negative portrayals of premenstrual women. PMS became something to be managed, yet it was not something that should get in the way of one's career or family. As one article advised:

> [M]enstruation need not adversely affect on-the-job performance. . . . With increasing numbers of women proving themselves to be admirably capable in top career positions, men can no longer point to "menstrual rages" or "irrational behavior" as reasons to relegate females to less responsible posts (Brody 1981:40).

Most articles provided explanations for the possible causes of PMS and offered women advice on how best to handle their symptoms. Premenstrual changes were problematized while the women who suffer from the changes were not. This is a crucial distinction and a dramatic change from the pre-1980 era. However, the popular literature often described PMS without distinguishing symptoms from a possible syndrome. Thus, the term PMS came to encompass everything from mild to severe symptomology.

THE FEMINIST LITERATURE

The feminist discourse began as a challenge to the various views of PMS presented in the popular and the medical literature. Significantly, only the feminist discourse attempted to analyze critically the emergence of PMS as a social problem, placing discussions of the syndrome within a socio-cultural context and examining the effect of changes in women's lives on the definition of and concern with PMS.

First, feminist writers were concerned about the apparent medicalization of another aspect of women's cycles (Riessman 1983). The implications of this medicalization and problematization of PMS went beyond women's bodies. It implied that the majority of women were "ill" each month and required possible medical care in order to control and cope with their "disease." Authors such as laws (1983) cautioned women that they

> must distinguish the medical men's construction of what I shall call PMT as they do, from a premenstrual state which is part of a woman's continuous

experience of cyclic change, and which is not inherently a medical problem (Laws 1983:20).

Secondly, feminists were concerned with the potential social, political, and economic implications of PMS. Chait (1986), who analyzes the use of PMS as a defense, cautioned lawyers to be aware of the "effects of mythology lurking in the court room." If PMS is used as a defense, attorneys need to "explode the sex-biased myths about menstruating women which if left dormant, could undermine the fairness of the defendant's trial" (291). Chait, like Laws, Hey, and Eagan (1985), felt that as women's social and economic opportunities expand, "the cry of 'raging hormones' due to PMS, especially raised in connection to female crime, easily can be seen as one more attempt to biologically justify the exclusion of women as a class from the mainstream of society" (272).

Finally, feminist authors did not forget about women who experienced premenstrual distress. They called for better research and treatments and stressed that providers need to listen to and legitimate women's concerns and experiences (Abplanalp 1983). This may sound contradictory with other statements such as those by Chait (1986); however, as Laws (1983) illustrated above, it is not that women do not have cyclical changes but that women need to define these changes.

Though feminist responses to PMS covered a wide range of areas, within each was a concern for the implications of various conceptualizations of PMS for women's private and public lives. During the mid-1980s feminists became less reactive to the medical and popular constructions and were creating their own. For example, anthropologists, such as Martin (1987) and Johnson (1987) analyzed PMS within the cultural context of the time. Johnson (1987:338) referred to PMS as a "western culture-specific disorder" which is a set of symptoms that have come to be defined within a given culture as a disease, "the etiology of which symbolizes core meanings and reflects pre-occupations of the culture; the diagnosis and treatment of which are dependent upon culture specific technology and ideology." According to Johnson, this disorder is culture specific and may be categorized differently within a different cultural context. PMS, as a culture-bound syndrome, can serve as a means of measuring women's roles and status within western society. Finally, Johnson (1987:351) asserts that the "ultimate fate of PMS in our culture should mirror quite accurately the resolution of conflicting role demands on women."

Martin (1987) agreed that PMS is linked to culture specific values. For her PMS is ultimately related to differing constructions of time and of the human capacities of men and women. Women's experiences of the world are not the same as men's. Martin's solution is a transformation of the current manner in which work and time are constructed. These authors took a step away from the early 1980s discussions and placed PMS within the cultural and social context of women's shifting roles in the 1980s, implying that PMS became an issue because of these changes not because it was a new and potentially dangerous "illness."

Discussion

From this analysis, it is clear that the debate over the definition, management, and treatment of PMS as a social problem was reflected in and shaped by the discussions occurring within the medical, popular, and feminist literatures. The interaction of these literatures during the 1980s shaped the constructions and meanings of the term PMS over time. The influences of these literatures upon one another is also evident. Prior to 1980, PMS was discussed in a few articles in research and popular journals. Its definition was limited to a singular view of what constituted premenstrual changes. After the trials in Britain, PMS became a major issue in the popular press. Debates began within the popular press over what this issue meant for women and their lives. In response to this, feminists mounted a challenge to the popularized medical construct and attempted to link the emergence of PMS to social and cultural factors, including but not limited to women's increased demands for equality.

Feminist writers challenged the existing view of premenstrual changes as a medical construct and helped shift discussions within the popular and medical arenas. McCrea (1983) notes this same type of shift resulted from the feminist challenge to the "deficiency model" of menopause. In this case, menopause became defined as a deficiency disease by physicians in the 1960s, "requiring" treatment with synthetic estrogen. In response to this disease definition, feminists challenged the disease model "claiming that menopause is normal and relatively unproblematic" (112). These feminist arguments influenced the popular portrayals of aging women as well as influencing the debate over the use of estrogen replacement therapy (ERT) within the medical community.

We see a similar type of shift regarding the influence that PMS exerts over women's lives in the mid-1980s. In what appears to be a moderation of a singular construct of PMS, medical researchers began to differentiate between PMS as a possible "illness" category and premenstrual changes which many women go through each month with little or no adverse effects. The popular press also shifted their views of premenstrual changes and focused more on coping strategies and less on the unpredictable nature of women.

Social problems do not emerge in a vacuum, but instead various factors trigger and influence their construction and evolution. PMS as a social problem emerged initially due to a specific event which was linked to changes within the socio-cultural environment of the early 1980s. Discussions of PMS were published at a time when women were not only participating in increasing numbers in the paid labor force but were also proving themselves to be quite capable within this context. PMS brought back old stereotypic views of women's abilities to control themselves, with the trials presenting the extreme view of women being adversely influenced by their biology. Yet, over time this view changed as it was challenged by feminist writers who pointed out the dangers and myths behind these emerging images.

In light of this discussion, we may ask if PMS is a social problem today. As defined in this article, PMS is not a social problem but has been recognized as a difficulty affecting some women. Consistent with feminist arguments, there has been moderation in views about PMS. In contemporary popular articles and research journals, the focus of discussions is on ways to diagnose, treat, or cope with symptoms that some women experience. The public debate over PMS has subsided, though there is no resolution of disagreement about what exactly constitutes PMS and its related symptoms.

Feminist challenges to the early popular and medical conceptualizations of PMS, along with other influences, appear to have reduced extreme portrayals of "out of control" women suffering from PMS in the popular literature. Yet, these portrayals still appear within the popular culture—for example, in cards and calendars that depict women's shifting moods, food cravings, and energy level in negative, biologically determined terms. Thus, we can see the influence of cultural context, critical events, and alternative literatures on publications that influence the way that PMS is constructed as a social problem or comes to lose that status. But there is still evidence of the persistence of a cultural context in which "deep mythic themes" persist—the persisting theme being the deterministic quality of a woman's menstrual cycle.

Notes

1. See Baily (1987) and Hoisti (1969) for a detailed discussion of the strengths and weaknesses of content analysis.
2. Although I did not review legal literature and cases, several articles within both the popular (Press 1982; Cantarow 1983; Sommer 1984) and feminist (Chait 1986; Laws 1983; Laws, Hey, and Eagen 1985) literature covered legal matters. These articles discussed specific cases, such as the U.S. case of the *People vs. Santos,* as well as the implications of the use of PMS as a defense.
3. For each discourse, I reviewed a sample of literature from other journals for comparative purposes. My results represent a general picture of the field over time. Also, all of the major PMS researchers are represented in my sample.

References

Abplanalp, Judith. 1983. "Premenstrual syndrome: A selective review." Women and Health 8:107–124.

Acker, Joan, Kate Barry, and Joke Esseveld. 1983. "Objectivity and truth: Problems in doing feminist research." Women's Studies International Forum 6:423–435.

Angier, Natalie, and Janet Witzleben. 1983. "Dr. Jekyll and Ms. Hyde." Reader's Digest, February, 119–123.

Bailey, Kenneth. 1987. Methods of Social Research. New York: The Free Press.

Berlin, Fred, Gregory Bergey, and John Money. 1982. "Periodic psychosis: A case report." American Journal of Psychiatry 139:119–120.

Blumer, Herbert. 1971. "Social problems as collective behavior." Social Problems 18:298–306.

Brody, Jane. 1981. "Menstrual problems—Lifting 'the curse' at last." Ladies Home Journal, June, 40–44.

Brooks-Gunn, J. 1986. "Differentiating premenstrual symptoms and syndromes." Psychosomatic Medicine 48:385–387.

Cantarow, Ellen. 1986. "The truth about PMS." Mademoiselle, March, 216–217, 260, 262.

Chait, Linda. 1986. "Premenstrual syndrome and our sisters in crime: A feminist dilemma." Women's Rights Law Reporter 9:267–293.

Clarke, Adele. 1989. "Women's health: Life cycle issues." In The History of Women, Health and Medicine in America: An Encyclopedic Handbook, ed. Rima Apple. New York: Garland Publishing.

Eagan, Andrea. 1983. "The selling of premenstrual syndrome." Ms., October, 26–31.

Frank, Robert. 1931. "Hormonal causes of premenstrual tension." Archives of Neurology and Psychiatry 26:1053–1057.

Friedan, Betty. 1965. The Feminine Mystique. New York: Dell.

Fuller, Richard, and Richard Myers. 1941. "The natural history of a social problem." American Sociological Review 6:320–28.

Hilgartner, Stephen, and Charles Bosk. 1988. "The rise and fall of social problems: A public arenas model." American Journal of Sociology 94:53–78.

Hoisti, Ole. 1969. Content Analysis for the Social Sciences and Humanities. Ontario: Addison-Wesley Publishing Co.

Hopson, Janet, and Anne Rosenfeld. 1984. "PMS: Puzzling monthly symptoms." Psychology Today, August, 30–35.

Johnson, Thomas. 1987. "Premenstrual syndrome as a western culture-specific disorder." Culture, Medicine, and Psychiatry 11:337–356.

Koeske, Randi Daimon. 1983. "Lifting the curse of menstruation: Toward a feminist perspective on the menstrual cycle." Women and Health 8:1–16.

Lamb, Wanda, George Ulett, William Masters, and Donald Robinson. 1953. "Premenstrual tension: EEG, hormonal, and psychiatric evaluation." American Journal of Psychiatry 109:840–848.

Lauersen, Niels, and Eileen Stukane. 1982. "Premenstrual syndrome: Can you win the hormone war?" Mademoiselle, December, 148–149, 198–199.

Laws, Sophie. 1983. "The sexual politics of premenstrual tension." Women's Studies International Forum 6:19–31.

Laws, Sophie, Valerie Hey, and Andrea Eagan. 1985. Seeing red: The politics of pre-menstrual tension. London: Hutchinson Press.

Martin, Emily. 1987. The Woman in the Body: A Cultural Analysis of Reproduction. Boston: Beacon.

McCrea, Frances. 1983. "The policies of menopause: The 'discovery' of a deficiency disease." Social Problems 31:111–123.

Moos, Rudolf. 1968. "The development of a menstrual distress questionnaire." Psychosomatic Medicine 30:853–867.

Olesen, Virginia. 1986. "Analyzing emergent issues in women's health: The case of the toxic-shock syndrome." In Culture, Society and Medicine, ed. Virginia Olesen and Nancy Woods, 51–62. New York: Hemisphere.

Press, Ann, and Peggy Clausen. 1982. "Not guilty because of PMS?" Newsweek, November 8, 111.

Reid, Robert. 1986. "Premenstrual syndrome: A time for introspection." The American Journal of Obstetrics and Gynecology 155:921–6.

Reid, Robert, and S.S.C. Yen. 1981. "Premenstrual syndrome." American Journal of Obstetrics and Gynecology 139:85–104.

Riessman, Catherine. 1983. "Women and medicalization: A new perspective." Social Policy 14:3–18.

Rittenhouse, C. Amanda. 1989. The Emergence of Premenstrual Syndrome: The Social History of a Women's Health "Problem." Ph.D. diss. San Francisco, Ca.: University of California, San Francisco.

Ruzek, Sheryl. 1978. The Women's Health Movement: Feminist Alternatives to Medical Control. New York: Praeger.

———. 1980. "Medical responses to women's health activities: Conflict, accommodation, and cooptation." Research in the Sociology of Health Care 1:335–354.

Smith-Rosenberg, Carroll. 1972. "The hysterical woman: Sex roles and role conflict in 19th-century America." Social Research 39:652–78.

Sommer, Barbara. 1984. "PMS in the courts: Are all women on trial?" Psychology Today, August, 36–38.

Spector, Malcolm, and John Kitsuse. 1973. "Social problems: A reformulation." Social Problems 20:145–159.

Spector, Malcolm, and John Kitsuse. 1977. Constructing Social Problems. Menlo Park, Ca.: Cummings.

Appendix A

CITATIONS FOR ARTICLES REVIEWED

Abplanalp, Judith, Roger Haskett, and Robert Rose. 1980. "The premenstrual syndrome." Psychiatric Clinics of North America 3:327–347.

Abramowitz, Elliot, A. Harvey Baker, and Susan Fleischer. 1982. "Onset of depressive psychiatric crises and the menstrual cycle." American Journal of Psychiatry 139:475–478.

Angier, Natalie, and Janet Witzleben. 1983. "Dr. Jekyll and Ms. Hyde." Reader's Digest, February, 119–123.

Awaritefe, Alfred, Milena Awaritefe, F.M.E. Diejomaoh, and John Ebie. 1980. "Personality and menstruation." Psychosomatic Medicine 42:237–251.

Backstrom, Torbjorn, Diana Sanders, Rosemary Leask, David Davidson, Pamela Warner, and John Bancroft. 1983. "Mood, sexuality, hormones, and the menstrual cycle. II. Hormone levels and their relationship to the premenstrual syndrome." Psychosomatic Medicine, 45:503–507.

Bancroft, John, Diana Sanders, David Davidson, and Pamela Warner. 1983. "Mood, sexuality, hormones and the menstrual cycle. III. Sexuality and the role of androgens." Psychosomatic Medicine 45:509–517.

Behrman, S.J. 1961. "Current opinion-case presentation." American Journal of Obstetrics and Gynecology 81:606–609.

Berlin, Fred, Gregory Bergey, and John Money. 1982. "Periodic psychosis: A case report. American Journal of Psychiatry, 139:119–120.

Bickers, William. 1952. "Premenstrual tension and its relationship to water metabolism." American Journal of Obstetrics and Gynecology, 64:587–590.

Bray, Rosemary. 1980. "Menstruation: Lifting the curse." Essence, September, 56–60.

Brody, Jane. 1981. "Menstrual problems—Lifting the curse at last." Ladies Home Journal, June, 40–44.

Brooks-Gunn, J. 1986. "Differentiating premenstrual symptoms and syndromes." Psychosomatic Medicine 48:385–387.

Brush, M., S. Watson, D. Horrobin, D. Phil, and M. Manku. 1984. "Abnormal essential fatty acid levels in plasma of women with premenstrual syndrome." American Journal of Obstetrics and Gynecology 150:362–366.

Burtis, Grace. 1987. "Eat to beat PMS." Mademoiselle, May, 180.

Cantarow, Ellen. 1986. "The truth about PMS." Mademoiselle, March, 216–218, 262.

Casper, Robert, and Ann-Marie Powell. 1986. "Premenstrual syndrome: Documentation by a linear analog scale compared with two descriptive scales." American Journal of Obstetrics and Gynecology 155:862–7.

Chait, Linda. 1986. "Premenstrual syndrome and our sisters in crime: A feminist dilemma." Women's Rights Law Reporter 9:267–293.

Chevalier, Lois. 1965. "Now doctors can end 'monthly problems.'" Ladies Home Journal, August, 44–46.

Christopher, Gail. 1981. "Good nutrition beats menstrual blues." Essence, February, 36–37.

Cohen, Sherry. 1981. "The premenstrual syndrome." Mademoiselle, October, 57–58.

Coyne, Christine. 1983. "Muscle tension and its relation to symptoms in the premenstruum." Research in Nursing and health, 6:199–205.

Cruz, Tess. 1983. "PMS hype or the return of the hysterical woman." Second Opinion, September. (Published by the Coalition for the Medical Rights of Women, San Francisco, Ca.)

DeJong, Renate, David Rubinow, Peter Roy-Byrne, M. Christine Hoban, Gay Grover, and Robert Post. 1985. "Premenstrual mood disorder and psychiatric illness." American Journal of Psychiatry 142:1359–1361.

Deleon-Jones, Frank, Eduardo Val, and Charles Herts. 1982. "MHPG excretion and lithium treatment during premenstrual tension syndrome: A case report." American Journal of Psychiatry 139:950–952.

Eichner, Eduard. 1983. "Clinical uses of 17 hydroxy-6-methylprogesterone acetate in gynecologic and obstetric practice." American Journal of Obstetrics and Gynecology 86:171–176.

Endicott, Jean, Uriel Halbreich, Sybil Schacht, and John Nee. 1981. "Premenstrual changes and affective disorders." Psychosomatic Medicine 43:519-529.

Faratian, B., A. Casper, P.M.S. O'Brien, I.R. Johnson, G.M. Filshie, and P. Prescott. 1984. "Premenstrual syndrome: Weight, abdominal swelling, and perceived body image." American Journal of Obstetrics and Gynecology 150:200–204.

Friedman, Richard, Stephen Hurt, John Clarkin, Ruth Corn, and Michael Aronoff. 1982. "Sexual histories and pre-menstrual affective syndrome in psychiatric inpatients." American Journal of Psychiatry 139:1484–1486.

Gaylin, Jody. 1978. "Learning to suffer—The cultural side of menstruation." Psychology Today, May, 36.

Golub, Leib, and Hyman Menduke. 1963. "Teen-age dysmenorrhea and social adjustment." American Journal of Obstetrics and Gynecology 85:433–436.

Golub, Leib, Hyman Menduke, and Samual Conly. 1965. "Weight changes in college women during the menstrual cycle." American Journal of Obstetrics and Gynecology, 91:89–94.

Greenblatt, Robert. 1955. "Pre-Menstrual tension: The needless misery." Reader's Digest, May, 36–38.

Hopson, Janet, and Anne Rosenfeld. 1984. "PMS: Puzzling monthly symptoms." Psychology Today, August, 36–38.

Howard, Lucy. 1986. "Psychiatry and the courts." Newsweek, June 23, 5.

Janowsky, David, Stephen Berens, and John Davis. 1973. "Correlations between the menstrual cycle: A renin-angiotensin-aldosterone hypothesis of premenstrual tension." Psychosomatic Medicine 35:143–154.

Koeske, Randi Daimon. 1980. "Theoretical perspectives on menstrual cycle research: The relevance of attributional approaches for the perception and explanation of premenstrual emotionality." In The Menstrual Cycle, ed. Alice Dan, E. Graham, and C. Beecher, 1:8–25.

Kotin, Leslie. 1986. "Preventing PMS." Essence, December, 14–15.

Lake, Alice. 1969. "Advice to women who are 'once-a-month witches.'" Reader's Digest, August, 117–120.

Lamb, Wanda, George Ulett, William Masters, and Donald Robinson. 1953. "Premenstrual tension: EEG, hormonal, and psychiatric evaluation." American Journal of Psychiatry 109:840–848.

Lark, Susan. 1986. "Stretch away PMS." Mademoiselle, October, 46.

Lauersen, Niels, and Eileen Stukane. 1982. "Premenstrual syndrome: Can you win the hormone war?" Mademoiselle, December, 148–149, 198–199.

Laws, Sophie. 1983. "The sexual politics of premenstrual tension." Women's Studies International Forum 6:19–31.

Laws, Sophie, Valerie Hey, and Andrea Eagan. 1985. Seeing Red: The Politics of Pre-Menstrual Tension. London: Hutchinson Press.

Leon, Gloria, Phyllis Phelan, John Kelly, and Sonia Patten. 1986. "The symptoms of bulimia and the menstrual cycle." Psychosomatic Medicine 48:415–422.

Logue, Camille, and Rudolf Moos. 1986. "Perimenstrual symptoms: Prevalence and risk factors." Psychosomatic Medicine 48:388–414.

Maddocks, Sarah, Philip Hahn, Frederick Moller, and Robert Reid. 1986. "A double-blind placebo-control led trial of progesterone vaginal suppositories in the treatment of premenstrual syndrome." American Journal of Obstetrics and Gynecology 154:573–81.

Magos, A.L. and J. Studd. 1986. "Assessment of menstrual cycle symptoms by trend analysis." American Journal of Obstetrics and Gynecology 155:271–7.

Magos, A.L., M. Brincat, and J. Studd. 1986. "Trend analysis of the symptoms of 150 women with a history of the premenstrual syndrome." American Journal of Obstetrics and Gynecology 155:277–82.

Malkin, Nina. 1986. "The taming of the shrew (inside you): Eat to beat PMS." Mademoiselle, September, 162–163.

———. 1986. "Your bodyguard: A get-wise guide to the top 14 female health hazards." Mademoiselle, October, 138, 140, 142.

Martin, Emily. 1987. The Woman in the Body: A Cultural Analysis of Reproduction. Boston: Beacon Press.

Moos, Rudolf. 1968. "The development of a menstrual distress questionnaire." Psychosomatic Medicine 30:853–867.

Morrison, Maggie. 1983. "Beating the premenstrual blues." Mademoiselle, August, 116.

Morton, Joseph. 1950. "Premenstrual tension." American Journal of Obstetrics and Gynecology, August, 343–352.

Oian, Pal, Anne Tollan, Hans Fadnes, Harald Noddeland, and Jan Maltau. 1987. "Transcapillary fluid dynamics during the menstrual cycle." American Journal of Obstetrics and Gynecology 156:952–5.

Pariser, Stephen, Stephen Stern, Myron Shank, James Falko, Richard O'Shaughnessy, and Chad Friedman. 1985. "Premenstrual syndrome: Concerns, controversies, and treatment." American Journal of Obstetrics and Gynecology 153:599–604.

Parlee, Mary Brown. 1973. "The premenstrual syndrome." Psychological Bulletin 80:454–465.

Parry, Barbara, Norman Rosenthal, Lawrence Tamarkin, and Thomas Wehr. 1987. "Treatment of a patient with seasonal premenstrual syndrome." American Journal of Psychiatry 144:762–766.

Parry, Barbara, and Thomas Wehr. 1987. "Therapeutic effect of sleep deprivation in patients with premenstrual syndrome." American Journal of Psychiatry 144:80–810.

Paulson, Morris. 1961. "Psychological concomitants of premenstrual tension." American Journal of Obstetrics and Gynecology 81:733–738.

Perr, Irwin. 1958. "Medical, psychiatric and legal aspects of premenstrual tension." American Journal of Psychiatry 115:211–219.

Posthuma, Barbara, Martin Bass, Shelley Bull, and Jeffrey Nisker. 1987. "Detecting changes in functional ability in women with premenstrual syndrome." American Journal of Obstetrics and Gynecology 156:275–8.

Press, Ann, and Peggy Clausen. 1982. "Not guilty because of PMS?" Newsweek, November 8, 111.

Prior, Jerilynn. 1984. "Is premenstrual syndrome exaggerated molominia? Letter to the Editor, American Journal of Psychiatry 141:1495.

Reeves, Billy, James Garvin, and Thomas McElin. 1971. "Premenstrual tension: Symptoms and weight changes related to potassium therapy." American Journal of Obstetrics and Gynecology 109:1036–1041.

Reid, Robert. 1986. "Premenstrual syndrome: A time for introspection." American Journal of Obstetrics and Gynecology 155:921–6.

Reid, Robert, and S.S.C. Yen. 1981. "Premenstrual syndrome." American Journal of Obstetrics and Gynecology 139:85–104.

Riessman, Catherine. 1983. "Women and medicalization: A new perspective." Social Policy 14:3–18.

Rome, Esther. "Premenstrual syndrome (PMS) examined through a feminist lens." Boston Women's Health Collective, unpublished manuscript.

Rosenthal, Jesse, Abbey Strauss, Lawrence Minkoff, and Arnold Winston. 1985. "Variations in red blood cell proton T relaxation times that correspond to menstrual cycle changes." American Journal of Obstetrics and Gynecology 153:812–813.

Roy-Byrne, Peter, David Rubinow, M. Christine Hoban, Gay Grover, and David Blank. 1987. "TSH and prolactin responses to TRH in patients with premenstrual syndrome." American Journal of Psychiatry 144:480–484.

Rubinow, David, and Peter Roy-Byrne. 1984. "Premenstrual syndromes: Overview from a methodologic perspective." American Journal of Psychiatry, 141:163–172.

Rubinow, David, Peter Roy-Byrne, M. Christine Hoban, Philip Gold, and Robert Post. 1984. "Prospective assessment of menstrually related mood disorders." American Journal of Psychiatry 141:684–686.

Saford, Henry. 1984. "Tell me doctor." Ladies Home Journal, July, 20–21:107.

Sanders, Diana, Pamela Warner, Torbjorn Backstrom, and John Bancroft. 1983. "Mood, sexuality, hormones and the menstrual cycle. I. Changes in mood and physical state: description of subjects and method." Psychosomatic Medicine, 45:487–501.

Shaver, Joan, and Nancy Woods. 1985. "Concordance of perimenstrual symptoms across two cycles." Research in Nursing and Health 8:313–319.

Smith, Stuart, and Cynthia Sauder. 1969. "Food cravings, depression and premenstrual problems." Psychosomatic Medicine 31:281–287.

Spicer, Betty Coe. 1963. "Help for the 'monthly blues.'" Ladies Home Journal, March, 16.

Sommer, Barbara. 1984. "PMS in the courts: Are all women on trial?" Psychology Today, August, 36–38.

Stout, Anna, Tana Grady, John Steege, Dan Blazer, Linda George, and Mary Lou Melville. 1986. "Premenstrual syndrome in black and white community samples." American Journal of Psychiatry 143:1436–1439.

Wong, Woon, Robert Freedman, Norman Levan, Chester Hyman, and Edward Quilligan. 1972. "Changes in the capillary filtration coefficient of cutaneous vessels in women with premenstrual tension." American Journal of Obstetrics and Gynecology 114:950–953.

Woods, Nancy, Ada Most, and Gretchen Dery. 1982a. "Estimating perimenstrual distress: A comparison of two methods." Research in Nursing and Health 5:81–91.

———. 1982b. "Recollections of menarche, current menstrual attitudes, and perimenstrual symptoms." Psychosomatic Medicine 44:285–293.

———. 1982c. "Toward a construct of perimenstrual distress." Research in Nursing and Health 5:123–136.

PART V

RACE, CLASS, AND HEALTH CARE

Substantial inequalities in health and health care exist in U.S. society, particularly by race and by class. These inequalities exist at all stages of the life course, beginning before birth and continuing through old age. The infant mortality rate for whites is about half of the rate for infants of all other races, with African-American infants having substantially higher mortality rates, about two and a half times that of whites. In some poor inner cities in the United States, the infant mortality rate rivals that in developing countries. Inequalities exist at the other end of the life course as well. Even though life expectancy in the United States is at a record high (76.9 years) and even though life expectancies have converged somewhat across races, substantial differences in health and life expectancies still exist by race and income. Likewise, the provision of health care is distributed unequally by race and by class—that is, having greater income and being white are associated with greater access to health care.

In "Race versus Class in the Health Care of African-American Elderly," Steven Wallace analyzes patterns of health care provision to African-American elderly in St. Louis, Missouri, through hospitals and nursing homes. His analyses document continued segregation of elderly patients by race. Wallace finds that while class is important in the economic life chances of African-Americans, class position does not fully explain racial segregation—in other words, race has an effect independent of class.

Elizabeth Armstrong's article "Lessons in Control: Prenatal Education in the Hospital" examines the prenatal education portion of one hospital's implementation of a national demonstration program entitled "Healthy Start," which was developed in response to the high rates of prematurity, low birth weight, and infant mortality in the United States. Through her observations of prenatal classes, Armstrong finds that the hospital has designed its prenatal and childbirth services to meet its own needs for patient compliance. First, the poor, working-class, predominantly African-American women who attend the classes are socialized to comply with the institutionally defined therapeutic regimen for birth. Second, the staff minimizes or ignores the concerns and questions women articulate regarding childbirth. Armstrong points to the gap between individual needs and institutional needs in the provision of health care, as well as the burden of responsibility placed on individuals, regardless of the social and economic constraints under which they make choices about their health and health care.

243

CHAPTER 13

Race versus Class in the Health Care of African-American Elderly

Steven P. Wallace

This paper examines patterns of health care for older African-Americans in St. Louis, Missouri, to determine the relative importance of class and race in the delivery of such care. Specifically, I ask whether race had an independent effect on older African-Americans' medical care in St. Louis during the 1980s. The resurgent debate over national health insurance makes this question particularly timely and its policy implications important. If race has an effect on the medical care of African-American elderly independent of the effects of class, then health policies that are color blind will fail to solve inequities in medical care. If, on the other hand, race is important in structuring health care delivery primarily because so many older African-Americans are poor, then health policies that address the needs of all poor persons equally would eliminate racial differences in medical care delivery.

In the following, I document continuing racial segregation in the institutional medical care of the elderly in the St. Louis metropolitan area. I then review the economic and social position of the elderly and examine the patterns and trends in institutional segregation, drawing on and evaluating available explanations of such continued segregation. A discussion of the policy implications of the findings concludes the paper.

Methods and Data

I use several sources of data to document racial variations in the institutional patterns of medical care. Nursing home facility[1] data are from the annual Missouri Department of Health mail survey of long-term care facilities. Initiated in 1980, it usually has a high response rate. The survey provides facility level data, including sources of payment, client characteristics, and staffing characteristics. For this paper I use data from facilities in St. Louis City and County (122 in 1988) in which most of the residents were age 60 or over. Facilities for children or disabled young adults are excluded. By focusing on the institutional level, we can better understand how race and class act as structural constraints on the life chances of African-American elderly.

Hospital data by race are not easily obtained. The state does not collect such data and the industry's data center refused to provide hospital level discharge data by race. I therefore had to develop a proxy that is sensitive to the distribution of older persons by race within each hospital. A common demographic technique for estimating the number of elderly in a geographic area uses the number of deaths of older persons. This is a reliable measure because death rates of the elderly are relatively high and stable (Shryock et al. 1971). In a similar manner, I use the number of deaths by hospital as an indicator of hospital use. Most deaths of those age 60 and over who live in St Louis occur in St. Louis area hospitals (Missouri Department of Health 1988), and the death rate per admission for the elderly in St. Louis hospitals falls within a narrow range (about 12 percent). Thus, the number of deaths of persons age 60 and over is a valid proxy for the racial distribution of elderly in hospitals. The Missouri Department of Health (1988) provided a special run of the death certificate data tape for deaths of persons aged 60 and over who had resided in St. Louis City and St. Louis County during 1961, 1970, 1989, and 1987.

Bias could be introduced into the proxy in two ways: if hospitals varied widely in the percent of elderly users who died while in the hospital and/or if older African-Americans died at a significantly different rate than older whites. Variation between hospitals in death rates should not affect the validity or reliability of the proxy. According to published Medicare death rates (U.S. Health Care Financing Administration, 1988a), St. Louis hospitals in 1987 had a mean death rate for Medicare patients (regardless of place of residence) of 12.4 percent, with a standard deviation of 2.1 percent. Only one hospital had a death rate more than two standard deviations above the mean (Normandy Osteopathic North at 18 percent) and only one had a death rate more than two standard deviations below the mean (Barnes at 8 percent). These figures were similar to the 1986 figures.

To assess the effect of the death rate variation, the dissimilarity index for 1987 was recalculated using "discharge" figures calculated by multiplying the number of deaths by the reciprocal of the hospital specific death rate (i.e., a hospital with 100 deaths and a 10 percent death rate was given a "discharge" number of 1000). The unadjusted dissimilarity index using the raw death numbers was 0.5497, while the adjusted dissimilarity index that accounts for the different death rates was 0.5432. Thus, the dissimilarity index is barely affected by the moderate death rate variations between hospitals.

The death rate variation by hospital had a larger effect on the proportion of city residents using city hospitals (vs. county hospitals). African-American elderly city residents using city hospitals fell from 91.9 percent to 86.2 percent using adjusted deaths, and white elderly city residents using city hospitals fell from 71.5 percent to 61.5 percent when adjusted to account for the variations in death rates. The data for county residents remained relatively constant. The moderate bias in the city data is consistent and somewhat magnifies the trends discussed below, so the proxy is useful.

The other potential bias is in the assumption that African-American and white hospital death rates are the same. National data confirms that the hospital death rates are comparable. In 1988, the hospital discharge status of patients was "dead" for 6.9 percent of whites and 7.5 percent of non-whites, which is not statistically different (U.S. National Center for Health Statistics 1990).

Further validation of the measure comes from a rank order list of hospitals used by African-Americans in St. Louis provided by the St. Louis Hospital Association. That list corresponds to the rank ordering of hospitals by number of deaths to older African-Americans. This further increases confidence in the validity of using deaths as a proxy.

Quality of nursing home care is measured using the published facility licensing and certification surveys conducted annually (U.S. Health Care Financing Administration 1988b). They contain data on 30 possible health and safety violations. There are no standard measures to adjust for the severity of each type of violation, so I weighted facility violations by the percentage of nursing homes reporting the violation statewide. This deflates common violations in comparison to rare violations. The weighted scores are summed for each facility to provide an overall weighted number of violations.

Quality of care in hospitals is more difficult to measure that for nursing homes. The federal government publishes Medicare death rate data for use as a quality of care indicator, although there are limitations to that approach. Another available indicator is the proportion of physicians on staff who are board certified (U.S. Congress 1988). These data are published by Medicare and the Missouri State Center for Health Statistics.

Data on the noninstitutionalized older population of the city of St. Louis are from a random population phone survey (N = 1,000) of residents age 60 and over conducted in 1987. The survey contains 368 variables on service utilization, social supports, and demographic variables (Smith et al. 1988).

Since I focus here on a single area—the city and county of St. Louis, Missouri, I control for variations in public policies (e.g., Medicaid) and availability of services (e.g., number of nursing home beds) that influence hospital and nursing home use. St. Louis is a midwestern industrial-metropolitan area of 2.4 million people. It includes a central city of about 400,000 that has been losing population to the suburbs since the 1950s. African-Americans have increased as a proportion of the city population at the same time, reaching 46.2 percent of the population in 1988 (Farley 1989). The proportion of African-Americans in suburban St. Louis County had increased to 11.3 percent of the population by 1980 (U.S. Bureau of the Census 1982). Similarly, African-American elderly have increased from 16 percent to 34 percent of the elderly population in the city and from 3 percent to 5 percent of the elderly population in the county between 1960 and 1988 (Table 13.1).

Table 13.1.   Population, Age 65 and over, St. Louis City and County, 1960–1988

	1960*	1970	1980	1988
St. Louis City				
African-American	14,791	20,842	23,088	23,213
White	77,393	65,901	56,398	45,664
St. Louis County				
African-American	1,646	2,387	4,751	4,900 (est)
White	47,539	70,776	97,206	100,200 (est)

Notes:
  * White-nonwhite
Sources:
  U.S. Bureau of the Census (1963, 1973, 1982).
  St. Louis County. 1988. Department of Community Health and Medical Care Annual Report. Clayton, Mo. Department of Community Health and Medical Care.
  University of Missouri, Urban Information Center, special run of data from the 1988 Census dress-rehearsal census.

St. Louis remained formally segregated until the 1960s; federal courts ordered interdistrict school desegregation in 1980 (Monti 1985). Medical care was segregated until the 1960s with one public city hospital serving African-Americans and a different city hospital serving primarily whites. In 1988 the city remained strongly segregated residentially, with the north side of town being primarily African-American and the south side primarily white. A central corridor was more integrated (Farley 1989). Middle class African-Americans began moving to suburbs in the 1970s, leaving a more impoverished African-American population in the city.

The suburbs are also highly segregated and segregation in the metropolitan area as a whole remained about the same between 1970 and 1980 despite high African-American residential mobility (Farley 1983). Segregation decreased only slightly between 1980 and 1988 in the city of St. Louis (Farley 1989). Massey and Denton (1989) have identified St. Louis and nine other U.S. metropolitan areas as "hypersegregated" (the others are Baltimore, Chicago, Cleveland, Detroit, Gary, Los Angeles, Milwaukee, Newark, and Philadelphia). These ten cities contained 29 percent of metropolitan African-Americans in 1980. The findings from St. Louis, therefore, can help us better understand the situation of older African-Americans in the large, segregated cities that exist across the United States.

Patterns of Segregation in Institutional Medical Care

This analysis focuses on nursing homes and hospitals because they are the central institutions in the American medical care system for the aged, accounting for about two-thirds of all personal health care expenditures for the elderly. Public programs pay for almost all (88 percent) hospital care for the elderly, and almost half of nursing home care (Waldo and Lazenby 1984).

Table 13.2 shows an indicator of the racial segregation in the St. Louis area, the index of dissimilarity. The index of dissimilarity is commonly used in looking at residential segregation (Massey and Denton 1989). It is defined as $D = (0.5) [| (x_i/X) - (y_i/Y) |]$, where x_i is the number of minority group X members in facility i, y_i is the number of group Y members in facility i, and X and Y are the total number of institutionalized residents of each respective group. The index can be interpreted as the proportion of residents of one race that would have to change facilities to make all facilities in a given area have an equal proportion of minorities. I calculated the dissimilarity index separately in the city and county for nursing homes,[2] while the city and county are combined for hospital care because of the high proportion of elders from the county who cross the county line to seek care in the city.

Segregation of the aged in nursing homes, as shown in Table 13.2, was roughly stable during the 1980s in both St. Louis City and County. During this time, between two-thirds and three-fourths of either African-American or white residents would have had to move to another nursing home to achieve full integration. Segregation of the aged in hospitals was significantly less, but also relatively stable between 1970–1987, with just over half of the elderly of one race having to change

Table 13.2.   Indexes of Dissimilarity, St. Louis City and County, Various Years

Nursing Homes[a]	Year				
	1980	1983	1986	1987	1988
St. Louis City	0.6674	0.6552	0.7545	0.7686	0.7405
St. Louis County	0.6428	0.717	0.698	0.7308	0.6995

Hospitals[b]	Year			
	1961	1970	1980	1987
St. Louis City and County	0.6896	0.551	0.541	0.5497

Residential Areas[c]	Year				
	1940	1960	1970	1980	1988
St. Louis City	0.846	0.845	0.838	0.838	0.798
St. Louis County	—	—	0.869	0.799	—

Notes:
a. Includes only those homes where over half of the residents are age 60 or over.
b. For those age 60 or over who were residents of St. Louis city or county prior to hospitalization.
c. Includes residents of all ages, calculated using census blocks.

Sources:
Hospital data calculated from Missouri Department of Health (1988) death certificate data.
Nursing home data calculated from Missouri Department of Health, *Missouri Nursing Home and Residential Care Facility Profiles*, various years. Residential areas from Farley 1989 and Farley 1983.

hospitals to fully integrate them. In general, there are clear racial patterns in nursing home and hospital use. Residential segregation levels in the city and county are similar to the nursing home segregation rates and have been relatively stable for 50 years (Table 13.2).

In addition to the general sociological interest in explaining racial segregation, the concentration of African-American elderly into a subset of medical institutions is problematic because there is evidence that the quality of nursing homes used by African-Americans is lower than those used by older whites. Using the annual nursing home licensing and certification reviews for skilled nursing facilities (SNFs) and intermediate care facilities (ICFs) in St. Louis city (U.S. Health Care Financing Administration 1988b), it is possible to compare general quality of care standards by facility. State nursing home examiners found the primarily African-American nursing homes (50 percent or more African-American residents) have more quality of care problems than those serving mostly whites. In the 1987 survey, six skilled and intermediate nursing facilities (SNF/ICFs that accounted for 88 percent of African-American residents in such facilities in St. Louis) had a mean adjusted violation rating of 7.22. This is over twice the adjusted violation rating of 3.17 of the seven primarily white SNF/ICFs evaluated in St. Louis. This shows that nursing home care is not only largely separate but is also unequal for African-American elderly in St. Louis.

For hospitals, quality indicators include the hospital death rate for older persons and the proportion of hospital house staff who are board certified (U.S. Congress

1988). In 1987, the 22 hospitals in St. Louis city and county had a mean death rate for Medicare clients of 12.45 percent, with a standard deviation of 2.09 percent. The death rates were statistically equivalent for the five hospitals accounting for 58.6 percent of elderly St. Louis African-American deaths and the seven hospitals accounting for 56.9 percent of elderly white deaths (12.6 percent and 12.3 percent respectively [U.S. Health Care Financing Administration 1988a]). African-American elderly were well represented in hospitals with the lowest death rates as well as in those with the highest.

The proportion of physicians who are board certified also shows no statistically significant difference between the hospitals that most African-American elderly use (82.2 percent board certified) and those that most elderly whites use (77.7 percent). The mean for all city and county hospitals was 69.9 percent with a standard deviation of 12.3 percent (U.S. Health Care Financing Administration 1988a). These indicators raise concerns about the quality of nursing homes, but not hospitals, used by older African-Americans. The racially patterned use of hospitals and nursing homes also has policy implications because nursing homes and hospitals are public accommodations, and integration of those facilities was mandated by the Civil Rights Act of 1964. Understanding why African-American elderly use a subset of medical institutions is important therefore for both theory and public policy.

Explaining Segregation

THE AVAILABLE THEORIES: INCOME, CLASS, CULTURE, AND RACE

Analyses of African-American/white disparities in health care frequently focus on individual behavior (such as the number of doctor or hospital visits per person) and draw on individual level explanations such as income or cultural traits. When considering institutional patterns such as those discussed above, however, we also should consider structural variables such as race and class. The following briefly outlines four approaches that have been used to explain continued racial disparities in health care: income, class, culture, and race.

Income explanations treat economic resources as a continuous variable in a fluid context. Differences between individuals are commonly conceptualized as the result of human capital differences, and frequently viewed as the result of individual initiative (Sowell 1981; Murray 1984). Contextual influences, such as government policy, are important to the extent that they corrupt normal incentives (such as cost-benefit calculations that shape an individual's actions).

There is a large literature showing how income influences the use of medical care (e.g., Fuchs 1986; Eastaugh 1987). These studies show how each additional dollar of income or expense for a patient (or additional dollar of revenue or expense for a provider) affects behavior. To the extent that older African-Americans are significantly poorer than older whites, differences in medical care between the groups may simply be a function of their incomes.

A class analysis argues that the basic economic structure of the nation perpetuates the position of African-Americans as a source of low-waged labor, preventing them from enjoying the same life chances as whites (Marks 1989; Marable 1983; Bonacich 1976). The issue is not one of income or economic incentives as a continuous variable, but of the structured operation of a capitalist economy as it undergoes historic transformations. One version of this theory suggests that in the past racism independently placed and kept African-Americans at the bottom of the economy, but since the Second World War the structure of the economy alone has impeded the mobility of poor African-Americans (Kasarda 1985; Wilson 1987). Other class analyses view racial divisions as a result of a capitalist economic system within which race is an ideological force that benefits capitalism. The state reproduces these race relations because it must stabilize productive relations for its own survival (Miles 1982; Wolpe 1986).

The class position of the aged is determined in large part by their pre-retirement class position and is reinforced by state policies involving retirement income and social services that recreate class disparities (see Estes 1986, 1981). Class theory highlights how economics creates structural barriers to health care for many elderly. The health problems of older African-Americans are seen as primarily a function of their disproportionate presence in the lower class, subsuming the effects of racial differences under those of class.

A cultural analysis argues that differences in life chances between African-Americans and whites are primarily the outcome of individual initiative and preferences, that is, of values and attitudes (Baca Zinn 1989; and see Lewis 1959; Moynihan 1965). While culture is a group pattern, policy analysts conceptualize it as residing in individuals, making individuals the targets of corrective actions. Public policy perpetuates poverty and social inequality by encouraging detrimental values and stifling individual motivation (e.g., Mead 1986; Murray 1984). As a result, ghetto problems have been worsened rather than improved by antipoverty efforts.

A cultural approach to health and medical care uses feelings of alienation from society and skepticism toward medical care to explain the lower use of preventive care and other services by African-Americans (Bullough 1972). Similarly, lower levels of knowledge about cancer and greater pessimism about a cure are cited to explain why African-Americans seek cancer treatment later than whites (National Cancer Institute 1984). Folk healing practices that may substitute for formal medical care also have been identified by researchers using this approach (Spector 1985). A cultural preference for family care is a common explanation of why older African-Americans use nursing homes significantly less than older whites (Morrison 1983).

Theories that give race an independent causal force in explaining the life chances of African-Americans focus on institutional barriers rather than individual characteristics (Boston 1988; Wellman 1977; Willie 1989). While this theory does consider the economic structure of the United States and the world system (Willie 1989), racial dynamics are seen to operate independently of class. This theory suggests that the medical care system is structured so as to treat African-Americans differently than whites, regardless of their class position (see Miller 1987; Okada and Wan 1980; Blendon et al. 1989).

EVALUATING THE ALTERNATIVES

Economic and social data on older individuals provide background information used by each of the four theories. Table 13.3 shows the economic statuses of African-Americans and whites age 60 and over living in the city of St. Louis in 1987. Older African-Americans were three times as likely as older whites to have low incomes (under $7,200/year), four times as likely to receive supplemental security income (SSI), and one-tenth as likely to have income from investments. African-American educational levels were also significantly lower. These are similar to national trends (Wallace 1990a). Income theories would draw on this resource difference to hypothesize that racial segregation in health care is a result of economics.

From a class perspective, the disproportional lifetime occupational position of older African-Americans in semi-skilled and unskilled jobs (Table 13.4) is more important than income, since an individuals' position in the production system is conceptualized as the critical factor influencing life chances. Almost three-fourths of older African-American men were in unskilled or semi-skilled occupations during their working lives, twice the rate of older white men (Table 13.4). This reflects the segregated occupational and educational structures of the area during the adult lives of the elderly (Korbett and Seematter 1987). Similarly, older African-American women who worked were primarily unskilled (mostly domestic workers) and semi-skilled (Table 13.4). While most members of both races were members of the working class, these data show that older African-Americans were in a marginal class segment while whites were more likely to be in an economically stable class segment.

Table 13.5 shows some of the differences in the social characteristics of older African-Americans and whites in the city of St. Louis. A statistically equal percent of older African-Americans and whites live alone. African-American elderly who live with others, however, follow a different pattern than whites. Older African-Americans are less likely to be living with a spouse, and more likely to be living with children or other

Table 13.3. Economic and Education Characteristics, St. Louis City Residents Age 60 and over, by Race, 1987

	African-Americans	Whites
Family Income under $7200/year	38.9%[a]	9.1%
Source of Income		
Social Security	85.8%[a]	91.6%
Private Pensions	34.8%[a]	45.5%
SSI	12.1%[a]	3.0%
Wage Income	7.8%[a]	9.7%
Investments	2.1%[a]	24.6%
8th Grade or less education	51.4%[a]	33.2%
	(N = 373)	(N = 629)

Note:
   a. African-American-white difference significant at the .01 level.
Source:
   St. Louis Area Agency on Aging Needs Assessment Survey.

Table 13.4. Lifetime Occupational Distribution, St. Louis City Residents Age 60 and over, by Gender and Race, 1987

			Occupational Category				
	Professional	Sales/ Technical	Skilled	Semi- Skilled	Un- Skilled	Homemaker	Total	N

Men

	Professional	Sales/ Technical	Skilled	Semi- Skilled	Un- Skilled	Homemaker	Total	N
African-American	9.5%	9.5%	9.5%	40.5%	31.0%		100%	(84)
White	20.2%	18.5%	23.4%	33.1%	4.8%		100%	(124)

Chi-Square df = 4, value = 34.678, p < .000

Women

	Professional	Sales/ Technical	Skilled	Semi- Skilled	Un- Skilled	Homemaker	Total	N
African-American	14.6%	4.7%	3.2%	17.4%	33.6%	26.5%	100%	(253)
White	8.4%	31.2%	3.7%	17.3%	8.8%	30.6%	100%	(490)

Chi-Square df = 5, value = 119.68, p < .000

Source:
St. Louis Area Agency on Aging Needs Assessment Survey.

Table 13.5.   Social Characteristics, St. Louis City Residents Age 60 and over, by Race, 1987

	African-Americans	Whites
Living alone		
Women	47.3%	52.4%
Men	33.3%	31.0%
Living with spouse		
Women	24.6%	30.8%
Men	39.8%[a]	54.6%
Living w/o spouse but w/children[c]	15.8%[b]	9.2%
Living w/o spouse but w/other family[c]	15.3%[b]	6.9%
Having children in area	72.4%	72.9%
Mean monthly visits with area children	37[d]	21

Notes:
   a. African-American—white difference significant at the .05 level.
   b. African-American—white difference significant at the .01 level.
   c. The number of men in this category was too small to analyze separately, but the trends were the
      same for both men and women.
   d. African-American—white difference significant at the .001 level.
Source:
   St. Louis Area Agency on Aging Needs Assessment Survey.

relatives. Potential access to family help, as measured by having children in the metropolitan area, is the same for African-American and white elderly (Table 13.5). Visiting
frequency, however, is significantly higher for African-Americans. These data are consistent with the literature on the strong helping networks that extend beyond the marital dyad in the African-American community (Taylor 1988), a frequently cited key
cultural difference between African-Americans and whites.

African-American elderly in St. Louis are in higher need of medical care as shown
by different measures of health status shown in Table 13.6. They are significantly more
likely to report fair or poor health status than older whites, which is consistent with
national trends (Wallace 1990a). They are also more likely to report greater activity
limitations, conditions that generally result from chronic illnesses. Finally, older
African-American women report more medical conditions than older white women.
The trend is similar for men, though it is not statistically significant.

The differences between African-American and white elderly in economic resources, class position, social support, and medical needs have to be taken into account
when considering alternate explanations of racial segregation in medical care.

NURSING HOME PATTERNS

As shown earlier, nursing home segregation in St. Louis is as strong as residential segregation. In the African-American north side, the average private nursing home is 75 percent African-American, while the average private nursing home in the white south side
is only 4 percent African-American. Central corridor nursing homes average one-third
African-American patients, about proportional to the number of African-American elderly in the city as a whole. The presence of nursing homes with many public pay patients in the south side argues against a purely income based interpretation of these dif-

Table 13.6.   Health Status, St. Louis City Residents Age 60 and over, by Race and Gender, 1987

	Race			
	African-American		White	
	Gender			
	Women	Men	Women	Men
Self Reported Health Status Fair or Poor	55.9%[a]	45.1%[b]	38.0%	29.5%
Mean Number Limitations[c]	1.21[b]	1.21[a]	0.81	0.42
Mean Number Conditions[d]	2.6[b]	2.2	2.2	1.9
Percent Reporting 4 or more Conditions	26.1%[b]	18.4%	16.5%	15.4%

Notes:
  a. African-American—white difference significant at the .01 level.
  b. African-American—white difference significant at the .05 level.
  c. Needing help with: using the phone, arranging transportation, shopping, preparing meals, doing housework, arranging home repairs, doing laundry, getting upstairs, getting around the house, taking a bath or shower, taking medicines, handling money.
  d. Arthritis/rheumatism, lung problems, high blood pressure, circulation problems, vision problems, hearing problems, urinary tract disorder, anemia, diabetes.
Source:
  St. Louis Area Agency on Aging Needs Assessment Survey.

ferences, since African-Americans would be better represented in the south side if the only barrier to care was ability to pay.

The data in Table 13.7 confirm this analysis. Since there are different public payment sources for skilled facilities (primarily Medicaid) and residential facilities (primarily a state funded "nursing care grant"), those two groups are analyzed separately in the regression analysis. For both types of facilities, the strongest predictor of the percent of residents who are African-American is the racial composition of the neighborhood of

Table 13.7.   Regression of Percent African-American in St. Louis City and County Nursing Homes, Skilled and Residential Facilities, 1988

	partial r^2	model r^2	b value	prob > f
Skilled Facilities				
SNF and ICF; (N = 76)				
Zip Code (% black)	0.4265	0.4265	0.4582	0.0001
Public Pay (%)	0.1421	0.5686	0.3032	0.0001
Intercept = −0.0604				
Residential Facilities				
(N = 40)				
Zip Code (% black)	0.6166	0.6166	0.5540	0.0001
Nonprofit facility	0.0526	0.6693	−.2192	0.0202
In city	0.0281	0.6974	0.1583	0.0755
Intercept = 0.0617				

Note:
  Information from the 1987 survey was used when a facility failed to respond to the 1988 questionnaire (N = 27).
Source:
  Missouri Department of Health, 1989. Missouri Nursing Home and Residential Care Facility Survey, 1988. Machine readable data file. Jefferson City, Mo.: State Center for Health Statistics.

the nursing home. The percent of African-Americans in a zip code predicts 62 percent of the variance in the racial composition of residential facilities and 46 percent of the variance in skilled facilities.

This finding supports the inclusion of culture or race in the analysis. The strong relationship between the racial composition of an area and the racial composition of nursing homes could be explained either by the preferences of residents and their families, or by racial discrimination. Cultural theories would suggest that families place their elderly in nursing homes that are closest to home so that it is easier to visit. Racial theories would hypothesize that the professional referral network "steers" African-Americans away from white nursing homes, and/or that African-Americans fear south St. Louis because of its racist reputation.

In residential care facilities (RCFs), the only other significant predictor is a dummy variable for non-profit status of nursing home that explains only five percent of the variance. African-American elderly are *less* likely to be in nonprofit residential homes (and more likely to be in for-profit homes) than white elderly after controlling for other variables. This suggests that for-profit residential facilities may be willing to accept anyone who can pay the minimum rate, while the nonprofit facilities may use nonfinancial criteria. The variables for percent public pay in facility, church ownership, corporate ownership, private individual ownership, and city versus county location were not significant predictors of the percent African-American residents in RCFs. This supports a class analysis that would predict that profit making facilities would not avoid patients based on race as long as it did not affect profits.

In skilled facilities (SNF/ICFs), the only other significant variable was the percent public pay, which explained 13 percent of the variance. Older African-Americans are on Medicaid more commonly than whites, so this finding supports the theory that some racial discrimination is simply a result of economics. Extended private pay is more likely by whites because at least one-quarter of older city whites have investment assets that could be sold to pay for care, while almost no older African-Americans have such investments (Table 13.3). The lean economic resources of African-American elderly could also be used to explain the fact that most of the nursing homes that only have mainly private pay patients are almost exclusively white. Even the Medicaid beds in south St. Louis, however, are filled primarily by whites. This contradicts a strict income interpretation because Medicaid beds should be randomly filled by race in the city as a result of the severe shortage of such beds. Overall, economic discrimination in SNF/ICFs, which are more expensive than RCFs[3], apparently accounts for some of the observed racial composition of skilled facilities, but it explains much less of the difference than does the racial composition of neighborhoods.

Other data support either a culture (preferences) or race (institutional barriers) analysis. Closer family ties among African-Americans would be expected to make distance from family a more important factor for African-American elderly seeking a nursing home. While African-American and white elderly in St. Louis have the same chance of having children in the area, African-American elderly see their children almost twice as often (Table 13.5). This would suggest that African-American families would be more sensitive to the distance they have to travel than whites. African-Americans, therefore, might be expected to prefer nursing homes in the African-American north side because it is closer to their families.

Other data contradict a strict cultural explanation of nursing home segregation. A public nursing home in the white south side is all Medicaid and half African-American. Obviously, African-Americans are willing to have family members in homes outside of their immediate neighborhoods. African-Americans do not have a cultural preference that *prevents* them from placing family members outside their immediate neighborhoods when necessary to obtain a Medicaid bed.

The small number of African-American elderly in white areas might be the result of hospital discharge planners and other referral sources "steering" African-Americans away from primarily white homes. Institutional referral sources are important because homes with mostly African-American residents obtain about 80 percent of their admissions from other institutions (primarily hospitals) and those with primarily white residents obtain about 70 percent of their admissions from other institutions (Missouri Department of Health 1989).

Another racial factor that could deter older African-Americans from seeking nursing home beds in the south side is the racism of that area. White south side residents can be openly hostile to African-Americans, a fact that is regularly reported by the media (e.g., Jackson and Smith 1988). Even African-American service workers can face harassment when they work in white south side homes (Wallace 1990b). This probably makes African-American families uncomfortable with the thought of placing their elderly in that area.

The data indicate that nursing home patterns are influenced primarily by racial forces, and secondarily by economics and possibly by cultural factors. Confirming the exact processes by which race, economics, and culture create this nursing home pattern would require further study of referral patterns, the perception of the south side by African-Americans, and the decision making process involved in selecting homes by African-Americans and whites.

HOSPITAL PATTERNS

As noted earlier (Table 13.2), hospital segregation was lower than the nursing home or residential patterns during the 1980s, but was still high and had remained relatively constant for almost 20 years.

Hospital data are available starting in 1961 when the medical facilities in St. Louis were still formally segregated and race was clearly the dominant factor in determining the distribution of patients in hospitals by race. The dissimilarity index for hospital use (using the death proxy) by residents of St. Louis city and county begins at .69 in 1961 as a result of formal segregation (Table 13.2). Almost two-thirds of older African-Americans were found in one segregated public hospital, while forty percent of older whites were in totally white hospitals. Desegregation laws and Medicare in the mid-1960s led to a broadening of the hospitals used by older African-Americans, and a corresponding drop in the dissimilarity index to .55 by 1970. Only 12.5 percent of older white were in all-white hospitals in 1970. By 1980, none of the city and county hospitals were exclusively white (although some had only a handful of African-American elderly). The simple discrimination that barred all African-Americans from some hospitals was no longer a force, but the dissimilarity index changed little between 1970 and 1987 regardless.

The pattern of hospital use by older county residents changed during the past 25 years. While city residents mostly used city hospitals between 1961 and 1987, county residents used both city and county hospitals in a proportion that differs by race and year. Figure 13.1 shows where older city and county residents died (the utilization proxy). In 1961, almost all older city residents used city hospitals. In contrast, only 35 percent of older whites living in the county stayed in the county for hospital care (they mostly traveled into St. Louis city), and the small number of older African-Americans living in the county primarily stayed in the county (Figure 13.1). By 1987 the trend for county elderly was reversed, with older whites more likely to stay in the county and older African-Americans more likely to travel to the city. The general level of segregation persisted through this shifting pattern of hospital use by county residents.

As population moved from the city to the county between 1961 and 1987, so did hospitals. At least seven hospitals in the city closed and an additional seven moved from city to county locations. The number of nonpsychiatric, nonfederal hospital beds per 1,000 persons doubled in the county during this time and remained relatively constant in the city (Missouri Department of Health 1959, 1970, 1980; U.S. Bureau of the Census 1963, 1973, 1982). If proximity were the most important factor in hospital use, the increasing availability of hospital beds in the county should have resulted in both African-American elderly as well as white elderly using county facilities. Instead, African-Americans increasingly used city facilities during the time that county hospitals became more accessible. From class and income perspective, it is significant that African-Americans are well represented in both the most and least profitable hospitals in the city and county (Steyer 1989). Thus, serving African-American elderly does not appear to have a specific economic outcome that might influence the willingness of hospitals to serve African-American elderly, contradicting an explanation of segregation based only on class or income theories.

The racial differences in the use of hospitals by the elderly are most obvious when examining the consolidation of the county and city public hospitals into a single facility in the 1980s. The county public hospital served large numbers of both white and African-American elderly in 1980, accounting for almost one-third of older African-American county resident deaths and 14 percent of older white county resident deaths. When the facility closed, elderly users of the public county hospital shifted to different types of hospitals depending on race. Older African-Americans shifted in equal parts to city teaching hospitals, private nonprofit hospitals, and the new public facility. Older whites shifted primarily to private nonprofit hospitals. A similar pattern occurred with the closure of the city public hospital during the regional consolidation, with older whites avoiding the new public regional hospital and using private nonprofit hospitals instead. The result was a continuation of the level of segregation in area hospitals.

This cannot be explained by income or class theories alone because of the sorting by race of poor elderly into different facilities. A step-wise regression found that the racial composition of the zip code area where a hospital is located predicts 79 percent of the variance in the percent African-American elderly in city and county hospitals (β = .66) in 1987. The percent of discharges paid by Medicaid predicts only 7 percent (β = .53) and the percent discharges paid by Medicare predicts 2 percent (β = −.39).

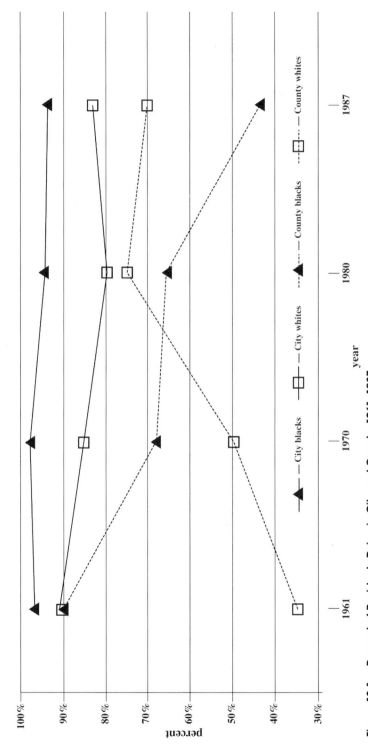

Figure 13.1. Percent of Residents Dying in City and County, 1961–1987

As with nursing homes, this finding could either be the result of cultural preferences for convenient care or an outcome of racial forces. For hospitals furthest out in the county, it is likely that their inaccessibility to African-American neighborhoods limits their use by older African-Americans. For hospitals only a few miles from African-American neighborhoods, however, distance cannot be the only factor. With few hospitals in primarily African-American areas, most older African-Americans have to travel a moderate distance to reach any facility. One method that might reduce African-American use of hospitals in exclusively white neighborhoods would be for those hospitals to avoid having outpatient clinics that might attract African-Americans from further away. At least four hospitals near African-American neighborhoods have no or limited clinic facilities and a low percent of African-American elderly. It is also possible that some hospitals resist giving admitting privileges to doctors who have many poor and/or African-American patients.

The dramatic loss of public hospital beds in the city and county mirrors national trends. This closure of public hospitals is consistent with a class analysis of the privatization of government functions (Wallace and Estes 1989). A class analysis, however, is not capable of explaining why older whites have essentially abandoned the public system—only 0.2 percent of county older white and 2.4 percent of city older white deaths occur in the regional public hospital. The resegregation of the public hospital has followed a pattern seen in residential areas where "white flight" occurs. Race is a central force because whites are avoiding a public hospital because it is located in an African-American part of the city. Ironically, Medicare and Medicaid's freedom of choice provisions in the use of hospitals has given white elderly the ability to avoid the new public hospital and maintain a relatively constant level of segregation.

Discussion

Most research during the 1980s on the differential life chances of African-Americans and whites has focused on residential, school, and occupational inequality. Less attention has been given to medical care even though health is a prerequisite to the other opportunities. This paper has documented the continuing and steady segregation by race of the elderly in nursing homes and hospitals in St. Louis, Missouri. Since almost one-third of metropolitan African-Americans live in similar cities across the county, the data analyzed here can illustrate forces affecting the life chances of a significant segment of African-American elderly in the United States. Competing theories would explain the medical segregation as the outcome of individual level attributes of culture or income, or structural level forces of class or race. The data presented provide a complex picture of the causal forces in the continuing medical segregation, with the structural influence of race having an independent effect.

Table 13.8 summarizes the evidence presented concerning each of the theories. Nursing homes, and to a somewhat less extent hospitals, remain highly segregated by race. The economic impact of older African-Americans' lower income and class cause some of the segregation of medical care, but the data do not support economics as the only or even primary force. Data that support the economic interpretation include the fact

Table 13.8. Summary of Evidence that Explains Segregation of African-American Elderly, by Theoretical Approach[a]

	Income	Class	Culture	Race
Background	African-Americans 3 times as likely to be low income	African-Americans in lowest segment of working class	African-American kin networks stronger	Neighborhoods are racially segregated
Nursing Homes	(+) public pay predicts some variance in percent African-American, suggesting simple economic discrimination as a secondary force (+) Nursing homes that are exclusively private pay are all white (−) public pay residents in south side are disproportionately white	(+) African-Americans are more likely to be in for profit RCFs	(+) neighborhood percent African-American is best predictor of African-American nursing home use—prefer closeness to family and/or race barriers (+) stronger family would make African-Americans more concerned with close facilities, but (−) public facility w/many African-Americans in south side suggests location is not primary factor	(+) 80 percent of nursing home patients come from other institutions (+) fear by African-Americans of harassment in south side
Hospitals	(−) Medicare & Medicaid reduce economic barriers & make the poor more desirable patients (−) white elderly avoid regional public hospital despite poverty of some	(−) most profitable and least profitable hospitals include both low and high proportions of African-American elderly patients (+) privatization of health care previously provided by public hospitals	(+) preference for close facilities, but (−) more African-American than white elderly travel from county to city for care	(−) all hospitals have at least a few African-American elderly patients (+) stable dissimilarity index over almost 20 years despite residential mobility (+) African-Americans from county disproportionately use city hospitals (+) Older whites avoid new regional public hospital (+) Poor use different facilities by race

Note:
a. (+) = evidence supports theory; (−) = evidence contradicts theory

that African-American elderly are low income and from the lowest segment of the working class, limiting their options. The proportion of a nursing home that is public pay (primarily Medicaid) explains a statistically significant but numerically small (5 to 13 percent) amount of the variance in the racial composition of nursing homes. While this supports the interpretation of an income or class bias, even the Medicaid beds in the white south side are filled almost exclusively with whites while the opposite is not true in the African-American north side.

The analysis of hospital use is less supportive of an economic interpretation, in part because essentially all elderly, rich and poor, pay for their hospitalization with Medicare. While the observed privatization of public hospital care is consistent with a class analysis, there is no significant correlation between profitability of private hospitals and the racial composition of the hospital. White flight from the reorganized public hospital system indicates that noneconomic forces play an important role in where the elderly obtain hospital care. The steady level of segregation in hospitals demonstrates that simply equalizing the ability to pay for care does not necessarily eliminate racial patterns in the distribution of patients among medical facilities.

The most important predictor of the racial composition of nursing homes and hospitals was the racial composition of the facility's zip code (accounting for about half to 80 percent of the variance). The closer family ties demonstrated by African-American elderly would suggest that a cultural preference for care close to home is involved. In both nursing homes and hospitals, however, African-Americans are found in facilities outside their neighborhoods. Both older African-Americans and whites show a willingness to travel within the city-county area to obtain medical care, but their ultimate locations vary substantially by race.

The data suggest that there is an independent racial factor in the sorting that occurs in facility use between older African-Americans and whites. While the overt racial exclusion of the early 1960s does not appear to have persisted, African-American elderly continue to be concentrated in a subset of area medical facilities. The high level of residential segregation in the area contributes to an ongoing concern by African-Americans about their safety in historically white neighborhoods. Because nursing homes obtain most of their patients from hospitals and other institutions, it is possible that hospitals are involved in steering patients into same-race areas. White patients also play a role in perpetuating segregation by their changing choices of hospitals.

Overall, the patterns of institutional medical care for the elderly in St. Louis suggest that race has an independent effect, one that is larger than class factors in determining the pattern of institutions used. While class may be increasingly important in the economic life chances of African-Americans, this research shows that medical care for the elderly is similar to housing, where wealth and class position alone fail to fully explain continued segregation (Farley and Allen 1987).

These findings have important implications for health policies for the elderly. Public policies that focus only on eliminating financial barriers to medical care will not fully open the doors to nursing homes or change the patterns of hospital use. Race conscious efforts in the planning and provision of medical care services will be required to assure that medical care is provided equitably to both African-Americans and whites. This is as important in national policy initiatives as it is in local health planning. Since most proposals for a

U.S. national health insurance focus on the economics of health care rather than institutional patterns, this analysis suggests that the proposals will fail to eliminate racial segregation in the health care provided to those who need it most—older African-Americans.

Notes

1. "Nursing homes" include highly skilled nursing facilities and intermediate care facilities (SNFs and ICFs) as well as more custodial residential care facilities (RCFs).

2. Combining the city and county provides similar results, but there are so few African-American elderly in county nursing homes that there appears to be separate markets for nursing home care in the two areas.

3. Many RCFs set their minimum fees at the SSI payment level, meaning that poor elderly can afford care by signing over their monthly aid checks. SNF/ICF care, on the other hand, typically costs a minimum of 4–5 times more.

References

Baca Zinn, Maxine. 1989. "Family, race, and poverty in the eighties." Signs 14:856–74.

Blendon, Robert J., Linda Aiken, Howard Freeman, and Christopher Corey. 1989. "Access to medical care for black and white Americans." Journal of the American Medical Association 261:278–81.

Bonacich, Edna. 1976. "Advanced capitalism and black/white race relations in the United States: a split labor market interpretation." American Sociological Review 41:34–51.

Boston, Thomas. 1988. Race, Class and Conservatism. Boston, Mass.: Unwin Hyman.

Bullough, Bonnie. 1972. "Poverty, ethnic identity and preventive health care." Journal of Health and Social Behavior 13:347–59.

Corbett, Katharine T., and Mary E. Seematter. 1987. "No crystal stair: black St. Louis, 1920–1940." Gateway Heritage (Quarterly Journal of the Missouri Historical Society) 8:8–15.

Eastaugh, Steven R. 1987. Financing Health Care: Economic Efficiency and Equity. Dover, Mass.: Auburn House.

Estes, Carroll L. 1981. "Public policy and aging in the 1980s." In Empowering Ministry in an Ageist Society, ed. Dieter Hessel, 23–38. Atlanta, Ga.: United Presbyterian Church, U.S.A.

———. 1986. "The politics of ageing in America." Ageing and Society 6:121–34.

Farley, John E. 1983. "Metropolitan housing segregation in 1980: the St. Louis case." Urban Affairs Quarterly 18;347–59.

———. 1989. Black-White Housing Segregation in the City of St. Louis: A 1988 Update. Edwardsville, Ill.: Southern Illinois University Regional Research and Development Services.

Farley, Reynolds, and Walter R. Allen. 1987. The Color Line and the Quality of Life in America. New York: Oxford University Press.

Fuchs, Victor R. 1986. The Health Economy. Cambridge, Mass.: Harvard University Pres.

Jackson, Andre, and Bill Smith. 1988. "White racism here is blunt and bitter." St. Louis Post-Dispatch 110 (December 12):1.

Kasarda, John. 1985. "Urban change and minority opportunities." In The New Urban Reality, ed. Paul E. Peterson, 33–67. Washington, D.C.: Brookings Institution.

Lewis, Oscar. 1959. Five Families: Mexican Case Studies in the Culture of Poverty. New York: Basic Books.

Marable, Manning. 1983. How Capitalism Underdeveloped Black America. Boston: South End Press.

Marks, Carole. 1989. Farewell, We're Good and Gone: The Great Black Migration. Bloomington, Ind.: University of Indiana Press.

Massey, Douglas S., and Nancy A. Denton. 1989. "Hypersegregation in U.S. metropolitan areas: black and Hispanic segregation along five dimensions." Demography 26:373–91.

Mead, Lawrence. 1986. Beyond Entitlement: The Social Obligations of Citizenship. New York: Free Press.

Miles, Robert. 1982. Racism and Migrant Labor. London: Routledge and Kegan Paul.

Miller, S.M. 1987. "Race in the health of America." Milbank Quarterly 65:500–31.

Missouri Department of Health. 1959. Missouri Hospital Directory. Jefferson City, Mo.: Division of Health.

———. 1970. Missouri Hospital Directory. Jefferson City, Mo.: Division of Health.

———. 1980. Directory of Hospitals and Related Health Services. Jefferson City, Mo.: Bureau of Licensing and Certification.

———. 1980. Missouri Nursing Home and Residential Care Facility Profiles (Various years). Jefferson City, Mo.: Missouri State Center for Health Statistics.

———. 1988. County of Residence by Institution by Race: 1961, 1970, 1980, 1987. Unpublished death certificate tables. Jefferson City, Mo.: State Center for Health Statistics.

———. 1989. Missouri Nursing Home and Residential Care Facility Survey, 1988. Machine readable data file. Jefferson City, Mo.: State Center for Health Statistics.

Monti, Daniel. 1985. A Semblance of Justice. Columbia, Mo.: University of Missouri Press.

Morrison, Barbara Jones. 1983. "Sociocultural dimensions: nursing homes and the minority aged." In Gerontological Social Work Practice in Long-Term Care, ed. George S. Setzel and M. Joanna Mellor, 127–45. Binghamton, N.Y.: Haworth Press.

Moynihan, Daniel P. 1965. The Negro Family: The Case for National Action. Washington, D.C.: U.S. Department of Labor.

Murray, Charles. 1984. Losing Ground. New York: Basic Books.

National Cancer Institute. 1984. SEER Program: Cancer Incidence and Mortality in the United States, 1973–1981. Bethesda, Md.: National Institutes of Health.

Okada, Louis M., and Thomas T.H. Wan. 1980. "Impact of community health centers and Medicaid on the use of health services." Public Health Reports 95:520–34.

Shryock, Henry S., Jacob S. Siegel, and Associates. 1971. The Methods and Materials of Demography. Washington, D.C.: Bureau of the Census.

Smith, L. Douglas, Robert J. Calsyn, Anna J. Biggs, Joan Hashimi, and Judy Musick. 1988. An Assessment of the Needs of Elderly Residents of the City of St. Louis. St. Louis, Mo.: University of Missouri-St. Louis.

Sowell, Thomas. 1981. Ethnic America. New York: Basic Books.

Spector, Rachel E. 1985. Cultural Diversity in Health and Illness. Norwalk, Conn.: Appleton-Century-Crofts.

Steyer, Robert. 1989. "Profits and charity in the balance." St. Louis Post-Dispatch. November 6, 1989:1.

Taylor, Robert J. 1988. "Aging and supportive relationships among black Americans." In The Black American Elderly, ed. James S. Jackson, 259–81. New York: Springer.

U.S. Bureau of the Census. 1963. 1960 Census of Population. Characteristics of the Population, Missouri. Vol. 1, Part 27. Washington, D.C.: U.S. Government Printing Office.

———. 1973. 1970 Census of Population. Characteristics of the Population, Missouri. Vol. 1, Part 27. Washington, D.C.: U.S. Government Printing Office.

————. 1982. 1980 Census of Population. General Population Characteristics. PC80-1-B27. Washington, D.C.: U.S. Government Printing Office.

U.S. Congress, Office of Technology Assessment. 1988. The Quality of Medical Care. Washington, D.C.: U.S. Government Printing Office.

U.S. Health Care Financing Administration. 1988a. Medicare Hospital Mortality Information, 1987. Washington, D.C.: U.S. Government Printing Office.

————. 1988b. Medicare/Medicaid Nursing Home Information, 1987–88. Missouri. Washington, D.C.: U.S. Government Printing Office.

U.S. National Center for Health Statistics. 1990. Discharges from Short-Stay Non-Federal Hospitals. Unpublished data from the National Hospital Discharge Survey, 1988. Hyattsville, Md.: National Center for Health Statistics.

Wallace, Steven P. 1990a. "The political economy of health for older blacks." International Journal of Health Services 20:665–80.

————. 1990b. "The no-care zone: availability, accessibility, and acceptability in community-based long-term care." The Gerontologist 30:254–61.

Wallace, Steven P., and Carroll L. Estes. 1989. "Health policy for the elderly: federal policy and institutional change." In Policy Issues for the 1990s. Policy Studies Review Annual, no. 9, ed. Ray Rist, 591–613. New Brunswick, N.J.: Transaction Publishers.

Waldo, Daniel, and Helen C. Lazenby. 1984. "Demographic characteristics and health care use and expenditures by the aged in the United States: 1977–1984." Health Care Financing Review 6:1.

Wellman, David. 1977. Portraits of White Racism. New York: Cambridge University Press.

Willie, Charles. Caste and Class Controversy on Race and Poverty. Second Edition. Dix Hills, N.Y.: General Hall.

Wilson, William Julius. The Truly Disadvantaged. Chicago, Ill.: University of Chicago Press.

Wolpe, Harold. 1986. "Class concepts, class struggle and racism." In Theories of Race and Ethnic Relations, ed. John Rex and David Mason, 110–30. New York: Cambridge University Press.

CHAPTER 14

Lessons in Control

PRENATAL EDUCATION IN THE HOSPITAL

Elizabeth M. Armstrong

Over the course of the last century, childbirth has become a hospitalized event in the U.S. Although initially women and doctors sought to hospitalize birth for somewhat different reasons, they also shared such aims as making birth safer and more "modern." However, as labor and delivery became increasingly medicalized, the goals and needs of women and hospitals for childbirth began to diverge. The ways in which the techniques and procedures of hospital birth evolved to meet the needs of staff and physicians, rather than laboring women, have been well documented in social histories of childbearing (Arney 1982; Leavitt 1985, 1986; Mitford 1993; Oakley 1984; Wertz and Wertz 1989). These include the division of labor into discrete phases which must take place in different rooms or areas of the hospital, the adoption of the lithotomy position for delivery, the application of restraints to laboring women, and more recently, the use of electronic fetal monitors (Arney 1982; Wertz and Wertz 1989). Even as hospitals today move ever more self-consciously towards adopting a market-oriented service model, referring to patients as "clients" or even "customers," the gap between what institutional efficiency mandates and what human dignity requires nevertheless yawns ever wider. Most recently, that gap captured widespread attention and generated political action in the form of federal legislation designed to end "drive-through" deliveries by mandating a minimum maternity stay.[1] However, the gap between institutional and personal goals for the birth process takes a variety of forms.

Offering prenatal education is one way that hospitals seek to bridge the gap between their institutional demands for birth and women's personal expectations. In addition, in an economic environment in which hospitals compete fiercely with each other through lavish advertising, luxurious birthing suites, and up-to-date neonatal intensive care units for the lucrative baby business, which they also see as building a loyal customer base,[2] hospitals routinely offer a variety of prenatal and birthing classes as additional services to draw expectant parents (League and Novelli 1994; Lindsay and Phillips 1992). Sometimes these classes are offered free; sometimes there is a nominal charge. Sometimes these classes focus on specific techniques to get through labor and delivery, such as the Lamaze or the Bradley methods; other times, the classes offer a more general introduction to health and nutrition in pregnancy. These two trends have led to an increasing proliferation of prenatal instruction; about half of women report attending some kind of class prior to delivery (Cogan 1980). However, such classes may, in fact, serve the institution better than the individuals by providing a forum to educate women about how labor and delivery will proceed in the hospital setting and foster their compliance with these routines.

The tendency of hospitals to operate according to their own interests, rather than their patients', has been well documented (Annas 1974), as have the social control functions of medicine (Conrad 1979; Freidson 1970; Parsons 1951; Zola 1972). However, Erving Goffman, in *Asylums* (1961), provides the best sociological description of the process by which organizational needs are defined as therapeutic needs. In his articulation of the "medical service model," along which mental hospitals are organized, Goffman describes the ways in which the institution comes to define what is in the patient's best interests; consequently, the patient's ability to do so is at best compromised, at worst lost. Moreover, he notes the institution's power to define the terms of treatment and to cloak its self-interest as being necessary or even good for the patient.

I argue in this paper that childbirth services as offered by hospitals in the late twentieth century fit Goffman's description of the medical service model. Like psychiatric services in the mental hospital, prenatal and childbirth services in hospitals are primarily organized and designed to meet institutional needs. Nonetheless, they are proffered as being in the patients' best interests. With pointed irony, Goffman (1961) described this conflation of organizational mandate with therapeutic benefit or necessity as "a wonderful prearranged harmony" in which "what is good for the profession is good for the patient" (p. 371).

Background

To understand the role of prenatal education today, it is necessary to understand four interrelated historical processes, which I review briefly here. These are, first, the medicalization—and specifically hospitalization—of childbirth that has occurred over the last two centuries; second, the emergence of various alternative models of childbirth that originally evolved to counter the pressures of medicalization; third, persistent rates of adverse birth outcomes that appear resistant to medical amelioration; and fourth, the consequent belief in personal behavior change through prenatal education as a "magic bullet" to improve birth outcomes.

Delivery in the hospital is a relatively new phenomenon in the span of human history, but it has led to profound changes in the experience of birth. From the earliest instances of hospitalized birth, the needs of the institution and the best interests of the woman diverged. In 17th century Paris, for example, women at the Hôtel Dieu delivered in a special room called "the stove" and then walked themselves to the recovery wards (Eccles 1982). In the U.S., change in the process of childbirth unfolded rapidly. By the last quarter of the 19th century, the newly formed, predominantly male, profession of obstetrics had replaced female midwives as birth attendants, and by the 1920s, the push to deliver in the hospital had accelerated. In 1900, less than five percent of all women gave birth in the hospital; two decades later, half of all births in major cities were in the hospital. And by 1939, half of all women and 75 percent of urban women delivered in the hospital (Wertz and Wertz 1989). Thus, within a generation, the venue for birth shifted from the woman's own home under the care of a female midwife and the woman's own kin, to the maternity ward under the supervision of a male physician. In turn, the centralized process of hospitalized birth necessitated—in the eyes of obstetricians—such dehumanizing interventions as routine enemas, shaving, douching, disinfection, and restraint during labor. Hospital birth also made possible the nearly universal use of anesthesia during labor. Moreover, the routinization of prenatal care encouraged obstetricians to adopt a view of childbirth as a pathological process (Arney 1982; Wertz and Wertz 1989). "By the 1920s, doctors believed that 'normal' deliveries, those without convulsions, deformed pelves, protracted and difficult labor, the threat of sepsis or of tears in the woman's perineum, were so rare as to be nonexistent" (Wertz and Wertz, p. 141). However, many observers from both within and without the medical establishment have cast doubt on the wisdom or effectiveness of treating all normal pregnancies as high risk, arguing that "birth is not an illness" (WHO 1985, 1997).

In addition, many feminist scholars have argued that as birth was increasingly controlled and dictated by male obstetricians, women lost the ability to articulate choices in labor, or even to participate actively, in birth (Arney 1982; Davis-Floyd 1992a; Martin 1987; Oakley 1984; Rothman 1991). Many routine obstetrical interventions appear to be iatrogenic, even potentially disastrous for the laboring woman and the child to be born. The use of epidural anesthesia, for example, has been linked to increased cesarean sections and depressed neurological response in neonates (Humenick 1995; Morton, et al. 1994; Murray, et al. 1981; Newton, et al. 1995; Richard and Alade 1990; Sepkoski, et al. 1992; Thorpe, et al. 1993; WHO 1997).

Partly in response to this "over-medicalization" of birth, various alternative models of the birth experience emerged over the latter half of the twentieth century, flourishing in the U.S., in particular in the 1960s and 70s. These include Grantly Dick-Read's "childbirth without fear," Fernand Lamaze's "childbirth without pain," Robert Bradley's "husband-coached" childbirth, Frederick Leboyer's birth method, which involves soft lights and a warm bath for the newborn, Michel Odent's underwater birth, and even home birth and midwife-attended birth.[3] These models of birth are typically grouped under the umbrella terms "natural childbirth," highlighting their distinction from medical (and presumably "unnatural") birth. These alternative childbirth movements often involved an educational component; pregnant women and their "birth partners" might attend, for example, "Lamaze classes" to learn the breathing technique integral to this mode of childbirth. Thus, as these alternative birth models proliferated, particularly Lamaze, education or classroom instruction became an important element of the prenatal experience in the U.S.[4] In addition, even as these models sought to empower women, responsibility for birth outcome began to shift towards the individual woman.

Indeed, pregnancy itself has become increasingly medicalized over the course of the late century. Delivery in the hospital was rare at the advent of the 20th century; rarer still was any prenatal contact between a pregnant woman and a doctor. The concept of medical supervision of *pregnancy* (as opposed to birth) was simply unheard of.

However, the crusade to reduce infant mortality in the early decades of the last century included pioneering efforts to increase women's access to medical care, not only at pregnancy's end, but throughout gestation as well. The U.S. Children's Bureau, founded in 1912, conducted an ongoing public education effort from 1913 through 1935 to inform women about prenatal hygiene and birth, stressing the importance of routine medical supervision throughout pregnancy (Barker 1998). One of the first actions of the new federal agency was the publication and dissemination of a handbook called *Prenatal Care* to millions of American women. The booklet signaled a significant shift in medical and popular thinking since one of its major messages was the importance of medical supervision throughout pregnancy as a way to reduce adverse outcomes, primarily infant mortality. Moreover, the Sheppard-Towner Act of 1921 provided federal funds for states to establish "hygiene stations" dedicated to women's and infants' health. These efforts were the beginning of a massive sea change in American medical and lay attitudes towards pregnancy. By the 1980s, prenatal care had become an article of faith in American society and the cornerstone of efforts to improve maternal and infant health: witness Congressional expansions of Medicaid eligibility to pregnant women during this period. Indeed, at the close of the 20th century, prenatal care was nearly universal in the U.S.[5]

Yet, despite widespread medical prenatal care and increasing levels of technological intervention in pregnancy and birth, in recent decades, the U.S. has been troubled by persistently high rates of low birth weight and infant mortality, particularly among the African-American population. Recently, downward trends in both infant mortality and maternal mortality have stagnated and progress in narrowing the black-white gap in infant mortality has stalled, arousing acute concern (CDC 1998, 1999; NCHS 1999). As the limits of medical intervention to reduce infant mortality became apparent, attention shifted to the individual behaviors of pregnant women. By the mid-1980s, a consensus had emerged that not only medical prenatal care, but prenatal education, was necessary to improve birth outcomes. The Institute of Medicine recommended in 1985, "health education should be an important component of low birthweight prevention" (IOM 1985, p. 7) and that:

> Health education for women who are pregnant or contemplating pregnancy should be expanded to include greater emphasis on behavioral risks in pregnancy; early signs and symptoms of pregnancy complications such as pre-term labor; and the role that prenatal care plays in improving the outcome of pregnancy. *Childbirth education classes could play an expanded role in the prevention of low birth weight births.* To do so, these classes should begin earlier, place greater emphasis on the prenatal period and the risk factors described above, and make a greater effort to enroll women from lower socioeconomic groups (IOM 1985, p. 13, emphasis added).

Four years later, the United States Public Health Service Expert Panel on the Content of Prenatal Care echoed this recommendation, urging that education become a more integral part of prenatal care (PHS 1989). According to *Healthy People 2000*, the federal government's goals for the health of the nation, "Improving the health of mothers and infants is a national priority. . . . Further, reductions in infant mortality and morbidity will require a focus on strategies to modify the behaviors and lifestyles that affect birth outcomes" (NCHS 1999, p. 137). This focus on prenatal education was itself precipitated by another significant shift in public health thinking. For the last several decades, medically supervised prenatal care has occupied center stage in efforts to improve birth outcomes; increasingly, prenatal education to alter individual women's behavior is seen as an integral means of reducing risk in pregnancy and consequently improving outcomes. Prenatal education has, thus, been proposed as a solution to one of the most troubling social facts of contemporary America: despite the billions of dollars lavished on health care, despite ever-higher concentrations of medical technology, babies continue to die in this country at a much higher rate than elsewhere in the industrialized world.

Thus, the "childbirth education" spawned by alternative birth movements collided with the mandate to reduce infant mortality and low birth weight through personal behavior interventions, giving rise to "prenatal education." By the early 1990s, an educational movement that had its roots in empowering women and transforming the experience of hospitalized birth, became an educational movement geared toward modifying behavior at the individual level. Like other forms of health education, prenatal care classes have been touted as a way of "empowering the consumer," particularly those who are disadvantaged in other ways. However, there remains an inherent conflict between the medical model that prevails in hospital birth and the pregnant woman's status as an autonomous being. Prenatal classes offer another means of "encoding the patient" to act according to dictates of the medical model. As Rothman (1991) points out, "the goal of a 'natural' childbirth has been replaced by the goal of a 'prepared' childbirth" (p. 31). These classes offer institutions a vene in which to persuade women to adopt the values, expectations and orientations of the hospital, and of what Davis-Floyd (1992a) calls "technocratic birth." Moreover, prenatal education seeks to devolve responsibility for achieving major *public* health goals onto the shoulders of *private* individuals.

Pregnancy Scholarship and Social Problems Work in the Hospital

Before I turn to a discussion of my findings, I pause here to discuss briefly the significance of "education" in the contemporary experience of pregnancy and the role of such education—formal and informal—in framing the "social problem" of adverse birth outcomes. The key elements of this frame are notions of control and individual responsibility for outcome. Women have always been held specially accountable for birth outcomes, though the shape and expression of that accountability has ranged from Aristotle's contentions that "foolish, drunken and harebrained women most often bring forth children like unto themselves, morose and languid," to the 19th century doctrine of maternal impressions (cf., Gardner 1994a). Today, pregnant women are subject to social, moral, and even legal sanction for their behavior during pregnancy. The public health shift from an emphasis on societal responsibility for ensuring healthy babies to individual responsibility (and especially culpability for unwanted outcomes) has been accompanied by a vastly expanded attention to the fetus and the rise of a paradigm of maternal-fetal conflict, in which the welfare and "interests" of the pregnant woman and the fetus she carries are imagined to be oppositional rather than mutual, making women's behavior during pregnancy the target of intense personal and political scrutiny. A "rhetoric of fetal endangerment" (Gardner 1994b) permeates cultural representations and the experience of pregnancy today.

It was precisely as women's actions as individuals (rather than as group members located within a social hierarchy) grew in prominence, both as an explanation for inequalities in birth outcomes and as the policy lever imagined to hold the key to achieving public health goals, that prenatal education rose to sudden prominence. That is, as women's behaviors were seen to be crucial determinants of outcomes, it became extremely important to educate them about how to behave in pregnancy. In fact, the rise of prenatal education in recent decades illustrates the increasing demands placed on pregnant women to be actively pregnant; to engage in what Gardner (1994b) calls "pregnancy scholarship." She notes that women today "train" themselves to be pregnant, in large part by seeking and applying the knowledge of experts (Gardner 1995, p. 31). Pregnancy, today, is a mental, as well as a physical endeavor, requiring that women master a specific body of knowledge and set of concepts, ranging from appropriate behavior in the prenatal period, to dietary prescriptions and proscriptions; from stages of fetal development, to stages of labor. "Implicitly, women are promised—in exchange for judicious bodily attention and management—that they can participate in the prevention of the 'social problem' of damaged fetuses who will eventually be born to become unsatisfactory members of society" (Gardner 1995, pp. 32–33). Along with the explosion of printed material on pregnancy that Gardner (1994b, 1995) analyzes, prenatal education has become an expected—even "required"—aspect of the contemporary pregnancy experience.

In fact, pregnant women today are expected not only to consult experts, but also in a sense, to become experts themselves. Indeed, much of this prenatal education is expected to take place at the individual level, in the quasi-institutionalized form of self-tutoring through "recommended" reading. (The popular book, *What to Expect When You're Expecting*, for example, promotes itself as a "pregnancy bible.") Prenatal education is an instance of what Holstein and Miller (1997) call everyday "social problems work"—the quotidian process of "accomplishing reality" that we all engage in. Social problems work describes the process by which social actors—often people who are ostensibly concerned with detecting and rectifying a particular social problem—make such problems real through such interpretive activities as communication, categorization, organization, and persuasion. The participants in the "Baby & Me" class described below—and most especially the instructor acting on behalf of the institution—were united in the ostensible goal of improving birth outcomes for high-risk women. In the classes, the participants learned how to have "a positive pregnancy," in the words of the health educator who led the class. The class, thus, served as a venue for the social problems work of preventing unwanted birth outcomes by providing a forum in which responsibility could be made explicit. Women were taught how to be pregnant. However, although the course advertised itself primarily as prenatal instruction, it, in fact, focused on teaching women how to be accountable for the hospital birth process itself. In practice, the course seemed to emphasize "Getting Ready for Delivery" over all other topics.[6]

Data and Methods

This paper reports on participant observation of prenatal education classes at a large urban tertiary-care hospital associated with a major research university. I will call the hospital Prestige Hospital. About 3,000 women of all social classes deliver annually at Prestige Hospital. In 1991, Prestige joined "Healthy Start," a nationwide demonstration project aimed at improving birth outcomes among low-income women. "Healthy Start" was initiated by President George Bush in response to widespread concern (and considerable national chagrin) about persistently high rates of pre-term birth, low birth-weight, and infant mortality in the U.S., particularly as compared with other developed countries.[7] Prestige Hospital's "Healthy Start" initiative included expanding clinic hours in the evening one night a week, making certain physical improvements to the clinic site, distributing tokens and vouchers for transportation to and from the clinic, and initiating a prenatal health education program for expectant women, called "Baby & Me." According to a grant report prepared by the hospital in 1996, the class series officially included the following topics: "Fetal Growth and Development," "Staying Healthy for Two," "Eating for Two," "Drug and Alcohol Education," "Getting Ready for Delivery," "Closer to Motherhood," and "Now I'm a Mom, Yikes!"

The women who were enrolled in Prestige Hospital's Healthy Start program were regarded as "high risk" for adverse outcomes. During the period of observation I report on here, 74 percent of the Healthy Start participants at Prestige had family incomes below the federal poverty level; 86 percent were African-American and 24 percent were less than 20 years old. Many of the women showed evidence of substance use and STD infection, risk factors for adverse outcomes. During this period, among women who participated in Healthy Start, 19 percent experienced pre-term delivery (<37 weeks gestation) and 25 percent had a baby with low birthweight (<2500 grams) (1996 hospital grant report).

The "Baby & Me" classes met for an hour and half one evening a week for eight weeks and promised to include discussion of "fetal growth and development; nutrition during pregnancy; breathing exercises; childbirth, plus more" (clinic notice advertising "Baby & Me"). The women in the class cycle that I report on here were all in their 20s, poor or working-class, and all were having their first child; many were unmarried. Most relied on some form of public health insurance. Women joined the class, which was offered for free, at a range of points in their pregnancies, so that some women were not due for 13 weeks, while others were due four weeks from the start of the class. The hospital encouraged women to bring partners to the class; however, not all of them did so. The hospital provided "healthful snacks . . . generally made with WIC-allowed foods" at each class (1996 Prestige Hospital grant report). In addition, the instructor distributed "incentive gifts"—baby clothes donated by a local department store—at the end of each class.

Although about a dozen women were enrolled in the "Baby & Me" classes, attendance at any given class ranged from six to ten pregnant women; about half of them were accompanied by a partner—sometimes the father of the baby, sometimes the woman's mother, and in one case, the mother of the father of the baby. There were both native-born and immigrant women in the class and the women and their partners represented several racial/ethnic groups, including white, African-American, Russian, and sub-continent Indian. Attendance fluctuated each week and there was some modest attrition over the course of the eight weeks. Two women, for example, gave birth before the completion of the course.

The analysis proceeds along a grounded theory approach, in which participant observation of the class led to development of an interview guide (Strauss and Corbin 1990). I attended all sessions of the class, which was led by the "Health Educator," a white woman in her forties I will call Cathy.[8] I had informal discussion with Cathy after each class. I also frequently observed the waiting room of the prenatal clinic, where I had informal conversations with both pregnant women and hospital staff. At the conclusion of the course, I interviewed eight women (all of the regular participants except for the two who had delivered before the conclusion of the class cycle) about their experience in the class and their expectations for labor and delivery, as well as their experience of pregnancy more generally. I conducted these semi-structured interviews in the women's homes; the interviews covered such topics as the woman's choice of Prestige Hospital, her impressions of the "Baby & Me" classes and her reports of what she learned there, her feelings about pregnancy, particularly her worries and fears, and her behaviors and actions during pregnancy. The observations I report here are drawn from field notes and interview transcripts.

Observations—Strategies of Socializing the Patient

The "Baby & Me" classes took place at the hospital inside a room labeled, "Patient Education Room." A picture of an African-American baby cut out from a magazine and a sign reading, "Learning Begins Here," were taped to the door of the patient education room. Cathy, a health educator, led each class. In one class, a hospital nutritionist came to speak to the women and in another class, two labor nurses visited briefly. Like Cathy herself, each of these women spoke with the "voice of the institution" (Goffman 1961, p. 380) and reflected its priorities in their interactions with the pregnant women. Cathy often used props, such as a model for the female pelvis, or videos to illustrate the lessons. At most of the classes, women were given printed materials; sometimes these were photocopies of hospital-written instructions or information, sometimes photocopies of information from books, often pamphlets or materials prepared outside the hospital, such as a brochure on "heart-healthy cooking" from PAM cooking spray. The lessons for the "Baby & Me" classes consisted of instruction and exhortation. Women were told what to do, how to do it, and when. I will focus, first, on the four principle ways in which the course sought to prepare women for birth according to the dictates of the hospital.

Labor as Industrial Production

First, the course sought to persuade women that labor was a routine and even quantifiable process. Cathy presented labor along a model of industrial production. All discussions of labor in the class emphasized not the sensate experience of it, but rather the measurement and abstraction of that experience. For example, Cathy labored to teach women to count their contractions and to estimate the stage of labor they were in. As Cathy and the labor nurses presented it, this ability was necessary, in part, to determine when it was time to come into the hospital, information that is important for pregnant women to know so that they will avoid cluttering the labor ward with false alarms. Cathy emphasized in every class how women would know when to come to the hospital. That knowledge was presented as a precise mathematical formula: the frequency of contractions, measured in the *number* of minutes between each one; the duration of contractions, measured in the *number* of seconds each one lasts; and the extent of cervical dilation, measured in the *number* of centimeters. Note that the third component of this formula is invisible to women, yet Cathy repeatedly told the women, "Come to the hospital when your contractions are 3–5 minutes apart and last about a minute each." She always added, "They'll send you home again if you're not dilated enough." Of course, it is impossible for women to gauge the extent of dilation. One message implicit in this formulaic treatment of labor is that all pregnancies are alike; none is special. All pregnancies follow the same rules of progress. Contrast this with Sharon's assertion that "Different women have different labors, so I just have to see for myself." The formulaic, mechanistic, and highly routinized model of labor presented in the class denies the kind of human individuality that Sharon believes inherent in the birth process.

The second and more troubling message is that, while women may dutifully count the spacing and duration of contractions, it is only the hospital that can truly assess whether the woman is preparing to deliver. As Rothman (1991) points out, in the medical model, "the state of being in labor, like illness or any deviance, is an ascribed status: that is, it is a position to which a person is assigned by those in authority" (p. 166). This focus on bodily measurement—and in particular, cervical dilation—can eclipse, and even transform, a woman's sensate perceptions of her pregnancy and labor, as illustrated in an episode from the class. After his wife delivered, Ricky returned to the class to describe her birth experience.

> I walked into the room and she shouted, "I'm having a baby, hon!" But then the doctor came in and measured her and told her she wasn't 10 centimeters dilated yet, and she yelled at me, like I did it! Like I came into the room and made her shrink!

In other words, the medical assessment of her labor precipitated a sudden, dramatic, and detrimental shift in Theresa's self-perception, as she veered from an image of herself in labor, "having a baby," to an image of herself as stalled, as not in labor.

Moreover, the prominence accorded to review of this formula in every class illustrates an incipient conflict between what women want and what the institution requires. "When to come to the hospital" is, in face, a source of tension, or at the very least, difference, between the institution and the women in labor, particularly those giving birth for the first time. Women seek reassurance by coming to the hospital early, perhaps as soon as *they* judge contractions to have begun in earnest. Hospital staff, on the other hand, are reluctant to admit women "too early" since they may crowd the maternity ward and exert additional demands on hospital staff and resources. Thus, the importance of impressing upon women the appropriate time to come to the hospital from the perspective of the institution. As I will describe in greater detail later in the paper, women in the class always responded with confusion, uncertainty, and trepidation, to Cathy's query about when it was time to come to the hospital, reflecting the gap between their anticipation of their birth experience and the hospital's institutional parameters for that experience.

Loss of Privacy

Second, in the classroom, women began to experience the degradation and denial of privacy that delivery in the hospital—particularly delivery in a teaching hospital—requires. Cathy began each class by asking women how they were feeling and what problems they had experienced over the last week. She routinely expected them to discuss intimate details of their bodies and physical functioning. These questions were asked, not in the relative privacy of a consulting room, but in the public atmosphere of the class attended by both men and women. At first, women seemed quite hesitant to discuss their gas, their indigestion, and their vomiting in front of strangers. In the first several classes, Cathy's questions were met with guarded silence as women shifted in their chairs and looked down at the floor. However, later, as they become more comfortable and more frank, "the teacher censured Theresa who, when prompted by the teacher, described her vaginal mucus thus: "excuse my language, but it was like cum." Cathy responded sharply, "I prefer to say it's like egg white, like the albumen when you crack an egg," and the next week told Theresa, "After what you said last week nothing you say could surprise me." Frankness about the physical aspects of pregnancy is extorted from women, but only up to a point: again, it is the teacher, and not the women themselves, who set the parameters of this discussion.

Another latent function of this aspect of the class may have been to "rehearse" women for delivery in a teaching hospital: women in the Healthy Start program had no reasonable expectation that the obstetrician who delivered them would be one whom they had seen during prenatal care. Thus, it is important for them to learn to describe physical symptoms and feelings to a "stranger." Moreover, in the absence of a sustained or consistent relationship with a single medical care provider who would be present at their deliveries, it becomes all the more imperative for women, themselves, to master knowledge of their symptoms and to be able to describe them in terms intelligible to the hospital staff.

Laying Down the Rules

Third, the discussions of labor and delivery in the class sought to establish the "rules" of birth at Prestige Hospital. Power is a pervasive dynamic in the doctor-patient relationship, particularly in obstetric encounters (Arney 1982; Fisher 1986; Rothman 1991; West 1993). In this setting, the instructor assumes the authority of the doctor; therefore, she "possess[es] the voice of the institution" and presents definitions "of the hospital's action upon the patient" (Goffman 1961, p. 380). It is she who outlines the medical service model to the future patients, explaining the rules that will govern their birth experiences. Hospital policies were presented in the "Baby & Me" class as unalterable. Many of the women voiced considerable concern that they would be allowed to stay in the hospital no longer than 24 hours, fearing that complications might arise after their discharge. Cathy emphasized again and again that Prestige would allow women to stay as long as their insurance permitted. "They won't send you home with a fever. But if you go home and develop a fever, you can always come back," she said. When Tracy asked if she could stay an extra night if she paid for it out of pocket, Cathy told her, "Oh, you couldn't do that. It's like $600 or $800 a night here." Choices—or rather their absence—during labor and delivery also troubled many of the women in the class. When Kimberly asked, "Do you get any say in whether you have an episiotomy?" Cathy answered, "Well, it's something they need to do. Like if you have surgery, you have to have an incision. . . . .It's pretty standard." Yet vaginal delivery is not surgery and many women are able to give birth without an episiotomy. In fact, there is considerable debate about the wisdom or efficacy of routine episiotomy (Belizan and Carroli 1998; Ecker, et al. 1997; Helewa 1997). However, options other than the hospital's "standards" were not discussed, nor are they, in fact, even options. Moreover, as I describe in the next section, not only does the hospital seek to erase choice, it also seeks to silence protest.

Staying Calm

Fourth, the class presented what might be called the etiquette or protocol of hospital delivery. Cathy reminded the women over and over to call the special hospital shuttle number, not an ambulance, when they were ready to come in. (An ambulance would take them to the nearest hospital, not necessarily Prestige, thus losing the birth for Prestige and subjecting women to an unfamiliar environment.) Cathy reminded the women "to bring what you need," i.e., toothbrush, toothpaste, hairbrush, even pillows. "Anything you need, you need to bring with you. Like a little vacation kit," she instructed. She led the class on a tour of the labor and delivery floor, where a labor nurse explained the check-in procedures. Most importantly, she impressed upon the women again and again the necessity of "staying calm." Both Cathy and the labor nurses they encountered on the tour reminded women often to avoid "adversarial situations" and that "staying calm makes things go smoother." As Cathy put it, "Whatever your expectations are, it's really important to remind yourself to stay calm. In a lot of situations, staying calm helps a lot."

Likewise, addressing the partners in the class, Cathy said one night, "Men, you've got to know your limits. Sit down if you think it's getting to be too much for you. Keep a peppermint or a candy in your pocket so you can just pop it in your mouth if you start to feel woozy. Remember, you don't want to get in the way, or create another problem." A checklist of "things to help keep your labor and delivery in order" that Cathy passed out in class concluded with the reminder, "*Stay calm*. Remember to breathe and relax" (emphasis in original). This point was stressed so often that some women told me in interviews that the most important thing they learned in the class was "If something goes wrong, not to panic, really," as Janelle put it. Of course, calm patients are significantly more compliant and require less staff time and attention than distraught ones. Thus, women are taught to subordinate their own distress, fear, or even anger—no matter what their expectations are, or how far their experience strays from those expectations—in obeisance to the institutional mandate to maintain order and control in the labor and delivery suite at all times. Exhorting women to stay calm thus becomes a powerful tool not for enhancing women's own experience of labor and delivery, but rather for preserving order in the institution. By impressing upon women the need to repress their own distress and to stay calm, the institution gains the ability not only to violate women's wishes, but also to do so without penalty of protest. Not only does the message to stay calm seek to silence protest before women can voice it, this stress on staying calm and avoiding panic may arouse unnecessary fear and anxiety on the part of the women. The implicit message beneath the constant exhortations to maintain calm seems to be that there may very well be good reason to panic.[9] Thus, the constant injunctions to stay clam may provoke fear as much as quell it.

Omissions and Silences

In fact, what was left undiscussed in the "Baby & Me" classes is as important as the information that was presented. The ways in which this course of prenatal education left women's needs unaddressed are manifold. First, the instructor frequently and explicitly failed to address women's direct questions, as illustrated in the following two vignettes. In the first, a nutritionist who came to speak to the class clearly ignores Meena's questions:

> *Meena*: What about liver? I've heard very bad things about liver during pregnancy.
>   *Nutritionist*: Oh no, organ meat is good for you.
>   *Meena*: Really? I've heard that because it's an organ, pesticides accumulate. . . .
>   *Nutritionist, interrupting her*: No, organ meat is good for you. Do you like liver?
>   *Meena*: I've never tried it, I was just wondering. . . .
>   *Nutritionist*: It's real good for you, lots of iron.

Not only does the nutritionist cut off the woman asking the question, she never answers Meena's concern about the potential accumulation of pesticides in organ meat. Meena's efforts to educate herself about what she believed to be a significant hazard were thwarted by the closed set of information the institution sought to transmit.[10] In the next vignette, Cathy herself initiated a discussion about why in old movies people always call for newspaper when a baby is born. "It's because an unread newspaper is sterile. Something about the thermodynamic printing process," she explained. "And it's also warm. Newspaper is a great insulator." Then, turning to one of the fathers-to-be in the room, she said, "So, John, when you're on the way to the hospital and the baby pops out, you know what to look for—some unread newspaper." However, when John's girlfriend, Sharon, who seemed genuinely intrigued and curious about this information asked, "How much newspaper do you need? Like how many sheets to keep the baby warm?," Cathy replied coolly and dismissively, "You know what? I really don't think you need to worry about that." Thus, women's concerns were occasionally met not only with evasion, but with contempt.

Second, the mechanistic and routinized view of labor the class presented was confusing and alienating to the women. Modern hospital birth rests on the notion of bodies as machines, a mechanistic view of what many women regard as a highly organic and holistic experience (Martin 1987), one that is sacred even (Balin 1988). In the medical model, labor and delivery become wholly quantified experiences and it is up to women to describe and evaluate their stage of labor in terms of numbers, rather than sensations or intuition. Yet women in the class had a difficult time remembering the complex calculus (number of contractions, duration of contractions, centimeters dilation) dictating when it was time to come to the hospital. One night in class Cathy asked, "Janelle, let's say you feel a big contraction. What would you do?" Janelle blurted out, "I have no idea! Panic!" In fact, when Cathy asked, as she did at every class, "How do you know when it's time to come to the hospital?," women often answered with references to the amount of pain they would feel: "You know by the pain," or "When the pain gets too bad." Tracy put it plainly: "I just can't imagine remembering all this stuff when you're in pain." Significantly, Cathy, herself, had never been pregnant or given birth, though she had two adopted children, and she frequently expressed discomfort with experiential descriptions of childbirth. When participants offered vivid descriptions of birth, Cathy was quick to censor them, as in the episode described earlier. In other words, women might be expected to learn the term "episiotomy," but to hear Ricky, whose wife delivered a few days before the class ended, describe it (at Cathy's own prompting): "Oh, that was awful! Cut, cut, cut (making giant scissor motions with his hands). I couldn't watch it. That grossed me out. There was so much blood," was an educational moment that happened outside the instructor's parameters for the class. She also objected to a couple's description of their nephew, delivered by forceps, as "a cone head," acknowledging only that forceps might leave "a mark" on the newborn's head. (In fact, as a result of prolonged time in the birth canal, babies delivered with forceps sometimes exhibit elongated heads that return to normal shape within a few days after birth.) There were limits to the knowledge offered women in the class. The knowledge Cathy presented was abstract and technical, rather than experiential; it consisted of facts, rather than feelings. Ironically, Cathy herself admonished women, "I think it's easier to know what to expect; that a lot of the fear is fear of the unknown." However, women also expressed considerable anxiety about pain in birth and about complications and the potential iatrogenic consequences of some of the obstetrical interventions they feared they would be subject to. Kimberly repeatedly voiced her concern about episiotomy and several women and their partners expressed fear of epidural anesthesia. Lilya seemed to express what many women were feeling when, after watching a video of childbirth, she said, "That looks pretty scary."

Moreover, a significant consequence of this mechanistic view of labor was the way pain and suffering in childbirth were neglected as topics worthy of attention. Discussion in the class tended to focus on defining the techniques and terms associated with birth: episiotomy, epidural, forceps, rather than on describing what those experiences would be like. (In fact, it was precisely this terminology that women most often reported as what they got out of the class.) This abstraction elided pain, as though labor were merely a mechanical process and not something that took place in flesh-and-blood bodies. Yet, in my interviews with them, women frequently expressed great trepidation about the pain they anticipated experiencing.

>*Interviewer*: Is there anything that scares you?
>
>*Sharon*: The pain of having the baby is the only thing that scares me. Only thing that scares me.
>
>*Lilya*: I don't know what to be concerned about. I'm concerned about everything! I don't like all this idea of surgery that may happen. I never had anybody cut me.
>
>*Kimberly*: I hate that whole idea about the episiotomy. I really, really don't like that. I really get the impression that at Prestige, they do them unnecessarily, and, I mean, I'm not a doctor or anything, but I just really get this feeling they do them to make their job easier more than to make it easier for you. I mean, I'd kinda like to go as long as I can without having to have one because I know they're painful. My sister had one and I KNOW THEY HURT. And I really don't want one unless it's absolutely necessary, and I have a feeling, like if I'm in labor too long—"that patient's been here twelve hours, let's get this baby out"—and I don't want one. The more and more I read—I bought all these pregnancy books—it seems like the kind of thing that should be an option, unless it's medically necessary, the baby's absolutely, positively, not going to fit. But I think, with enough time and coaching and that sort of thing—women have been doing this forever, I mean, I think it's possible. But I think they'll do it if it's taking too long and I just won't have a say about it. And I know it's going to hurt! And I can see myself going to work and sitting at my desk for eight hours with episiotomy stitches. I hope . . . I don't want one. But I'll probably have one. I really think it's standard at Prestige. I really don't want one.

Kimberly's comments illustrate not only that she perceives episiotomy will be a painful experience, but that she believes the procedure is performed not for her benefit, but for the benefit of the hospital staff. Moreover, as she revealed to me in our interview, she was in the probationary period of a new job, without any accrued sick leave or vacation time, and hoping to deliver on a weekend and return to work the next Monday. In other words, the pain of the episiotomy that she so feared represented to her, not only discomfort, but a threat to her livelihood as well. Although she frequently tried to introduce these concerns in class, they were never directly addressed. Cathy only reiterated that episiotomy was "necessary."

Finally, constructing patients as "consumers" and making information the foundation of preparation for childbirth places a potentially heavy burden on pregnant women. The educated consumer is a pillar of the free marketplace, which requires "perfect information" on the part of participants to function smoothly—hence, the perceived need to "educate" patients. If women present at the hospital for birth "uneducated" about the regimen they are to face there, their ignorance will impede the workings of the organization and make the tasks of the hospital staff more difficult. When Theresa repeatedly violated this rule and presented to the hospital multiple times when she thought she was in labor only to be sent home again, the instructor made an example of her, ominously warning the other women, "Do you know what I think? I think she's going to get a C-section. And I would say the same thing if she were here in the room!" as if the operation were a punishment for failing, repeatedly, to understand her labor in the terms the hospital dictated.[11] To be uninformed is to be a bad patient and by extension, a bad mother. However, the women themselves often expressed feelings of being overwhelmed by the information they were expected to master. "You cannot learn everything!" Lilya exclaimed plaintively.

Yet, as Goffman (1961) notes, "when the client fails to follow common-sense precautions or expert advice . . . the server inevitably begins to have a moral role" (p. 330). While it ignored some kinds of knowledge, or rendered experience inaccessible, the "Baby & Me" course often worked to moralize other kinds of knowledge and likewise to stigmatize certain kinds of ignorance. This element of moral instruction in the prenatal course is illustrated in another episode in which Cathy turned a patient into an occasion for moralizing. During the group's tour of the labor and delivery ward, we encountered a woman in a hospital gown, pushing an IV stand ahead of her. Cathy began to question the woman and learned that she had delivered a few days earlier and was on her way to feed her baby. She asked whether the baby was a boy or girl, what its name was, how much it weighed. After a few minutes of chatting, the woman parted from the group and pushed open the heavy doors of the neonatal intensive care unit. As soon as she disappeared behind the NICU's doors, Cathy asked the group in a stage whisper, "Did you hear how much her baby weighed?" She waited for responses; a few people volunteered, "Four pounds." "Only four pounds," Cathy said solemnly. "And now the baby has to be in intensive care. She can't take her baby home." The message was clear: if you have a low birth weight baby, you are an unfit mother. You cannot take your baby home. Good mothers take their babies home after a night or two in the hospital.

In addition, women's fears about birth were frequently trivialized, as we saw in Cathy's dismissal of the newspaper question. For example, when several women queried about the risks of epidurals, Cathy answered, "Well, I don't want to brag about the hospital, but you are delivering at *Prestige Hospital*. The doctors here are really good. The anesthesiologists are really good here. They know what they're doing. You really don't need to worry about that." Women's fears were made to seem inconsequential in light of the institution. On a tour of the labor and delivery floor, Cathy assured women, "It's all very medically sophisticated. There are lots of trained people looking out for you. It's not at all like you're at the river and you squat and you pass your baby ad go back to the cornfield." This ethnocentric view of childbirth presents an image of the hospital as the modern and civilized way to give birth.

The instructor's normative comments about birth illuminate the class and power differential that existed between her and the women who attended, a division that moreover reflected the power of the institution itself as a social organization over the lives of these women. It is the hospital that defines what constitutes a "good" or "normal" birth experience. Expectations and desires regarding the progress of labor and birth may vary by class and cultural subgroup (Davis-Floyd 1992b; Lazarus 1994; Nelson 1986; Sargent and Stark 1989), yet these differences were ignored in this diverse group. For example, every week Cathy asked each woman whom she had chosen as her birth partner to accompany her during labor and delivery. Lilya, a recent émigré from Russia, always answered, "I don't know," an answer Cathy assumed meant she lacked social support. (Outside of class, Cathy frequently expressed to me her fears that Lilya was without a social network.) However, in her interview with me, Lilya revealed that she found the notion of being accompanied in birth by anyone other than medical professionals culturally alien. She explained:

> I didn't expect that many people would be allowed to assist during labor and delivery. Doctors in our country don't allow anybody [in the birth suite]. Fathers, grandmothers, all that, all the relatives, they are outside, and when the mother comes out from the hospital, only then, they will see her and the baby.

Other women also told me in interviews that they "did not want to be seen like that" or thought their male partners "couldn't handle it." regardless, Cathy interpreted their reluctance to adopt a birth partner as a lack of social support or as a sign of an uncooperative partner.

In fact, the issue of "birth partners" provides one of the starkest illustrations of the gap between institutional expectations for the experience of birth and the realities of these women's lives and their own feelings about their birth experiences. Like the question of when to come to the hospital, the matter of who to come with received special emphasis in almost every class. The notion of a specific "birth partner" or "labor coach" is, itself, a product of earlier waves of alternative childbirth education (especially the Lamaze and Bradley methods), as well as a significant shift in the experience of birth. Nonetheless, the idea of choosing a birth partner has become firmly ingrained in American culture, particularly among the middle class. The hospital clearly expected women to be accompanied during birth. Not only did Cathy raise the subject in every class, she viewed the birth partner as essential. She made a point of asking each woman individually whether she had chosen a birth partner yet and who that person was. When women voiced anxiety about remembering the rules surrounding labor, particularly when they were in pain, Cathy reassured them by saying, "You'll be fine. You'll remember it. You'll have your birthing coach there to remember a lot of it for you. Always listen to your birthing coach. He or she is in control."[12] Yet, the participants in the class expressed very different expectations of the role of the birth partner in their interviews with me. Many had not chosen a birth partner for reasons that ranged from cultural background, as in Lilya's case, to personal preference, to socioeconomic reality. When I asked Janelle, for example, who would accompany her to the hospital, she answered flatly.

> It all depends. 'Cause if I go in during the day, I'll have to do everything myself, like call the ambulance, get my bags. But since my boyfriend's mother works across the street [from the hospital], when I get there, I will call her,

or I'll call her before I get there, and she'll just go across the street. Most likely, during the day, she'll be there. But during the night, it'll probably be her or my boyfriend.

Since her boyfriend worked at a hotel during the day, she reported he would "get there eventually." Thus, as Janelle's case illustrates, the very notion that a woman's birth partner is available to accompany her to the hospital at any time reveals a significant class bias.

Some women also expressed a desire not to be seen by their partners in the degraded and out-of-control state they imagined labor to be. Others felt their partners were unequal to the task. When I asked whether her boyfriend would be her birth partner, Tracy told me, "Well, he says he doesn't want to be in there because he can't take all the blood and stuff, and he wouldn't know what to do and stuff, being that he just went to a couple of classes. 'Cause he'll be just as nervous as I am. 'Cause this is his first [child] too."

Kimberly, on the other hand, who had recently moved to this city from another state and whose boyfriend remained behind, expressed considerable trepidation about coming into the hospital alone, without a birth partner, fearing she would be stigmatized as a "single black mother," a label she firmly rejected in her own mind. Sharon, whose boyfriend came with her to most of the classes, nonetheless, told me that she did not expect him to accompany her through labor and delivery. "He can't take it," she said.

Even when women did have birth partners as expected, the experience did not always match the scenario Cathy tried to present. As I noted above, Cathy often reassured women when they expressed trepidation about remembering how to know when to come to the hospital by reminding them that their "birth coach" would "remember a lot of it for you." Ricky, Theresa's husband, came to the class one night to announce that Theresa had given birth earlier in the day. Cathy asked him to describe the birth: "How did you know when to go to the hospital? What did you do to help her?" she asked. Ricky recalled that Theresa had been very upset during labor, yelling and calling him names and cursing both him and the anesthesiologist. "She asked for every drug in the book, street drugs, anything," he reported. Cathy said, "So what did you do?" Ricky exclaimed indignantly, "I didn't do nothin'! I left her alone!" Ricky, who seemed to find Cathy's question surprising, as well as ingenuous, did not think he was "in control" of his wife's labor.

Moreover, the prenatal education offered through the "Baby & Me" classes served a broader social control function as well, in as far as it attempted to ameliorate class and cultural differences and encouraged women to adopt the mores and practices of the dominant culture. The class worked to impose a particular model not only of birth, but also of motherhood, more generally. In this sense, the "Baby & Me" class carried on the tradition of "Friendly Visiting" established by social charity agencies over a century ago. Friendly visitors, reform-minded upper-class women, sought to teach poor and predominantly immigrant women "domestic science"—how to save, to practice thrift, to adopt "American" standards of cleanliness and orderliness, to forgo their native cuisine and to prepare healthful American meals. To the charity agency volunteers who were friendly visitors in the nineteenth century, "right living meant living like the American middle-class lived, or aspired to live" (Ehrenreich and English 1978, p. 173). Like the friendly visitors, Cathy herself was overtly middle-class and often expressed a bourgeois domesticity that may well have been beyond the reach or taste of the women in the class. She openly embraced what Ehrenreich and English (p 173) call "the entire ideology of 'right living.'" She encouraged them to "shop for bargains" and was openly disdainful of one of the husbands who acknowledged that he paid $100 for a pair of brand-name sneakers. She urged the women to make their own bread, as she does in her bread machine. She praised Disney movies like *Aladdin* for the way they have introduced "exotic" names like Jafar into the mainstream. However, when one woman said she was thinking of naming her baby Caprice, Cathy's swift rebuke clearly expressed her own class status: "Caprice is the name of a car. You want Caprice, go get a Chevy Caprice." Moreover, for immigrant women in the class, names such as Jafar may hardly seem "exotic." Cathy's moralizing extended far beyond expectations for women's behavior during pregnancy and childbirth, and into the broader realm of mothering and household production. Moreover, as her opinions on names suggest, the racial difference between Cathy and many of the women in the class magnified the social distance between them.

Yet, in may ways, Cathy was as constrained as the women themselves in her ability to re-interpret or re-invent the experience of pregnancy and birth outside the institutional parameters she operated within. Not only do her interactions with the women in the class illustrate what Waitzkin (1991) calls "the micro-politics of medicine," they also bear the imprint of the macro-politics of organized health care. In denying an alternative to episiotomy or a 24-hour hospital stay, she was echoing institutional priorities that treat women not as individuals, but as sources of revenue. The focus in the "Baby & Me" classes on preventing births that are in any way troublesome—whether because the woman presents at the hospital "too early" or whether because the baby ends up in the NICU—reflects an institutional and societal emphasis on the bottom line. While it is through Cathy's words that women learned the lessons in control that I have described here, it is important to remember that, in this course of prenatal education, women "heard" not only Cathy, but "the voice of the institution" (Goffman 1961) as well. Moreover, these lessons were shaped not only by the particular institution of Prestige Hospital, but also by the corporate structure of health care in the U.S. today.

Beyond Medicalization: Functions of the Class for Participants

Yet, despite all its flaws, most women did come to the "Baby & Me" class week after week. Why, if the prenatal course served the institution more than individuals, did women continue to attend? There are at least three immediate answers. First, the women saw the classes as an essential element of their prenatal care. Like most women, these women were highly motivated to have healthy and successful pregnancies and were eager to do what they could to ensure a good outcome. When asked why she took the class, Tracy, for example, replied, "'Cause it was my first [child], and I didn't want to go in there and not know what to do, if something was to happen." Lilya likewise answered, "I didn't know much about [pregnancy]! At least it gives some idea what you can expect, what you can pay attention to." Moreover, although they were not required to attend "Baby & Me" classes, the same general sense of "compliance" that brought them into the clinic for their prenatal visits led them to the classes. Second, at least a few women seemed to expect the class to teach specific labor techniques. Several women indicated that they expected the class to be more along the lines of a childbirth preparation course instructing in specific techniques, like Lamaze. "I thought we would be more into sitting on the floor with pillows, breathing, practicing," said Janelle. (That she is able to conjure such a vivid and specific image of prenatal classes reveals how deeply ingrained and therefore familiar the notion of childbirth education has become in our culture; women expect such classes to be a normal part of the experience of pregnancy.) Third, the class did provide some useful information to women and gave them a forum in which to ask questions about their physical symptoms, nutrition, and other concerns they may have hesitated to bring up during hurried routine clinic visits. "I got a lot of information out of it, like about breastfeeding and—I'm having a boy—so how to take care of the navel and where the little baby is circumcised, and which side is better to sleep on and why," reported Sharon. Of course, women also sought additional information from the class, though they did not as frequently receive it. Several women told me in interviews that they had "looked things up" or "read up" on subjects outside the class. "If she said a term or something I didn't understand, I would go find it in a book," Tracy recalled.

However the most important reason that women attended the course was that it provided social support and a tenuous social network for the women, many of whom were unmarried. Particularly for the women who did not have active partners, the class offered an opportunity to be in the company of others making the same life transition.

> *Lilya*: It's always interesting, you know, to be with people in a similar position. . . . You don't have to do *everything* by yourself.
> *Kimberly*: That's one of the main reasons I joined the class. . . . It was nice having somewhere to go every week just to unload about the baby, because I can't do it at work.
> *Tracy*: I was alone. . . . I thought it would be a good thing to get together with a bunch of people in a similar situation. I figured I wouldn't be the only woman who was by myself.

Certainly in part, the class functioned as a quasi-support group. Women did come to know each other in a limited way and were genuinely interested in hearing the stories of the labors and deliveries of their two classmates who gave birth before the class ended. Becoming a mother for the first time connects women to a new social world—that of parents—and being pregnant initiates this process. Some women, in particular, seemed to need this social contact and sense of belonging particularly acutely. Kimberly repeatedly suggested that the class have a reunion in the summer to meet each other's babies and to stay in touch. When she learned that another participant in the class lived in the same neighborhood as she did, she insisted that they exchange phone numbers. On the last night of the class, Tracy brought a present and a card for each of her classmates.

Moreover, Cathy, for all her sermonizing, did evince a genuine caring for the women in the class. She made an effort to learn their names and something about their social situations. She often referred to them as "my girls:" and it was she who solicited local stores to make donations of the baby clothes she distributed at the end of every class meeting. For women who may have received disjointed prenatal care, seeing a different provider at each prenatal visit, Cathy's presence in the classroom each week may have seemed reassuring.

Conclusion

In recent years, prenatal care has been proposed as the solution to one of the most troubling social problems of our time: persistent rates of low birth weight and infant mortality, despite one of the most advanced medical systems in the world. Public health history—both distant and recent—suggests that we need to look to changes in social structure and to the relief of social misery, deprivation, and inequality as the surest routes to sustained gains in maternal and infant health (CDC 1999; Link and Phelan 1995; McKeown 1979), yet, as a society we continue to expect that changing how people act as individuals is sufficient to bring about desired change in health outcomes. Prenatal care is an article of faith in the U.S. today. However, the narrow medical model on which prenatal care rests both blinds us to the social embeddedness of the behaviors that are today constituted as the major threats to maternal and infant health and severely limits the potential of this intervention to reduce further the rate of adverse birth outcomes in the U.S., or the disparity in outcomes among different social groups in this country.

Moreover, the extension of the medical model of prenatal care described here—namely, prenatal education—reflects a significant shift in public health strategy. This study is the first to examine the process of prenatal education in depth and in detail. Despite the prominence of prenatal education in policy rhetoric, there have been precious few studies of its effect on birth outcomes and no attention to its impact on the experience of pregnancy among American women. Current policies that make prenatal education the keystone of efforts to improve maternal and infant health seek to locate in individual patterns of behavior the most cogent explanations for the distribution of prenatal and perinatal health, as well as the most powerful lever to affect these outcomes. However, as this analysis suggests, prenatal education threatens to narrow even further the scope of public health endeavors. Rather than emphasizing institutional innovation or social reform, as did earlier efforts to improve maternal and child health, prenatal education reduces civic responsibility for birth outcomes, eclipsing the obligations of society to care for its present and future members. Despite a rhetoric of empowerment, patient education serves to transfer responsibility for health outcomes from the medical profession to the patient. Moreover, patient education such as that exemplified by the "Baby & Me" classes serves not only to transfer responsibility, but to shift the actual burden of care work as well, from the hospital to the pregnant woman.

Certainly not all prenatal education is so constrained in its ability to prepare the woman herself for the experience of birth as that described here. The extent to which this study may be generalizable is limited, most importantly by its small size, but also by the extent to which it is bound by social class. Because the Healthy Start classes at

Prestige Hospital were targeted to disadvantaged women, this study cannot comment on the process of prenatal education among all women. However, other studies of childbirth education have reported similar findings (Freda, et al. 1993; League and Novelli 1994; Monto 1996; Nolan 1997; Zwelling 1996). Zwelling (p. 429) observes that one of the prevailing goals of childbirth education is "to prepare the parents to be better patients in the maternity care system." Studies of childbirth education in Australia (O'Meara 1993), Great Britain (Cliff and Deery 1997; Nolan 1997), New Zealand (Gunn, et al. 1983) and the U.S. (Maloney 1985) find that such classes often fall short of expectant parents' expectations.

Moreover, although I observed only one cycle of classes and interviewed only a small sample of women, my findings are echoed by other sociological observers of pregnancy and birth. Wertz and Wertz (1989) note that prenatal care is geared towards coaxing women to follow a particular model of pregnancy and to conform to prevailing medical notions of a "healthy" pregnancy; for example, in the 1950s and 1960s, strict regimens concerning weight gain in pregnancy were essentially a form of "obedience training" for prenatal patients, teaching them to be subservient to the dictates of the care provider. Therefore, medical supervision of pregnancy functions not only to prepare the woman medically for birth, but prepare her for a "successful" *medical* birth as well. Likewise, critics of childbirth education have long noted that it often functions not so much to empower women to experience an alternative, non-medicalized birth as to convince them to act "within the framework of institutional rules," as Rothman (1991, p. 175) puts it. Lamaze training, Rothman contends, teaches women to maintain self-control, all the while deferring to the obstetrician's demands and wishes. "In essence, the method keeps the woman quiet by giving her a task to do, making being a 'good'—non-complaining, obedient, cooperative—patient, the woman's primary goal" (p. 93). Thus, even such supposedly "empowering" techniques as Lamaze may be subverted to achieve goals of socialization and social control. Rothman also reports the "considerable time" spent in childbirth education classes on defining labor and instructing women how to distinguish it from "false labor." Moreover, she notes, "'real' labor is defined, not in terms of sensations the woman experiences, but in terms of 'progress'—cervical dilation" (p. 167).

In their study of communication between obstetricians and pregnant women, Shapiro et al. (1983) found that women often did not obtain the information that they wanted from their doctors and that, moreover, this communication gap was wider for socially disadvantaged women. A more recent study by Markens, Browner, and Press (1997) of women's eating habits during pregnancy found that women struggled to accommodate their diets to clinical advice. In fact, they argue that medical management of pregnancy has been "normalized" and that "this normalization indicates acceptance of the growing emphasis on the exclusive, or nearly exclusive, role of maternal responsibility for fetal outcome" (Markens, Browner, and Press 1997, p. 369). Gardner finds that the lay literature on pregnancy emphasizes the importance of "mental and emotional self-control" (Gardner 1994b, p. 78) during pregnancy and focuses as well on consciousness of bodily conditions: "the woman's own unconscious and untutored understanding of pregnancy is devalued" (Garnder 1995, p. 37). Finally, Balsamo's (1996) multi-layered analysis of "public pregnancies" suggests that the processes of socialization and social problems at work in this class mirror the broader culture of pregnancy in this period of American history.

The contemporary medical model of pregnancy and birth equates personal knowledge with personal control. Yet women have differing tastes and different expectations of control during birth. As Lilya put it, "Well, no matter how you are prepared, or how worried you are, it will happen like it will happen." In seeking to elevate self-control to a paramount achievement of the birth process, this model both threatens to elide women's personal preferences for this significant life event and to impose responsibility on them for a process and an outcome that is in fact manifestly not under their control. As a flyer passed out in the "Baby & Me" classes asserts, "The more you know, the more in charge you will be!" Yet little I observed in this class supports this claim. The knowledge offered in the class was not directed at placing women and their wishes at the center of the birth experience; rather, the class delivered the message that the institution, ultimately, was in charge.

What Goffman (1961) argues about the mental hospital is equally true of the maternity ward of many hospitals: "some of the hospital routine would be dictated not by medical considerations, but by other factors, notably rules for patient management that have emerged in the institution for the convenience and comfort of staff" (p. 347). Moreover, Goffman notes, "the success of the patient in making this assimilation [to the medical service model] necessarily resides in his being deceived about certain procedures" (p. 346). The "Healthy Start" prenatal education at Prestige Hospital obfuscated as much as it illuminated. In fact, there were limits to the knowledge offered in the class and the instructor, who had never experienced birth herself, expressed disapproval or discomfort when participants offered each other experiential knowledge that strayed beyond these boundaries. Goffman contends that what the mental hospital offers and professes to be "a service" "is not necessarily a service, especially not a medical service, to the inmate" (Goffman, p. 353). Likewise, the service of the "Baby & Me" classes offered at Prestige Hospital was not necessarily a service to the women who attended the class. Moreover, this model of prenatal education subverts the axiom that "knowledge is power." What the class offered was not so much knowledge as information. In the "Patient Education Room" women were allowed to learn only so much.

However, there are really two stores in this fieldwork. Both are about power. One is about the power of medical institutions to define human experience—what birth ought to be like—and to absorb challenges to medical authority—in this care, hegemony over the process of birth—and to transmute these challenges in such a way that institutional mandates are reconfigured as patient needs or patient interests. The prenatal education described here accomplishes one of the class of functions of medicalization—that of "securing adherence to social norms" (Conrad and Schneider 1992, p. 242) Thus, childbirth education becomes prenatal education, which purports to teach pregnant women an alternative way to experience childbirth, one not dominated by the dictates of medicine or hospitals, but really functions to prepare them for compliance with the institutional regime.

The other story in this fieldwork is about the power of people to extract meaning and value from the processes of medicalization perpetrated upon them. The dynamics of the "Baby & Me" classes illustrate a process of medicalization that women both participated in *and* rejected. These pregnant women may be complicit with the medicalization of their pregnancies and births (Riessman and Nathanson 1986), but what drew them back week after week to the classes was what they found *outside* the realm of medicalization to make their course of prenatal education worthwhile. These women saw themselves not only as "patients" expected to report their physical symptoms or learn to recognize labor according to a medical formula, for example, but also as individuals experiencing a significant life transition. Thus, women found camaraderie and fellowship with other women who gave them reason to return to the weekly "Baby & Me" sessions. Although this course of prenatal education operated in many ways to prep the patient without teaching—or empowering—the woman, women who attended the class were, nevertheless, able to find and extract other functions that better served their needs. *What* they reported learning—"to stay calm, how to know when to come to the hospital"—is significantly different from *why* they reported coming—"to be with other women like me." In other words, women's complicity with the medicalization inherent in the class reflects not only powerful forces of socialization, but also the extent to which the prenatal classes enabled women to achieve their own goals of social interaction with peers and of locating social support for their experience of pregnancy and birth within the often tenuous circumstances of their own lives. It is not only the hegemony or social dominance of organized medicine that permits medicalization. Rather, this study suggests that medicalization may at times proceed and become integrated into expectations of the life course precisely because it accomplishes extra-medical tasks.

Nonetheless, there is no gainsaying that prenatal education offers yet another avenue to achieve social control and medicalize human experience. Goffman (1961) concludes *Asylums* with the distressing and all-too-prescient observation that "To be made a patient is to be remade into a serviceable object, the irony being that so little service is available once this is done" (p. 379). Despite an abundant rhetoric of client satisfaction and customer service, the current health care environment in the U.S. only threatens to widen the gap between individuals in need of care, particularly those who are disempowered, and the institutions that purport to serve them. Although the analysis presented here suggests that would-be patients may find some meaning in the medicalization of life events such as birth and becoming a mother, certainly it is only in the interstices and at the margins that they are able to do so. Not only do institutions retain their overwhelming power to overshadow individuals in the dawn of the new millennium, social establishments like public health and medicine increasingly seek to persuade individuals to accomplish goals that ought more properly to be in the purview of our society as a whole.

Notes

1. Congress enacted legislation in September 1996 requiring insurance companies to cover at least 48 hours in the hospital after vaginal birth and 96 hours after birth by cesarean section. Prior to Congressional action, many state legislatures had passed similar laws.

2. The OB/GYN clinic at the hospital observed in this study advertised its services with a brochure picturing a young woman holding a toddler. The woman says, "My grandmother had my mother here, my mother had me here, and now I'm having my baby at Prestige Hospital."

3. Note that many of these alternative forms of childbirth are designed and promoted by men.

4. Both the American Society for Psychoprophylaxis in Obstetrics (APSO/Lamaze) and the International Childbirth Education Association (ICEA) were formed in 1960 and continue to be active today.

5. Virtually all pregnant women in the U.S. receive some prenatal care; however, 16 percent of women do not begin receiving care until after the first trimester and one in ten women receives inadequate care (CDC 2000).

6. The focus on delivery reflects both women's anxieties about the birth process and institutional priorities.

7. When "Healthy Start" was launched, the U.S. ranked 24th among industrialized countries in infant mortality. The infant mortality rate that year was 8.9 per 1,000 births: among African-Americans, it was 17.6 (NCHS 1999).

8. The names I use to identify the instructor and all the participants in the class are pseudonyms.

9. I am grateful to an anonymous reviewer for this insight.

10. Moreover, note the focus on individual behavior—the woman's diet—rather than the environmental hazard.

11. Theresa later delivered her baby vaginally.

12. It hardly bears pointing out that such a conception of the birth partner's role places control with someone other than the delivering woman.

References

Annas, George J. 1974. "The hospital: A human rights wasteland." *The Civil Liberties Review* 1, 4:9–29.

Arney, William Ray. 1982. *Power and the Profession of Obstetrics*. Chicago: University of Chicago Press.

Balin, Jane. 1988. "The sacred dimensions of pregnancy and birth." *Qualitative Sociology* 11, 4:275–301.

Balsamo, Anne. 1996. "Public pregnancies and cultural narratives of surveillance." In *Technologies of the Gendered Body: Reading Cyborg Women*. Durham: Duke University Press.

Barker, K. K. 1998. "A ship upon a stormy sea: The medicalization of pregnancy." *Social Science and Medicine* 47, 8:1067–1076.

Belizan, Jose M. and Guillermo Carroli. 1998. "Routine episiotomy should be abandoned." Letter. *British Medical Journal* 317, 7169:1389.

Centers for Disease Control and Prevention (CDC). 1998. "Maternal mortality—United States, 1982–1996." *Morbidity and Mortality Weekly Report* 47, 34:705–707.

———. 1999. "Achievements in public health, 1900–1999: Healthier mothers and babies." *Morbidity and Mortality Weekly Report* 48, 38:849–858.

———. 2000. "Entry into prenatal care—United States, 1989–1997." *Morbidity and Mortality Weekly Report* 48, 38:849–858.

Cliff, D. and R. Deery. 1997. "Too much like school: Social class, age, marital status, and attendance/non-attendance at antenatal classes." *Midwifery* 13, 3:139–145.

Cogan, R. 1980. "Effects of childbirth preparation." *Clinical Obstetrics and Gynecology* 23, 1:1–14.

Conrad, Peter. 1979. "Types of medical social control." *Sociology of Health and Illness* 1, 1:1–11.

Conrad, Peter and Joseph W. Schneider. 1992. *Deviance and Medicalization: From Badness to Sickness*. Philadelphia: Temple University Press.

Davis-Floyd, Robbie E. 1992a. *Birth as an American Rite of Passage*. Berkeley: University of California Press.

———. 1992b. "The technocratic body and the organic body: Cultural models for women's birth choices. *Knowledge and Society: The Anthropology of Science and Technology* 9:59–93.

Eccles, Audrey. 1982. *Obstetrics and Gynecology in Tuder and Stuart England*. London: Croom Helm.

Ecker, Jeffrey L., Winona M. Tan, Raj K. Bansal, Judith T. Bishop, and Sarah J. Kilpatrick. 1997. "Is there a benefit to episiotomy at operative vaginal delivery? Observations over ten years in a stable population." *American Journal of Obstetrics and Gynecology* 176, 2:411–414.

Ehrenreich, Barbara and Deirdre English. 1978. *For Her Own Good: 150 Year of the Experts' Advice to Women*. New York: Doubleday.

Fisher, Sue. 1986. *In the Patient's Best Interest: Women and the Politics of Medical Decisions*. New Brunswick: Rutgers University Press.

Freda, Margaret C., H. Frank Andersen, Karla Damus, and Irwin R. Merkatz. 1993. "Are there differences in information given to private and public prenatal patients?" *American Journal of Obstetrics and Gynecology* 169, 1:155–160.

Friedson, Eliot. 1970. *Profession of Medicine: A Study of the Sociology of Applied Knowledge*. New York: Dodd, Mead and Co.

Gardner, Carol Brooks. 1994a. "The social construction of pregnancy and fetal development: Notes on a nineteenth-century rhetoric of endangerment." In *Constructing the Social*, T. R. Sarbin and J. I. Kitsuse, eds., 45–64. London: Sage Publications.

———. 1994b. "Little strangers: Pregnancy conduct and the twentieth-century rhetoric of endangerment." In *Troubling Children: Studies of Children and Social Problems*, Joel Best, ed., 69–92. New York: Aldine de Gruyter.

———. 1995. "Learning for two: A study in the rhetoric of pregnancy practices." *Perspectives on Social Problems* 7:29–51.

Goffman, Erving. 1961. "The medical model and mental hospitalization: Some notes on the vicissitudes of the tinkering trades." In *Asylums*. New York: Anchor Books.

Gunn, T. R., A. Fisher, P. Lloyd, and S. O'Donnell. 1983. "Antenatal education: Does it improve the quality of labour and delivery?" *New Zealand Medical Journal* 96, 724:51–53.

Helewa, Michael E. 1997. "Episiotomy and severe perineal trauma: Of science and fiction." *Canadian Medical Association Journal* 156, 724:51–53.

Helewa, Michael E. 1997. "Episiotomy and severe perineal trauma: Of science and fiction." *Canadian Medical Association Journal* 156, 6:811–813.

Holstein, James A. and Gale Miller. 1997. "Social problems as work." In *Social Problems in Everyday Life: Studies of Social Problems Work*, Gale Miller and James A. Holstein, eds., ix-xxi. Greenwich, CT: JAI Press, Inc.

Humenick, Sharron S. 1995. "The impact of epidurals on infants including breastfeeding." *Journal of Perinatal Education* 4, 4:65–68.

Institute of Medicine (IOM). 1985. *Preventing Low Birth Weight*. Washington, D.C.: National Academy Press.

Lazarus, Ellen S. 1994. "What do women want? Issues of choice, control and class in pregnancy and childbirth." *Medical Anthropology Quarterly* 8, 1:25–46.

League, J. and L. Novelli. 1994. "Going, going, gone?" *Childbirth Instructor* 4, 4:30–33.

Leavitt, Judith Walzer. 1985. "'Science' enters the birthing room: Obstetrics in America since the 18th century.: In *Sickness and Health in America: Readings in the History of Medicine and Public Health*, Judith Walzer Leavitt and Ronald L. Numbers, eds., 81–97, Madison: University of Wisconsin Press.

———. 1986. *Brought to Bed: Childbearing in America, 1730–1950*. New York: Oxford University Press.

Lindsay, Douglas C. and Celeste R. Phillips. 1992. "Choosing a maternity care system." *Trustee: The Magazine for Hospital Governing Boards* 45, 4:12–13.

Link, Bruce G. and Jo Phelan. 1995. "Social conditions as fundamental causes of disease." *Journal of Health and Social Behavior*. Extra Issue:80–94.

Maloney, R. 1985. "Childbirth education classes: Expectant parents' expectations." *Journal of Obstetric, Gynecologic, and Neonatal Nursing* 14, 3:245–248.

Markens, Susan, C. H. Browner, and Nancy Press. 1997. "Feeding the fetus: On interrogating the notion of maternal-fetal conflict." *Feminist Studies* 23, 2:351–372.

Martin, Emily. 1987. *The Woman in the Body: A Cultural Analysis of Reproduction*. Boston: Beacon Press.

McKeown, Thomas. 1979. *The Role of Medicine: Dream, Mirage or Nemesis?* Princeton: Princeton University Press.

Mitford, Jessica. 1993. *The American Way of Birth*. New York: Penguin Books.

Monto, M. A. 1996. "Lamaze and Bradley childbirth classes: Contracting perspectives toward the medical model of birth." *Birth* 23, 4:193–201.

Morton, Sally C., M. S. Williams, Emmett B. Keeler, Joseph C. Gambone, and Katherine L. Kahn. 1994. "Effect of epidural analgesia for labor on the cesarean delivery rate." *Obstetrics and Gynecology*, 83:1045–1051.

Murray, A. D., R. M. Dolby, R. L. Nation, and D. B. Thomas. 1981. "Effects of epidural anesthesia on newborns and their mothers." *Child Development* 52, 1:71–82.

National Center for Health Statistics (NCHS). 1999. *Healthy People 2000 Review, 1998–1999*. Hyattsville, MD: Public Health Service, 137–144.

Nelson, Margaret K. 1986. "Birth and social class." In *The American Way of Birth*, Pamela S. Eakins, ed., 142–174. Philadelphia: Temple University Press.

Newton, Edward R., Barbara C. Schroeder, Kelly G. Knape, and Bari L. Bennett. 1995. "Epidural analgesia and uterine function." *Obstetrics and Gynecology* 85:749–755.

Nolan, Mary L. 1997. "Anenatal education—where next?" *Journal of Advanced Nursing* 25, 6:1198–1204.

Oakley, Ann. 1984. *The Captured Womb: A History of Medical Care of Pregnant Women*. Oxford: Basil Blackwell Publisher.

O'Meara, C. 1993. "An evaluation of consumer perspectives of childbirth and parenting education." *Midwifery* 9, 4:210–219.

Parsons, Talcott. 1951. "Social structure and dynamic process: The case of modern medical practice." In *The Social System*, Chapter X. Glencoe, IL: The Free Press.

Public Health Service, Department of Health and Human Services. 1989. *Caring for Our Future: The Context of Prenatal Care. A Report of the Public Health Expert Panel on the Content of Prenatal Care*. Washington, D.C.: Public Health Service.

Reissman, Catherine Kohler and Constance A. Nathanson. 1986. "The management of reproduction: Social construction of risk and responsibility." In *Applications of Social Science to Clinical Medicine and Health Policy*, Linda H. Aiken and David Mechanic, eds. New Brunswick: Rutgers University Press.

Richard, Lennert and Margaret O. Alade. 1990. "Effect of delivery room routines on success of first breastfeed." *Lancet* 336, 8723:1105–1107.

Rothman, Barbara Katz. 1991. *In Labor: Women and Power in the Birthplace*. New York: W. W. Norton and Company.

Sargent, Carolyn and Nancy Stark. 1989. "Childbirth education and childbirth models: Parental perspectives on control, anesthesia, and technological intervention in the birth process." *Medical Anthropology Quarterly* NS 3, 1:36–51.

Sepkoski, Carol M., Barry M. Lester, G. W. Ostheimer, and T. Berry Brazelton. 1992. "The effects of maternal epidural anesthesia on neonatal behavior during the first month." *Developmental Medicine and Child Neurology* 34, 12:1072–1080.

Shapiro, M. C., J. M. Najman, A. Chang, J. D. Keeping, J. Morrison, and J. S. Western. 1983. "Information control and the exercise of power in the obstetrical encounter." *Social Science and Medicine* 17, 3:139–146.

Strauss, Anselm L. and Juliet Corbin. 1990. *Basics of Qualitative Research: Grounded Theory Procedures and Techniques.* Newbury Park, CA: Sage Publications.

Thorpe, James A., Daniel H. Hu, Rene M. Albin, Jay McNitt, Bruce A. Meyer, Gary R. Cohen, and John D. Yeast. 1993. "The effect of intrapartum epidural analgesia on nulliparous labor: A randomized, controlled prospective trial." *American Journal of Obstetrics and Gynecology* 169:851–858.

Waitzkin, Howard. 1991. *The Politics of Medical Encounters: How Patients and Doctors Deal with Social Problems.* New Haven: Yale University Press.

Wertz, Richard W. and Dorothy C. Wertz. 1989. *Lying-In: A History of Childbirth in America.* New Haven: Yale University Press.

West, Candace. 1993. "Reconceptualizing gender in physician-patient relationships." *Social Science and Medicine* 36, 1:57–66.

World Health Organization [WHO]. 1985. *Summary Report on the Joint Interregional Conference on Appropriate Technology for Birth.* Geneva: Regional Office for Europe of the WHO.

———. 1997. *Care in Normal Birth: A Practical Guide. Report of a Technical Working Group.* Geneva: WHO, Department of Reproductive Health and Research.

Zola, Irving Kenneth. 1972. "Medicine as an institution of social control." *Sociological Review* 20:487–504.

Zwelling, Elaine. 1996. "Childbirth education in the 1990s and beyond." *Journal of Obstetric, Gynecologic and Neonatal Nursing* 25, 5:425–432.

Part VI

MEDICAL ACCOUNTABILITY

Sociologists have often pointed out how medicine developed a "professional dominance" that gave physicians an unusual amount of autonomy and insulation from outside regulation. For example, physicians restricted entry into the profession by controlling the educational curricula and the licensing boards for medical practice. Until the last two decades, physicians controlled their independent practices, and medical mistakes received relatively little public recognition and response. Their work was largely insulated from any kind of public oversight. In this period, medicine functioned as perhaps the most independent profession, largely unencumbered by bureaucratic and governmental demands. With the rise of the insurance industry, the preponderance of managed care, and the large governmental contributions to financing health care (especially through Medicare for older Americans), this independence and professional dominance has been severely eroded in recent years.

One issue that remains important is medical accountability. To whom, for what, and under what circumstances is medicine accountable? Public accountability has long been limited: How can organizations or consumers hold medicine accountable for what they do or do not do? How can the public know about and deal with incompetent physicians? Doctors, like everyone else, make mistakes. How can they be held accountable for their actions? In a society where patients are increasingly defined as "consumers," accountability become a more central issue. Much of the current focus is on accountability for medical costs, but there are other important issues as well. The three articles in part VI present different faces of the medical accountability issue.

Carol Klaperman Morrow, in "Sick Doctors: The Social Construction of Professional Deviance," considers the conceptualization of "substandard performance" as a social issue. She shows that physicians who are found to be drug addicted, alcoholic, or suffering from psychiatric disorders, are often deemed "impaired physicians." Rather than questioning the social and cultural components of self-governance, we see a neutralization of public accountability by medicalizing the professional deviance.

In the second article, "Changing Doctor-Patient Relationships and the Rise in Concern for Accountability," Michael Betz and Lenahan O'Connell examine public distrust of physicians, contrasting professional and patient perspectives. Their prediction that third-party controls will deprofessionalize the medical profession has not material-ized, although it is clear that physicians are more accountable today for financial and quality-of-care issues then they were previously.

In the final selection, Stephen L. Fielding explores the relationship between "Changing Medical Practice and Medical Malpractice Claims." While most people think malpractice is mostly related to the number and severity of medical mistakes, Fielding examines the statistics of medical malpractice claims and argues that medical malpractice claims are associated with medical work in particular kinds of practice set-tings. Moreover, he shows how the different patient and physician perspectives on what constitutes "medical outcomes" affect what gets called "malpractice."

CHAPTER 15

Sick Doctors

THE SOCIAL CONSTRUCTION OF PROFESSIONAL DEVIANCE

Carol Klaperman Morrow

The boundaries of professional self-governance in medicine are shifting, and traditional notions of deviance and social control are being re-evaluated. A new interpretation of misconduct and a new strategy for controlling misconduct have been "discovered" and widely promoted within the profession. In the early 1970s, organized medicine in the United States for the first time officially recognized the extent to which drug addiction, alcoholism, and psychiatric disorders among doctors undermine the competent and scrupulous practice of medicine, and proposed that treatment of such disorders be provided within the context of professional discipline and public accountability.

The scope of disorders among doctors was first documented in the 1950s when the United States Commissioner of Narcotics reported an addiction rate of one in 100 doctors, as compared with one in 3,000 for the general population (Anslinger and Chapman, 1957). Later studies confirmed that one to two percent of doctors develop drug abuse problems at some point in their careers, and found that an additional six to eight percent of doctors develop alcohol problems (Blachly, *et al.*, 1968; Modlin and Montes, 1964; Vaillant *et al.*, 1970). While the distribution of such disorders within the profession has not been determined, studies suggest that most drug addicts are general practitioners and general surgeons, while most alcoholics are psychiatrists (Bissell and Jones, 1976; *Medical World News*, 1972).

Before organized medicine acknowledged the extent of the problem and its implications for professional performance, doctors shunned, humiliated, or routinely covered for addicted and alcoholic colleagues; medical societies either ignored sick doctors or, infrequently, brought them before all-purpose ethics and grievance committees; hospitals and state disciplinary agencies considered only cases of blatantly unprofessional conduct, substandard performance, and disregard for patient welfare. The typical fate of severely addicted or alcoholic doctors was loss of hospital privileges or revocation of license. Since 1973, however, sick doctors have become a growing concern of the American Medical Association (AMA) and its component medical societies, hospitals, and state disciplinary boards. The emerging mechanisms of professional social control reject moralistic notions of addiction and alcoholism, underscore the sick doctor's right to nonjudgmental treatment, and firmly integrate rehabilitation with the peer review of professional performance and the protection of patient welfare.

The concern with *physician impairment*, as it is called within the profession, signals a change in professional self-governance. Previously, self-governance has been either educationally oriented, as in the case of hospital medical audits and continuing medical education courses, or punitive, as in state disciplinary proceedings against a doctor's license. These latter regulatory controls emphasize the ignorance, moral weakness, or malice of offenders, and call for their retraining, moral condemnation or legal punishment.

Physician impairment, however, suggests that professional deviance (incompetence, unscrupulous conduct, illegal practices) be understood as the symptom or outcome of a medical condition for which the deviant is not to blame. Efforts to control impairment thus constitute "a new approach to an old problem" of substandard performance (Palmer, 1975:1) in which doctors are assumed to become unqualified through illness and the problem doctor's medical condition is "given priority on the assumption that appropriate handling and treatment of his disorder will lead to amelioration of his other difficulties" (Steindler, 1975:30). Problem doctors who come to the attention of so-called impaired physician programs are, broadly speaking, treated medically, rather than controlled legally, censured morally, or retrained. Such programs are characterized by concerned physician advocacy, a commitment to confidential, nonjudgmental confrontation and medical rehabilitation, early paternalistic intervention in the name of health, and monopolization of the management of the problem doctor by medical experts (Morrow, 1981).

The growing tendency to interpret deviations from the rules of good medical care and professional conduct as the symptom or outcome of illness, and the establishment of programs to control these deviations by "treating" their underlying cause, signify the medicalization of professional social control. This paper describes the social, political, and legal context in which interest in physician impairment emerged and the diffusion of programs and policies based on this concept.

Method and Data

This study is based on data collected in 1979 from several sources. First, I sent a seven-page questionnaire and request for information to the 54 U.S. medical societies in all the states and jurisdictions. Twenty-eight societies returned questionnaires. These represented 53 percent of those surveyed and 90 percent of the 31 societies with identifiable impaired physician programs at the time. Second, I interviewed, in person or by telephone, 23 individuals knowledgeable about peer review in general or physician impairment in particular. Twelve had founded or directed impaired physician programs, representing 38 percent of programs active at the time. Third, I examined the actual management of problem doctors by preparing six case studies of selected types of problem doctors, including the drug addict, sexual offender, and senile doctor. Finally, I reviewed some 100 published articles and various unpublished and previously unanalyzed documents, including transcripts of state disciplinary hearings, and in-house materials provided by impaired physician programs.

Political and Social Context

The concept of physician impairment emerged in the early 1970s when consumers, journalists, and state legislators were challenging medicine's claims of competence and dedication to public welfare, and trying to limit professional autonomy and require practitioners to account for the effectiveness and efficiency of their services. As I outline below, increased government intervention, consumer activism, media exposés of medical fraud and abuse, soaring rates of malpractice litigation, and expanded concepts of legal liability for malpractice litigation, exerted enormous pressures on doctors to monitor themselves in ways that secured the public's health and trust in the profession while protecting the profession's welfare and reputation.

In the swelling U.S. consumer movement of the late 1960s and mid-1970s, patients voiced their distrust in medicine by arming themselves with a "bill of rights" and "shoppers' guides" to health care, forming self-help groups, and suing doctors for professional incompetence and negligence (American Hospital Association, 1973; Denenberg, 1972; Ferguson, 1977; Lander, 1978). Medical malpractice claims became increasingly common in the mid-1960s and early 1970s, with the sharpest increase coming between 1970 and 1973 (Lander, 1978). By 1975, 26 percent of doctors had been sued at least once during their career, up from 17 percent in 1971 (Scott, 1975).

The public's decreasing trust in medicine and its willingness to seek restitution through the courts led to an economic crisis in the professional liability industry, which in turn prompted a flurry of reforms in professional discipline. Increases in the number of malpractice actions and the size of damages led in the early 1970s to hikes of up to 500 percent in malpractice insurance premiums, withdrawal of some insurers from the field, and more difficult access to insurance coverage for practitioners and institutions. By 1975, "a crisis atmosphere prevailed nationwide, both in states that faced real availability problems and those that did not" (Law and Polan, 1978:195). Doctors threatened work slow-downs, while medical societies and hospitals negotiated frantically with insurers and state legislatures held emergency sessions. In 1975 and 1976, more than 30 states enacted legislative reforms authorizing new forms of insurance companies especially for the medical profession and modifying legal requirements for proving negligence, filing suit, determining awards, and otherwise revising how much and under what circumstances victims of malpractice could recover (Law and Polan, 1978).

Having thus soothed the medical community, legislators demanded that professional groups do their part to deal more effectively with incompetence. The federal and state commissions established in response to the malpractice crisis identified substandard professional performance and the ineffective control of problem doctors as important factors affecting the overall quality of medical care and the medical malpractice situation (New York State Assembly, 1977; Otten, 1973a). State disciplinary boards were strongly criticized in the widely cited report of the federal Department of Health, Education and Welfare's commission on medical malpractice (Department of Health, Education and Welfare, 1973), which found that most boards were either unable or unwilling to act against incompetent doctors.[1] In what Chapman (1978a) called an "explosion of legislation," every state legislature in the country reorganized its licensing and disciplinary machinery and revised its medical practice act. Forty-one states did so between 1974 and 1976 alone. The new state laws expanded the grounds for disciplinary action to include incompetence, broadened disciplinary powers to include continuing education, medical rehabilitation and supervised practice, required mandatory reporting by medical practitioners and institutions of suspected professional misconduct as well as malpractice claims, settlements, and judgments, and granted reporters of misconduct immunity from civil suit (Chapman, 1978a).

The AMA joined the attack on problem doctors by designing a model reporting and immunity bill (AMA, 1977), lobbying for increased power to discipline problem doctors—particularly those proved guilty of medical malpractice (*New York Medicine*, 1974)—and appointing, in 1975, an Ad Hoc Committee on Medical Discipline to determine "if there is a relationship between the medical disciplinary system and the incidence and cost of malpractice claims" (AMA, 1976:49). The committee concluded that medical discipline had improved since the previous AMA study in 1961, the first of its kind, but advised state medical societies to further strengthen medical discipline and reduce the number of malpractice claims by improving techniques for evaluating competence and cooperating with state boards in revising existing state disciplinary machinery.

In addition, organized medicine addressed the problem of incompetence by continuing to support recently developed programs in continuing medical education. A 1965 report of the AMA had identified the need to provide incentives for voluntary continuing education and encouraged professional associations to develop educational requirements for membership privileges and design educational programs that awarded participating doctors (Derbyshire, 1965). These initially voluntary efforts soon became compulsory. In 1971 New Mexico became the first state to make proof of continuing medical education necessary to renew a doctor's license; by 1979, 23 states had followed suit (Derbyshire, 1979).

This flood of state legislative reforms followed on the heels of federal legislation designed to revamp medical peer review. Professional Standard Review Organizations (PSROs), enacted in 1972, were authorized to review the cost and indirectly the quality of care provided to federally funded patients. Both the government and the profession perceived the new controls as a last chance to establish professional credibility and accountability and the PSROs thus aroused a great deal of controversy, confusion, and anxiety among doctors (Hicks, 1974; Somers, 1973).

These various consumer and legislative challenges to professional self-governance coincided with a succession of spectacular cases of misconduct which were widely reported in the press and popular journals, and investigated by legislative bodies and task forces. In 1972, a highly publicized series of articles in the *New York Times* accused Dr. Max Jacobson, a 73-year-old Manhattan general practitioner, of indiscriminately (and illegally) dispensing mood-altering amphetamines to a large clientele—many of whom were rich and powerful—and abusing such drugs himself (Brody, 1972; Rensberger, 1972). The articles raised serious questions about the profession's ability to police itself and protect the public's health. The county medical society, which had previous knowledge of the allegations against Jacobson, responded to the furor created by the articles by launching an extensive and unprecedented investigation, soliciting information from government agencies, recruiting witnesses, and convening special meetings (Altman, 1973a). In addition, the Jacobson case sensitized the medical society to the more general problem of chemical abuse among doctors and contributed to the decision to found, in 1974, a "sick physicians' committee."

One year later, the *New York Times* publicized the case of Drs. Cyril and Stewart Marcus, obstetrician-gynecologists at the prestigious New York Hospital (Rensberger, 1975a). The twin brothers were found dead of drug-related causes days after their hospital privileges were withdrawn; the state disciplinary board had been preparing to serve them with charges of unprofessional conduct. The county medical society, which had been conducting a related investigation into the Marcuses' failure to complete insurance forms, called a meeting of all local hospital leaders and issued guidelines to help them deal with disabled staff members. New York Hospital itself introduced formal administrative mechanisms providing for monitoring systems, mandatory reporting by hospital personnel of suspected disability, and medical rehabilitation and/or termination of hospital privileges for disabled staff members, Dr. E. Hugh Luckey, president of the hospital, explained that "recent articles lead one to the conclusion that we must find better ways of dealing with the competency of all individuals holding the type of precious private trust which anyone in the public service holds" (Rensberger, 1975b:29). Finally, state authorities, who in retrospect viewed the Marcus case as a "political dividing line" (Gitlow, 1979:1019), moved to reorganize the state's disciplinary machinery to create a new medical disciplinary board separate from other professional boards.

A third widely publicized case forcefully demonstrated the inadequacy of the profession's regulatory efforts and raised the possibility of professional and hospital liability for ineffective peer review (Law and Polan, 1978; Sheridan, 1974). In 1973, California Superior Court Judge B. Abbott Goldberg fund former Sacramento orthopedic surgeon Dr. John Nork and the city's Mercy General Hospital responsible for negligent surgery on Albert Gonzales, a grocery clerk (*Gonzales v. Nork*, 1973). The court ordered them to pay equal shares of compensatory damages totaling $1.7 million and Nork to pay an additional $4 million in punitive damages. The court found that Nork acted maliciously and incompetently in performing dozens of unnecessary, substandard operations, persuading patients with threats and false diagnoses, writing fraudulent progress notes, and altering recommendations of consultants. Judge Goldberg condemned the state medical board, the county medical society, and the local hospitals for their ignorance of Nork's behavior, for participating in a "conspiracy of silence," and for not disciplining Nork for repeated incidents of malpractice over an eight-year period.[2]

The president of the local medical society was "shaken" by "this historic attack on peer review," and launched an investigation into possible canon-of-ethic violations in the reporting of peers' misconduct (Otten, 1974:3). Three months later the state disciplinary board, which first learned of Nork's activities from the newspapers, revoked the doctor's license on the grounds of unprofessional conduct. Such actions did little to allay the acute embarrassment of the state medical association and state board, each of which had publicly asserted several weeks before the Nork decision that they were "cracking down" on negligent and incompetent doctors who were not, in any case, a problem in the state (*Medical World News*, 1974).

Clearly, professional disciplinary bodies were ineffective in detecting and controlling substandard professional performance. Moreover, the apparent need for litigation to protect patient welfare led state legislative committees and the public to question whether the profession's right to police itself should be curtailed (Altman, 1973b; Cater and Rosenfeld, 1976; *Medical World News*, 1975; New York State Assembly, 1977; Otten, 1973b; Rosenfeld, 1977; Sheridan, 1974). In addition, the Nork case introduced the possibility of holding medical practitioners and institutions legally liable for failure to practice effective peer review. An earlier landmark decision in *Darling v. Charleston Community Hospital* (1968) held the hospital liable for failing to comply with the standards of state licensing agencies or the Joint Commission on Accreditation of Hospitals, a private trade organization, in establishing policies that provide a setting for acceptable medical care. The Nork case expanded that decision by holding that compliance with such standards did not sufficiently demonstrate that the hospital practiced reasonable care in protecting its patients against medical incompetence and fraud, and held the hospital responsible for the conduct of its attending staff, whether it knew of malpractice, had reason to know, or should have known. In *Corleto v. Shore Memorial Hospital* (1975), a New Jersey Court of Appeals further expanded the concept of corporate liability by ruling that the entire hospital staff could be held liable for negligence in improperly awarding staff privileges.

It was within this context of widespread, intense concern with professional performance and ineffective professional discipline that organized medicine officially recognized and addressed the special challenge to accountability that was believed to be posed by physician addiction, alcoholism, and mental disorders. It is important to note that the AMA's recognition of sick doctors and the subsequent development of impaired physicians programs and statutes were not associated with an escalation in the incidence of physician addiction and alcoholism. Virtually no discussion of the problem and its solution suggests or documents increasing numbers of sick doctors. As Parker (1977:731) observed: "the need had been apparent for many ears . . . but programs for the detection and recognition of physicians with disabling problems . . . did not previously appear to be an urgent obligation to those 'in charge'." Indeed, as far back as 1958, the Federation of State Medical Boards in the United States identified drug addiction and alcoholism among doctors as a pressing disciplinary problem and called for the development of a model program of probation and rehabilitation that could be adopted by individual state boards (Glaspel, 1958). A decade later, the federation approved a resolution calling for a nationwide program, to be developed in cooperation with the AMA and other professional groups, that would educate doctors about the frequency and dangers of narcotic addiction. Yet the resolution, introduced by the Oregon board, received scant attention at the AMA's annual meeting. The federation recalled: "Every effort to excite interest in the problem (even the recognition that there was a problem) failed" (Casterline, 1973a:30).

It was not the perceived changes in the dimension of the problem, but the prevailing political, social, and economic climate of the 1970s that set the stage for the medicalization of professional self-governance. The problem of sick doctors was brought into focus by external pressures which forced the profession to discipline its members more effectively, or at least symbolically demonstrate its commitment to such a task. Thus, of the 24 impaired physician programs responding to the particular survey question, 47 percent referred to general pressures for accountability stemming from the malpractice situation (including legal liabilities of practitioners and institutions) and state and federal regulation of health care services. Speaking at the third AMA conference on physician impairment, one physician warned:

> As a profession, we accept the principle of monitoring ourselves, realizing that if we do not do this effectively, it will be done for us. Much is at stake— the public's life, health, and trust in the profession; the welfare and reputation of the impaired physician; and the welfare and autonomy of the profession (Robertson, 1978:38).

A strong public outcry for the control of sick doctors does not fully account for the profession's interest in them. Of the 21 impaired physician programs responding to the particular survey question, 28 percent linked the founding of their program to an increased number of complaints about sick doctors; only 19 percent said that the public interest in the specific problem of impairment was important. Moreover, while respondents referred to the malpractice situation, several also acknowledged that malpractice actions rarely allege physician impairment.[3] Finally, even had there been a distinct and widespread public outcry for the control of sick doctors, that would not explain how and why the profession chose to conceptualize and manage such doctors as "impaired physicians" rather than incompetent or unscrupulous malefactors. It was, in the final analysis, organized medicine and not consumers or government watchdogs that systematically drew attention to—indeed, discovered—the special problem of physician impairment, and, in doing so, proposed a comprehensive, systematic, and distinctly medical approach to problem doctors.

Medicalizing Professional Social Control

THE "DISCOVERY" OF PHYSICIAN IMPAIRMENT

An important landmark in the history of the organized campaign to identify and control physician impairment was a policy paper prepared by the AMA Council on Mental Health entitled "The sick physician: Impairment by psychiatric-disorders, including alcoholism and drug dependence" (AMA, 1973). The report, which was prepared for the board of trustees and adopted as policy by the House of Delegates in November 1972, marked the AMA's first official recognition of the problem and the extent to which sick doctors challenged the profession's ability to prevent, detect, account for, and control substandard professional performance.

Of the nine doctors serving on the Council of Mental Health, the psychiatrist Rogers Smith was instrumental in alerting the AMA to the problems posed by impaired physicians. As co-founder of Oregon's fraternal organization, Friends of Medicine,

Smith had become sensitive to the personal suffering, the risk to patient welfare, and the sheer waste of human resources associated with physicians impairment. He became committed to rehabilitating sick doctors with "minimal loss of self-esteem, professional status, and service to his community" (Crawshaw, 1977:3). Smith revived the issues raised by the neglected Oregon resolution of 1967, and won praise from the Federation of State Medical Boards as "the leading contender for the reward for opening the eyes (and the minds)" of the AMA (Casterline, 1973a:30).

Smith, together with his colleagues and staff at the AMA, began investigating the problem by surveying the activities of the nation's state medical associations. They found that seven associations had an identifiable committee dealing with he problem and another seven indicated some interest in the problem. Twenty-three states reported that they lacked any program to deal with the problem, and three vehemently denied that the problem existed. Almost one-third of the associations did not respond, suggesting to the AMA either indifference or denial or the problem (AMA, 1973). Notwithstanding most states' lack of interest in the problem, the survey, together with available clinical reports and the statistical experience of three state boards, convinced the council that "we did, indeed, have a problem on our hands" (Smith, 1979:260).

The subsequent report firmly located the problem of sick doctors within the context of professional self-governance, outlined a systematic and comprehensive program for dealing with physician impairment, and urged doctors to support the new effort, claiming it was a "physician's ethical responsibility to take cognizance of a colleague's inability to practice medicine adequately" by reason of medical impairment (AMA, 1973:684). The council recommended a sequence of disciplinary interventions, beginning with informal personal efforts to persuade sick colleagues to enter treatment. But if these efforts failed, colleagues should refer sick doctors to a special committee of the hospital medical staff. If the hospital could not act effectively or chose not to, concerned colleagues should refer cases to a special committee of the medical society. In either event, colleagues were urged to persuade sick doctors to enter treatment voluntarily, for in addition to the impact of physician impairment on professional accountability for patient care, "an equally important issue is the effective treatment and rehabilitation of the physician-patient so that he can be restored to a useful lie" (AMA, 1973:684). Given the profession's dual commitment to physician rehabilitation and patient welfare, sick doctors who could not be persuaded to enter treatment voluntarily should, according to the council, be referred to the coercive state disciplinary board which could compel them to seek treatment at the risk of losing their license.

Thus, colleagues were urged to route sick doctors through an increasingly formal, coercive, and punitive series of disciplinary agencies, moving from the hospital to the medical society and, finally, to the state disciplinary board. Throughout, the emphasis was not on punishment, but rehabilitation. Punitive measures, such as loss of license, were to be invoked only when a sick doctor refused treatment and continued to endanger patients.

Given the absence at the time of any systematic program by organized medicine to identify, rehabilitate, and control sick doctors, the AMA policy paper in effect "discovered" impairment as a disciplinary problem that needed to be managed within the context of professional self-governance. The discovery galvanized the medical profession into action. Indeed, the profession's campaign to identify and rehabilitate impaired doctors has proceeded at so fast a pace that one doctor I interviewed likened the momentum to the spread of the Bubonic plague.

THE DIFFUSION OF THE CONCEPT OF PHYSICIAN IMPAIRMENT

The new approach to sick doctors has been the subject of five national conferences sponsored by the AMA since April 1975. The conferences clarified the scope of the problem of physician impairment and its implications for professional performance, reviewed the relevant activities of medical societies, licensing boards and hospitals, and discussed specific aspects of prevention, case finding, confrontation techniques, law enforcement, and the adjustment problems of the recovering physician (Hugunin, 1977; Robertson, 1978, 1980; Steindler, 1975). Together with numerous regional and state conferences, the national meetings helped arouse professional and public interest in the problem, provided a setting for interpersonal exchanges and influence, and fostered the development of information and support networks within the campaign's band of devoted pioneers and champions.

The new approach to physician impairment was further promoted and clarified in policy papers issued by state and local medical societies which, characteristically, duplicated sections of the AMA's 1973 report. Newsletters such as the AMA's *Impaired Physician Newsletter,* launched in 1978, and the California Medical Association's *What You Need to Know about Physician Impairment*, begun in 1977, disseminated information to doctors and interested lay people. Medical societies sponsored education drives, urging that "members of medical groups and their families must be made aware that alcoholism and other addictive diseases and most psychiatric disorders are treatable diseases, not moral weaknesses and not synonymous with social disgrace" (Talbott *et al.,* 1977:777). Articles in professional journals, trade magazines, and the popular press investigated the scope and significance of physician impairment (Bloom, 1978; Luy, 1976; Rensberger, 1977), considered its ethical, legal, and social aspects (Annas, 1978; Ludlam, 1978), and examined the activities of new impaired physician programs (Clinger, 1977; Rosenberg, 1979). Finally, confessionals by recovered or currently addicted and alcoholic doctors appeared as a new genre of professional literature and hammered home the lesson that the profession could not afford, morally and politically, to ignore sick doctors (Chapman, 1978b; Miller, 1977; Newsom, 1978).

By clarifying the scope of physician impairment and emphasizing the medical roots of substandard professional performance and the importance of rehabilitation, these policy statements, conferences, educational campaigns, articles, and confessionals together promoted the new medical perspective outlined in the AMA's pioneering paper.

LEGITIMATION AND INSTITUTIONALIZATION OF THE NEW PERSPECTIVE

Physician impairment quickly became accepted as a disciplinary problem that deserved a significant share of the profession's disciplinary resources. At its second national conference in 1977 the AMA officially recognized the "psychiatrically disturbed physician whose professional competence is undermined by his failure to recognize his own physical disability, his irrational or psychotic behavior, his senility, or his addiction to sedative or narcotic drugs" (Palmer, 1977:1). This definition was part of a broader classification scheme used to distinguish varieties of problem doctors and patterns of management; also included were "incompetent" doctors who needed to be retrained and "malicious" doctors who performed "unethical acts for their own reward" and who were to be dealt with through legal channels (Palmer, 1977:1). Journal articles and scholarly reports appeared with such titles as "The unethical and the impaired physician: Distinguishing criteria" (Homlish, 1979), "Medical discipline: Dealing with physicians who are unscrupulous, disabled, and/or incompetent" (*New York State Journal of Medicine*, 1979), and "Medico-legal implications of the incompetent, errant, and 'sick' physician" (Hirsh, 1977).

The concept of physician impairment was further institutionalized through bureaucratization; organizations were founded which implemented the medial perspective directly, by engaging in medical diagnosis and making referrals to treatment, and indirectly by promoting and seeking support for their activities. By 1980, less than a decade after the AMA's pioneering policy appear, all but three of the 54 U.S. medical societies of all states and jurisdictions had authorized or implemented impaired physician programs, a sharp increase from the seven societies reporting some type of program in 1972 (Robertson, 1980). The programs confront sick doctors with their problem, persuade them to enter treatment and monitor their rehabilitation and re-entry into practice.

The new medical perspective was also codified in so-called "sick doctor statutes" or amendments.[4] Given the state's legal jurisdiction over problem doctors and its exclusive right to apply the ultimate disciplinary sanction (license revocation), state government support for the concept of physician impairment and the associated changes in professional self-governance was an important force in the impaired physician campaign.

The sick doctor amendments to state medical practice acts are based on the model Disabled Physician Act prepared by the AMA (AMA, 1975). They expand the powers of the state regulatory agencies which had up until the time of amendment been authorized to restrict a doctors' practice for reason of illness only upon proof of fault, or in the case of mental illness only when the doctor had been legally declared incompetent or committed to an institution. The new state laws radically revise disciplinary procedures by broadening the states' jurisdiction to include cases in which sick doctors have not actually caused injury to patients, but give probable cause to believe that they are unable to practice medicine with "reasonable skill and safety because of "physical or mental illness, including deterioration through the aging process or loss of motor skill, or abuse of drugs, including alcohol" (AMA, 1975). The statutes emphasize early rehabilitative intervention and authorize the state to perform diagnostic physical and mental examination of suspected doctors, determine their fitness to practice medicine, and impose a variety of protective or corrective measures, including counseling and restriction of practice.

By October 1980, sick doctor amendments had been enacted in 39 states, a dramatic leap from the two states having such statutes in 1972 (*Legal Aspects of Medical Practice*, 1980). While it is too early to assess the effects of the amendments, it appears that instead of losing their license sick doctors are being placed on probation while receiving rehabilitative treatment monitored and approved by the state board (AMA, 1976).

Leaders in the Impaired Physician Campaign

The widespread enactment of sick doctor statutes and the establishment of impaired physician programs signify the relative permanence of the new medical perspective on professional social control. This successful institutionalization of the medical model reflects the vigorous efforts of a small band of dedicated individuals, virtually all of whom were physicians. In the language of Becker (1963:162), these doctors acted as "moral entrepreneurs" who worked vigorously to arouse interest in physician impairment, make people "feel that something ought to be done about it, . . . supply the push necessary to get things done, and direct such energies as are aroused in the proper direction to get a rule created."

For the purpose of this survey I defined leaders in the impaired physician campaign as those who were official speakers at the AMA's first national conference on physician impairment in 1975 and those who funded or chaired medical society impaired physician programs. While both groups of leaders were instrumental in promoting and institutionalizing the concept of physician impairment, the latter acted largely at the local level while the former participated in a nationwide information and support network and provided guidance across the nation. These individuals took time off from busy professional practices to volunteer their efforts; medical societies reimbursed them to various degrees for out-of-pocket expenses such as travel. They lectured, led workshops at national and regional conferences, served as advisors to fledgling programs, and published or were cited in journal articles discussing the newly identified challenge to professional accountability. Using these criteria I identified 67 leaders: 21 national, 46 local, and four working at both levels.

PSYCHIATRIC LEADERSHIP

Forty-six percent of all leaders (44 percent of local, 40 percent of national) were either certified psychiatrists or certified psychiatrist-neurologists. No other single specialty was as heavily represented. In addition, of a total of 313 members of 21 impaired physician programs, 25 percent were psychiatrists, compared with 18 percent in family practice, 14 percent in internal medicine, 10 percent in surgery, and 4 percent in obstetrics-gynecology.

Psychiatric leadership may be explained in part by psychiatrists' presumed effectiveness in establishing rapport with the mentally and physically disabled, assessing their self-destructive tendencies, and persuading them to seek treatment. Given their training and experience, psychiatrists probably make good confronters and consultants helping confronters "anticipate and handle sick doctors' reactions" (Robertson, 1978:28). In addition, psychiatrists' research interests in emotional disturbances and strategies of intervention in denial systems fostered their involvement in impaired physician programs. Much of the literature on the etiology, incidence, and treatment of behavioral and emotional disorders in doctors derives from research conducted by psychiatrists and presented at annual meetings of the American Psychiatric Association.

The involvement of psychiatrists also reflects the AMA's position that the impaired physician requires psychiatric intervention. In its 1973 position paper the AMA recommended that impaired physician programs "should comprise examining physicians including, but not limited to, psychiatrists and neurologists" (AMA, 1973:684). Four years later at is second national conference on physician impairment the AMA officially declared that impaired physicians need psychiatric attention (Palmer, 1977). As Gitlow (1979) later explained, while doctors may be physically disabled, the disability becomes a disciplinary problem only if they do not appreciate reality—that is, the extent to which their disability affects their professional performance. Following the AMA's recognition of impairment, the American Psychiatric Association which had, since 1958, included sessions on the problem at its annual meetings, broadened its involvement by appointing task forces on physician suicide (1973) and physician impairment (1979), educating district branches about the problem, and assessing available psychiatric services and insurance coverage for physicians (Robertson, 1980).

THE INFLUENCE OF THE FORMERLY IMPAIRED

A second group of doctors who strongly influenced the character of the emerging response to sick doctors were recovered addicts and alcoholics. While data on the backgrounds of local and national leaders were not available, I was able to document the participation of recovered doctors in impaired physician programs. The survey that I conducted in 1979 found that of the 19 state medical societies responding to the particular question—more than half of all societies with active programs at the time—only five did not include at least one recovered doctor; of 274 program members, 19 percent were formerly impaired.

The personal experience and insight of formerly impaired doctors and their living demonstration of the possibility of recovery and renewed professional respectability are believed to make them especially effective in healing sick colleagues to enter treatment. In addition, the openness of recovered doctors promotes a view of impairment as unfortunate but morally neutral, thereby reducing the stigma of sick doctors and improving in turn their chances of recovery. In light of the contribution that the formerly impaired may take to the recovery of others, a number of impaired physician programs encourage and in some cases require recovered doctors to participate in the program as confronters.

The disclosure of former impairment and active participation in the rehabilitation programs can benefit the recovered doctor as well. In several cases disclosure has boosted colleagues' respect for the doctors' frankness and fortitude and increased their credibility as confronters and consultants (Cruse, 1978; Miller, 1977; Newsom, 1978). In addition, maintaining physician impairment as a problem of high priority, educating the professional community about the non-volitional character of alcohol and drug abuse, and carrying the message of recovery to troubled colleagues are ways the many doctors associated with Alcoholics Anonymous can spread the word about AA—"twelfth step work" it is called. Indeed, critics and admirers alike recognize the missionary fervor of the formerly impaired and commonly refer to them as crusaders or zealots.

Professional Ideology and the Appeal of the Medical Model

Given the widespread and rapid diffusion of the concept of physician impairment, we need to examine its appeal not only for such special interest groups as psychiatrists and the formerly impaired, but for the general professional community as well. Acceptance of a medical approach to problem doctors reflects in part the presumed effectiveness of medical treatment in alleviating pain and suffering. However, acceptance of a medical model of deviance depends on more than the presumed or demonstrated benefits of medical technology.[5] As Friedson (1970:251) has demonstrated, medicine's jurisdiction "over the label illness and anything to which it may be attached [is awarded] irrespective of its capacity to deal with it effectively." As such, we need to consider the extent to which the model in question not only effectively controls deviance but also serves other ideological and political functions (Chambliss, 1964; Currie, 1968). Specifically, the unprecedented and dramatic interest in sick doctors, the numerous national and regional conferences and articles, and the rapid enactment of impaired physician programs and statutes, point not only to the presumed effectiveness of the medical model, but also its compatibility with professional beliefs, values, and interests. The new approach to professional deviance constitutes not only a practical means of protecting patient welfare and rehabilitating sick doctors, but also a symbolic affirmation of basic professional ideas and norms

Clearly, a medical model of professional self-governance articulates the profession's basic mandate and mission to identify and control illness through medical treatment: "As practitioners of the healing arts, we more than any other group, should favor treatment and/or rehabilitation of our disabled colleagues above any other alternative" (Kansas Medical Society, n.d.) . In their commitment to medical diagnosis and treatment, doctors redefine as nonculpable illness what may alternatively be viewed as moral weakness, ignorance, or malice.[6] In this case, by interpreting behavior along the health-illness dimension rather than the good-bad dimension, the medical model does not blame problem doctors, viewing alcoholic and addicted doctors as victims of "a disease that's no more shameful than a bout with pneumonia" (Miller, 1977:192). "There is no room here for the moralistic judgmental attitudes that often impede discussions of such problems," the chair of one impaired physician program cautioned. "We are concerned here with sick physicians rather than bad physicians" (Ayres, n.d.).

A nonjudgmental approach means that doctors may acknowledge substandard performance as undesirable, while retaining faith in colleagues' basic trustworthiness and integrity, and participating in a regulatory system which treats problem doctors with respect and dignity and protects them from (presumably) ineffective punitive sanctions and unwarranted moral criticism. A system of social control that is based on the medical model does not challenge doctors' natural reluctance to criticize fellow members of the professional guild; indeed, it builds upon doctors' fellowship and brotherly concern.

An additional appeal of the medical model lies in its individualization of the problem. As it has been developed by the medical profession in the United States, the traditional medical model locates the causes of and solutions to problems in the attributes of the individual rather than the surrounding structure or context. In the case of sick doctors, impaired physician programs recognize the extent to which addiction, alcoholism, and mental disorders constitute "occupational hazards." However, they have (especially in their early years) focused corrective efforts on providing referrals for individual therapy and counseling rather than restructuring stressful patterns in medical practice and training. By focusing on the individual problem doctor, the programs discourage both doctors and the public from feeling that addiction, incompetence, and unethical conduct are inevitable outcomes of medical education and practice (Weinstein, 1978).

Finally, the medical model pairs misconduct with illness and defines substandard performance as a medical problem to be treated by medical experts. It extends the profession's mandate as healers to include the management of problem doctors whose misconduct may be construed as an outcome or symptom of illness. Such a system of self-governance, based on the medical model, safeguards the profession's control over its members and discourages intervention by government and other would-be regulators.

Impaired physician programs could reduce the scope of official state control over problem doctors who are defined as sick. In its 1973 policy paper, the AMA cast state board action as a "last resort." Medical societies and hospitals were to have initial jurisdiction over impaired doctors, and medical societies were to retain advisory powers even after state boards entered the case. As later outlined in the AMA's model Disabled Physician Act, the state board was to authorize the state medical society to determine the doctor's fitness to safely practice medicine and make recommendations concerning the doctor's continued practice.

Reducing the state disciplinary board to a "last resort" ruffled the feathers of the Federation of State Medical Boards, which initially argued that "hospital staff and medical society committee persuasion . . . seldom has adequate muscle to move the deviant physician toward proper management of his problem," producing a greater risk of self-treatment, unsupervised low quality of medical practice, and delayed entry into treatment. In contrast, by "acting with compassion, yet firmness," and by judiciously using their authority to compel examination and treatment upon pain of license revocation, state boards, it was claimed, could successfully rehabilitate the addicted and alcoholic doctors (Casterline, 1973b). The federation's protests reflected their concern over jurisdiction and over the absence of effective activities by organized medicine. In some states, disciplinary boards and medical societies have not resolved their differences, and physicians and legislators regularly debate the limits of autonomous self-governance. However, the survey that I conducted found that 81 percent of the 24 medical societies responding to the particular question reported satisfaction with the board's support of their efforts on behalf of impaired physicians. Where the relationship is harmonious, medical society programs derive strength from the very existence of coercive state disciplinary bodies; moreover, understaffed, underfinanced disciplinary boards appreciate outside support.

Many impaired physician programs now act in an informal or official advisory capacity for state boards, and a handful have been formally authorized to reroute impaired doctors from state board proceedings into their medically oriented treatment programs. Characteristically, the so-called "diversion program" is empowered to evaluate the extent of impairment, prepare a treatment program, monitor treatment, and recommend when and under what conditions the doctor should resume practice (*LACMA Physician*, 1980). By persuading doctors to enter treatment on pain of referral to the state board, and by implementing diversion programs, medical societies have assumed the very role envisioned by the federation for state boards—that is, a compassionate yet firm approach that rehabilitates sick doctors while safeguarding public welfare. By deferring disciplinary action for as long as the doctor continues to receive effective supervised treatment, state boards narrow *their* jurisdiction to recalcitrant or severely impaired doctors who pose a manifest danger to patient welfare.

In sum, diffusion of the medical model of social control has been hastened by the model's compatibility with the profession's mandate as healers, doctors' natural preference for nonjudgmental rehabilitation rather than punishment of colleagues, medicine's tradition of individual explanations for deviance, and the profession's commitment to self-governance. The language of medical social control summarizes these beliefs, perceptions, and expectations, and structures appropriate actions. "Impairment" commonly connotes a medical, nonculpable disability. And the names of impaired physician programs—"Assistance Program for Troubled Physicians" (Iowa), "Physicians' Concerned Committee" (Maine), "Physicians' Care Committee" (Oklahoma), to cite some representative examples—and such slogans as "physician advocacy" and "brother's keeper" evoke compassion, tolerance, and concrete collegial help.

At this point it is important to note, as Schur (1979:21) has observed, that the compatibility that exists between the medical model and professional culture and interests does not mean that medicalization must necessarily "represent some kind of conscious conspiracy on the part of doctors." The point is that, to the profession, the concept of physician impairment and the associated mechanisms of social control seem logical and meaningful. Indeed, for some doctors the rehabilitation of sick doctors has acquired the character of a moral imperative: "there are . . . a number of compelling reasons why we must confront the problem of the sick physician. But the basic reason, the one which we cannot ignore, is simply that it is Right" (Stewart, 1977:329).

The Social and Cultural Components of Professional Self-Governance

The newly designed impaired physician programs, policies, and statutes highlight the extent to which self-governance is not only a practical activity, but also a symbolic expression of the basic professional beliefs and values that underlie medical practice and influence colleagues' relations with each other, with patients, and with the public. Doctors' humanitarian and political motivations have shaped a new disciplinary policy that allows concerned colleagues to help and rehabilitate problem doctors while also protecting patients and safeguarding the profession's privilege of autonomous self-regulation.

The emerging mechanisms of professional control described here differ in important ways from the peer review processes documented in the research of the past decade. Professional values and attitudes have previously shaped a system of self-regulation that maximizes the autonomy and independence of the individual practitioners and minimizes their accountability to colleagues and the public. Conceptions of professional work and workers have reduced the visibility of doctors' performance, discouraged doctors from using the formal sanctions at their disposal, and led colleagues to avoid open criticism of their peers and maintain formal courtesy even under such trying conditions as mortality review conferences, where the management of deceased patients is scrutinized (Arluke, 1978; Burkett and Knafl, 1975; Freidson, 1975; Goss, 1961; Light, 1972; Millman, 1977; Morrow, 1976). In contrast, impaired physician programs view the problem doctor as a morally innocent patient and cast the disciplinary agent as medical diagnostician and healer. As such, the act as advocates *for* the doctor, and commit themselves to early identification, frank confrontation, and nonjudgmental rehabilitative intervention. Their concerned rehabilitative posture encourages otherwise reluctant doctors to identify impairment, identify misconduct that is a symptom or outcome of impairment, report that condition to an impaired physician program, and confront the sick doctor.

The unique impact of a medical model of professional social control derives from the extent to which it complements, rather than challenges, basic professional beliefs, values, and interests. The drive to identify and rehabilitate impaired physicians, which grew under the threat of public criticism and increasing government restriction is an ideologically convenient way to humanely control errant colleagues, promote public trust, and strengthen professional autonomy.

Notes

1. In fact, critics found that state disciplinary boards were extraordinarily lax. Between 1964 and 1974 state boards took less than 2,000 formal actions ranging from reprimand to license revocation against a physician population of about 300,000. Between 1970 and 1975 no more than eight doctors were disciplined for incompetence (Derbyshire, 1974; Law and Polan, 1978).

2. Nork was later named as defendant in more than 40 malpractice cases.

3. Evidence from the California and New York State medical boards suggests that there is no relationship between impairment and the likelihood of being sued for malpractice (Robertson, 1980).

4. Legitimation and institutionalization as stages in the acceptance of new deviance designations, and codification and bureaucratization as two general types of institutionalization, are discussed in Conrad and Schneider (1980).

5. See, for example, Conrad and Schneider (1980) on medical conceptions of madness and homosexuality, and Sutherland (1950) on the development of sexual psychopath laws.

6. See Bittner (1968) for a more general discussion of the processes by which social control professions seek and find manifestations of the problems lying within their jurisdiction.

References

Altman, Lawrence K. 1973a. "Medical society faces discipline issues." The New York Times, February 25:1, 48.

———. 1973b. "A.M.A. urges discipline of incompetent physicians." The New York Times, October 29: 1, 7.

American Hospital Association. 1973. A Patient's Bill of Rights. Pamphlet. Chicago: American Hospital Association.

American Medical Association (AMA). 1973. "The sick physician: Impairment by psychiatric disorders, including alcoholism and drug dependence. " Prepared by the Council on Mental Health of the American Medical Association. Journal of the American Medical Association 223 (February 5):684–687.

———. 1975. "Disabled physician act." A model legislative bill prepared by the Legislative Department of the American Medical Association. Pp. 40–48 in Emanuel M. Steindler (ed.), The Impaired Physician: An Interpretive Summary of the AMA Conference on "The Disabled Doctor: Challenge to the Profession." Chicago: American Medical Association.

———. 1976. "Final report of the ad hoc committee on medical discipline." Proceedings of the AMA House of Delegates (December): 49–56.

———. 1977. "An act relating to the improvement of medical discipline." A model legislative bill prepared by the Legislative Department of the American Medical Association. Pp. 78–84 in Mary B. Hugunin (ed.), Helping the Impaired Physician: Proceedings of the AMA Conference on "The Impaired Physician: Answering the Challenge." Chicago: American Medical Association.

Annas, George J. 1978. "Who to call when the doctor is sick." Hastings Center Report 8 (December):18–20.

Anslinger, Harry, and K. W. Chapman. 1957. "Narcotic addiction: An interview." Modern Medicine 25 (October 15):170–171.

Arluke, Arnold. 1978. "Beginner's license: Problems of social control in the context of professional education." Unpublished Ph.D. dissertation, New York University.

Ayres, Perry n.d. "Physician effectiveness program: Ohio State Medical Association." Mimeograph. Columbus, Ohio: State Medical Association.

Becker, Howard S. 1963. Outsiders: Studies in the Sociology of Deviance. New York: Free Press.

Bissell, LeClaire, and Robert Jones. 1976. "The alcoholic physician: A survey." American Journal of Psychology 133 (October):1142–1146.

Bittner, Egon. 1968. "The structure of psychiatric influence." Mental Hygiene 52 (July):423–430.

Blachly, P.H. W. Disher, and G. Rodner. 1968. "Suicide by physicians." Bulletin of Suicidology 118 (December):1–18.

Bloom, Mark. 1978. "Impaired physicians: Medicine bites the bullet." Medical World News 19 (July 24):40–51.

Brody, Jane E. 1972. "Medical society to ask Jacobson to meeting." The New York Times, December 8:16.

Burkett, Gary and Kathleen Knafl. 1975. "Judgment and decision-making in a medical specialty." Sociology of Work and Occupations 1 (February):82–109.

Carter, A.J., and Neill S. Rosenfeld. 1976. "Ex-Suffolk MD leaves legacy of malpractice." Newsday, February 8:5, 19.

Casterline, Ray L. 1973a. "Rogers Smith and the hot potato resolution." Federation Bulletin [Federation of State Medical Boards in the United States] 60 (January):29–30.

———. 1973b. "Physician, heal thyself." Federation Bulletin [Federation of State Medical Boards in the United States] 60 (January):31–33.

Chambliss, William J. 1964. "A sociological analysis of the law of vagrancy." Social Problems 12 (Fall):66–77.

Chapman, Stu. 1978a. "Medicine cleans its house." Legal Aspects of Medical Practice 6 (November):30–40.

———. 1978b. "I am a reformed alcoholic and I am a doctor." Legal Aspects of Medical Practice 6 (November):47–49.

Clinger, Robert D. 1977. "The OSMA physician effectiveness program: How it operates." Ohio State Medical Journal 45 (November):734–735.

Conrad, Peter, and Joseph W. Schneider. 1980. Deviance and Medicalization: From Badness to Sickness. St. Louis, Missouri: C.V. Mosby.

Crawshaw, Ralph. 1977. "The friends of medicine." Unpublished paper presented at the 6th World Congress of Psychiatry, Honolulu, September.

Cruse, Joseph. 1978. "The conspiracy of silence." Pp. 79–85 in California Medical Association, Conference Proceedings: What You Need to Know about Impairment in Physicians. San Francisco: California Medical Association.

Currie, Elliot P. 1968. "Crimes without criminals: Witchcraft and its control in Renaissance Europe." Law and Society Review 3 (August):7–32.

Denenberg, Herbert. 1972. A Shopper's Guide to Surgery: Fourteen Rules on How to Avoid Unnecessary Surgery. Pamphlet. Chicago: Blue Cross Association.

Department of Health, Education and Welfare. 1973. Medical Malpractice: Report of the Secretary's Commission on Medical Malpractice. Department of Health, Education and Welfare Publication No. (OS) 73–88, January 16.

Derbyshire, Robert C. 1965. "Report: What should the profession do about the incompetent physician?" Journal of the American Medical Association 194 (December 20):1287–1290.

———. 1974. "Medical ethics and discipline." Journal of the American Medical Association 228 (April):59–62.

———. 1979. "Physician competence: What is the problem? What are the answers?" New York State Journal of Medicine 79 (June):1028–1031.

Ferguson, Tom. 1977. "The self-care concept." Medical Self-Care 2 (1):4–5.

Friedson, Eliot. 1970. Profession of Medicine: A Study of the Sociology of Applied Knowledge. New York: Dodd, Mead.

———. 1975. Doctoring Together: A Study of Professional Social Control. New York: Elsevier.

Gitlow, Stanley E. 1979. Opening remarks to "Medical discipline: Dealing with physicians who are unscrupulous, disabled or incompetent. A symposium." New York State Journal of Medicine 79 (June):1019–1021.

Glaspel, C. J. 1958. "Problems in narcotic addiction." Federation Bulletin [Federation of State Medical Boards in the United States] 45 (July):200–207.

Goss, Mary E. W. 1961. "Influence and authority among physicians in an outpatient clinic." American Sociological Review 26 (February):39–50.

Hicks, Nancy. 1974. "A.M.A. faces rift on peer review." The New York Times, June 24:8.

Hirsh, Harold. 1977. "Medico-legal implications of the incompetent, errant, and 'sick' physician: Changing times." Southern Medical Journal 70 (April):421–425.

Homlish, John S. 1979. "The unethical and the impaired physician: Distinguishing criteria." Newsletter of the Kansas District Branch of the American Psychiatric Association 3(Fall):6–10.

Hugunin, Mary B. (ed.). 1977. Helping the Impaired Physician: Proceedings of the AMA Conference on "The Impaired Physician: Answering the Challenge." Chicago: American Medical Association.

Kansas Medical Society. n.d. Education, Advocation, Rehabilitation. Pamphlet. Topeka, Kansas: Kansas Medical Association.

LACMA Physician. 1980. "BMQA's new diversion program: Rehabilitation, yes, recrimination, no." 119 (January):33.

Lander, Louise. 1978. Defective Medicine: Risk, Anger and the Malpractice Crisis. New York: Farrar, Straus, Giroux.

Law, Sylvia, and Stephen Polan. 1978. Pain and Profit: The Politics of Malpractice. New York: Harper and Row.

Legal Aspects of Medical Practice. 1980. "What can you do about an impaired physician?" 8(April):40–49.

Light, Donald W. Jr. 1972. "Psychiatry and suicide: The management of a mistake." American Journal of Sociology 77 (March):821–838.

Ludlum, James E. 1978. "The legal perspective: Helping the impaired physician." Trustee (October):17–22.

Luy, Mary Lynn M. 1976. "How you can spot—and help—your troubled colleague." Modern Medicine 44(February):28–32.

Medical World News. 1972. "Getting addicted MDs off the hook." 13 (December 15):21.

———. 1974. "How well does medicine police itself?" 15 (March 15):62–72.

———. 1975. "Sex 'malpractice' costs MD $350,000." 16 (May 5):37–40.

Miller, T. Rothrock. 1977. "My life as an alcoholic doctor." Medical Economics 54 (December 12):192–208.

Millman, Marcia. 1977. The Unkindest Cut. New York: Morrow.

Modlin, Herbert C., and A. Montes. 1964. "Narcotic addiction in physicians." American Journal of Psychiatry 121 (October):358–365.

Morrow, Carol Klaperman. 1976. Health Care Guidance: Commercial Health Insurance and National Health Policy. New York: Praeger.

———. 1981. "Sick doctors: The medicalization of self-governance in the profession of medicine." Unpublished Ph.D. dissertation, New York University.

Newsom, John. 1978. "Too young to be an alcoholic." Pp. 69–78 in California Medical Association, Conference Proceedings: What You Need to Know About Physician Impairment. San Francisco: California Medical Association.

New York Medicine. 1974. "State society to ask for power to discipline MDs." November: 381–383, 386–388.

New York State Assembly. 1977. First Interim Report on Medical Problems in the State of New York. Committees on Health and Insurance, New York State Assembly, Albany, N.Y., May 10.

New York State Journal of Medicine. 1979. "Medical discipline: Dealing with physicians who are unscrupulous, disabled and/or incompetent. A symposium." 79(June):1018–1041.

Otten, Michael. 1973a. "The costly burden of malpractice." Sacramento Union, December 24:sec. A, pp. 1–2.

———. 1973b. "State criticized over Nork." Sacramento Union, December 21: sec. A, pp. 1, 3.

———. 1974. "Nork judge scored for broad attacks." Sacramento Union, January 7:sec A, p. 3.

Palmer, George S. 1975. "The sick doctor statute: A new approach to an old problem." Paper presented at a conference of the American Medical Association on "The Disabled Doctor: Challenge to the Profession." San Francisco, April 11–12.

Palmer, Richard E. 1977. "The three impairments." Pp. 1–3 in Mary Hugunin (ed.), Helping the Impaired Physician: Proceedings of the AMA Conference on "The Imparied Physician: Answering the Challenge." Chicago: American Medical Association.

Parker, Milton. 1977. "The OSMA physician effectiveness program." Ohio State Medical Journal 73 (November):731.

Rensberger, Boyce. 1972. "Amphetamines used by a physician to lift moods of famous patients." The New York Times, December 4:1, 34.

———. 1975a. "Death of 2 doctors poses a fitness issue." The New York Times, August 15:1, 32.

———. 1975b. "New York Hospital defends its actions on Marcus twins." The New York Times, August 19:1, 29.

———. 1977. "The doctors who need the care of other doctors." The New York Times, May 1:sec. E, p. 8.

Robertson, Janice J. (ed.) 1978. Proceedings of the Third AMA Conference on the Imparied Physician. Chicago: American Medical Association.

———. 1980. The Impaired Physician: Building Well-Being. Proceedings of the Fourth AMA Conference on the Impaired Physician. Chicago: American Medical Association.

Rosenberg, Charlotte. 1979. "Doctor rehabilitation: It is working." Medical Economics 51 (November 26):114–117, 120–122.

Rosenfeld, Neill S. 1977. "When a medical exam is abuse." Newsday, February 21:5, 30.

Schur, Edwin M. 1979. Interpreting Deviance: A Sociological Introduction. New York: Harper and Row.

Scott, B. 1975. "A survey of medical opinion: The malpractice crisis is worse than we thought." Medical Opinion 4 (July):40.

Sheridan, Bart. 1974. "Why the lawyers caught Nork and the doctors didn't." Medical Economics 51 (July 22):91–109.

Smith, Rogers J. 1979. "The boards and rehabilitation of impaired physicians." Federation Bulletin [Federation of State Medical Boards in the United States] 66 (September):259–265.

Somers, Anne R. 1973. "PSRO: Friend or foe." New England Journal of Medicine 289 (August 19):321–322.

Steindler, Emanuel M. 1975. The Impaired Physician: An Interpretive Summary of the AMA Conference on "The Disabled Doctor: Challenge to the Profession." Chicago: American Medical Association.

Stewart, David. 1977. "About those sick physicians." Journal of the Kentucky Medical Association 75 (July):328–329.

Sutherland, Edwin H. 1950. "The diffusion of sexual psychopath laws." American Journal of Sociology 56 (September):142–148.

Talbott, G. Douglas, Hank Holderfield, Kenneth Shoemaker, and Earnest Atkins. 1977. "The MAG disabled doctors' program: A two year review." Journal of the Medical Association of Georgia 66 (October):777–781.

Vaillant, G. E., J. R. Brighton, and C. McArthur. 1970. "Physicians' use of mood-altering drugs." New England Journal of Medicine 282 (February 12):365–370.

Weinstein, Deena. 1978. "Fraud in science." Paper presented at the annual meeting of the American Sociological Association, San Francisco, September.

CASES CITED

Corleto v. Shore Memorial Hospital, 350 A. 2d 534, 1975.

Darling v. Charleston Community Memorial Hospital, 211 N.E. 2d 253, 1968.

Gonzales v. Nork, No. 228566, Superior Court of Sacramento County, California, November 19, 1973.

CHAPTER 16

Changing Doctor-Patient Relationships and the Rise in Concern for Accountability

Michael Betz and Lenahan O'Connell

People in the United States have become increasingly distrustful of politicians, doctors, lawyers, teachers, social workers, and other professionals (Burham, 1982; Cihlar, 1974; Manning, 1974; Miller, 1974; *Time*, 1980). The public is asking whose interests the professionals are serving and who is benefiting most from those services—the professional or the client. The distrust of professionals is reflected in decreased confidence in institutions. Opinion polls from 1966 to 1975 show a decline of confidence in Congress from 42 to 13 percent; in colleges, from 61 to 36 percent; and in medicine from 72 to 43 percent (Harris, 1976).

The rise of distrust is puzzling. Sociologists predicted that the growth of a professional and technical class dedicated to the service ethic and rational standards of performance would integrate modern industrial society (Carr-Saunders and Wilson, 1933; Durkheim, 1964; Halmos, 1970). Parsons (1939) argued that professionalization carries a scientific and service orientation. Indeed, the number of people in the professional class is growing: from 1950 to 1980 the number of professionals rose from nine percent to 16 percent of the workforce (U.S. Bureau of the Census, 1981). Yet conflict between professionals and their clients is also growing.

Functionalists such as Durkheim (1964) and Parsons (1939) assume that professionalizaton[1]—the process by which the members of an occupation gain greater power over their area of work—contributes to social integration, consensus, and trust. We disagree. This paper uses the example of doctor-patient relationships to show that professionalization, in conjunction with other trends, has transformed the exchange between doctor and patient in such a way that dissension, conflict, and distrust have emerged.[2] As a result, professionals and clients have become separated into two communities: (1) producers of services, who are oriented toward technical performance standards enforced by their occupational association; and (2) consumers, who often have little power. While clients respect the professionals' expertise, they do not assume that "expert" decisions are made always with the clients' best interests in mind.

We believe that traditional conditions supporting trust and mutual answerability (i.e., accountability) in professional-client relationships have changed dramatically. First, we examine changes in the doctor-patient relationship. Second, we identify two very different structures of exchange which have operated historically. Third, these types of exchange are examined against the backdrop of historical changes in population mobility, professionalization, bureaucratization, and specialization. Fourth, we contrast the ideology of the medical profession with that of the patients. We suggest that patient discontent is so widespread as to warrant being called a movement, which we contend is rationalizing the exchange relationship. Finally, we conclude that the pressures for more accountability will decrease the power and autonomy of the medical profession.

Changes in Doctor-Patient Relationships

The public's confidence in, and respect for, doctors has declined markedly since 1950 (Gallup, 1972). Fully 72 percent of the public expressed confidence in doctors in 1966, compared with only 43 percent in 1975[3] (Harris, 1976). Burnham (1982:1475) calls the period between 1910 and 1950 when doctors enjoyed public respect "the golden age of medicine." We argue that the decline in public respect after 1950 coincided with the call for accountability of the medical profession[4]—in itself a symptom of the changing structures of exchange relations in medical care.

Why did distrust and the call for accountability arise? Some believe that the increase in distrust reflects an increase in cost (Etzioni, 1977; Gaines, 1973). But while both physicians' incomes and cost of health care have outpaced the Consumer Price Index in the United States, the cost of an office visit has not. From 1935 to 1980, the Consumer Price Index rose from 38.8 to 246.8, while the index of doctors' fees rose from 41.1 to 269.3 (1967 = 100; U.S. Bureau of the Census, 1981:102, 467). Thus, increases in cost do not necessarily produce dissatisfaction with the financial terms of the exchange, because fees have remained stable relative to the Consumer Price Index while the quality of service has increased dramatically. Moreover, third-party payers (government and insurance carriers) have reduced out-of-pocket expenses for patients from 54.9 percent of total cost in 1960 to 32.4 percent in 1980 (U.S. Bureau of the Census, 1981:101). Yet, patient satisfaction and trust have still fallen.

In 1930 most doctors were general practitioners and the services they provided could be observed and sanctioned by members of a stable community. By 1980, however, most doctors were specialists seeing patients in settings where others cannot sanction the transaction. This movement away from community-based medicine in the United States is reflected in the decline in home visits. Between 1957 and 1971, home visits declined from 10.2 percent to 1.7 percent of all doctor/patient contacts. By 1971, 69.9 percent of patient consultations occurred in the doctor's office, 10.2 percent in the hospital, and 13.3 percent over the telephone (Rowland, 1978:342).

Unfortunately, there has been little research on the doctors' role in the community. But as early as the 1930s, Lynd and Lynd (1937) noted the declining prominence of doctors in Muncie, Indiana, where patients were already shopping around for a doctor. Specialists in the 1980s see patients only for the duration of a specific illness, make few housecalls, and spend little time with a patient per visit (U.S. National Center for Health Statistics, 1982:7).

Changes in the conditions under which doctors and patients meet have led patients to be more concerned about fairness and immediate benefit, even where no evidence of inequity exists.[5] Why, after all, should patients distrust doctors who are better educated and who have more effective treatments at their disposal than their predecessors? What is the connection between this sense of distrust and the changes that have taken place in the doctor-patient relationship? We believe that the sense of trust is diminished as the doctor-patient relationship becomes more specialized, impersonal, and short-lived.

Structures of Exchange

GENERALIZED EXCHANGE

Generalized exchange occurs within normatively defined settings such as kinship groups, work groups, and tightly knit communities in which three or more parties participate (Levi-Strauss, 1969; Sahlins, 1963), the prototype of generalized exchange is a one-sided transfer of goods between members of a family. The transfer may be temporarily unbalanced or one-sided, and so for a brief time is not characterized by mutual reward. For example, A gives to B, but A may receive from B or frequently from some third party. The exchange may be direct or indirect; parties to the immediate transaction do not know how or when the exchange will be completed. The exchange is open-ended and therefore risky, since there is no guarantee that the first two parties, A and B, will ever balance their accounts. When the exchange involves three or more parties, it is difficult to keep track of transactions among all the parties.

During multi-party, generalized exchange, the transaction is governed by the norm of generalized reciprocity, under which one actor benefits another, from whom no immediate or direct benefit is expected in return. "[Generalized reciprocity] requires the deferment of the exchange, so that the settlement is not to the benefit of the same person who sacrificed" (Levi-Strauss, 1969:448). Unlike Gouldner's (1960) norm of reciprocity (any benefit one receives from another implies a duty to reciprocate that person), the norm of generalized reciprocity holds that one has a duty to reward others, but not necessarily the specific person who first rendered a benefit. Generalized reciprocity always entails an element of one-sidedness: one party gives without certainty of return (Caplow, 1982).

The social group implicitly insures the long-term balance of the benefits from the transactions; in consequence, partners are less likely to worry about exploitation. Hence, time horizons are longer and partners are far less likely to experience negative emotions which can destroy a relationship.

Concern with answerability in tightly knit communities is less formal, transpires over a longer time period, and generates more trust in the system of exchanges. Since the social unit (in this case, community) can elicit trust in the eventual fairness of all the exchange relations within, it engenders bonds of solidarity among members.[6] Hence, generalized exchange furthers social relationships because trust created by the social unit serves to strengthen the social bond as exchange relations emerge.

RESTRICTED EXCHANGE

Restricted exchange entails a direct transfer of rewarding activities or items between two people motivated by self-interest. The prototype of restricted exchange is the market transaction, in which two parties seek maximum utility. The two parties (and only two) profit directly from the exchange of psychological or economic rewards. The motivation for restricted exchange is the norm of reciprocity which fosters a *quid pro quo* mentality (Gouldner, 1960). People react with anger when the norm of reciprocity (or its companion principle, the rule of distributive justice) is not honored (Homans, 1974:37).

Concern with the proportionality of return is a significant aspect of restricted exchange. Since each party expects not only to benefit, but also to benefit according to a standard of distributive justice, each closely scrutinizes the reward of the other. The structure of restricted exchange encourages interpersonal rather than intrapersonal comparisons. In an *interpersonal* comparison, an individual believes that both partners are rewarded in proportion to their costs; thus, it encourages a conscious search for short-term fairness, because each party seeks proportional returns, that is, distributive justice. Since the outcome is often unfair, restricted exchanges frequently produce dissatisfaction. In an *intrapersonal* comparison, an individual is satisfied that he or she will receive some benefit, though not necessarily a proportional benefit. The individual does not appraise the relative costs and rewards of the exchange partner (Ekeh, 1974).

Given this association of restricted exchange with dissatisfaction, it is not surprising that concern for accountability arises when there is a change from generalized exchange in a community setting to restricted exchange in a bureaucratic setting. Since a bureaucratic setting fosters interpersonal comparisons, dissatisfaction is more likely. It is always difficult to arrange a perfectly balanced exchange. And when exchange partners are strangers who are not embedded in a shared network of social contacts, trust is unlikely. Trust is a structural product, and not merely a function of the communication skills of exchange partners.

The Historical Changes and Exchange Type

Historically, doctors in the United States worked in stable communities where patterns of generalized exchange operated. The two most important structural features of the community were: (1) the existence of long-term social relationships; and (2) a group of more than two members. These features made it possible for doctors and their patients to accept imbalances in the exchange processes without experiencing the anger and disruption that would result typically in restricted exchange. At least four historical changes have transformed the structure of exchange relations, creating concerns with the trustworthiness of the exchange partners.[7] These are: the impact of population mobility, professionalization, bureaucratization, and specialization. We discuss each in turn.

1. POPULATION MOBILITY

Greater population mobility has increased the number of interactions governed by rational and calculative, rather than emotional, criteria. The process of urbanization loosened the ties of the local community and thus freed the average citizen for geographic and social mobility.[8] As a result, short-term transactions with strangers became increasingly common. Simmel (1950:410) describes the relationship between strangers as one in which each participant "reacts with his head instead of his heart." Participants calculate their own self-interest and seek to achieve their own goals, with the relationship becoming simply a means to an end.

After the Second World War the proportion of persons in the United States who move increased to 20 percent a year; hence, one person in every five lives in a different household than they did the previous year. From 1965 to 1970, 47 percent of the U.S. population moved; 45 percent moved from 1975 to 1980 (U.S. Bureau of the Census, 1982).

Face-to-face relations created primary modes of social control which helped ensure trust in the system of exchange. To avoid gossip, rebuke, or expulsion, persons had to live up to obligations, that is, be answerable to the larger community's standards of fairness. In sum, mobility of the population has loosened the ties within the local community, increasing the incidence of short-term, two-party transactions in which primary modes of control are less effective.

2. PROFESSIONALIZATION

Early in the 20th century, as the importance of community in the geographical sense declined, the importance of occupational community increased. After the American Medical Association gained legal control over licensing and admissions to medical school in 1912, doctors increasingly turned to their peers for standard of conduct and norms of performance. Thus, the profession gained more power to regulate itself, and even limit entrance into the field. Ironically, self-regulation has insulated doctors from the very people whom they claim to serve (Weinbach, 1976).

Occupational association forged stronger ties with occupational peers, with the decline in the importance of community in the geographical sense.

> As advances are made in history, the organization which has territorial groups as its base (village or city, district, province, etc.) steadily becomes effaced, i.e., . . . the bonds attaching us there became daily more fragile and more slack. . . .Now it is impossible for this organization to disappear without something replacing it. . . . We have just shown how occupational groups are suited to fill this role, and that is their destiny (Durkheim, 1964:27).

Allegiance to the welfare of the client, as defined by the community, became superseded by an allegiance to the professional association. The effect on the doctor-patient relationship was great. What was previously a more intimate, multi-faceted relation became increasingly an impersonal, single-faceted relationship. Doctors took fewer cues for interacting with patients from either the patients themselves or the community; instead, their attitudes and values were determined more by their colleagues. Even the price of their services was recommended by the profession.

Figures on the supply and demand of medical services in the Untied States highlight the change in doctor-patient relationships in the 20th century. While the number of doctors per 100,000 people has fluctuated from 157 in 1900, to 125 in 1930, to 1,977 in 1979 (U.S. Bureau of the Census, 1975:34; 1981:104), the demand for doctors' services increased dramatically. The number of visits to a doctor per person per year increased from 2.6 in 1928 to 5.1 in 1975 (Andersen and Anderson, 1979). The medical profession responded to the shortage of doctors by shortening the time doctors spent with patients. In 1975, 66.7 percent of patients spent less than 15 minutes with their doctors per visit; by 1980, 72.8 percent did so (U.S. National Center for Health Statistics, 1977:7; 1982:7).

Professionalization widens the social distance between the client and the professional. This separates the parties to the exchange, creates a social void, and cultivates distrust. After professionalization replaced the moral authority of the community with the legal authority of the American Medical Association, patients had reason for dissatisfaction with this form of social control. Because the professional association serves as an agent of the doctors' self-interest, clients lost the impartial third party of the community. Under normal circumstances of exchange, clients might look elsewhere for medical services. The importance of medical care to the patient and the legal monopoly of the profession severely limited clients' alternatives (Carrolla and Gaston, 1974; Friedman and Kuznets, 1954). Consequently, clients felt trapped in a relationship they could neither alter nor do without.

With the rationalization of technique and accompanying professionalization, doctors also became more oriented toward technical treatment of illness, ignoring the supportive, confidence-building, and trusting dimension of the helping relationship. A split between technical rationality and interpersonal rationality developed. As technical rationality increased, clients were less able to judge whether their doctors' responses were meeting the patients' goals. Ben-Sira (1976) notes that patients who cannot understand the technical reasons for treatment rely more upon doctors' personal demeanor or interpersonal style to evaluate performance.

In an encounter between doctor and patient today there is little concern with the patient's sentiments and emotions. Consequently, to the patient, the doctor appears less sensitive. Thus, since the new formal etiquette of interaction is anything but personal, clients see professionals as increasingly unresponsive. Actually, the nature of a restricted exchange precludes responsiveness and influences the utilitarian and impersonal quality of the interaction. In sum, the process of professionalization has eroded patients' satisfaction with the doctor-patient exchange, thereby stimulating the demand for accountability.

3. BUREAUCRATIZATION

The U.S. health care system has become increasingly bureaucratic[9] since health care has moved from the office of the family practitioner to the office of a group practice, or to a clinic, or hospital (Duff and Hollingshead, 1968; Freidson, 1970; Fuchs, 1974:56; Mechanic, 1976a). The percentage of doctors in group practice has increased from less than 1 percent in 1932 to 20 percent in 1975 (Goodman, 1978). While 10 percent of doctors were employed full-time in hospitals in 1970, 46 percent of doctors saw their patients in the hospital, making if the major work setting for medical practice (Freidson 1970:109).

The growth of malpractice litigation in medicine reflects the growing segmentation and impersonality of doctor-patient relationships. Malpractice suits were uncommon when stable, face-to-face, long-term relationships in a single community facilitated the effectiveness of primary modes of social control. Whereas the old structure of generalized exchange insulated doctors against the threat of malpractice suits (Mechanic, 1976:273), the more recent exchange structure encourages such litigation. A 1963 editorial in the *Journal of the American Medical Association* states:

> Often . . . whether or not a disappointed patient files a claim is determined by his feelings toward the physician, since a liability suit is frequently a symptom of the breakdown in the patient-physician relationship. A patient who has a feeling of friendly trust toward his physician, and who believes that everything possible has been done for him, is not likely to sue—even when a bad result does ensue (Committee on Medicolegal Problems, 1963:696).

Trust is related to the structure of exchange relationships. When an exchange takes place between people who share a common identity in a long-term relationship, trust is more likely.

> Patients may believe that faults have been committed in their cases as much because they think the physician lacks interest in them or has treated them discourteously as because of the objective quality of the medical care received. Many patients who are aware that physicians have been negligent in their care would not consider litigation because of their personal relationship to a physician whom they feel tried to do the best he or she could. Whatever the result, the intentions are viewed as good. In contrast, litigation often follows disputes about fees or an experience in which the physician is perceived as callous, unresponsive, and without humility (Mechanic, 1976a:272).

Another effect of impersonal, bureaucratic medical service is the development of "patient consciousness," as patients are thrown together in "groups, clinics, health centers, and other mass production locations" (Haug, 1975:208). In another, but similar, context Marx argued that concentration of workers in the factory system was one basis for recognition of their common fate and a subsequent pursuit of class interests.

4. SPECIALIZATION

Modern medicine is practiced increasingly by specialists. In 1948, 80 percent of doctors in the United States were in general practice, whereas by 1968, 84 percent were specialists (Goodman, 1976). Medical specialization fosters distrust; it breaks down the structure of generalized exchange by replacing a long-term relationship with one general practitioner with several short-term relationships with specialists. Because specialists deal with a narrow range of symptoms and problems, they are more concerned with disease than with people. This fact increases the likelihood of miscommunication, discontinuity, and higher cost.

Specialization has helped create a crisis in the U.S. health care system by both fragmenting and depersonalizing the doctor-patient relationship (National Advisory Commission on Health Manpower, 1967). Since medical care is distributed over a greater number of doctors, patients have fewer contacts with the same doctors. Specialization further separates the professionals from the lay public because geographical and occupational communities rarely overlap. Doctors and patients no longer rely on the same agents of social control for their norms and standards. As a result, earlier modes of social control have become less effective in regulating the doctor-patient relationship.

These four historical changes in the structure of exchange relations have helped precipitate an accountability movement.[10] The movement's decentralized ad hoc organization reflects a diffuse, episodic dissatisfaction with medical services. The movement's tactics and goals are varied: they range from such isolated, individual actions as demands for more consultation and information, to organized campaigns for change, including positions on policy-making boards and legislative changes. A unifying theme of all these actions is patient ideology; it is common beliefs which transform a collection of discrete groups into a social movement with a common cause.

Opposing Ideologies

Social groups which contend for scarce resources develop ideologies. While ideologies are usually explicitly political, they apply equally to non-political social relations characterized by power and domination. Dolbeare and Dolbeare (1973:7) define ideology as "an integrated system of belief in which definitions of reality bear a relation to a goal and methods of achieving it." Ideologies have three components: (1) a world-view describing how a particular system works and why it is either fair or unfair; (2) the values that are central and the goals it holds out in its quest for fairness: and (3) "an image of the process of social change . . . . and the tactics that it deems appropriate" (Dolbeare and Dolbeare, 1973:7).

THE MEDICAL PROFESSION

In the predominant world-view of doctors, the medical system is fair. The ideal relationship between doctors and patients is a two-party transaction in which fee-paying patients defer to the judgment of doctors. Although doctors dominate the exchange, they consider the relationship to be fair because they have both expertise and ethics. This world-view is based on three beliefs about the medical profession: (1) doctors possess expertise; (2) doctors have responded to a "calling" and work for intrinsic as well as monetary reasons; and (3) doctors are committed to service; that is, their judgments are based not on self-interest but on the best interests of patients (Berlant, 1975; Freidson, 1970; Larson, 1977; McKinley, 1973; Parsons, 1963).

The strategies used to protect this fee-for-service relationship are: (1) opposition to group practice and any organized third-party payers; (2) idealization of the benefits realized by submissive patients; (3) encouragement of professional referral systems and fee splitting; and (4) institutionalization of ethical codes to assure the public of proper conduct (Berlant, 1975:36). The medical profession's ideology contends that doctors can be trusted because they pursue a calling for the sake of service to the patient, unlike merchants, who pursue profit. To enhance this claim to trustworthiness, the medical profession instituted licensing and a code of ethics for self-policing. These in turn promote the monopolization of medical practice. With monopoly comes power. Not surprisingly, all elements of the medical profession's ideology—even those emphasizing vocation and service to the patient—reinforce the doctors' power in the relationship.

Since this ideology asserts that doctors pursue the best interests of their patients, it also asserts that the interests of the two groups are identical: both seek the patients' health and well-being. Yet this ideology ignores cost. In sum, it denies the existence of structural conflict between doctors, and patients, as well as the marketplace aspect of the exchange.

THE PATIENT

The advocates of accountability argue that doctors are not disinterested experts dedicated to serving patients. In the world-view of patients, doctors are self-interested vendors of a service, and as unworthy of trust as merchants. Patients seek fair exchange by actively participating in consultation and treatment. This involvement expresses the accountability movement's basic values: equity and participation. In the interest of fair exchange, patient consumers pursue three objectives: (1) more information about alternative therapies and costs; (2) more precise performance standards which stipulate benefits to be delivered; and (3) redress of grievance whenever a transaction is deemed unfair. Among the movement's concerns: Professional Standards Review Organization (PSRO), relicensure bills, requirements for continuing education, the articulation of new patient rights such as patient consultations, positions on hospital boards, death with dignity in an hospice, and, of course legal redress through malpractice suits (Betz 1981; Matek, 1977; May, 1976).

Because the medical profession's ideology holds that doctors' and patients' interests are the same, it cannot address effectively such patient concerns as the possibility of excessive treatment. The patient ideology can and does, because it assumes that doctors and patients may have different interests. The patient ideology seeks a proportional return—the type of return mandated by the nature of restricted exchange.

Contrary to the claims of the medical profession, trust between doctors and patients depends on more than personal demeanor. It also depends on the existence of local third parties who serve as agents of social control. As the practice of medicine is removed from the social control of the local community, doctors are trusted less. Thus, the rise of the accountability movement was inevitable, given the fear of exploitation inherent in the circumstances of restricted exchange.

Summary and Conclusion

Patient distrust of doctors has increased as the doctor-patient relationship has been altered by professionalization, specialization, bureaucratization, and population mobility. The causal sequence is mediated by a structural transition from a three-party to a two-party exchange, and from a long-term to a shorter-term relationship; both the time dimension and number of actors help generate a change of norm. Whereas exchange was once guided by the norm of generalized reciprocity, it is now guided by the norm of reciprocity; the latter generates a *quid pro quo* mentality and discomfort with powerlessness. In addition, the need for reciprocation leads to a greater concern for short-term balanced exchange (proportional reward). Partners to the exchange make more interpersonal comparisons to insure that the other person is not benefiting more than is necessary to obtain balance. This, too, heightens the pervasive feeling of distrust. Thus, under the conditions of restricted exchange, patients are more likely to fear that doctors will exploit their power. Consequently, patients are more likely to become part of the accountability movement in an effort to find a third party or legal mechanism capable of insuring fairness of exchange.

Given the structure of both industrialized society and modern medicine, we cannot return to an earlier era in which medical practice was regulated by the local community. When complex, technical performances are required, face-to-face modes of control (gossip, ostracism) no longer effectively insure fair exchanges.

Distrust of doctors is a dialectical response to the dominance of organized medicine. Like Galbraith (1956), who pointed to the labor union as a countervailing power to the dominance of the corporation, we believe that the call for accountability in medicine is a countervailing power in response the power of doctors. The changing structure of exchange has led to distrust despite the ideological statements of the medical profession and the expertise of its members. Distrust promoted a counter organization and ideology. Professionalization in medicine, instead of promoting social integration, produced a suspicious and antagonistic social movement. Increasingly the public has turned to both law and public agencies to control and regulate transactions in health care. Conflict, not integration, has followed the change from general practice in the community to specialization in impersonal settings.

Haug (1975) argues that the public's increasing access to medical knowledge will undermine the power of doctors. She stresses the role of knowledge and belief, while slighting the role of organization and political power in the process of deprofessionalization. We stress the changing structure of the exchange, the decline of trust in medicine, and the creation of a counter organization as important factors in causing a decline in doctors' control of the medical decision-making process.

The accountability movement in health care can also be viewed as the rationalization of exchange relations, in that patients are pursuing greater predictability and advantage through various channels. We expect the movement to result in the rationalization of the exchange relation in the following ways: (1) greater clarity of goals and procedures to reach those goals; (2) more patient or client contribution to the health exchange (whether that occurs directly within the doctor-patient relationship or in the planning counsels and boards which deliver health care); and (3) a new structure of controls on the delivery of health care which are more formal and more oriented toward results.[11]

What has happened in medicine is probably symptomatic of wider social trends. We believe further research will reveal that the conditions of exchange between producers and consumers in a number of fields have undergone similar changes. If so, we expect to see these changes translated into social movements demanding accountability. Indeed, the broad "consumer movement" probably reflects specific calls for accountability generated by the changing exchange relations in a number of different markets.

Notes

1. We emphasize the political process by which occupational groupings change their economic and prestige positions within the larger family of occupations. The more powerful professions have located their training within universities, formed a professional association, obtained exclusive power over licensing, and adopted ethical codes. Other usages of the term include the demographic change in the number of persons working in fields classified as "professional occupations" and a simple process by which occupations acquire a list of traits designated as "professional" (Johnson, 1972:21).

2. Haug (1975) offers a similar thesis while emphasizing the demonopolization of the knowledge base. We emphasize the more general role and importance of organization as a political resource.

3. We focus on patient trust of the doctor rather than doctor trust of the patient because, in an exchange between an expert and a client, the key issue is the client's belief in the expert's implicit assertion of competence.

4. We use Passos's (1973:18) conceptualization of accountability as the "assessment of performance, that is, determining what the professional has done, how much it has cost, and ultimately whether the result was worth the cost." As evidence of this public pressure on doctors we point to the increased use of the term *accountability* in academic and popular literature. The Social Science Citation Index (SSCI), which arranges all published materials in social science literature by subject area of the title, first used this term in 1969, when there were two articles. In 1974 there were 89 references. A total of some 700 articles and books on accountability were indexed from 1969 to 1981.

5. Some of the rise in concern for accountability reflects the public's increased knowledge about medical matters (Haug, 1975:203; Lorber, 1975). We believe, however, that knowledge cannot account entirely for distrust; it may, in some cases, increase trust. Both knowledge without distrust and distrust without knowledge can increase the call for accountability.

6. Several studies suggest a connection between trust and social relationships. Blau (1964) posited a connection between social exchange and the creation of trust. Bar-Tal *et al.* (1977) found that expectation is positively related to the closeness of relationships. Litwak and Szeleny (1969) found that while technological change leads to new forms of primary group structure, the more we are tied by sentiment or blood, the more we expect. To the extent that we expect help from others, we trust them.

7. Because we focus on the exchange relation, we are more interested in residential stability of population than in urbanization and size of place as a factor in the rise of distrust.

8. In 1920, 48.8 percent of the U.S. population lived in rural or non-urban areas; in 1950, 36 percent; in 1980, 25 percent.

9. By bureaucratization we refer to the process by which activities become coordinated into more formal and routine modes of organization. This process is in the direction of attaining the ideal characteristics of the Weberian model of rationalizing the way in which goals are more efficiently pursued by specialization of task, hierarchy of command, record keeping, formalization, and an impersonal orientation to work relations.

10. By a movement we refer to a collectivity acting with some continuity to promote a change in the society or group of which it is a part (Turner and Killian, 1972). The accountability movement has many scattered groupings or cells which have no central command (Gerlach and Hines, 1970).

11. As doctors become subject to third-party controls, we expect their stress level, alienation, and job dissatisfaction to increase (Karger, 1981). Doctors have used autonomy to cope with or camouflage their problems, such as stress and drug abuse, but if the demand for accountability limits their autonomy, they may be less able to cope.

References

Andersen, Ronald, and Odin Anderson. 1979. "Tends in the use of health services." Pp. 371–391 in Howard Freeman, Sol Levine, and Leo Reeder (eds.), Handbook of Medical Sociology, 3rd edition, Englewood Cliffs, NJ: Prentice Hall.

Bar-Tal, Daniel, Yaakov Bar-Zohar, Martin S. Greenberg, and Margarette Hermon. 1977. "Reciprocity behavior in the relationship between donor and recipient and between harm-doer and victim." Sociometry 40(3):293–298.

Ben-Sira, Zeev. 1976. "The functions of the professional's affective behavior in client satisfaction: A revised approach to social interaction theory." Journal of Heath and Social Behavior 17 (March):3–11.

Berlant, Jeffrey Lionel. 1975. Profession and Monopoly. Berkeley: University of California Press.

Betz, Michael. 1981. "From whence accountability." Nursing and Health Care 2(9):482–486.

Blau, Peter. 1964. Exchange and Power in Social Life. New York: John Wiley and Sons.

Burnham, John C. 1982. "American medicine's golden age: What happened to it?" Science 215 (March 19):1475–1478.

Caplow, Theodore. 1982. "Christmas gifts and kin networks." American Sociological Review 47 (June):383–392.

Carr-Saunders, Alexander M., and Paul A. Wilson. 1933. The Professions. Oxford, England: The Clarendon Press.

Carroll, Sidney, and Robert Gaston. 1974. "A proposal to conduct a study: Applied research on public regulation and economic productivity." Unpublished paper, The University of Tennessee.

Cihlar, Carroll. 1974. "Consumer views." Hospitals 48 (April 1):189–191.

Committee on Medicolegal Problems. 1963. "Professional liability and the physician." Journal of American Medical Association 183 (February 23):695–703.

Dolbeare, Kenneth M., and Patricia Dolbeare. 1973. American Ideologies: The Competing Political Beliefs of the 1970s. Chicago: Rand McNally.

Duff, Raymond S., and August B. Hollingshead. 1968. Sickness and Society. New York: Harper.

Durkheim, Emile. 1964. The Division of Labor in Society. New York: The Free Press.

Ekeh, Peter. 1974. Social Exchange Theory. Cambridge, MA: Harvard University Press.

Etzioni, Amitai. 1977. "Accountability of health administrations." A preliminary report to the Commission of Education for Health Administration. Unpublished.

Friedman, Milton, and Simon Kuznets. 1954. Income From Independent Professional Practice. New York: National Bureau of Economic Research.

Freidson, Eliot. 1970. Professional Dominance: The Social Structure of Medical Care. New York: Atherton.

Fuchs, Victor R. 1974. Who Shall Live? Health, Economics, and Social Choice. New York: Basic Books.

Gaines, Edythe. 1973. "The future of accountability." Pp. 425–434 in Richard Hostrop, James Mechlenburger, and John Wilson (eds.), Accountability for Educational Results. Hamden, NJ: Shoe String Press.

Galbraith, John. 1956. American Capitalism: The Concept of Coutnervailing Power. Boston: Houghton Mifflin.

Gallup Poll. 1972. The Gallup Poll: 1935–1971. New York: Random House.

Gerlach, Luther, and Virginia Hine. 1970. People, Power, Change. Indianapolis: Bobbs-Merrill Company.

Goodman, Leo. 1978. "Growth of group practice." Profile of Medical Practice. Chicago: American Medical Association.

Gouldner, Alvin W. 1960. "The norm of reciprocity: A preliminary statement." American Sociological Review 25 (April):161–179.

Halmos, Paul. 1970. The Personal Service Society. New York: Schocken.

Harris Survey. 1976. Yearbook of Public Opinion. New York: Louis Harris and Associates.

Haug, Marie R. 1975. "Deprofessionalization of everyone?" Sociological Focus 8(3):197–212.

Homans, George C. 1974. Social Behavior: Its Elementary Forms. New York: Harcourt Brace Jovanovitch.

Johnson, Terence. 1972. Professions and Power. London, England: Macmillan Press.

Karger, Howard. 1981. "Burnout as alienation." Social Science Review 55 (June):270–283.

Larson, Magali S. 1977. The Rise of Professionalism: A Sociological Analysis. Berkeley: The University of California Press.

Levi-Strauss, Claude. 1969. The Elementary Structures of Kinship. Boston: Beacon Press.

Litwak, Eugene, and Ivan Szeleny. 1969. "Primary group structures and their functions: Kin, neighbors, and friends." American Sociological Review 34(4):465–481.

Lorber, Judith. 1975. "Good patient and problem patients: Conformity and deviance in a general hospital." Journal of Health and Social Behavior 11:213–225.

Lynd, Robert S., and Helen M. Lynd. 1937. Middletown in Transition. New York: Harcourt, Brace, and World.

McKinley, John B. 1973. "On the professional regulation of change." Pp. 67–68 in Paul Halmos (ed.), Professionalization and Social Change. The Sociological Review Monograph. Keele, Staffordshire: The University of Keele.

Manning, Bayless. 1974. "Just why are lawyers so unpopular?" Los Angeles Times, September 1:Sec. 4, p. 3.

Matek, Stanley J. 1977. Accountability: Its Meaning and Its Relevance to the Health Care Field. Hyattsville, MD: U.S. Dept. of Health, Education, and Welfare.

May, Judith. 1976. Professionals and Clients: A Constitutional Struggle. Beverly Hills: Sage.

Mechanic, David. 1976a. The Growth of Bureaucratic Medicine. New York: John Wiley and Sons.

———. 1976b. "Some social aspects of the medical malpractice dilemma." Duke Law Journal 6 (January):1179–1196.

Miller, Arthur. 1974. "Index of trust in government." Institute for Social Research Newsletter (Winter):5.

National Advisory Commission on Health Manpower. 1967. Report of the National Advisory Commission on Health Manpower. Volume 1. Washington, D.C.: U.S. Government Printing Office.

Parsons, Talcott. 1939. "The profession and social structure." Social Forces 17 (May):457–467.

———. 1963. "Social change and medical organization in the United States: A sociological perspective." The Annals of the American Academy of Political and Social Science 346 (March):21–33.

Passos, Joyce. 1973. "Accountability: Myth or mandate?" Journal of Nursing Administration 3(3):17–22.

Rowland, Howard. 1978. The Nurse Almanac. Germantown, IN: Aspen Systems Corporation.

Sahlins, Marshall. 1963. "On the sociology of primitive exchange." Pp. 139–227 in Michael Banton (ed.), The Relevance of Models for Social Anthropology. American Sociological Association monograph 1. London: Tavistock.

Simmel, Georg. 1950. The Sociology of Georg Simmel. Translated by Kurt H. Wolf. New York: Free Press.

Time. 1980. "The busting of American trust." Time, October 29:106.

Turner, Ralph, and Lewis Killian. 1972. Collective Behavior. 2nd edition. Englewood Cliffs: Prentice-Hall.

U.S. Bureau of the Census. 1975. Historical Statistics, Colonial Times to 1970. Washington, D.C.: U.S. Government Printing Office.

———. 1981. Statistical Abstract of the United States. Washington, D.C.: U.S. Government Printing Office.

———. 1982. Current Population Reports, series p-20. Washington, D.C.: U.S. Government Printing Office.

U.S. National Center for Health Statistics. 1977. Vital and Health Statistics, Series 13. Washington D.C.: U.S. Government Printing Office.

———. 1982. Vital and Health Statistics, Series 13. Washington, D.C.: U.S. Government Printing Office.

Weinbach, Robert. 1976. "Accountability crises: Consequences of professionalization." Sociology and Social Welfare 4(7):1011–1024.

CHAPTER 17

Changing Medical Practice and Medical Malpractice Claims

Stephen L. Fielding

Medical Malpractice Claims

Medical malpractice claims have increased from 3.2 claims-per-hundred physicians before 1981 to a high of 10.1 by 1985 (American Medical Association 1984, 1987). Since then, claims decreased to 7.7 claims-per-hundred physicians in 1990, increasing to 8.2 in 1991 (American Medical Association 1993). The difference in claim rates across specialties is evidence of the impact of medicine's structure on malpractice claims (Brennan et al. 1991). For example, in 1991 primary care providers such as family practitioners, internists, and general pediatricians had 5.7, 5.5, and 6.4 claims-per-hundred physicians, respectively (American Medical Association, 1993). In contrast, tertiary care physicians such as surgeons and obstetricans/gynecologists[1] had 14 and 11.6 claims-per-hundred physicians, respectively. The overall rise of the claims rate reflects a social problem. As Mills (1961) might have said, the private troubles of patients have become the public issues of health care. As medicine has "advanced" so has it increasingly subjected patients to risk (Dutton 1988). The ability to cure disease has increased the chances for unexpected failures (i.e., maloccurrences).

Brennan et al. (1991) estimate that there were 98,609 maloccurrences in New York State in 1984, and of these, 27,179 (1 percent of acute care, non-psychiatric hospital admissions) were due to negligence. However, Localio et al. (1991), using these 1984 data and the New York malpractice claims data, show that only 3,570 malpractice cases were filed on the estimated 27,179 maloccurrences involving negligence. Thus, patients with injuries due to negligence often do not file claims.

Only those maloccurrences that result from negligent acts are eligible for malpractice claim compensation. In order for a plaintiff to win a malpractice case in court it must be reasonably demonstrated that: a) the provider deviated from generally accepted medical practice; and b) the injury was the result of the provider's action or failure to act. The problem for physicians and their insurers is that claims are often difficult or costly to defend. As a result, some cases are settled out of court for expediency.

Most studies of medical malpractice do not focus on the issue of error. Instead, they focus on the economic, legal, and insurance aspects, which I have previously discussed

331

(Fielding 1990a, b). One recent study by the Congressional Budget Office (CBO) (1992) indicates that medical malpractice premiums amount to less than 1 percent of national health care expenditures. Additionally, much of what is referred to as *defensive medicine* would probably still be provided for other reasons, according to the CBO. However, physicians claim that they cannot afford the cost of malpractice insurance, even though their mean net income after all expenses (including liability insurance) and before taxes has increased well ahead of inflation, from $97,700 in 1982 to $155,800 in 1989 (American Medical Association 1991).

Two studies have focused on medical errors from the physician's perspective. While attending morbidity and mortality conferences Bosk (1979) observed that mal-occurrences were presented by the attending physician as a learning process for himself and his colleagues. However, no mention was made at these meetings about the personal or social impacts of these mistakes on patients. Paget's (1988) work examines medicine as an *error-ridden* activity. As she listened to physicians talk about their work she discovered that errors were the norm rather than the exception.[2]

Only two studies (May and Stengel 1990; Imershein and Brents 1992) examine malpractice claims from the patients' perspective. May and Stengel conducted a survey of dissatisfied patients that included suers and non-suers in Wisconsin. The investigators found that patients were not greatly affected by many of the procedural niceties (e.g., bedside manner) often taught as part of the risk management programs sponsored by insurance companies and hospitals. More importantly, those who filed a claim sought more input from friends, family, and other confidantes than those who did not. Presumably this social support enabled them to redefine their medical outcomes as iatrogenic (injury caused by their medical treatment). Imershein and Brents interviewed 16 Floridian medical malpractice plaintiffs who received awards in excess of $250,000. Among their key findings were that claimants suffered few harmful side effects from litigation, and factors other than money played a role in their decision to sue. Many respondents reported that they felt better for having "told their story." Retribution or deterrence were also important reasons for suing. They felt angry and betrayed by the medical profession and they did not want anyone else to go through the same thing.

In this study I analyze in-depth physician and claimant interviews, based on grounded theory (Glaser and Strauss 1967). After reviewing these data, several themes emerge. The first is the distinction between the biomedical and the sociomedical definitions of medical outcomes. Physicians judge medical outcomes in terms of whether they acted according to generally accepted medical practice. In contrast, patients judge medical outcomes in terms of how their lives have changed. A second theme involves the uncertainty of medical practice for physicians. Marginalization is a third theme and occurs when physicians push their patients' social concerns related to their treatment to the periphery. A fourth category contains several related themes involving the emotive and behavioral reactions of litigants. These include anger, distrust, defensive medical practice, vindication, and deference towards their physicians. Finally, some respondents view medicine more as a business rather than a humanistic institution.

Methods

The data for my research include closed (i.e., cases reaching verdict/settlement) malpractice claims from the Massachusetts Board of Registration in Medicine (N=4,353), closed malpractice claims from New York State's Office of Professional Medical Conduct (N=30,516), audiotaped in-depth interviews with physicians (n=17) and claimants (n=16), and a survey of sued Massachusetts physicians (n=129). The Massachusetts Medical Board data include those closed claims originally reported under state law from December 1981 through February 1992. The New York data include those claims reported under state law and closed from 1982 to 1992.

I obtained the in-depth interview respondents by placing announcements in newspapers in Massachusetts and New York.[3] I also used a list of physicians from the Massachusetts Board of Medicine who had at least one case that went to court. Since only 117 of the 1,840 physician names on the Massachusetts Medical Board list were women, I over-sampled this group in order to get the same number of men and women physicians for the in-depth interviews. This was necessary in order to get enough women physicians for a more detailed analysis.

The purpose of the survey is to provide socioeconomic information not available in the Massachusetts closed claims data and provide criterion variables for comparing a probability sampling of Massachusetts claims to claims from other data sources (see Table 17.1). However, the claimant data in this survey are likely to be less reliable than the physician data since the former are based on physician reports. I collected these data by systematically drawing 758 of the 1,840 names from the list mentioned above and mailing the survey along with a cover letter. I sent a post card reminder to the non-respondents two weeks later, producing a response rate of 17 percent. The low response is probably due to the sensitive nature of the topic and the fact that physicians are both very busy and frequently solicited to fill out questionnaires. Physicians generally have lower response rates than other professionals (Sudman 1985). I instructed the physicians to fill out the questionnaire in reference to their most recent claim only.[4]

The in-depth interviews were semi-structured. Ten physician interviews took place in their offices and lasted about an hour. Seven interviews were conducted via phone. Eight of the claimant interviews were conducted at home and 8 via phone. The claimant interviews took about 90 minutes. I asked respondents to discuss their city or town and neighborhood, their occupation, their malpractice case, and possible solutions to malpractice. The respondents were asked to recall past events. In several cases the events took place more than 15 years ago. The respondents' memories were likely to be selective given that they were recalling painful issues. Finally, the opportunity for exploring the details of each case from both sides was precluded since I was advised by counsel not to interview claimants and physicians who were parties to the same case. Doing so might increase the likelihood of either litigant reopening the case and subpoenaing my interview data as new evidence.

Table 17.1.   Comparison of the Modal Responses and Median Among the Four Data Sets[1]

Variables	In-depth Interviews[2]		New York State Closed Claims (N = 30,516)	Massachusetts Physician Survey[3] (n = 129)	Massachusetts Closed Claims (N = 4,353)
	Physicians (n = 17)	Claimants (n = 16)			
Type Error	35% Performing (17)	44% Performing (16)	31% performing (22,076)	42% Diagnostic (113)	63% Performing (4,267)
Award Made	53% Yes (15)	75% Yes (16)	40% Yes (30,490)	44% Yes[4] (81)	43% Yes (4,353)
Median Severity[5]	$62,500 (8)	$28,500 (12)	$12,224[6] (15,189)	$150,000 (39)	$110,000 (1,882)
Physician Sex	53% Men (17)	38% Men[7] (16)	95% Men (19,685)	95% Men (129)	92% Men (3,963)

Notes:
1. Numbers in parentheses are cases with non-missing data from which the percents were computed.
2. Claimants and physicians are not parties to the same suit.
3. All claims, unless otherwise stated.
4. Closed claims only.
5. Includes only those cases where an award was made.
6. Includes only those claims awarded since 1982.
7. Sex of claimants.

Claims' Characteristics

Although my research relies primarily on the in-depth interviews, the statistical data are of importance. Using in-depth interviews with the quantitative data is vital because each have different strengths for understanding malpractice claims. The statistical data are necessary for describing the populations (Fielding and Fielding 1986; Denzin 1989).

The Massachusetts closed claims data show that the top five categories comprising 27 percent of all medical malpractice claims are: improper performance, improper treatment, failure to diagnose cancer, improper choice of treatment, and improper management of obstetric delivery. (All categorical series in this paper are listed in descending order of frequency.) These categories are relatively similar to New York where 55 percent of the claims are based on improper performance and failure to diagnose. The general pattern in both states is that physicians tend to be sued more for diagnostic errors while surgeons tend to be sued more for performance errors. Malpractice claims also take a long time to resolve. The median duration of malpractice claims in New York is seven years (there is no information on this in the Massachusetts data).

I found the in-depth interview group similar to the New York and Massachusetts populations in terms of: the incident location (the modal category is operating room), the final disposition (nearly half of the claims were settled out of court), the proportion appealed (less than 10 percent), type of practice (a slight majority sued are non-surgeons), and age (physician mean are at the time of occurrence is the mid-forties, and late thirties for patients). The differences between the interview groups are summarized in Table 17.1. The Massachusetts survey data show that the modal type of error on which the claim was based is diagnostic (42 percent) rather than performing. Awards are more common among those interviewed than among those surveyed (see Table 17.1). The size of the award is difficult to interpret because one or two large awards can strongly skew the data, particularly when there are few cases. In order to minimize this I report the median size of claims where an award was made ($62,500, $28,500, $12,244, $150,000, $110,000, respectively in Table 17.1). Only 5 percent of the awards were more than $350,000 and $1,000,000 in New York and Massachusetts, respectively. Women comprise a greater proportion of those interviewed because I over-sampled women physicians, and more women claimants volunteered for interviews.

In terms of socioeconomic status, claimants in New York State and Massachusetts are less educated than the claimants interviewed. For example, 65 percent of the claimants in New York, and 74 percent of the claimants reported by physicians in the Massachusetts survey had a high school education or less. In contrast, 87 percent of the interviewed claimants reported a bachelors or higher level of educaiton.[5] I conclude that those interviewed are reasonably similar to the claimants in the New York and Massachusetts data set with the exception that awards, though smaller, were more often paid; my respondents are disproportionately female, and they are more highly educated. Therefore, while I will not generalize from the interview data, I believe that the in-depth interviews represent reasonably typical cases and therefore the experiences reported are probably similar to the populations.[6]

The Medical Versus Social Definition of Medical Outcomes

The accounts that follow are public issues since they are closely related to changes in the structure of health care outlined earlier. However these accounts also reshape the existing social contexts over time (Giddens 1984). Certainly the major question of interest is why the claimants decided to sue their physicians. This question led me to look at how my respondents defined medical outcomes. Mishler (1990) notes the distinction between the *voice of medicine* and the *voice of the lifeworld* in his study of physician-patient communication. The former is based on the professional authority of the physician and focuses on establishing the diagnosis. This process involves physicians asking specific questions of patients. I noted that physicians defined patient outcomes using the voice of medicine, that is, on the basis of medically oriented assumptions (i.e., did I do the right thing or did I negligently harm the patient through my act or omission?). In contrast, the voice of the lifeworld is the voice of the person within his illness, which is embedded within the person's social context (did the outcome change my life?). In this model the physician would learn about the patient's symptoms and how they affect the person's life, via a more open-ended discussion.

But just what factors influence people to pursue a claim? Although there can be no conclusive answer to this question, Hickson et al. (1992) conducted a survey of mothers in Florida whose infants had experienced permanent injuries or death to determine why they sued. The most common reasons for suing were: advice from acquaintances (33 percent), recognizing a cover-up (24 percent), and financial need (24 percent). Stimpson and Webb (1975) found that it takes time after a visit to the physician to make sense of what happened. The authors found that the visit itself was characterized by the patient's deferential behavior towards the physician, whereas the period after the visit involves making sense of what happened—possibly bringing the doctor's judgment into question. They also noted that when recounting visits patients tended to be negative towards their doctors and portrayed themselves in a more active, assertive light.

CLEAR-CUT NEGLIGENCE

Some of the claimants I interviewed found the decision to sue straightforward because they perceived gross negligence, which was corroborated by others involved. Claire's account unfolded when problems developed in her mother's leg due to an artery blockage.[7] She was admitted for an angioplasty. When the angioplasty failed to clear the artery the surgeons decided to administer blood anti-coagulants in efforts to dissolve the blockage. Anti-coagulants were contraindicated because they would dissolve not only the targeted clots, but the clots that sealed the punctures from the angioplasty procedures. Expert testimony during the trial indicated that the correct treatment would have been a thrombectomy that would physically remove the occluding clot. Furthermore, the physicians were found negligent in not closely observing their patient for hemorrhaging during post-op. A thrombectomy was performed later and the hemorrhaging stopped. Nevertheless, Claire's mother was critically ill from the loss of blood and had to be admitted to intensive care, where at one point she had to be resuscitated.

Claire and her husband decided to sue on behalf of her mother while she was still in the hospital. The decision was aided in major part because another physician told them that things did not go the way they were supposed to and some of the nurses said that they believed errors were made. This legitimated their decision to sue. Henry and Claire recalled:

> *Henry:* Well and one of them [nurses] said, "This should never have happened." I can remember those words, "This should never have happened."
> *Claire:* Now that could have been a general expression.
> *Henry:* Yeah, but the signal that we were getting was that the nurses felt that this was (*Claire:* Bad medicine.) bad medicine. Ah and I think some of the doctors, some of them like Dr. — who was so helpful they were almost too helpful. You know, they were, as if they were making up for somebody else's error. So you got a very strange sense at the time.

They spoke to a lawyer who advised they do nothing until her mother was released a few months later. A jury eventually awarded her mother an award in excess of my sample median of $41,000.[8]

UNCERTAIN NEGLIGENCE

However, most claimants did not sue immediately. Instead, they socially reconstructed their reality over a longer period (Becker 1970; Glaser and Strauss 1967; Berger and Luckmann 1967), transforming themselves from patients to claimants. Their decision only unfolded as they spoke with others and had time to assess whether their conditions adversely affected their lives. One such case involved Diane, who was recovering from surgery. A resident began making advances towards her and, soon thereafter, sexually assaulted her. Recalling her decision to sue, she said:

> it was a little over a year when I was watching [a talk show] and, it was a program about doctors and dentists who molest. I thought, My God! This has happened to somebody besides me! I thought I was the only person in the world this had happened to. And the next day I went and saw a lawyer.

But friends had been encouraging her to sue before this:

> And I think I was ready to [sue] because a number of people had said to me, mostly men, Why don't you see a lawyer? I remember saying that I'm just not emotionally strong enough.

She won a small award.

Another example is Michael and Rose and their infant son. Rose had originally noticed a lump in her son's scrotum and, suspecting cancer, took him to their physician. The lump was diagnosed as a benign hydrocele (an accumulation of fluid) and a routine surgical procedure was scheduled. Rose was with her son after the surgery and noticed that once he regained consciousness he became less responsive over the next couple of hours. She alerted the nursing staff several times that he did not look or respond well, but her fears were downplayed. Tragically, he died as a result of hemorrhaging as his internal sutures had failed. Although Michael and Rose's family pressed them to sue right away, they did not initiate a claim until several months later:

> We also waited [several] months before we went to an attorney because we were in so much emotional pain that we didn't want to lash out at the wrong people. We weren't sure what had happened, let alone whether someone should be responsible for what had happened. But we were being urged by a lot of our friends and family members to go to an attorney and sue right away, even though they did not know all of the particulars of the case, because we didn't talk to them a lot about it.

Their case was eventually settled out of court for less than the median award. This case is interesting because it illustrates that it is not the severity of the case alone that determines whether or not a malpractice claim is filed. In some cases even catastrophic outcomes take time to socially construct as malpractice. People need time in order to get past the feeling of shock and disbelief that is likely to accompany a catastrophic outcome.

Another case in which the passage of time was important for the social construction of malpractice is Richard, who had a tumor on his spinal cord that was misdiagnosed as a parathyroid adenoma. This condition involves tumors on the parathyroid gland that interfere with gland's ability to produce hormones regulating calcium in the blood. He had been experiencing pain the upper right side of his chest that prevented him from working. Surgery later revealed no adenoma. Richard then went to a neurologist who suspected, by Richard's gait, that he had a tumor on the spinal cord. A month later Richard had surgery, which eliminated the problem. He returned to work a few months later. He was awarded less than the median award in an out-of-court settlement. When I asked Richard about how he made the decision to sue he said:

> Well, I took a number of months, I didn't go back to work until November. . . . And then I spoke to a friend of mine whose brother-in-law had a malpractice suit and had an attorney. I went to see this attorney and he said he thought that I had a case. . . . We sued the hospital, the internist, and the surgeon. . . . I think after 5 or 6 years we got a settlement.

Richard's subsequent interpretive process centered on the pain, inconvenience, and the disruption of his job. His decision was aided by finding a physician who was successful in treating him and speaking with a friend whose brother-in-law was party to a malpractice suit. These provided the social support that contributed to the definition of Richard's life and context.

In contrast, physicians define treatment outcomes from a biomedical perspective. Physicians view themselves as working within an uncertain environment and even a skillful performance cannot guarantee expected outcomes. Dr. Greer, an orthopedic surgeon, treated a young man who was the victim of a head-on automobile collision, sustaining internal injuries and leg fractures. He alleged that his leg was treated improperly. On admission, the patient was in critical condition, and it took two weeks to stabilize him before his fractures could be treated. Greer decided on a conservative means of treating the fractures, using traction instead of surgery. This resulted in an expected shortening of the patient's leg as a result of bowing. Had he decided to treat the patient more aggressively with surgery, the leg would not have bowed. However, surgery would have put the patient at excessive risk, according to Greer. He recalled:

> Well, I thought this patient was very ungrateful for what we had tried to do and the fact that we had to save his life. And I thought that I had a very good relationship with this man. I spent a great deal of time when he would come here to the office. I used to spend a great deal of time talking with him. And I never had any inkling that he was contemplating suing me. I don't really think at the time he was coming here to the office that he was thinking about this. I think it's something that maybe evolved over time. But when you talk with some of the older physicians they will tell you that sometimes these things will come from very unexpected sources. You can't tell, you can't predict a suit.

Greer raised an important point. It is hard to predict when a claim will be made. Greer believed that he did a good job because he saved the patient's life and his leg. Should he have used more aggressive treatment? To do this would constitute a gamble. The patient might have had a straight leg, but in Greer's judgment the patient was more likely to have died. However, the patient's social context was far removed form the medical context in which Greer had to contend. A jury found for Greer a few years later.

Uncertainty

From the physician's perspective the medically correct action is often uncertain. Physicians today continue to have the same fundamental problems with uncertainty that Fox (1957) discussed in her study of medical students at the Cornell Medical College. There, she noted that uncertainty was related to a lack of knowledge or skill of the individual, as well as the limitations of current medical knowledge. The implication drawn from my interviews is that uncertainty expands at a faster rate than the accumulation of knowledge. This is supported by Paget (1988) in her phenomenological analysis of mistakes. She found that physicians viewed medicine as *error-ridden*. Physicians also believed that errors involving judgment (excluding catastrophic outcomes resulting from gross negligence) did not happen at one point in time, rather they unfolded as changes took place within the patient's body. Dr. Rosen, an internist, is a good example. He was involved in a case alleging delayed diagnosis of meningitis in a toddler. Meningitis is an infection of the membranes that surround the brain and the spinal column.

The patient presented with a fever that had been running for 2 or 3 hours. Rosen examined the patient and found no extraordinary symptoms. He prescribed aspirin, which was generally accepted medical practice at the time. The parents returned the next morning because the child appeared much sicker. Rosen was away for a few days and his practice was covered by his partner who also believed the child was not seriously ill. However, Rosen's partner told the parents that should she become worse to bring her in the next day. The child did become worse, but her parents did not bring her in until Rosen returned. Rosen took one look at the child and immediately knew that the child was seriously ill. She clearly presented symptoms of meningitis: stiff neck, listlessness, and lethargy.

He promptly sent the patient to the hospital where the diagnosis was confirmed. They started intensive antibiotic therapy and the child responded favorably. Unfortunately, 20 to 30 percent of children with meningitis lose some or most of their hearing. This problem is well documented and not preventable once meningitis is beyond its early stages. The child lost all of her hearing in one ear and most of her hearing in the other. In retrospect the initial decisions made by Rosen and his partner were wrong because they failed to diagnose and treat the meningitis. This case went to trial, but shortly before the jury would have rendered a verdict, it was the insurance company's decision to settle for more than the median award.

A similar case involved Dr. Conran, a cardiologist, who failed to diagnose pulmonary emboli, even though he and his colleagues considered that possibility. The patient died suddenly shortly thereafter.

> I should have instituted treatment. My feeling is the following: I do feel that I missed [the diagnosis], you know in retrospect. I sit down and I look at it, and it screams pulmonary emboli but you know it's a difference between knowing the answer to the question and sitting down and looking at all the data and saying, oh my God, sure it is, and looking and looking at a patient, listening to their symptoms and watching the data evolve.

Each of these cases illustrates Paget's (1988) argument that acts only become mistaken as time unfolds. Paget states, "Action as it is acted out—that is, in the moment of its externalization—risks error" (1988:48). She concludes:

> A mistake follows an act. It identifies the character of an act in its aftermath. It names it. An act, however, is not mistaken; it becomes mistaken. There is a paradox here, for seen from the inside of action, that is, from the point of view of an actor, an act becomes mistaken only after it has already gone wrong. As it is unfolding, it is not becoming mistaken at all; it is becoming (1988:56).

Perrow (1984) would describe these errors as *normal accidents*, which result from the unforeseen interaction of two or more subsystems that create a system failure. Physicians refer to these as untoward events. They use their best judgment, but it's wrong in retrospect.

Uncertainty is not only part of the practice of medicine itself, it is also a part of how medicine is organized on a day-to-day basis. The following case of Dr. Shah, who is an obstetrician/gynecologist, illustrates this point. He was sued for a drug treatment error. He is an unusual case since he admitted to being negligent. After performing a colposcopy (endoscopic examination of the cervix) on a patient who, unbeknownst to him was pregnant, he negligently signed an order authorizing a rubella vaccination, which has a theoretical potential for causing birth defects. This mistake was due to a lack of coordination among himself, his nurse, and his physician assistant. When this error was discovered the woman was alerted to what had happened. She then had an abortion elsewhere and filed a claim, which was settled out of court for less than the median award. Shah described the nature of his daily medical practice:

> and at the time that the order was brought to me I didn't connect who was getting it. But I kind of assumed, you know we often times sign orders for all sorts of reasons, and again, that's no excuse because when something goes wrong you can hold yourself to the letter of the medical practice and say, that's not good medical practice. But, it's like everything else. You cut corners to some extent with anything you do. Most of the time things go well and nothing ever comes of it and occasionally things do come of it and you say, well, maybe I should be a lot more compulsive and do everything according to the way it should be done. But I also realize that in the practice of medicine and most lines of work you just can't do that. You'd spend so much time doing all sorts of stuff that really was not productive at all, plus you have to have a certain amount of trust and ability to delegate responsibilities.

Physicians face even greater problems of coordinating patient care with in-patient admissions. A great deal of uncertainty in medical work is related to its bureaucratic organization. Physicians face uncertainty because many people proceed on the basis of imperfect knowledge as they perform medical services.

Marginalization

While uncertainty was an important theme among physicians, marginalization was a central theme among claimants. Physicians were more concerned with the medically correct course of action (i.e., producing the desired outcome). Although patients ultimately want the same thing, they are more immediately concerned with the process of care. Marginalization occurs when physicians push their patients' personal and social health concerns to the periphery (Waltzkin 1991). Some examples are: not listening to or discounting what patients have to say; patronizing the patient; ignoring the patient's personal concerns; and, avoiding patients or withholding information after a maloccurrence. Marginalization is most common in tertiary care medicine. Brody (1987) argues that tertiary care is guided by a short-term decisional ethic whereby the physician as technician robs the patient of autonomy. In contrast, primary care is guided more by a long-term relational ethic in which the physician decides not whether to provide information to the patient but when, thus bringing the patient as person to the center stage of treatment. Thus a health care system emphasizing tertiary care will facilitate a greater incidence of marginalization. Todd (1989) notes marginalization in her critique of the biomedical model. She taped encounters between physicians and patients that revealed how physicians controlled the flow of information. Patients outwardly accepted this control; however, in follow-up interviews Todd discovered that patients either withheld information or changed physicians. Physicians ultimately were never aware of how patients had defined the visit. Michael and Rose's case illustrates the medical staff's failure to listen:

> When they [surgeons] came back [to see their son after the surgery] I said that [he] had a very bad color, that he seemed yellow. The doctor said, "Well that's because of the shot we gave him, he's just recovering from that." I said well he seems like he's not reacting, he seemed very clumsy to me. I mentioned that his eyes seemed to be dilated. I also saw him [her son] pant once and I mentioned that to the doctor but he didn't seem to've heard what I said because he was talking to the other doctors . . . they had sort of casually dismissed my questions twice saying that was the shot they had given him . . .

The surgeon and the rest of the staff believed that they fully understood the situation and that Rose was just a worried mother whose observations had no medical significance.

There was little material in the physicians' accounts suggesting marginalization. However, I told some physicians about this claimant theme and asked if they agreed with it. One physician told me:

> Oh I think it's a valid patient complaint [patronize and don't listen], I think we're trained that way. If a patient gives a few things and they start to click, that's what we're taught in medical school. We come to a conclusion. Perhaps if we listen a little bit longer, that's always good, but that's hard to do when you're up against a twenty minutes office visit and have things to do. (Dr. Tibbets)

Another physician, speaking on behalf of his colleagues, said:

> No, I think they [patients] are right. I think doctors tend to be arrogant and they, when they are talking to the stupid, stupid public they tend to be condescending in that how could you possibly understand this complex medical situation? How can I explain it to you? It took me all of my life to learn this and you just have to take my word for it. Neither am I going to take the time to sit down and translate this into common [language] so you just have to accept what I say. (Dr. Greer)

Another example of marginalization occurred in the 1950s. Lisa had been experiencing severe cramps during menstruation that were caused by the early stages of endometriosis. She had developed a fibroid tumor on her uterine wall, which could potentially spread outside the uterus and lead to cancer. As she wanted to have more children, she distinctly and repeatedly told the surgeon that the surgery was to be limited to the removal of the fibroid tumor. However, upon recovery from surgery the surgeon said that he had performed a compete hysterectomy because of the advanced spread of disease. He and his assistants ignored her concerns about bearing more children. She became extremely upset, which the surgeon interpreted as a need for psychiatric care. She recalled being patronized by the psychiatrist dispatched by her surgeon:

> This strange doctor comes [He said,] "How are we today?" [patronizing voice] And I said, Who the hell are you and what do you want? And he said, [patronizing tone] "Well you're a secretary. If you went to a file cabinet and found some trash in it, what would you do?" Inferring that my insides were all trash I said, Are you a psychiatrist? And he said, "Yes, how did you know? Have you been to one before?" I said, No, you're just like the ones in the movies. Now get out of my room.

When Lisa's case came to trial her surgeon contended that it was not only medically necessary to perform the hysterectomy, but that they had awakened her from general anesthesia to get her consent to proceed with the hysterectomy, which they alleged she gave. According to the testimony of Lisa's surgeon under cross examination:

> She [Lisa] had nembutal, three grains, the evening before [surgery], three grains three hours before operation, a quarter of a grain of morphine, 1/100 grain of scopolamine one hour before operation, and intravenously eight grains of morphine as often as the anesthetist and I thought. (Court transcript)

In the final deliberation the jury could not accept the surgeon's argument and found for the plaintiff. The jury determined that the award should be $2,000, which included pain and suffering. Lisa noted how low this figure was in light of women's primary roles as mothers in the 1950s.

Emotive and Behavioral Reactions

Several themes involving emotive and behavioral reactions emerged from my interviews and the Massachusetts survey. As illustrated below, the physicians' interviews contained themes of anger, distrust of patients, and defensive medicine; the patients' themes included anger, vindication, and deference.

PHYSICIANS

Physicians believe they are often sued for non-negligent maloccurrences and they get angry when it happens (Poole 1989; Smith 1987; Drimmer 19889). There is evidence to support this. Taragin et al. (1992) conducted a retrospective cohort study of closed malpractice claims in New Jersey and concluded that physicians charged with malpractice provided defensible care in most cases. They also found that cases that they identified as defensible were rarely awarded—regardless of the severity of the patient's injury. In order to find out whether physicians ever saw justification to the claims filed against them I asked physicians participating in the Massachusetts survey, "To what extent do you believe the plaintiff was justified in filing her or his suit?" In those cases where an award was made 44 percent of the physicians responded that they perceived at least some justification on the part of the claimant, compared to only 22 percent of the respondents in those cases where no award was made (Chi-Square = 4.76, P < .05, Phi = .22, n = 116). This finding lends support to Taragin et al., since this suggests that most awards arise from legitimate claims.

Higher malpractice claims rates cause physicians to trust patients less than they once did and to practice defensive medicine. This lack of trust is magnified after being sued. Dr. Adler is an internist who was sued for a delayed diagnosis of lupus, an autoimmune disorder causing inflammation to the connective tissue.

> It makes me feel like she's [the patient] not as nice a person as I thought. I guess it makes me feel a little bit like she's a threat. Now everybody who walks in, I guess I'm unconsciously sort of sizing them up. Are they a potential enemy?

Dr. Manning, also an internist, voiced the same sentiment. She was sued by a patient she had treated for a lacerated arm. The patient later claimed that Manning was responsible for nerve damage and a partial loss of function. Manning won, saying ". . . every patient is a potential threat. You can't see patients as patients, you have to see them as potential liabilities." These experiences have a strong impact on physicians so they seek to limit their future liability as best they can through defensive practices.

One example of defensive practice is ordering medically unwarranted tests. Dr. Manning said ". . . you play the defensive medicine game and you order some stuff [tests] that are kind of silly."

Dr. Greer said, "I think when any doctor practices defensively it means that they are more likely to order unnecessary studies."

Detailed chart documentation is another form of defensive medicine. Dr. King, an internist, was sued by a patient whom she had treated for renal failure and other problems over a four-year period. She finally diagnosed a benign pituitary tumor, which, according to the patient's medical records, was diagnosed many years earlier and forgotten. Her diagnosis was made difficult by the multiple medications that the patient was taking. She won that case and emphasized the importance of recovering herself:

> . . . judgment counts for nothing anymore in the medical profession. Nobody cares what your opinion really is. They just want to see that you document it. You document justification for your opinion.

Dr. Rosen made the same point:

> Now I write [in the medical chart] a whole big deal. You know it takes longer because I always have to worry that someday somebody is going to come back and say, "Well, gee I see that you checked that the child didn't have a stiff neck, that you checked to see that the belly was nice and soft and that the chest was clear . . ."

These forms of defensive practice present no problems for patients since they offer the potential for more accurate diagnoses. However, from the physician's perspective they represent the erosion of clinical autonomy (Fielding 1990b). This involves how a patient's care is managed (in this case covering oneself against liability by doing things that are not considered medically necessary). Physicians view this as a threat to their professional expertise.

A final example of an emotive reaction is Dr. Boyd, an obstetrician who was sued by a woman in her second pregnancy. Dr. Boyd used an epidural to anesthetize the patient before delivering her baby. This requires a large needle to introduce anesthesia into the spinal column. In so doing she punctured the spinal membrane, allowing some of the spinal fluid to escape. This is a self-correcting condition, but it causes severe headaches for several weeks or more. Boyd had to pay an award that was less than the median amount. She told me:

> Well, it [being sued] makes you angry at everything. It makes you angry at the legal system and in particular the lawyers who do this for a living, who, you feel are living of everybody's pain. Your pain, the patient's pain or perceived pain to them, and it makes you feel like they're a bunch of sleazy parasites.

Although this should not have happened, this mistake was non-negligent. Physicians argue that no one performs their job flawlessly at all times. Patients should be able to accept the fact that things do not always proceed as expected.

CLAIMANTS

Anger was certainly felt by the claimants. Lisa is an example. She was outraged over her unauthorized hysterectomy. This was exacerbated by the nursing staff's lack of support during her stay in the hospital. They did not appreciate her attitude. Lisa recalled:

> I mean the nurse came in and she was so nasty. There were a couple of nurses that I used to lie in bed thinking, oh, when I get the strength I'm going to kill them! The hospital was terrible.

Lisa still feels anger: "I would swear that I was just vindictive. . . .I still am, vindictive. Forty years later I still think that way." She went to a newspaper in a major city hoping her story would be published so others could read about her experience. The paper refused to report it on the grounds that it would be too damaging to the medical profession.

Withholding information after treatment, or avoiding patients, also presents problems from the patient's perspective. Physicians and institutions withhold information because they fear liability. However, in withholding information they deny patients information about their social context. In effect, they deny patients a degree of access to something of themselves and this adds to their patients' emotional distress. This is why some claimants told me they sued, not just for money, but because they wanted to learn the truth. Rose recalled:

> . . . we were suing because we wanted information, and we didn't want to let this [her son's death] be able to happen without knowing what had happened to him. When we got the autopsy report, it was so inadequate and what they called the death—it wasn't bleeding to death, it was therapeutic misadventure. It meant nothing to us. . . .

Claire's husband Henry recounted the same problem of not being able to learn about what had happened: "We didn't really get a full explanation of what happened until we went to trial and then because the doctors had to explain it to a jury . . ." A good example of how avoiding patients after a maloccurrence can trigger a suit is told by Suzanne, whose then obstetrician relied on another physician's prior typing of her blood, which was incorrect. A blood incompatibility resulted in a stillbirth. She had been unsuccessfully trying to find out about the details of what happened:

> So then I decided, "That's it [decided to sue]!" The son of a bitch, you know what I mean? He hasn't even contacted me. He's been, you now, hiding from me . . .

She won her case, and received an award of $5,000.

One physician continued to see his patient but did not acknowledge her reported problem. Tanya had a hip replacement that resulted in damage to the peroneal nerve, causing pain and her foot to extend downward. She lost her suit.

> I wanted somebody to say, lookit, somethin' happened and we're gonna try and get to the bottom of it. . . . I can accept a mistake. What I couldn't accept is them sendin' me home saying' the operation was fine . . . I was half out of my mind! . . . they ignored the aftercare.

The irony is that while these defensive strategies are designed to minimize any evidence that can be used against physicians in a suit, they may increase the very likelihood of being sued.

Some respondents said that vindication was also one of the benefits of suing. When I asked Claire and Henry about how they felt after winning Claire's mother's case, they replied:

> *Henry:* What was important is the vindication. The fact that she felt that.
> *Claire:* Everything that could have gone wrong, went wrong . . .
> *Henry:* She suddenly was vindicated. She wanted the money but only [because] we had personally put out a fair amount of money during her recovery period and she was very anxious that we get, she repay us.

Some claimants felt that providers should beheld responsible for clear cut iatrogenic injury. John fell and broke his hip. During his recovery from surgery his nurses failed to raise the rails on the side of his bed. He fell out and reinjured his hip.

> I wasn't doing it for the money. I was doing it that someone should face the responsibility that those side gear those side panels, should have been absolutely [up].

Yet in spite of what many claimants had been through, there were a number of claimants who still felt deference regarding their former physicians. For example, Tanya told me, "I don't want to rip this man [the orthopedic surgeon] apart. My husband says, 'Don't talk about him, he's probably a good doctor . . .'"

This is a striking statement in light of what Tanya had been through. Claimants often emphasize that they were not out to attack their physicians. They do get angry and some may want revenge, but most just wanted to recover their emotional and financial losses. Contrary to what the media and physicians say, filing a malpractice claim is an anxiety producing experience. Many of my claimants were apprehensive about using the legal system to challenge the professional dominance of the medical profession.

Medicine as a Business

The context in which medicine is practiced has changed greatly over the past 25 years. Today most medical procedures are practiced within an increasingly business oriented context (i.e., medicine as a commodity) (Lander 1978; Relman 1980, 1991; Fielding 1987, 1990a, b; Hay 1992). Thus as medicine moves away from a humanitarian or service ideal it becomes more subject to the expectations for providing standardized service and is thus vulnerable to liability. A few claimants and physicians felt that some of the problems associated with malpractice claims were the result of medicine's changing service ideal. Suzanne said:

> I think the old attitude, you know, the old system of having a family doctor and having a relationship like it's your distant uncle, or . . . that paternalistic, family attitude, and trust. That no longer exits, that's one thing. But um, I think there's several [other] reasons. I think it's [medicine] more and more a business. And the people are seeing themselves as consumers of a business, rather than this lofty, almost like, as if a [sic] person were a rabbi or a priest. I think it's now, just as if you were buying a car, and the car screws up. And the consumer, if you want to call it that now, instead of the patient, is becoming more savvy and more sophisticated, and is more willing to change doctors . . .

Dr. Abrahams saw malpractice claims as a symptom of a structural problem whereby medicine is increasingly run as a big business. He is an ophthalmic surgeon who attempted a cataract removal on a woman in her sixties. A medical device failed and the operation had to be terminated and continued at another time. She ended up with 20/60 vision instead of the expected 20/20. Abrahams and the device manufacturer each settled for less than the median award. Abrahams said:

> I mean medicine has become a big business. The multi-person groups I would assume have a higher risk because one doctor is taking two days off

a week, and you're [the patient] seeing different doctors each time. I think that the general trend toward medicine is toward these larger health plans and away from the private practitioner. And I think as soon as you make medicine impersonal . . . they're not suing a person, they're suing an organization. It's much easier to do that.

Dr. King looked at the financial problems from a structural perspective. When I asked her why she thought these were more claims she said:

I think the way we have used technology it's becoming more and more of a [medical] liability because we [patients and insurers] can't afford the technology.

She implies that medical technology is a double-edged sword. Although it has enhanced the stature and income of members of the medical profession, its high cost of acquisition and operation is a major reason for the intrusion of new actors into medicine. Although the physician historically has been the dominant player in medicine, physicians have always had intimate relationships with their patients. This is no longer true, particularly among tertiary care physicians. The physician of today is much more a technician and a manger, and the setting in which he or she works is more like a business office than a physician's office or a patient's home.

The high cost of medical care is closely related to the medicine as a business theme. Manuel is a good example. His thumb was improperly set after an accident. When he learned this he refused to pay the added expense of correcting the problem:

I said but if it's not [a non-negligent outcome], if somebody screwed up then why should I have to pay for all this stuff? And I says all I want to do is talk to somebody who will give me some straight answers. But if you don't want to talk to me, I said my attorney says he thinks we got a malpractice suit and we should go to town on them . . .

They settled for a very small award.

Conclusions

Physicians and claimants are greatly constrained by the health care system. Biomedical definitions of outcomes, uncertainty, anger over seemingly frivolous claims, distrust of patients, defensive practice, and medicine as a business were the major concerns of physicians. Although some claimants agreed with physicians that medicine has become more of a business, their concerns centered on marginalization, anger, distrust of physicians, lack of information and acknowledgment of their problem, vindication, and deference. The interviews do provide a sense of physicians and patients as strangers. The most interesting findings stem from the differences between how the physicians and claimants defined medical outcomes. Physicians define treatments from a biomedical perspective. According to this view, if they act according to generally accepted medical practice they should not be held liable for maloccurrence since they are clearly beyond the control of medicine. This is true legally. Individual physicians justify maloccurrences by arguing that the practice of medicine is filled with uncertainty. However, this argument is inconsistent with the history of the medical profession, which has vigorously publicized its achievements. Both the terms *science* and *miracle* have often appeared in their public announcements, strongly implying the notion of certainty. *Science* implies precision and understanding while *miracle* implies a supernatural event. Taken together, less than perfect outcomes become unacceptable. Thus, the promotion of medicine, and consumer education, are the primary reasons why patients have high expectations. This inconsistency is something that the medical profession must address, should there be continued emphasis on high-tech care.

In contrast, the claimants I interviewed define their treatments from a sociomedical perspective. They socially construct (or reconstruct) their medical treatments and outcomes in relation to their social context. The perception of malpractice and the decision to sue are more social than individual and not always immediately evident to patients. This finding is consistent with May and Stengel (1990), Stimpson and Webb (1975), and Hickson et al. (1992), who find that claimants seek extensive input from others about whether to sue. The patient's decision process may also be influenced by the physician's distrust of patients and the defensive practice of withholding information after a maloccurrence. By withholding information physicians deny patients the social context necessary for making sense of what happened. Withholding such information may be a strong factor influencing the decision to sue. Claimants certainly sought money but they also sued for emotional losses. They wanted to learn the truth and be vindicated.

I conclude that marginalization is of lesser importance to the decision-making process among those I interviewed, even though it was the most frequently occurring theme. While the claimants wanted to be treated as mature and feeling people, they did not expect it, and did not consider this a legitimate basis for suing. This is not to say that marginalization is not a serious problem. Marginalization could certainly "tip the scales" towards suing in some situations. In extreme cases, such as Lisa's, it can be the driving factor behind a claim. Furthermore, avoiding the marginalization of patients is not only important humanistically, it is important medically. The case of Michael and Rose clearly and repeatedly telling the staff that their son was becoming less responsive during recovery is a good example.

The theme of medicine as a business is particularly poignant given the specter of managed competition. This creates a dialectical tension. Medical care is moving towards a more systematic analysis of medical procedures, and greater accountability and efficiency. These should standardize care and reduce the likelihood of iatrogenic injury. However, this rationalization of medical care threatens the intimate relationship between physicians and patients. Thus, medical care is reduced from the status of a humanistic institution to a commercial commodity. Such a status legitimates and encourages recovery for damages.

The increasing number of medical malpractice claims is rooted in the practice of inherently risky medical procedures and the organization of the health care system. Malpractice claims have been poorly understood because of the contrasting assumptions used by physicians and patients in defining medical outcomes. The most effective way to control malpractice claims is to emphasize prevention, provide more humanistic primary care, and reevaluate the social policies that mold the structure of the health care system.

Notes

1. Although obstetricians are primary care specialists, many of the procedures that they perform are invasive, such as fetal monitoring and Caesarean sections. Gynecologists perform fewer invasive procedures but they are included here because many obstetricians practice in both areas.

2. There is a tragic irony here since she died in 1989 as a result of the failure of her physicians to diagnose a rare cancer (Paget 1993). Several mistakes were made in the course of her care. At Northwestern University her physicians failed to order spinal X-rays as indicated by her symptoms of back pain. Later, while in Florida, a second physician did order an X-ray, but he failed to detect a clear shadow indicating Paget's pathology. Subsequent care then proceeded on the false assumption that her pain was due to soft tissue injury.

3. Fourteen interviews resulted from author queries placed in the *New York Times Book Review*, 10 interviews came from the Massachusetts Medical Board list, 6 interviews were respondents from announcements placed in upstate New York papers, and 3 interviews were from announcements placed in Boston newspapers.

4. The major claim dispositions in these data include 29 percent open cases, 29 percent settled out of court (31 of these 37 cases resulted in awards to the claimants) and 15 percent jury finding for the defendant. The other categories include: no attorney accepted the claimant's case, case was dropped, case was settled before judgment, jury found for the plaintiff, summary judgment for the defendant, and other.

5. Seventy-five percent of the claimants in New York State reporting income earned $30,000 or less (n=2,541).

6. However, I can generalize findings form the Massachusetts survey to that population with moderate confidence because the survey is similar to the population on the criterion variables mentioned in text, except that the survey defendants were less likely to drop their claims. Additionally, the modal error type in the survey was diagnostic rather than performing. Having said this, the physicians interviewed in-depth were as likely to own their homes as those in the physician population. Ninety-six percent of the physicians in the survey reported owning their homes. In contrast, claimants interviewed in-depth were less likely to own their homes. Sixty-seven percent of the claimants reported owning their homes.

7. Names of all physicians and claimants have been changed throughout this study.

8. In most cases I report awards relative to the median, since the size of an award is a potential identifier. However, I do report the exact size of the award in those cases more than 25 years old.

References

The American Medical Association. 1984. Socioeconomic Characteristics of Medical Practice. Chicago: AMA.

———. 1987. Socioeconomic Characteristics of Medical Practice. Chicago: AMA.

———. 1991. Socioeconomic Characteristics of Medical Practice. Chicago: AMA.

————. 1993. Socioeconomic Characteristics of Medical Practice. Chicago: AMA.

Becker, Howard S. 1970. Sociological Work. Chicago: Aldine.

Berger, Peter L., and T. Luckmann. 1967. The Social Construction of Reality. New York: Doubleday.

Bosk, Charles. 1979. Forgive and Remember: Managing Medical Failure. Chicago: University of Chicago.

Brenna, Troyen A., Lucian L. Leape, Nan M. Laird et al. 1991. "Incidence of adverse events and negligence in hospitalized patients." New England Journal of Medicine 324:370–376.

Brody, Howard. 1987. Stories of Sickness. New Haven, Conn.: Yale University Press.

Congressional Budget Office. 1992. Economic Implications of Rising Health Care Costs. Washington, D.C.: United States Congressional Budget Office.

Denzin, Norman K. 1989. The Research Act. Englewood Cliffs, N.J.: Prentice-Hall.

Drimmer, Jack. 1989. "My malpractice ordeal is over—after only 26 years." Medical Economics (October 2):50–52.

Dutton, Diana B. 1988. Worse Than The Disease: Pitfalls of Medical Progress. New York: Cambridge University.

Fielding, Nigel, and J. Fielding. 1986. Linking Data. Beverly Hills: Sage Publications.

Fielding, Stephen L. 1987. Physicians Under Crossfire: Medical Malpractice Suits and Cost Containment in Massachusetts. Ann Arbor, Mich.: University Microfilms; 87–13, 298.

————. 1990a. "The social construction of the medical malpractice crisis: A case study of Massachusetts physicians." Sociological Forum 5:279–295.

————. 1990b. "Physician reactions to malpractice suits and cost containment in Massachusetts." Work and Occupations 17:302–319.

Fox, Renee C. 1957. "Training for uncertainty." In The Student Physician, eds. R.K. Merton, G.G. Reader, and P.L. Kendall, 207–41. Cambridge, Mass.: Harvard University.

Giddens, Anthony. 1984. The Constitution of Society. Berkeley: University of California Press.

Glaser, Barney, and Anselm L. Strauss. 1967. Discovery of Grounded Theory. Chicago: Aldine.

Hay, Iain. 1992. Money, Medicine, and Malpractice in American Society. New York: Praeger.

Hickson, Gerald B., E.W. Clayton, P.B. Githens, and F.A. Sloan. 1992. "Factor that prompted families to file medical malpractice claims following perinatal injuries." Journal of the American Medical Association 267:1359–1363.

Imershein, Allen W., and A.H. Brents. 1992. "The impact of large medical malpractice awards on malpractice awardees." The Journal of Legal Medicine 13:33–49.

Lander, Louise. 1978. Defective Medicine: Risk, Anger, and the Malpractice Crisis. New York: Farrar, Straus and Giroux.

Lawthers, Ann G., A.R. Localio, N.M. Laird et al. 1992. "Physicians' perceptions of the risk of being sued." Journal of Health Politics, Policy and Law 17:463–482.

Lieberman, Jethro K. 1983. The Litigious Society. New York: Basic Books.

Localio, Russell A., Ann G. Lawthers, Troyen A. Brennan et al. 1991. "Relation between malpractice claims and adverse events due to negligence." New England Journal of Medicine 325:245–251.

May, Marlynn L., and D.B. Stengel. 1990. "Who sues their doctor? How patients handle medical grievances." Law & Society Review 24:105–120.

Mills, C. Wright. 1961. The Sociological Imagination. New York: Grove Press.

Mishler, Elliot G. 1990. "The struggle between the voice of medicine and the voice of the lifeworld." In The Sociology of Health and Illness: Critical Perspectives, eds. Peter Conrad and Rochelle Kern, 295–307. New York: St. Martins.

The National Center for Health Statistics. 1993. Monthly Vital Statistics Report. V 42(2).

Paget, Marianne A. 1988. The Unity of Mistakes. Philadelphia: Temple.

———. 1993. A Complex Sorrow: Reflections on Cancer and an Abbreviated Life, ed. M.L. De-Vault. Philadelphia: Temple.

Perrow, Charles. 1984. Normal Accidents. New York: Basic Books.

Poole, Anthony G. 1989. "Never think you've got a lock on a malpractice victory." Medical Economics (July 3):40–43.

Relman, Arnold S. 1980. "The new medical-industrial complex." New England Journal of medicine 303:963–970.

———. 1991. "The health care industry: Where is it taking us?" New England Journal of Medicine 325:854–859.

Smith, Michael S. 1987. "Getting sued renewed my faith in medicine." Medical Economics (December 21):50–53.

Stimpson, Gerry, and Barbara Webb. 1975. Gong to See the Doctor. Boston: Routledge & Kegan Paul.

Sudman, Seymour. 1985. "Mail surveys of reluctant professionals." Evaluation Review 9:349–360.

Taragin, Mark I., L.R. Willet, A.P. Wilczek et al. 1992. "The influence of standard of care and severity of injury on the resolution of medical malpractice claims." Annals of Internal Medicine 117:780–784.

Todd, Alexandra. 1989. Intimate Adversaries. Philadelphia: University of Pennsylvania.

Waitzkin, Howard. 1991. The Politics of Medical Encounters. New Haven: Yale University.

Sources

The chapters in this volume originally appeared in *Social Problems* and are copyrighted by the Society for the Study of Social Problems. These works are reprinted with the permission of the publisher and authors.

Chapter 1. Joseph W. Schneider. "Deviant Drinking as Disease: Alcoholism as a Social Accomplishment." *Social Problems* 25, no. 4 (1978): 361–372.

Chapter 2. Herb Haines. "*Primum Non Nocere*: Chemical Execution and the Limits of Medical Social Control." *Social Problems* 36, no. 5 (1989): 442–454.

Chapter 3. Peter Conrad and Deborah Potter. "From Hyperactive Children to ADHD Adults: Observations on the Expansion of Medical Categories." *Social Problems* 47, no. 4 (2000): 559–582.

Chapter 4. Stephen J. Pfohl. "The 'Discovery' of Child Abuse." *Social Problems* 24, no. 3 (1977): 310–323.

Chapter 5. Michael P. Johnson and Karl Hufbauer. "Sudden Infant Death Syndrome as a Medical Research Problem since 1945." *Social Problems* 30, no. 1 (1982): 65–81.

Chapter 6. Robert S. Broadhead. "Officer Ugg, Mr. Yuk, Uncle Barf . . . Ad Nausea: Controlling Poison Control, 1950-1985." *Social Problems* 33, no. 5 (1986): 424–437.

Chapter 7. Josh Gamson. "Silence, Death, and the Invisible Enemy: AIDS Activism and Social Movement 'Newness.'" *Social Problems* 36, no. 4 (1989): 351–367.

Chapter 8. Ernest Quimby and Samuel R. Friedman. "Dynamics of Black Mobilization Against AIDS in New York City." *Social Problems* 36, no. 4 (1989): 403–415.

Chapter 9. Maren Klawiter. "Racing for the Cure, Walking Women, and Toxic Touring: Mapping Cultures of Action within the Bay Area Terrain of Breast Cancer." *Social Problems* 46, no. 1 (1999): 104–126.

Chapter 10. Frances B. McCrea. "The Politics of Menopause: The 'Discovery' of a Deficiency Disease." *Social Problems* 31, no. 1 (1983): 111–123.

Chapter 11. Diana Dull and Candace West. "Accounting for Cosmetic Surgery: The Accomplishment of Gender." *Social Problems* 38, no. 1 (1991): 54–70.

Chapter 12. C. Amanda Rittenhouse. "The Emergence of Premenstrual Syndrome as a Social Problem." *Social Problems* 38, no. 3 (1991): 412–425.

Chapter 13. Steven Wallace. "Race versus Class in the Health Care of African-American Elderly." *Social Problems* 37, no. 4 (1990): 517–534.

Chapter 14. Elizabeth M. Armstrong. "Lessons in Control: Prenatal Education in the Hospital." *Social Problems* 47, no. 4 (2000): 583–605.

Chapter 15. Carol Klaperman Morrow. "Sick Doctors: The Social Construction of Professional Deviance." *Social Problems* 30, no. 1 (1982): 92–108.

Chapter 16. Michael Betz and Lenahan O'Connell. "Changing Doctor-Patient Relationships and the Rise in Concern for Accountability." *Social Problems* 31, no. 1 (1983): 84–95.

Chapter 17. Stephen L. Fielding. "Changing Medical Practice and Medical Malpractice Claims." *Social Problems* 42, no. 1 (1995): 38–55.

Index

A.A. *See* Alcoholics Anonymous

A.A. *Grapevine*, 16, 20n6

accountability: doctor/patient relationships and, 317–19, 320–27; professional deviance and, 297–98, 299–303; professionalization and, 4, 295–96. *See also* medical malpractice

action, 168–69, 176–78, 180

ACT UP. *See* AIDS Coalition to Unleash Power

addiction, 16–19

Addiction Research and Treatment Corporation (ARTC), 152

Adelson, Lester, 89, 90, 91, 92

Adult Attention Deficit Foundation, 47

adults, 44–59, 109

advertising, 195

African Americans: AIDS and, 131, 141n4, 145–56; childbirth and, 270; culture and, 251, 252–54, 254–57, 260, 261, 262; health care and, 245, 248–63; income and, 252, 254–57, 258–62; life expectancy and, 2, 4, 243; social class and, 245, 251, 252, 254–57, 258–62; social movements and, 124, 145–46, 148–56. *See also* race

African-Americans Against AIDS, 148

ageism, 198–200, 201, 202, 211, 221. *See also* elderly

The Ageless Woman (Kaufman), 196

AIDS: African Americans and, 131, 141n4, 145–56; blood and, 136–37; boundary-crossing and, 125, 129–30, 137–38;

control and, 126–27, 132–41; culture and, 129–30, 134–38; death and, 136; discrimination and, 133, 149; disease and, 140; education and, 155–56; government and, 133, 134, 137, 148–49, 150, 155, 156; health care and, 153; homosexuality and, 129, 131, 134–38, 139, 148, 152–53, 156, 170; labels and, 126–27, 129, 132–41, 149; media and, 135; medical profession and, 135; morality and, 134–35, 154–55; normalization and, 126–27, 132–41; pharmaceutical companies and, 134; plague metaphor and, 125, 140; politics and, 129, 131, 134, 139, 140, 141n2, 155; prescription drugs and, 134, 150–52, 152–54, 155, 156; public attention to, 123–24, 153; rates of, 146–48; religion and, 150, 154–55, 156; social class and, 154, 156; social movements and, 123–24, 125–27, 128–30, 140–41, 145–46, 148–56, 170; stigma and, 134–36, 138; symbols and, 136–38; women and, 130, 152

AIDS Coalition to Network, Organize and Win (AIDS NOW), 126, 152

AIDS Coalition to Unleash Power (ACT UP): blood and, 136–37; boundary-crossing and, 125, 129–30, 137–38; breast cancer and, 173; control and, 126–27, 132–41; culture and, 129–30, 134–38; death and, 136; enemies of, 131–33, 134, 135–36, 138;

163–64, 166, 167, 169–70, 174–75, 179, 180, 181–82; bureaucratization of, 322–23, 326, 341; cost of, 1, 2, 59, 209, 213, 318, 348; culture and, 251, 252–54, 254–57, 260, 261, 262; diagnostic expansion and, 57–59; elderly and, 248–49, 249–50, 251, 252–54; income and, 250, 252, 254–57, 258–62; menopause and, 191; patients and, 4; poison control and, 107–9, 112–14, 119–20; race and, 243, 245, 248–63; social class and, 3, 243, 245, 251, 252, 254–57, 258–62; social problems and, 2–5; upstream/downstream approach and, 3, 4; whites and, 248–63; women and, 174
health insurance: breast cancer and, 184n10; diagnostic expansion and, 59; inequality in, 1; race and, 245, 262–63; universal, 3. *See also* insurance companies; managed care
Healthy People 2000, 270–71
"Healthy Start," 243, 273
Helpern, Milton, 93
Henderson, L. J., 1
Heritage, John, 219
Hickson, Gerald B., 336
Hippocratic Oath, 30, 32, 33
Hispanics, 131, 141n4, 145–48
HIV. *See* AIDS
Holstein, James A., 272
homosexuality: AIDS and, 129, 131, 134–38, 139, 148, 152–53, 156, 170; AIDS Coalition to Unleash Power and, 130–31; breast cancer and, 170, 171, 172, 184n11; domain expansion and, 41; labels and, 133, 134–38; politics and, 131, 133, 134, 139
hospitals: poison control and, 68, 108, 112–13, 114–20; segregation in, 249–50, 257–62. *See also* prenatal education
house of refuge movement, 69, 70–71, 72, 73
Hufbauer, Karl, 67–68
humanitarianism, 28–29
Hunter, Jehu C., 97, 99
The Hyperactive Child, Adolescent and Adult (Wender), 45
hyperactivity, 41, 42–45. *See also* attention deficit hyperactivity disorder

ideology, 324–25
illness, 2, 4, 192, 269, 275. *See also* disease; health
Imershein, Allen W., 332
Imperial Chemicals Industry, 175–76
IMS National Disease and Therapeutics Index, 203n5
income, 250, 252, 254–57, 258–62. *See also* economics; social class
Inebriate Association, 12–13
inebriate asylums, 12–13
infant mortality, 243, 270–71, 273, 286
Ingalsbee, Timothy, 164
insanity, 35
institutionalization, 73, 305–7
insurance. *See* health insurance; insurance companies; malpractice insurance
insurance companies, 2, 4. *See also* health insurance; managed care
International Guild for Infant Survival, 95, 97, 98, 101–2

Jacobson, Max, 300–301
Jellinek, E. M., 13–14, 16–18
Jellinek model, 13, 16–19
Jenness, Valerie, 41
Jern, Herbert, 194
Johnson, Michael, 67–68
Johnson, Thomas, 234
Johnson, Timothy, 47
Joseph, Stephen, 150
Journal of Inebriety, 12–13
Journal of Studies on Alcohol, 18, 20n3
juvenile courts, 69, 70, 72–73

Kaufman, Sherwin, 196
Keller, Mark, 16, 18–19
Kennedy, Edward M., 98
Kennedy, John F., 113
Kinney, Eleanor Roberts, 90
Kitsuse, John, 132, 133
Klawiter, Maren, 124
Komen, Susan G., 166, 169
Kramer, Peter, 53
Krenzelok, Edward, 107

labels, 79–83, 126–27, 129, 132–41, 149. *See also* stigma
Landau, Theodore, 192

About the Editors

Peter Conrad is Harry Coplan Professor of Social Sciences at Brandeis University. His major research interests are in health and illness, social problems, and deviance. He served as president of the SSSP during 1996–1997. He is currently completing a book on "the medicalization of society."

Valerie Leiter is assistant professor of sociology at Simmons College. Her work focuses on disability, sociology of childhood, and family sociology. Currently, her research examines children's access to health care, and formal and familial systems of care for children with disabilities.